YACHTING

A Turn of the Century Treasury

YACHTING

A Turn of the Century Treasury

Edited by
Tony Meisel

CASTLE

Yachting
A Turn of the Century
Treasury

Copyright © 1987 Castle,
a division of Book Sales, Inc.
110 Enterprise Avenue
Secaucus, NJ 07094

Printed in the United States of America

ISBN: 1-55521-208-5

Contents

Introduction

From its beginnings in the eighteenth century, yachting has been perceived as a sport for the wealthy. And, except for the eccentric who sailed for personal gain or challenge in a small boat, most pleasure boating in the nineteenth century was devoted to racing under a variety of rules or rather grand cruising from harbor to harbor in comfort and safety.

There were exceptuions to this, of course: Commordore Vanderbilt's grand tour of Europe replete with servants, marble vanities, evening song fests; Howard Blackburn's small boat voyages across the Atlantic; and, most famous of all, Joshua Slocum's pioneering circumnavigation in a re-built oyster smack. But to most sailors, this was out of sight, if not out of mind!

Remember, this was still a time of commercial sail, when the fishing fleets on the Georges Bank were still dominated by Portugese and New England schooners. The technique and vocabulary of sail was a commonplace to those who manned these ships. If you worked at something, little chance that you would undertake the same activity for pleasure! But it was from these ships and the experience of their crews that many of the models for yachting's finest vessels were derived. From the time of Edward Burgess on through John Alden in the 1940's, the schooner was a model for all that signifies the best plying the seas under sail.

Small boat cruising and racing--and small is a relative term, anything under 100-feet was considered unseaworthily small before WW I--for most meant Sunday afternoon sails around the bay or, occasionally, a month's leisurely cruise along the New England coast. After all, boat ownership was rather more onerous at the turn of the century than it is today. Real wood, hemp and manila, flax and canvas sails, iron strapping and wood blocks demanded a degree of sacrifice usually delegated to a paid hand.

But development was all, even then. The latest advances in rigs and hull forms, sails and go-fast gadgets preoccupied the sailor of the 1890's as much as it does the weekend yachtsman of today. And let's not forget the constant search for greater ease of handling and more comfort. The true sybarite is never satisfied!

Cruising, when it took place, was a rather majestic affair compared to nowadays. Stewards, crews, expert captains coddled the "amateurs" on board. Blue blazers and white flannels enrobed the scions of the family yacht. What a life! But others, ever more intrepid, followed their own curiosities and embarked on more strenuous and probably more fulfilling voyages. Along the coast of wild Florida, Down East through fog and gale, into new areas these men (and occasionally women) charted, discovered and thrilled to the contest of man and boat versus sea and wind.

The greatest numbers--of a small group, to be sure--raced. Small boat one-design classes sprung up, allowing the family of modest means to participate in the sport. New racing rules constantly were developed, oft-times resulting in extraordinarily unseaworthy craft. But the great designers--Clinton Crane, Nat Herreshoff, William Hand and Burgess, among others--led the way to increasingly seaworthy and offshore-capable designs.

And then, the motorboat arrived on the scene. Here was a marvel to enthrall the mechanical age! It could go any-where, independent of wind and, to a degree, weather. It came in a bewildering variety of forms: steam, naptha, gasoline, make-and-break and more. It made lots of noise, and it actually worked... sometimes.

Turn-of-the-century yachting was a period of enormous energy, development, transformation. It was a time which changed the face of the sport forever. And though some of it may seem horribly old-fashioned and hypercautious by today's standards, one must remember that then it was but an extension of a common commercial pursuit. At least there were thousands of working sailors who could handle any vessel. You can't find that anymore!

Tony Meisel
New Suffolk, NY

A Storm at Sea
(1898)

A STORM AT SEA.

BY H. PHELPS WHITMARSH.
Author of "The Mutiny on the 'Jinny Aiken.'"

THE writer of the following sketch, after many stirring adventures in Australia, had become a pearl-diver on the northwest coast. The season was nearing its close, and the pearl-fishermen were anxiously awaiting the arrival of the supply-ship, from Singapore, when the annual cyclones broke before their time, and wrecked the fleet almost to the last vessel.—EDITOR.

IT was the early part of November. The cyclone season was approaching, and every man in the fleet was looking forward to the two or three months' rest and recreation which lay before him; for in "willy-nilly time," as the natives call it, diving is suspended. A few of the divers had planned to run their boats far up the creeks during the stormy term, but the greater number were bound for Cossack and for a taste of civilization. We were all anchored a little to the southward of Cape Bossut, where a new patch had kept us busy for a fortnight, waiting for the Singapore steamer. Six weeks had elapsed since she had passed through the fleet on her way north, and we were short of provisions and overloaded with shell. A good ending to a good season had put the pearlers in excellent humor. All hands were like school-boys on the eve of breaking up for the holidays, and as soon as the overdue *Cockatoo* arrived, there promised to be fun.

Among my friends on the grounds was a Captain Blake, of the schooner *Dolphin*. He was the owner of a fleet of five luggers, a successful man, and, strange to say, a gentleman. Like most of the white men on the coast, Blake had a "past." That, however, did not concern me; he was a good fellow, a marvelous story-teller, and he kept a certain brand of Scotch whisky which I have not yet seen equaled. On the pearling-grounds any one of these things was enough to make a man popular. Blake was perhaps forty-five years old, tall, spare, and with iron-gray hair and mustache—a man who, in spite of his yellow, East Indian complexion and somewhat dissipated look, was still handsome.

While we were waiting for the *Cockatoo*, I spent most of my evenings aboard Blake's hospitable schooner. I usually sculled back to my own boat about ten o'clock, but one night I got caught. It came on to blow from the eastward. Unprotected as we were, a choppy sea rose at once, and, as the night was unusually dark, and my dinghy only a cockle-shell, I decided to remain aboard the *Dolphin* for the night. We sat up talking and smoking until late. Then Blake lent me a suit of his pajamas, and we turned in. James, Blake's mate, being in Lagrange Bay repairing one of the luggers, I took his bunk. There was nothing alarming about the situation, and I soon fell asleep.

Crack! Rattle! Bing!

The last sound rang and reverberated through the schooner's timbers like the stroke of a bell.

Awakened by these unusual sounds, the captain and I instantly sat bolt upright in our bunks. We looked at each other inquiringly, and listened. The sides of the vessel were hissing softly, and through the open companionway came the flutter of ill-stowed canvas and the hum of much wind. Yet the schooner was quiet—strangely so.

"Chain parted, eh, captain?" I said, leaping to the deck.

"Yes, curse it; that 's the third this season," he replied, following suit. "Here, you know your way about, boy. Run up and let go the heavy-weather anchor. It must be a pretty stiff squall."

As he spoke, a gust of cold, damp air descended the hatchway, and drove from the cabin its previous mugginess. The sound of hissing at the vessel's side changed to a series of little spats, and she began to roll.

"Broadside on," said the captain, as I jumped for the ladder.

Routing out the Malay crew, I cut the lashings of the great iron mud-hook, and fell to prying it from its chocks.

"Heave!" cried Orang, the Manila boatswain. "Heave and sink her! Heave!"

There was a splash, the rusty roar of eighteen fathoms of cable tearing through the hawse-pipe, then a lull. The heavy-weather anchor had found bottom.

Snubbed short, like a down-stream trout when fairly hooked, the schooner flung her stern round, and faced the eye of the wind with a new tune in her rigging. For she no longer went peaceably with her enemy, but stopped and defied him. She laid her nose down closer to the water, and all her ropes, from the double-bass forestay to the shrill-piping signal-halyards, joined in a song of insolence.

After I had paid out cable to the forty-fathom mark, and seen that everything was shipshape forward, I went aft again. On the top steps of the cabin I paused and scanned the horizon. It was a wicked-looking night. The sky was low, and like black wool. The sea, too, was black, all but the snarling crests of the waves; and they by contrast were a ghastly white. Up to windward the masts of the fleet were outlined against the lighter tone of the sand-hills, over which the wind came down in fast, fierce puffs. Two luggers, with a foot or two of sail showing, were trying to beat their way into the creek beyond the cape. It was a futile attempt, however, as they were being blown bodily to leeward. Among the crowd of boats ahead I tried in vain to distinguish the *Norma*. I felt it to be fortunate that she was anchored close inshore and was well supplied with chains and anchors.

Descending into the cabin, I found the captain standing on the settee, examining the barometer.

"Falling, Blake?" I inquired.

"Fast," he answered, with a grave face. "How does it look on deck?"

"Pretty bad," I admitted. "It 's more than a cockeyed bob,[1] I 'm afraid."

"Yes; by the look of things, we are in for an easterly blow, if not worse."

"Surely it could not be a cyclone at this time, could it?" I asked.

"According to general belief, it 's a month too early for a willy-nilly," said the captain; "but as that is based upon the statements of a lot of —— niggers, I don't know whether we can depend on it or not."

I wished then that I had remained aboard my own boat. Malays are poor heavy-weather sailors; and the *Norma*, moreover, was deeply laden. Though I knew that the

chances of there being a great storm were in our favor, yet I was fearful for the *Norma's* safety.

Returning from a visit to the deck, the skipper said: "You 'd better turn in and get some sleep. As long as James is away, I 'll have to press you into service. I will take the first watch, and you can relieve me. Orang is standing by, forward."

Accustomed, by my sea-service, to obeying orders, I vaulted into my bunk, turned my face from the lamp, and went to sleep. I was too restless, however, to remain so long. Within an hour I was wide awake again. The captain, with an unlighted cigar between his teeth, was seated in full view of the barometer. Though his face was calm and his attitude easy, I could tell by his eyes that he was listening—that he was expecting something.

By this time the shrouds were pitching their song in a higher key, the waves had changed their snarl to a sullen roar, the schooner creaked and groaned, and her cable twanged like a harpstring.

Of a sudden, a strange rumbling noise vibrated through the vessel, and she trembled from stem to stern. It lasted for about three seconds, then stopped; then continued at short intervals. She was dragging her anchor.

The captain sprang up the companionway and hurried forward. I could hear his voice shouting orders to the crew, and later a prolonged rattle of cable. With ninety fathoms of chain out, the rumbling ceased. Blake came down the cabin steps, muttering. He lighted his cigar and returned to his chair to listen.

Louder and louder waxed the sounds of the approaching storm. The *Dolphin* leaped and dived and tugged at her chain, as a great fish might. She thrashed the sea with her stanch, bluff bow, till she rose in an acre of foam. Gust after gust in quick succession swept down upon her from the sand-hills, and she crouched before their fierce onslaught. The scroll-like waves were making deeper, darker hollows. She tried in vain to bound from one ridge to another. The captain began to pull on a suit of oilskins. Jamming his sou'wester on his head, he looked again at the barometer, and then turned toward my bunk.

"I 'm awake, Blake," I said. "Time to turn out?"

"Yes," he replied. "There 'll be work for us, unless I am mistaken. James's oilskins

_____
[1] Westralian for squall.

and sea-boots are under the bunk. I'm going on deck."

His tall form had hardly disappeared through the black square of the hatchway when, above the clamor of the elements, there rang out a deep-toned "Clang!" The cable had parted again.

As I tumbled out, I heard a rush of bare feet overhead, the rapid flinging down of coiled ropes upon the deck, and Blake bellowing like a bull. Without looking for more clothes, I scrambled up the ladder, to find the hands taking a double reef in the mainsail, preparatory to hoisting. The foretopmast staysail had already been set, and the schooner was scudding before the wind.

Feeling my way aft to the captain, I shouted: "What are you going to do—run?"

"Aye; there's nothing for it but to run now," he answered. "You had better take the wheel. That shaking orang-utan there is giving her her eight points each way."

Going behind the Malay, I laid hold of the spokes, and soon had the yawing schooner steadied. Since she was merely running before the wind, without a set course, no compass was needed, and I steered by the "feel" of the wind at my back. No sooner was the mainsail on her than the *Dolphin* took wings anew, and flew over the seething seas as though she were alive to the impending danger. I thought of my little lugger and wondered how she fared. But my forebodings in regard to the *Norma* were only momentary.

The noise, the speed of the vessel, and the great amount of air, exhilarated me beyond measure. I was brimming over with strength, with laughter, with daring. Hatless, shoeless, and with my pajamas fast blowing to rags, I felt no discomfort, but only a sense of power and exultation. I talked to the vessel as I steered, praised her extravagantly when she slipped away from the fast-following waves, swore at her when she answered the helm slowly, and sang between times at the top of my voice. I was, indeed, intoxicated.

Dawn broke with a hurrying, tattered sky and a rising sea. The great breath which had so suddenly come upon the peaceful fleet now backed into the northeast, and momentarily grew in strength. Frequent rainsqualls, in narrow black lines, rose from the vague horizon, and, outstripping the upper clouds, flew swiftly across their ashen-hued faces, and deluged the racing schooner.

By this time the hatches were battened down with double tarpaulins, extra gaskets had been passed around the furled sails, the water-casks and other movables had been stowed below, and all preparations made for a gale.

About six o'clock I was relieved by Orang. All hands drank their coffee on deck, for the weather looked still more threatening. The closed arch of the heavens was becoming darker and darker. The gathering of dense cloud masses in the northeast was spreading fanwise across the sky, lowering the dome, and having the appearance of great black brush-marks upon a gray canvas. On they came, until all the sky was lined with straight, sooty smudges. Then they joined, and gradually formed a solid roof of darkness. It was an eclipse, depressing, ominous.

Suddenly, out of the sky immediately overhead, there came a blinding flash and a terrific thunderclap. A shock was felt by every soul aboard. The dog forward howled dismally, the Malays set up a wail to Allah, and the schooner's maintopmast fell in splinters about her deck.

Blake and I, who were standing together under the lee of the poop, looked at each other with blanched faces.

"That makes a man think there is a God," said the captain.

The tempest fell upon us then in all fury. There was a continuous crash of thunder, a ceaseless blaze of lightning; and the wind swept over the boiling sea with shrieks of blind destruction. At the first gust the few yards of canvas on the vessel left the bolt-ropes, and flapped away like birds to leeward. A heavy, slanting rain, which stung like whip-lashes, came with the new wind; and clouds of salt smoke, blown from the ruffled backs of the monster waves, befogged everything and drew the horizon close about us.

Faster and faster flew the *Dolphin* before the wrath of the storm. Her speed was slow, however, when compared with that of the clouds, the waves, or the wind. Unless one looked at her swirling wake, indeed, one might have thought her without headway, so easily did the waves overtake and pass her. At one moment she trembled in a dark valley before the onward rush of a white-streaked, slaty-hued mountain; at another she was riding buoyantly on its foaming crest; again, the mountain fell away, and she slid down into a valley.

And as the wildness of the gale increased, so did the tumult of it grow louder and louder. The rain and the salt spray hissed in unison; the wind whirred, whistled, howled, and shrieked; the clouds opened their ports and cannonaded incessantly; and the ocean gave tongue in one long, magnificent roar. Added to these chief chords of the storm symphony were many minor strains—strange mutterings, and the voices of the sea. Wind, wave, and sky had combined their uproar, and the result was a deafening clamor. It was fearful; we looked at one another with eyes that asked, How will it all end?

The morning wore on. Still the storm grew more and more furious. To stand and watch the towering, angry ridges that ever rose astern; to see them come rushing after the little schooner, each one threatening to engulf her; to hear them roaring as they came; to feel the sting of their salt spray as they went boiling along the top-rail—these were things, indeed, to make the stoutest heart quake. Although we had set a storm-trysail, and the *Dolphin* ran before it like a frightened thing, we could no longer escape the sea. We had been expecting it for some time. It came at last. One frightful billow, higher, fiercer, hoarier than the others, reared itself above the stern. The schooner hung a moment in the shadowy abyss before it. Then she rose quickly toward the raging crest. But too late. It toppled with a crash over the heads of the men at the wheel, and swept her like an avalanche.

We were all carried forward with the rush of water. I found myself swimming abaft the forecastle-head. The deck was filled to the rails, and the vessel seemed to be sinking. She rose, however, gave a few quick rolls, like a big dog shaking himself, spilled the greater part of her weighty burden, and hurried on again.

Looking aft, I saw the wheel spinning madly. The steersman had been washed away. I yelled at one of the Malays to follow me, and clawed my way to the poop. When I reached it, the schooner was almost broadside on. Luckily the succeeding waves were not so large, or she must then and there have foundered.

The captain, pale and trembling, limped to my side a few minutes later. He had been hurt; his leg had been badly wrenched, blood was streaming from a gash in his temple, and he feared several of his ribs were broken.

As it was evidently unsafe to try to keep the *Dolphin* before it any longer, we decided, dangerous as it was in such a sea, to heave her to. The crew, in the meantime, had fled below, and it was only by force that the brave little Manila boatswain and I routed them on deck again. After we had hauled

aft the sheet of the trysail, all hands were ordered into the main-rigging. Then, waiting for the right moment, I jammed the wheel over, shipped a becket over one of the spokes so as to hold it, and sprang aloft with the others.

It was a wind-blown, fearful little crowd that clung in the schooner's rigging that day waiting for her to come round. As I watched the *Dolphin's* nose swing, and saw the great gray combers lift high their foaming crests abeam, I appreciated for the first time in my life how risky a thing it was to heave to in a big sea. One, two, three of the mountains the *Dolphin* passed in safety; the fourth leaped her rail amidships and buried her. I heard the thundering of tons upon tons of green water falling on her decks; I felt her tremble and settle beneath us; I looked down upon a white waste of water, and I said in my heart, "She is gone!" But it was not so. She had only caught the thin top of the wave, after all, and though its weight and force had leveled the bulwarks to the deck on both sides, this very thing enabled her to rid herself quickly of water. A few moments more and she thrashed her spars to windward, screaming like a fiend. She had accomplished her task in safety.

Although the vessel now lay over until the water reached her hatch-coamings, and in spite of her frightful pitchings, lurchings, and the stinging, hail-like spray that flew continually over the weather bow, we all felt much relieved at the change; for under the new conditions she behaved beautifully, riding buoyantly over the ever-advancing ranges, and shipping few seas.

About noon the sky lightened, and the wind went down somewhat. We rejoiced in the hope that the gale had spent itself. Vain hopes; vain rejoicings; in less than half an hour the wind flew round suddenly to the northwest, and blew harder than ever. The storm-trysail disappeared at the first puff. Even under bare poles, however, the schooner careened at such an angle that we feared she would capsize. Four o'clock came, and still the gale grew and grew. The waves, their crests lashed into fury, rose higher yet; and the troughs between were valleys of terror.

The captain and I, meanwhile, had established ourselves abaft the high cabin skylight, where we were sheltered from the wind and yet could keep a lookout. Blake, poor fellow, was suffering so intensely from his side that he was obliged to lie down. I tried to induce him to go below, but he would not.

Seeing that he had made up his mind to remain on deck, I passed the bight of a rope under his arms, and nailed a piece of wood at his feet, so that he might not slip to leeward. From time to time I made a trip into the cabin to examine the barometer, which continued to fall. No one, fortunately, was needed at the wheel. As long as it was lashed hard down, the schooner steered herself. With the exception of morning coffee, we had eaten nothing all day. The excess of wind, moreover, and the constant strain we had been under for fourteen hours, were most exhausting. Our troubles, too, were increased by the discovery that the schooner had three feet of water in her hold. Although, owing to the unusual straining of the vessel, this was not altogether unexpected, the knowledge gave us some alarm, for the Malay crew had lost their courage and become ungovernable. Like a lot of frightened sheep, shivering and wild-looking, I found them huddled in the galley. Ketchong stood outside, under the lee of the same little structure, with an expression of disgust upon his broad yellow face. He showed his white teeth when I told him to get the men at the pumps. For a minute, perhaps, he stood at the galley door yelling. Then, no one coming forth, he drew his sheath-knife and dived into the dark interior. Fearing trouble, I laid hold of a belaying-pin, and waited.

A series of howls issued from the cook-house door; there were sounds of a fierce struggle going on inside; then, like sheep chased by a fierce collie, the crew pressed out on deck. Ketchong, grinning horribly and still prodding the laggards with his pointed blade, followed closely at their heels, and between us we drove them to the pumps. But we could not make them work satisfactorily. Not only was the slant of the schooner's deck against us, but fear seemed to have driven the men's strength away, and at every wave that broke over us they dropped the handle-bars and fled. We gave it up at last, and I went aft to the captain again.

Night was approaching, and the situation showed no signs of improvement. The seas broke over the little vessel more and more, and with every gust she heeled dangerously.

Blake looked up at me as I stood clinging to the skylight beside him. "How does it look now?" he asked.

"No better, I 'm afraid," I admitted. "We 've got to lighten her somehow."

He groaned. He knew what I meant, but the *Dolphin's* sticks were dear to him. He said, however, after a pause: "Well, go ahead, old man. Cut away if you must."

"It 's safest," I replied; and I started forward.

As I reached the weather rail of the poop, I ducked involuntarily. A high, dark wall of water was approaching, which I felt we could not escape. I had scarce time to call, "Hold on, Blake!" when it fell upon us with a dull crash. We were half drowned by the flood that rushed over us. I rose to my feet, gasping.

Sliding down to the skylight to assure myself that the captain was safe, I heard above the din a faint cry; and at the same instant I saw the galley, with half a dozen black heads about it, floating alongside. Under the weight of water, the wire lashing which had secured the galley to the deck had parted, and the whole house, occupants included, had slid down to the railless side, overboard. I rushed to the lee side, and threw several ropes toward them. But all fell short. Dazed, helpless, horrified, I stood and watched them drift away, beheld them writhing like a mass of black snakes amid the foam of the next wavetop, and saw the edge of the galley rise on the back of another. Then they vanished, swallowed up in the grayness of the evening and the smoke and smother of the storm.

The sea again broke heavily upon the *Dolphin's* deck. I realized that no time was to be lost; and, watching my opportunity, I made a dash forward. In the boatswain's locker, under the forecastle-head, I found the ax. It was not very sharp, and I wondered whether it would serve. Even at that moment, when the gale was screeching overhead, and death seemed so near, I was proud of my task. For years I had read and been told of blows in which it was necessary to cut away the masts; in my sea-training I had been instructed how it should be done, and, now that this thing had actually come into my experience, I felt rather vain, and said to myself that I must do it in a seamanlike manner.

Down in the lee scuppers, always up to my waist in water, and often overhead, I hacked away at the slack forerigging. It cut more easily than I had expected. Shrouds and backstays were soon flying to leeward. Next I "ringed" the foremast as high as I could reach, for I hoped to rig a jury-mast on the stump later. Then I tackled the weather rigging. The taut wire ropes parted like threads at the first blow. When only two of the shrouds were left standing, there came a fierce squall upon us. Instantly the remaining splices drew, and the foremast, with a mighty crack and splintering, toppled overboard. When, in addition to this, the jibboom went of its own accord, the schooner righted perceptibly.

With only her main lower mast standing, the *Dolphin* made comparatively fair weather of it, and for a time I was tempted to let her go as she was. The remembrance, however, that Blake and I were now alone, that the vessel had an unusual amount of water in her hold, and that the night was before us, decided me to continue my work. I therefore laid low the remaining mast.

After this my strength seemed to leave me. I trembled all over, and with difficulty dragged myself aft. Reaching Blake's side, I dropped on the wet deck beside him, and hooking my arm through the bight of his rope, slept the sleep of exhaustion. Once or twice I half awakened and edged closer to Blake for warmth, but I was not brought to full consciousness for six hours, when Blake's voice in my ear caused me to rouse with a start.

The gale was still howling furiously, a heavy rain was falling, and the night was intensely dark. Both the captain's teeth and mine were chattering, for it had grown very cold. Blake, who was faint from fasting, wanted me to go down into the cabin for a bottle of brandy, which, he told me, was stowed in one of the lockers. Now thoroughly awake, I discovered that I too was ravenously hungry, and gladly went below.

Feeling my way to the hatchway, I cautiously let myself down into the warm, stuffy atmosphere of the cabin. It was pitch-dark, and everything was awash. Chests, stools, clothes, bedding, crockery—all had been flung upon the deck, where they swished and smashed from side to side. The swinging lamp, and the telltale compass, which had hung above the table, were both broken; and the weather side of the skylight was stove in so that a cataract of water poured down at every sea. Only the barometer was intact, and that, I noted, by the light of a match, had ceased to fall. It was a good sign, and I yelled the news to Blake with a feeling of extravagant joy. In the darkness and the confusion into which the lockers had been thrown, I failed to find the brandy. I laid hold of some bottled ale, however, and two tins of sardines, and with these I ascended to the poop.

Lashed up to the windward, under the lee of the low rail, we sat and ate our midnight meal. We knocked off the necks of the bottles with a sheath-knife and opened the sardines with the same instrument. We used our fingers to eat with, and drank from the jagged edges of the bottles. The liquor was warm and bitter, but it made us feel more comfortable when it was down; and when we had finished we took a few more turns round our bodies with the ropes, and curling down together, fell asleep. We had reached that point where we really did not care what happened. We ached for a little warmth, a little comfort, a little rest.

The schooner, meanwhile, kept to the wind by the flying rags of the stowed sails, ascended the heights, slid down into the gullies, and rode on into the blackness of the awful night.

About four o'clock we were awake again. The barometer was rising, the sky was broken and lighter in patches, and the wind seemed to have abated somewhat. We shook hands, and laughed childishly over these signs of a dying storm. Ale and some half-soaked biscuits served for our breakfast, after which I bound Blake's side and legs with strips of blanket soaked in liniment. Though the unceasing motion of the vessel must have kept him in constant pain, the brave fellow never complained.

Seated close up under the weather bulwarks, with our backs against the stanchions, we waited hopefully for the coming day. It came, not suddenly, as it was wont to do in that tropical latitude, but with a slow changing of black to dark gray, and dark gray to a lead color. Sea, air, and sky were all the same dismal tone. We saw it reflected in our own pale faces. We saw it, too, in the appearance of the *Dolphin*. As human beings are said sometimes to do, she had turned gray in the night. Here the color transition stopped. It was daylight.

With the daylight, however, came the realization of our worst fears. Though the wind was dropping fast, the schooner no longer floated buoyantly as on the previous day, but moved in a tired, sluggish way. She wallowed in the dark troughs each time, and it seemed as though she could not climb the ridge that ever rose before her. The waves, finding her defenseless, broke with cruel force against her battered bow; they rolled across her railless deck unceasingly; they pounced upon her unawares, and buried her to the break of the poop. They did not race with ruffled backs and smoking crests before the gale now, but swept on in a deliberate, lumpish fashion, more than ever dangerous.

The *Dolphin* was sinking. Her hold was half full of water, and her deck almost on a level with the sea. Sooner or later—it might not be for half a day, or it might be within half an hour—she would go down.

Up to this time I had looked forward to the end with hopeful certainty. We should pull through it all right, I felt sure. Now I could see nothing ahead of us but death. No matter which way I turned, the grim specter rose before me, cruel and inevitable. I did not seem to care very much. It was not so hard to face death as I thought it would be. My principal feeling was one of rebellion. It was unjust that we should die then, just as the storm was over. It was not right to be treated so after all our efforts. Why had not she gone down in the night, when we were asleep, if she was going down? It was an infernal shame! In my heart of hearts I did not even then believe it.

It began to rain again—a heavy tropical downpour, though strangely cold. By comparison, the salt water that broke over us every few minutes was warm, and we wished that it would come oftener. From time to time I crept below and brought up more ale. It kept us from getting hungry, but otherwise had no effect. Returning from one of these trips, I found Blake in an attitude that he had doubtless learned at his mother's knee. His eyes were closed, the palms of his hands were placed together, and his lips were moving. He was praying. Not wishing to intrude upon him, I sat down on the top step of the companion, and waited. It was evident that the *Dolphin's* captain had given up all hope; yet, in the face of this grave acknowledgment (for so I took it), I could not forbear an inward smile. It was so funny to see Blake, of all men, praying. As I sat there, I fell to wondering whether it would be any good for me to pray. After due reflection I decided that it would not be any good. I argued that as I had not prayed for years, God would know that fear was my only reason for taking it up again, and would therefore take no notice of any supplications of mine. Thus I reasoned and thought in the hours which I felt were my last.

I took my place beside Blake again, and drearily watched the gray, foam-streaked surges that bore down upon us in such an endless regiment. How long should we have to wait before they swallowed us? I asked myself. I tried to imagine how it would all end, and I resolved that when it came I should not swim. Then my thoughts turned toward home. The picture of a dear old midland vicarage with climbing roses upon its walls, and an ancient cedar of Lebanon on its lawn, grew out of the gray, and in and about it moved the forms of those who were nearest to me. Yet, strange to say, I saw them only in one place. Thus my mother ever sat at a table pouring tea from an old silver tea-pot that I remembered from childhood. The ornament on top of the lid had been lost, and a huge black-velvet cozy with red embroidery stood close to the tea-pot stand. My father, with his coat-tails flying, appeared taking a short cut over the graves to the vestry door. The last bell had tolled, and the processional had begun. My sisters I also saw in some equally singular way. Aye, and there was a girl, too, a fair-haired, blue-eyed sweetheart of mine, who sat in the stern of a boat with a counterpane sail, and steered boldly into forbidden reaches of the river.

We grew unutterably weary as the day advanced. Weak, stupefied, aching in every muscle and shivering with cold, we sat waiting for the end. For my own part, nothing but pride kept me up. I would have given worlds to creep into one of the cabin berths and go to sleep. The schooner, meanwhile, sank lower and lower. It would not be long now. We imagined that the fear of death had left us, and we were calm.

In the midst of this somehow boastful acquiescence of ours, however, the *Dolphin*, now slow and lubberly in her movements, plunged headlong into the belly of a quivering green sea. Instantly our tranquillity forsook us, and we sprang to the highest point, —the main-boom,—blanched and trembling with fright. The wave closed over us with a seething sound, and, with the weight of molten lead, it flattened us upon the spar as though it would crush our lives out.

When it had passed, we saw that a yawning hole had opened up in the main-hatch. It could now be only a few minutes before she would fill and founder.

In a frenzy of self-preservation, we turned to the small dinghy that lay on the poop. The schooner's largest boat had been knocked to splinters long before, and but for the fact that the dinghy had been placed bottom up directly abaft the mainmast, and had been partly sheltered by the cabin skylight, it would also have been demolished. I do not think that either of us believed that such a cockle-shell would live in that sea. We took to her merely as a last resort—a staving off of the termination. Hurriedly we cut the lashings, turned her upon her keel, and saw that she was firmly plugged. Oars we could not find, but we threw a bailer into her, and an old rope fender to act as a sea-anchor. Then we slid her down to the side, intending to launch her over the rail with our hands, for she was very light. All being in readiness, I turned to dive below for some food, and as I did so the *Dolphin* plunged again. I had scarce time to throw myself over the gunwale of the dinghy before it was afloat and whirling on the crest of the advancing wave. I expected that we should be swamped immediately, but as the wave passed without our shipping much water, I gained courage, and, making the fender fast to the end of the painter, threw it overboard. Looking round, I then saw that Blake lay at the bottom of the boat, behind me, face downward. Over-

come by pain, my companion had fainted. I raised his head a little, and placed a stretcher under his forehead. More than this, however, I did not dare.

As the dinghy rose again, I looked anxiously on all sides for some signs of the *Dolphin*, but could not see her. The sea, gray, and streaked with wavering lines of foam, filled my vision. It was monstrous, awful, terrifying, and I dropped cowering at the bottom of the boat.

Beyond this point my memory fails me. I remember hazily starting up once or twice, and madly bailing. I recollect also looking up into a blue sky, and wondering if it were a dream. But, for the rest, I know nothing.

[THE writer and his companion, after being in the dinghy for eighteen hours, were picked up by the supply-ship *Cockatoo*.]

Racing in
Small Sailboats
(1911)

RACING IN SMALL SAIL-BOATS

BY L. DE B. HANDLEY

Illustrated with Photographs

A SPINNAKER BREEZE

EVER since the introduction of the power boat into the field of racing, alarmists have been predicting the early disappearance of the competitive sailing yacht, but somehow, as season follows season, there appears no indication of the ill prophecy coming true. In fact, interest in the sport seems to be growing yearly; more and more men are taking it up, and the number of racing sailboats is increasing instead of decreasing.

One has but to glance over the newspaper files of 1910 to verify the correctness of this statement. Not only was the season the most successful in history, but the Larchmont Week Regatta, which may well be taken as the barometer of yaching matters, brought together a record fleet of one hundred and twelve boats, the greatest ever chronicled.

It may suit the pessimist to see in the abandonment of the huge racing freak of former days a sign of the decadence of the sport, but the growing popularity of the smaller classes proves conclusively how biased is his judgment. The gigantic speed machine is an anomaly, justifiable only under the plea of international competition, as a test of world supremacy, if at all; it has no place in everyday sport. The cost of building and running it is out of all proportion to the pleasure it affords. Besides which, the constant changes in rating rules, brought about by a praiseworthy effort to develop sane and seaworthy types of racing craft, make its period of utility problematic and often very short.

But, apart from these considerations, yachtsmen have come to realize that other advantages are derived from the change to smaller boats. Chief among them is the securing of absolute command of one's craft, which is neither practical nor advisable in the larger classes. The great spread of canvas on anything above a forty-footer makes it almost imperative for the helmsman to entrust to another the task of directing the setting and trimming of sails, and this division of authority often proves a cause of annoyance, for it is not in human nature to share power without disagreement, and differences of opinion lead to argument and impair one's chances of victory.

On craft of, say, the P class size, or below it, the owner or skipper is absolute master. While at the tiller he can form and carry out his plan of campaign without aid or interference, and he knows that upon his skill and generalship must depend the issue. This is a great source of satisfaction, for every man likes to feel that, win or lose, he is in full control of his ship and all credit and blame must go to him.

Plenty of Competition

Another good feature of small boat racing is the assurance one has of keen competition and plenty of it. The big fellows could never rely on more than one, or possibly two opponents. In the smaller classes, instead, several starters are the rule rather than the exception. Take, for instance, the New York Yacht Club thirty-footers and the new Larchmont Yacht Club monotypes launched last year; it is a rare occurrence when half a dozen of the former and a dozen of the latter fail to report for a regatta, and the majority are so well handled as to make the contest a fine battle of wits in which every trick of seamanship has to be brought into play and the least error may be responsible for defeat.

And what racing it is! At start a sharp tussle in close quarters for the honor of crossing the line first; then an exciting neck to neck struggle over the course, with every sense on the alert to anticipate unexpected moves from one's rivals and to take advantage of every opportunity; a thrilling fight to the end, with every antagonist a probable factor until the home mark is reached. To the keen sportsman such racing is ten times more exciting than the dual encounters of the lordly ninety-footers.

The belief, once deeply rooted, that to race yachts enjoyably and successfully one must have unlimited means no longer obtains. Its fallacy has been demonstrated; the game is open to all. There are seen everywhere, nowadays, enthusiasts who, though unable to afford expensive craft, follow the sport with as much zest and pleasure as their more fortunate brother yachtsmen. They own little open dories, diminutive decked-in sloops, and other tiny cockles that require but a few hundred dollars to build and can be maintained at really nominal expense, yet they have as much fun with them as if they were handsome yachts. There is evidence of it in the regularity with which the dories attend in full force the regattas of Massachusetts Bay, Long Island Sound, and New York Bay. Indeed, the keen rivalry among skippers is hardly surpassed in the larger classes. And, after all, it is the spirit of competition which appeals to the true sportsman, not the size or type of the craft.

It is indicative of the development of sailboat racing that many confirmed cruising yachtsmen have of late taken it up. Nor can one feel surprise at their conversion. There is a fascination about racing totally lacking in cruising. Sailing quietly from port to port, with no greater incentive than to get there, is at best a tame pastime. One is often too lazy or unconcerned even to trim sheets or set light sails, and a boat comes to be a mere means of transportation. How different in racing! There is no room on board here for the drones. Every man's services are in demand as crew, he is raised to the dignity of able seaman with particular duties allotted to him, and the voice of the skipper keeps him constantly on the jump, for there is something to be done every blessed moment.

The handicap classes have done a lot to popularize small boat racing, particularly among the cruising men, for they have made it possible for craft of almost any build to compete with prospects of success. Time allowances are not calculated on hull measurement and sail area in these classes, but on actual or estimated performance, and boats sail in separate divisions, determined by and according to their speed. At first the system did not meet with general favor, for it was at times necessary to match a big under-rigged cruiser with an out-classed racer half its size, and this incongruous pairing caused ridicule that men were often unwilling to face. Some braved it, however, and reported such good sport that little by little the ranks grew

LETTING HER HAVE IT

A WELL BUNCHED START IN A LIGHT BREEZE

until it was possible to give a certain homogeneity to the divisions, then prejudice fled and the membership increased rapidly.

There are at present handicap classes in all Eastern yachting centers. That of Long Island Sound is the most flourishing. Last year its fleet numbered forty-four sails, formed into five divisions, and they gave three hundred and sixty-seven starts and won one hundred and seventy-two prizes. Rather a healthy organization.

There are two different and distinct kinds of races indulged in by sailboat men: Short ones, around triangular courses; and long, or cruising ones. They are totally apart from each other, require different attributes in skipper and crew, and as a rule are fostered by different men, though a few enjoy both.

Triangular racing appeals most to those who cannot afford to leave their interests for any length of time and to yachtsmen who do not care to subject themselves to any inconvenience. It takes but a few hours of the afternoon to cover the ten or twelve mile courses prescribed and one can generally count on getting home for dinner. Also the regattas are usually held on Saturday so that little or no time has to be taken from business.

It is a most pleasant way of spending the half holiday. There is something very attractive, even gay, about the reunion of the fleet around the committee boat before starting. It is like a big social gathering. Most of the skippers and crews know each other and one notes on every side a friendly exchange of greetings, a jolly bandying of quip and repartee, as the boats cross and re-cross, or move along rail to rail, awaiting their signal. And all about are non-racing craft of every description, often dressed in multicolored flags in honor of the occasion, that give to the scene a festive and striking appearance.

Not the least charm of racing lies in its uncertainty and ever-changing phases. You may find a bright, sunny day, with smooth sea and gentle zephyrs, or you may run into lowering skies, rough water, a howling gale, and possibly drenching rain. And while one enjoys the fair weather it is the battle with the unchained elements, the close proximity of danger that really fascinates. One learns to love the sound of the wind

A START LIKE THIS TAKES NERVE

shrieking through the rigging and the feel of the salty spray cutting the face, as the boat plows along with deck awash, every rope straining to the breaking point. It is a man's game, then, a game that appeals wonderfully to anyone with a drop of fighting blood in his veins.

Success in triangular racing depends a great deal on the watchfulness and promptness in action of skipper and crew. It is often necessary to meet the unexpected move of a rival on the spur of the moment and rapidity in maneuvering is essential. The crew, which is frequently composed mainly of corinthians, is an integral part of the racing machine and unless it is well trained and working in perfect harmony, good results cannot be hoped for.

I once witnessed crew-work in its ideal form in a race aboard one of the Massachusetts twenty-two-footers and it was a revelation. The men, all amateurs, had been sailing together so long that they did things instinctively, almost unconsciously, and they went about it with a vim that was inspiring. The only order one heard from the skipper was, "Ready about" or "Ready to jibe." For

the rest, whether it was to set spinnaker or ballooner, trim sails, or anything else, everyone knew so accurately when and how to do it that it was quite unnecessary to tell them. This boat won almost every race she entered with the original crew handling her, but never showed at all after changing owner.

And looking on the other side of the medal, an episode of the season of 1909, in Long Island Sound, will illustrate how a slight error on the part of a crew may account for defeat. The *Crescent* and *Bobtail* had been fighting all summer for supremacy in their class and met off Larchmont in one of the late and deciding regattas. It was one of those days of steady breeze in which flukes are unlikely to occur, and the two boats made a great race of it. Side by side they covered the course, not fifty yards dividing them at any time.

On approaching the last mark, from which it was a reach home, both carried spinnakers. The *Bobtail* was leading by a few feet, but the *Crescent* could outreach her and it looked like a sure thing for her. The order to take in spinnakers came simultaneously from both skippers. On the *Bobtail* it dropped neatly and she rounded the mark nicely, but on the *Crescent* the man who was to lower the halyard allowed a couple of feet of it to slip through his hands before the pole was in and the next minute the stick had caught the water and was jammed against the shrouds.

At the speed the boat was traveling it was a difficult thing to free it and some time elapsed before the big sail was gathered in. By then the *Bobtail* had gained a big lead and although the *Crescent* cut it down considerably on the reach home she was beaten by fifty-eight seconds. Barring the accident, she would undoubtedly have won. Of course, this is but one of the hundreds of things which a crew man can do to handicap and hurt a boat's chances.

Coolness and Nerve Demanded

A racing skipper must have presence of mind, know every trick of boat-to-boat sailing, be able to see opportunities at a glance and know how to take advantage of them, have perfect control of his crew and craft, and possess the cool head and nerve necessary safely to take a risk when the occasion demands. One is working so close to an adversary, at times, that only inches separate when one alters course or goes about, and it takes a sure eye, a steady hand, and plenty of courage to maneuver in such instances. The slightest miscalculation will cause a collision that is punished by disqualification and may also do considerable damage.

Presence of mind is a very valuable asset. Most sailing men know what they ought to do under given conditions, but it is the man who thinks first and acts quickest who secures the advantage. An instance, out of the thousands which might be cited, will illustrate. If memory serves me, it was in 1903 that the Herreshoff thirty-footer *Alert* entered the field against the *Oiseau* and *Flosshilde,* then the leaders of the class. In one of the mid-summer regattas the *Oiseau* came late to the line and the other pair were a few hundred yards away before she crossed.

A light air from the west enabled the fleet to lay the mark and make slow progress against the incoming tide. Off the turning buoy the wind petered out completely and the boats began to fall back. Elementary seamanship should have told every skipper to anchor and hold his ground, but somehow only the *Oiseau's* captain seemed to think of it. He quickly dropped a small hook and the others soon drifted back to him. They then saw their mistake and followed suit, but it was too late. When a fresh afternoon southerly sprang up the *Oiseau* was first to get it, and the lead she gained by it brought her home in front. Her victory was due solely to presence of mind.

Trickery, or let us say strategy, also plays an important role. Every experienced racing man has an infinity of little dodges stowed away in his head, which he makes use of when the chance presents. I saw Billy Swan win a race with the American Yacht Club monotype *Hobo* in a manner that demonstrated the value of a fertile brain. On the latter part of the last leg, a spinnaker run, he was rapidly overhauled by the *Jolly Tar* and it looked as if he would soon be blanketed and passed. Swan waited until his rival was nearly alongside then dropped spinnaker and rounded up, forcing the other off his course. Thus they proceeded until in range with the committee boat when the *Hobo* suddenly jibed and found herself nearest to the line and to windward so that she had no difficulty in crossing first. Had Swan held his course he would probably have been beaten.

Knowledge of conditions, ability to anticipate changes in tide and wind, and constant watchfulness are often deciding factors. Fluky breezes predominate in Eastern waters during the hot months and one needs to be perseveringly on the *qui vive.* Over and over again events have been won by those who were on the lookout. Only last season, in one of the Larchmont regattas, the fleet was lazily drifting from Red Spring buoy to a dory off Sands Point, with hardly breeze enough to fill the sails, when a dark line on the water, near the shore, heralded the arrival of the usual southerly.

The yachtsmen who were watching

CLOSE WINDWARD WORK WITH THE NEW YORK 30-FOOT ALL DESIGN CLASS. ALL THE "TRICKS OF THE TRADE" ARE NEEDED HERE

for it saw it first and unhesitatingly went to meet it. A few minutes later they were speeding along with rail under, while those who had held to a straight line were left helplessly behind and were beaten beyond hope by the time the wind reached them. A good sailor will go a long way out of his course to find wind on such a day.

Sound judgment and perfect control of one's craft are indispensable not only to success, but to safety. A racing skipper often finds himself in very nasty holes, particularly in jockeying for a start and rounding a mark, and it takes a level head and a firm hand to avoid setbacks and possible accidents. In the elimination trials held at Oyster Bay in 1907, in anticipation of the Jamestown Q class races for the King's Cup, nine boats reported and found a half gale blowing. Some pretty work was seen while they waited for the early signals, but it became sensational as the time for the start approached. All nine boats were aiming at reaching the extreme windward end of the line at exactly the same second and the way they maneuvered in close formation, heeled to a dangerous angle, in a smother of foam, was a sight to behold.

Fifteen seconds from the gun the *Vingt Trois* was under the lee of a rival, close hauled, and seemingly hopelessly pocketed, for she hadn't room to go about and jibing was out of the question. It was one of those cases when a chance had to be taken and the skipper realized it. Bearing off a trifle he opened the gap a little, then jammed the tiller down hard and spun around. It was so close that an involuntary cry escaped both crews, but it was calculated to the inch. The bowsprit swung within a hair of the other's mainsail, without touching it, and as the gun boomed, the *Vingt Trois* went over in splendid position. It was as pretty a piece of work as the writer ever saw, and as dangerous, for at the rate both boats were traveling a collision would have meant disaster.

It is the wise man who can estimate when to take a risk and when not to. Recklessness and foolhardiness are the negation of good seamanship and seldom do one any good. In a race I witnessed in 1910 a reckless skipper lost a prize and a spinnaker by poor judgment, and hundreds of others have probably fared worse. In this case four of the New York Yacht Club thirties were tearing before a gale on the last leg of the course, almost on a line. It was a question which would get over first. It was blowing entirely too hard to set light sails and none carried spinnaker, but as the finish floats hove into sight the captain of the second boat decided that to win he must do something unusual and the only thing that occurred to him was to crowd on sail, so the order went forth to set spinnaker.

It was madness to attempt it, and the crew protested, but to no purpose, so up went the sail in stops and out the pole. As might have been predicted, no sooner did the huge bit of canvas break out than the howling wind got hold of it and tore it to ribbons. In a minute all was confusion on board and before the wreckage had been cleared the foolhardy skipper found himself relegated to fourth place and so he crossed the line. It is a wise saying of old salts that any landlubber knows when to put on sail, but only a good sailor when to shorten it.

A PICK-UP MEAL WHILE RUNNING BEFORE THE WIND

The spirit of sportsmanship is prevalent among racing yachtsmen and makes things very pleasant. There are, of course, a few black sheep, as there are in every sport, but not many. One will often see a class wait for a belated member after the signal to start has been given, and I have had several personal experiences which show how general is the feeling of not wanting to take unfair advantage of an opponent. Last year, for instance, I went to the line shorthanded one day during Larchmont Week, and mentioned my plight to the owner of *Wander IV,* a rival craft. He immediately asked me to take one of his own crew men and generously deprived himself of the latter's services to help me out.

The season before I lost the *Crescent's* jib in one of the Oyster Bay regattas, on Saturday, and it looked as if I would be kept out of Monday's race, at Larchmont, but the skipper of *Bobtail,* a feared opponent, promptly tendered one of his and enabled me to compete. Again while sailing on the raceabout *Rascal* we split our spinnaker on the first round of the course and the owner of the *Busy Bee,* racing against us, magnanimously came alongside to offer an extra one that he had on board, although he lost considerable ground in so doing. Doubtless every racing man has had similar experiences.

In long distance or cruising races, trickery does not play a conspicuous role, for the simple reason that the boats are seldom grouped. They often part company soon after the start, to follow different routes and at times do not come together during the entire contest. Some look upon this feature as a most unsatisfactory one and claim that it detracts from the zest of competition, but anyone who has waited for the first clearing of

LETTING GO THE LEE RUNNER WITH THE RAIL UNDER

dawn to scan the horizon with glasses, in search of the rest of the fleet, knows how keen is the interest throughout.

To be successful in long-distance racing, the most essential attribute is understanding of at least pilot water navigation. This knowledge many have acquired practically in pleasure cruising, and it stands them in good stead. Familiarity with tides, lights, fog signals, winds, charts, and compass sailing gives a tremendous advantage. But above all it is necessary to be able to steer by feel, on the wind, during the hours of darkness. It is a rather rare accomplishment that only comes after long practice.

Endurance is also indispensable. The men are most valuable who can stand the strain of continued work at the tiller without allowing their attention to wander from their task and who will shoulder without a murmur the burden of changing and trimming sails when tired. It is no sinecure to be in harness

ALL KINDS OF LIGHT CANVAS

day and night, ever ready to respond to the call of "All hands on deck," and frequently with only a snatch of sleep taken now and then, and no solid meals. The time comes when nature clamors for rest, and no end of will-power is needed to stick to one's duties. Particularly in heavy weather, when skipper and crew have no respite, there are hours when drooping lids and aching muscles cry out for mercy and it becomes punishment to perform even the slightest task.

It is poor policy to waste too much energy in the early part of a long-distance race. Human endurance has its limitations. You will usually see the veteran leave the work to the eager novice, at first, for he knows where overanxiety leads. It is when the other begins to give out that he jumps into the fray. And it is the wise skipper who establishes rigorous discipline on board, and after dividing his crew into two watches insists on each being below deck during the hours off duty. A crew that remains fresh to the end increases the likelihood of victory tenfold.

It must not be imagined, however, that it is all work and no pleasure. A few congenial companions manage to knock no end of fun out of these trips. Men who sail are generally of the happy-go-lucky type who can take with a smile good fortune and ill, and after all, with a light heart and a fair sense of humor it is not hard to turn small inconveniences and even mishaps into a laugh.

And there are compensations. What of those wonderful days when the sky is blue, the sunshine bright, the water sparkling, and the wind steady and true? What of those incomparable nights, soft and mellow, when the white sail glistens in the moonlight and one lies comfortably on deck drinking in the beauty about and listening to the gentle swish of the water under the bow? What of those thrilling sails in the darkness, when the wind sings a mad song through the shrouds, the waves crash over the side, and one feels the boat leap like a living thing through the inky blackness, seemingly eager herself to rush on to victory? Sport? Why there is nothing like it.

The sport is still in its infancy, but it is developing fast, and rapidly making recruits. Time was, and not many years ago, when one spoke with befitting respect of the few who dared venture outside of sheltered waters in supposedly

AGILITY MEANS MUCH IN SMALL BOAT RACING

frail and unseaworthy racing craft. But things have changed. Yachtsmen have come to appreciate how much a well-built little boat will stand, if properly handled, and it has given them confidence. They have also perfected themselves in the art of navigation and lost all fear of unconfined horizons. One has but to compare the early fleets that took part in the Block Island race of the New York Athletic Club, now the classic small-boat feature of the Eastern season, with those of to-day, to note the remarkable progress made. Six boats took part in the event at its introduction, and nearly fifty crossed the line last year.

But even more conclusive was the contest for the yachting cups of 1910, which were competed for over a two-hundred-and-ten-mile course that circled Long Island. Most of the distance was covered in the open ocean in sight of a dangerous coast which for some seventy-five miles offers no harbor or shelter to put into in case of storm. Nevertheless, thirteen boats under forty-two feet on deck, most of them of an out-and-out racing type, completed the long journey successfully.

The memorable trip of the thirty-foot-er *Mimosa III,* in the Cape May Race of 1908, afforded a striking example of the seaworthiness of the modern racing craft and of the ability and fearlessness of our corinthian sailors. Manned entirely by amateurs, the little ship went out bravely into weather so fierce that several larger and heavier-timbered boats had to put back to port, and for an entire night beat into the teeth of a tearing gale, hammered by seas that tested the best staying qualities of the big schooners against her. Yet she stood it undaunted and emerged from the test without showing a mark of the terrific pounding she had received.

There are now held yearly in the East about a dozen important long-distance races open to all, besides many club cruises which are also competitive, and the boats that take part in them are drawn principally from the triangular racing classes. In some of these events professional crews are allowed, but in others only corinthians may be used. Skippers seem to prefer good amateurs, anyhow, when they can get them, for they take keener interest in the contest and are generally more willing to spare no pains to win.

A SCRAP FOR THE WINDWARD BERTH

There is evidence of the growing popularity of long-distance racing in the number of yachtsmen who will any day abandon triangular courses for it, and it is not difficult to explain the preference, for there is a great deal more to it, a far greater variety of happenings. Conditions are often met which one seldom, if ever, encounters in afternoon racing, and weather of several different kinds may be one's lot in the same race.

A brief outline of last summer's contest for the Brooklyn Yacht Club's Ocean Cup, in which the writer sailed on the *Waialua,* will serve to give a good idea of the diversity of experience one may enjoy on such trips.

The course lay from off Echo Bay to Vineyard Sound Lightship and around it, then outside Block Island and Long Island to Sheepshead Bay, a distance of two hundred and eighty nautical miles. The first part of the journey was covered under spinnakers, with a moderate breeze and ideal fair weather. Up to Horton's Point the wind held and the fleet kept together. Then came night and a dead calm of several hours. Morning brought fluky light airs from every point of the compass, and the boats scattered in every direction. By evening a dense, blinding fog had closed in, and for nearly five hours skippers had to sail dangerous waters entirely by dead reckoning, for lights could not be seen and fog signals were indistinguishable in the babel of horns, sirens, and whistles, sounded by passing steamers.

The course lay along the route of vessels plying between New York and Eastern ports and an infinity of them seemed to be seeking the lightship about the time we approached it. For a stirring and exciting experience commend me to beating up to a light that cannot be seen a hundred yards off on such a night, with the danger ever present of being annihilated by one of the nearby monsters whose deep-throated bellows and throbbing engines can be heard on every side. We escaped, however, and finally located our mark about midnight, got safely around it, and struck for the open sea, anxious to get out of harm's way.

By dawn the fog had lifted, but ominous clouds on the horizon and a falling barometer gave promise of storm. It came sooner than we expected, and a healthy young squall it proved to be. For about an hour the wind kept us on the jump, while the rain poured down on us. Then the storm passed swiftly, leaving a heavy swell and a light head wind, a combination against which it was almost impossible to progress. Before noon a spanking breeze set in, though, and took us in short tacks to Montauk Point, off which we found big-crested waves that it was necessary to go through. They gave us a bad quarter of an hour and an alarming pounding.

Outside Long Island we ran into a half gale sweeping over the hills in such ugly puffs that we had to reef. Then the wind moderated and allowed us to resume full sail, only to blow harder than ever about an hour later, forcing us to cut down the canvas to the second points. Even so it was heavy going and the tiller pulled so hard that we had to take turns at it and make the tricks very short. But all's well that ends well. By sundown a nice, steady, reaching breeze had set in and with ballooner kiting we tore off the miles under perfect conditions throughout the night, hardly touching a sheet until the bend in the coast made us round up close-hauled. We crossed the line at daybreak with the wind still holding true.

There may be more fascinating sports than small sailboat racing, but it is not the yachtsman who has experienced its thrills who will admit it.

Captain
Joshua Slocum
(1902)

At Home on Martha's Vineyard.

CAPTAIN JOSHUA SLOCUM

THE MAN WHO SAILED ALONE AROUND THE WORLD IN A THIRTY-SEVEN-FOOT BOAT

By CLIFTON JOHNSON

PHOTOGRAPHS BY THE AUTHOR

THE *Spray*, as I first saw her, lay gently rocking in a little cove on the Massachusetts coast near Woods Hole. No one could fail to recognize her as an unusual craft at once—such breadth of beam, such homely simplicity, such sturdy strength. Yes, that was the very boat, thirty-seven feet long and fourteen wide, in which Captain Joshua Slocum had sailed around the world. There were other vessels about—catboats, sloops, and yachts, but beside this one they appeared like playthings. The *Spray* could not compete with them in grace and style, yet she had an attractive air of domesticity and was evidently built for a sea home suited to all seasons and all waters and not simply adapted to fair summer weather along shore. It was a pleasure to set foot on her and note her snug appointments. It

was a pleasure to eat with Captain Slocum a rough and ready lunch that he deftly prepared in the little galley, and it was a pleasure when night came to bunk in under a deck awning and sleep on board. But, best of all, was a sail the next morning in " the old *Spray*," as her owner affectionately calls her, from the mainland across to Martha's Vineyard.

On the island at the village of West Tisbury is his home. This is not, however, his native region; for his birthplace was in Nova Scotia. There he began life fifty-eight years ago on a little clay farm overlooking the Bay of Fundy. The sea was two and a half miles distant, but it was in sight, and when the wind was right the boy could hear the waves breaking against the rocky coast. The sea was fascinating to him from the first, and he liked to watch

37

the ships sail up and down the bay. The Slocums were nearly all sailors, and Old Ocean was always beckoning to the lad and claiming him as its own long before he began to cruise on its waters. But as a child he was a farm boy, and Nova Scotia farm life was then only one remove from pioneering. Cabins of logs were still occasionally in use, though they were considered rude and behind the times, and those who dwelt in them were looked on as "low down."

The houses all had big chimneys and depended on open fires for heat and cooking. "Yes," said the captain in relating this to me, "and what good things to eat came from those old fireplaces—oh! those barley cakes and those buckwheat flapjacks—oh!"

Captain Slocum's earliest experience as a navigator was gained on a placid mill pond about a mile down the hill from his home. Here, when he was nine or ten years old, he constructed a raft. It was customary among the farmers to use a knotty spruce log for the bottom rail of the zigzag fences, and three of these with boards nailed across made quite a substantial craft. Joshua rigged up a mast and sail and the rustic vessel carried him many a lagging voyage before the breeze; but he always had to pole back.

Shortly after he built his raft he began to go out on the sea fishing for cod and mackerel in a small schooner with a crew made up among the neighbors. He continued at home working as a desultory fisherman and farm laborer until he was seventeen, when he "slithered off" and started life on his own account in a Yarmouth tannery. He did not, however, find the change congenial and was often down on the wharves nights and Sundays climbing over the vessels. In a few months he had shipped for Dublin as an ordinary seaman and the next four years were spent on the Atlantic. Then he voyaged to California, tried salmon fishing in Oregon, went to China and Australia, and suffered shipwreck on the coast of Borneo. He was not long in becoming an officer and at the age of twenty-three was master of a California coaster. A dozen years later he had command of the *Northern Light*, one of the finest sailing vessels of its time. As a whole he had been remarkably fortunate and prosperous, and presently he bought a ship for himself—the *Aquidneck*—and

engaged in trade on the coast of Brazil. But things now began to go wrong and they culminated in the wreck of the vessel. It was not insured and he lost all he had gained in his long years of voyaging. He had come to consider New England his home, and to return thither with his wife and two boys who had been his companions on the ill-fated *Aquidneck* he concluded to build and navigate his own boat. So he constructed the *Liberdade*, a craft not much larger than a good sized rowboat, and in this the family made one of the most interesting and original voyages ever sailed.

They came safe to port and the captain started life anew. But misfortune dogged his heels and nearly every venture he made, whether on land or sea, turned out a dismal failure. He recalled many times that happy voyage on the *Liberdade*. It seemed as if the only way to be care free was to go on another voyage of that kind. The idea harmonized with his innate love of adventure, and he soon set to work building the *Spray* and at length started off around the world. The project had become known and through the kindness of interested well wishers he left Boston fairly well equipped except in the matter of money. In cash he possessed scarcely ten cents. This financial weakness several times threatened to cut short his voyage in the earlier part of it, but always some one came to his aid in the nick of time. Then he discovered that everywhere he went there was great curiosity with regard to the boat and its owner's adventures and plans. At a number of ports he charged a small admission fee. As a show the *Spray* was very profitable; but it was a severe task to handle the crowds and answer the multitude of questions. "I never worked so hard in my life," he says. "I would be dog-tired at night and drop right down."

To escape this labor he finally, in Tasmania, hired a hall and told his story to an audience, instead of repeating it to individuals on his boat. The lecture was a success and he frequently repeated it as he continued his wanderings. The result was that he returned from his cruise with a bag full of sovereigns and a new vocation. He had hardly set foot on his native soil when he began to get requests to relate his adventures for publication. These

The Lonely Lookout of the *Spray*.

he wrote out one winter living on the *Spray* in the Erie Basin at Brooklyn. He became intensely interested in the work and could do nothing else, often sticking to his task in the tiny cabin of the boat until after midnight.

The story, both in its magazine printing and in book form, was exceptionally successful and won for him a wide reputation. It is not only unique in itself, but it is told in a most engaging way. Its evident

loss of the *Aquidneck* and his subsequent hard luck that made him a writer, and he now declares that his troubles were all good fairies in disguise.

Of late the captain has become a thoroughgoing landsman and has cast anchor on a little Martha's Vineyard farm, where he lives on the outskirts of a rural village with several old sea captains for neighbors. His house is one of the most ancient on the island—an oak-ribbed ark of

The Crew at Breakfast.

faithfulness to the facts, its lucidity, and its never failing vim and humor are charming. The wonder is that a man with such a limited boyhood education, and who had been knocking about the sea nearly ever since, should be able to turn to authorship and express himself so forcibly and fluently. The only hint of a literary turn of mind that showed itself in his youth was a habit he had for a time of copying jokes and anecdotes that pleased him from the newspapers into a blank book. It was the

a dwelling with warped floors and tiny window panes and open fireplaces. Its aspect is at present rather forlorn and naked, but the captain knows how to wield the hammer and the saw, and will soon make it snug. In a single season he has become an enthusiastic agriculturist, is proud of his flourishing garden and would like to own and make fruitful all the land round about. He delights to point out the beauties of the sturdy oak woods which overspread much of the region, the prom-

The Slocums' Pleasure on Shore.

ising condition of the abounding huckleberry bushes, the possibilities of the wet hollows for cranberry culture and of the protected slopes for fruit trees, and he is sure the island water is the sweetest and purest in the world. Martha's Vineyard looks to him like Eden, and it seems likely the sea will know him no more.

So much the better for the rest of us if, as a consequence, we shall see and hear him oftener. The aroma and salt spray of Old Ocean are in his conversation and his writings. He has the power to invigorate and refresh, and the records of that round-the-world-voyage on the *Spray* and of that other long voyage on the *Liberdade* rank among the most enchanting sea narratives ever written.

A Cruise
in a Pilot Boat
(1887)

A CRUISE IN A PILOT-BOAT.

AT THE LIGHT-SHIP.
UNDER STUDDING SAILS.   PILOT-BOAT UNDER FULL SAIL.   BOUND OUT.

FEW of those who have heard of, or have seen, the trim pilot-boats of New York Bay are aware what a thorough preparatory education and experience is required of a New York pilot. Nor is it generally known how systematic is the organization which regulates the movements of these pilots, and what hazards they must encounter in plying their vocation on the boisterous Atlantic.

Having accepted a cordial invitation to take a cruise in the *Caprice*, Mr. Burns and myself were notified to keep ourselves in readiness to sail at a moment's warning. The schooner was then at sea, but was expected back at any hour to pick up her pilots and provisions. More than a week passed, however, before we were notified to be at the pier on the following morning. The *Caprice* had been detained by severe weather, which gave us the promise of a boisterous trip. When we reached the office of the Pilot Commissioners,—a low-studded, elbow-shaped room, on the corner of Burling Slip,—everything portended a storm. A massive antique mahogany desk, at one side, served partially to conceal the busy secretary of the department, whose position is by no means a sinecure. All the multifarious accounts, together with most of the shore business of the pilots, pass under his eye. Between two windows stood a large and elaborate chronometer clock, including with it a barometer and thermometer, and around the room were ranged a number of closets or lockers. One by one the pilots straggled in, took a look at the glass, and discussed the prospects of the weather, which

45

was pronounced to be unusually foreboding, with the mercury ranging below twenty-nine degrees and a sky of the most sinister aspect.

By half-past nine, the pilots who belonged to the *Caprice* having arrived, we started for the pier where she was lying. I confess the prospect of a cruise in such a graceful little craft filled me with enthusiasm. She was ninety-six feet long and twenty feet beam, and drew eleven feet aft. Not over-sparred, like too many of our yachts, her masts were beautiful sticks and admirably proportioned, without a knot or a crack. The cabin was coziness itself; nothing can exceed the comfort of a snug little cabin when all hands but the watch are below, the swinging lamp is lit, and the long steady howl of the gale and the boom of the seas breaking on deck blend in a sublime organ-peal—the tumult of the storm often rising above the jests and yarns of the men gathered around the table or lying in their bunks with feet dangling over the side. A stove was firmly fixed in the center, on a brightly burnished plate of brass. On each side were a state-room and two berths that could be closed by slides. The galley and quarters of the crew were amidships, and were divided from the cabin by a bulkhead. The crew included four able seamen, a swarthy lascar cook, a cabin-boy, and the boat-keeper. The latter commands the schooner, and takes her back to port after all the pilots have been put on board other vessels. But before that, the boat is under the direction of the pilot whose turn it is to board the next ship.

We put to sea with six pilots, the full complement being seven. These formed a joint-stock company, but while all were licensed pilots, they were not all of equal rank. This matter of rank underlies the whole principle involved in piloting according to the laws of the State of New York, and a *résumé* of the regulations is therefore pertinent, while the schooner is making sail. The number of pilot-boats licensed to run out of the port of New York is fixed by law; it is now twenty-eight, and they register from forty to seventy tons. Each boat is obliged to carry its number in enormous black figures on the mainsail. These boats are owned by about one hundred and seventy pilots, but, strange to say, they are never said to be manned except when left in charge of the boat-keeper. Including pilots and crews, this fleet of schooners gives employment to nearly four hundred men. In this survey we do not, of course, include the New Jersey pilots who sail out of New York Bay, but are subject to the laws of the other State. This number is by no means excessive when we consider that the

foreign entries and departures of vessels in the port of New York are at present over ten thousand a year, while the coastwise entries and departures are nearly four times that number. Coasting vessels, though they often find it expedient to employ a pilot, are at liberty to decline to take one. But vessels coming from, or bound to, foreign ports have no option in the matter. If a pilot-boat can get near enough to hail them, they must either accept a pilot or pay the full charges he would be entitled to receive if he boarded that ship. This law is by no means so unfair as some might regard it. The pilots must devote much time and expense to qualify themselves for their business, and are exposed to great perils. Unless they are protected by the laws from the whims of sea-captains, the profits of pilotage would be so reduced that it would be impossible to induce capable men to enter the service. While it may be alleged that in fine weather their services are often not needed, on the other hand, emergencies frequently arise when a good pilot is indispensable.

The responsibility devolving on a pilot, and the extent of his qualifications, may be partly appreciated when one learns that, immediately on boarding a vessel, he takes command, and is answerable for any accident until he has discharged his duty of taking the vessel in or out of port. If any mishap befall the ship at that time, he is liable to have his license revoked, and thus lose all further opportunity of plying his vocation. The New York pilot must, therefore, for the good of all concerned, pass through a long and rigorous course of training. He must serve, man and boy, before the mast till he masters every problem in the management of every form of rig. To this he must add a thorough knowledge of navigation. Then he must contrive to obtain the position of boat-keeper or pilot's mate. In that capacity, he must serve three full years on one pilot-boat before he can be admitted for his examination for a license. If through ill-fortune he lose his position, he must begin *de novo*, and serve the full time on another boat. Sometimes, a boat-keeper serves nine or ten years on various boats before his apprenticeship is complete. After all this, he must pass a most rigid examination on all points of seamanship and navigation before the Board of Pilot Commissioners, and exhibit a thorough knowledge of the tides, rips, sands, and all other phenomena for hundreds of miles out from the piers of the East and North rivers. But even after receiving his license, he is sometimes forced to wait years, until some pilot happens to die and leave a vacancy for him. The first year

ICED UP.

of pilotage, he is granted a license to pilot vessels drawing less than sixteen feet. If he give satisfaction, the following year he is permitted to take charge of ships drawing eighteen feet. If he pass a satisfactory examination the third year, he then receives a full license, entitling him to pilot vessels of any draught, and is then first called a branch or full pilot.

This matter of draft often gives rise to amusing maneuvers between captain and pilot—the former sometimes endeavoring to evade a correct statement of the actual draft of the vessel at the time, and the latter in turn employing his wits to get at the truth without appearing to doubt the word of the captain. Vessels drawing under fourteen feet pay three dollars and seventy cents a foot; the rate increases by degrees, until ships drawing twenty-one feet and upward pay six dollars and fifty cents per foot.

On receiving his license, the pilot must give bonds for the proper discharge of his duty, and he is liable to heavy fines if he declines to fill a vacancy or to board a vessel making signals for a pilot. He is also required to be temperate in his habits and of reputable character. The proper execution of these regulations is to a large degree insured by the great competition among the boats, and the consequent vigilance of each to detect delinquencies in his rivals.

It is evident that to be a New York pilot is no sinecure, and that the position is one of great responsibility and trust.

In a few moments the *Caprice* was stealing past Castle Garden, and leaving behind her the towering roofs and spires of the lower part of New York. Nothing could be more disheartening than the pall of sullen clouds that hung over the bay. There was scarcely any wind, but the glass and the sky indicated that we were either in the center of a revolving storm or that one was rapidly approaching. But there were also signs of a shift of the wind into the north-west, and a few vessels bound south had concluded to venture out, and were gliding with the tide toward the Narrows.

No sooner had we put off into the stream than the pilots began to look about for a possible prize. Their keen enterprise was illustrated sooner than I expected. Scarcely had we shoved off from the pier when we saw a schooner putting to sea a mile away.

"Johnnie, head her for that schooner," said one of the pilots, to the man at the wheel.

"You can't catch her," said another.

"Yes, we can. She's only got her foresail and jib up."

"She'll have her mainsail up in a minute. They're hoisting it now."

"I don't care if they be. We'll catch her, anyway."

And catch her we did, by making all sail with man-of-war speed. Hauling under her stern, we hailed her, and sent a pilot on board to guide her past Sandy Hook. We then took some provisions from Staten Island, and glided through the Narrows. We picked up our pilot at the station-boat. This leads us to notice that one of the pilot fleet is always stationed off Sandy Hook, to serve as a rendezvous to pilots when they leave vessels, after having piloted them out of New York. The boat anchors between the lightship and Sandy Hook for four days, when another boat takes her place. When the weather is very bad, the station-boat lies off and on. Sometimes she is forced to make a harbor herself, but it is wild weather indeed when she is obliged to do that. A penalty of one hundred dollars a day is enforced on every boat that delays to appear at the station when its turn has arrived.

The storm signal was flying at Sandy Hook, but it is not for pilots to observe its warning, and we ran out to sea and headed south. At night-fall we double-reefed the mainsail and hove to. We were now in the water where the *Caprice*, at Christmas-time two years ago, encountered the most frightful dangers. Every sea that came on board froze, until the ice on deck was twelve inches thick, and it was feared she might founder with the weight of the ice. Great blocks of ice grew on the furled jib, and could not be detached without tearing the sail. On New Year's Eve, William Wright, the boat-keeper, entered in the ship's log-book: "January 1st and a happy New Year!" Five days after that, another hand entered on the pages of the same logbook the following terse but tragic record: "Thursday, 6th. Blowing hard from N. E. At 4 A. M. hauled the jib down. Lost a man off the bowsprit. Hove the yawl out and lost two men and the yawl; then hove the other yawl out and lost her. Lay around tacking till daylight, and kept a lookout on the mast-head till 8 A. M. Then started for town at 1 P. M." One of these poor fellows was Wright, the boat-keeper. One month more, and he would have been licensed as a pilot!

Two years before this, the *Caprice* was hove on her beam-ends in a terrific squall, losing both masts and a man who was in the rigging. On still another occasion she was tripped by a huge wave and nearly filled. Momentarily expecting her to go down, the crew took to the boats and were picked up. The schooner survived the gale, however, was towed into port by a passing vessel, and

was repurchased at auction by her former owners. On another occasion she was run into by a steamer, cut down to the water's edge and sunk in shoal water, from which she was raised again. She seems to lead a charmed life, but her career well illustrates some of the hazards of piloting—which are so well appreciated by the underwriters that they charge ten per cent. premium for insuring pilotboats.

Nothing of note occurred during the first night, and after running south for a few hours after daylight, we had just hove to again with the helm lashed, when the lookout at the mast-head cried:

"A pilot-boat on the weather bow, sir."

Immediately the order rang out, in quick, sharp tones:

"Shake out the reefs of the mainsail and keep her away!"

An exciting race followed between the two pilot-boats, several miles apart, to reach a large ship standing north. Now rising, now plunging over the gray seas, and staggering under a press of canvas, we neared the prize only to see it snatched from our grasp by the other boat. No sooner was that fact ascertained than we shortened sail, the lookout was sent aloft to his usual eyrie at the fore cross-trees, and the pilots, without so much as a word of regret, returned to studying the chart, reading a threadbare novel, fingering the well-thumbed cards, or snatching a little sleep in their bunks. This is about the ordinary routine in a pilot-schooner during good weather—intervals of seeming quiet broken by sudden alternations of the utmost excitement, together with a feverish, endless vigilance from mast-head and deck.

Nothing of note occurred on the third day; the recent prevailing winds had kept vessels out at sea. The third night it blew half a gale, and we hove to under close reefs about forty miles south-east of Barnegat light. About ten o'clock, the lights of a steamer heading northward were faintly descried in the mysterious gloom that overhung the sea.

"Give her a torch!" was the order that instantaneously followed the discovery. A tub containing turpentine was brought on deck; a ball of cotton was dipped into this and set on fire. It resembled the contrivance used to light cigars, except on a larger and ruder scale. The torch was so held as to illuminate the large numbers on the mainsail. Nothing more picturesque can be imagined than this contrast of light and shade—the dark figure in uncouth oil suit standing on the low, reeling deck, fiercely whirling the ball of fire over his head, and the ruddy sail and rigging clear-cut against the impenetrable blackness

ON THE LOOKOUT.

of night, while the wind whistled through the cordage and the foam seemed to turn into blood as it washed on board.

The steamer, which proved to be a coastwise craft, gradually drew nearer and passed by, heedless of the signal. The excitement was over, and all hands but the watch turned in. At four we signaled a second steamer, and discovered the torch of another schooner in our vicinity.

On the following morning, a wild scene presented itself to view when I went on deck. The gale which had been blowing around us, and of which we had had a taste during the night, had suddenly shifted into the north-west, and was shrieking out of that quarter, with every prospect of increasing. The quick, short, emerald waves, smitten with the gold of the sun bursting over the low shores of New Jersey, were streaked with foam and were rising fast. As it was useless to look for inbound vessels with this wind, and as its force might increase to a dangerous degree, we de-

cided to beat in under the land, where we should find smooth water. It was a long and arduous pounding with the seas, but finally we found ourselves close under the sand dunes of Little Egg Harbor. Then we wore ship, and trimmed the sheets to run up the coast to Sandy Hook. Several other pilot-boats were in company, and an impromptu race immediately ensued. Not to speak too technically, it suffices to say we were under very short sail. The sky was a clear, crisp azure, flecked with swiftly scudding wind-clouds. The blasts swept off the land with exceeding violence and suddenness, laying the little vessel over on her side and burying her lee rail under a mass of boiling foam, the spray smoking under her bow the while, and blowing off to leeward in sheets. Thus hour after hour went by in this stimulating race. Hour after hour, also, we threaded our way through a fleet of coasting schooners, that were taking advantage of the northerly gale to run down the coast in ballast. Their swelling sails gleamed like flakes of flame over the intense amethystine blue of the sea, that was ridged with long crests of foam. We flew past the lofty light-house of Barnegat and its whitening reefs, past the cedar-tufted banks of Manasquan, the sloping cottages of Elberon, the spacious hotels of Long Branch, the pointed gables of Seabright, and the twin watch-towers of the Highlands, until the sentinel shaft of Sandy Hook loomed grandly in the north, and the splendor of the setting sun suffused land and sea and sky with indescribable beauty. Then we headed up into a cove behind the Hook, dropped anchor close by the beach, and went below to a smoking supper. Though the quartering moon shone gloriously that evening, we all snatched a much-needed slumber before venturing out once more to encounter the wild March winds on the gray wastes of the Atlantic.

At dawn we made sail, and stood due east along the shore of Long Island before half a gale of wind. At ten o'clock we discovered a pilot-boat ahead, and crowded on sail to overhaul her. While she was in sight our movements would be necessarily influenced by her own. Finding that we were overhauling her, she finally put her helm down and headed south.

We kept on to the east, deciding to go as far as Saint George's Bank after steamers. These vessels are the great prizes in the pilot lottery, because their draft averages more than that of sailing ships. To secure an inbound steamer also insures piloting her out again. Ocean steamers are therefore very desirable game, and great risks are encountered in order to intercept them. The opposite ex-

STEADY!

treme are Norwegian barks, for they are small and generally come to this country in ballast. "To get a Norwegian bark" is therefore considered a good joke on the poor fellow whose luck it is to board one. Steamers which are exclusively freight boats, and are irregular in their sailing days and slow in their movements, are called "tramps," and are also not held in high esteem by the pilots. The cruises to the eastward are sometimes, although rarely, protracted to twenty or thirty days. But the average luck is good.

The following evening, when we were well eastward of Nantucket light-ship, a steamer was reported heading directly for us. Immediately the cards were flung aside, and in a moment every soul was on deck. The pilot whose turn it was to board the next vessel, after a hurried survey of the steamer, exclaimed:

"Boys, good-bye. Finish the game for yourselves!"

He then dashed below, and in all haste put on a "boiled" shirt and a Sunday-go-to-meeting suit, and packed his valise. It should be remembered that these steamers are rather more "swell" than sailing ships, and seem to demand a corresponding difference in apparel. In the meantime, the torch was blazing on deck in the liveliest manner. The needle-like points of light representing the steamer gradually approached, and at last the huge, vague form of the vessel herself could be defined. But she already had a pilot, and paid no attention to us. The game in the cabin was resumed at once, and the

"boiled" shirt was once more folded up and laid away carefully in the locker. The precariousness of steamer-catching is well illustrated by this matter of dressing to board them. One of our pilots told us that he had actually shaved and dressed six times in one trip, for a steamer, before he had succeeded in boarding one. There is a tradition of a pilot who dressed seventeen times before success crowned his perseverance.

Morning broke on a savage scene; enormous mounds of water, crested with foam, swelled up against the sky and tossed the little *Caprice* like an egg-shell. The gale increasing with great fury, we hove to under try-sails—sails scarcely larger than a table-cloth, showing a spread of canvas so moderate that, as they say at sea, we were under "a three-reefed mitten with the thumb brailed up." The squalls were tremendous, and were accompanied by blinding sheets of snow, which seemed to sweep from the horizon in a moment and envelop the sea in impenetrable gloom; the decks and rigging were robed in ermine. The gale increased to a hurricane. The little schooner for the most part rode easily, but sometimes a sea, that seemed to go bodily over her, would strike her, and might have sunk her but for the low bulwarks, only a foot high, that allowed the water to run off; sometimes, too, she was carried over so far that there was danger of her rolling com-

A GLIMPSE OF THE SUN.

LAUNCHING THE BOAT.

pletely over. Three times during the day we wore ship in order that we might not be driven out of the track of the steamers; whatever the weather, business was never forgotten. This maneuver was, under the circumstances, one of extreme peril, and required the greatest skill and circumspection.

The sun went down over one of the wildest scenes I have ever witnessed at sea. With some difficulty we managed to get supper, while the deafening roar of the howling winds and the thunder of the surges pounding on deck almost deadened the conversation that went on uninterruptedly below; yarns were told, and intricate problems with cards were discussed by men in oil jackets and sou'-westers, while the cook served out rations of hot coffee. Any moment a terrific catastrophe was likely to overwhelm us, but it is not in the nature of the sailor, after he has taken every precaution, to borrow trouble about

possibilities. A vivid flash of lightning at long intervals indicated that the gale was approaching its height, and it was decided to put up stanchions, or posts, in the cabin. These were firmly fixed between the timbers of the deck and the cabin floor, to keep the ballast from shifting in case a sudden lurch should throw the schooner on her beam-ends. If the ballast had shifted, it would have been all over with us in a moment. So violent was the lurching and creaking of the little vessel, all that long, dreary night, that no one slept until toward dawn, when the weather moderated slightly.

But while the wind was less violent, it blew hard at intervals, and the temperature was so low that the deck was covered with a layer of ice. At noon we succeeded in getting an observation, the pale sun flashing for a moment through the scud and causing the heaving deep to look like molten silver. We were in longitude 66° 30′ and in 48 fathoms of water, and were heading south-west, under very short sail, when a fearful squall darkened the horizon and rushed toward us with appalling rapidity. At the same instant the lookout discovered two steamers and a pilot-boat to the eastward. The wildest excitement ensued. Reefs were shaken out, notwithstanding the squall, and the little schooner flew before the blast as if bewitched. The "boiled" shirt was put on again, winds and waves were defied, and everything was forgotten except the great fact that we must snatch the steamers from the clutches of the rival pilot-boat under our lee. When the dense pall of gloom finally passed off to leeward, the southernmost steamer was discovered to have been boarded by our rival. Every effort that skill could devise was then put forth to catch the other steamer. As we lessened the distance, the *Caprice* was hove to and awaited her approach. Slowing up, the great Cunarder gradually drew toward us, majestically mounting and plunging on the vast surges, while cataracts poured from her hawse-holes as the bow soared skyward. At this exciting moment an enormous whale, little, if any, shorter than our schooner, arose close alongside the *Caprice*, and, spouting as if to salute her, dived again into the depths.

The yawl, only sixteen feet long, was now launched over our lee side into the frothing waters, and with two seamen and the pilot started for the steamer, then a quarter of a mile distant. I confess it was a thrilling spectacle to see this mere cockleshell, with her precious freight of three lives, now lifted far above us on a mountainous billow, and now descending out of sight into the depths of a hollow vale, and hiding there until it seemed as if she would never appear again.

By slow degrees the yawl succeeded in reaching the lee side of the steamer. There again the greatest prudence was required to prevent her from being swamped by the action of the mighty hull, rolling deep in the turbulent sea. At last we saw the pilot, the merest speck, spring on the ladder and creep up the side of the steamer. Then came the yet more difficult task of picking up the yawl. The way it was done was by keeping her head to the wind, and allowing her to drift down toward the schooner. By wearing, we kept directly in the track of the yawl; she slipped across our stern, and pulling up under the lee side, was hauled on board.

As can be easily imagined, one of the pilot's most arduous duties is to board a vessel in heavy weather. Each pilot-schooner is provided with two yawls. They are lashed to the deck, bottom upward, and are lifted and launched over the low side of the schooner by means of a light tackle reaching down from the mast-heads, and hooked into the stem and stern. The pilot-yawls differ from other boats in that they are short, broad, and deep, and are thus very buoyant. It is not an uncommon circumstance for men to be lost when boarding vessels. Both yawls of one of our New York pilot-boats were successively capsized last winter, when trying to board the *Arizona* in a gale of wind. Happily the men were picked up by the lifeboats of the steamer, after great exertion.

It is with regret that I must add that the pilots are sometimes unfairly treated by the captains of the regular transatlantic lines. There is too often a disreputable reason why these steamers give the go-by to pilot-boats that are almost within hail, and pick up another that is beyond. Almost every passenger who has crossed on the regular lines has had experience of the various black-mailing schemes that are sprung on the passengers toward the close of the voyage. Now it is to make up a purse for the captain, who has simply done his duty for a good salary, and no more requires a testimonial than other men who fulfill their duty in their chosen pursuits; or, again, money is solicited for some absurd or imaginary scheme, generally in the name of charity. Only those who have crossed a number of times discover that this is black-mail pure and simple under disguise, and that it is generally engineered by blatant and officious passengers, who have axes of their own to grind. It is black-mail because it is generally brought forward in such a manner that even those who see through the business are forced to contribute, in order to avoid the charge of stinginess. But the worst form of this vile business which assails the luckless passenger on board these steamships is the system of gambling called betting on the number of the pilot-boat that shall board the steamer.

I remember a minister, inexperienced in matters of real life, who urged me to subscribe to the list of those who were betting on the number of our prospective pilot-boat. "My dear sir," I replied to him, "don't you see that this is nothing more nor less than gambling?" But he could not be convinced, and lost his money. Why he lost, and why others lose on such a wager, is explicable in a few words. The captain and some of his officers often join in the betting—of course through other persons—or they have friends among the betters whom they are willing to favor. The passengers, on the other hand, are generally so ignorant of nautical matters that the captain can do as he pleases with little risk

BOARDING A STEAMER.

of detection. For this reason, he can steer out of the way of a pilot-boat that is not the one on which he has staked his money, and go out of his course to take a pilot from the boat on which he has staked his money. It is true that, sometimes, he may not come across that one; but, in most cases, the game is in his hands, while the passenger, on the other hand, little knows that he is so heavily handicapped. We have heard that the master of one of the largest steamers going out of New York had a serious altercation, growing out of a transaction of this sort, with one of his passengers, who was sharper than the majority of the class.

On the eighth day out, we were four hundred and fifty miles east of New York, on the southern edge of Saint George's Bank. At one time, we passed off soundings into blue water for a few hours, a fact proclaimed in sonorous tones by one of the pilots, when he sang out :

> " No sound,
> 　No ground,
> 　　No bottom to be found
> With a long pitch-pine pole, daddy."

The day was gloriously beautiful, the sky cloudless, and the swell remaining after the gale was scarcely dimpled by the zephyr-like cat's-paws.

One of the crack boats of the New York pilot-fleet loomed above the western horizon, carrying every stitch of canvas. Her shapely sails gleaming in the morning sun, she gradually crept up in our wake, while another pilot-boat was also visible in the eastern board. Circumstances being thus against us, we hauled to the wind on the starboard tack, and headed south until we had run them both out of sight.

"Our policy is to scatter," dryly remarked one of our pilots, a tall, slender Scotchman, of large intelligence and an inexhaustible stock of dry humor.

A standing reward of two dollars for the discovery of a steamer was now offered to the crew, whose vigilance was thus greatly stimulated, although it would have been impossible to sharpen their sense of sight.

"Sail ho!" rang from the mast-head at noon. It proved to be a sailing-ship far to the southward. The wind was so light we could not hope to reach her except by sending out a yawl. But the uncertain nature of the season made this inexpedient. This hazardous method is, however, quite frequently followed by our pilots in calm weather. Its nature is well indicated by the following adventure, which befell one of the pilots of the *Caprice* some years ago :

It was on a summer day. A dead calm prevailed. They were forty miles south of Long Island. A bark lay eight miles away, motionless. The pilot-schooner was also unable to move. But it would not do to allow the prize to escape, as she might do if a breeze should strike her sails first. It was decided to row in the yawl to the bark. Eight miles, as every one knows, is quite a distance with oars, or, as it is called, with a "white-ash breeze." But the weather promised to continue fine, and the pilot and his two men started off without water, provisions, compass, or sail. Gradually they gained on the chase. But night was creeping on; the cat's-paws stealing along the horizon suggested, too, that they had better hasten their strokes or the bark would get away from them. By great good fortune, as it seemed to them, they finally came almost within hailing distance of her. Five minutes more and they would have boarded her!—when the coming wind

filled her flapping sails, and they had the mortification to see her slowly glide away. Their frantic shouts, if heard, were unheeded. They found themselves alone on the wide ocean, parched with thirst, and weary and hungry. Night was coming on apace. A low, wailing wind was moaning from the south, and as soon as the sun sank out of sight the sea began to rise, and storm-clouds obscured the hazy light of the stars. At that juncture their schooner, which had been following, came not far from them ; but, supposing they had been picked up by the bark, did not perceive them, and again their shouts were unheard. Then, indeed, they gave themselves up for lost. The nearest land was forty miles away. As the wind was blowing it would sweep them toward it, while the increasing violence of the gusts foreboded a sea so wild that they must almost inevitably be swamped and drowned in making a landing. Yet their only course was to drive before the wind, and trust to luck to extricate them from their perilous situation. As night wore on, the storm increased ; often the little boat shipped water and seemed on the verge of destruction. Every moment was bringing them nearer to the crisis of their fate. Toward dawn, when the night is darkest, they heard the thunder of surf on the reefs, and faintly discerned, in the gloom, the ghostly pallor of the upward-driven foam. Exhausted as they were, they yet kept their wits about them to seize any possibility of escape that might offer. In one spot there seemed to be a break in the ridge of foam. Skillfully guiding the boat toward it, in another instant they felt the yawl lifted up on the crest of an enormous breaker rushing with lightning speed toward the land. A deafening roar succeeded, a crash, a whirl, and a torrent of foam. In a twinkling the boat was capsized, and the men were borne far up on the beach. One struck a rock and was drowned. The others, as the wave receded, ran up the sand. When the next wave followed, they dug their hands into the beach and held on, lest they should be swept away by the under-tow. But for the fortunate break in the reef through which they had guided the boat, they would all have been lost.

TWO DAYS of perfect weather, each closed with a sunset of magical splendor, were followed by a change. The glass began to fall ; cloud-streamers arched over the zenith from horizon to horizon. A sad wind moaned over the heaving deep, and a mist gradually closed us in. Then came fitful showers, and, between the flaws, the little schooner flapped her slatting sails with foreboding dreariness.

REEFING THE MAINSAIL.

Another storm was stealing upon us. During the day—it was Sunday—we saw a number of steamers, bound eastward, which had left New York on the previous day. I should add that for two days we had been heading westward, and were now not far from the Nantucket light-ship. An inbound steamer was also seen from the mast-head, and we flung out all the kites and let our little schooner fly at her wildest rate. Here seemed a fair chance at last, for we were apparently south of the pilot-boats we had previously seen, while the whole horizon round revealed not a boat in sight. But, after another mad chase, our hopes were blasted in a moment when the steamer hung out her signal to inform us she was provided with a pilot.

That night there was a snow-ring around the moon, and the glass was still slowly falling. On the following day we had a very exciting chase after a White Star boat. But she, again, had been already boarded. At four P. M. the wind, which had been whiffling about in a dubious manner to all points of the compass,

settled into a strong, steady breeze from the east, and by night-fall it blew half a gale.

"Call all hands to reef!" rang through the ship, and soon the crew were ranged along the booms, shortening sail. A wild night was before us. For a while we hove to, in order to be in the track of steamers, reasoning that as the wind was likely to hold awhile it would prevent other boats from getting far east of New York, and thus we should have a fair chance of not being interrupted in our chances by interlopers. But, as the gale freshened, it seemed unlikely that we should board any vessel in the weather now threatening, and the helm was put up and we stood west again. We had now been out twelve days.

At sunset the sky was completely obscured by a dense canopy of cloud. Just as the sun rested on the ocean's verge, the clouds lifted enough to allow the sun to burst forth and illumine the horizon with a line of vivid fire, below which the ocean rolled intensely sullen and livid. But who can describe the awful magnificence which irradiated the entire heav-

HOVE TO FOR A PILOT.

ens with a volcanic glow! The sky was like the dome of a vast oven heated to the last degree. At the same moment a shower fell on the sea, and immediately two perfect rainbows spanned the firmament. Then, as if a curtain had been drawn across the scene, night closed in, and the wild winds howled over a little ship tossing alone on a dreary waste of waves.

It blew very hard that night. A dangerous cross-sea set in, and twice the *Caprice* was nearly thrown on her beam-ends with terrific lurches. We kept a bright light at the masthead and a double lookout, for it was an uncanny time for a collision, and we were directly in the track of ships.

On the following day it moderated, but the wind, which had only "backed in," shifted from north to east after dark. This brought a corresponding change of weather. Rain and fog set in, and a very puffy breeze that settled into a gale before morning. We ran westward all night under short sail, taking casts of the lead at intervals. Soon after ten,

the atmosphere being thick, but not so much so as to prevent us from discerning objects the distance of a mile, we discovered a sailing-ship ahead, evidently running for New York, and probably in need of a pilot. Edging away toward her, we lit our torch, and had the satisfaction of seeing her send up a couple of rockets in response. At the same time she backed her reefed main-topsail and hove to. Running down on her lee side, we also hove to very near to her, and proceeded to launch the yawl. It was a wild scene as the little boat vanished into the darkness, perhaps never to be seen again. But her crew carried a lantern with them, and after they had left the pilot on board the ship, we were able to shape our movements by this little glimmer bobbing up and down like an *ignis fatuus* in the misty dark. As the night wore on, the fog grew so dense that we brought up our six-pound brass piece from the fore peak, and fired it at short intervals; this was done, not, as one might suppose, to keep vessels from coming into collision with the schooner, but to inform them there was a pilot-boat in the vicinity. But this very fact required redoubled vigilance on our part, in order that we might not be run down. In the middle watch we were startled, just after firing the cannon, by the answering whistle of a steamer hoarsely coming down the wind, and close at hand. The excitement of the moment was intense. Again we fired the cannon. The whistle drew nearer, and all at once the colored lights of a steamer loomed out of the dripping mist, and her huge bow emerged from the gloom, so near that it actually seemed to overhang our deck. Passing close alongside, she slowed up the palpitation of her mighty engine a moment to make sure of our position, and then vaguely glided out of sight.

On the following morning, the sun was invisible. The war of the elements was raging with increasing fury. The wind had shifted to south-east. The fog was less dense, and we could see some distance. We were running under a bit of foresail, and hardly needed that. It seemed, at times, as if the following seas would founder the schooner as they towered over the low taffrail. Not a sail was in sight, not even a solitary gull; it is a curious fact that, excepting the petrels, seabirds keep near to the land in bad weather. By means of the patent log towing astern and from casts of the lead, we knew we could not be far from Sandy Hook light-ship.

About ten, the light-ship hove in sight. We rushed by it at the rate of thirteen knots. An enormous sea was rolling over the bar, but the depth of water was enough for vessels like the *Caprice*, and by skillful steering she passed over handsomely. The fierceness of the wind was now terrific, and, dowsing the foresail, we ran up the Lower Bay and flew through the Narrows under bare poles. Thus ended a most delightful and entertaining cruise.

Through an Autumn Gale (1896)

THROUGH AN AUTUMN GALE.

By "Windward."

IT all happened simply because we wanted to add one more first prize to our winnings for the season. But the best laid plans "gang aft agley"; and so it was with us. The season was well along, the little *Flora Lee* had put a good year's work to her credit ; and we were feeling especially jolly, over winning first in the Fourth of July open race — the little sixteen-footer sailing in the class above her usual one and beating out the twenty-one-foot cats in a howling gale from the north-west, — when the City of Gloucester announced its open race for the latter part of August, and it was voted unanimously to make the run to Gloucester and try again. We decided to take a larger boat along as convoy, for sleeping accommodations, and fate — and a most perverse one — led us to the choice of the *Bonito*, a twenty-five-foot cabin cat. The skipper facetiously remarked that the name was a good omen, probably derived from the Latin through the Spanish, meaning good eating, from *bon*, good —*ito*, to eat. (This derivation will not bear examination.) This thought immediately caught the attention of the mate (whose capacity for grub was phenomenal), and although we had other boats in mind, the happy signification of *Bonito* so caught his fancy, that we yielded to his persistency and finally selected that craft.

The Sunday preceding our proposed start was such a beautiful day, with a gentle breeze, east to south-east, that the skipper and mate decided, in short order, to take the smaller boat down as far as "Skipper Ireson's Town" and let her lay there to await the arrival of the convoy, on Wednesday. There was a long, high roll outside, the remnants of a week's hard "sou'easter," and the skipper soon gave up the helm to the mate and took to studying the heavens, insisting that he was simply showing the devotional spirit appropriate to the day. Curiously enough, when we slid in by Marblehead Rock and rounded the light into the smooth waters of the beautiful little harbor, the devotions of the skipper came to a sudden end and he proceeded to stow away what little grub the others, taking a mean advantage of his devotions, had left for him. Tying up to a mooring and making everything snug on board, we started up through the endless paths of the quaint old town and were soon on the way back to "Bean Town," our souls filled with pity for those benighted land-lubbers who travel along shore by cars.

But the cruise proper began on Wednesday, when we took the *Bonito* in hand. Tearing ourselves away from business cares in the early afternoon, the clan assembled; and, after the usual hurry of preparation, during which the skipper tried to sail her over one of the Club rafts, we started off. It took only a couple of tacks to the windward for us to find out that the *Bonito* was not a "wind-jammer." But we finally worked out by Scarecrow Light, and, the breeze favoring us by hauling to the southward, we eased sheets and cracked on the jib for the run to the town of lost paths and endless streets. Seeing the forty-six-footer *Alborak* standing out of the harbor, with Captain Haff at the helm, we deluded ourselves into thinking we could race with her, and, although the breeze was freshening, we laid the old *Bonito* out and drove her through the growing sea as hard as we dared. We slid rapidly down by Nahant, and, the *Alborak* running in there, our attention was given to our own craft for the first time since the start. If memory serves, the discovery was caused by the command of the mate to the cabin boy to bring up some grub from the cabin. As the latter started to go below, he cried out that the boat was leaking; and, sure enough, we found that while we had been racing, the sea had been coming into the old craft. We pitched the things out of the cabin, on deck, in a vain effort to get them dried before we got into Marblehead. But the prospect was not pleasant; for the incident had given us some wet clothes and bedding, a damp cabin and, worst of all, the prospect of spending three or four days in a leaky boat. Naturally, our spirits were rather dampened as we ran into Marblehead a little after sunset. But after we got our ground tackle down and snugged things up for the night, and especially when we had stowed away our supper, we began to feel a little more cheerful, things took on a brighter hue, and it was finally determined to wait till morning before deciding whether to give up the *Bonita* and take solely to the *Flora*, quietly resting in North Shore waters.

Morning broke beautiful and clear, with a gentle breeze still from the east; the gaily colored cottages on the Neck shining, and the blue waves of the harbor sparkling in the beautiful, bright sunlight. Marblehead Harbor on such a morning is as unique and picturesque as must be some of the bold refuges and coves on the rocky shores of Brittany. Despite the changes that wealth has wrought on the Neck, and business progress in the old town by the water; the sharp outline of the little bay; the bold peninsula stretching like a protecting arm into the sea, holding in its hand a beacon light ; the massive gray rocks blocking the entrance to the harbor, stretching down the North Shore and seeming to oppose their quiescent power to the strength of all old Ocean's force—irresistibly carry the mind back to those earlier days when the life of the town was primitive and quaint, when strength and courage were the essential virtues of the Marbleheader, as the hard-hearted old skipper learned to his cost.

The beautiful morning and the glimpses of the bright blue waters to the northward soon put away all thought of giving up our trip, and notwithstanding a leaky boat and a damp cabin, we determined to stick by the old craft and carry out our original programme.

The little *Flora* we found none the worse for her rest, and, dividing our crew—the professor and skipper going aboard the *Flora*, which we double reefed,—we stood out to the northward. Few stretches of shore, of equal length, can equal the beauty of that between Marblehead and Gloucester. Standing down inside of Baker's Island, the view seaward or landward is one seldom equaled, and certainly very rarely surpassed. Toward the sea, the view to the " open " is broken by the ragged islands; here and there stands a lighthouse or tall, gaunt, spindle, silent but constant warnings upon dangerous paths; beyond, variously shaped buoys mark jagged rocks, around which the swirling waters rise and tumble and pound with angry violence; while as far as the eye can reach stretches the great ocean in its blue infinity. Shoreward, the eye looks over the inner islands. They, too, are rough and jagged, but more sheltered and timbered,—a strip of golden beach between the ocean's blueness and the dark, restful green of the forest stretching almost to the water's edge. Surely summer cruising in such waters is yachtsmen's bliss, and a rare treat for even the most careless observer of the beauties nature scatters round us.

The sail to Gloucester was to windward, and we soon had the *Bonito* a long distance astern. It was a test, too, of the windward qualities of the " skimming dish;" for the wind began to freshen as the clouds banked up in the east, and when we were as far as Kettle Island, the *Flora* with double reefs and a crew of only two, had all the wind she wanted. When we ran in by Norman's Woe, the bell buoy was ringing violently in the rising sea, as if to warn all of the gale then brewing in the sky, and, joining the *Bonito* as she came in, we ran up round Ten Pound Island and, choosing a good berth in the inner harbor, we planted our mud-hooks.

The freshening wind and threatening sky were ominous of unpleasant weather, and soon boats from our home port came running into the harbor, all hands wet and hungry—for it had begun to rain now, some pretty well played out, but all voting the run down from Boston great fun. Among them were the *Exile*, a twenty-one-foot flyer, which had come across the bay at a steamer rate. The *Scamp,* the *Flora's* consort and rival, came in with all hands drenched and with one of her crew so played out with seasickness that he had to be held on all the way across the bay. The rain was getting decidedly frequent and wet; but we refused this time to let our spirits get dampened in the least, and all hands gathered on the *Bonito,* which became, for the rest of the cruise, a sort of rendezvous. When we turned in, each and every one offered up a fervent petition to the clerk of the weather, that he might send bright skies and favoring breezes on the morrow.

But it was not to be; for it seemed as though we were hardly asleep, when we were awakened by that indescribable feeling which tells the sailor, at once, that the vessel is dragging her anchor. It was just about two bells. Here was a pretty mess! There was no great danger, except from collision; but that one danger was quite enough; for in the small inner harbor, hardly a mile long by one-third of a mile wide, there were anchored considerably over two hundred sail, from the big fisherman down to the sixteen-foot racer.

Our first thoughts had to be directed to the safety of the boat we were on, the *Bonito*; afterwards would be time enough to look after the *Flora,* which we had anchored some little distance from the larger boats.

The wind had swung around from south-east, through the west, into the north-east, and was now coming in savage squalls, the forerunner of a north-east gale. The rain, driven by the gale and falling in torrents, made it almost impossible to see about the deck. The night was black as ink; but now and then there came a blinding flash of lightning, followed by deafening thunder. We had left an awning over the standing room and this, filling with wind, was pulling us astern at a lively rate. So far we had struck nothing; and getting the awning off and putting out our other ground tackle, we brought up temporarily. All was commotion about us; the crews on deck, getting down topmasts, putting out extra anchors, paying out scope, and making everything snug; lanterns

flashing about deck, and red coston lights flaring forth and casting weird, dancing shadows; all with confused shouting, muffled by the howling of the gale through the rigging. It was romantic;—but also uncomfortable. We made out the *Flora* riding the gale all right and soon had her in a good berth. But the *Bonito* we could not hold; she drifted alongside of a big white sloop and, having no more ground tackle, we lashed on to her and turned in once more to try and get a little sleep before morning.

Morning brought no change. The wind was whistling through the rigging and the rain was still coming down as though the weather clerk was bound to drown us in fresh water if not salt.

The inner harbor is well protected, but the number of boats scattered along the shore bore witness to the strength of the gale and the poor holding ground on the bottom. Two or three of the big fishing schooners were on shore on the southerly side of the harbor, and the anchor cables of the whole fleet were in a confused snarl, owing to the shifting of the boats in the gale. We found that the fouling of ours had been the cause of our dragging after we had put out our best bower. Casting off from our neighbors and straightening out our ground tackle, we snugged things up to ride out the gale.

And a gale it surely was! Such a one as the month of August seldom brings to our New England coast.

This was the day of the race. But for once, our crew was not anxious for a tussle with the wind and water. Clothes, boots and oilers were all wet, soaking wet; and what with poor sleep and considerable excitement for a couple of nights, we were not feeling quite in racing condition.

As the starting time drew near, some of the larger boats stood out toward the line under close reefs, and we soon learned that the Regatta Committee had shortened the course, giving all except the fishing schooners an inside course. But even this could not tempt us. The truth of the matter was that the weather and exposure had not had a very good effect. The skipper had left home with a severe cold, but with a trustful faith that a few days' outing on the water would do his cold good; but a damp cabin, and rowing around the harbor in a driving rain and howling gale, with nothing on but wet oilskins, had not had a good effect. The professor, too, was somewhat of a wreck. Even the alluring interest of some light reading he had brought with him, to wit, a professional treatise on "The Properties of Floating Bodies," had no attraction for him.

The race inside, for the yachtsmen, passed off with the usual accompaniment of broken spars and torn sails; with few competitors, however, except from the home ports, visiting yachtsmen being mindful of the long sail home and the need of spars and sails. But the fishermen's race of that day will always be remembered as "The Race" by all familiar with the racing annals of Massachusetts Bay.

When we had entered the harbor, the preceding afternoon, we had found some of the schooners taking sand aboard to ballast them, and when morning came the crews were early astir, getting their craft ready for the struggle. Never was there a day better suited to test the staunch schooners and the steady nerve, dauntless courage, and wonderful skill of the skippers and crews. Whoever has seen the handling of these schooners in crowded harbors, the nice judgment, the luffing and waring, has learned to admire the fisherman's skill—a skill more remarkable as the crews seldom have any great discipline or organization. And that day, above all others, would test their nerve and courage. They well knew the conditions they would meet outside, and life lines stretched around each schooner told the onlooker what they expected. A fifty-mile race in the bay in such a wind and sea as there was that day, is no child's play, but the stout little schooners went through it all in fine form, running off to leeward at railroad speed, jibing around Harding's Ledge bell buoy, reckless of sails, rigging and spars, and after a ten-mile sail in the trough of the sea, with lee rails and decks covered with solid water, they hauled to weather around Davis Ledge and battled out to windward, riding the huge seas bravely, but now and then plunging bows in so that the water ran

aft and to leeward in miniature Niagaras, causing all hands to hang on to the lines for dear life. The winners might well feel that they had won what was indeed a race and a test of seamanship.

Late in the afternoon, all the boats were again at their anchors, and when we turned in that night, though the gale was still whistling through the rigging and the rain driving against the house, we knew that our anchors were now planted deep enough to hold us, and that, unless the unexpected happened, we could put in a good night's sleep.

When we tumbled up on deck in the morning, we found the conditions still the same. The day drizzled away without a great deal of excitement. The streets of old Gloucester looked lifeless and desolate, even for a place then two hundred and fifty years old. Bunting, scattered profusely about, hung limply from the buildings, adding to the drenched appearance of the city; only the lofty flags floating in the gale showing any signs of animation. "Oilers" were the fashionable dress. The hotels had many visitors who had come to enjoy the celebration, but who were now forced to keep in-doors, and everybody felt that we needed a new weather bureau, even if we had to overturn the ruling administration to get it.

Before we turned in, it was agreed to start for home the next morning if the weather should moderate at all, so that the sea outside, which had been so heavy that the rollers broke, would go down some. All but the skipper turned in on the *Bonito ;* but the three days had been too much for him. Even the skill of old Dr. Barleycorn had not made him comfortable, and he took his traps ashore and put up at the hotel.

Sunday morning came, and, gathering on board, we decided to run home, the wind having moderated some and the breaking of the clouds indicating a cessation of the storm and clear weather later in the day. We were soon out by Norman's Woe. And now we could begin to appreciate the force of the gale. We noticed that the White Squadron had put to sea, but the great monitor *Miantonomah* was compelled to put back, the tremendous seas dashing over her making it impossible for her to proceed. It was a grand scene, seated in the stern of the *Flora Lee*, hardly a foot above the level of the water, to see the mighty walls of water roll up behind us, seeming as though about to overwhelm us; and then to be raised quickly, the little boat rushing ahead as if to escape the pursuer, and then, overtaken, to drop down into the hollow of a wave—down into a valley where we could hardly feel the wind, so lofty were the rollers. As nearly as we could estimate, they were running from eighteen to twenty-two feet in height—so high as to practically shut off the wind when we were in the trough of a wave. At such times, the boat would almost lose her headway, and when she rose on the top of the following wave and suddenly felt the force of the wind, it was necessary to put the helm sharp across in order to keep her on the course. It was exciting, for a broach-to, in such conditions, would have been disastrous. The *Scamp* soon left us, going in-shore; and we afterwards learned that it had been impossible to steer her. We did not see her again on our run home. We found a better breeze by keeping across the bay, although much rougher water. As we neared the ledges to the northward of Halfway Rock, the rollers ran higher still and were just on the verge of breaking, and it seemed for some time as though it would have been wiser if we, too, had run in-shore, for, if even one sea should break under us, we should probably fill in a moment, the boat being entirely open. We began to recall the professor's "Properties of Floating Bodies," and figured out that we still had the air-tanks to hold on to if worst came to worst. Finally, to keep steerage way while in the trough of the sea, we had to give the boat more sail, and the mate soon had the reefs out of the *Bonito*, and we ran along together. The sight, as we ran by Halfway Rock, was one long to be remembered. The mountains of water seemed to rush angrily and irresistibly against the lonely boulder, as if to push it under or dash it in pieces. Breaking on it with a dull roar, like distant thunder, they would dash into spray and fly into the air, glistening in the sun; while, as the waves rushed on, the old rock would seem to rise out of each contest like some disdainful, gray old leviathan, de-

spising his antagonist and contemptuously shaking himself free from him. Inside the rock, toward the shore, the water showed here and there masses of white foam, where the waves rushed over some half-sunken reef. As we looked, we could not help thinking that it is only at such times that the difficulties of early navigators can be appreciated; and surely no path was ever more beset with all the dangers that the sailor has to meet than that of the early Salem Puritans from this Halfway Rock, through the tortuous channels that lead to the "City of Witches."

As we neared Marblehead, the wind moderated, we shook out our remaining reefs, and soon ran into smoother waters. The sailing became delightful; the breeze, still east and of moderate strength, giving us a fair wind all the way home. We ran by the Outer Pigs, then by beautiful Nahant, summer residence of ultra Boston, and in by Deer Island Light, familiarly known as "Scarecrow," and were once more in the familiar waters of the Hub's most beautiful harbor.

The sail to the anchorage off the Clubhouse was soon ended, and after reporting some of the boats behind us to inquiring friends, we hauled our traps ashore, and our cruise was something of the past.

That night we "bunked" in our own rooms, each unquestionably saying to himself that, though cruising is great fun, yet after four days on a leaky, twenty-five foot boat, in such weather as we had experienced, "there's no place like home." And yet, the cruise added one more to those pleasures which the past has for us, in the remembrance of the good times and exciting experiences that went with all our old, warm, boyhood friendships; for though our yachting experience has been long and varied, though our racing has brought prizes not a few, and our cruising pleasures we shall always remember; yet we all think that no four days of ours can ever quite equal the memory of that trip along shore. We did not get the prize that was nominally the reason of our cruise, but the "Discovery of the Leak," the "Midnight Squall," and the "Sail Home," none of us will ever forget.

The Yachting Circuit of Lake Erie (1897)

OHIO Y. C. HOUSE, PRESQUE ISLE.

THE YACHTING CIRCUIT OF LAKE ERIE.

By G. F. Flannery.

ROGUE.

"READY about! H-a-r-d-a-l-e-e!" sang out the captain of the *Nox* late on the evening of the 28th of July, as the little craft made her last tack in beating out of Charlotte harbor at the mouth of the Genesee River. The twenty-seven-footer had just left her anchorage near the house of the Rochester Yacht Club, starting out for a five weeks' cruise, round the racing circuit of Lake Erie.

A light breeze and a cloudless sky brought the *Nox* to Port Dalhousie, where, anchored at the mouth of the canal, was found the *Euroclydon*, in command of Rev. C. E. Whitcombe, Commodore of the Royal Victoria Yacht Club of Hamilton. The *Nox's* crew were old friends of the Commodore, and it was a joyous meeting, to be made even more so by the arrival soon of the *Myrna*—a winner of quite a few prizes—in charge of her owner, William Briggar, and Hugh Weir as sailing master, also of Hamilton.

The usual yachting courtesies were exchanged between the captains and crews, and at eight o'clock that evening the three boats—two twenty-seven-footers, *Nox* and *Myrna*, lashed side by side, and *Rocky John*, as the Commodore's twenty-five-foot craft was dubbed, following behind—began a tow through the canal. Each boat paid a nominal toll-fee of fifty cents, and each paid five dollars toward a team to furnish the motive power.

The Welland Canal, as is well known, connects Lakes Erie and Ontario, and

NOX.

SCUD, OF TOLEDO.

from the lake, while a northerly wind will lower it nearly as much, forcing the water in the channel out into the lake.

That trip through the canal was deeply interesting, through a night of ceaseless activity. No one went below for more than a few minutes at a time. The boiling water which churned and tossed the boats in the locks, kept all on the lookout. One man walked ahead on the tow-path, blowing a large fog-horn to warn the bridge and lock tenders of the approach of the boats. Three men ashore carried snubbing-lines with which to check the boats in the locks; and the balance of the party handled fenders, boat-hooks, etc., to keep the craft from pounding against the smooth and slimy sides of the great masonry lifts. At first it was a rather pleasant and novel experience; later it began to grow a little monotonous, and by midnight it had degenerated into the hardest kind of hard work. The only uninterested party was the boy driver. As soon as the boats entered a lock, and the team stopped, the lad sat calmly down beside a snubbing-post, and went to sleep. When the boats were raised to the upper level he seemed to awake, simultaneously with the opening of

VIVIA.

overcomes the barrier to navigation presented by the great fall and rapids of the Niagara River. It was built by the Canadian Government. In 1882 it was enlarged to a width of one hundred feet at the bottom, and deepened to allow vessels of fourteen feet draft an easy passage. Part of the old canal was abandoned, and new locks—270 by 45 feet—were constructed. This new canal is twenty-seven miles long, and has twenty-seven locks, each with an average rise of fourteen feet. Twenty-six of the locks are within a distance of ten miles of Lake Ontario, and are of very massive gray limestone masonry. The twenty-seventh, a guard-lock, is at the Lake Erie end of the waterway, and is rendered necessary to keep the water at the head of the canal deep enough to allow the free passage of boats. A heavy southerly blow will at times raise the water in the Port Colburne channel at least five feet, driving it in great masses

ARAB.

the upper gate, and proceeded a few hundred feet to the next lock, where he repeated the performance.

The sun just showed his red rays above the horizon as the last of the series of locks was left behind; and regular watches were once more set upon the boats as they entered the upper or seventeen-mile level.

When the guard-lock at Port Colburne was passed, the sides of the Ontario boats were for the first time lapped by the blue waters of treacherous Lake Erie, waters which later were to land *Rocky John* high and dry on a lee shore, to cause almost the destruction of the *Myrna*, and to put *Nox* in the condition of a badly used-up prize-fighter. Friday afternoon and night were passed in Port Colburne, where we were joined by the Toronto racer, *Canada*, the *Vivia, Nadia, Dinah,* and several others — all on their way to "make the circuit."

It was at Port Colburne that *Nox's* crew first struck their appetites, along with the crews of the other boats from the lower lake, appetites which put fifteen pounds of flesh on each man before the five weeks' cruise was up. And the crew lived well, if they were, all five, compelled to cook, eat, and sleep in a cabin six by nine by four-and-a-half feet high.

It was only necessary to forego meals on one or two occasions — once when the commissary forgot to procure fresh supplies of food before a forty-

SPRITE, OF TOLEDO.

MIRIAM.

IRIS.

mile run, and the others when rough weather, after a daylight start from port, prevented cooking even with coffee-pot and frying-pan lashed to the range with numerous pieces of marline. Those runs on empty stomachs were the most disagreeable experience of the whole cruise; and the crews—sullen and half sick — vented their spleen by vigorous abuse of their skippers.

There being no yacht club at Port Dover, the regatta was gotten up in the hope of booming the sleepy little Canadian village and causing the formation of such an organization, although there is no suitable harbor or anchorage at that port for even a small fleet, Silver Creek, the stream on which the port is located, being only a couple of hundred feet wide and navigable for not more than an eighth of a mile from its mouth.

To the visiting yachtsmen the most interesting feature at this stopping-point was a Port-Dover-built yacht—the *Harriet*—the like of which none of the strangers had ever seen before. Lying at anchor close to the sedgy bank of the creek, just at the base of a high hill, she was found on a Sunday morning, her captain and owner engaged in "washing down decks." He, a kindly, eccentric and well-to-do gentleman of the old school, designed and constructed her, and he spends about three months a year on her, cruising about in neighboring waters. The yachtsmen, after a visit to her moorings, christened craft and captain "Moses in the Bulrushes," a very appropriate name considering the spot he had chosen for an anchorage. An inspection showed the boat to be about eighteen feet long, with a yawl rig and provided with a cabin like a very large blacksmith-bellows. When the captain wishes to turn in he fastens a halliard to the after end of the cabin and raises it up, thus securing sleeping - room. When he clears up for sailing he simply drops his bellows-top affair and has a nearly flush deck. His dinghy—also home-made — is a veritable curiosity. It is constructed of several yards of paraffine-soaked canvas stretched over four pieces of bent hickory, and is about five feet long. When on a cruise, the owner takes out a few bolts, folds up his dinghy like a broken accordion, stows it in his cabin, and is ready for sailing. To the yachtsmen he appeared to be very proud of his little *Harriet*, apologizing for her lack of a single coat of paint to "slick her up ;" and, after exhibiting her good points to a couple of hundred visitors, gave them to understand that if she wasn't quite as comely as the *Priscilla* or the *Canada*, or as speedy as the steam-yacht *Enquirer*, still she was a very nice little home-made craft, on which, during the season, he took more real pleasure than any other sailorman in the fleet. As he walked along the dock, neatly dressed in an old-fashioned way and wearing an old-fashioned set of large gold seals on his watch-chain, he was the cynosure of all eyes in the fleet ; and his sturdy figure and weather-beaten features, from which shone a pair of bright, sharp and kindly blue eyes, secured for him a warm clasp of the hand and a friendly word from the wealthiest owner as well as from the poorest "Jackey" in port.

The first racing of the circuit on Erie waters was off Port Dover, in Long Point Bay—a broad indentation of Lake Erie, on the Canadian shore. The bay is protected on the southwest, whence come the prevailing winds, by Long Point ; but, while a good racing ground, it has seldom been used for a regatta, owing to poor harbor accommodations at the Port. The races of 1896 will probably serve to bring the good points of the bay into more prominence.

To the man who has never sailed in a yacht race, his first experience in such an event is one he will never forget—especially if the wind be strong enough to keep the boat's lee-rail under water. And it is very hard work for the crew ; not a moment's rest from the time they "strip" their craft, removing every portable article to shore, till the race is over, everything placed in position aboard again, and the last rope coiled down. It is pull on a halliard, ease off or flatten down a sheet, set a spinnaker, reef a sail, or something of the kind that will keep the sailormen at it the whole time. The landlubber who sails in a race for the first time will be busy enough, keeping out of the way of skipper and crew, and calculating the chance of getting safely ashore. But after one or two trips, he also will feel the thrill that excites the regular sailors. As he begins to tend backstay, and occasionally to give a pull at the main or jib sheet, and sees the boat heel over a little, his confidence increases and his fear decreases. He prays for more wind, and, as the water comes into the cockpit and he is called on to bail it out, he really begins to enjoy the excitement. What if his oilskins do not keep out the water, and his every stitch of clothing is in a drenched condition ! What if he is obliged to rush forward on a wet and slippery deck, or to climb out on the horn, where he is plunged again and again into the water up to his armpits ! It only makes the blood course more quickly through his veins. He may become wet and bedraggled, he may become hungry and half sick, but if his boat lands a winner, he is amply repaid for all inconveniences with which he has put up ; while if he crosses the line too late to take a place, he as readily finds a legitimate excuse for failure as do the more experienced sailors.

The first experience of a real heavy Lake Erie sea by the Ontario boats was on the run over to Erie, sixty miles directly across the lake from Port Dover. Tuesday evening, after the regatta ball, some of the craft started out for the trip, the remainder getting away at intervals during the night. There was a piping breeze from the southwest and quite a sea on in Long Point Bay, till the Point, eighteen miles distant, was reached about noon. The wind had gradually been increasing in strength all the morning, and *Nox*, one of the late arrivals at the Point, found a couple of dozen other craft at anchor, sheltered by the outreaching land, not caring to cross the open lake in high wind and heavy sea. However, *Nox*, with canvas reduced to a triple-reefed mainsail, all cabin fixtures carefully stowed, the extra anchor lashed to the centerboard pipe, the dinghy brought up on deck, and the cabin hatch battened down tight, made a start shortly after one o'clock.

It was not till Long Point had been left a couple of miles astern that the full size of the undertaking dawned on the minds of the mariners, and then it was deemed safer to go on than try to go back. The wind seemed to increase in strength each moment, while the waves piled up higher. In the middle of the lake occasional rollers would be met with at least twelve or fourteen feet high, while the average was fully eight or ten. All alone, without a single sail in sight ahead or astern, to port or starboard, *Nox* ploughed along in grand style, her lee-rail a foot under water. A couple of hours served to raise the high bluffs of the American shore; and late in the afternoon, with a gradually dying breeze, the little cutter ran into Erie harbor, Presque Isle Bay, under full sail, making the trip of thirty-two miles in a little over four hours. The other boats did not leave Long Point anchorage till late in the afternoon, arriving at Erie at intervals between midnight and six o'clock in the morning.

What American has not heard of Presque Isle Bay? What youth or maiden conning over the history lesson assigned by the teacher fails to connect this pretty landlocked harbor with one of the stirring events of the War of 1812 which gave American sailors a glory whose luster will never dim? Was it not in Presque Isle Bay that Perry fitted out his little fleet which demonstrated the superiority of the Americans on Lake Erie? And it is on the south shore of this beautiful bay that the youngest yacht club on the Great Lakes has erected a very pretty club-house. Only two years old it has a membership of nearly a hundred of the best people of Erie, with able officers; and its fleet of yachts, though small, will be increased by quite a number of new and speedy ones during the coming season.

The club has two courses for its regattas—one in the bay, for light-draft boats; and the other outside Erie light, in the lake, for boats that draw seven feet or more. In this matter of choice the club is extremely fortunate, and the inner course has a decided tendency to develop the "little fellows," to give men of moderate means and young men an opportunity to own and sail half-raters or twenty-five-footers before undertaking the management or ownership of larger craft.

In the management of its regatta of two days, the Erie Club won many warm commendations from all visitors, who wished members and officers the fullest measure of success, before starting for the next "stand" at Cleveland; for had not the Keystone Club done its best to make it pleasant for the non-club sailormen, and had they not succeeded beyond their fondest anticipations!

Fairport, O., was our next stopping-place, over Sunday, and early Monday morning we started for Cleveland. Scarcely had the open lake been reached when threatening clouds appeared in the west. The yachts pressed on, and after sailing about four miles and when two miles from shore, a storm broke and lasted perhaps ten minutes, but they were the liveliest ten minutes of the five weeks' cruise. When the squall struck the *Nox* she had prepared for it by reducing her canvas to a reefed staysail. That was found altogether too much, and the skipper ordered it furled. The three mates rushed forward and, in water up to their knees, worked for dear life trying to smother the flapping duck, while the skipper, hanging on to the tiller with both hands, alternately shouted orders to hurry and blamed the crew for being so slow. The boat heeled over under the pressure of the wind until her cabin combing was under water and her cockpit rail was just awash, while the non-sailor scrambled up the deck, fast approaching a fearfully perpendicular position, and clambered over on to the outside of the boat. When joked about it afterward he stated his opinion very freely that, as he could not swim, it was much pleasanter if the *Nox* went down, to drown on top of her than under her. The *Nox*, *West Wind*, and a couple of more boats were the only ones to receive the benefit of this squall, the other boats in the convoy not being called on to take in a single cloth. The sudden changes of the fickle weather on Erie were illustrated on this run by the passage of the squall and the immediate succession of a dead calm. For an hour two men of the five on the *Nox* were busy with boat-hooks preventing the dinghy smashing into the counter of the yacht, as the small tender was tossed hither and thither by the sea that had been stirred up by the short-lived storm. Later on a good sailing breeze sprang up, and the twenty yachts that could he counted within a distance of four miles, hurried

there being no breakwater east of the river; the second thing that struck them, a few hours later, was the squall.

In the anchorage were gathered together nearly a hundred yachts of all sizes and descriptions, their crews resting in fancied security. Some boats were entirely deserted, while on others the crews lazied and read upon the decks in the shade of the awning. About four o'clock, after a terribly oppressive morning, it grew suddenly cool. To the northwest great banks of cloud and mist gathered together in an incredibly short time, while from them came vivid flashes of lightning and ter-

ERIE Y. C. HOUSE.

on toward the Cuyahoga River, dropping anchor in the western harbor.

Cleveland, the Forest City, but better named the smoky and dirty city, will be remembered by all the stranger yachtsmen for two things—the record-breaking squall that played havoc with the boats at the anchorage, and the exceedingly kind treatment of the visitors by the Cleveland Club. The first thing that struck the non-Cleveland sailors was the fact that, while the beautiful club-house was elegantly situated on the lake shore at Lakeside Park, the anchorage for the yachts was a mile to the westward, inside the breakwater,

rific reports of heavenly artillery. To the large number of guests on the balcony of the club-house the sight was indescribably grand and impressive, and no one thought for a moment that anything was about to happen to the little pleasure craft. Almost before any idea that trouble was ahead entered the minds of the onlookers, with a rush and a shriek a gale, which the Weather Bureau recorded as fifty-five miles an hour, began to toss the yachts at its mercy. Out on the lake the rain could be seen descending in sheets, while glass in the club-house windows began giving way under the terrific force of the blast. Over behind the breakwater, first one, then another, of the white-winged racers dragged her anchor—even where a second hook had been put out—and went ashore ; while *Nox*, her crew all ashore, began to give way to the pressure of the wind and was slowly forced against a large house-boat, the collision carrying away her bowsprit, forward rigging and port-rail, tearing her staysail to tatters and opening up her stem half an inch. Fortunate for her crew was it that she fouled the house-boat badly ; and, her standing rigging becoming fastened to the larger boat, the smaller one was saved from total loss.

Word of the disaster was telephoned, and the United States life-saving crew, located only a few hundred feet away, put out in their surf-boat and saved the lives of the crew of the *Crescent*, which had gone down in thirty feet of water off the west pier. As soon as possible the officers of the club were at hand with a large steam-tug, and the work of pulling off the stranded boats was begun. The *Dinah*, *Hiawatha*, *Myrna*, *Sprite*, *Viking*, *Eva* and several others, which had been cast on a bed of sand a few hundred feet west of the river, were slowly worked off into deeper water, where the injuries were investigated by their crews. It was found that the damages—beyond wet clothing and bedding—consisted only of broken rigging, which was, in all cases, repaired within a couple of days.

The Cleveland Yacht Club is the largest and wealthiest on the Great Lakes.

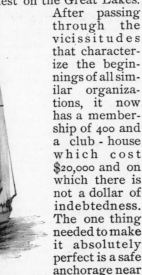

SCORPION.

After passing through the vicissitudes that characterize the beginnings of all similar organizations, it now has a membership of 400 and a club - house which cost $20,000 and on which there is not a dollar of indebtedness. The one thing needed to make it absolutely perfect is a safe anchorage near

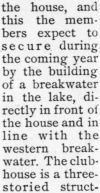

MARIE.

the house, and this the members expect to secure during the coming year by the building of a breakwater in the lake, directly in front of the house and in line with the western breakwater. The club-house is a three-storied structure of artistic design. On the lake front of each floor is a capacious balcony affording ample accommodations for a hundred guests who may be interested in a race or in watching the incoming and outgoing of the craft.

To the visitor two little couplets over the entrance to the café and ladies' reception-room, respectively, appear very appropriate. On entering the café the guest is reminded that

" With orange peel and lemon sliced
    The mainbrace very oft is spliced."

And how his sense of the beautiful is appealed to by the lines that face him at the reception-room :

" How very like a full-rigged cutter
    Balloon - jibbed sleeves our hearts make flutter."

Do they not recall to him visions of pretty maids in the ball-room or on the deck of a white-winged yacht ? Does not the social side of the sailor's life come out in bold relief, as he thinks of the club receptions and hops, with soft music and gliding feet, and the ladies' days when the gentler sex are given an idea of the brighter side of the yachtman's life ? Such, indeed, were the feelings of the visitors to the Cleveland Club's home, as "splicing the mainbrace" and talking over the pith and point of the rhymes, they toasted the officers and the members, and said many pretty and heartfelt things about the courteous manner in which each individual clubman had done his utmost to render happy those who had come many miles to attend their celebration. And more than heartfelt were the good wishes of those who had had the ill-luck to be wrecked and who had been so considerately assisted out of their misfortune. On the run from Cleveland to Put-in-

Bay, fifteen or sixteen of the yachts stopped in Lorain over Sunday, where some went to church in one of the prettiest little towns on the south shore of the lake. The harbor is a very good one, and here, as in most other Ohio lake-ports, iron-ore storage and shipment is probably the greatest industry. To load or unload a vessel of three thousand tons takes but a short time.

The run from Cleveland to South Bass Island was marked, as was every run after leaving Erie, by the encountering of one of the greatest nuisances, next to rocks and shoals, that a seafaring man can meet with, and that is pound-nets. They lined the American shore far out into the lake. They were everywhere — close to harbors and far from harbors. They were two miles from shore, and they were ten miles from shore. A pound-net, as discovered by the sailors, is an invention of his Satanic Majesty for the express purpose of ruining the souls and bodies of the yachtowners and wrecking their boats. It consists of rows of thirty or forty telegraph poles driven ten or a dozen feet apart into the bed of the lake, and projecting about five feet above the surface in a calm — the finest apparatus imaginable on which to tear rigging or smash the bottom out of a boat so unfortunate as to run into them in heavy weather. Why the United States government allows them to obstruct navigation is a conundrum that none of the yachtsmen could solve to the satisfaction of themselves or any one else.

Put-in-Bay, situated on South Bass Island, the great summer resort of Northern Ohio and Southeastern Michigan, the place whence Perry sent his famous message, "We have met the enemy and they are ours," is an ideal spot for yachting. Within a radius of three miles are a dozen beautifully wooded islands. Put-in-Bay itself is a typical summer resort — a second Coney Island. It has its swell hotels, its second-grade hotels, and its "hash-houses," and it has fakirs of all kinds by the score. It is enlivened by daily excursions from Toledo, Sandusky, Detroit, etc.; and the excursionists fill the coffers of the permanent and temporary business men of the bay. Yet, with all its natural advantages, with an anchorage in lee of Gibraltar Island superior to any other on the lake, it has no active yacht club,

and depends for its aquatic sport on the boats from other points on Erie, Michigan and Huron, which annually gather here for a week's good time. But the bay has a boat whose style is peculiar to the place. It is called a "sanpan," and is an eight-foot punt, made of a few pine boards, which in light winds simply skims along the surface of the water. Many of these sanpans are sailed by small boys, and their skill and daring opened the eyes of some of the elders, who were heard to repeat the old saying, "There is a special Providence that watches over small boys, drunken men and fools."

It was with feelings of pleasure that on Saturday morning all the boats — some sixty in number — started, in a driving rain, for the last contest of the series, a cruising race to Toledo, thirty miles away. The race was sailed with a reefing breeze, which died down to almost a dead calm at the end of the course. Here, as fast as a dozen or fifteen boats crossed the line, they were met by a tug — as the Toledo sailors had promised — which towed them twelve miles up the Maumee River, of Indian fame, to the city of Toledo. The people of this place, and the officers of the International Yacht Race Association, outdid themselves in the manner in which they received the visitors. Each day of the races a dozen tugs towed all the yachts out to the course on the lake, and towed them back after the event of the day. It was a pretty sight from the deck of the press-boat as the latter passed string after string of sailing craft, each astern of a bustling, puffing, little tug. And what a racket the tugs and steamers and even the crews of the sailing yachts with their foghorns did raise as the two rival flag-defenders, the *Canada* and the *Vencedor*, crossed the home line! And how disappointed the Americans were at the result of the third day's race — the loss, by twenty-six seconds, of the trophy! But better luck another time. The story I need not give; it is old, though glorious, and, moreover, was chronicled in detail in OUTING for September last.

Two yacht clubs — the Ohio and the Toledo, if they be not yet consolidated — exist in this city on the Maumee; and to their credit may it be said that they are flourishing, for the disadvantages — situated as they are, twelve miles from an open racing course — are great. Canoes and boats drawing a few feet can race in the river, but craft of any draft are obliged to go out on the lake; and a twelve-mile tow or sail two ways in a narrow channel is anything but conducive to good manners, good morals or good yachting spirit.

The yacht-club ball held by the Toledo club in honor of the visitors was the social affair of the whole trip; and a prettier lot of maids and matrons could not well be imagined, as they waltzed and chasséed with duck-suited yachtsmen at the Pythian Temple.

The international races were over, the circuit was ended, the yachts departed

by two inch-and-a-half lines of her own, brought over the bow and running down *Nadia's* stern, forward to the latter's mast. That tow was, as the colored man said, "the most wakefullest time" the six crews ever saw. Shortly after reaching the open lake, a northeast breeze sprang up which raised quite a sea. As it grew dark, *Nox*, much the smallest boat and the worst-placed one in the fleet, began to labor heavily, and every now and then would ship a barrel of water forward. The later it grew, the rougher became the sea, and the less buoyantly did all the boats meet the surges. Toward midnight, with a full moon occasionally peeping through

BUFFALO Y. C. HOUSE.

in little groups early in the day, and by ten o'clock on Thursday, Toledo was practically deserted. *Nox's* crew took their places at the end of the tow of six boats—which included the victorious *Canada* and the *Vivia*, of Toronto, the *Merle*, of Buffalo, the *Miriam*, of Erie, and the *Nadia*, of Hamilton—headed by the large steam barge *Russell Sage*.

At three o'clock the tow was started, each boat being fastened by a bow and stern line to the hawser, *Canada* leading on the port side, *Vivia* following on the starboard; and then *Merle* and *Miriam*, with *Nadia* at the end of the six hundred feet of cable. *Nox* was fastened

dark masses of clouds and illuminating a wild night-scene, it was a question whether to cast the little cutter loose from the tow-line and sail home, but every hour of hanging on brought the boat ten miles nearer Ontario. The great danger was that a bow-line breaking on one of the boats forward, this would swing round on the stern-line, smash into the boat next astern and, fouling, result in the wreck of the whole fleet, with consequent great disaster. Wave after wave would completely submerge the *Nox*, and the men on deck, though clad in oilskins and sou'-westers, were wet to the skin.

The situation was serious, and at twelve o'clock an awning was lashed to the deck just abaft the mast and carried over the cabin roof, where it was fastened to the backstays a couple of feet above the deck. It made quite an effectual breakwater, keeping the fluid from entering the cockpit and cabin, in which latter place the fifth hand on the boat was obliged, once an hour, during the night, to bail out a barrelful of Erie's liquid. Still an occasional wave would break over the awning, and at 2:30 A. M. an enormous billow appeared at the bow of the boat. *Nox* could not ride it, the towing pace was so fast, and went through it, the whole boat being a foot under water for what seemed an age It brought the two men in the other watch out of their bunks with a bound, and startled every one aboard. The same wave swept the *Vivia* from stem to stern, and gave the *Miriam's* crew a bad shaking-up. The pounding of the seas on the deck and sides and the groaning of the boat prevented sleep ; and sunrise, with a slowly-abating wind and sea, was never more welcome to mariners than it was Friday morning to the *Noxites*, as well as to the other amateurs. No coffee could be cooked, and recourse was had to Jamaica ginger to warm the blood into circulation. By noon the wind had died down to a dead calm, and, though the boat made considerable water through the centerboard pipe, her counter being under the surface all the time, the bedding was gotten out on deck and dried, and all except the wheelman slept. At four o'clock the *Russell Sage*, amidst the

cheers and well - wishes of the yachtsmen and the blowing of its own whistles, dropped the sailing craft off Port Colburne, into which place they slowly drifted about eleven hours later, the *Miriam* having parted off Erie, and the *Merle* dropping off at Port Maitland.

A few hours' rest in Port Colburne, and the *Nox* started through the Welland Canal on the home trip. This was easier than the journey up, as there was less trouble in locking down at the various levels. A short stop at Dalhousie and a husky run down old Ontario in a gale from the west brought *Nox* into Charlotte harbor after an absence of five weeks lacking two days.

During these five weeks she carried her happy crew of five over eight hundred miles. She had met with many storms and some calms. She had been tossed by the winds and battered by the seas. She had met with partial shipwreck and she had won her owners some prizes, and had lost them others. She had been in strange waters, and had carried the Rochester pennant where it had never been carried before. And now the close companionship was to be broken. While delighted to be at home, it was with feelings of sadness and regret that, before a final parting, the members of the crew, on the captain's invitation, dropped into the cabin to "splice the mainbrace," and gave a last handshake ere they parted. For yachting as well as other ties must be broken, and the burdens of life must be resumed even by those who for pleasure "go down to the sea in ships."

HOMEWARD-BOUND.

The Larchmont Regatta Week (1897)

THE LARCHMONT YACHT CLUB-HOUSE.

ASTHORE.

I AM not quite positive of the identity of the man who invented the Larchmont week, but whoever it was he deserves to be immortalized in the archives of the club. Whether a member of the "sea-going contingent" or a leading light of the renowned "rocking-chair fleet," whose headquarters ashore is on the shady side of the piazza, within easy call of the soda-water fountain, and whose rallying point afloat is the majestic flagship *Flub-Dub*, he ought to be commemorated in some graceful manner commensurate with the value of his inspiration.

For several years the annual cruises of the club had been crowned with but scant success. Handicapped by thunderstorms and dead calms on the stagnant Sound, the squadron generally found its way to Shelter Island, and sought solace in the mild diversions and dissipations of summer hotel life.

In 1895 the allied squadrons of the Larchmont and Atlantic Yacht Clubs went on a cruise together, but the combined efforts of both fleets could not achieve anything remarkably note-worthy. So, one evening in January, 1896, in one of the cozy snuggeries of the Larchmont Club, when the sparks of the hickory logs on the tiled

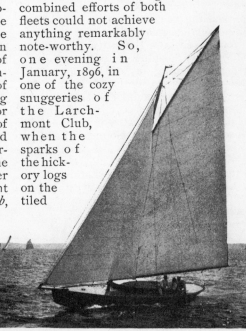

RACCOON.

hearth were reflected in certain steaming glasses of potent, soul-inspiring grog, it befell that the divine afflatus made itself manifest in one of the

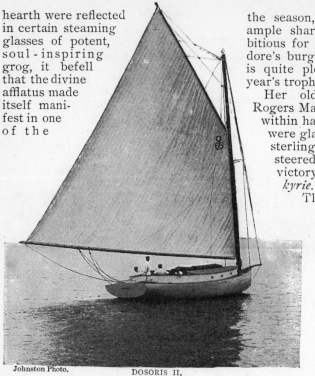

DOSORIS II.

jovial circle, and the Larchmont week was then and there resolved upon.

The yachting carnival of 1896 was brilliant, but its luster was dimmed by the dazzling splendor of this year's fête.

The picturesque grounds of the club never looked more beautiful than they did on the morning of Saturday, July 17th, the opening day of the race week. The close-shaven emerald lawns, the well-kept flower beds, the trim gravel walks made a fitting foreground for the handsomest and best equipped clubhouse on Long Island Sound. The snug harbor was filled with a fine fleet of pleasure craft, including the contestants for the prizes, and an ample squadron of steam yachts, naphtha, vapor, and electric launches destined to be filled later in the day with eager sightseers.

The flagship *Colonia*, owned by Commodore Charles A. Postley, looked the pink of racing perfection. She was in commission early in the season, and had already won an ample share of prizes, but was ambitious for more to fill up the commodore's burglar-proof plate vault, which is quite plethoric with this and last year's trophies.

Her old antagonist, *Emerald*, J. Rogers Maxwell, owner, was anchored within hailing distance, and all hands were glad to see aboard of her that sterling veteran, "Hank" Haff, who steered *Volunteer* and *Defender* to victory against *Thistle* and *Valkyrie*.

There was only a light air blowing from the southward and westward when colors were made at eight bells in the morning watch. The Regatta Committee, Messrs. Lovejoy, Wintringham and Coates cast anxious eyes to windward. One young irreverent yachtsman yelled out: "Blow, good devil, and you shall have the cook!" But even this generous offer failed to bring any responsive breeze from the bellows of the wind god.

The crews of the yachts set their lower sails, saw their head sails clear for hoisting,

ACUSHLA.

and hove short on their anchors. The shining white wings were stretched in the hope of wooing the fickle breeze, but as yet the flags on the lofty mast beside the club-house scarcely fluttered in the still and drowsy atmosphere. Light and fleecy clouds sailed slowly across the lilac-hued heavens. Sluggish coasters drifted idly with the tide. The churning of the mirror-like waters of the Sound by the wheels of passing steamers could plainly be heard though distant fully a mile.

And now the fair yachtswomen flocked to the club float, and there embarked in gigs and launches boun to the larger yachts, from whose decks they were to be spectators of the sea-fight. I can promise you they looked pretty in their nautical costumes, which, in my judgment, always serve to set off the graceful

coming out of the harbor in all the pride of racing canvas, and with balloon muslin ready for hoisting to the capricious wind. The flotilla of steam and naphtha craft took up commanding positions from which to witness the start, while the racing yachts, moving marvelously fast in so faint a breeze, with sharp bows furrowed the glassy surface of the placid Sound.

The wind began to freshen slightly at one o'clock, and the signal for the schooners to start

Johnston Photo. NOROTA.

figures of our charming countrywomen to an advantage such as no other garb affords. Golf and bicycle uniforms are all very well in their way, but they cannot compare with the really smart yachting rigs of the incomparable American girls. They were present, too, in large numbers, for the Larchmont Club is immensely popular with the sex, and the hops and entertainments given by the club are always well patronized by sea-nymphs.

At noon the Regatta Committee consulted the glass, and decided that a breeze was due at one o'clock. Then they sailed forth in one of the club launches to the tugboat Luckenbach. Meanwhile the fleet got under way,

sent *Emerald* and *Colonia* away at 1h. 05m. *Emerald* had the best of the flying start by about seven seconds, and spreading her light "ballooners" with seamanlike smartness, romped away on the first leg of the course, which was a broad reach with the wind on the starboard quarter. Somehow there seemed a delay on *Colonia* in spreading her flying kites, and this naturally gave her rival considerable advantage. *Amorita*, owned by Mr. W. Gould Brokaw, also crossed the line, but having no competitor, excited no interest.

The course for all classes was triangular, that for schooners being thirty miles and the smaller vessels in proportion. *Vencedor* and *Syce* followed at 1:20,

AMORITA.

Vencedor leading and unfolding a bal-loon jib of enormous size, under whose influence she glided along with great swiftness, to the delight of Mr. Gillig's friends. The others followed in order.

Cutters—36-foot class, 1h. 30m., *Acush-la, Surprise, Pawnee.*

Sloops—30-foot class, 1h. 35m., *Musme, Raccoon, Carolina, Penelope, Goblin, Kite.*

Sloops—25-foot class, 1h. 40m., *Va-quero, Houri, Quantuck, Skimaug.*

Sloops—20-foot class, 1h.45m., *Asthore.*

Cats—30-foot class, 1h. 50m., *Volsung, Onaway, Kit, Uarda.*

Cats—25-foot class, 1h. 55m., *Presto, Grace, Rob Roy.*

Cats—20-foot class, 2h., *Minnetonka, Dorothy, Byna Jane.*

It was a reach to the eastward marks, a beat across the Sound, and a reach to the finish-line off the club-house. *Emerald* maintained her lead to the first mark, beating *Colonia* 1m. 5s. on the reach of six miles. *Vencedor* also did her little four-mile reach 50s. faster than *Syce.* But when *Emerald* and *Vencedor,* flattened in sheets for the dead beat, the schooner's center-board got hopelessly jammed in the trunk, from which it declined to budge for the rest of the day ; and the Chicago boat, owing to her sails, was not in condition for a thresh to windward in spite of the efforts of Mr. H a z e n Morse who sailed her. B o t h were thus com-pelled to play second-fiddle to the finish.

There was a trifle more wind in the second round, but nothing to brag of, all the contestants finishing before six o'clock in the evening.

The winners were: *Colonia, Syce, Acushla, Raccoon, Kite, Houri, Volsung, Presto* and *Dorothy. Amorita, Pawnee* and *Asthore* had sail-overs. The ex-act details of this and the remain-ing races of the week will be found in the Yachting Depart-ment of Monthly Review at the end of this issue.

There was a musical frolic, which did not end until midnight, to which the jovial members of the rocking-chair fleet l a r g e l y con-tributed. And thus ended the first day of the Larchmont week.

The weather was by no means prom-ising on Monday, the wind being east, the sky cloudy, with occasional showers. The steam yachts did not offer so many attractions to the ladies as they did on Saturday, so "stag parties" were rather the rule than the exception. There were only six starters, *Colonia* and *Emerald* in the schooner class, *Raccoon, Musme,* and *Carolina* in the special 30-foot class, and *Shark* in the 20-foot class. The courses were the usual club triangles, and the breeze was true and steady from start to finish, the water being smooth throughout.

Capt. Haff, the famous Long Island s k i p p e r, was at the *Emerald's* wheel, while Charles Barr, formerly of Scotland, but n o w hailing from Mar-blehead, Mass., steered the

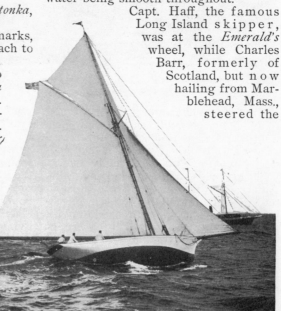

Johnston Photo.   AWA.

Colonia. The starting signal was sounded at 11:35, and Haff, securing the weather berth, forced *Colonia* to give *Emerald* room at the stake-boat and crossing the line 57 seconds ahead. The course was east ¾ north, six miles dead to windward, with a strong flood tide to buck against.

The "thirties" were sent off at 11:40, with *Raccoon* in the lead, followed by *Musme.* These boats crossed on the port tack, but *Carolina* was on the starboard tack, making a sluggish third.

By dint of the sea-jockey's art *Colonia* was kept under *Emerald's* lee for half an hour, before her skipper could extricate her from her demoralizing position, but just as soon as she got clear of her blanketing she displayed her saucy stern to the *Emerald,* ate out to windward in capital style, and also outfooted her clever opponent in spite of all the artful dodges of Capt. Haff. Hammer and tongs it was until the easterly mark was reached. It was rounded as follows: *Colonia* 1h. 11m. 30s., and *Emerald* 1h. 12m. 50s., *Colonia* being 1m. 20s. ahead of her antagonist. It must be said that *Emerald* made a better turn than *Colonia,* but the last-named was by far the smarter of the two in setting the spinnaker and the balloon jibtopsail, thus reversing the order of affairs in Saturday's race, when *Emerald's* crew was particularly active in setting and shifting her flying kites. With the tide in their favor the six-mile run down the wind was soon accomplished.

Meanwhile the 30-footers had been enjoying a lively little tussle of their own, with *Raccoon* in the lead, *Carolina* second, and *Musme* third. In the 4-mile thresh to windward, the elapsed times

ON THE LAWN AT THE BOAT-RACES.

of the three boats were: *Raccoon,* 1h. 17m. 1s.; *Carolina,* 1h. 19m. 4s., and *Musme,* 1h. 19m. 12s.

Colonia rounded the Hempstead mark at 1h. 52m. 11s., and *Emerald* at 1h. 53m. It was now a broad reach to the home mark, three miles distant across the Sound, with the wind on the starboard quarter. The times at the conclusion of the first round of 15 miles being: *Colonia* 2h. 8m. 59s., and *Emerald,* 2h. 9m. 57s., *Colonia* being 58 seconds in the lead.

The elapsed times of the 30-footers at the end of their first round of eleven miles were: *Raccoon,* 2h. 12m. 11s.; *Musme,* 2h. 13m. 58s.; *Carolina,* 2h. 14m. 40s. The wind was a trifle brisker on the second round, but there were few changes in the relative positions of the boats, except that *Colonia* steadily increased her lead, finishing at 4h. 38m. 8s., while *Emerald* crossed the line at 4h. 43m. 5s.

Colonia thus beat *Emerald* 3m. 41s. *Raccoon* beat *Carolina* 3m. 46s. and *Musme* 5m. 4s., while *Shark* enjoyed the barren honor of a sailover.

From the point of view of the ladies, the most enjoyable day of the carnival was Tuesday, July 20th, when the fleet lay at anchor, and all the lovely afternoon was devoted to the racing of small boats and naphtha launches and some rollicking water sports. It was ladies' day, and the sex was well represented.

At noon all the yachts in the harbor, at a signal from the flagship, dressed ship, the flags being displayed in rainbow fashion and fluttering gayly in the light and balmy southwest breeze. The effect was lovely and artistic, and was hugely admired. At one o'clock the Seventh Regiment band assembled on the lawn, and to the inspiriting strains of the "Star Spangled Banner," the American flag, the club burgee and a host of other flags were broken out on the flagstaff.

SYCE.

The boat-races came next, and mighty interesting they were, the first contest being a spirited bout, in which eight naphtha launches, 21 feet and under, from *Colonia*, *Emerald*, *Sachem*, *Pawnee*, *Trochilus*, *Marietta*, *Viola* and *Amorita* contested. *Colonia's* launch won by 36 seconds, *Emerald's* being second and *Sachem's* third.

A four-oared gig race followed, for the Hen and Chickens, colored. Boats from *Colonia*, *Sachem* and *Amorita* were the competitors, *Amorita's* gig winning by 24 seconds.

Pair-oared gigs from the *Duquesne*, *Syce*, *Viola*, *Emerald*, *Sachem*, *Viator* and *Huron* rowed a capital race for the *Dauntless* colors, *Syce's* crew being successful, with *Emerald* second, *Viator* third.

Dinghies from *Trochilus*, *Emerald*, *Oneonta*, *Lydia*, *Marietta*, *Viator*, *Liris*, *Duquesne* and *Amorita* rowed for the Execution colors, *Marietta* winning, with *Amorita* second, and *Oneonta* third.

At four o'clock the water baseball game was called, between "Fortunates and Unfortunates," as the programme put it. The married nine were Theodore R. Hostetter, Harry M. Gillig, F. S. Schlesinger, Thomas Van Dusen, Frank Fullgraff, George Hatton, Will-

iam Barton, Dr. C. W. Stimson and E. B. Sanger. The single men were G. G. Milne, C. Baird, H. L. Currie, Herbert Seeley, Archibald Dally, Harold Spencer M. Clarke, George Singer and Willie Caldwell.

This was simply a "larky" frolic in the water, carried on by men who were good swimmers. The umpire, Captain West, was, of course, thrown overboard, and Frank Fullgraff, in a woman's yachting costume, fell into the water with a scream, shrill as a locomotive's shriek, and created a momentary scare among the uninitiated. Swimming matches and tub races brought the water-sports to an amusing close, and then all hands got ready for the ball, which was held in the dining-hall of the club, which was decorated with bunting. Mr. Augustin Monroe was master of the ceremonies, and he was ably assisted by Messrs. Murray and Sterling. All were conspicuous with brilliant silken sashes of blue and white stripes—the colors of the club.

The scene out-of-doors was enchanting. The fleet was brilliantly illuminated. The grounds of the club were ablaze with light. Prismatic fountains played ; Chinese lanterns swung from trees, and fairy lamps twinkled in the verdant foliage.

A strong sou'wester, with frequent showers, a nasty jump of a sea, with prospects of hard squalls, were the meteorological features of Wednesday, July 21st. Out of fifty yachts entered only twenty-seven faced the music when the starting signal was given at 11:35. *Emerald* made a splendid start, crossing the line on the instant the whistle blew. *Colonia* crossed too soon, and had to put back, losing 1m. 43s. by injudicious haste. In spite of the weight of wind, both schooners lugged their clubtopsails from start to finish. It is likely that *Emerald* would have done better under a working maintopsail, as she didn't seem to stand up so well as *Colonia*. It was a reach to the first mark at Matinnecock, which was rounded thus : *Emerald*, 12h. 5m. 23s.; *Colonia*, 12h. 6m. 34s. When sheets were flattened in for the beat of six miles *Colonia* soon took up a commanding position to windward and gained steadily every tack she made.

Emerald clewed up her foretopsail in a puff, and did not set it again until the thresh to windward was over. In the first round *Colonia* beat *Emerald* 5m. 27s.

Vencedor's starboard spreader was carried away before the start, but Mr. Hoyt, of the *Syce*, agreed to wait an hour for Mr. Gillig; but the repairs were not effectual, and as *Vencedor* was making her way for the line, the spreader snapped in two, so there was no race in that class.

Most of the smaller craft had reefed down and even then some had as much muslin set as they could stagger under; and what with salt spray and drenching showers of rain the yachtsmen got pretty wet. But all sailed plucky races and none withdrew until they had to.

Colonia in the second round increased her lead though the breeze had lightened considerably, which should have helped *Emerald* materially. The contest was keen in all classes, and none were sorry when the race was finished.

Colonia beat *Emerald*, 12m. 39s. *Norota* had a sailover. *Surprise* beat *Acushla*, 6m. 54s. *Pawnee* beat *Fidelio*. *Raccoon* beat *Musme*, 1m. 19s. *Goblin* beat *Penelope*, 43m. 42s. *Houri* vanquished *Quantuck*. *Shark* defeated *Keneu*. *Kit* beat *Volsung*, 39m. 37s. *Win or Lose* beat *Grace*, 11m. 5s.

Thursday morning dawned dismally. Heavy rain pelted down and a dense mist settled over the Sound like a great white pall. Only the smaller classes were to compete, but the little fellows always get good treatment at Larchmont, where their value is highly appreciated. After a dreary wait a pleasant little s a i l i n g breeze came out from the south-southwest, and the yachts were started at 12h. 35m., over triangular courses of twenty-two and eleven miles.

The first leg was a reach, with the wind on the s t a r b o a r d quarter, the second a beat, and the third a reach, with the breeze on the port quarter. *Awa* and *Choctaw*, in

the 51-foot cabin trunk class; *Musme* and *Raccoon*, in the 30-foot class; *Kit, Win or Lose, Dosoris II.* and *Grace*, in the cabin cat class, and *Shark* and *Asthore*, in the 20-foot class, were the starters.

The race was uneventful, except that *Asthore* fouled *Shark* soon after the start and withdrew. *Grace* and *Win or Lose* retired after the first round. *Musme* easily vanquished *Raccoon*.

Choctaw beat *Awa*, 2m. 56s.; *Musme* defeated *Raccoon*, 4m. 51s.; *Kit* beat *Dosoris II.*, 10m. 29s., and *Shark* was victorious over *Asthore*.

There was a good breeze from the southwest on Friday with pleasant weather. It was hoped that *Emerald* and *Colonia* would start in the open regatta, but both craft remained idle at their moorings. *Vencedor* and *Syce* were ready, however, and so were *Raccoon, Carolina*, and *Musme* in the 30-foot class, and *Shark* had a competitor in the *Wave*, an imported 1-rater, built by Sibbick, and sailed in good style by Captain James C. Summers. She wasn't in it with the home craft, a more powerful and able little ship.

The starting whistle was blown at 11:40, the course being o v e r the eleven-mile triangle, the leg to the eastward being sailed first. *Vencedor* led for a time, but in windward work was no m a t c h for *Syce*. The times of the first round were: *S y c e*, 1h. 37m. 21s.; *Vencedor*, 1h. 39m. 26s.; *Raccoon*, 1h. 46m. 28s.;

Johnston Photo.

THE FLAGSHIP COLONIA.

Musme, 1h. 46m. 38s. *Carolina* had withdrawn.

Syce beat *Vencedor,* 4m. 8s.; *Norota* had a sailover; *Raccoon* beat *Musme,* 4s.; *Shark* beat *Wave,* 22m. 39s.

The races concluded on Saturday, when a capital breeze piped up from the westward, and to its merry music thirty-two yachts crossed the line. *Emerald* appeared to have had enough of defeat, so *Colonia* sailed over the course alone, and so did *Norota* and *Acushla.* Mr. John F. Lovejoy, chairman of the Regatta Committee, sailed the *Vencedor,* but her spreader gave way again and although she was kept at it in her crippled condition, she was no match for the *Syce,* which soon overtook her.

As the leaders were approaching the finish line of the first round an accident occurred which might have been attended by tragic consequences. The cat-boat *Dorothy,* with her owner, Mr. John E. Sanborn, steering, and her crew, Messrs. C. C. Wright and Henry E. James, sitting up to windward, was romping along under as much muslin as she could lug, on the port tack. Mr. Burnham's cutter, *Norota,* also under a press of canvas, was approaching on the starboard tack, thus having the right of way. Neither boat observed the other until it was too late. *Dorothy* crashed into *Norota's* port bow about six feet forward of the mast, carrying away a big chunk of the cutter's rail. By the force of the collision the bows of the *Dorothy* were stove in and she began to sink. Mr. James made a successful jump for the *Norota's* deck, but Mr. Sanborn knowing that Mr. Wright was unable to swim stuck to his boat.

The judges' tug, Edward Luckenbach, hurried to the rescue. Mr. Wright was hauled aboard by a line, and Mr. Sanborn swam to the tug. A hawser was made fast to the wreck, but after being towed a little way she went to Davy Jones's locker.

Most of the smaller boats were sailed under snug canvas. In the result *Syce* beat *Vencedor,* 19.36; *Pawnee* beat *Fidelio,* 2.48; *Carolina* beat *Musme,* 7.13; *Houri* beat *Quantuck,* 6.45; *Shark* beat *Wave, Jester* beat *Alice,* 13.43; *Dosoris* beat *Kit,* 1s.; *Win or Lose* beat *Gracie,* 7.02; *Minnetonka* beat *Willie B.*

The successful week wound up with a great display of fireworks on the club grounds and a concert. From a social, as well as from a sportsmanlike point of view, the Larchmont aquatic carnival week of 1897 could not have been more brilliant.   A. J. KENEALY.

Johnston Photo.

MUSME.

Catboating on Jersey Inland Waters (1899)

SUNSET ON BARNEGAT INLET.—"WE WATCHED THE SHADOWS LENGTHEN INTO NIGHT."

CATBOATING ON JERSEY INLAND WATERS.

BY HENRY TATNALL BROWN.

IT had been hopelessly contemplated for a year; it had been vaguely discussed for months; and now at last the Admiral and I stood upon the Beach Haven dock, smothered in baggage, on a fair summer morning, realizing that the proposed excursion to Bay Head was indeed something more tangible than a wild, bright dream.

The voyage in contemplation was not a very extensive one, in all perhaps a hundred miles, while the craft in which we proposed to cover the distance was the writer's small twenty-footer of the genus Cape Cod cat. A necessary adjunct to the successful handling of a sailboat is wind; therefore, on this occasion, the situation was not devoid of sorrow, for if there ever was a calmer morning it has not been the writer's privilege to witness it. In no way discouraged, however, by a circumstance so trifling we stood among our baggage, gazing wistfully out over the glassy, listless surface of Tuckerton Bay, the attainment of liberty being as yet too recent for aught

else to have much place in our thoughts. Arousing at last to the needs of the occasion and realizing that, when wind is wanting, the blessings of a favoring tide must be embraced while they exist, we began the task of conveying the baggage aboard the *White Wing* and stowing it in preparation for departure.

First in importance, as also in size, loomed up the 75-pound basket of provisions, filled to overflowing with things eatable, and, as was afterward found, with some things uneatable. By its side and trotting in the same general class, came the water cooler; an unpretentious little article whose general air of meekness and self-abnegation had been increased by the loss of the knob on the lid, which had gone off at the invitation of a saw in the hands of the Admiral.

The wisdom of this piece of vandalism, however, appeared later when it was barely possible to push the cooler under the forward deck.

Next in the procession appeared a telescope satchel, and then in formidable array the writer's three cameras, large, medium and small, lined up for action. As representing the crowd of inevitable small boys who are ever to be found at

91

THE BEACH HAVEN YACHT CLUB

the heels of a circus, the rear was brought up by the double-barreled gun, the field glasses, the coast survey in a tin case, a paper box filled with the flag cards of the Beach Haven Yacht Club, two sticky, oil-skin suits of woe-begone appearance, and "lastly, but not leastly," a small chip basket, which, like the marvelous bag of the "Swiss Family Robinson," contained everything not found elsewhere.

Such was the manifest of cargo that it was proposed to stow in a twenty-foot catboat with a cockpit 6 x 10, and yet leave room in which two able-bodied men could live and move and have their being. It was a scientific problem and a warm one, but it was satifactorily accomplished with no evil results to note, except that the cargo stowed under forward put the yacht perceptibly down at the head ; and at last we gladly cast off the painter, resigning ourselves to the tender mercies of a strong flood-tide and to the onslaught of gnats by the million.

The voyager from Beach Haven to the drawbridge at Martin's usually has two courses open to him. The longer and deeper channel runs westerly, and then around by Long Point on the mainland, while the shorter and shallower runs in a more northeasterly direction and hugs the shore of Long Beach. The latter alternative was selected for two reasons. Firstly, and mainly, because, with no wind and a tide running strongly in that direction, we could hardly have done otherwise ; and secondly, because, our boat drawing but fifteen inches of water, depth of channel was no great object where time and distance might be saved. In the words of the poet, whose nautical acumen and gallantry are unquestionable :

ON TOMS RIVER.

" A sail-boat 'thout a sail
Ez like a comet 'thout a tail,
Ez like a gal 'thout a beau
An' like a winter 'thout a snow."

For these reasons, and because if there had been any wind it should undoubtedly have been fair and southerly, we hoisted the sail of the *White Wing* and trimmed it accordingly. The writer took the tiller, not that he could be of any particular service there, for the craft had no steerage way, but on the general principle that it is much better form always to have some one at the helm of a boat, even though the said boat be going stern foremost. The Admiral, when not engaged in drinking ice water, stood like the proverbial boy, forward upon the almost burning deck, pole in hand, ready to sheer her off the flats at bends in the channel, sound for shoals, and make himself generally useful. When almost abreast of Spray Beach a faint breeze came in from off the ocean, bringing with it the roar of the surf and the promise of better things.

About a mile further up came the realization of our hopes in the shape of a fair and fresh sea breeze, making life once more worth living, and starting the *White Wing* ahead of the tide and over the bottom at about a five-mile gait. Our hope was to reach Harvey Cedars, a point about ten miles north of Beach Haven, at dinner time.

The course up among the thoroughfares past "Pehala" and the "Ship Bottom" life-saving station, although tortuous was uneventful. By noon the "Cross Channels" and first drawbridge were reached and passed. The channel at this point makes in short to the northeast, and it is necessary after passing the draw to point almost for Long Beach City if you would escape going hard aground. The writer had, on a former occasion, experienced the pleasure of an enforced sojourn of this kind upon the flats just northward, until a kindly flood-tide had lifted him on its gentle bosom and assuaged his grief, not, however, until he had fallen overboard, head first, in an attempt to pole into deeper water. Another hour brought us abreast of Harvey Cedars, and we tied to the dock.

After dinner the writer went off to photograph the fine old cedar trees from which the place partially obtains its name, and became engaged in an instructive conversation regarding the traditions of the place. I was told that a long time ago, before even the main shore of New Jersey was settled, some whalers from Long Island came down and started up in business on the northward end of Long Beach. The fellow who selected that particular slice of wilderness on which the hotel is now located, was named Harvey, and the cedar grove at the place therefore has since become known as the Harvey Cedars. So far so good ; had our host stopped there all had been well, but he plunged still deeper into the subject and finally swung around into a dissertation on the cherished tradition of the Barnegat Pirates, expressing scepticism of their very existence, characterizing them as mere sneak thieves, and throwing a pall over all the romantic associations of the theme as treated by Vansant, and others.

About 3 P. M. we again went aboard the boat and soon had her under way, this time with Island Heights as an objective point, twenty miles northward. The breeze still held from the southeast but had freshened considerably, and, coming over the starboard quarter, could not have suited better for our needs. And here let me state that, from this time until we once again reached home, the wind was favorable to us no matter in what direction we might purpose to go. The last time we had undertaken a similar journey the wind had headed us off in every direction, until finally in despair we went ashore and walked home. In the words of the poet :

    " The tide ever flowed,
      And the wind always blowed,
        From the place where we goed."

Not only was the wind invariably ahead, but it was one of those exasperating "wide winds" that came from no-where in particular. It was therefore no wonder that we were pleased to have things this time all our own way. It was, to say the least, remarkable, for go north or go south, go east or go west, we would always have wind in plenty and from such a quarter that we could lay our course with started sheet. In fact with the exception of perhaps two hours, we were not close-hauled on the wind during the entire trip.

The course from Harvey Cedars to the mouth of Toms River was less familiar to us than the part of the bay already passed, but an inspection of the chart supplemented with information pumped from the natives by the Admiral, pulled us through in good shape. At four o'clock we opened up Barnegat Inlet on the starboard beam, and knew that we had still remaining fourteen miles to cover before dark. The channel from this point to off the mouth of Cedar Creek, according to the chart, is the better part of a mile wide, and from six to nine feet deep, so that a craft as small as ours and drawing perhaps fifteen inches can romp around 'most anywhere. In fact one party whom we consulted regarding channels, etc., after inquiring the *White Wing's* draught, replied, " For mercy sake just keep off the dry land." The wind continued to freshen, so that by 5 P. M. full sail was all the yacht could stagger under, and we reached and cleared the drawbridge at Barnegat Pier by about 5.30. The wind having by that time increased to almost the dignity of a gale, made things rather lively. The yacht already loaded down at the head and running free showed some disposition to kick up in the rear and push her bow under. Now and then a sharp squall would smite her from above, a big following sea would get under her stern below, and the combined efforts of the two would stand her on her nose. Having shipped one good healthy sea since leaving the draw, we concluded things were wet enough and eased her off by slacking the peak. Doubtless we could actually have made better time and in more comfort had we shaken up and reefed, but, as every yachtsman knows, it is always a temptation in a free wind and going like a race-horse to let her slide and take the chances. By 5.45 we opened up the mouth of Toms River and laid our course in for Island Heights.

As we sailed past the river's mouth

we noticed a small boat anchored apparently in the channel, with a white flag flying from a pole in the stern. Further up we encountered another of the same description. These phenomena we construed to indicate that a regatta had been in progress, a supposition that we afterwards learned to be correct. High bluffs beautiful in their leafy greenness line the northern shore, and it is upon these bluffs about two miles from the river's mouth that Island Heights is situated. As we approached, the water around and about the dock seemed literally covered by a multitude of rowboats of all sizes and descriptions. Our preconceived ideas of a regatta led us to believe that we were about to witness the start of a rowing contest, and, we therefore, stood well across to the south shore in order not to interfere with the probable course, and dropped our anchor in line with the dock. The boats, however, showed no disposition to line up for a start, but continued their seemingly aimless and endless movements to and fro over a given space. It was a curious combination and baffled all reasons we could marshal to meet the occasion.

The wind, as is frequently the case, died down at sunset into a gentle air, and we proceeded peacefully to eat our suppers from the stores in the commissary basket and watch the evening shadows lengthen into night.

We then went ashore and to arrange for quarters over night, and during the evening made the acquaintance of a nice old captain named Dorsett, who is skipper of and part owner in the schooner yacht of the Commodore of the Island Heights' Yacht Club. Meeting him again in the morning he gave us an invitation aboard the flag-ship, which we accepted; and he accordingly rowed us out to the schooner, which, he told us, being a boat builder by trade, he had himself constructed. The *Rosamond* proved to be an exceedingly roomy and well-appointed craft, having evidently been constructed more with a view to solid comfort than beauty. The large cabin with convertible bunks, the convenient toilet arrangements, and the galley complete in all appointments, formed a combination with which one could feel as supremely contented and comfortable as in his own good house at home. So much attention is in these days paid to speed and beauty

at the expense of comfort that it is indeed refreshing to find now and then an exception. After leaving the *Rosamond*, our friend the Captain rowed us along the water front, showing us the various boats constructed by himself and initiating us into the history of others. By 10 A. M. we felt our mission at Island Heights to be about accomplished, and therefore weighed anchor for a run up to the town of Toms River. Just above the Heights we passed through our third drawbridge, on one end of which the station is located.

The breeze was so fresh that we had tied in one reef, and under this sail we quickly covered the two miles and a half to our destination. After tying up to the south end of a small dock, we went ashore and walked up the street by the river toward the center of the town on a hunt for the post-office, where we might satisfy our conjugal obligations to report progress.

It was nearly noon when we finally left Toms River for Bay Head, distant a full afternoon sail, going down through the draw past Island Heights, and on out into Barnegat Bay. The wind seemed to be working more southwesterly, and the sky in that direction looked somewhat squally. A short distance above the mouth of Toms River, concluding that dinner time had arrived, we put into a small cove on the main shore, dropped sail and anchored. After a lengthy investigation into the mysteries of the commissary basket, somewhat to the detriment of salmon, sardines, peanut paste and canned goods generally, we weighed anchor and again started on our journey.

The course from the mouth of Toms River is not what the Bowery boy would characterize as "dead easy" for a greenhorn. We were told that after leaving the River we should do well to hug the main shore until we opened up a good-sized creek, and then keep hard off into the bay in order to clear a shoal running well out from there, after which we could again keep in close until pretty well up toward the driveway across the bay. The wind was puffy and at times uncertain; at one point in particular we experienced the peculiar phenomenon of sailing with a strong free southwesterly wind, while another yacht but a little way off on the starboard quarter had a full breeze from eastward. This is not entirely a pleasant situation, as it keeps one guessing as to just how soon the conflicting wind will prevail, gybe over the boom and raise Hail Columbia generally. We had looked at Berkeley, Ortley, Lavallette City and the other settlements along the eastern shore with longing eyes, but as the weather seemed unsettled and time was limited we thought best to pass them by. Mantoloking, however, presented attractions too strong to be resisted, so we went ashore there for a little while, and felt repaid for so doing. The place is certainly very attractive with its high, bold shore, its artificial pond and splendid railway accommodations. The small pavilions on the beach, artistically made of unbarked trees and

THE DOCK AT SEASIDE PARK.

roofed with brush, looked particularly enticing.

On returning to the dock we realized that the wind had worked itself into a gale, with a squall coming up from westward, and profiting by the experience of the day before, we tied in three reefs and found them none too many. Just as we reached the drawbridge in the driveway across the bay, a short distance above Mantoloking, a handsome knockabout (or perhaps I should more correctly say sloop, as the bowsprit was longer than knockabout regulation allows) appeared, coming through from the other side. Desiring to give her good clearance we changed our course more to the windward. The sloop was on the port tack close-hauled, and in order to go through the draw her helmsman luffed up, trusting to her headway to carry her well past. The force of this headway was, however,

almost killed by the heavy head wind and sea, so that by the time she had cleared, her steerage way was gone, her head fell off to port, and she made leeway broadside into the piling, where the sheet became hitched over a post and things generally tangled up. Much as we sympathized with her crew, we saw that, although helpless, she was in no particular danger, and feeling that our assistance would be worthless we put the *White Wing* again on her course for Bay Head.

After passing the draw we held a straight course through a small thoroughfare running between two islands, and then hauled on the wind hard to westward. It is said that many unacquainted with the channel go aground at this point in the attempt to hold a direct course for Bay Head. The squall in the west rapidly grew nearer and blacker, until we began to wonder if, after all, we could reach Bay Head before it was upon us. Near to the main shore were several yachts sailing pleasure parties up and down in the greatest unconcern. We passed near to one particularly lively party in a large black cabin catboat, who, we afterwards learned, rode out the storm at anchor. It was not, however, until we found ourselves entering the cove in which the Bay Head Yacht Club is located that the first drops fell, and we fortunately had time to moor, drop sail, and scoot for the shelter of the club-house porch, where other refugees were gathered, before the full fury of the squall broke upon us. When the floodgates finally were opened it proved a full-sized old stager, and made things so generally interesting that we felt indeed most heartily glad to have in time gained a kindly shelter, and shivered at the thought of weathering such a confusion of the elements in our little open boat. Things having quieted down a bit, we made for "The Bluffs," a lovely hotel situated in the south end of the town, and, tired and hungry as we were, never was a meal more enjoyed than the supper to which we sat down that night. The next morning after breakfast, from which the Admiral was finally persuaded to tear himself away, we went to the dock and prepared for our homeward voyage. It was our desire to stop at Seaside Park, Barnegat City and Long Beach City, on the way down. A moderate breeze

THE BAY HEAD YACHT CLUB ANCHORAGE

THE BEACH HAVEN YACHT CLUB.

was blowing from the northwest and we hoisted the sail to dry. Everything wettable and unprotected was thoroughly soaked.

We set sail at 9 A. M., having had an exceedingly pleasant stay, retracing our course of the day before to the mouth of Toms River, and then standing across the bay eastward to Seaside Park, arriving there without happenings of special note by dinner time. We dined at the Manhasset Hotel, kept by some friends of ours, and after a look around went aboard again and started for Barnegat lighthouse, where we expected to spend the night. The wind had worked around to eastward until when abreast of Barnegat Inlet it drew off the light.

The best way to find the mouth of the

DRAWBRIDGES LOOM UP AT ALL POINTS OF THE COMPASS.

channel into Barnegat City was, we were told, to hug the western shore closely until abreast of a large building said to be in Waretown, and then to bear off sharply to eastward, keeping Barnegat light over the bow and the large building on the main, dead astern. This we did, easily finding the channel, which is fairly well staked out, and following another and larger yacht working in the same direction. Even with the tide in our favor part way, it was a long beat to windward, but being about the only close-hauled work we had yet encountered it was enjoyed rather than otherwise. By sunset the wind had almost died out, but it held on long enough for us to lee-bow the tide and make a landing in the mouth of a small creek, which seems to be the best accommodations afforded by the place. Here we lay moored to the bank and ate

our suppers, watching meanwhile the fading colors in the afterglow of a particularly beautiful sunset. We were rudely aroused from our contemplation of nature's sublimity by a horde of ravenous mosquitoes that swooped down upon us by the thousand and followed us in a hasty flight to the very doors of the Oceanic Hotel, which opened to rescue us from an untimely end.

Next morning we left our moorings at about 8:30, fully an hour later than we had calculated, some time having been consumed in the purchase of a can-opener and in other ways. The breeze was still easterly but exceedingly light, and as we moved slowly past Clam Island flats it became apparent that a friend whom we were to pick up at Long Beach City would not only reach there by the appointed time, but at the rate we were moving the poor fellow would in all probability wait for us some two hours.

If we had only made the connecting point, Harvey Cedars, instead, it would not have been so bad. We coaxed and doctored the *White Wing* by all means at our command, but if anything she seemed to go the slower. When the Admiral steered the writer found fault, and when the writer had the tiller the Admiral complained; but at last we were able to distinguish Long Beach City dock, and by the aid of the glasses some people at its end. As we drew still nearer two of the group could be recognized—one, the long-looked-for lost, and the other a little shaver who calls the Admiral "Dad." It was fully ten o'clock when we finally jammed the yacht's nose into the dock, and those dear saints had patiently waited two straight hours and were good-natured still. We went ashore for ice and were well repaid in another direction, for behold! there, at but a little distance from the shore end of the dock. That most welcome of sights, to a farm-raised youth at the seaside, a cow—yes, two cows, chewing and blinking and wabbling their ears, in total oblivion of admiring eyes.

At last, about eleven A. M., we broke away from this our last halting place and started for our last drawbridge. This is indeed the drawbridge paradise. They loom up on all occasions and at all points of the compass. Every set of directions received from chance acquaintances was heavily tinctured with drawbridges. The principal characteristic of the scenery had been drawbridges. They were like the "Morro Castle," in Spanish domain, bewilderingly innumerable. We had passed through their yawning depths no less than seven times, and now we were nearing an eighth encounter, and verily it seemed that at last we had met our fate. The drawbridge below Long Beach City refused to open. On our approach we hallooed and fired the double-barrel gun to make our presence known, but all to no purpose. Apparently the monster had struck for a raise. Our interest in the subject of an "open door" in China was supplanted by an overwhelming desire for an open draw at Martin's.

A closer inspection revealed the fact that the fastenings which hold the bridge closed were jammed, and that two men, looking like mere flies in comparison with the mighty structure, were straining every nerve to get them free. In the end, however, mind conquered over matter, the ponderous thing opened slowly its huge yawning throat and we slid quickly through. As we proposed to have dinner aboard the boat and our hymeneal leave of absence had not yet expired, there seemed no good reason why we should hurry homeward. We therefore concluded to reach Beach Haven by way of Long Point, and not by the way we had come.

The day was a most beautiful one; in fact, with the exception of the Bay Head squall, the weather on the entire trip had been ideal. The breeze had increased to a good, healthy strength, that pushed the *White Wing* southward

at a strong, steady gait, like an old warhorse that once more smells home. At our start from Beach Haven, drifting northward with the tide and lacking wind, we had gone aground just above the dock. From that time until the Beach Haven water tower once more arose in view we had not grounded, unless a touch or two on the centerboard may be so considered. And now, with surroundings perfectly familiar, in an at-

THE ADMIRAL STOOD, POLE IN HAND.

tempt at a short cut into the Little Channel, we again ploughed the earth. It was no serious matter, but demonstrates the strange idiosyncrasies of man, where confidence kills caution. At 1:30 P. M. we once more stood on the old Beach Haven dock, lightened in larder, riper in experience, two healthy, happy, sunburned husbands

On the
Big Sea Water
(1900)

ON THE BIG SEA WATER.

By Stewart Edward White.

The Skipper.

The Dog Watch.

The Red Rover.

MOST of the Lake Michigan and Lake Huron yachtsmen either sail majestically up the middle in schooners, or dodge past sand-bars between ugly piers in smaller sloops.

Neither course is pleasant. In the schooner you have a sailing-master, a sideboard, and many friends. You hoist flags in a punctilious manner when the crew eats pie, or the skipper takes a drink; you bestow much thought on the advisability of shooting small breech-loading cannon; the failure of one of the A. B.'s to coil a line Flemish causes uneasiness, and the boarding of shore visitors on the captain's side of the yacht is a matter of agonized mortification. This is interesting, just as is the purchase of neckties of approved stripe, or the donning of the proper shoes with the proper trousers. But it is not cruising.

Nor is the small boat in much better case. Therein you dodge large short seas which break over with considerable weight; you are constantly reefing for black squalls; above all, you are on a continual rack of anxiety as to whether you will miss the shoal or whether you can make the next harbor before dark —usually a sandy little river, lumber-flanked, dirty.

We avoided both horns of the dilemma, and this is how we did it.

Just forty-five miles from the Island of Mackinac you may enter Potaganissing Bay. This, in turn, opens into the North Channel. The North Channel contains many islands and a harbor every few miles. It conceals various bass of sporting proclivity, and it leads to the Georgian Bay.

All these waters are deep. The chart of the British Government estimates that the islands which spangle them number "from thirty to one hundred thousand," which is near enough to the truth not to be troublesome. There are very few shoals, and these few are visible in the clear water many miles. Most of the shores can be dived from, or, what is more to the point, can be tied to with a six-foot draught. The scenery is beautiful. The Chippewa and Ottawa inhabitants are interesting. Up the north rivers are a number of Hudson Bay posts, some of which are still trading. There are no summer resorts. You can sail on open water, with more space abeam, forward, and astern than in Long Island Sound, or you can wind in and out of the island channels, just as you happen to please. Sometimes it seems you are in a great lake eight or ten miles across, the shores of which open before you and close silently behind you as you advance. Again, you need a fair wind and a steady eye, as in the forty-foot passage of the Little Detroit. Or still again, you may be out of sight of land entirely. In that country to the west hangs a horizon of smoke, faintly aromatic, pleasing, and to the north a brown horizon of mountains, rock-browed, bold. The afternoon sun becomes a great red ball, whose track on the waters is of blood, and whose last glance causes the north hills to blush a glowing purple. Above all, it is the northland, and the air is like wine.

Yet, strangely enough, yachtsmen continue to carry out their punctilious etiquette, or to seek their sawmill harbors, while the bays are solitary, save for the Indian fishing boats and the few, the very few, of the elect.

We are of the elect. We claim it with the arrogance of bigotry, if you will, but we claim it emphatically.

The summer of which this narrative speaks we foregathered from several points of the compass. The mate, possessed of a fly-book which he worshiped idolatrously, and a fund of theoretics which everybody else distrusted, arrived on the *Manitou* from Chicago. The dog watch was a lank individual of skillful pencil, small reverence, and ready excuse, summering on the island. The scullion was a fair-skinned, jolly, good-natured young artist from Baltimore. The skipper now speaks.

Our boat was a cutter sloop, twenty-eight by eight, drawing just six feet, and carrying much outside ballast. She was put together for business. Her decks were flush, with the exception of a low deck-house and a small self-bailing cockpit. Her horn was housable. She could be battened down and driven through anything. Her spars were lofty, and her spread of canvas great. She could, moreover, beat under the staysail, which is an unusual and desirable accomplishment.

For six days we ballasted, rove halliards and sheets, slaved in interior depths, and astounded the resorters by

Near Clapperton.

our disreputable appearance. At the end of that time we found our work good. The cutter was stocked and equipped.

The skipper distinguished himself just before the start by getting knocked overboard by the boom. He made desperate efforts to save himself, but disappeared amid frantic cheers from the entire crew, who, along with winds, waves and marine gods, were most liberally "cussed" when he climbed over the rail. The wind was light and dead ahead as we tacked, and after getting along a few miles it died entirely, so the best we could do was to haul aft the main-sheet snugly and slap about. The crew made bets as to whether or not the yacht would beat the dingy going sideways. On examination of our exchequer we found several pennies, one of which the mate threw overboard with the appropriate whistling and scratching of the mast. The gods were at once appeased, and a moment later we heeled over with gunwales awash. The mate turned a pale green. The dog-watch became a dull yellow brown, and lay down.

And now the skipper had his jest.

Directly across the noble reach of Detour Passage (through which each year passes a greater tonnage than through any like waterway in the world), north of Drummond, the waters open out. Near at hand, far away, to the right, to the left, rise hundreds and hundreds of little islands. They are all wooded to the water's edge; they all drop off into deep soundings. Between them are glimpses of distant blue seas and other islands. As the yacht slowly and steadily cut her way forward, more and more of these dots of rock and earth opened up, revealing enchanting possibilities of

At Anchor—Farthest North.

exploration. With a northerly gale abeam we bowled along through the islands only too swiftly. We had reefed away down, stowed the staysail, even dropped the peak, not because she would not carry the canvas, but in order to reduce speed. You see, we had never been there before, and though we had charts no one could tell whether they were reliable.

So we sped along, disputing about islands, keeping a sharp lookout for yellow water, and hoping fervently that Providence had its eye on us. Somebody had heard somebody say that a man he knew had heard that Harbor Island was a good place.

Suddenly in a long island some miles ahead, a bight opened up, under the lee of which we perceived a narrow opening. Through the opening there appeared another bight. The chart fiends agreed that this must be Harbor Island, and that in the narrow opening—about a hundred and fifty feet wide—was much water. We derided, but crept in under the jib, sounding energetically, when on a sudden came a sarcastic voice from the shore: "There is twenty-two feet of water all through there"—and we abstained from further sounding. After a little we rounded a point, the anchor bit, and we drew a long breath and looked around us.

The passage opened into a great lake or bay situated in the very center of the island. The high woods surrounded it on all sides—even the entrance seemed closed by the point of the outer bay—and in one elbow nestled a house, a workshop, and a dock. We had just dodged in from a three-reef gale, yet here the water was hardly riffled, and we could hear various frogs, tree-toads, and birds assuring each other sleepily that it was almost evening. We stayed days, and even the business man grumbled only softly. Such is Harbor Island.

Now, on Harbor Island there is a king, and his name is Church. He is grizzled and gray. He lives in a house on the knoll. His wife is Ojibway, and his children half-breeds, therefore the Indians do him homage in some sort. King Church knows the language of the native, and can sing therein; he possesses a fund of information concerning Indian customs and manners, which he imparts quaintly between puffs of his pipe; he has much lore of ancient times, and can tell you of the old raid the peaceful Ottawas (accent the second syllable, if you please) made on the Iroquois, and how even to this day they occasionally get into a panic for fear of retaliation, and flee incontinently to the headwaters of the creeks. And then he will pour out into a tin cup near a half a pint of raw Canadian Club. After this he wipes his mouth on his checkered shirt, and discourses of Epictetus and the pronunciation of *Thule*. The capt'n surprises you somewhat.

We floated gently out of the narrow passage, and, turning sharp to port, cruised down a little channel between Harbor and Maple Islands. Navigation at this point became interesting. The mate sat in the cock-pit with the charts spread out before him, keeping an eye on ranges, and the skipper held the stick. We wound in and out between beautifully wooded islands, over waters so clear that shoals fairly stared at us, and we couldn't have run against them if we had tried. In a little while the islands widened out, and soon after leaving Indian Village astern, we gybed and headed up the more open waters of Potaganissing. Some little time later we rounded Chippewa Point and emerged into the north channel of the Georgian Bay, finally dropping anchor behind the peninsula of Thessalon.

On the east side of the peninsula we discovered a cove, surrounded by huge old Laurentian rocks, rounded by the action of water and cracked in symmetrical parallelograms by the frost. In a hollow between several of these some Indians had pitched their wigwams and built kettle tripods. The rover and dog-watch had been so long deprived of feminine society that they hailed with eager delight the advent of two girls on the beach. With a view to moonlight boating, they became clamorous to borrow the dinghy. *Vetoed:* the skipper and mate wanted to turn in.

Next day we made a direct run across open waters under a southeasterly breeze. The air was cool, the sun warm. All the ship's sewing and patching was done, the rover in especial toiling long and loud over his private wardrobe. The mate kept an eye on the chart, and all took tricks at the helm.

About four bells we dropped anchor in Sitgreave's Bay, a large bight of

The Dog-watch Takes a Bath.

The Rover Mends His Wardrobe.

The Rover Sleeps on Deck.

The Scullion Goes Shopping.

water, hugging a smaller bight under the arm of one of its points. The latter made an ideal harbor, sheltered in every direction. The mate exhumed from his war-bag that precious fly-book and had a try for trout.

The mate was always convincing himself that he had left that confounded fly-book on the beach somewhere. He usually attained that conviction about midnight, at which time he would rout us all out and detail his suspicions.

" Well," said we with forced calmness, " we're anchored. It can't be any farther away by morning."

"Ah, but I could not sleep until I know where it is !"

He would then haul from his war-bag the following articles, which he distributed over us in our bunks : Two undershirts, two pairs drawers, six pairs socks, one pair shoes, a sweater, a flannel shirt, two pairs ducks, a suit of oil-skins, fish-lines, soap, towels, brushes, medicine case, pistol, cartridges, and, last of all, the fly-book. Then putting them all back again, he would sink to sleep like a tired child.

Near the head of a cove we passed through a zone of echoes, remarkable even for this country of many voices. At one place a pistol-shot gave back seven distinct reports. All day long we loafed through the open water, passing successively the False Detour Passage, Cockburn's Island, Mississauga, and the first point of Grand Manitoulin—a huge island, which was to lie to our starboard for many days.

The only breeze we struck next day struck us about breakfast time. It had been perfectly calm, and the skipper was trying to get breakfast. On the oil-stove he had a kettle of "stirabout"; on the alcohol lamp a pot of coffee. The puff in question wandered idly over the hills of Mildrum Bay, sought what it could devour, and leaned against our mainsail to rest. The coffee emptied into the starboard bunk-locker ; the stirabout was saved at the last moment. The alcohol distributed itself impartially and began to blaze. At this the skipper seized a coat (the rover's) and entered earnestly into the business of extinguishing small flames. To accomplish it he leaped madly back and forth soliciting assistance. The crew, puzzled and anxious, could not for some time make out the seeming madman. Their final comprehension arrived about the time the last flame was smothered, and the skipper then had difficulty in averting a deluge of water.

Somebody believed the squall hit pretty hard, but none cared.

One day we beat down Gore Bay, around another point, into a beautiful land-locked harbor. On one side the bluffs rose to a height of over two hundred feet, palisaded like the Hudson. In the curve of the other lay the town, a dusty-streeted little affair, whose establishments were adapted to the needs of farmers.

The dog-watch, the rover, and the skipper climbed the high bluffs, wherefrom they obtained a beautiful view of the bay and the surrounding country. The latter is well cleared into organized farms, in sharp contrast to the trackless wilderness everywhere else in this northland.

Clapperton Island is what the part above water is called. Thereabouts are large rounded bowlders, bigger than houses, wherefrom you could slide on a shovel direct into nine fathoms. Near at hand are the Sow and Pigs, brown-skinned, foam-flecked, threatening. Underneath are bold reefs to be dodged by means of puzzling ranges.

We did these things, and, besides, we managed to admire the great ragged hills to northward, the green islands ahead, the queer, straight-up-and-down formation of Clapperton itself. We took a moment to cuss the dog-watch for letting the jib-sheet run at the most critical moment of all, and to wonder frantically about the location of Reynolds' Rock, water a fathom and a half, big sea. That sea was nasty, three-cornered, wet. It slapped us, and twisted us, and yawed us until the helmsman's life was a burden to him because of the great fear of jibing.

However, once that rock was dodged and that point rounded, we found ourselves boiling along down the lee of Clapperton in a flat sea, but with a puffy wind that often buried our dead-eyes. The rover distinguished himself by sitting calmly on the stern in the height of the nervousness sketching the effect of some old lumber schooners against the sky. The wind now swooped over the hemlocks of Clapperton, and fell upon us suddenly. This disgusted the dog-watch, for the sporadic and decided heeling of the craft disturbed his habitual reclining posture.

As we proceeded, we became aware that the objects toward which we were tending, notably a range of perpendicular cliffs and a deep V-shaped bight, were larger than we had at first supposed them to be. The cliffs rose; the bight opened. We consulted the chart. The land proved to be some six hundred feet in height, and the bay eighteen miles deep and five miles broad. Later we learned from the Indians at its foot that we were the first yacht to enter it for twenty years, which goes far to show the unexplored character of these waters. The Indian village just mentioned consisted of perhaps a score of little log-houses scattered over a mile or so of country. They were arranged quite without order. Instead of flanking the road, the road went to them. They seemed to be fairly clean for Indian huts, owing probably to the fact that these were not "backwoods Indians," but enjoyed the advantages of Christianity. These advantages consist mainly of *ex post facto* marriages, a church with a small tin steeple, and the usual brilliant Roman Catholic prints. That is to the external man. But they mean moreover industry, child-like faith, and a blind trust in the priest. The monthly visits of the latter measure time for the villagers.

In the early morning the wind backed to the north. The skipper paid out cable and let go the second anchor. Later a big sea was rolling down that thirty-mile sweep. We tugged and plunged. "Kismet," said we, and hung on. The rain drove down and we had to eat a cold breakfast within the cabin. "Hell!" said we, and curled up variously, trying to read. The mate took bismuth for a weak stomach. The yacht tried to pull her nose under water by the bitts. The wind shrieked in seven keys.

For untold ages thus it endured. Then with many strange oaths the mate and dog-watch donned slickers and departed in the dingy. "We will stretch our legs on the beach, and return anon," said they.

We issued premonitory advice as to returning into cabins with damp clothes.

Two hours later the skipper uncoiled and looked out the hatchway.

The scuds were scurrying by in ragged gray wisps so low down that they swept the face of the great cliffs opposite. A mist obscured all distant objects. Rain drove in fitful gusts. Great white-crested waves rolled majestically down, lifted the yacht, and finally dashed against the coast with a mighty boom.

The skipper crawled forward. Both anchors held. The yacht rode the great surges easily. He returned to the cabin. The rover and the skipper conversed concerning the mate and the dog-watch. After looking out, the rover gave it as his opinion that both were drowned. The opinion was received with indifference. Both then ate of cold lunch.

Finally, about sunset, those base deserters reappeared, one at a time, wetly and with danger.

They reported much. They had penetrated to the sanctums of sugar-makers, the fashioners of snow-shoes and blanket-weavers and builders of baskets. In one hut the dog-watch had been requested to dance with an Indian maiden of sweet sixteen, but, overcome with sudden and strange timidity, had declined, whereupon the squaws did guy him in strange polysyllables. The mate was hailed as a *Musk-a-wah-wah-ninney*, or doctor, by virtue of his medical studies. The dog-watch agreed to endorse the title, provided the accent was placed on the last syllable. Said *Musk-a-wah-wah-ninney* dosed sick Indians with great satisfaction to himself and them.

During the day on which we left this quaint harbor we shifted canvas just eleven times. We had all kinds of weather, from a vicious black squall to a dead calm. We wore everything, from our skin-tight "swimming suits" to full lines of slickers.

But when it was all over, how pleasant it was to slip quietly along under the influence of a soft fair wind that scarcely rippled the water! The bird songs of late afternoon sounded clearly as we glided past an occasional little island or skirted the miniature coast of a larger bit of land. Directly astern the sun was setting in the usual blood-red haze. The water was taking to itself the peculiar deep

amethyst tinge of the northland, the color seeming to belong in the very substance of the liquid rather than to be merely reflected from the surface. The yacht cleaved her way onward without a sound. Point after point opened up silently. The dusk of evening fell, and we did not care, for we knew that in the narrow channel of Little Current were situated lighthouses, well ranged, and that with this fair, sweet wind we could nose our way to a little cove we wot of at the head of Goat Island, where the channel turns, and thence by one more easy stage to Killarney.

We went through Little Current like a shot out of a gun, but without mishap. Below the passage the water opens out into many broad reaches, island-starred. With the exception of the North Passage, which we did not attempt this trip, it is the most beautiful portion of the channel. From one point you could look up an opening, mathematically straight, twelve miles long, and but a quarter of a mile wide, composed of many islands ranged side by side. To the south, on Manitoulin, open bays as deep as that in which we had weathered the norther. And toward the pole-star were great ranges of precipitous mountains.

All day long we made time through the islands under a fresh fair wind. Almost before we knew it we were picking our way among shoals off Killarney.

We rather expected letters at Killarney, so we sought out the post-office. It was located in an Indian woman's kitchen cupboard. She presented us with the assortment, with the request that we return what we could not use. From her grandmother's maiden aunt we ordered moccasins, most excellent heavy-weather foot-wear for gripping on slippery decks. On the docks was much Indian bark and quill work, indicative of tourists. Inquiry disclosed that the Collingwood boats touched here twice a week, and our letters made it necessary for our scribe to return to civilization by their friendly aid.

"There is a King and his Name is Church."

Navigation
for Yachtsmen
(1900)

NAVIGATION FOR YACHTSMEN.

By W. J. Henderson.

SOME years ago, it is not necessary to say how many, I was cruising on a certain sloop yacht. We lay in a harbor, which shall be nameless (for names lead to identifications), and were to sail in the morning for another port; that being the manner of cruising yachts the world over. There was a young moon in the western heavens, and a light breeze out of the direction in which lay our port of destination. Winds in such directions are apt to evoke improper language from skippers, so when the brass-buttoned gentleman, who gave the sailing orders on this particular craft, came up the com-panion-way audibly grumbling, I thought nothing of it. But he walked up to me, and said:

"That's a sweet run we've got to make to-morrow."

"A very sweet run, indeed," I answered, with all the civility I had on board.

"Seventy-six miles!" he snorted.

"Oh, I think not quite so far as that," I replied, with some confidence.

"Why," said he, "I've just measured it on the chart."

"That's rather curious," I responded, "for I did the same thing myself a few minutes ago, and made it fifty-four miles."

"Well, it's seventy-six," he declared, with the air of one in authority.

I then cordially invited him to come below and show me how he made it, and the owner of the yacht confessed that he would like to see us reconcile our difference of opinion. So we went below and the sailing-master proceeded to lay off the distance on the longitude scale at the bottom of the chart, a method which was never right on sea or land. I complimented him on his ingenuity in augmenting distances, and then proceeded to teach him how to measure courses on a chart, with the result that the owner of the yacht, amazed at the ignorance of his captain, asked me to take charge of the navigation for the rest of the cruise. I need hardly add that the yacht went faster after that, as she did not have to account for quite so many miles a day, and she left port more frequently than she had previously done when runs seemed to be too long to make in a sailing day without more wind or a fair tide, or some one of the other things which anchor-loving sailing-masters need before they are willing to get under way.

This story teaches us that the owner of a yacht should always know navigation. Other things also teach it, but it is an undisputed fact that the ignorance of navigation on the part of yachtsmen leads to a considerable amount of imposition by skippers. Furthermore, I have read somewhere, I forget where, that a yacht owner can never hope to sail his yacht better than the professional sailor, but he can hope to beat him at navigation. This is a fact. It is a real joy to see how easily an intelligent man gets hold of the practice of navigation. And he is always ready and willing to pursue the study to the end, and to master it, while the average skipper is content with a little rule-of-three work, just enough to carry him from port to port. Few have any idea how many chances are taken at sea in navigation. For instance, Capt. Howard Patterson was once called as an expert witness in a suit of a discharged captain for wages for the remainder of the season. The defense was that the man was incompetent, and had proved himself so by piling the yacht up on a rock off the San Domingan coast, when he supposed himself to be more than fifty miles away from it. Capt. Patterson examined this

gentleman's log, and found that in sailing due south, on a line of no variation, he had changed his longitude more than a degree to the eastward. And yet this fellow had the audacity to ship as master of a seagoing yacht, bound for a cruise in foreign waters! Another skipper, showing me the chart of a cruise of a friend's yacht among the Windward Islands, pointed to his position by dead-reckoning one noon, and said:

"I thought that was where I was, but when I got the sun, I found I was away over here."

And he pointed to a position some thirty miles away. I asked him if he had not been able to get any stars in the early morning to give him a better fix, and he answered, with a distant look in his eyes:

"I don't never use no stars."

I learned that this man, who had been a lime-juicer from boyhood, and had been master of an ocean steamer, knew only two sights—the sun at noon, and at nine o'clock in the morning. He could not take an "ex-merid," nor a sunset sight, and knew nothing about the use of the stars, and was totally ignorant of the existence of Sumner's method. He could not take an azimuth for deviation, and he was unacquainted with great circle sailing. Nothing serious had ever happened to him, because he had had luck. He had made some pretty wild landfalls, but that was about all. I am confident that any yachtsman will agree with me that it is much better to be one's own navigator than to take chances with half-educated skippers. The sailing-master can sail the yacht better than the owner. There is no question about that. But the owner can, after a few months of attention to the subject and a reasonable amount of practice, give the average sailing-master cards and spades at navigation. And if the owner chances to be a good Corinthian, the time is not far away when he will be able to take the entire command of his yacht.

And think of the comfort of it! I do not need to tell yachtsmen of the tricks of skippers to avoid doing the work for which they are engaged. There is no news in the statement that if the sailing-master has his way, the mud hook will seldom rise from the bottom of the deep. But let the owner demonstrate to his captain that he can sail his own yacht fairly, and navigate her excellently, and from that instant the skipper is what he ought to be—the owner's humble servant.

Now, there is no copper-bottomed mystery about the art of navigation. It is not a thing that is incomprehensible to all but skilled mathematicians. I have frequently been surprised to find that men thought that only one who could construct his own logarithms, and was a past-master of spherical trigonometry, could be a navigator. It never seems to have occurred to these gentlemen that if their idea of navigation was the correct one, it would be something entirely beyond the reach of the captain of a collier or a coasting schooner. The truth is, that in order to become a navigator one has only to know how to handle decimals and compound numbers, and any man can do that much. The mathematical part of the subject is easy. Of course, it is a good thing for a man to have studied geometry and trigonometry, for a knowledge of these subjects will make comprehensible to him many things which otherwise he must take on faith. But he can learn to navigate his vessel without any heavy cargo of mathematics, and in the picturesque language of the day, get there just the same. The trigonometrical data requisite to the solution of the problems of navigation are all worked out in the tables found in the epitomes. All that the navigator has to do is to know out of which tables to pick certain figures, and after that it is only a matter of addition and subtraction.

That is all of the mathematical mystery. But, of course, the computation is only a small part of the work. A good navigator must thoroughly understand the theory of the science. He must know just when and how to use the different kinds of sights in order to get the best results. He must not only know that the sun or any other heavenly body will give him the most certain longitude when it bears directly east or west, but he must know why. He must not only know that he must take the sun for latitude when it bears due north or south of him, but he must know the reason of the operation. To get at the theory of navigation is not at all difficult. Any intelligent man can learn it without trouble, and the process of learning is simply fascinating. This is not merely the declaration of an enthusiast, which I confess to being, but a statement founded on the observation of many men in the act of studying this charming part of the seaman's calling.

How can the yachtsman learn navigation? Well, he can go to a teacher, if he so desires, or he can work the thing out for himself with patience and a little help. I have never known a man to make a successful navigator of himself without any help, because there are some few points, especially in the management of the sextant, that need illustration. The man working by himself never knows when he has these things right. As for text books, there are several. I need not name them, but I must caution the student to let the big epitomes alone. They are not for him. Bowditch's "American Navigator" is useless to any one but a skilled mathematician. The tables contained in this, the standard American work, can be bought separately under the title of "Useful Tables." With these tables, a nautical almanac, a text book, and his charts, the student will be equipped with sufficient printed matter. He will need also a sextant, a pair of parallel rules, a pair of dividers, a protractor, and for sea work a chronometer. I am presuming that his yacht is equipped with a lead, a log line, and a compass.

This article cannot pretend to lay down a course of study, but, perhaps, it may not be amiss to offer one or two suggestions. Put the sextant and the chronometer away till you have thoroughly mastered dead-reckoning. And before you attack dead-reckoning make sure that you know all that can be known about the information to be obtained from a chart. In clear weather you can sail the whole length of the Atlantic coast-line of the United States with a chart, a log, a lead, and a compass. Make up your mind that you have learned all that before you undertake to go any further. Now, dearly beloved, you cannot learn all that out of the book. The book will tell you how the different things are to be done, but, when you come to do them in practice, you will find that two things will trouble you— the ship won't wait for you, and the fellow at the helm won't keep her straight. While you are trying to locate your yacht by the position of certain objects on the shore, the yacht will run so far past these objects that by the time you have your position marked, you will need a new one. And if the helmsman does not keep her on a straight course, your second bearing will not have the true relation to your first one.

Do not let such things discourage you. What you need is practice, plenty of practice. In working along a coast everything has to be done pretty quickly, especially if you are close to it. To work expeditiously requires a dexterity, and a mental speed which can be acquired only by familiarity with the various processes, and this familiarity comes only with experience. In the very beginning the navigator must make himself a past-master of the compass. Hs must have the rules for correcting compass courses and bearings for deviation and variation at his fingers' ends. He must be able to apply them without stopping to compute. He must perform the processes mentally, and he must always perform them right, or else he will get into trouble. Now I have no hesitation in saying that the solution of compass courses is the most confusing, and, therefore, the most difficult thing in navigation. It comes right at the beginning, but when it is mastered the comfort of the navigator in dealing with the subsequent problems of dead-reckoning is something that can only be imagined. I have seen students of navigation, who had advanced beyond mere chart work, struggling hopelessly in the mazes of working out the course to be sailed from a given position to a new latitude and longitude, and all because they were not thoroughly sure of the rules for correcting courses. Yet this is a thing that comes up every time you shift your helm.

After you have thoroughly learned chart-sailing, then master dead-reckoning. Do not allow yourself to fall into an error, by no means uncommon, that dead-reckoning is not of much value. To the yachtsman it is of especial use, because he is more likely to have opportunities for its employment than for that of observation. Here, again, I can not too urgently proclaim the need of practise. Dead-reckoning is often called, and with justice, a stupid old pilot. Its results are so easily affected by insidious errors that only the man familiar with the conditions under which mistaken calculations are likely to creep in can avoid serious misfortune.

These fundamental parts of the science being at one's fingers' ends, he may attack the work of fixing the position of the ship by observation. And here let me caution the student about one or two things. Do not let any one, no matter who he may be, persuade you to burden your mind with every one of the formulas to be found in the epitomes of navigation. Do not permit some smart naval officer to put you to the blush by making you confess that you don't know how to work latitude by double altitudes, or longitude by lunars. Learn the subject in such a way that you can tell him flatly that the man who uses such worn-out methods is an ignoramus and does not understand the theory of navigation. When you can take a meridian altitude of the sun and a star, and also an ex-meridian altitude, and know the use of the Polar star, you will have all the latitude you need in your business. Equally when you can take a chronometer sight of the sun and a star, you will be pretty well off as regards longitude. It is well to learn, also, the method by a sunrise and sunset sight. It is infrequently used, but the chances are that when you want it you will want it badly.

When you have learned these methods, give yourself up with all your heart and all your mind to the Sumner method. By the Sumner method one gets his latitude and longitude and his deviation all out of one problem. And the thing is capable of so many and such various applications that there is hardly any situation in the experience of the navigator to which it cannot be applied. For example, the old-fashioned way of making the noon position of a ship at sea is this: Take a chronometer sight of the sun in the morning. Do not work it out, but set it aside till after you have your latitude at noon. Then work the latitude back to the time of the morning sight and with the resultant latitude compute the morning longitude. Then carry the longitude forward by dead-reckoning to noon, and thus you have the correct latitude and longitude of the ship at that time. If you are a smart worker, you can get this job completed in about three-quarters of an hour. If you are a little slow at figures, it will take an hour.

Now, by the Sumner method, one uses his latitude by dead-reckoning for working out the morning sight as soon as the altitude is obtained. From his result he constructs in about five minutes what is called a Sumner line of position. When he has obtained the noon latitude, he simply measures on the chart the course and distance sailed since he made the line of position and rules another line parallel to the first. Where this second line cuts the noon parallel of latitude, the ship is at noon. This computation can be completed in ten minutes after the noon altitude is obtained, and it is quite as accurate as the old-fashioned way. Yet the local inspectors are still requiring candidates for the master's license to work the thing out in the primeval style. The Sumner method is of the greatest value in approaching a coast. The results to be obtained from an intelligent application of it are indispensable, and I would heave overboard at once any treatise on navigation which did not discuss this topic very fully.

Finally, let me repeat to the yachtsman that there is only one way to become a good navigator, and that is to keep practicing all the time. Use your sextant constantly. Learn to take the angular height of lighthouses with it, and to compute from this the distance of the ship from them. Learn to measure horizontal angles with it, and to ascertain from them the distance of your vessel from certain known points. Familiarize yourself with the methods of taking cross-bearings and bow and beam bearings, as you run along any line of land. If you find that at first you cannot take bearings fast enough to help you as the yacht passes the land, heave your vessel to; or, if she is a steamer, stop her. Never mind the smiles of your self-satisfied sailing-master. He will be walking on his hands and knees before you in a few months when some night you work a time-sight of a star.

And when you come to practicing observation work, do so in known positions. If you are running into Newport near noon and find yourself abreast of Beaver Tail at twelve o clock, shoot the sun for latitude. You will find the latitude of the light on the chart, or in the lighthouse list. See how near you can come to it. If you are passing Point Jude about nine o'clock on a clear summer's morning, when the point bears due north of you, and your longitude should be the same as that of the light, take a chronometer-sight of the sun. You will find a good sea horizon to the eastward. Work out your sight and see how near you come to the real thing. If you are not correct, you can ascertain the reason. If you try to practice at sea, out of sight of land, you will not know whether you are right or not. By practicing in known positions, you will acquire an absolute certainty about your work and a confidence in yourself which will be worth millions to you in the time of need. Do the same thing with your dead-reckoning. Keep it in clear weather and along the shore. You can tell precisely how much and of what nature your errors are, and thus learn to avoid them in the future.

And buy good instruments. A cheap sextant is not worth the trouble it takes to heave it over the side. A cheap chronometer is the biggest liar on earth. A poor compass is worse than a bunco-steerer. The first outlay on these things is the largest. But it is a good investment. It will save you a lot of money in the end. When you have your good instruments and have learned how to use them, go down to the local inspectors and take out a license to command your own yacht. Then, when you go over the side and set your foot on your own quarter-deck, let it be understood that there is just one captain on board of that ship, and that he will nominate the hour when the mud hook is to come up, and will also give out the course and the daily noon position of the ship. After that you will feel like a man who has just come into a fortune and moved out of a fourth floor furnished room into his own house.

Yachting on the Great Lakes (1900)

YACHTING ON THE GREAT LAKES.

By John B. Berryman.

FROM the head of Lake Michigan to the outlet of Lake Ontario, stretches a continuous waterway of more than eleven hundred miles, with a maximum breadth of one hundred and five miles, in Lake Huron. This is all open water, with the exception of sixty miles through the St. Clair and Detroit rivers, between lakes Huron and Erie, and some thirty miles through the Welland Canal, which cuts the narrow peninsula dividing Lake Erie from Lake Ontario. The maximum depth varies from 275 to 1,000 feet.

As Lake Superior does not boast a yacht club, its vast expanse has not been included in this purview, but the enthusiastic cruiser may, if he so desire, add to his itinerary the 60,000 or 70,000 square miles of water covered by that lake and the Georgian Bay.

These arid facts are given simply to show that should yachting not flourish between the Chicago River and the Thousand Islands, it is not from lack of water. And water, so a well-known commodore informs me, when intelligently blended with other components, is absolutely essential to a proper enjoyment of the sport.

The people of the cities on the Great Lakes have an environment conducive to maritime development; and the marvellous growth of inland shipping in the past ten years witnesses that, commercially, the middle west has been fully alive to its opportunities. The volume of tonnage passing through the Sault Ste. Marie Canal, in a season is greater than that of any waterway in the world, and vastly in excess of the tonnage of the famous Suez Canal.

At the first blush this seems to have little bearing upon yachting. The 7,000-ton freighter is a very distant relative of the jaunty steam yacht, yet the development of commercial shipping has an appreciable effect upon the growth of shipping for pleasure only. A maritime nation is a yachting nation. People accustomed to the sight of ships and habituated to water travel, take great interest in everything pertaining to the sea. The spirit of the old Vikings is latent in most of the Anglo-Saxon family, and needs but suitable environment to germinate.

Yachting, as an organized sport, had its inception about half a century ago. Pleasure craft there were before then, and possibly races between single boats, but no organizations with fixed rules such as we have to-day, and as the communities on the shores of the lakes were only in the formative period fifty years ago, we could hardly expect much interest in a sport, which, more than all others, demands leisure and money, among a people possessing neither the one nor the other. Fifty years, however, have worked many changes. The oldest and largest yachting organization on the Great Lakes is the Royal Canadian Yacht Club, of Toronto, Canada, founded in 1852. The membership at the present time is slightly in excess of 800. The club has waxed fat in the forty-eight years which have passed since. Dr. Hodder, Major McGrath, J. J. Arnold, and a few others, made a modest beginning, but, like the faithful Adam, time has not shorn it of its virility. The club maintains a town home on the city side of Toronto Bay, and a second house beautifully situated among shady trees on the island which forms the natural breakwater of the harbor. The fleet is large and of excellent quality for either cruising or racing.

The ambitious city of Hamilton boasts two clubs — the Royal Hamilton and the Victoria—both flourishing organizations. Hamilton has a splendid natural harbor

Cleveland Y. C. House.

especially well adapted for small boat sailing, and this has tended to build up the sport among the younger element.

Canada has, also, a strong club in the venerable city of Kingston, noted for its good sailors. Yachting all along the Canadian shore is "fashionable," and, consequently, flourishing. What fashion approves thrives. Were it the correct thing to own a yellow dog, we would have yellow dog clubs in every hamlet, each with a waiting list a yard long.

The year 1886 was made more or less memorable by the founding of the Rochester (N.Y.) Yacht Club, an aggressive organization with a decided taste for racing, owning a commodious house on the Genessee River, and a fleet of fifty-eight boats.

The Oswego Yacht Club shares with Rochester the burden of carrying the Stars and Stripes to the front at the annual meetings of the Lake Yacht Racing Association. They have some excellent sailors at Oswego, and a respectable list of boats.

Upon Lake Erie, there are clubs at Buf-

falo, Cleveland, Toledo, Erie and Sandusky—all doing well, and holding every year a regatta at Put-in-Bay, which is always well attended.

Sandusky seems entitled to the distinction of being one of the yachting pioneers. The Sandusky boats, *Mist, Witch* and *Winona*, were in the habit of carrying off nearly every prize in sight in their day, which was somewhere between 1856 and 1861. The yachting men there went to sleep for many seasons, content with past glories, but the interest has revived during the last few years.

The Erie Yacht Club is the youngest on the lake, having been formed in 1896. There has never been any real yachting at Erie, but there must be a hereditary seafaring strain in the old town which should make sailing popular. It was at this port Commodore Perry built, equipped and manned his fleet in 1812 or 1813. From Erie, he sailed to the immortal encounter which earned for him a place among the nation's heroes, and at Erie the bones of his old flagship, *Niagara*, rest peacefully on the bottom of Misery Bay.

The tars of Detroit have two organizations — the Detroit Boat Club and the Citizens' Yachting Association, the latter formed by merging the old Detroit Yacht Club and the Michigan Yacht Club.

The Detroit Boat Club, as its name implies, was originally an oarsman's organization; the yachting feature has grown gradually. The club was founded in 1839, and is, I believe, the oldest aquatic club on the chain of lakes. Had yachting been a feature from the first, the club would antedate any other yacht club by many years. It has a very handsome home on Belle Isle, an island in the river opposite Detroit.

The Detroit boats are sailed principally upon Lake St. Clair, a broad, shallow sheet of water formed by the widening of the river of the same name; but they are usually well in evidence at the Put-in-Bay regattas of the Interlake Yachting Association.

On Lake Michigan there are a number of very creditable organizations. The Chicago, Columbia and Jackson Park clubs, all of Chicago, and the Milwaukee, Sheboygan, Green Bay, Little Traverse Bay and Grand Rapids clubs, at the ports thus named.

The oldest of them is the Chicago Yacht Club, founded in 1875. The club owns a unique building, modeled after an ancient galleon, but as the membership has outgrown the present accommodations, plans are making for a new house to cost in the neighborhood of $25,000. The club fleet is composed principally of large boats, seven of the number measuring over fifty feet racing length.

The Columbia Club has a large fleet, especially strong in the classes below twenty-five feet, and a new club-house has just been completed.

It is very lamentable, however, that Chicago should, when her wealth and population is considered, be so far behind other lake cities in yachting matters.

Not that the number or quality of the boats is insignificant, but with a population equal, or in excess of, all the cities on Lake Ontario or Lake Erie combined, one naturally looks for plethoric rosters of both men and yachts. The truth is, there are at least two clubs on the lakes, each with a membership larger than that of the three Chicago clubs combined. I do not think this condition will exist for any great length of time. The sport seems now to be in the hands of the right people, who are going about the matter in the right way to popularize it, and the increased interest is apparent.

The Milwaukee Club has a large membership and excellent quarters overlooking the splendid artificial harbor. The fleet is far from what it should be, but this will be remedied in time, probably.

To sum up, there are some twenty-two clubs on the lakes, with a membership of about 5,500, and possibly 600 to 700 yachts of all sizes.

The clubs on Lake Michigan belong to the Lake Michigan Yachting Association; those in Detroit and upon Lake Erie to the Interlake Yachting Association, and those on Lake Ontario to the Lake Yacht Racing Union.

These organizations are again consolidated into the Yacht Racing Union of the Great Lakes. Each association sends three delegates to the central body, and these delegates are known as the Council. The president of the Council for the current year is Mr. Chas. E. Kramer, of Chicago, who was secretary of the Chicago Yacht Club a quarter of a century ago. The serious business of Mr. Kramer's life is making post prandial speeches and attending yacht club meetings. As a recreation he practices maritime law. The secretary is the inimitable J. Edmund Burroughs, of Rochester, N. Y., known far and wide as the gentleman who walked the mast of the old *Madge* from the hounds to the deck. The *Madge* was heeled so far over at the time, that he

Rochester Y. C. House.—*Genesee* in Foreground.

could not get in any other way, and he had become tired of sitting in the raging surge.

At present the rules are practically uniform on all the lakes, but a local association is privileged to make rules for its own members, irrespective of the central body.

The system of measurement now in force is the well-known girth rule,

$$\frac{L.W.L + B + .75\,G + \frac{1}{2}\sqrt{S.A.}}{2}$$

in which

$L.W.L.$ = Load water line.

$B.$ = Beam at its greatest point.

$G.$ = Girth.

$S.A.$ = Sail area.

Girth is the length of a line drawn around the immersed surface of a hull from water-line to water-line at a point six-tenths of the distance between the fore-and-aft ends of the water-line measuring from the forward end.

For centreboard boats the girth is taken around the hull as above, and to this is added twice the distance between the underside of the keel and the centre of area of the board. The centreboard must not be ballasted except to overcome flotation, ballasted boards, or those made of metal, if they weigh more than an oak board two inches thick of the same superficial area, are measured as fixed keels.

This rule has practically been tried only one season, but the test given last year, when six challenging and six defending yachts were built for the trial races, preceding the contest for *Canada's* Cup, crowded much experience into a limited time. On the whole, the rule worked satisfactorily, especially in the direction of equalizing the elements of speed in divers types. It is not productive of such a large-bodied boat as the 35 per cent. midship section rule which preceded it, but it seems to make a fast craft with

Chicago Y. C. House.

body enough to permit as fair accommodations as a rational man would look for in a boat intended primarily for speed.

These trial races demonstrated that a very undesirable craft could be built under the girth rule, but the fact remains that of the twelve built, the three (*Genesee, Beaver, Minota*) which undoubtedly stood first, second and third in point of speed, were all good, wholesome boats, built on sane lines.

The end of racing is to win. If a rule be so framed that an honest boat stands a fair chance of winning, then honest boats will be built and the sport be the gainer. After all, is not speed the result of a careful balance between all elements rather than an exaggeration of any one?

In order to build up a fleet of substantial seaworthy yachts, the Yacht Racing Union, three years ago, adopted a table of scantling setting forth in detail dimensions of the stem, sternpost, keel, keelson, frames, floors, clamp, bilge, stringer, deck beams and planking for each class. All boats constructed since the adoption of this table, to be eligible to Association regattas, must be built in accordance therewith. This was a decided step in the right direction, and its wisdom will be clearly apparent as time goes on.

During the summer

Detroit Boat Club House.

season the lakes are comparatively free from destructive storms. Of course, fierce squalls are not unusual (what body of water is free from them?), but their duration is short, and, as a general thing, their coming may be seen in ample time.

Any well-built, ballasted yacht may cruise all summer with perfect safety, provided that insanity does not develop in the skipper. When the wind blows fresh it kicks up a short, steep sea which makes the berth of the lookout forward rather damp, and if the wind happens to have been blowing strongly in another part of the lake, we sometimes have a heavy ground swell.

Upon Lake Michigan a heavy blow

centreboard is a necessity. I never could become very enthusiastic over the type, but the world would be deadly monotonous if we all thought alike.

Since the first club burgee was hoisted the lake yachtsmen have fought out hundreds of friendly contests with boats of every conceivable design. Deep English cutters—planks on edge—have been tried out against beamy sand-baggers; compromise centreboard boats have met fin keels; cutters of diverging lines have met each other. Every successful yacht on salt water has had its prototype upon the inland seas, and many have been floated which were never dreamed of in old Neptune's philosophy. On these waters, in

Milwaukee Y. C. House.

from the northeast brings down a vicious sea which is liable to seriously strain a vessel not well put together.

For anything except afternoon sailing, the best kind of boat on the lakes is one with good freeboard, beam and outside lead. The cutter and schooner are probably the most desirable types—the cutter is, in fact, the predominant type on lakes Ontario and Michigan. The fin keels also have shown themselves excellent sea boats when well built. Some of them have passed safely and easily through tremendous weather.

Upon Lake Erie boats do not run so much to fixed keel; probably owing to local conditions, the centreboard sloop is very popular at Detroit—of course, the

fact, American and English designers have had their best opportunity to study and adopt what was desirable in the product of the other.

This has followed, naturally, through the presence of a large Canadian yachting interest on one side of Lake Ontario looking to England for designing talent, and of an American contingent on the opposite shore enlisting the services of the naval architects of our own country.

In the earlier days, McGiehan, of New York, was one of the more prominent American designers, and contemporary with him was A. G. Cuthbert, of Coburg, Ont., who built *Atalanta* and *Countess of Dufferin,* which made very unsuccessful attempts to "lift" the *America's* Cup. It may be remarked in passing, that other designers of great reputation, and with far better financial backing than old Capt. Cuthbert ever dreamed of, have failed in the same way.

Following Cuthbert and McGiehan, came a remarkable series of high-class yachts from designers of the modern school. The late Edward Burgess sent *Merle* and *Vilueth,* both successful, but the former particularly so. Wm. Fife, Jr., the designer of *Shamrock,* contributed *Zelma, Yama* and *Canada.* The yacht last named defeated *Vencedor,* of Chicago, a Poeckel design, for an international lake trophy in 1896. This trophy is now known as *Canada's* Cup. Watson, the designer of the *Valkyries,* who will design the new challenger for Sir Thomas Lipton, sent many years since *Verve I.* and *Verve II.,* and later on that splendid cutter, *Vreda.* Cary-Smith is known through the sloop *Cinderella,* and schooners *Clorita* and *Sallie.* Last year, Arthur Payne, of Southampton, who designed, I believe, the successful English cutters *Saint* and *Penitent,* sent the lines of the graceful cutter *Beaver,* the defeated defender of *Canada's* Cup, while Hanley, of Quincy Point, Mass., had the victorious challenger in *Genesee,* undoubtedly the fastest 35-footer on fresh water, if not in the country.

There is one challenge cup on the Great Lakes which is truly international in a broad sense. This is *Canada's* Cup, previously referred to. The cup had its origin in 1896, when E. C. Berriman, through the Lincoln Park Y. C. of Chicago, challenged the Royal Canadian Yacht Club of Toronto to a match race between two boats in the 45-foot class.

The challenge was accepted, and the contestants, *Vencedor* and *Canada,* met upon neutral waters at Put-in-Bay, Lake Erie. For this match the Toledo International Yacht Race Association donated a handsome sterling silver trophy, designed by Tiffany. The cup bears the emblematic figures of the eagle and the lion, and is artistic in conception and execution.

The match was decided in favor of *Canada.*

The owners of *Canada,* afterward, by deed of gift, transferred the cup to the Royal Canadian Yacht Club, to be held as a perpetual international challenge trophy.

In 1899 the Chicago Yacht Club challenged, selecting the Rochester yacht *Genesee* after a series of trial races. The holders defended with the cutter *Beaver,* choosing her after a number of trials, in which six boats competed. *Genesee* won in three magnificent races, and the cup is now in Chicago. The two contests which have taken place for this trophy have been the cause of some remarkable boats being built, and the future contests, for contests there will be, as the Canadians are too good sportsmen to let matters rest as they are, will of necessity bring out the highest skill of American and English designers.

There is yet another the Fisher Cup, which originated in Chicago in 1882, and has been the cause of much exciting racing, but it is open to yachts belonging to the Lake Yacht Racing Association only, so that the contests are limited to clubs on Lake Ontario.

It is the misfortune of the lake yachtsmen to have ports of call very far apart. Our shores are not indented by harbors, nor enlivened by summer resorts every few miles.

Flagship *Thistle,* Chicago Y. C

It is this feature, more than any other, which has whitened the waters of Long Island Sound and the Massachusetts coast with sails.

This stimulus we shall never have, but so long as the free winds blow in the halls of heaven and the blue waters dance in the summer sun, we shall not lack for men who appreciate the witchery of the deep.

The America's Cup
(1885)

ITS PAST EFFECT ON YACHT—BUILDING AND THE COMING CONTEST FOR ITS POSSESSION.

We have the prospect of a visit, in the coming season, of a British yacht with the purpose of getting back that much-treasured emblem of victory so gallantly won by the *America* nearly thirty-four years ago. To those of us old enough to remember the event, there comes up also a recollection of the wonder, interest, and enthusiasm which preceded, attended, and followed it, the like of which no yachting incident of the future can reasonably ever be expected to equal; as from any such there must be wanting several elements that gave *eclat* to the *America's* advent into British waters. The project of an international yachting-contest was not hackneyed; it was new as the vessel which was to take the premier part in it; it had all the freshness and force of its novelty. The British people, even those not familiar with yachting matters, were intent with interest.

Some knowledge of the purpose to try the yacht against English vessels must have existed in England even while the *America* was being built, for illustrated papers showed the vessel as she stood in the builder's yard put up in frame, and to such an extent was her peculiar form considered an innovation at that time that the writer, who was then living in England, and little more than a boy, remembers that after the *America's* victory all sorts of attempts were made to produce models like that yacht, some of which had no better aid than the perspective representations of the vessel given in the illustrated papers. We have it on the authority of the *Field* that "the yacht *America* turned everything topsy-turvy at Cowes," and "that in three years one hundred yachts had been lengthened forward," "or altered;" and all this when, for eighteen years preceding the arrival of the *America* in English waters, at least one English naval architect had been advocating just those features which were realized with so much beauty and effectiveness in her.

It may be interesting at this time, in view of the promised visit of the *Genesta*, and perhaps also of other contestants for the treasured cup, to note some of those changes, improvements, and developments which have been effected in modern yachts, and in doing this to give some attention to influences which have served to effect them. Owing to the very important changes which had their inception immediately before the building of the *America*, it will be best to go back to 1845.

About this time the New York Yacht Club was organized, and held its first regatta on July 16 of that year. Six schooners and three sloops were in the race, of sizes varying from forty-five to seventeen tons, O.M., and the *Cygnet*, according to the records of the Club, "won the cup of the value of the entrance-money."

In this race were several yachts of George Steers's build, including the winner; and to those who are privileged to inspect the models preserved in the large room of the New York Yacht Club, and carefully arranged by Mr. Olsen in chronological order as nearly as practicable, there will probably be nothing that he can see that will more surprise him, nothing for which he will be so little prepared, as the radical change in the character of models before 1850, and after that date. These will not show a gradual development of the long bow, easy and hollow, and the graceful form. The change is not progressive by moderate degrees, but sudden and complete. It is the change from the caterpillar to the butterfly. So far as George Steers's models are referred to there is nothing in the collection of the New York Yacht Club of date preceding 1851 which shows the long bow, hollow lines and graceful shape, of which, among yacht-builders, he would appear to have been in this country the pioneer. The *Una*, built in 1847, and shown with a long bow, is there; but the model shows her as she was after being altered in 1854. The *Sybil*, *Syren*, *La Coquette*, and other of George Steers's models of yachts built previous to 1848, are there to be seen; but none of these, any more than the model of the *Cygnet*,

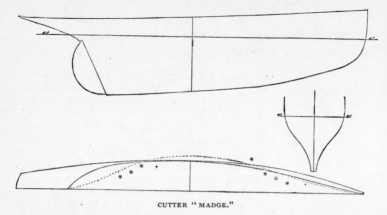

CUTTER "MADGE."

contain any suggestion of the features of the *Sylvie* and the *America*. There is, however, a missing link to be found in the pilot-boat *Mary Taylor*, built elsewhere, according to Mr. Henry Steers, in the summer of 1848; according to others, a year later. This boat was built for Mr. Richard Brown, who sailed the *America* in the Cowes races, and whose son afterward sailed her when that vessel took part as one of the fleet put against the *Cambria* in 1870. In the *Mary Taylor*, George Steers took a new departure.

The model of this vessel was lately shown to the writer by Mr. Henry Steers, and a table of offset is given in "Griffith's Naval Architecture," published in 1851; but a good representation of her may be found in "Marett's Yacht Building." For the purpose of showing the kind of yacht that was built in New York between 1840 and 1848 I here give the lines of the *Cygnet*, built about 1844. The lines were taken from her model.

I also give the outlines of the *Mary Taylor* and the *America*, those of the last-named vessel being taken from an unpublished drawing. These will be sufficient to show, so far as any professional yacht-builder in this country had to do with it, the inception of a change in yacht-modeling then unprecedented, and not since equaled, nor likely to be, in the extent of attention which was secured from yachtsmen, or of influence exerted on yacht-designers. Between the great improvement which George Steers made in the *Mary Taylor* and the celebrity which he gained in the yacht *America*, I only know of one intermediate effort on this class of vessel, and that was on the pilot-boat *Moses H. Grinnell*, which vessel, as might be expected, had strong points of resemblance to the pre-

ceding as well as to the following design. While it does not seem to be disputed that the *America* converted the yachting fraternity everywhere to a strong belief in long bows and hollow lines, it seems equally incapable of contradiction that the *Maria*, owned by John C. Stevens, of Hoboken, had an extremely long and hollow bow put upon her two years or so before the *America* was launched. As the *Maria* and her owner are intimately connected with early yachting history, and with the building of *America*, some notice of both may be interesting here.

The *Maria*, as first built, in 1845, was modeled with a full bow, and after the style of a fast North-river sloop. She had about eighty-eight feet water-line length, and twenty-six-and-a-half feet beam, and two center-boards. She was sloop-rigged, and a number of ingenious devices that originated with the owner, or his brothers, were used upon her. She had a hollow mast, and a hollow boom made from staves. She had a big sail-plan, and a boom seventy feet long on the foot of her jib. She anticipated, by many years, the modern practice of using outside lead; about twelve tons of lead were used outside her planking, and about eight tons more were let into her thick center-board, which was fitted with powerful springs, so as to admit of its being raised with little effort. An interesting fact to modern "Corinthians" is that the first race the *Maria* sailed in was on October 6, 1846. There were six yachts in the race, all manned by amateurs, and the *Maria* won handsomely.

Herewith I give water-line and cross-section of the *Maria*, which will show the character of the boat. She was lengthened twice at the bow, altered about the free-board of the stern, and, finally, her rig was changed to a schooner's in 1865. The character of the alteration made at the bow is shown by dotted lines.

The model on the premises of the New York Yacht Club shows the yacht after she was finally lengthened, about 1849, and represents, I believe, the only really

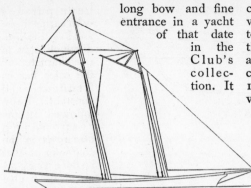

SAIL PLAN OF "AMERICA."

long bow and fine entrance in a yacht of that date in the Club's collection. It is on record, however, that early in the century, Mr. R. L. Stevens, after vainly trying to overcome the opposition and fear of ridicule of a firm of shipbuilders whom he asked to put a long false bow on a river steamer to increase her speed, finally had the work carried out under his own immediate direction, and with results very advantageous to speed.

The *America* was built for Mr. John C. Stevens under a stipulation that an extra price was to be paid for her if she beat the *Maria;* but she was not to be accepted if she did not do it. This, it is said, she failed to do, which is, perhaps, not to be wondered at when it is considered that the *Maria*, having now been lengthened, was about twenty feet longer than the *America*, sloop-rigged, and in smooth water. Though she failed to equal the *Maria* under the conditions of trial, she sailed so well that she was bought by five gentlemen (including two of the Stevens family), who clubbed together for the purpose. She was sent to England, with the result known to everybody. A true, but, at the same time, misleading, statement has occasionally appeared in print, that the *Maria*, which could beat the *America*, was beaten in 1846 by a schooner called *Coquette*, a vessel sixty-six feet long. It should here be explained that in this rough-water contest it was not the *Maria* lengthened, but the original full-bowed craft, that suffered defeat.

Having noticed the salient point connected with the introduction of the modern long bow in this country, it may be stated that the late J. Scott Russell, N.A., had, as early as 1833, made some experiments with forms and models, and, as a result, he advocated a wave-line bow, with concave entrance, and a fore-body six-tenths the whole length of the vessel, and had given good reasons and able argument in favor of these features and proportions. Moreover, according to Marett and other authorities, including Lloyd's Register, the *Mosquito* cutter, an iron yacht, was built in 1848. This vessel had a long bow, of about the proportion recommended by Mr. Russell. The water-line of the bow was fine, and had some concavity in it; and the character of her lines and model must, at the time of her first appearance in British racing waters, have shown a strong and striking contrast to the vessels she appeared amongst. One or two yachts having the same new features were launched into English waters between this time and the arrival of *America*, in 1851; but it does not seem that these created any great enthusiasm, or that the British yachtsman was yet ready to abandon the cod's-head and mackerel-tail principle. Perhaps, had the *Mosquito* sailed over from New York, and been as successful as was the *America* upon her first appearance, her influence might have been different. For two or three seasons, however, and until after a change of ownership and captains, the *Mosquito* was not the signal success which she then became.

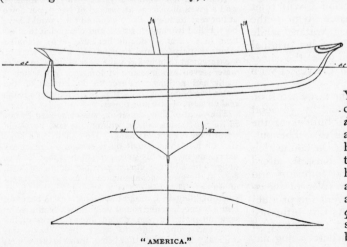

"AMERICA."

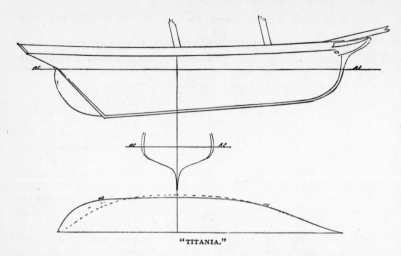

"TITANIA."

In the mean time the America entered upon the scene, and that hybrid fish that was neither cod nor mackerel ceased to be any longer the trusted pattern after which the aspiring yachtsman must fashion his craft. The *Mosquito* was a cutter of about sixty-two and one-half feet water-line, and in 1852 and 1853 was, according to Marett, engaged in sixteen races, and in that time was beaten only once, and then only by a few feet. The midship section and water-line of this famous yacht are given here as taken from "Marett's Yacht Building," and will serve to show the general character of this innovator. I do not find the name of this yacht in the list of those which raced with the *America* for the cup in 1851; but she appears to have raced with that vessel round the Isle of Wight for the Queen's Cup in July, 1852, and to have beaten her then by one minute and forty-nine seconds.

Before leaving this period I will refer to the only private match which the *America* sailed in British waters while she remained in the hands of her original owners; and I will also give the sheer plan and other outlines of the vessel with which she competed.

These are taken from the large work on naval architecture published by J. Scott Russell, the designer and builder of the *Titania*, the yacht referred to. The outlines of this vessel, studied in connection with the remarks of Mr. Russell, afford the strongest proof of the fettering and pernicious influence which rules of measurement may have, to prevent the production of the best forms. As this influence has always been present in the history of yachting, more especially where racing has

been pursued with earnestness, and as the frequent changes in the character of the rules has as frequently and constantly been followed by corresponding changes in the character of that influence, as shown in the features of yachts built under the rules, the zealous yachtsman will doubtless find interesting reading in the following words of Mr. Russell: —

The *Titania* was the only English yacht that would accept the challenge of Mr. Stevens's famous yacht *America*. The *Titania* accepted the challenge scarcely in the hope of winning, for she was over-matched in size, sail, area, and every element of racing; but the English engineer was chivalrously unwilling that the American engineer should leave Cowes without the courtesies of a tournament. . . .

These two yachts serve as landmarks to record an important revolution which came over the ideas of Englishmen, and especially of yachtsmen, in reference to the whole question of yacht-building and yacht-measurement.

The *Titania* represents the old straight waistcoat, in which the naval architect was compelled to work previous to the great challenge of the *America* in 1851. The yacht clubs who have earned the reputation of being great advancers of naval architecture had, nevertheless, until that date, obstinately adhered to antiquated theories of yacht-measurement. These theories compelled the builder to narrow the beam of the yacht to the utmost, even at the expense of ugly forms and bad qualities.

If he did not do this a yacht of a given tonnage and a given displacement, instead of being put down at her real tonnage of one hundred tons, would have been called two hundred tons, and compelled to allow time to a yacht of double her size. For a similar arbitrary purpose, and to meet the absurd laws of measurement then in force, the keel of the ship under water served as a measure of tonnage, with which it really had nothing whatever to do, instead of the water-line being taken for that purpose, which is the real element of size and power.

The yacht-builder, therefore, was compelled by law to do two things, which, without the law, he would never have dreamt of doing. He had to cut a large slice off his lateral longitudinal section by giving an enormous rake to his stern-post, and to that he was obliged to add the utmost possible depth of keel, even at the great inconvenience of excessive draught of water. The *Titania* is a type of this system of yacht-building in a straight waistcoat. The beautiful round water-lines and round body-lines which may be seen on plate 32 (see dotted lines) represent the ideal and proper lines to which the *Titania* was originally drawn; but, after being drawn to these lines, the builder was forced to cut two large slices off her on each side, at the load water-line, to make her extreme breadth come within the law for tonnage. He had to cut off the water-lines where they would have had a gentle swell in the middle, and make them straight and flat; and he had to cut off from the keel of the vessel a large amount of the area of longitudinal section, which was absolutely necessary to make the vessel windwardly, — all this having been done to make the vessel square with this irrational law of tonnage. . . . Mr. Stevens's yacht, *America*, was a pure wave-line vessel, built without the trammels of measurement tonnage.

In America a ship of one hundred tons is called one hundred tons whether her keel be cut off or retained, or whether the natural form of her water-lines be contracted or left free. The *America* was not larger, had no more weight to carry, and no more water to displace, than the *Titania*; but she was left with her broad shoulders in the water unmutilated, to enable her to stand up under press of sail; and she retained her full length and depth of longitudinal immersed section in the water to enable her to lie close on a wind.

In other respects her lines were like those of the *Titania* below water-lines. She was built on the wave principle, carried out without modification on lines very similar to those in plate 32. (See dotted water-line and cross-section.)

For the Americans adopted for many classes of vessels, yachts as well as clippers (including the famous sailing-clippers of Mr. McKay), the wave principle of construction.

The consequence of the race between these two rivals on the same system — one free and the other in fetters — was as might have been expected. Before the wind there was scarcely a difference in their speed, except that arising from the larger sail area of the *America*. On a wind on the contrary, the *America* stood up under canvas, by virtue of her uncurtailed shoulders, while the *Titania* keeled over. The *America*, with her uncurtailed longitudinal section, weathered the *Titania* at every tack. This challenge of America to England was of incalculable benefit to England. America reaped a crop of glory; England reaped a crop of wisdom.

The yacht-builders of England at once adopted the wave-line principle for their new yachts and called them, with rigid self-denial, American lines; and they instantly swept from their books those legislative en-

" GENESTA."

actments which compelled their yacht-builders to dance in fetters. It was worth the loss of a race to gain so much.

With reference to these same matters, we may find that Mr. Marett has written, —

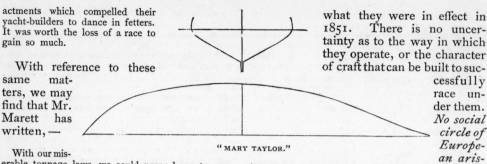

"MARY TAYLOR."

what they were in effect in 1851. There is no uncertainty as to the way in which they operate, or the character of craft that can be built to successfully race under them. *No social circle of European aris-*

With our miserable tonnage laws, we could never hope to compete with the untrammeled American; our fastest vessels were such small cutters as were able to avail themselves of a shuffling evasion of tonnage. Applied to larger craft, this evasion was inadmissible; hence little or no improvement is to be traced in the construction of large-class yachts for many years prior to 1851. However, the *America* set our builders to work, and nothing was to be seen but long bows, or lengthened bows.

With an object in view, which I shall notice further on, I have quoted somewhat more largely than I might otherwise have done. It is, perhaps, as strong a showing as could be made for the meddlesome, mischievous, and cramping influence of a measurement-rule, that it could have influenced the author of the wave-line system to sacrifice the long, easy bow and rounded sides, which formed an essential part of that system, and which he had then advocated for near a score of years to the exigency of the rule's requirements.

It is not so easy to see, however, where Mr. Russell finds ground for the statement that the legislative enactments, which compelled the English yacht-builder to dance in fetters, were swept instantly from their books. The very absurd regulation which required that the measure of length should be taken on the keel was changed, and not very promptly; and length was taken from the extreme outside of stem to extreme outside of stern-post, until the yawl *Jallanar* was built with her stern-post situate at a point a very long way forward of the after termination of her water-line. The very simple and natural method was at last adopted of taking the actual length on the water-line into account, provided that no part of the boat under water exceeded this length.

This change made it no longer needful under English rules for the builder to rake his stern-post excessively; and when he does it now it is to a less degree, and for the purpose of insuring quick movement in stays chiefly. In other respects, the English rules remain to-day pretty much

tocracy was ever half so arbitrary and discriminating in the selection of its company as is the club which adopts an English rule of measurement; only the long, lean, narrow, and deep yacht, with lead ballast outside, or equivalent to this, will ever be found among the privileged company of its racers. The only variety is between this kind and more so. More money, by far, is being spent in Great Britain in the production of racing-yachts than in any country in the world; more, perhaps, than in all the rest of the world put together, and more trained skill and energy are being used there in this direction; *but if there are any undeveloped possibilities in the direction of a yacht of different character and proportions than the present English racing-yacht, which, nevertheless, shall be fast, serviceable, and desirable, this will never, I think, be shown on an English race course by a yacht produced under their present rules.*

I shall have occasion to notice some features of rules in use here, and the effect of them, but for the present will leave this part of my subject to allude briefly to changes and improvements effected, in our own waters and abroad, in yachts and their equipment since 1851.

In looking back over that time it is scarcely possible to point out any startling innovations, great novelties, or striking improvements. New features, changes, and improvements are more easy to name. In respect to models very many yachtsmen could be found who would claim that the old *America* is equal to any schooner of her size to-day, in rough water or smooth, and in any kind of weather. It would certainly have added a lively interest to many regattas, and have gladdened the eyes of spectators to have had her in them. The old boat certainly did well in the great race of the yacht fleet over the New York course, with the *Cambria*, in 1870, coming in, as she did, fourth; and if a mishap in setting her light canvas had been avoided, she might have done better. Three or four years ago cherished memories were entertained of the sloop *Julia's* old-time performances, and the wish was often expressed that the schooner-rig should be changed back to the old rig and trim, when she would show the newer craft that she was more than good for them yet. The wish was commonly father to the thought; sympathies were with the old sloop; but somehow when the change was made she failed to keep alongside the boats that had no history; and the *Julia* is no more; but the *Nirvana*, like a modernized phenix, rises from her ashes.

Whatever conclusion may be reached by a comparison of the best model of thirty-four years ago with the yachts of to-day, I think it will be admitted by common consent that there are fewer old tubs and monstrosities now than then; that crude productions are now the exception; that the work of yacht designing is generally in more capable hands; and that, if George Steers were alive to-day, he would find all his skill needed to equal, not to say excel, the symmetry, grace, and speed of some of our modern craft.

That which is true here is at least equally true of our trans-Atlantic friends; in both places, to a very great extent, the whittler-out of a model has been superseded by the capable and tasteful architect, whose work is the result of well-considered calculations which leave only a

always opportunity in yacht-modeling, as in anything else, and such a man necessarily stands less in need of extraneous aids than other men; even such a man, however, cannot always resolve the lessons of experience and experiment out of his own inner consciousness; while on the other hand, to the man of ordinary sense and judgment who is acquainted with the observations and experiments, and the facts of special experience, which have come under view within the past few years, and with the formulas which have been founded on some of these, such knowledge cannot fail to prove a safeguard from error and a help toward success in yacht designing.

Among notions held as governing-beliefs at one time, which have been now swept into the rubbish of the past, are such as the cod's-head and mackerel-tail theory — that of the area of midship section being a measure of resistance; that because the pressure in water was greater at lower depths, a deep-draught vessel was more difficult to propel; that a deep forefoot was an essential requisite to windwardly qualities. Mr. Stevens's *Maria*, with her ten-inch draught forward, was the first radical exponent of an idea opposite to the last that I am acquainted with.

Though our knowledge of what constitutes resistance to bodies passing through water is not so precise and definite as it is to be hoped that it yet will be, the wave-line theory of Mr. Russell, the writings of Pro-

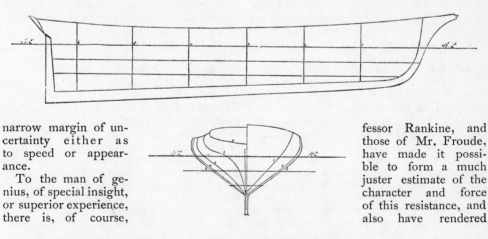

narrow margin of uncertainty either as to speed or appearance.

To the man of genius, of special insight, or superior experience, there is, of course,

fessor Rankine, and those of Mr. Froude, have made it possible to form a much juster estimate of the character and force of this resistance, and also have rendered

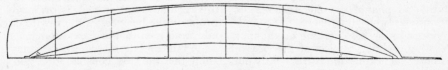

"CYGNET."

it more practicable to escape the largest measure of its influence.

The difficulty, or I may better say the impracticability, of using Mr. Russell's beautiful and valuable conception of the wave-line theory, no longer remains, since it has been shown that it can be used without abridgment, and without other modification than is involved in its application through a curve of areas. A form of use, that, in the design for a yacht, involves no constraint or sacrifice whatever, except it may be under some unnatural and cramping measurement rule (like those of the English yacht clubs), and which, while it furnishes a safe guide and standard for the distribution of bulk through the underwater body of the yacht, fore and aft, dictates only such bulk and proportion as would have been used by the best modelers without its requirement. As to shape of lines and sections it does not dictate at all.

While no very startling novelties have appeared among the yachts of either Europe or this country within the past few years, the character and success of some alterations, and also some new appearances, have been incidents well worth notice. Of such was the alteration of the *Sappho* here, and the launching of that very interesting subject for study, the *Jallanar*, in England.

But I must pass by these to notice the very striking differences between the rigging and sails considered needful for a racing-yacht to-day and thirty years ago.

A look at the picture of any yacht of that period will show the American vessel to be without foretop-mast (if a schooner), with a short maintop-mast, short gaff, no crosstrees or mast-head spreader, and a small topsail,—in all cases sent up from the deck.

This description applies equally to the sloop of the time. Balloon sails were not then used, neither was wire rigging. The first balloon gaff-topsail or balloon jib-topsail that Mr. Sawyer, the sail-maker, remembers to have seen was on the *Psyche*, in 1867; and since then have come the immense balloon maintop-mast staysail for schooners, and the spinnaker, an English contrivance of comparatively recent date.

The sail plan of the schooner-yacht *Fortuna*, which shows the outlines of the light sails in dotted lines, will, in contrast with the sail plan of the old *America*, exhibit an interesting difference.

I must now say a something on the most engrossing yachting subject of the present time here. The question is frequently put, and never answered satisfactorily, and in the nature of things cannot be, — Can we keep the *America's* cup? It has, as we all know, been often successfully defended, and usually there has been little apprehension of the result of a contest for it. But this time there is a difference. A cutter is coming, a big cutter, over eighty feet long, with about sixty tons of lead hanging on to her keel. If it were a schooner that was coming it would be different. England has been neglecting the schooners, has built few of them in recent years, and raced little with them; with scarce an exception those she has are a little out of date. The precise reverse of this represents our case; and, of single-masted vessels, of the proper size, we have not a single example. Besides this the cutter is, and always has been, the Englishman's pet rig, on which he lavished his fondest care, and money without stint, and which he feels that he knows just how to handle. He certainly ought to, as he carefully picks his men out of a choice lot that he usually knows something about, and then gives them enough practice to get acquainted with the minutest detail of their work. The *Genesta* was, it appears from the records, in thirty-four races during the season of 1884, and took either first or second prize in just one-half the number.

The late Robert Fish, after one of his visits to England in connection with the *Sappho*, said to the writer: "I don't think so much of their schooners, but I do of their cutters;" and the old man had the necessary experience and judgment to entitle his words to more than the weight of a casual expression.

Of course, in the absence of any existing one-masted yacht of the proper size and power, it is interesting for yachtsmen to learn that wealthy and public-spirited members of the New York Yacht Club are likely to build one or more boats of the proper size; but in respect to the direction in which opportunity lies, and to the kind of craft that should be produced to meet the English cutter, there is necessarily a wide variety of opinion, and an impossibility of demonstrating by mathematics or other process that any one is more correct than the rest. As to whether the new boat should be wide or narrow, deep or shallow, center-board or keel, is primarily and properly the business of those who pay the cost, and next that of the custodians of the cup; but an interested outsider may presume that the first consideration will be to accept the kind of model and proportions which, all things considered, will give most promise of success. Taking into consideration the fact that the cup was won by a sharp-floored keel yacht, there can certainly be no impropriety in meeting the challenge with such a boat rather than with a centerboard boat, if the first-named gives greater promise than the last; and looking at the only contests over the New York Yacht Club course in which a British cutter has been opposed by centerboard yachts in weather of various kinds, the results were not such as to afford much encouragement for the building of the latter kind to put against a first-class English racer. For it must be remembered by those who would belittle the excellence of the *Wave* and the *Schemer*, that no boats of their class have, up to the present time, ever shown as marked superiority over these boats as did the *Verve* and the *Neptune* over the *Madge* before she left her native waters.

Much has been said since these races of the faulty rule of measurement then in use, under which these races were sailed, and which gave a large and unreasonable allowance of time to the *Madge*. The rule was an old one, first used by the New York Yacht Club, in which length and beam were multiplied, and allowances were made on differences in the product of these quantities. The rule was seen and acknowledged to be an unfair one, and was soon afterwards abandoned; but every one of these races would have been won by the *Madge* on a simple water-line measurement.

I have already quoted Mr. Russell's remarks respecting the disadvantage to the yacht-designer of working under measurement-rules, which, as he expresses it, put him in a straitjacket; and in the outlines of the *Titania* as she was built, and again by

"MOSQUITO."

dotted lines showing how he would like to have built her, I have illustrated his meaning. In seeking to answer, in part, the question as to what are the limits within which opportunity exists to design a vessel to beat the coming cutter, I must repeat any former statement, that the rules under which British racing-vessels are built, except that they now supply no reason for cutting away the stern-post, have pretty much the same kind of effect as they had in 1851. In many of the most recent cutter-designs that have been illustrated, an unmistakable straightness in the vertical line of the frames is discernible, and the water-lines are less rounded in the middle body, and less fine and easy at the ends than they, in all probability, would have been if designed under a different rule, such as is that of the New York Yacht Club. If the extreme features which present themselves in the *Titania* are not now seen in modern English yachts it is because it has been long since found that these do not pay. The British designer finds beam so dear that he takes the smallest quantity of it that he can make do; length, he finds cheap, and he takes a lot of it; depth, he finds, has no price at all, and, if he can make two or three feet of it do duty for one foot cut off the beam, of course he will do it. Having now reduced the width of his load water-line to the narrowest limits, to preserve the needed area within it, and furnish a fulcrum of the needed strength to lift the heavy weight on his keel, he makes his ends somewhat fuller than he likes, and leaves his middle body as nearly like a wall as he dares to, varying his work as he appreciates, respectively, the value of fine form, or the need of stability and other qualities. Of all men, the British yacht-designer, doubtless, best understands the peculiar work he has to do. His task is not, however, our task:

"MARIA."

he is fettered by mischievous rules, and we are free. It is not easy to see how he is ever going to get experience in building racing-vessels of other than one kind, under his present rules; but, give him those of the New York Yacht Club and I am very much mistaken if he would not very soon contrive a yacht

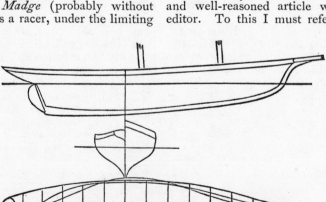

and in close agreement with a trochoid at the stern.

In this respect she represents many well-known English racers; and, as a general thing, the forebody of an English racing-yacht is somewhat fuller than that of an American vessel. A slight expansion in the width of beam of such a vessel would enable the designer to give somewhat finer ends

SAIL PLAN OF THE "FORTUNA."

of the same length of the *Genesta*, and with a smaller sail plan, that, with equally good equipment and handling, would soon leave that craft astern. Nor is the task more difficult for our own designers, excepting as these are less familiar with the craft they have met. While, for some reasons, it may be most desirable that the stranger should be met by a vessel having no unnecessary likeness to the challenger, it may be doubted if a center-board yacht, even if built of iron, can realize the full advantage of the lead keel, which forms such an important feature in the deep English yacht. I give the outlines of the cutter *Madge*, and also of the *Fortuna*, schooner.

The curve of sectional areas of the latter (shown by a dotted line) form almost a perfect wave line, a slight difference only being notable in the trochoid of the stern, indicated by three crosses. —† † †. The curve of the *Madge* (probably without disadvantage as a racer, under the limiting alternative which the British rules present, and the effect of which has already been referred to), is decidedly fuller than a curve of versed sines at the bow,

without loss of stability, or increase in the propelling power; and, carrying out this modification, he could reduce the depth moderately, and obtain the same power to carry sail that he now has with a lessened amount of wetted surface, and, consequently, of resistance. He would, in fact, have made it possible to get a higher speed out of his vessel when driven, and also have improved her in light winds, by reducing the amount of both kinds of resistance, which affect the speed of vessels under those different conditions; and it would be hard to prove that such modifications, carried out in proper degree, would not make in every way a better vessel than one of the extreme type.

That views similar to those which I have expressed are shared by others who have a most competent knowledge of the English cutter may be seen by any one who will refer to the *Field* of the date of January 31, in which may be found a very impartial and well-reasoned article written by the editor. To this I must refer all who are interested, and will here only make one short quotation: —

But assume that length, or length and displacement, or length, breadth, and depth, formed the rule, and in a very few years we should begin

"FORTUNA."

to regard some other type as the type *par excellence*.

In conclusion, I may say that conviction that has obtained in some minds that because some yachts very long, deep, and narrow, like the *Jallanar*, have gained a wide reputation as sea-boats, and have moreover been speedy in heavy weather, that therefore, the longest, deepest, and narrowest proportions are best, seems to be a broad conclusion on a somewhat narrow basis. It seems indeed possible that the most important facts of the case are not even named. The *Jallanar* has a form that would be apt to impress any student of naval architecture as that of a perfect sea-boat. The fine ends, convex frames, swelling middle body, the easy form to drive, and the small length and weight of her spars relative to the length of the boat,— all these furnish reasons why she should be a good sea-boat, and none perhaps more than the last. It is the absence of any discouragement to the use of a moderate sail-area, which makes the rules (of the Seawanhaka, New York,

Eastern, and such other of our clubs as have adopted rules) based upon sail-area and length less meddlesome and mischievous than any rules which have preceded them. These do take into account that with which they are concerned, the representative of power, and the length the boat sails on, and they leave everything else alone.

There can be no want of true yachting spirit, no want of dignity or propriety, in the New York Yacht Club building any such vessel of whatever proportions as may seem to suit best its purpose to meet the coming cutter, and there would certainly seem to be no want of opportunity under its own free measurement; and a lesson no less valuable and telling than that given by the *America* may be repeated to our British friends as to the cramping effect of their rules. If, however, we lose the cup, the nature of these rules will leave no longer any doubt or discretion as to the character of vessel that must be built to compete for it with any likelihood of success.

J. Hyslop.

The
Lake Champlain
Yacht Club
(1888)

THE LAKE CHAMPLAIN YACHT CLUB.

FREDERIC G. MATHER.

"THIS is a great day for Lake Champlain," said a rustic who had been discussing with his fellow the difference between a cat-boat and a sloop. "I may not know the difference, but there's plenty about here who do — and I say, 'Hurrah for old Champlain! anyhow.'"

The rustic, like many others who are right, spoke better than he knew. It was a mild morning in September last. Rain had fallen all through the neighborhood, and more was to come according to that never failing test — the low-hung clouds which still covered the eastern slopes of the Adirondacks and refused to lift even when an occasional ray of sunshine gave them every chance. From the opposite shore of New York the early morning hours were watched with intense interest. The alternate layers of mist and mountain showed also stretches of lake, and the larger objects in Burlington appeared through the rifts—the whole making nature's *mise en scène* for what was to come.

And, indeed, it was a great day. The Lake Champlain Yacht Club was organized May 16, 1887, with a constitution, by-laws and sailing regulations patterned closely after those of the New York Yacht Club. Its rules for sailing were no stricter than its rules for uniforms. In a word, at the time of the regatta everything that experience and enterprise could suggest had been in preparation for sixteen months under the guidance of such gentlemen as W. Boerum Wetmore, commodore; W. A. Crombie, vice-commodore; J. Gregory Smith, president; W. S. Webb, first vice-president; Henry Ballard, second vice-president; Joseph Auld, secretary, and Horatio Hickok, treasurer. An executive committee of thirty included not only the above but also such names as H. J. Brookes, H. Le Grand Cannon, H. H. Noble, Jacob G. Sanders, J. A. Averill, A. C. Tuttle, W. H. H. Murray and Alvaro Adsit—all of them well-known sailors upon fresh water; while the total membership of two hundred took

in navigators as far to the southward as Albany and New York. In fact, it will be noticed that many of the names are those of New Yorkers who spend the summer months along the shores of Champlain, and one enthusiastic member, Robert W. Rogers, comes all the way from New Orleans. Among the members who have not, according to popular belief, made any aquatic record is G. F. Edmunds, the U. S. Senator from the State of Vermont.

Thus all that hard work, good discipline and natty uniforms could do had been done. The day was a great one because it would bring what had been attempted to a practical test. The lake is about one hundred miles long with a breadth varying from half a mile at the southern end to twenty miles (including islands) at the northern end, so that the greatest stretch of clear water from east to west is ten miles, and the longest unobstructed sweep lengthwise is forty miles. There is no perceptible current, although the drainage is northward into the valley of the St. Lawrence. The prevailing winds are from the south, with occasional winds from the north and, near the shores, frequent puffs that come down through the notches in the Green Mountains on one side and the Adirondack Mountains on the other. Given, then, such a lake not so steady for sailing purposes as Long Island Sound, the chain of the Great Lakes, or even the inland lakes of Chautauqua, Seneca and Cayuga with their low-crowned banks, and yet less treacherous than smaller mountain lakes, like George and Memphremagog— to find the craft that will sail it best with speed and safety. This was the problem that had been discussed and solved and solved over again for months, and which had now come to the point where all theories must show their value or cease to be entertained.

Yachting on Lake Champlain was a plant of slow growth. It was hardly an exotic, because some kind of craft had been known there for 250 years. The xebecs of the early French gave way to the sloops and schooners of the English; and the latter, in the decline of commerce, have been followed by the "long-lakers," and the Canadian square-sail galleys of to-day.

143

THE "GYPSIE,"
PHELPS & SON, BURLINGTON, VT.

spects, it has outgrown what he developed and contended for at the first. So Mr. Murray shall have the credit in these pages.

It had occurred to Mr. Murray that the type of oyster-boat known on Long Island Sound as the "sharpie," would fill all the conditions on Champlain noted above. The sharpie was the successor of the old V-shaped punts, or "flat-iron" scows, that brought the earlier oysters to market. When the demand for more bivalves led to the transplanting of Southern oysters to Long Island Sound, the larger boat, the sharpie, was produced, as the one which would combine cheapness, light

Sail boats of uncertain age, and still more uncertain origin, have flitted about the lake for generations; but nothing was ever evolved from them that met the requirements of the modern yacht. It was reserved for the Rev. W. H. H. Murray to bring thither some of the ideas that he had gathered among the oystermen along the coast of Connecticut and to adapt them to a fresh-water lake. Everyone credits Mr. Murray, better known as "Adirondack," with calling attention to the broad expanse of lake opposite Burlington that had not been used as it might be by sails and hulls of modern cut; and everybody agrees that the present yacht club is the outcome of his earlier efforts, although, in many re-

THE "VIRGINIA"—PETER THUST, ST. JOHNS, CANADA.

THE "FLYAWAY"—DR. W. S. WEBB.

draught, broad bottom, ready handling with the sail or oar, sea-worthiness, and fair sailing qualities.

So Mr. Murray constructed the *White Wings* in Connecticut, and brought it to Burlington to show his faith in his new theory. We may quote liberally from his description of a sharpie adapted for use on Lake Champlain. The length over-all is 50 feet; depth, 4 feet amidships; extreme width of deck, 12 feet; length of center-board, 16 feet; width, 5 feet; distance between masts, 30 feet; sail-area, 200 to 300 yards; length of foremast, 50 feet; length of mainmast, 47 feet. The sails are laced to small booms, or the sprit can be used. The sails can be of strictly "leg-o'-mutton" shape or "clubbed" in form, which is desirable when a large spread of canvas is demanded, because it allows a large sail area, and, at the same time, keeps the major section of the sail low down, where the wind-pressure should be located. These boats are decked and staved in hard woods — oak, cherry, birch or Southern pine. White pine is of course allowed, but it is soft and liable to be marred by indentations. The sides are of white pine plank, 2 inches in thickness, 8 inches wide,

and from 16 to 20 feet in length. Such plank-work is easily shaped, and makes a strong boat. The bottom is of Southern pine, finest quality, 2 inches thick and 6 wide, and the stern-piece of best white oak, with plenty of size to it. Fourteen feet abaft the stem is the front of the cabin, and the length of cabin is adapted to suit service. If for home sailing, it can be twelve feet, divided amidships into two apartments—one for men, the other for women. The front section of each apartment, say 4 x 5, is fitted with a lavatory like a Pullman car; height of cabin, six feet in the clear. This gives an elevation of sides above deck-line of, say, two feet, three sides to be built in two or three panels which can be opened inward in fair weather, and buttoned to cabin roof. The cabin is thus converted, at will, into a charming sitting-room, in which ladies and children can be protected from the sun, and yet enjoy the sight of water and mountains beyond. If the boat is intended for cruising, the cabin can be made longer, say twenty-two feet. This would still leave a large cockpit, and accommodate a party of a dozen with berths and tables for sleeping and eating, whether the weather was fair or foul. The table-leaf can be hinged to the center-board case, so as to hang vertically to it and take up no room when not in use. Berths, on bed frames, made of wicker, 6 x 2 feet, are hinged to the cabin sides, and like the table, hang pendant when not in use. Cook's galley, immediately ahead of the cabin, is entered by a hatch of large size, say 3 x 4 feet, built to be slid forward in close-fitting grooves, so that in rough weather it would be practically water-tight. The cabin should be of quartered oak or cherry, or any desirable wood. Fifty chairs

COMMODORE'S LAUNCH "DOLPHIN."

can be placed in the cabins and cockpit.

Such were the boats of which Mr. Murray wrote: "They are well adapted to meet the wants of amateurs, and will do much to make yachting a popular recreation to a degree never hitherto realized." The appearance of the *White Wings* led to the building of other sharpies, and an organization under the name of the Sharpie Yacht Club of Burlington became the nucleus of the present yacht club.

Since Burlington boasts no canoe or rowing clubs, it was Mr. Murray's idea to combine all the boating interests as a part of a general scheme which should take charge of all kinds of sports and pastimes natural to such a magnificent body of inland water, and yet the boating section of the club was to be devoted to sharpies — the model to which Mr. Murray still pins his faith. As the club grew it showed decided tendencies toward a regular yacht club. This carried with it the erection of a $5,000 clubhouse on one of the best wharves in the harbor at a point about which all the boating tendencies of the lake might rally, the expenses of membership being only $10 yearly with no financial responsibility beyond this figure.

As an illustration of the very effective and concise way of doing things, it will be of interest to repeat a statement that was posted upon the bulletin board: "The regatta committee will announce before each race in which direction the course shall be sailed, which will depend upon the wind. If the course is first to the north from the club-house, all yachts will pass to the right of all rounding marks, leaving them on their port sides. In case an overlap exists between two yachts when both of them, without tacking, are about to pass

a mark on the required side, then the outside yacht must give the inside yacht room to pass clear of the mark. A yacht shall not, however, be justified in attempting to establish an overlap and thus force a passage between another yacht and the mark after the latter yacht has altered her helm for the purpose of rounding. When a yacht is in danger of running aground, or of touching a pier, rock or other obstruction, and cannot go clear by altering her course without fouling another yacht, then this latter shall on being hailed by the former, at once give room, and in case one yacht is forced to tack or to bear away in order to give room, the other shall also tack or bear away, as the case may be, at as near the same time as is possible without danger of fouling."

The regatta should have taken place on the first Tuesday in August, and that will be the date hereafter; but last year it was postponed till September 21, in the hope that certain new boats might be finished and enter the races. The *Nautilus*, the most eagerly expected of all, failed to appear. We will make note of her later on.

It was required

SHARPIE YACHT "BURLINGTON"—JOSEPH AULD AND OTHERS, BURLINGTON, VT.

W. S. WEBB, FIRST VICE-PRESIDENT.
W. A. CROMBIE, VICE-COMMODORE.   JOSEPH AULD, SECRETARY.

in every instance that there should be three starters or no race. The club course of about $8\frac{5}{16}$ miles commenced on a line inside the breakwater and at right angles to the club-house, round the south end of the breakwater, south of Rock Dunder, south of Juniper Ledge buoy, west end of Juniper Island, north end of breakwater to starting line. This was the course for the first class sailing yachts (33 feet and upward), the time not to exceed $2\frac{3}{4}$ hours. The first prize was \$60, and the second \$20.

There had been a brush, a few days before, for the championship pennant. The *Flyaway*, a sloop built by Lawler, of Boston, for Dr. W. S. Webb, had covered the course in 1h. 30m. 42s. Next came the *Ripple*, a sloop built and owned by Adsit and Bigelow, in 1h. 32m. 50s.; and last came the sharpie, *White Wings*, built under Murray's eye, and owned by C. B. Gray, her time being 1h. 48m. 30s. The same boats started in the first class race,

except that the sharpie, *Burlington*, owned by Joseph Auld and others, having less freeboard and an improved stern, took the place of the *White Wings*. Time allowance was waived by the *Ripple* and the *Burlington*. The *Ripple* came over the line first and held the lead till, on rounding Juniper Island, she was passed by the *Flyaway*. Then came a very close contest, the *Ripple* afterward claiming she would have won if she had had the time allowance. The elapsed time was: *Flyaway*, 1h. 45m. 53s.; *Ripple*, 1h. 46m. 33s. The *Burlington* was becalmed and withdrew.

By this time a drizzling rain had set in; but the yachtsmen and their friends had had enough taste of the sport to want more. The second class race was for sailing yachts measuring between 20 and 33 feet. The prizes were \$45 and \$15. The course was the club course, omitting the turning of Juniper Ledge buoy—distance, $7\frac{1}{3}$ miles, to be covered in $2\frac{3}{4}$ hours.

There were five starters, and the prospects were for the best race of the day. But the rain beat down the wind ; the race became a drifting match, and was postponed till the next day. The starters were : the *White Wings*, sharpie ; the *Agnes T.*, a sloop owned by T. A. Taft ; the *Princess*, a sloop owned by R. W. Rogers ; the *Puritan*, a sloop owned by W. C. Witherbee, and the *Eagle*, a schooner-rigged keel-boat owned by W. S. Hopkins. The same yachts were allowed to sail in the postponed race on the following day, but only the *Agnes T.* appeared. She sailed over the course in 1h. 14m. 25s. Two entries of the day before were barred out because they did not start at that time.

There was still more rain and still less wind when the third class yachts (under 20 feet) were called. The course was 5⅛ miles, starting around the north end of the breakwater, thence about Rock Dun-

around the south end of the breakwater, a distance of 7 1-5 miles. The time limit was 1½ hours. Four of the starters finished the race ; the fifth, the *Idlewild*, owned by Averill & Kellogg, having passed the first buoy only. The starters, together with their owners and elapsed time, were these : the *Nymph*, Dr. W. S. Webb, 41m. 55s.; the *Cecil*, Myers & Clough, 49m. 33s.; the *Adonis*, J. B. Tressidder, 52m. 14½s. ; the *Comus*, R. W. Rogers, 58m. 17s. It was evident from the start that the *Nymph* would win—but there was a very exciting contest for second place, the *Cecil* finally leading the *Adonis*. In figuring the result the Isherwood rule was used, because the lengths of all the boats were less than 50 feet. If they had been more than 50 feet, the Emory rules of the American yacht club would have held. The Isherwood rules provide that the speed in knots per hour is divided by the cube root of the

THE BURLINGTON Y. C HOUSE.

der, and homeward around the south end of the breakwater. Two hours was the time limit ; and the prizes were $30 and $10. The only starter was the sloop *Goat*, owned by W. C. Witherbee—and so the race was declared off.

But no amount of rain or lack of wind could keep back the steam and naphtha launches of under 50 feet from racing for the $100 cup offered by Commodore Wetmore. The course was around the north end of the breakwater, north of Appletree buoy, south of Proctor's shoal buoy and

length on the waterline of the yachts respectively, and the quotients represent, relatively, the merits of the different yachts. Based on this rule, the ratios were : *Nymph*, 1.13 ; *Cecil*, 0.97 ; *Adonis*, 0.91.

The *Nymph* is 46 feet long, 8 feet beam, and 3 feet draught. She divides with the *Dolphin*, owned by Commodore Wetmore, the honor of being the fastest steam launch on the lake. The *Dolphin* is 42 feet long, with the same beam and draught as the *Nymph*. On October 15 there was a

COMMODORE B. WETMORE.

test of speed between the two for the champion pennant of the lake. The *Nymph* won by 11½s. over a 7-mile course, there being no time allowance. On November 1 another race over a course of 6½ miles was won by the *Dolphin* by 32½s. We may look for good time from both the *Dolphin* and the *Nymph* in the steam race of 1889.

The greatest race of all came off upon Saturday, September 22, the second and final day of the regatta. This was for the $500 cup made by Tiffany, and presented by the ladies of Burlington. It is an elaborately-made punch-bowl, with a fine engraving, on the outside, of the harbor of Burlington. According to the rules of the club, "the Ladies' Cup" shall be a perpetual challenge, and shall be sailed for each year by the yachts belonging to the members of the club at their annual regatta. The course shall be about ten miles, and the sailing allowances, etc., shall be governed by such rules of the club, as from time to time may obtain. The course, etc., may be changed from time to time by the regatta committee as the exigencies of the club may require. They, or their successors in office, are made custodians of the cup for the club, and shall award the same each year to the successful yacht; which yacht shall have its name and the date of the regatta engraved on the cup by the committee, and shall hold it until the next annual regatta, giving bonds to the committee in the sum of $600 for the safe

keeping of the same. Any damage or loss to the cup while in the possession of a yacht shall be appraised and deducted by the committee from the bond on the return of the cup, which shall be one week before the next annual meeting. Owners of yachts failing to return the cup at the time specified, shall sacrifice their bonds and cease to be members of the club. A yacht holding the cup and not competing for its possession, is considered as having competed and lost. In all races, at least three yachts must start or no race, unless a race has been postponed; but should the yacht which is in possession of the cup be a competitor, she may sail the course, without this limit as to the number starting.

The wind being from an unfavorable quarter, the course of 9⅞ miles was reversed. It led from the south end of the breakwater, south of Rock Dunder, south of Juniper Ledge buoy, west of Juniper Island, north of Appletree buoy, and around the north end of the breakwater. Eight yachts entered the lists: the *Flyaway*, the *Agnes T.*, the *Ripple*, the *White Wings*, the *Burlington*, the *Gypsie*, Phelps & Son, the *Surprise*, Joseph Labelle, and the *Virginia*, Peter Thust, the two latter being Canadians. There was a splendid start, the eight boats all crossing the line within a space of 1m. 14s. They kept well together, and on turning the Ledge buoy they were so closely bunched as to be in each other's way. Then came more than four miles of beating. The *White Wings* capsized in trying to house her jib, and the Canadian boats gave up the fight. The *Agnes T.* had led thus far with a prospect of winning, because she was allowed 2m. 10s.—a figure that would have given her the race over the *Flyaway* the day before. But her narrow beam kept down the area of her sails, and she dropped out, while the *Flyaway* spread her gaff-topsail and shot ahead. The *Burlington* held her port tack well into the broad lake, the *Gypsie* tacking nearly as long. It was evident the race belonged to the *Flyaway* or the *Agnes T.* The latter was 6½m. behind in turning the Appletree buoy. Then the race homeward was commenced. The *Flyaway* set her jib-topsail, and the *Agnes T.* set her spinnaker. It was to be a very close thing—for the *Flyaway* had allowed her rival 2m. 26s., and the *Gypsie* 9m. 50s. Had not the spinnaker gone overboard, the *Agnes T.* might have won.

The score stood—

	Elapsed Time.	Corrected Time.
	H. M. S.	H. M. S.
Flyaway	2 03 19	2 03 19
Agnes T.	2 09 10	2 06 44
Gypsie	2 17 20	2 07 30
Burlington	2 16 28	2 22 55

It should be stated that the *Burlington* was obliged to give an allowance of 6m. 27s. to the winner—thus making her fourth, although she was third in elapsed time. As soon as the *Flyaway* crossed the line there was a welcome from all the steam-whistles in and about the harbor, such as old Champlain had never heard before.

Now came an incident that showed the *esprit de corps* of the new yacht club. Many of the older clubs do not venture upon the Corinthian race, wherein every boat must be sailed by its owner, assisted solely by members of the club to which he belongs. Even if the members want a race of this sort, it is only after years of hard work and constant sailing contests, that it will be worth the trouble. But Commodore Wetmore had with him upon the *Dolphin* — the official boat — Col. W. A. Crombie, vice-commodore; Chester Griswold, fleet captain; Joseph Auld, secretary; Maj. M. B. Adams, U. S. Engineers; Captain Abbott, of the 6th U. S. Cavalry,

and one or two civilians, who were also land-lubbers. It was suggested to the commodore that it was of no use to start the Corinthian race because there could be none—the *Agnes T.* alone offering to sail. But the commodore blew his whistles, the proper flag appeared on the club-house, and the race was started in good form— all except the boats. Then the Commodore delivered himself : " I propose to let everybody know that we go through the forms of starting every race, whether there is anybody to start or not. Next year every boatman and every visitor will know just what to expect. It is better to start our first regatta right and educate everybody up to the proper way to do these things."

The final whistle was blown and the first annual regatta of the Lake Champlain Yacht Club was over ; and over with great credit, thanks more particularly to the energetic Regatta Committee, W. Boerum Wetmore, Chester Griswold and H. Le G. Cannon, of New York, and Elias Lyman and Lieut. A. S. Cummins, of Burlington. Then the sharpies, cutters, sloops and cats sailed away ; and if you were "handy there" you must have heard the old refrain taken up and echoed back from the hills !—

THE "AGNES T."—T. A. TAFT.

" Watch her ! catch her !
  Jump up in a ju-ba-ju ;
Give her sheet and let her howl,
  We're the boys to put her through.
Oh! you ought to hear her howling
  When the wind is blowing free."

Among the sailing-yachts that did not race, were—the *Emily*, Rev. C. H. Kimball, of Hartford, Conn. ; and the *Champlain*, J. Armoy Knox, of New York. The list would not be complete without a mention of three screw-yachts : the *Sappho*, owned and sailed by the ever-hospitable Dr. W. S. Webb ; the *Scionda*, which knows every reef and bay of Champlain, under the guidance of the genial commodore, Jacob G. Sanders ; and the *Alexandria*, upon whose decks and within whose cabins Mr. Alexander Macdonald, of St. Johns, dispensed true Canadian hospitality, and added much to the social features of the regatta by the presence of his guests, Mayor Macdonald, U. S. Consul Bertrand, and Mr. Charles Aspin, of St. Johns, and Judge Davidson, Col. and Mrs. Bond, Miss Bond, Miss Wood, and Miss Grant, of Montreal.

It is hoped, and rather expected, that another year we may see a race for steam yachts. The *Sappho* is 104 feet long, 15 feet beam and 7 feet 6 inches in draught. The *Scionda* is 98 feet long, 17 feet beam and 6 feet in draught. The *Alexandria* is about 85 feet long, with a beam and draught nearly the same as the *Scionda*. She is built not so much for speed as for porpoise and other fishing off the coast of Newfoundland, and all of her arrangements and appliances are of the most complete and compact kind. An engine, from Providence, R. I., gives the motive-power.

The new yacht club starts with all the advantages that the experience of the older clubs can offer. It is really the pioneer of strict yachting on the inland waters of the United States. Even on salt water the history of yachting commences with the New York Yacht Club less than fifty years ago ; and all the developments of the present day date from within the past twenty years. The pioneer of clubs in New England, the Boston, was not formed till 1865. The South Boston was formed in 1868 ; and the Bunker Hill and the Portland in 1869. At the latter date there were only fifteen clubs in the United States —all of them on salt water. So the new club enters the lists not much behind the others in age, and with every inducement and opportunity to avoid their mistakes, and to profit by their success. In these

days of steam-power the yachtsmen are the only ones left to keep alive the tone' and vigor of the old-time seamanship which was the theme of song and story. And when the American navy finds its reserve—as it surely will—in the well-trained yachtsmen of the day, then the Champlain Club will offer aid that is worth having upon a lake that saw the transit of arms for more than 200 years.

But the Lake Champlain Yacht Club is thus early in the process of changing from its original design and scope. We have already seen how it has grown beyond the sharpie. In spite of schooner or barque rigs and lower freeboards and more cutter-like sterns the sharpies that entered the races showed that they were both out-pointed and out-footed by the sloops. In other words, they failed to hold that grip upon the water that all boats must have when beating. Their narrow beams also keep down the area of their sails. As racers, therefore, the regatta showed them to be failures—although they are safe, roomy and comfortable boats for cruising. The accident to the *White Wings* should not tell against the sharpie model, for even a broader beamed boat is liable to go over when a gybe comes along and the booms and the ballast are on the same side of the keel. In running before the wind, however, the sharpie proves to be a safe and a fairly speedy boat.

The other extreme—to which the club seems to be tending—is the salt-water sloop of the latest design. Such an one, the *Nautilus*, was expected to be ready for this regatta, but it will surely be on hand next year, prepared to beat all comers, if what is claimed can be proved. The hull floats a mile or two down the lake, and the spars and boom are laid aside till another season. Burgess, of Boston, finished the lines, and they are very nearly those of the *Volunteer*, the defender of the *America's* Cup, but on a smaller scale. The length on deck is 53 feet, and on the waterline 40 feet. The beam is 15 feet and 3 inches, and the draught is 5 feet—or about 13 feet with the 12-foot center-board down. The color is white, but the gunwales are of oak, and the combings are of mahogany. Steel rigging is used. The mast is 42 feet high, and the topmast is 34 feet more, a total of 76 feet from the deck. From the step of the mast to the end of the bowsprit is 39 feet, while the boom is 47 feet long. This makes the lower edge of the sail-plan triangle 86 feet. With a single rig of sails spread the *Nautilus* will carry about 350 square yards, but if the flying-jib, the spinnaker, and other extra sails are included, the area will reach about 700 square yards.

Of course the building of the *Nautilus* is tentative. It remains to be seen whether as much sail area as can be spread to the steady breezes of salt water can be spread with profit, or even with safety, to the comparatively unsteady and uncertain winds of an inland lake that is surrounded by mountains. The American Canoe Association has proved, on a smaller scale, that big sails on a mountain-locked lake are to be avoided. Experience has shown that a moderate area of sail, well handled, wins the day; but there are times when a light wind gives the race to the man who has the largest area. The same experience is likely to come to the yacht club, and our prediction is that it will soon be shown that the *Nautilus* has too many and too large sails for her hull, and that by the time of the regatta in August she will appear with a smaller area. But if the *Nautilus* can go through the narrow pass in the lake known as Split Rock, with its varying currents of air and water, and its sudden and terrific squalls from off Whallon's bay, then she can do anything; for that is the test of seamanship, according to the old sailors on the lake. Such a severe trial, however, should not be asked of the *Nautilus*, or of any other new boat that is built for the same purpose. Her mission is not so much to tempt Providence as to mark an era in the advancement of yachting upon the unsalted waters.

Whatever may be thought of Burlington as a place of winter resort, it is certain that it is developing into a more popular place for the passing of the warmer months. Instead of the winter carnivals we have not only yacht-racing, but all the other pleasures that the water can afford. While the principal rivers of the New York shore are bounded by rocks, those on the Vermont shore are bounded by long bars of sand. To the northward of Burlington the Lamoille sends out a long sand-bar on which, with a little assistance by men, a drive has been formed to one of the larger islands. It goes by the name of the Sandbar Bridge. Then there is the Winooski, or Onion River, which empties into the lake seven or eight miles south of the Lamoille River, and a mile or so north of Burlington. The river rises close to the Connecticut River, on the southern bor-

ders of Vermont, breaks through the range of the Green Mountains and shows caves at Duxbury and many other points along the slope of the Camel's Hump. The river, in fact, runs through the valley between Mansfield and the Camel's Hump, and presents a series of surprises to the tourist.

Burlington was in the old seigniory of La Manaudiere on both sides of the Lamoille River, and belonged to Pierre Rainbault, who was one of the French victims at the time of the conquest of Canada by the English. Burlington has many beautiful spots, and the monuments to Lafayette and Allen are especially worth visiting. The isolated rock Dunder, only a mile or two off from the wharves, has always been an object of mystery, many claiming that it was the original boundary between the French and English Indians. Then there is Juniper Island, on which the United States has established a light-house, and the breakwater which forms the real harbor of the city except when, as occasionally happens, the waves break down the breakwater itself. Only a short distance down the lake are Shelburne town, and the neighboring resort known as Cedar Beach. Then we come to the extensive grounds, thousands of acres in area, recently purchased by the Vanderbilts and their connections, and now developed into most beautiful parks and all kinds of driveways, that would do credit to cities of much larger growth.

Indeed, Burlington is the city which Edward Everett Hale recently described as a fitting answer to Matthew Arnold's strictures upon the homeliness of Americans and their surroundings. Mr. Hale spoke of the new hospital in Burlington, and its fund of half a million dollars, and said: "If this be a commonplace monument, let us thank God that we live in a commonplace land." He spoke of the public library with its choice collections, and was informed that it was a question whether there were three or four paupers in the poorhouse. Then Mr. Hale went on to say: "This is so distinguished a condition of affairs that I should not dare tell that story in any social science congress in Europe. It would be set down as a Yankee exaggeration. People would say it was impossible. It is not impossible, because the men and women of Burlington have known how to give themselves to the administration of the wealth in common."

Memories of
Yacht Cruises
(1888)

MEMORIES OF YACHT CRUISES.

BY CAPTAIN R. F. COFFIN.

THE annual cruises of the New York Yacht Club have, since their first institution in the year 1854, been memorable events in its history; quite as much, and perhaps more so, than its annual regattas. Though only a portion of the fleet were generally entered for the races, as a rule, nearly every yacht in commission took part in the cruise.

The advent of the British schooner *Cambria*, in 1870, and her participation in the cruise of that year, gave to it an importance far beyond that of any previous, and no one who had the good fortune to witness it will ever forget the splendid finish of the fleet off Fort Adams at the close of the run from New London. A sweepstakes had been arranged, each yacht, if I remember rightly, putting up $25, and some residents of Newport went off the fort in a cat-boat and timed each yacht accurately as she arrived. It was about four o'clock on a very fine afternoon when the fleet, all "in a bunch," came along before a fine southwest wind, with all light canvas set, the *Tidal Wave* leading and

the *Cambria* either third or fourth in the race. There was, of course, no time allowance, and the start had not been accurately timed, all getting under way as best they could from the anchorage off the Pequot House at gun-fire. The whole fleet were schooners, the day of the single-sticked vessels not having come until some years later.

At that time Mr. Stebbins was the commodore, a conservative of the old school, and the younger element were inclined to chafe at the formality and etiquette insisted on by the commanding officer. They made up for it afterwards, under his successor, Commodore Bennett. Among the notables who were present on this cruise was Mr. Lawrence Jerome, or, as Mr. Ashbury was wont to call him, "Mr. Jeromy." "Larry," as he is more generally called among society men, quite astonished Ashbury, who never, I think, quite knew what to make of him. "That Mr. Jeromy," said he on one occasion, "is one of the most remarkable men I ever met in my life. He comes on board my yacht and drinks brandy and water all day long—not but what he's entirely welcome to it—but it don't seem to have any effect on him," and I don't think Mr. Ashbury was ever quite satisfied as to whether it was the brandy or the man that was responsible for this result.

It was on this cruise that the memorable series of match races were sailed, which have already been detailed in a former series of articles in OUTING.* Every schooner in the fleet wanted to measure speed with the British boat, and Mr. Ashbury was quite willing to accommodate them for his invariable stake, a fifty guinea cup. Mr. Ashbury was not much of a yachtsman, and the *Cambria* was practically run by two newspaper men who had come over in her from England. The owner's room was amidships, and he had his berth hung on "gimbals," so that, however great the inclination of the vessel, the bed was always level ; and in this bed Mr. Ashbury was wont to lie during the most exciting races, sending his steward up from time to time to ask Mr. Kemp or Captain Tannock how the *Cambria* was doing with

* This series of articles appeared in the successive numbers of OUTING, beginning with June, 1886, and closing with the November number of the same year.

her rival. He was a very quiet gentleman, and the convivial habits of some of the yachtsmen of those days were not to his taste.

While the *Cambria* was lying at Newport during this cruise, she was honored one afternoon by a visit from the President of the United States, and I think I never saw a prouder man than Mr. Ashbury was that day. I think he prized this visit more than he would have prized the America's cup had he won it. He had from the first been extremely courteous to the newspaper men who were attending the club, but this day, while the American ensign was flying from the *Cambria's* fore truck in honor of the distinguished visitor, the reporters, who, of course, were as obtrusive in the pursuit of news then as now, were sternly repulsed from the gangway and not allowed on board until the President had taken his departure. I shall never forget how indignant one of them was, and how he vowed he would never set foot upon the British deck again. After a time he was mollified, and we went on board to receive such details of the visit as Mr. Ashbury chose to give—which were not many—for Mr. Ashbury was a gentleman, and very properly thought that the conversation between himself and his guest was not a proper subject for a newspaper dispatch. He, however, made up in profuse hospitality for any seeming discourtesy in refusing the honor of our presence while his guest was there, and if either or all of us

CAMBRIA.

had chosen to have taken a champagne bath in honor of the occasion, I think Mr. Ashbury would have been only too happy to have furnished the wine. I ascertained the other day that the old schooner had been sold for a coaster or fishing vessel, or something of that kind, and I thought of the glory of that afternoon at Newport and felt sad.

I fear that the New York yachting men never appreciated Mr. Ashbury at his real worth. Few if any of them ever became intimate with him, and his unfortunate protests during his second visit embittered them against him. These protests, I am convinced, he made under a sense of duty, and in one instance I know he was correct in the view he took. The *Cambria* was a better boat than the *Livonia*, and her model in the New York Yacht Club collection compares favorably with any that is there. Among the incidents in her history, it may be noted that she was the first British yacht to pass through the Suez Canal.

The cruise of 1871 to Marblehead was memorable as being the first in which both the New York and Eastern Yacht Club fleets joined. Bennett was the commodore and took with him, on one of the *Herald* news yachts—the *Jeanette*, I think—a brass band, and there was a very lively time for the whole cruise. Some fine races were sailed at Newport; and it was while the fleet was there that it received the second notification of challenge for the America's cup.

As something that probably will never occur again in its history, I note that in 1873 the Brooklyn Yacht Club, under commodore Jacob Voorhis, had a cruise, in which a fleet of four schooners of the largest class—among them the *Madeleine* and *Tidal Wave*—and ten sloops, started. During the cruise the fleet increased to seven schooners and seventeen sloops, a large fleet for those days. At that time the Brooklyn club was second only to the New York in importance, and it seemed as unlikely that it should ever come to grief, as it is now that the New York or Atlantic clubs will; but who can tell what the future may have in store?

At that time fleets used to make Glen Cove Harbor their rendezvous, and would probably have continued this down to the present day had not the hotel been burned. The first night in Glen Cove was indeed a night of jollity. The proprietor of the house always made great preparations, and there was a hop, attended not only by the regular guests of the house, but by the gentry of the neighborhood, and the festivities were kept up with great perseverance until it was time to go on board in the morning, the long run to New London always necessitating an early start. It is notable that on these cruises, which many join ostensibly for the improvement of their health, men are, as a rule, in better condition on the first night than at any time during the remainder of the sail. Generally, about a week is enough for a novice, and he suddenly discovers that business requires his presence in New York.

Glen Cove was a bad rendezvous for the reporters. In many instances the scribe would be assigned to this duty on the day previous to the assembling of the yachts at Glen Cove, and would go to the spot by the afternoon boat or by train, an entire stranger to all in the fleet. In most cases the owner had on board all whom his yacht could accommodate so far as sleeping quarters were concerned, and as there was always a probability of a night on the Sound between Glen Cove and New London, there was no room for any more. Besides, in many instances, then, perhaps, more than now, the owner provided the boat and the guests the provisions, and the owner did not feel justified in adding a "dead-head" to the party. If the guests were men of means, they naturally preferred this arrangement, which made them feel more independent. In one case, the guests of the cruise contributed enough provender, cigars, wines and liquors, to not only carry the yacht comfortably through the rest of the season, but to supply the owner's house for the winter. The owner, therefore, did not feel at liberty to invite the reporter to eat his guests' provisions, and the guests did not like to invite him to a yacht which was not theirs.

Again, the presence of a stranger was a restraint, and even if the owner knew him, the guests did not, and at times things occurred on the yacht that it was not advisable to have reported. Personally, I think that the owners were quite right. If I owned a yacht on a cruise with a cabin full of guests, I would not have a reporter on board, unless it were a man on whose discretion I could confidently rely.

Although everybody wanted the cruise reported, no one desired to carry the reporters, and there was sometimes considerable skirmishing before all got berths. If the reporter was left behind he could only

reach New London by returning to New York and taking a fresh departure. Once on the other side of the Sound, however, all difficulty was over, and the reporter who was left behind could reach the next stopping-place of the fleet by rail before its arrival.

Generally, however, after the first day's sail, the reporter made acquaintances and had more invitations than he could accept, for "my ship always sails fast." It is impossible for any one to write of a cruise without giving more prominence to the yacht on which he is than to any other. The relative position of all the fleet is stated with reference to the writer's temporary boarding-house, and, whether he desires it or not, that craft will have a good show. Usually, however, he does desire it, for the change from Hitchcock's *menu* to the "plain and simple fare" of the ordinary yacht is an agreeable one, and the writer feels inclined to extol his host and his ship.

Still, while Glen Cove is not for the reporter a good place to "emigrate from," I think the fleet misses a very interesting stretch of Sound sailing by starting from New London. If, however, the fleet intends going round Cape Cod, it is better to start from New London, or it will be difficult to hold the men together for the final port ; and, indeed, it is difficult, anyhow, to carry a fleet beyond Martha's Vineyard.

This is another very inconvenient place for the reporters. When the cable to the main land is not broken, as it is frequently, there is but one operator, and to send six or seven long "specials" is impossible. The "boys" have to agree to send each a

brief dispatch, or else to "pool their issues" and send one long one, to be duplicated in New York to each office. I remember well the trouble that was caused the first time this was done. Next day nearly every one received an inquiry from his office demanding an explanation. I may mention, while on this subject, that reports of yacht cruises were never telegraphed until 1870. Before this the scribe had an easy time, wrote a long letter when he felt inclined, and mailed when he could. Now, however, the job of reporting a yachting cruise may well be called hard work. Two or three years ago in the reports of the "Goelet" cup race—the most interesting of the season—all failed but two. The Associated Press got a report through from Providence, and the New York *Herald* man got his through from Newport. A severe tempest interrupted all the others.

I think it was in 1873, when Mr. Bennett was commodore, that the fleet arrived at Oak Bluffs, on Saturday evening, only to find the cable broken and the last steamer to the main land gone. There were but two reporters with the fleet, one, of course, a *Herald* man. Finding that for a $10 bill a cat-boat could be hired in which to cross the Sound, he communicated with his chief and received orders to cross and send the report at any expense. On the way over the two men lay prone in the bottom of the boat under a little half-deck forward, which covered them for about half their lengths, and there wrote reports. There was a stiff breeze and quite a bubble of a sea, and the spray poured down on the exposed portions of their persons in a steady shower, but they wanted to return with the boatman and desired to have their reports ready. Arriving at Wood's Hole, the operator was found to be a woman, and to leave their damp and nearly illegible reports, full of nautical *technique*, with her seemed out of the question. She, however, was more than equal to the situation. "With the yachts, hey?" said she, "and I don't suppose you've got half the terms correct. It's lucky for you that my husband was a sailor ; you go right back with the boatman, leave the reports with me, and if I find anything wrong—and I'm sure to—I'll make it right." The reports in the papers the next day were the most correct of any printed during that cruise.

Bennett was not a good commodore. Though brilliant, he was erratic. He spent money freely and entertained lavishly, but took no pains to conciliate any one. It requires great tact to preserve discipline in a fleet, when each subordinate feels himself the equal, if not the superior, in social position of his commanding officer, and is as sensitive as a child to any seeming slight. Mr. Bennett, if he possessed the necessary tact, did not care to exercise it. Owners of the smaller yachts found—or thought they found—themselves snubbed and slighted.

In 1875 Mr. G. L. Kingsland, an old Knickerbocker, was elected commodore, with W. A. Garner as vice, and S. Nicholson Kane for rear commodore. Commodore Bennett had remained abroad during 1873, but had given to the clubs many cups—more valuable than any before presented ; among them were the Cape May and Brenton Reef cups, which are now in England, and which will probably be the prizes in the next international contest.

On the strength of this liberality, he was re-elected and had charge of the fleet in 1874. It is extremely doubtful, however, if he could have been elected for another year, and so the "weatherly *Alarm*," as we used to call her, became the flagship, with the *Mohawk*—as fine a yacht as was ever built—as the yacht of the vice-commodore. It was after the return of the fleet from its cruise that year that the celebrated controversy of keel versus centreboard arose, which resulted in the *Resolute* matches and the great race between the *Mohawk* and *Dauntless*. The cruise that year was in no way remarkable. The club intended at the outset to go round the cape, but finally returned from Martha's Vineyard to Newport, where it sailed some very spirited races.

Commodore Kingsland was not popular. His old-fashioned conservative style did not suit the young and progressive element, and a determined effort was made at the annual election to make Mr. Garner the commodore. There were forty-nine yachts represented, and the vote stood 25 for Kingsland and 24 for Garner, Mr. Kingsland thus re-electing himself. Lester Wallack, at that time owner of the *Columbia*, was brought from the theatre in his character-costume, but Mr. Kingsland refused to allow him to vote, declaring the polls closed. Because these proceedings were truthfully reported in the papers, Commodore Kingsland ruled that for the future the scribes should be banished from the meetings, and that rule has

SCHOONER MADELEINE.

ever since been enforced. I think, perhaps, if the meetings of the club had been faithfully reported, some mistakes that have been made would perhaps have been avoided.

It sounds curious to hear of the New York Yacht Club being financially embarrassed, but under the Kingsland administration it was stated at the meeting of May, 1876, that at the close of the year the debt of the club would not be less than $3,000. Under these circumstances it was not to be expected that the cruise would be a particularly lively one. The *Mohawk* had capsized and Mr. Garner and his wife were drowned, and this had a depressing effect on yachting that not even the victory of the *Madeleine* and the retention of the America's cup could dissipate. Still there was a good assemblage of yachts at Glen Cove. Varying the usual programme, the fleet went to Shelter Island, Greenport, instead of New London. On arriving at Newport it numbered eleven schooners and five sloops, thus showing that the sloops were coming to the front. They were all of the old-fashioned type, however, with the exception of the *Vindex*, an iron boat called by courtesy a cutter. In those days the *Arrow* was considered a wonder, and in this run from New London to Newport she beat the *Vision*, which was second, by one hour and fifteen minutes. The fleet started with a most elaborate programme, including Marblehead, the Isle of Shoals, and possibly some port east of that, and a few of the yachts—seven schooners and three sloops—did go as far as Gloucester.

Those were dark days for the New York Yacht Club, and in the year 1877 it came very near going utterly to the dogs. At a meeting held February 16, at which there

were only nine votes, although there were sixty members present, it was decided by a vote of seven to two to do away with the club-houses, both on Staten Island and in the city, store the models, and hold the club meetings at some restaurant. Of course, had not this action been reconsidered, the non-yacht owners would have resigned. Wiser counsels prevailed, Mr. Kane was elected commodore, the club-rooms in the city were retained, and the club was saved. The home at Staten Island should have been retained also, for the club was not, perhaps, as near bankruptcy as its short-sighted committee alleged. At its dinner at Delmonico's, March 21, there were $50,000 worth of silverware in the shape of prize-cups doing duty as *épergnes*.

Kane was the best commodore that the club had had for many years. He was a thorough gentleman and yachtsman, able to sail and navigate his own yacht, and withal possessed of rare finesse and tact. The club, under his administration, took a new lease of life. The abandonment of the club-house and anchorage at Stapleton,

GALATEA.

however, was a grievous error and has forced the yacht-owners of the New York club to enroll themselves in other clubs. As, however, none have resigned from the old club, the result has been rather a gain to the other clubs than a loss to the New York. It has, however, placed the Atlantic Club in the front rank, second in importance in this country only to the New York ; and if any disaffection should arise in the old club from any cause, its members might readily transfer their allegiance to the Atlantic Club without losing caste. The Atlantic is not in any sense a rival organization, but it seems to me that it was impolitic by unwise legislation to force men to join other clubs in order to find the necessary facilities which should have been furnished by their own. However, the yacht owners did this themselves. I do not hesitate to assert that the great body of non-yacht owners, from whom four-fifths of the financial support of the club comes, would have cheerfully borne the expense of continuing the club-house at Staten Island, and I am quite sure that, great as has been the prosperity of the New York Yacht Club during this decade, it would have been far more prosperous had this club-house been kept up. Had this not been emphatically the international decade, the New York Yacht Club would, I have no doubt, have fallen to third place, and the Eastern and Atlantic would have supplanted it in importance. But during this decade the *Countess of Dufferin*, the *Atalanta*, the *Genesta*, *Galatea*, and *Thistle* races have all been sailed, and the attention of the whole nation has been directed to the New York Yacht Club. It is very distasteful to the members of the New York Yacht Club to be told that a possibility exists that a time may come when it will not retain its present proud position among the clubs of the world, and he who reminds them is apt to be regarded as an enemy ; but they have only to go back to 1876, and this 7 to 2 vote, to see how near to ruin it came on that occasion, frightened by the bugbear of a $3,000 deficiency. The only object OUTING has is to arouse the thought of the members on this subject and make them alert to the consequences of unwise legislation.

All this, however, is a digression, and only incidentally has to do with the memories of past cruises. I have called attention to the fact that the New York club changed its first stopping-place, after leaving Glen Cove, from New London to Shelter Island, Greenport Harbor. It was the Atlantic Club that first availed itself of the facilities of the harbor of Greenport, and at one time it seriously considered the advisability of establishing itself in that place. A member of the club donated land for a club-house, and another gave $500 toward the erection of a building. The offer was tempting, for the club then was small, its headquarters in an old canal-boat at the foot of Court Street, Brooklyn, and the idea of a fine club-house at Greenport was dazzling. Fortunately for the club it had long-headed men in control and the proposition was rejected. Had it been adopted, it would have been ruinous ; the club might as well have had a club-house in France as in Greenport, and would by this time have been extinct.

The only fit course for vessels such as those of the Atlantic, the New York, the Seawanhaka Corinthian and the New York Corinthian clubs is on the ocean. Nearly every year a proposition is made to transplant the New York Yacht Club to quarters on the Sound. It is urged that yachting means pleasure-sailing, and that, as most of the pleasure-sailing is done on the Sound, that is the most appropriate place for a club-house. To this OUTING replies, that yachting means racing, and that as soon as either of these four clubs puts Hell Gate and the East River between themselves and its racecourse, it will have accomplished its own dissolution.

I well remember when the Brooklyn Yacht Club first made Greenport a stopping place, and I think it must have been during this memorable cruise of 1873. The fleet ran over from New London with a fine breeze, arriving about two o'clock in the afternoon. It was saluted with guns from the shore in response to its own salutes, and by the display of flags all over the town, and nearly the whole population of the town was at the water-front. So fine a fleet of yachts had never before been seen there, for the Atlantic Club, which alone at that time had visited Greenport, was extremely insignificant compared with this fleet of the Brooklyn Club, and storekeepers, shipwrights, painters, sailmakers, etc., welcomed it with heartiness, anticipating a rich harvest. The hope was constantly expressed that the New York Yacht Club might be made cognizant of the manifold advantage of the port as a stopping-place. Well, the New York Club was informed, and went.

Somehow the realization of the advantages to be derived from the visits of a yacht club are not equal to the anticipation, and the citizens of Greenport soon came to the conclusion that the pecuniary advantage derivable from the visit was more than counterbalanced by its objectionable features. The welcome at first extended was soon succeeded by a reception decidedly cool. To the ladies of the place, however, the advent of the clubs has always been a source of especial gratification. The yachtsman's uniform possesses a peculiar fascination for them, and a visit to a yacht, with a sail down the harbor, is a joy to be remembered for months, as a contrast to the ordinary monotony of village life.

After the completion of the Manhansett House on Shelter Island, the New York Yacht Club found this a most agreeable place for a day's sojourn, and the different proprietors of this—one of the best hotels on the coast—have always welcomed the visit of the New York Yacht Club with pleasure. The communication with this city is direct and frequent, and business men like the place on this account. The anchorage, however, is inconvenient on account of the great depth of water, and on this account, perhaps, as well as for other reasons, the Atlantic Club makes its anchorage in Deering Cove and its headquarters the Prospect House, a quiet hotel, conducted on strictly temperance principles, more in accordance with the character of the members than its fashionable neighbor, the Manhansett.

The Pequot House, at the entrance of New London Harbor, where the New York Yacht Club makes its rendezvous, has never encouraged the visits of any other club. While it was under the proprietorship of the late Mr. Crocker, he, I understand, distinctly informed the commodore of the Brooklyn Club on one occasion that he would be better pleased by the absence of the club than by its presence, and whether or not the same intimation was given to the Atlantic I cannot say, but for a number of years its fleet has anchored on the opposite side of the harbor, and made the Edgecombe House its headquarters.

Newport is the real home of American yachts, and there is not a day during the season when its harbor does not contain some. They are such common and constant visitors that the entry of the largest and finest fleet does not cause a ripple of excitement. The storekeepers, however, along the harbor front advance their prices on the arrival of a large fleet, and the boatmen and truckmen seem to consider the visiting yachtsmen their especial prey. The New York Yacht Club, thanks to its enterprising member, Mr. Ogden Goelet, has a very convenient landing stage, and his annual gift is the occasion of a racing event, which, under the title of the Goelet cup race, has come to be considered one of the principal events of the season.

A proposition has been made to establish the headquarters of the New York Yacht Club at Newport on account of its central position, half way between the two great yachting ports of Boston and New York, and because it possesses avowedly the best racing courses in the United States. This would, I think, be unwise; but I do consider that it would be in the interests of yachting to establish a national club there, or a national association, for which members of other clubs should be eligible, either as a distinct and independent yacht club, or an association composed of delegates from all existing clubs. Yacht clubs have multiplied to such an extent, and the sport has attained such an importance, that the time is quite ripe for such a movement. A week's racing at Newport each year, in which different classes of vessels could have their days, from the largest schooner or steamer to the open sloop or cat-rigged boat, would be, I think, a good thing; and scarce any port other than Newport has the courses suitable to each. It has the ocean course to and round Block Island for the big yachts, and it has been the home of the cat-boat from its earliest history, and has a fine expanse of smooth water, practically tideless and free from shoals.

MEMORIES OF YACHT CRUISES.

BY CAPTAIN R. F. COFFIN.

ENTRANCE TO NEW LONDON HARBOR.

HE pleasantest form of cruising is, perhaps, on a single yacht, rather than with a squadron. Nevertheless, there is a charm in the association of a large body of men, united by a common purpose, that is lacking when an owner confines himself to the companionship of a few friends.

Yachting means racing, and the yacht off on an individual cruise seizes every opportunity to measure her speed with any craft she encounters. Singularly enough, the yachts of Mr. A. and Mr. B. will sail in company for a whole day, and at dinner in the evening, while Mr. A. is telling his friends how decidedly he beat Mr. B.'s yacht during the day's sail, Mr. B., at exactly the same time, is narrating to those who are gathered round his festive board, that he has been fortunate enough to encounter Mr. A.'s yacht in the cruise of the day —something which for a long time he had desired—and has beaten her terribly.

Men entirely truthful on all other topics will "enlarge their borders" a little when telling of the performance of their yachts, and the man has never yet been discovered who, when telling of the time of his run from port to port, or of the relative performance of his craft with other vessels, has been known to be strictly accurate. It was always so. "My ship" was always faster than any other man's ship, and records of remarkable passages must be taken with considerable allowance of "salt," for the temptation to leave out of the count the days of departure and arrival has been in most cases too strong to resist.

Now, the squadron cruise is a series of races from the time that the fleet leaves the rendezvous until it breaks up ; and during recent cruises measures have been taken to have the record exact by timing the yachts at the beginning and end of the day's run. Before the adoption of this system, the record did not mean much, for in a crowded roadstead, like the mouth of New London harbor, for instance, with the wind blowing in—as it almost invariably does in summer—the yachts farthest out would obtain a lead of a quarter or a half hour. Again, if the finish was in a small harbor, like Newport, a big fleet coming up with a cracking southwest wind—such as almost always is found there in the afternoon—would invariably have to divide, one half going in by Fort Adam and the other going round the north end of Goat Island, and, of course, the time of anchoring did not give a fair record.

Even in the case of the run of the fleet when it was accompanied by the *Cambria*, of which we spoke in the August article, while each yacht was exactly timed as it crossed a line from the Dumplings to Fort Adams, only the finish was recorded with accuracy, while the start from the anchorage off the Pequot House on signal, was manifestly unfair. The *Tidal Wave*, being well up the harbor, and in a poor berth, was just in the act of shifting to a better position, and was running down with anchor lifted, when the starting gun was fired. Of course she kept right on, and secured a lead which perhaps gave her the race.

To obviate this unfairness, starting by signal when under way was adopted ; that is, the fleet would be ordered to heave-to off a certain point, Brenton's Reef light-

ship, for instance, and at a signal from the flagship, start for the next port. It was found, however, that there were always some too impatient to wait for the signal, who would start on ahead in order to be reported first to arrive at the destined haven. With the very general introduction of steam yachts, however, it has been possible to accurately time start and finish, and since the present commodore took office he has been pleased to make of his flagship a regatta committee boat. From her deck it has been quite easy to time the yachts at the start when passing a given point, and then to go on, overtaking and passing even the most speedy, again timing them at some given point near the port of arrival.

All this has made the cruise much more interesting. Never had regatta committee such comfortable quarters before; never by any previous commodore were the representatives of the press so well cared for; seldom, if ever, had any of them an opportunity to live so sumptuously, and yet, although it seems ungracious to say it, I have some doubts whether committee and press men would not feel more at ease under the old system, when each man had

to care for himself, and a tugboat was deemed good enough for the regatta committee.

Year by year the annual cruise has grown in importance and popularity, and new and interesting features have been added. Besides the runs from port to port with accurately kept records, there are set regattas with allowance of time and valuable prizes; at Newport, New Bedford, Martha's Vineyard and Marblehead. For these regattas a very salutary rule has been adopted: that no yacht shall be eligible for entry to these cruise races which hauls out of water after the cruise has begun. This rule was put in force because a few of the owners used to keep their yachts at Greenport, where facilities for hauling out are admirable, so that on the eve of an important race the yacht would be stripped for racing, put upon the ways, cleaned and "pot-leaded." Then, in prime racing fettle, she would join the squadron on the evening previous to the race, enter for it, sail triumphantly over the course the next day, "scoop in the mug," and then "top her boom and sail large," remaining with the squadron no longer. This sort of "funny work," a kind of leg-

Fred. S. Cozzens

ESTELLE.

acy from the old days of " sand-bag " races, " gin regattas," etc., when all tricks of the " boat sharp " were considered legitimate, has been stopped.

The formation of clubs, with fair, fixed rules ; the encouragement given to Corinthian sailing, and the introduction of a more intelligent, better educated and more respectable element in yachting, has dethroned the professional sailing-master entirely, and on board of many of the yachts he occupies his proper position of

cessfully oppose the autocrat of the engine-room. Steam-yachts, as a rule, are about half the time at the machine-shop, to the great pecuniary advantage, it is hinted, of the engineer. A well-known constructor of steam machinery is reported as saying : " Guarantee me the repairing of the engine and boiler, and let me have the appointment of the engineer, and I'll put the machinery into a new yacht for nothing." All this will be changed by and by, as gentlemen who own steam-yachts become better acquainted with the mechanism of the engine, but unless they become practical machinists, the engineer will always have a decided " pull."

The formation of the American Club devoted almost entirely to the interest of the steam-yacht will do much for the better education of steamboat owners, and in the interest of the yachting of the future it is a good thing that it was organized. Though it was a serious mistake for the New York Yacht Club to have permitted this organization to come into

Fred. S. Cozzens

CLYTIE.

executive officer, the owner being captain of his own craft.

While this is true to a great extent in the sailing fleet, in a majority of instances the engineer is the ruling power on board the steam-yacht, neither captain nor owner knowing enough about machinery to suc-

existence, it is doubtful if the interests of steam-yachting could have been as well conserved in the New York Yacht Club, where the sailing yacht must always hold the front rank, as in this new club, which cares for nothing else but steamers.

Here inventors flock and "machine

cranks" of every description, but all may be sure that if they present anything possessing germs of promise, the intelligent and wealthy men of this club will gladly aid in its development. In the city rooms of this club, steam-yacht owners meet nightly, and talk valve and "cut-off," expansion and different shapes of propeller wheel, while in the summer, at its elegant quarters on Milton Point, the discussion is continued and practical test is made on the quiet waters of the Sound. The cruises of this club so far have been simply races over a stipulated course, with an expensive steamer for members and guests, but in the cruise of the future, a fleet of forty or fifty steam vessels, in the course of a three weeks' cruise, will visit every harbor of note between this city and Portland. This will be a pleasure cruise, indeed, and dwarf the present cruises of sailing yachts to nothingness.

The racing of the future will be done by the small sloop, the owner of which will luxuriously view the contest from the deck of his magnificently appointed steam-yacht. In the reaction from an exclusive regard for the "single-stick" vessel, several fine schooners were built at the beginning of the present season, but I doubt if they will hold their own for cruising yachts

steam fleet, and are being turned out as rapidly as the company can make them.

All this, however, is somewhat of a digression, as the object of this article is to continue the reminiscences of past club cruises.

I think that the last which the Brooklyn Club made was in July, 1877, and it was a decided failure. Mr. Dickerson was the commodore at the time and did what he could to keep up the club prestige. The schooner *Madeleine* was his flagship, and there mustered in Glen Cove Harbor beside her, the schooners *Estelle*, *Comet* and *Playful*, and the sloops *Niantic*, *Ada* and *Kate*.

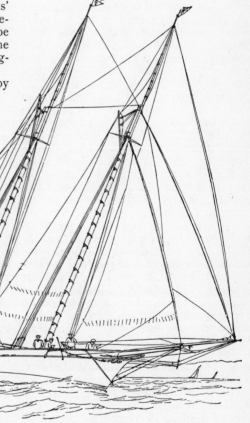

Fred. S. Cozzens

COMET.

with the steamers, more and more of which are being built every season, constant improvements in machinery making them cheaper and more fitted for pleasure craft. Light naphtha launches are now to be seen hung at the davits of nearly all of the large sailing-yachts as well as of the

It was a melancholy cruise. From Glen Cove, *en route* to Greenport, the fleet touched for an hour or so at Black Rock, and then foolishly left that harbor at four P.M. and proceeded in a pouring rain to arrive at Greenport about three o'clock the next morning with all hands thoroughly disgusted. Here there was a division of sentiment, part of the fleet stopping at Block Island, on the way to Newport, and the others going direct. Thence two schooners and four sloops made their way to Vineyard Haven and there disbanded.

Commodore Dickerson was not popular for some reason, but no man could have arrested the downward course of the Brooklyn Yacht Club at that time. It was badly managed ; jealousies had arisen, and there was a party opposed to members of the club who had been identified with it for years and had always studied its best interests. The cry was raised that these men ran the club and had too much to say, and they at once retired in disgust and left the management in untried hands. Driven from its headquarters at the foot of Court Street by the encroachments of commerce, it went to Gravesend Bay and put up a club-house at Guntherville. There was too little water for the large yachts, no shelter for the small ones, and the place was difficult of access—even more so at that time than now. Still, as long as it held on to its club-house at the foot of Court Street, some of its older members, John Dimon, Henry Wood, and others of that sort, stuck by it. When, however, that was given up, these gentlemen joined the Atlantic Club, and the Brooklyn became a club without yachts or flag-officers.

The fleet of the New York Yacht Club in this year's cruise was a fine one, and the affair a great success. Commodore Kane had exerted himself in the matter personally, and the result was the presence at Glen Cove of fourteen schooners and three sloops. From Glen Cove to New London a sweepstake was arranged, which added, of course, to the interest of the occasion. The fleet had rather a tedious time getting to New London, having light and variable airs. The schooner *Estelle* led the fleet, ariving at 2.15 A.M., the *Clytie* being second.

This cruise was famous for the presence of the double-hulled schooner *Nereid*. The wonderful speed developed by the *Amaryllis,* the first of the Herreshoff " catamarans," at the Centennial regatta, caused a catamaran *furore.* Mr. Anson Phelps Stokes thought that the principle might be successfully applied to large yachts, and had the *Nereid* built on the north shore of Staten Island by Mr. Lou Town. She was a large vessel, and the idea was to have quarters for the crew in one of the hulls, while the owner and guests occupied the other. She frightened the owners of second-class schooners in the New York Yacht Club terribly, and a special meeting was called to bar her out, but finally this unsportsmanlike measure did not prevail. She was a flat failure. There was no foundation for her mast, and as the rigging was set up the mast and deck settled, nor had she any speed, owing to the rigidity of her construction. The ball-and-socket joint which is the secret of the speed of the Herreshoff boats was lacking. The next summer a third hull was put between the other two in order to hold the mast, but it did not improve her, and after the expenditure of a large sum, she was hauled up on the beach at Stapleton and abandoned.

This was a fine cruise, the fleet visiting Shelter Island, Block Island, Newport, Vineyard Haven, and New Bedford. At the last place, the club remained two days, having boat races in the harbor and a grand reception at the New Bedford club-house. Quite an extended programme was agreed upon, including two big squadron races at Newport, a second visit to Shelter Island and a return to New London, where there was to be a final race previous to disbanding. On arrival at Newport, however, the cruise was abandoned.

It has always seemed to me a mistake not to return to the place of departure to disband. In the first place, it would be nearer home, and then it would give the yachts some weather work in the passages from port to port. Going round Cape Cod is nonsense, unless the club desires to extend its cruise to the east, say as far as Mount Desert or Portland ; but it is a very tame affair to go from New London to Shelter Island, thence to Newport and New Bedford, disbanding at Vineyard Haven. The whole course has been down the wind and there has been no chance to try the yachts in weather work, which, after all, is the true test of excellence. If, however, after going this trip, the club returned over the same course, finishing at New London, or, better still, at Glen Cove or Larchmont, it would make a nice cruise, and at the end all hands would be within easy reach of home. It is difficult, however, to hold a fleet together for more than a week or ten days, as remaining with the fleet is purely a voluntary act on the part of the owners. A show is made of respect for authority, by hoisting the signal " Leave of absence is requested," but what would happen should the leave be refused ?

Heroes of the Deep (1907)

HEROES OF THE DEEP.

BY HERBERT D. WARD.

THE fishing-fleet is like a large wheel of life, of the three hundred and fifty spokes of which twenty-five pass in and out of the bay every day, a quivering procession, freighted with hope, with gain, with sorrow, and with disappointment. The beautiful harbor of Gloucester stretches from Norman's Woe to Eastern Point, and the fish that enter are daily measured by the hundred thousand weight.

There is no port in this country to which the Naval Department, in case of war, would sooner look for sailors to man the fleets than this old town which, in 1606, Champlain (the first white man to tread the shores of Cape Ann) called "Le Beau Port." For the great fishing-fleet holds nearly seven thousand souls under its gurried decks, and every one of these has faced, as a matter of course, dangers that would give the average reader many a nightmare, if he could experience but a touch of their reality. What novelist would think of sketching the story of a dried codfish? What novelist could do better?

It is always with a vague regret that we read the sagas, and are thrilled by the viking's exploits. It seems as if the deeds of daring had gone by forever, and as if the heroes of the deep were a myth of the past. Absorbed in the Norse romance, we forget that the vikings were only pirates, and that they dared for slaughter and for booty. If the Gloucester of to-day had only existed then, what heroic saga would it not have inspired! For to risk life for glory, or riches, or rescue, or love is in the heart of every man to do; but to risk life for a bare existence, for other people's profit, and for an anonymous end partakes of that commonplace sublimity which does not form the favorite plot of poets, although once in a while it is the subject of a daily paragraph.

For the vikings are not dead. From Portland to New Orleans, our harbors are full of them. They lounge upon our wharves, and we do not recognize them. They loiter on our streets, and we know them not. But if there is a more modest, unconscious, or braver fellow than Jack the Fisherman, our eyes have yet to rest upon his face. He is the hardiest and most daring, the best sailor in the world to-day. Any Continental kingdom would give its wealth to possess him for its defense. He is the envy of every maritime nation. Has he no value for us, beyond the halibut and the cod, the haddock and the cusk?

In the old days the wharves of Gloucester town were busy with the making of fish. The flakes were white with awnings protecting the drying cod from stain of sun. In the inner harbor the catch is still dexterously weighed, and pitched from dory to dory, till it is washed, and fit to be salted in platoons of savory hogsheads. But, comparatively speaking, the years of the great fares have gone by, and the harvest of "summer boarders" has come. Five women occupy the wharves for one full fare from Georges, or one long trip from the Banks. Too many of the awnings are replaced by the white umbrellas that shelter the aspiring impressionists. Facing the crumbling corner of a once prosperous wharf, you find a lone lady in bicycle-gaiters laying in water colors, not the color of the water, or of the dismantled vessel before her, or of any other dead or living thing. Little our modern artistling thinks that every quavering plank upon which she treads is charged with years of drama from the living sea.

Only the other day, seated upon the edge of a dory, on the deck of a vessel that had just discharged its small fare of fresh fish, I happened to get into conversation with a red, fat-faced Swedish lad. He was not much over nineteen. He had not outgrown blushing when you mentioned shave. He is of the kind that ships a boy and lands a man. Nor did Hans suspect the reason of the change. His was the majority given by experience, not by years. But I drew out his record from him as I draw a refractory charge out of a muzzle-loader. He was lying in a nest of dories, smoking lazily, and ravished by the July sun. He looked incapable of motion or ambition. He was the last fellow your popular novelist would pick out as a hero.

"No," he said, in his broad foreign accent, without deigning to look up; "I never see any one drowned or saved. The most courageous thing I ever did was to get drunk and get sober again. Yes; I saw my dory-mate saved by a plug-strap."

For the benefit of the reader who has not made his trip, it is necessary to explain that every dory has a plug in its bottom. This is like a large bung in a barrel. Through this plug runs a piece of buoy line, which ends in a loop about eight inches or so long on the waterside. This is the plug-strap, which is probably instrumental in saving twenty lives a year.

"Last winter," admitted Hans, reluctantly, "I was off Greenland, and me and my mate was about two mile baitin' up trawls. It was terrible cold, the water freezing where she struck. The dory was almost full of fish. All to once a big wave capsized the dory and threw us into the water. When the dory came up, I caught the grab-line; but my mate was too far off, so I let go, and swam off, and towed him, and we held hands across the bottom. Only one could hold on to the grab-line at once, so I put his other hand in it, and holt on to the other. He was growin' pretty weak. He was washed off twice, and I haul him in each time. They took us off in about an hour; another minute, and I guess we 'd 'a' both gone. It was the grab-line that saved him."

He stopped, and puffed with a languid unconsciousness which it seemed, somehow, bad manners to disturb.

"Don't you remember seeing anything really grand—that is—heroic?"

The questioner floundered helplessly before the young fisherman's puzzled look.

"Naw," Hans smiled contemptuously; "I don't think."

Yet the boy himself had artlessly confessed to what was as much a deed of heroism as that of the engineer in sticking to his throttle for his passengers' sakes at the moment of collision.

But the fisherman considers such an act as a matter of course. The average summer boarder, eagerly gossiping on the hotel piazzas, and idly watching the white schooners slip in and out of the harbor, is seldom awakened out of that spurious superiority which the pale-faced, well-dressed alien generally feels toward the weather-beaten, simple "native." Yet once in a while even this fond illusion is dispelled.

It happened not many summers ago that on a calm afternoon arose one of those sudden, virulent squalls that are common to Ipswich Bay and Gloucester Harbor. It seemed as if the barometer had not time to fall. The dory fishermen had long since returned home. Only those were left who go down to the sea for pleasure. All these sloops, large or small, were in charge of experienced sailors who had, at the first signs of danger, scudded for moorings, or had run down the sails—all but one little party. It was the smallest keel of the pleasure fleet, and this time manned by four children. As the squall began to threaten, upon the eighteen-foot jib-and-mainsail boat the eyes of the Point and the Cove were anxiously fixed. The children, two girls and two boys, belonged to two families, and their mothers ran to the nearest point of land to watch them. The clouds were racing like black warhorses, their manes taking frightful shapes. Large schooners were now under bare poles, dropping quick anchors. Alas! in the mouth of the bay that crazy little boat braved the portent with both sails spread, and wabbled like one bereft of reason. Boyish figures were dimly seen rushing frantically to the mast and back to the cockpit. Then a groan of anguish arose from our group; for, without further warning, the squall burst. The foam, the rain, and the spray, with angry teeth, advanced from the west, enveloped the boat, passed on, and hid the tragedy from sight.

When the spray cut our faces, and the wind made ears almost useless, I heard a voice bellowing from windward:

"It 's no use! They 're goners! Nothing in God's heaven can save 'em now! Their halyards are fouled."

Kind hands bore the mothers into the house; for their children were, for them, already dead.

The man who howled at us was one of the "natives." He was an offshore fisherman. He had a trap and a few lobster-pots, and earned a living in the easiest, safest possible way. He stood there, bracing himself against the hurricane. He was "oiled up," alert; he had a new look upon his face: the heavens had fallen, and he was in his own element.

At that moment there was a break in the clouds. To our amazement, by some freak of Providence the crazy craft was still in sight. Now head on, now head off, with her jib blown out, careening fearfully, the tiny boat still lived. But the worst of the squall was yet to come.

"If I only had my dory!" cried the fisherman, with the tears running down his face. But his dory was far out on his hauling-line, and the waves were dashing high upon the rocks. His dory was impossible.

"Take my boat, Joe."

Now that keel tender of mine, well built for its purpose,—that of pleasure-sailing on smooth seas,—was too narrow and cranky for a man to trust his life to in a gale like that, and the fisherman shook his head mournfully. Just then another gust swept down.

"There she goes!" some one cried, in horror. The sail-boat was rapidly drifting down upon the rocks, and in danger of upsetting at any moment. A white, fluttering speck could be seen on the reeling deck. One of the little girls was waving her handkerchief at her father, who was pacing the beach in the helpless, aimless fashion of one dazed by agony.

Then the fisherman looked at me. He had children, too,—a good many of them,—and he loved his wife. But there was a look upon his face that perhaps had never been there before, that might never come there again.

"Get me the oars," he commanded, "and help me to shove her off!"

We started down to the dancing float. He jumped into the cockle-shell, and I shoved him off. Now it seemed as if he would go upon the rocks, but he did not strike. Twenty times the sea smote him, and he looked engulfed, but he rode free. In the jaws of the squall, he got to the driving, careening boat, and boarded her—no one knew how. In a moment the refusing halyards, tangled by ignorant little fingers, were in his strong, skilled hands; and before night it was all down the coast that the boarder children were saved, and that there had arisen a new hero.

A few weeks after, the Massachusetts Humane Society, gave him a silver medal, and I have no doubt whatever that the little episode has passed almost out of his mind, and clean out of that of his neighbors, by this time. It sometimes takes a squall to make a hero. Yet perhaps now and then, on a winter's night, he looks at the gleaming white badge of honor within its velvet case, and rubs it up to keep it bright. And his children and his children's children will turn it with wonder in little fingers, and treasure it with puzzled reverence. For by

its argent the fisherman's family are ennobled, and enter the aristocracy of the Massachusetts coast.

This is only one of a few cases where the man gets the medal. But there are a hundred more who have done deeds as brave as this, and braver, whose names have drifted out of easy memories, even as the scud drifts to the lee. A newspaper-file may hold them embalmed, but that is only another proof of their obliteration.

The men who go forth upon the sea to fish have, beyond all other mariners of peace, extraordinary opportunities of showing hardihood. Theirs is the most dangerous calling upon the ocean. Perils of fog are their daily bread. The dangers of drift and collision, when the gale tears them from their shoal anchorage, or when the liner plows through their puny fleet, are the dead reckoning of their calling. Then the squall that heaves the vessel down till her masts lie level with the foam, the lee shore at night in the winter hurricane, the iceberg, and the chance comber—these are fearful experiences to the fishing-schooners of from eighty to a hundred tons. From these causes alone about six vessels and at least seventy-five lives a year are offered up by the Gloucester fleet upon the altar of fish.

But there is one other peculiarity of this vocation, which, I believe, for pure hazard or undiluted danger has not its equal in any other department of labor—that is, the necessity of fishing with trawls. It is bad enough to dare the worst seas in the hemisphere in a vessel the decks of which do not rise more than two feet above the level of the water; but to add to that the hauling and baiting of trawls in heavy-laden dories, in the gale and fog and ice—this is throwing sixes for life, with only the gambler's luck or habit in one's favor.

The dory is the gull among small boats, with its flat bottom, its flaring sides, its movable thwarts, its plug. It is the fisherman's home, his refuge, and often his coffin. It is so light that it takes only a little sea to catch it unawares and tip it completely over. No matter how heavily laden, it will, cat-like, when sunk, turn itself over and rise to the surface. It affords no protection from the sea save through the skill of its occupants; no shelter from the icy gale but the oilskin and mittens of the man at the buoy-line. While it is the fisherman's best friend, it is also a treacherous one.

At least a half a dozen instances are recorded of a vessel having sent out its whole crew, two by two, in dories, to set or haul the trawls, and not one having returned, and the captain and the cook being left to bring their vessel back home as best they could.

On the morning of January 25, 1893, the schooner *Grace L. Fears* lay at anchor on Burgeo Bank. She had ventured that far north to catch halibut. The crew jumped over her sides into their dories to haul their trawls. In one of these boats were Howard Blackburn and his mate Tom Welch. As they left the vessel's side it began to snow lightly.· These men were too used to this kind of sea hazard to mind it at all. Their business was to get fish, and not to worry about the dangers of the process.

So they stuck to their trawls, unmindful of the fact that the storm had grown thick and had long since shut them in a little white circle beyond which nothing could be seen. They knew their peril, but to go back to the vessel without their gear would subject them to forecastle sarcasm.

When they did start to go back, the squall had changed the wind so that now they lay to the leeward of their vessel. This confused the men. They pulled to windward, but the vessel was not to be found. No bell, no horn, no sound but the swish of the wind and snow upon the rising sea could be heard.

As the gale increased, unable to hold their own, they anchored, and lay there till after dark, when the clouds cleared. Far to windward they saw the faint flicker of the schooner's riding-light.

"Now up with the anchor, Tom," said Blackburn, "and one more pull will get us there!"

But the sea, which had arisen as well as the wind, baffled them, and they lost water. Again they threw out the anchor. This time it did not hold, and as the dory rose on crest after crest in her swift drift to leeward, the fishermen caught agonizing glimpses of the flaring torch which is always kept burning at night on the deck of a vessel to guide stray dories back.

There came another gust of snow, a surge of seas, a scramble to bail the water and save the dory from filling; then, when they looked, the flare was gone from their sight.

Now began a desperate struggle for life which has not been surpassed in dory misadventures. A hundred times that night a curler filled the boat. What a wild scurry to bail it out with the little wooden shovel and the hat before the next deluge came!

At last the gale increased so that a drag became imperative, or they would inevitably swamp. So Blackburn broke in the head of a trawl-keg, tied it to an iron winch known as a hurdy-gurdy, made fast a stout piece of dory-line, and threw it.· Just as the drag went by the board, a sea broke clean over the dory. Welch dropped his oars, and bailed for his life; and with the first scoopful, over went Blackburn's mittens. This was a fatal loss.

With nothing to drink or eat, with freezing hands, in a frail open craft, exposed to the coldest and severest of winter storms— here was a situation terrible enough to appal the bravest heart. To hope against despair is the elemental quality of heroism. Such courage is not easy of conception. It is the viking's trait.

Now Blackburn thought and decided quickly. His hands were beginning to freeze. They were already numb and whitening. What were they most useful for, frozen? Without a word of complaint, he bent his stiffening fingers at the knuckles until they curled about the handles of the oars. Whatever might happen, his only chance of life lay in rowing; that he knew. Thus he calmly sat down and waited for his hands to freeze in this position, and began to encourage his dory-mate:

"We'll be picked up; this can't last long."

By this time the wind was so sharp that the men could not look to windward, so that even if a vessel had passed near them they might not have seen it. Ice had formed rapidly on the sides and gunwales of the dory, and the two took turns in clearing the boat of water and ice, which weighted it down.

On the morning of the second day it had come to be Welch's turn to bail. Blackburn told him to jump to his work so. as to keep his blood moving. Welch answered that he could not see.

"Tom," said Blackburn, "this won't do. You will have to do your part. Your hands are not frozen and beaten to pieces like mine." The speaker showed his right hand, with all one side and the little finger beaten off by pounding ice.

But this sight did not encourage Welch, who lay down in the bottom of the dory, absolutely disheartened.

"What is the use, Howard?" he moaned. "I can't live till morning, and I might as well go first as last."

In order to protect him as much as possible, Blackburn lay down beside him so as to keep him warm. Welch's mind began to wander. He thrust his feet over the sides of the dory, moaned, and begged in the most piteous tone for water. He broke off the ice from the sides of the boat; but it nauseated him, and he threw it away.

Blackburn, in the mean time, must bail busily in order to keep the dory from sinking. As he stopped, he heard his dory-mate whispering and pitifully trying to articulate. Blackburn called, but received no reply. When he went to the bow, in the dark of the morning, and touched his mate, he found that he had, as sole companion, a frozen corpse.

He took the body of his friend, and gently placed it in the stern. His first thought was, "The mittens!" They were too precious to be wasted on the dead.

He pulled one off; but his hands were now so swollen that he could do nothing with it.

Now Blackburn stood up in the middle of the boat, defying the icy storm and the waves with indomitable courage. He would not allow himself even to sit down, for fear that the drowsiness which overtook his mate would slay him. He hauled in the drag, and pulled for his life.

The third day found the sea somewhat moderated. The undaunted man had come up against his last resources of strength and will.

Oh, for one morsel of food, one drop of pure water! But the dory fisherman is provided with neither.

Now that it was possible to do so, the castaway hauled in his drag, sat down on the thwart, and began to row. It was then that the ingenious wisdom of his stiffening fingers began to be apparent. He was able to grasp the oars with firmness. He had no feeling in his hands, and the friction of the oar-handles upon his frozen flesh began to crumble his palms away like powder. He rowed all that day until night. The wind began to rise again. He threw out the drag; the dory did not ship any water now. It was too cold for him to go to sleep; had he done so, he would have been frozen in fifteen minutes. The only way for him to keep awake was to fold his arms about the thwart, and allow the rocking of the dory to lift him backward and forward all night long.

All the next day he clung to his oars, pulling toward the land. On the fourth night he found himself still a long way off.

Sunday morning opened calm, with an unruffled sea. There was a slight rise in the temperature, which inspired the hopeful man to renewed exertions. He determined to reach the shore, and he put his last strength into a powerful stroke of the oars.

In the afternoon he struck the tide-rip at the mouth of a small river, and landed at a little wharf near a deserted house. The floor of the house was covered knee-deep with snow. He turned over the boards of the floor, and the bottom of the bedstead, in order to be able to lie down on the dry side. He gathered together a few old nets and lines for a pillow, and a net for a blanket. He tried to sleep now, for the first time; but such was the pain from his swollen limbs and from his terrible thirst that he could not sleep. He spent the long night munching snow and walking the floor.

That night the dory swung against a rock and filled. The next morning Blackburn rescued his dory-mate's body, all shrouded in ice as it was, from the sunken dory. He took it in his arms, and tried to lift it upon the wharf. But he was too weak for this, and the body slipped, and fell into twelve feet of water. Lying down upon the wharf, the fisherman could peer to the bottom of the river, and there he could see the cold face looking up at him plaintively, as if begging not to be deserted. Then the living man vowed not to neglect his dead mate.

He spent that day renewing his boat and rowing out again into the open in search of life. He saw no vessel, no house, no sign of life, not even a column of smoke; and almost for the first time disheartened, he turned his sinking dory back to the place whence she had started in the morning.

This was the evening of the fifth day after leaving the *Grace L. Fears.* It is difficult to understand how he survived without food.

As he was struggling up the swift current, he noticed outlines which he had not seen before—the roofs of three houses. It took him two hours and a half, and the last remnant of his strength, to reach the spot. It was moonlight, and the people saw the strange dory coming up, and waited for it.

Then Blackburn knew that he was saved. But even then he refused to eat or drink, or go into a house and be cared for, until they promised him to rescue the body of his mate, sunk beneath the wharf.

Blackburn lost his hands and most of his toes, but came back to Gloucester in safety. The story of his courage, of his unparalleled suffering, of his devotion to his dory-mate, is well known along the old fishing-wharves, and will be told for many a day.

How does such a tale of valor end? Does the heroism "strike in" and last through?

The closing pages in the stirring story are unwritten, but the capacity for bearing hardship is not exhausted, nor is the love of adventure. Captain of a stout crew, rounding ing and the heroism of the fishermen. Such stories might be multiplied by the score once every year. It is only when a survivor with an instinct for the dramatic tells of his own

DRAWN BY GEORGE VARIAN.

"'HE WAS GROWIN' PRETTY WEAK.'"

the Horn on a midwinter voyage, beating up the California coast toward the gold-frosted tributaries of the Yukon, the hero of the Burgeo Bank may be found in the wild current that sweeps to the Klondike.

I have enlarged upon this experience because it is typical of one half of the suffer-

agony, or that of his mate, that we know anything about it at all, except from the tragic head-lines found in the files of the "Cape Ann Advertiser."

In the face of the appalling proportion of deaths from drifting dories, averaging anywhere from two per cent. to five per cent. a year, where is the Massachusetts legislature? Gentlemen, pass a law compelling every owner and skipper to provision every dory with at least five days' rations for two men. Such a law would probably save twenty lives a year.

rode heavily, with the breakwater to leeward. A diabolic magnet, it dragged the reluctant victim close and closer. Men watching on shore, seeing that it was only a question of a short time before the boat would break up, started to Rockport to get

DRAWN BY GEORGE VARIAN.

"ALL THE NEXT DAY HE CLUNG TO HIS OARS."

To one of my yachting skippers I owe a story of a practical joke which may help to lift that form of pleasantry out of the disrepute into which it has fallen.

In 1880 a coaster, bound from the eastward to Boston, came to anchor off Pigeon Cove in the teeth of a howling gale. She

a life-boat and rescue the crew. Among the watchers were three fishermen who, by their own experience, knew too well what that lee shore meant to the poor exhausted sailors on the ill-fated coaster. They saw at a glance that the life-boat would never get there in time. So the two brothers Zacharie and Constance Surette, and George Saunders, started on the run for the schooner *Cora Lee*, tied up safely at the wharf. From her they borrowed a dory, and jumped in. As they began to row out, they talked cheerfully:

"Hurry, boys! We must n't let those fellows in that life-boat get ahead of us."

"Won't they feel cheap! See?"

They had passed the breakwater, and were facing the furious gale. By this time the schooner was riding bows under, and drifting rapidly. The three men could hardly hold their oars; it was difficult to keep the dory from swamping. After almost superseaman efforts, they reached the vessel. It was so rough that the men on board had to leap into the sea and be picked up. Every one was saved but a dog, which refused to jump. It was none too soon. There was a desperate backing of water, a perilous turning, a pull to the harbor, a magnificent bending to the oars—then came the dull crash upon the rocks; the vessel was kindling-wood in about five minutes after the men were rescued.

When they were safely landed, one of the three heroes said:

"That 's a darn good joke on that life crew."

It was the only comment upon the situation; and, as far as I can learn, no one ever bragged about the exploit, or mentioned it again. The fishermen treated it just as if it were an every-day occurrence. But a few days later the Massachusetts Humane Society sent these plucky fellows twenty dollars each, thus recognizing them as fit men to be enrolled upon its brilliant scroll.

The life-boat, it is just to add, was doing her best. She had too far to go to get there in time.

On April 25, 1895, a fishing-vessel came out from the harbor of Dyre Fiord, Iceland, to bait up and set its trawls. It became calm at night, but in the morning, when the dories went out to haul, it began to breeze up. The gale came up so rapidly that the head dories, in order to save themselves at all, cut their gear and made for the vessel, which was drifting astern so that the men could get aboard. Soon all the dories were in but one, and the skipper was in the rigging, looking for it anxiously. It was not long before he discovered it to windward, bottom up, with the two men on top.

Volunteers offered instantly. By this time the gale was a hurricane, and the sea had made rapidly. The great danger was apparent. One of the men who went to the

rescue as a matter of course, at the peril of his life, was Carl Eckhoff, an indomitable Swede. I have been unable to discover the names of the other two.

The wind, as well as the tide, was against the rescuers. Again and again they were almost swamped; but rapid bailing and skilful handling carried them on in the white hell. At last, well-nigh spent, they reached the dory just in time to save one man alive. But the other was dead. His head was fouled in the gear where he had fallen over, benumbed by the icy water. They carried him back to the vessel, and worked three hours in vain trying to resuscitate him. Then they made for the harbor.

On the following day a procession of the crews of three vessels wended its way to the churchyard. Uplifted upon the stalwart arms of mourning mates, the dory led the way. It was the assassin dory, and in it, in simple state, lay the man it had killed.

Up through the churchyard, into the plain church, the man was carried in his strange bier. There he was laid before the pulpit while the minister said over him the prayer for the dead. The freezing grave was ready. In it John Jacobsen was buried. No longer will he risk the gale or the ice. The dory that had slain him was his coffin; and the cold earth of warm-hearted Iceland has covered both man and boat in an eternal peace.

It is to be borne in mind that the majority of the fishermen are young men in their prime. Again, the greater part of them have never seen an accident. Theirs has not been the vessel to be "hove down." The memory of seventy-three vessels that were lost or damaged on the Labrador coast during the gale of October 11, 1885, and of the one hundred and fifty men or more who were drowned, has no part in their happy-go-lucky life. In truth, they look upon their lives as happy. To pity a fisherman is to administer the final insult. Precipitous seas, waves the crests of which are as carded wool, are monotonous to them. Thus the idea of rescue, which is, after all, a secondary feature of heroism, becomes to the seaman as much a reflex action as the unconscious tripping of the fingers of a pianist.

It was off the Horn. Waves such as are encountered only there in all the world raced irresistibly. The ship labored mightily through the night. In a lull the cry, "Man overboard!" rang from stem to stern. Without hesitation the helmsman put the wheel "hard up." The watch peered over the sides of the ship into the foam. All at once a man

DRAWN BY H. REUTERDAHL.

AN ICELAND BURIAL.

rushed up the companionway. He was in his night-clothes. Without waiting a moment, he leaped the rail and plunged overboard. There was only death to be found in the boiling, benumbing waters. By some witchery of Neptune, a cross sea tossed the two men to leeward, and the ship dipped them up. They were both unconscious, and the hero had his man clutched by the hair. Even to the old sailors used to miracles of the sea the safety of the two was not so great a marvel as the fact that the man had dared to jump at all; for he was a timid, seasick landlubber making his first voyage, and his seeming cowardice had been the butt of savage scorn. How, then, had he outdared them all in recklessness? He was asked the question. How could he do it?

He answered simply that he had lain awake nights planning just what he would do if he heard the cry, "Man overboard!" It was so hard for him to overcome his instinctive fear of the water that he had mentally and systematically schooled himself to action. Thus, while his body cringed, his soul was heroic. This habit of mind made opportunity impossible to pass by. The intuitive response to his training swept him over the rail before he knew where he was.

In this way nerve is ingrained in many a nature, through self-training, before the man realizes that it is there. Chance does not make a hero: it simply translates him to himself and to the world.

This was well illustrated, a number of years ago, by a veteran fisherman.

Addison Davis was riding on the top of a coach across the old Beverly Bridge. This was in the days prior to the iron road. As the lumbering coach approached the middle of the bridge, Addison's trained ear heard a gurgle below. He bent over, and saw a boy's head disappearing in the water. Without waiting even for the inspiration, he leaped from the top of the coach over the rail, and before the vehicle could come to a stop he had the drowning boy by the hair. When asked later how he dared to do it, his reply was:

"Oh, that 's nothing. I had to do it; that 's all."

To him, as to every other hand-liner or trawler, the instinct of rescue was as simple as that of hunger, and called for no comment.

Even the babies in Gloucester are not without this instinct, although they do not count among their playthings medals from the Humane Society. It happened, this last summer, that a couple of children were playing in a spar-yard. They had ventured out upon the rolling logs floating on the tide. The older boy slipped. He was six. Down he went, head first, of course. The other one, a child of three, ran over to where he saw his playmate disappear between the logs, lay down at full length, and grabbed him by the hair when he came up. But the logs were coming together, so the baby put one of his chubby legs between the closing of the crush, and began to shriek. Without that spontaneous coolness and ability to rescue, which he probably inherited from generations of seamen, there would have been another procession of mourning-hacks in the old town.

A child who is taught, at six months, to sit up in the stern of a dory, and who rows alone at three years, is whipped if he does not show a little common sense upon the water. I saw a rigger send his son, a boy of seven, up to the top of a hundred-foot mast to hook a block, and threaten him

with the rope's end if he tumbled off. Such is the kind of training that made Captain Sol Jacobs the "high-line" of the Gloucester fleet.

At one time, when mackerel were scarce, a school was located from the crosstrees. Captain Jacobs was determined to set the seine before they scattered. He hurried off the seine-boat, and he himself steered her with an oar, standing on the stern thwart. Almost on the edge of the glistening school, —whether it was the response of nature to strong language, or a cross wave, who could say?—Captain Sol was hurled overboard. Now there is no other skipper on the coast more beloved by his crew than old Sol Jacobs, and the men immediately began to back. It was a clear choice between skipper and fish. But the skipper, who came up puffing, all "oiled up" and weighted down, decided for himself.

"What do ye think you came out here for?" he cried, with some expressive and, under the circumstances, valuable remarks not intended for print. "Set that seine quick, and don't ye wait for me!"

In about a quarter of an hour, almost dead with exhaustion, the skipper was helped over the side of the boat. But the crew had by this time set and pursed up a hundred barrels. No wonder Captain Sol always has his pick when he ships a crew.

Nothing stirs the blood or the imagination more than stories of promotion on the field of battle. War seems almost worth while, and slaughter expiated, when the general in command rides up amid the roar and smoke, and addresses a private, "Well done, corporal!" Or when, after the successful charge, he singles out the heroic lieutenant before all the regiment, and, saluting, says, "You have done well, captain!"

The exploits of peace, generally more heroic because on a less dramatic plane, have a scant gallery, little applause, and result in few promotions. A man, like a cyclone, emerges from the clear sky, but, unlike the whirlwind, performs some great feat of construction, and then melts back again into the firmament that gave him life, and the world knows him no more.

Such is Hans Slate. He has been a common, every-day fisherman for some years. During the latter part of 1896 he shipped on the schooner *Smuggler* with Captain Antoine Courant. On the night of December 30, 1896, the vessel drove ashore in a gale of wind at Cahoon's Hollow, Cape Cod. In an instant

"HE LEAPED FROM THE TOP OF THE COACH."

the seas began to break over her. The crew had to hurry to the rigging, and it was only a question of time when the masts would go by the board and all be drowned.

It seemed hours to the men, though in point of fact it was soon enough, before a flickering light on the beach told that the patrol had discovered their peril, and that the life-saving crew was at hand.

The first shot went wild, far over the

vessel. The masts creaked and bent under every onslaught of the waves. Would they hold out? But the second shot was better. The line was caught on the vessel, but far down the preventer-stay, and, besides all that, it was fouled on the hawser. It was virtually useless, for no one could step foot on deck and live. The men gave a groan of despair, for their last hope was gone.

At that moment a dark figure, like a wraith of the storm, slid down the jib-stay from the masthead. The white foam bit at him. The twanging wire threatened to jerk him off at any moment; at every heave of the surf it would come up taut with a jerk, like a gigantic bowstring. Every man of the crew breathed a prayer as Hans Slate reached the bowsprit safely. Then he was lost in a terrible sea. But Hans was imperturbable. With desperate skill and with unparalleled coolness (considering that he was engulfed by iced water every few seconds), he finally succeeded in freeing the life-line from the clutches of the hawser. He tied the rope about his neck, and started back up the swaying stay. This he had to

DRAWN BY GEORGE VARIAN.

"HANS SLATE'S EXPLOIT."

do hand over hand. Try this on a warm summer day on a motionless boat, and experience what the feat means. Now add numbed and bleeding hands, a drenched body, an icy hurricane, lashing waters, darkness, a wire whipcord, to a swaying mast that is liable to give way at any moment, and you get an inkling of Hans Slate's modest exploit. At last he secured the precious line at the masthead,

and then the breeches-buoy was busy on its merciful errand.

Soon only three were left. Hans was one, of course. Another was a boy, who was helpless on the ratlines far below the masthead. He had no strength to move; so Hans took him in his arms, carried him to the masthead, and lashed him safely to the buoy and sent him over. Now only he and the captain were left, and the captain was a heavy man, I am told. Ominous sounds told that the wreck was fast breaking up under the assaults of the sea.

"You go," said Hans, quietly.

"No," said the captain; "you first, I last."

"By —, no! You go; I stay here."

The skipper tried to go aloft up the rigging. But he could not do it. Then Hans tried from under to boost him up. But that could not be done.

"It's no use," said the skipper, after another futile struggle. "Save yourself; I can't get up there. You'd better be quick! The masts will be overboard in five minutes."

But Hans uttered not a word. He climbed up under the captain, clasped the skipper's hands about his neck, and thus shouldering him, carried him aloft. The crew said things about it. They mentioned words like "impossible" and "superhuman." But Hans did it, even with the wreck of his strength, while his hands were raw, his body bruised and bleeding, and when the gale tripped the little strength he had.

After he had secured his captain, the hero

"THE SECOND BOAT."

remained alone upon the wreck, which was now rapidly going, waiting for the buoy to return. He did not expect to save himself, for the mast swayed horribly. Indeed, he had hardly enough life left in him to secure himself. Just as his feet had touched the land, a sound of a mighty crack overrode the thunder of the water and the wind, and the masts crashed into the surf.

"If it had not been for Hans Slate," the captain declared, "not a man of the crew would have been saved. If there ever was a hero, Hans is he." And when a fisherman says a thing like that, you may know that there is no peradventure in his estimate; for he is a judge of valor, and knows what he is talking about.

On the night of December 31, 1896, the British steamer *Warwick*, from Glasgow to St. John, New Brunswick, drove at full speed against Yellow Muir Ledge, Grand Manan. After futile attempts to save themselves in the howling gale, the crew, numbering fifty-two souls, launched the two remaining boats the next morning at daylight, crowded into them, and left the wreck. Ever drenched, ever bailing for dear life, in momentary peril of capsizing, becoming more numbed and discouraged, drifting farther from land, falling off into deeper troughs of the heaving seas, the poor men finally gave up hope; for survival was only a question of minutes, or, at most, of hours. At that crisis, when the tempest was at its height, out of the scud, the seas, and the foam, out of the hurricane, there appeared a savior. The fifty-two frozen men thought the materialization a miracle.

A few days before, when the gale was rising, the *George S. Boutwell*, a fishing-schooner from the port of Gloucester, anchored in a little sheltered spot called Seal Cove. The *Boutwell* was launched in 1869, and had been racked and tossed since the day of her birth. She was old and feeble, and her skipper, Zacharie Surette, was easing her up the coast. She had been creeping from shelter to shelter, escaping the winter storms. When this flurry arose, Captain Surette congratulated himself on his own safety; for the vessel was light, and to risk her in such a storm was sheer suicide, and he knew it. During a lull in the blow, the keeper of the North Head Light noticed the steamer grinding on the rocks. The *Boutwell* was the only vessel within twenty miles or more. The keeper ran down to the cove, jumped into a frail dinghy, and rowed out, with great danger to himself, and told the captain

what he had seen. There was not an instant's hesitation among skipper and crew.

"Don't wait to haul her up, boys! Buoy that anchor! Sharp, now! Lash the jumbo down! Three reefs in her mainsail, and let her go!"

Not a man on deck but knew it might be his last voyage. It was bad enough loaded—but light! A single cross sea would open her ancient seams. An unpropitious comber might sweep her clean. A chance squall would heave the light thing down. But Captain Surette—the same man who played his grim joke on the life-boat crew—stood by his wheel, and, regardless of the old vessel's groans and protestations, whipped her on. He was as careless of the punishing elements as the soldier who furiously, amid shrapnel, spurs his jaded horse into the enemy's trenches.

Steadily blown to leeward, at sea the two boat-loads made preparation to perish. Suddenly the *Boutwell*, like a huge gull, bore down upon them. Fearing she would go by, not knowing that she came to save, the men in the boats stood up, extending their hands, and shouting madly. It took no little seamanship to shoot up near the first boat, which, but for its air-tanks, would have long since swamped. Ropes with slip-nooses were thrown, and the men, one after another, were drawn to the *Boutwell's* deck, and immediately stowed below. Then came another three miles' battle for the second boat, and another rescue, that is simple enough to mention, but hard to accomplish and describe. Now the *Boutwell*, never before so laden, with her fifty-two saved on board, made a desperate fight to get under the lee shore, and for safety, twelve miles away.

The British government, never niggardly in recognizing noble deeds, presented Captain Surette with a magnificent pair of marine glasses, in acknowledgment of his humanity. I am glad that his crew have recently been remembered. It takes followers to make a leader. In reading the records of the last twenty years, I have found but one instance where the crew of a Gloucester vessel did not either initiate or eagerly second and invite the hazard for mercy's sake, although generally there is one man who arises in an emergency, tosses off discouragement like a feather, forgets his empty stomach, his bruises, smiles at his freezing limbs, dares the elements to murder him if they can, and then becomes the commandant of his own fate and that of his mates.

Around Cape Ann
(1881)

AROUND CAPE ANN.

ANNISQUAM TO MARBLEHEAD.

FISH-HOUSES AT ROCKY NECK.

It would seem that Nature, when at work upon the Massachusetts coast, intended to make an island of the larger part of Cape Ann, but for some reason left it hanging to the continent by a narrow ribbon of sand. The colonial government discovered this in 1638, but put no hand to the finishing touch. Rev. Mr. Blynman, a person " of a sweet, humble, heavenly carriage," the first minister of the town, was authorized by it, " 26th, 5 mo., 1643, to cut the beach through, and to maintain it, and to have the benefit of it to himself and his forever, giving the inhabitants of the town free passage." Thus the waters of Massachusetts and Ipswich bays, after a courtship of perhaps thousands of years, were joined in the bonds of matrimony by the Rev. Richard Blynman. Since that date these bays have been married and divorced many times, according to the humor of the sea or the people controlling town-meeting.

If we start from this point by water, we follow the channel down Annisquam River by Trynall Cove, up and down Mill River, in and out of Goose and Lobster coves, by beacon and light-house, in and out of Hogskin, Plum, Lane's, Folly, and Loblolly coves, by Halibut and Andrew's points to Pigeon Cove, by the harbor of Rockport and Bearskin Neck, Long and Gap coves, Straitsmouth, Thatcher's, Milk and Salt islands, into Starknaught and

Little Good harbors, and along their beaches, by Bass Rocks, Brace's Cove, and Eastern Point; rounding this into Gloucester harbor, the water-line still keeping its eccentric windings, hugging Ten Pound Island here, and there (once) Peter Mud's (now) Rocky Neck; by the old fort point, along Pavilion Beach, coming again to where the waters of the two bays mingle.

Sea coves are ever delightful, and the Cape is full of them. It always seems as if the sea went peering up into them to spy out the land, to seek a fortune, or a quiet dreaming-place, more or less succeeding in the search. It must often lose a nap, though, at Folly Cove, for this lies open to the fiercest gales.

Long before, in 1602, Captain Gosnold, in his ship the *Concord*, sailed by the Cape, pressing his weak little bark with all the sail he dared, to Cape Cod. Next year Martin Pring went sailing by, landing perhaps. Three years later, De Monts and Champlain sailed into what is now Gloucester harbor, naming it Le Beau Port. Again, a few years, and the " admiral of New England," John Smith, flitted by. (If he landed there is no record. The hotel registers of 1614 are notably incomplete.) With a few men in a small boat he ranged the coast, sounded harbors, made maps, and named everything his eyes lit on. One fair headland became Tragabigzanda,

ANNISQUAM.

but a prince renamed it Cape Ann, thereby rescuing the writer and innumerable other babies from being born Tragabigzanda-ans!

Now came the attempt to plant a colony. "Compassion towards the fisherman and partly some expectation of gain," raised in England three thousand pounds for the purpose. Fish were to be caught; some were to go across the sea to sell them, while others remained the winter through. Fourteen men, names unknown, were thus left in 1623-4, to await the return of their ship in the spring. When the departing vessel rounded the harbor-point, did they fail to go to the high rocky hill yonder and yearn after her until hull and sail sank from sight? Was ever spring looked for with more longing than by those fourteen? Hark! is that the clangor of wild geese? See! is it a sail or a cloud? Ah, a sail!—the same ship and master returned. These were the first flitting occupants of our soil,—forerunners of that multitude of watchers which this coast hath borne from that day to this!

Any history is sad, but the history of a sea-coast is the saddest of all records. Not a mile of Cape Ann shore but has a tale of wreck or memorable disaster. How frequent, too, the record is "They sailed and were never heard from!" On a coast, the landmarks in men's memories are the dates of some loss. It is the storms and wrecks that are recorded; the safe returns, the dropping anchors, the furling sails, are a thousand to one, yet the sunny memories of them lengthen no human history.

The loss of no single sail from this port ever equaled that of the brig *Gloucester*, which more than a hundred years ago entered the silent fleet of the "never heard from," making sixty widows. To their ears was borne the dismal tale that, on the night when the ship was supposed to have been lost, a ball of light (a corposant) was seen to move about the town, and stay briefly over the roof of each of the missing crew! So, we are told, the silent fleet signals the shore from its invisible decks.

Our dwellers in early days had to arm themselves against native witches and foreign ghostly marauders. One story has it that at Louisburg, in 1745, a Cape Ann soldier shot a crow with his silver sleeve-buttons, which brought down Peg Wesson, a witch here, with a broken leg, the soldier's buttons being found in the wound. Other cunning spirits would allow themselves to fall beautifully, when shot at by good powder and shot, but when the marksman, proud of his aim and happy, went to pick them up, they would vanish.

Those were the days of pirates, too. In April, 1724, the new sloop *Squirrel*, captain Andrew Harraden, came sailing into Annisquam harbor, whence only a short time before she had departed on a fishing voyage. Why this unlooked-for arrival? What is that at the mast-head—a bucket? Young eyes, what is it? The spy-glass, daughter; let me lean it on your shoulder; be spry! My God, a man's head! Ay, work fit only for a man-of-war, the deck of that simple fishing-sloop had seen. At sea, April 14th, had come John Phillips, the pirate, and taken possession of her. The *Squirrel* had caught Phillips's eye—she was a new craft, and needed only a few finishing touches. So the next day he transferred his company to her, and set skipper Harraden to work about the unfinished sloop. Here was sharp need of wit, will, and weapons; but the captured crew had the first

A "BIT" NEAR BAY VIEW.

and the second, and the third soon came with the occasion. At noon on the fourth day, while the *Squirrel* was speeding merrily on her way, Edward Cheeseman, a captured man, suddenly tossed John Nott overboard,—the agreed-on signal. Down went Phillips by the hands of Harraden; Burrell, the boatswain, was quieted by a broad-ax, and overboard, to join John Nott, went Jimmy Sparks, the gunner, whereupon the others surrendered. This gang of Phillips's had, within nine months, taken thirty-four vessels, and if the head of the leader hung as a trophy mast-high on the *Squirrel*, the thirty-fifth—why, perhaps skipper Harraden had no ensign.

The General Court of Massachusetts granted Harraden, Cheeseman, and Philmore (who laid the plan) £42 each, and Giles, Ivernay, Butman, and Lassen £32 each, for their day's deed. There is a low, dark, woody isle in Annisquam River, named Hangman's Island, which seems to have got a dark name from its gloomy look alone, as the pirates were not hanged there, though tradition connects it in some way with this event.

Another story has for years been told by Cape Ann firesides, of another sloop, and another Andrew—this time Andrew Robinson, a Cape Ann man, whose equal it never had. Once, far from home in a harbor, he with his two men and sloop, was captured by Indians. His men were speedily dispatched, but Robinson was reserved for a death-feast. That night he was guarded by the only sober Indian. When the others were asleep, the captain killed him, and, miles away, boarded his sloop and set sail. At daylight the Indians discovered their loss and gave pursuit. A sailing craft, in a light wind, with a helmsman only,—how easy for canoes to capture! As they neared him, Robinson dropped his gun; the Indians bounded on deck one after another, only to fall and be thrown overboard, tomahawked by the captain—seeing which, the others wavered and withdrew, convinced that his life was charmed. His salvation was due to scupper nails which he had scattered over the deck where the enemy

named Le Beau Port, and sincerely. Harbors differ as men do. Harbors are human and something like women; they have their own times for dainty and delicate attire. To know them, you must study them, under daylight, under twilight; at sunrise and sunset; under the full harvest moon; at low tide and high tide; in a storm and after it is over; then

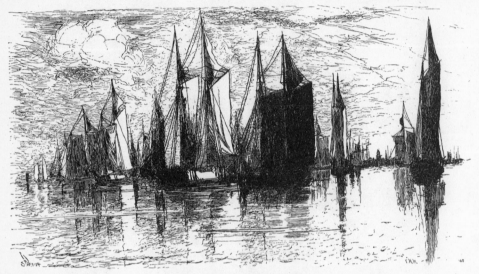

GLOUCESTER HARBOR—SUNSET.

would alight,—the short, sharp heads and points of which gave to naked feet no foothold, but only terror and pain.

Cape Ann seems to make good report of its ministers. One, dying at thirty-three, is pictured as "of a pleasant aspect and mien; of a sweet temper, inoffensive in his whole behavior; pious and peaceable in his conversation; his ministerial gifts superior, and his fidelity, diligence, and success answerable." His salary was sixty pounds per annum as long as he could live comfortably by it. Perhaps he lived as long as he could by it and then died, thus adding to the list of his virtues that of dying rather than ask for more salary. Of another minister it is stated that "on all proper occasions he always strove to excite childhood to laughter, youth to mirth, and mature age to cheerfulness." Another came to a divided parish, and for fifty years won the hearts of his hearers by "simplicity, sincerity, and meekness." Another, zealous, faithful, and excellent, died in the eighty-third year of his age and the fifty-eighth of his ministry. Still another, becoming aged and infirm, accepted a pension of *twenty shillings a month* from the parish, after a service of forty years.

In 1606, we have seen, our harbor was

will you find some mood to admire, new beauty come to sight. Our harbor, like every other, sulks sometimes, one must allow. A dog-day's fog has hung over it, or wrung itself dry into it, to-day. Open as the highway to all farers, many kinds of craft share its favor. The deeply laden collier with its sober mien; the lumber-coaster with her deck-load suggesting the heart of pine forests in Maine; the stranger ship with salt from Spain; the sloop or schooner yacht with every grace a marvel and every line a picture,—those lilies of the sea, which toil not, neither do they spin; the tug-boat eying every sail for a summons; the fisherman with her seine-boat ready for action, idle after toil; the ferry-boat going her way so often as to have it by heart; the light, clumsy wood-coaster from the provinces, sturdily maintaining her look of indifference to the finer company around her; a single skiff shooting among the dories and boats; all pointing different ways; some with sails partly set, expectant; some with minds made up, their anchors resolutely down, and all either grieving or sulking over the uncertain weather. One hint of farewell from the setting sun, and what a change! The somber collier and coaster look careless and happy, and the yachts share the gold that falls upon them with every

GLOUCESTER HARBOR—EARLY MORNING.

homely sister, till twilight creeps and creeps up every mast, like a miser, for every glint of it. The woods along the western shore grow like a deepening mystery. The tide is down, and the weed-hung rocks seem darkly to desire the night. One gleam is in the western sky, the light of which little pools of tide among the rocks sue for and obtain, by some bridge unseen.

Seldom seems a sky so bright
As the sunset sky to-night;
Yet it lieth far away,
While I walk in twilight gray!

Lo! but here a bit of tide,
Hemmed by rock on either side,
Gleams, and in itself content
With a gleam yon sky hath sent.

Bit of sky so far and bright,
Why doth thy forgetful light,

While the day is leaving me,
Think to bless that bit of sea?

Tide, thy wall of rock about
Cannot keep that gleam without!
Sky, couldst thou withhold thy mite
From that lonely pool to-night?

Golden sky, thou seem'st to be
Some illumined memory!
Bit of sea, thou seem'st some heart
From that memory apart!

By a bridge I cannot see
Comes that far-off memory;
Heart, that memory is thine!
Heart, thy memories are mine!

To see the summer day come into the harbor, one must rise early. The early evening most men know; but the early morning— what is it? How many of us know it? How

OLD FISH-HOUSE—GLOUCESTER.

many love it? One star is skipper and crew of the whole heavens, and, weary with its watch, "turns in," not curious to see what the day is like. The wind is sleeping. A boat here and there puts off to some vessel. "Schooner ahoy!" says a voice from the shore, and she *ahoys*. Sail and hull and rope and block are duplicated in the tide below. That was a yawn of the awaking wind. Notes of preparation deepen. Sail after sail is swayed up. Anchors break their hold; then comes the quickened clink, clink, of the windlass; the jib is hoisted, and the south-west wind, no longer napping, fills it and a hundred other sails that make their way out of the harbor in the morning sunlight, to and fro.

The first schooner-rigged craft that ever swam, it is claimed, was built by Andrew

posed the Cape Ann fleet in 1693; now it has nearly five hundred sail, of almost twenty-eight thousand tons, and Gloucester is the largest fishing port in the land. Its fleet is manned by men of every clime. A tide of young men, mainly from the Provinces, sets steadily toward this port. Many have the characteristic recklessness of the sailor, and earnings of weeks are spent between sunset and sunrise. There is among them no sailor cut of clothes, and ashore they follow the prevailing fashions, down to lager beer. All haunts are prepared for Jack, and he is prepared for all haunts. As in all other callings, thrift follows prudence and industry, though he seem to lie open to the changes and chances of luck. You will see his cottage commanding the finest sea view, for on the heights lie the

EAST GLOUCESTER.

Robinson at East Gloucester, in 1713, and named the *Schooner*. It was a handy craft for rig, but, even down to fifty years ago, a clumsy body. Cape Ann vessels are mostly built at Essex, a few miles from Gloucester; up a river or crooked creek, the builders construct and launch their faithful work for all sorts of seas to mock at and all sorts of weather to try. So they were building thirty years ago, when one, more venturesome, suddenly departed from the models of the day, sharpening the bow and hollowing the run. What talk among the fishermen! Who would go in her? What a —— of a rake! What a sheer! She was manned, though; became successful, and very soon others were on the stocks modeled after the *Romp*, the pet of the fleet.

Six sloops, one boat, and one shallop com-

cheapest lots. Alas! that the waiting wife can also look harborward on every coming sail, often to see the flag "half-mast"—for whom?

Here are no labor strikes. The sailor brings in a fare of fish, perhaps all he has caught, by themselves. They are weighed off, the vessel is put to rights, and he goes up to the counting-room for his check. The whole value of the fish is reckoned by the vessel-owner or his clerk; then is deducted cost of ice and bait bought; then, one-quarter of one per cent. for the Widows' and Orphans' Fund; one half the remainder belongs to the owner, the other to him. From his part is then deducted charges for wood-sawing and splitting, for water, medicine-chest, condensed milk, and any charge for labor on the vessel which belonged to him to do, but which has been hired done. His check is then handed him, and he presents it in person, or it finds its devious way to the bank by other—perhaps not cleaner—hands.

One of the most exciting scenes imaginable is that of a fleet of hundreds making the port in a storm. In a north-east gale they must beat in. All day long, by twos and threes, they come. It is luff, bear away, or tack ship to avoid a smash. Crack, snap, goes a jib-boom off. Crack, snap, there is one main-boom the less. Hoarse voices of the skippers howl in entreaty or command above the howling gale, and the shore is lined with listening lookers-on.

A visit to Cape Ann is hardly a visit unless one has driven around it. Almost every

named the "Poles." On an unguarded side it may be climbed. At the western base a rocky pasture rolls up hill and down, to the river.

Toward sunrise, across the creek, up beyond the green meadows, lies a bit of old brown road over a hill, leading only to the hearth-stones of a "vanished settlement," to what in old time was the town. If you sit down there, it will be to wonder what the dwellers fed on, and how babies ever grew to men on this uncertain soil. The multitude of stones seem like flocks and herds, held by some spell of enchantment, and one waits half expectant to see if haply they may not resume their wonted ways, and fall to grazing the little grass there is.

Now we descend from the "Poles" to the highway again, cross the bridge by the old mill,

MARBLEHEAD FROM THE HARBOR.

variety of scenery is met with and enjoyed during the fifteen miles' drive—miniature forests and mountains, and mimic seas. Out of the city we follow the highway northward. Many a by-way with its legend will entreat us to turn into it. The house on the left, with the upper story projecting over the lower, was in old times a tavern. Here the five select-men of 1740 met to be sworn in, on which occasion the bill against the town for their entertainment, including "licker," was £3 18s. 2d.

Now to the right lie orchard and meadow, with a salt-water creek winding between. On the left stands an old mansion, on whose walls hangs a portrait of a lady by Copley. Farther on, also to the left, a mass of gray rock lifts itself high above the way like a battlement,

by the church of Riverdale, rising as the road rises, until we catch again glimpses of river creeks and coves, making, as has been said, "the scenery bewildering in beauty." Now a quick turn of the road, and to the left, we look down a rocky vale to a river creek, and ahead into a vista of overarching willows; under them by an old mill and over Goose Cove bridge; then in a few minutes we are on the bridge that spans Lobster Cove. Our eyes rest on the rocky ridge where the first settlers of Cape Ann lived, and where they now lie with scarcely earth enough to cover them. One side of the cove is bordered by a hill-side of pine-woods. Along the other lies all the quaintness there is left in 'Squam. Olden buildings face divers ways, with their bits of land and ledge. One looking broadly to the southern sun,

THE TOWN OF MARBLEHEAD.

with a face partly dark and partly light, confesses to a divided ownership. Old wharves remain, which commerce has forsaken and forgotten, whereon the grass has only half a mind to grow, and the soil scarcely any mind to let it live. Only a decrepit boat or two abandoned to die, or dismantled just enough to show that the owner has in mind for them yet a voyage or two more—only these are left to tell of her sea-faring life. The days when the sloop *Squirrel*, to the old wives' wonder, sails in and drops anchor in Annisquam harbor, with a pirate's head for an ensign, are departed.

Farther on we hear the clink of the quarrymen's hammers: miles and miles of stone have been carried away from the heart of Cape Ann. Across the bay looms the eastern shore. Sea-coves invite the road down, or the road invites the sea alongside. One little nook—a cove of a cove—we look into from the road, or a bit of bridge that goes over it. From this nook, these two hundred years, the fisherman's encounter with the sea and fate has been hand to hand. His craft a dory, he wins his bread by hook and line, or sets his net and lobster-trap for luck. A mossy fish-house flanks one side; on the other, the home of the fisherfolk stands, almost within reach of the tide, with a tree or two to ward off the gaze of the curious passer-by.

On again, and we are at the end of the Cape, Pigeon Cove, where, it is said, in 1692, two young men built the first house as a refuge for their mother, who was denounced at Salem as a witch. Since that day, Pigeon Cove has had many a lover of its sea gleams and glooms, its crags, its forest-paths and pastures of fern and sweet-scented bayberry-bushes, its bird-songs, its tinkling tides, and the sea-flavored talk of its old fisher-folk. Dana, the poet, discovered its charms forty years ago. Then another poet, Bryant, gave to woods, and fields, and shores the added charms of his presence. Then came artists, authors, and divines, and after the few, the multitude. The old gambrel-roofed inn and cozy quietude was obliged to make way for the Mansard and the summer throng.

One thing the lounger and all his throng cannot take away—the old, old blue sea. Here it is, blue as far as the eye can go, and blue beyond. The many-handed sea! common carrier for all faring kind! Twice a day it fills, with the royal wine of its favor, the goblets it has hollowed out of the rock. Upon it east and west bound fleets come and go their silent way, all the more weird when they pass the silver wake of the moon. Happy vision if we chance to see a fleet of a hundred sail hover in the near offing!

Under the light of the full moon we ride on the remaining five or six miles to complete the tour, through the town of Rockport, and the farming suburbs of the city.

Vater and Gattin, whom these pages know, one summer day planned a row in their boat, the *Idler*, from Le Beau Port along the shore to Magnolia, a few miles. A fine thing to do at the best, but at the worst, not fine enough to tempt one twice. As they started, the wavelets, thinking it very jolly, no doubt, put little white feathers in their green caps and danced away to the shore. Vater rowed past Fishermen's Field, where Roger Conant and Miles Standish met, and the fourteen watchers waited; past Norman's Woe, where Longfellow wrecked the *Hesperus*—the wind rising, the little waves growing wilder with delight, or something which seems like it, and Gattin seated in the bottom of the boat. Higher the waves rise, higher the wind rises. "The rude and broken coast-line white with breakers" there to leeward gave no comfort to Vater at the oars, who headed the boat almost bayward, to keep out of the trough of the sea. Once or twice there came a little cry from Gattin, as a threatening wave higher than her head seemed about to break into the *Idler*. They took little thought of Whittier's lines:

"Of the marvellous valley hidden in the depths of
    Gloucester woods,
Full of plants that love the summer—blooms of
    warmer latitudes;
Where the Arctic birch is braided by the Tropic's
    flowery vines,
And the white magnolia-blossoms star the twilight
    of the pines."

However, they landed safely at Magnolia, and from the windows of the Hesperus house looked out upon the waves, which, now that the rowers were out of their reach, seemed to soften down.

There were boats and coast-scenery in Vater's dreams that night, and in them, after a perilous row in a dory, he found himself snug and safe climbing a stair-way in the harbor of Marblehead.

Marblehead!—it is no dream-land. Name it, and what stories of heroism, trial, and trouble throng to mind! Its old look is wearing away. Last summer a visitor found in the harbor but one old schooner; a coal-vessel was running in, and a few yachts were sunning themselves idly in its waters. The fish-houses and flakes are falling down; new houses look out from old places; but you look for the name of the street you are in, and it is that of a hero, or is historic in itself. Marblehead streets are crooked, but their names will wear.

The Deep Sea
Trawlers
(1912)

THE DEEP SEA TRAWLERS

By FREDERICK WILLIAM WALLACE

ILLUSTRATED WITH PHOTOGRAPHS

WINTER and summer alike thousands of hearty men from our down-east ports and from Nova Scotia are putting out to reap the harvest of the sea. They are the finest type of sailormen afloat and their vessels, though small and as fleet as a racing yacht, outlive the worst of North Atlantic winter weather. The author of this article tells from personal experience how their lives are lived and how their work is done.

"EVERYTHING stowed away?" queried the skipper of the oil-skinned gang loafing around the schooner's decks.

"Everything, Skipper," replied a man.

A FISHERMAN OF THE OLD SCHOOL

"Waal, I cal'late we'll swing off for home." The skipper sniffed at the fresh breeze blowing over the starboard quarter and gave a casual glance at the tumbling waste of foam-capped sea over which the big ninety-five-ton schooner was plunging hove-to under foresail and jumbo.

The glass was hovering down around the twenty-nine; the sky to windward was threatening, and there was an ill-concealed spite in the slap of the waves bursting in steam-like spray on the weather bow. The iron-jawed lineaments of the skipper showed no concern. "H'ist yer mains'l, fellers!" he said, and at the command twenty men tailed on to throat and peak halliards and up went the mighty sail with the great eighty-foot boom sweeping across the decks to all the play of the boarded main-sheet.

"Jig her up, boys!" is the next order, and with three husky men "fore-all" on the jig falls the wrinkles are smoothed out of the vast sheet of canvas and it sets as smooth as a board.

"Up on your jib now, boys!" And on the cry the jib halliards are manned and the triangular canvas climbs the stay with a rattle of hanks and thunderous flaps. "Jig up an' make fast!" And the jib is stretched until the luff bolt rope sets up as taut as wire rigging.

"Light sails, Skipper?" queries a man.

"Light sails next!" replies the skipper laconically. "Set your stays'l to

THE HELEN B. THOMAS—A FINE EXAMPLE OF THE MODERN TYPE OF
KNOCKABOUT-DESIGNED FISHING SCHOONER

loo'ard!" There is a scurry of the gang to the staysail box amidships and while three or four of the oilskinned crowd are overhauling the maintopmast staysail (to give it its full name) others are hustling a snake-like roll of canvas out over the bows to some of the crew on the bowsprit foot-ropes. With her canvas fluttering and shaking in the breeze, the schooner rears and courtesies to the big combers slipping under her copper-colored bilge and playfully fills the sea-boots of the men on the bowsprit engaged in bending the balloon jib.

With the aid of lurid anathemas the sail is quickly snapped to the foremost stay, and after shackling on the halliard and sheets and bending the downhaul, the crowd scramble in off the footropes as the big sail climbs the stay. "Sheet down!" bawls the skipper from aft, and as balloon and stays'l are swayed down and belayed to leeward pins, the skipper swings the wheel over. For a moment, as she swings off the wind, the schooner pauses as if in expectant hesitation, and then the canvas catches the pressure of the breeze and down she rolls until a cascade of green water

LOOKING AFT FROM THE
BOWSPRIT

they sense the fifteen knot clip the vessel is reeling off.

"Any sign of the *Uranus?*" queries the skipper, casting an eye around the horizon. A man clambers leisurely aloft, and he has scarce ascended above the shearpole before his hail has all hands on the alert. "Vessel jest off t' loo'ard," he cries. "Looks like th' *Uranus* . . . . Yes, it's her all right an' Jack Muise has all his kites hung out an' dustin' like th' mill tail of Tophet!"

No! Before I go any further I must explain that this is not a yacht race, but is merely the "swinging off" for home of an American fishing schooner. Just an ordinary, Banks fisherman, though to the uninitiated the foregoing description may have read like the start of a millionaire's schooner race off Marblehead or Cowes. The wealthy yachtsmen, however, cannot get any more pleasure out of their expensive racing machines than do the Bank fishermen in their able vessels when all the salt is wet, or the pens full below, and the schooner is dressed for the run for the home port. If there is another vessel also homeward bound and heading in the same direction, there commences a "hook" which would have a yachtsman enthusiastic one minute and scared stiff the next.

Reckless and jealous of their vessel's reputation as they undoubtedly are, yet the fishermen know exactly what their able craft will stand. In their design, the modern 90 to 120-ton Bank fishermen are a type evolved for the very worst of Atlantic weather, and deep draughted,

streams over the lee rail. The log trailing astern wakens from the apathy of a drift with a start and commences to spin out the watery knots. There is a sonorous booming of wind in the great white spaces aloft; an Aeolian minstrelsy in the tautened weather rigging mingles with the swish of spray and the tearing, roaring sound of seething foam. The lower dead-eyes of the lee rigging vanish from sight every now and again and the scuppers froth and spurt water inboard while drawbuckets and baskets and loose ends of gear dance in the boiling waterways.

The skipper, astride of the wheel box, glances over the bellying wind-filled canvas with an eye watchful and jealous as to set and trim, and the crew, lounging aft upon the house and kid, enjoy a feeling of elation as

DORIES TOWING ASTERN IN A FOG

well ballasted and strongly built, they are well fitted to combat the tremendous buffetings of a North Atlantic winter gale.

Though designed for commercial purposes, the Canadian and United States fishermen would have but little use for a vessel with only the ability to stand hard knocks; the general type of fishing vessel employed in off-shore service today is a craft of fine lines and easy, well-moulded hull. Owing to their depth and ballast they can carry an immense spread of sail, and it is blowing a "breeze of wind" before it is necessary to reduce any of it.

The men, too, are of a reckless, daring class and probably the finest seamen left in this latter day age of steam. No men can carry sail longer, or in the pursuit of their vocation endure more risks and hardships than these same fishermen of the American coasts. Canadians and Newfoundlanders the majority of them are—all from hardy British stock—Devon Englishmen, Highland Scotch and West Coast Irish who emigrated to Newfoundland, Nova Scotia and the New England States years ago and gave birth to a second generation of farmers and fishermen of a type hardier and more daring than their pioneer progenitors. There is also a sprinkling of Dutch, Scandinavian and Portuguese from the Azores to be found among them, and all, irrespective of their parent nationality, are distinctive as a class of seafarers who for hardiness, intelligence, resourcefulness and daring are unequalled.

"LOWER AWAY TOP DORY!"

And a singularly independent body of men are these harvesters of the shoal water banks of America's Atlantic coast. They own allegiance to nobody or to nothing but their skipper and their national flag, and in the former case it is a matter of respecting a chosen leader rather than a submission to the deep sea authority of the orthodox master mariner. These American and Canadian Bank fishing skippers have authority to command similar to their brethren of other craft, but it is enforced in such a way that the men do not feel it. If, by any chance, a skipper overstepped the unwritten limit and "hustled" his crowd too much he would be shortly minus a crew when he made port, and other fishermen would decline to ship with him.

It is the skippers who make up the crews for their vessels and the skipper with the good record and ability to

COMING ALONGSIDE WITH THE CATCH

BAITING UP THE TRAWLS

Some have been equipped with auxiliary gasolene engines but the majority of the vessels in the modern Banking fleets are of the 75 to 120-ton knockabout and semi-knockabout design. The actual work of the fishing is mostly carried on from small boats known as dories, which when not in use are carried nested upon the schooner's decks. A modern fishing vessel carries from six to twelve of these dories and each dory may be capable of carrying one or two men according to the method of fishing practised. In dory handlining, one man goes in a dory and fishes by means of the ordinary handline with

catch fish can always ship the best fishermen. Indeed, when fitting out for the season's fishing, he is generally overwhelmed with applications. Not so the fishing skipper blessed with only ordinary luck or on his first venture in command of a schooner. With him it is a case of appealing to personal friends; a cajoling of old shipmates; and in the latter circumstance, of being forced to take the gangs that the other skippers refuse. Once he makes good or brings home big fares, however, he will find good men waiting at the dockhead and eager to ship with him.

The steam trawler has not invaded the fishing grounds of the Western Atlantic banks to any great extent, and the craft who operate the fisheries upon them are all schooners.

HOVE-TO WITH MAINSAIL STOWED

two hooks in precisely the same manner as the seaside holiday maker does when he hires a boat for a day's sea fishing. There is this difference, however, that whereas the amateur is pursuing the piscatorial art within sight of the shore, the Bank fisherman is out on the open Atlantic some 50 to 150 miles from the nearest land and exposed to the ever present danger of getting astray in the steaming fogs of the Bank. Though the skippers have a wonderful faculty of remembering the locations of the little boats scattered over the miles of desolate sea, yet it often hap-

CLOSE-HAULED

pens that a sudden squall will separate the vessel from her smaller boats, and when that happens the dory men commence to examine the contents of the water jar with an anxious eye and nerve themselves for a pull to the nearest land.

Another (and the most common) method of fishing is by means of long trawl lines equipped with hundreds of hooks. These trawl lines are put up in tubs containing 2,100 feet of line with snoods or gangins spliced into it and containing some 600 hooks. Two men, dorymates, go in each dory, and between them they outfit themselves with

DORY ALONGSIDE VESSEL

A CREW OF TYPICAL FISHERMEN AT SEA

dorymates keep the deck on the watch-and-watch system. The watches are never of long duration, divided as they are among so many men taking turn in pairs, but whether it is from thirty to ninety minutes, each dorymate takes his half of the watch at wheel and lookout.

The surest way to gain an idea of the manner of life aboard an American or Canadian fishing schooner is to make a trip in one of them from any of the noted fishing ports — Gloucester, Boston, Portland, or Provincetown in the United States; or Lunenburg, Shelburne, Yarmouth or Digby in Nova Scotia.

If the trip is a salt fishing venture, the schooner will have filled her hold pens with a cargo of coarse salt to be used in salting down the fish caught; if

four to six tubs of trawl and when fishing take turn about at rowing, hauling the lines and coiling down in the tubs. This partnership is one feature peculiar to the Bank fishermen, and the men pay particular attention to the selection of a dorymate. In the majority of cases the two are close friends hailing from the same town, or relations, and between them they purchase and rig up the gear necessary for the fishing. Each man shares up in the work of baiting the trawl, hooking - up, overhauling gear; and in the work of handling the schooner two

DORY ON THE BANKS

WAITING FOR THE DORIES

cast over the buoy anchor. To this anchor the end line of the first tub of baited trawl is made fast, and after the anchor has dropped down the thirty to seventy fathoms of water, the tub of baited trawl is dexterously paid out by one of the fishermen while the other rows to windward or leeward, athwart or with the tide as occasion warrants. When the first tub has been cast over, the second, third and sometimes fourth tubs of trawl are bent on to the end lines and paid out and when the operation is completed another anchor is attached and by this means the mile long trawl is kept along the bottom, where the fish feed. For a space of twenty minutes to three-quarters of an hour the dorymates allow the trawl to "set," and making the dory fast to the last anchor, indulge in a smoke or forty winks.

After the fish have been given ample time to bite, the long, back-breaking haul on over a mile of line is commenced. Equipped with woolen circlets

for fresh fishing, the pens are filled with blocks of ice. On the run to the Bank— which is made as quickly as possible and under all sail the vessel will stand— the men overhaul their gear, stand their short watches and catch up on sleep. Arriving on the Bank—which may be Georges, Browns, Banquereau, Sable Island, La Have, St. Peters or Grand— the skipper finds his location by means of the sounding lead and determines upon what favorite spot he will make a set.

From then on, if the weather is favorable, the work is a hard grind. Roused out for breakfast at four in the morning, the dorymates bait up their lengthy trawls with herring, capelin, or squid, and at 5.30 a. m. the skipper passes the word for the dories to be launched and and in a few minutes all of them are astern and being towed over the grounds and dropped off one by one at sufficient distance from each other to avoid fouling the gear.

In the dory the first operation is to

SCHOONER ON THE FISHING BANKS

over the hands to protect them each man takes turns at hauling the heavy weight of line and captured fish over the hardwood roller placed in the bow of the dory. As the fish come wriggling up to the gunnel the trawl hauler by a dexterous turn of the wrist, slings the cod, haddock, hake, pollock, cusk or halibut into the pen placed amidships in the dory. Other useless or unmarketable fish are slatted off the hooks into the sea again.

How the Trawls are Hauled

While one man is hauling the trawl, the other is immediately aft of him coiling the line down in the tubs again, besides being ready to gaff any fish that should escape. In the meantime the schooner with only the skipper, cook and spare hand aboard is engaged in patrolling the string of dories, and when the tubs have all been set and hauled she commences picking the dories up.

As each swings alongside the schooner, the dory painter is caught by the cook or the spare hand; and held alongside, the dorymates commence to pitch out their fish into the pens on the schooner's decks. After the fish have been pitched out the men scramble aboard and hoist their dories in, clean them, and nest them, one within the other. Dinner is ready by that time, and the men, voraciously hungry, sail into the appetizing pots of grub with a rare zest. Huge pieces of boiled beef, baked halibut, potatoes, tapioca, doughnuts and ginger cake disappear with astonishing rapidity and after a short smoke, the men hasten on deck to prepare the gear for the afternoon set. At nightfall they come aboard again, and after supper start in dressing down the catch which litters the decks. Tables are rigged and with a steady monotonous series of operations on the part of the fishermen working in the glare of the flaring kerosene torches, the fish are gutted, cleaned and either salted or stacked away in ice down in the vessel's hold. In summertime a great batlike flock of Mother Carey's chickens hover around the vessel gorging on the offal, and these pretty little sea sparrows, blinded by the glare of the torches,

come flopping and fluttering against the huge mainsail flapping idly with a patter of reef points as we lie hove-to. In winter the petrels are not seen but their place is taken by the great Atlantic gulls which scream weirdly through the freezing night and daringly swoop down to the deck in the effort to purloin a fish.

When the catch has been dressed down and stowed away, the decks are cleared up and the watch set. Into foc'sle and cabin go the men with the exception of the two on watch, and after a yarn, a long smoke and maybe a card game the gang retire early in readiness for the work of the morrow.

Thus it goes on day after day until the bait or ice is exhausted or until the vessel has, in her skipper's opinion, "made her trip." The salt fishermen can take their time, but the shackers, fresh and market fishermen cannot afford to stay too long at sea. Ice melts fast and fish spoil rapidly, therefore when the skipper passes the word to "swing off for home" there commences an exhilarating drive for port not to be beaten for sail carrying or the thrill of an able vessel being driven by any of the best of the pleasure craft of the yachtsmen.

The monotony of aimless wandering over the various Banks in the quest for fish, the reeling, sickening lurches of the long days and nights hove-to on the swinging Atlantic seas have all been forgotten, as with her muslin on her and canvassed clear to her maintopmast truck, one hundred and twenty feet from the deck, she storms along with every timber in her fabric protesting at the tug-of-war between wind and sea.

In the foregoing, little has been said of the real hazards of the life of the Banks fishermen, but before illustrating what some of them are, the writer wishes to portray the peculiar individuality of the fishermen of America's Atlantic coasts. In the first place, it must not be imagined that these men are of the class of fishermen common to the European seas—heavily clad, clumsily booted, and carrying an odor of tar and stale fish, liquor and tobacco around with them. The writer's recollection of sundry specimens of the British smacksmen

serve to confirm him in the verdict that
the American fisherman is the gentleman
of his profession. He makes good
money—anywhere from $700 to $1,200
a year—and the skippers earn a great
deal more on an average than do the
masters of some of the liners in the
transatlantic trade to-day. They are all
able to read and write and discourse
intelligently upon subjects outside of
their vocations, and the majority of them
have enough principle to save their earnings.

As a rule, they are inclined to be total abstainers, and since they have a
great respect for themselves the fishing
ports are not thronged with nightly
crowds of carousing fishermen. They
are good customers to the various shop-
keepers in the fishing ports, buying the
best of everything in store clothes—
nothing less than twenty-five dollars for
a suit—and for use at sea they buy oilskins, mittens, sweaters and rubber
boots of the best quality. A representative crowd of Canadian or American
fishermen ashore on the conclusion of a
trip and dressed in their shore-going
clothes would be hard to recognize as
so-called "horny-handed toilers of the
deep."

In the fishing nearly all the men own
their own gear and ship aboard the
schooners on the share system—paying
for the hire of the vessel and dories and
engaging a cook, victualling and stock-
ing the schooner with ice, salt and bait.
When the fare has been realized, the
various bills for hire, ice, bait, stores
and cook's wages are paid and the balance left is divided among the crew.
The writer has been on trips where each
man realized considerably over $70 for
a two weeks' cruise, and when fish prices
are high they often earn over $100 apiece
inside of ten days.

Their remuneration is earned in every
sense of the word, especially in winter;
and winter on the western shores of the
North Atlantic is almost as bad as June
weather off Cape Horn. The schooners
are overhauled and prepared for the
buffetings of the heavy winter winds and
seas, the slender topmasts are discarded
and the light sails used in the summer
drives to and from the Banks are left in

port. Under four lowers, viz.: mainsail, foresail, forestaysail, or jumbo, and
jib she fares forth to open water, and
the men fish from the dories between
squalls.

It is man's work to stand for hours in
a rearing, reeling 18-foot dory hauling
on a heavy trawl line dripping icy cold
water. The oilskins become as stiff as
leather, the fingers become numb with
cold, and it requires incessant vigilance
on the part of the dorymates to avoid
being capsized or pitched out of the
boat by slipping on the ice-covered floor
of the dory. The schooner hovers jeal-
ously near her charges and the skipper
keeps a watchful eye upon the weather—
but sometimes it catches him. Sudden,
unheralded squalls come whirling down
and by the time the skipper and the two
men aboard have coaxed the schooner
through the howling snow-laden inferno
of wild wind and wilder sea the dories
have gone astray. Sometimes they are
all picked up again safely. Sometimes
men who have been astray for hours are
rescued by other craft, but very often in
winter fishing the men are lost forever.

The Toll of the Banks

Then the Bank fogs in summer are
a menace to be reckoned with, though
more from the steamers tearing through
them than from getting lost. Many a
vessel has been run down in the Bank
mists by liners running on schedule time,
and not slowing down for the fog, while
the number of dories run under will
never be known. Each year takes its
toll, and the Memorial Day at Gloucester, Mass., or the official returns of the
Canadian Government enumerate terse-
ly the number of men lost while prose-
cuting their vocations on the Banks.
"Lost in dory astray on Quero." "Capsized from dory on Western." "Washed
off main boom while reefing mainsail on
La Have." "Washed off bowsprit."
"Drowned in wreck of vessel." "Supposed lost in Gulf of St. Lawrence—
never heard of." Such are the records
which follow the toll of the drowned
in the Canadian and American Bank
fisheries. One hundred and sixty men,
Canadians and Americans, were lost in

a single gale upon Georges some years ago, and never a year passes but what has its tale of sacrifices to the spite of wind and sea.

The men themselves are the last to think about possible danger. It is a gamble with death—this dory work in open water—and a surprisingly small number of the Bank fishermen can swim, yet they think nothing of heavy seas in these frail craft. They realize the dangers of fog and getting astray in winter, but the wildest breeze that ever blew gives them absolutely no concern, and if making a passage they will hoist sail to it. The wind will be blowing a gale and the sea running in roaring, wind-whipped crests, but the fishing skipper will characterize it as "quite a breeze of wind" and be calmly "cal'latin' ef th' vessel kin stand th' whole mains'l!"

Brave seafarers and great shipmates all, they are men whom the highest in the land might be proud to know and name as friends!

Cruising
with the Yahgans
(1911)

THE OUTING MAGAZINE

FOUNDED 1882

EGBERT G JACOBSON

APRIL, 1911

CRUISING WITH THE YAHGANS

BY CHARLES WELLINGTON FURLONG

Illustrated with Photographs by the Author

SWIRLING around Cape Froward, the southernmost tip of the mainland of South America, now east, now west, through the Strait of Magellan, surge the mighty tides of the southern oceans, their huge combers ever battering against the mountain islands of the Fuégian Archipelago, and their icy currents swashing through them.

Never were men more isolated than Magellan and his crews when they passed through the Straits on what, to me, stands as the most remarkable voyage of exploration the world has known. Magellan undoubtedly took the archipelago south of the Straits to be a single land, perhaps the northernmost part of an Antarctic continent.

On either side of the Strait, he saw camp and signal fires. To starboard the smokes of the big Tehuelches' fires rose in great black volumes from the dry maté-negro bushes, breaking the long, level line of the Patagonian pampas.

To port, those of the wild Ona floated from the undulating northlands of their island. Then, further westward, among the steep, mountainous defiles of the Strait, on either side, the smokes of the treacherous canoe Indians, the Alaculoops and Yahgans, were stenciled blue against the dank, somber woods which clothe most of the mountains of these islands to the height of a thousand feet.

So Magellan called this land Tierra-del-Fuégo—Land of Fire. However, there is a tradition that he really called it Tierra-del-Huomo—Land of Smoke—but that, on the return of the expedition, the sovereign of Spain changed it to Tierra-del-Fuégo, saying, "Where there is smoke there must be fire." *

My purpose in these parts was exploration and the ethnic study of those little known Amerinds who have almost disappeared, and about whom the world

* Formerly the entire archipelago was called Tierra-del-Fuégo, now this name applies to its largest island. The other most important islands have their names, but the archipelago as a whole is known as Fuégia.

knows so little. One of my most important expeditions was among the Yahgan tribe, the southernmost inhabitants of the world.

The focal point of civilization in the Territory of the Magellanes and in all southern Patagonia is that interesting, little straits settlement of twelve thousand inhabitants—Punta Arenas (Pūntā'-rênas)—P. A., they call it there. As it is the Mecca of the Patagonian and Fuégian settlers, so it is the center of the most deserted territory of the disappearing tribes.

Passing of the Aborigines

The Patagonians (Tehuelches) have shrunk back to the high pampas, and no longer come to trade at Sandy Point (Punta Arenas); the Onas have retreated, fighting the ranchers, to the impenetrable mountain fastnesses of Tierra-del-Fuégo; the Alaculoops secrete themselves in the western archipelago, rarely coming east of Cape Tamar, while the Yahgans, farthest south of all, are found only in the region of Beagle Channel and those lonely, dangerous reaches in the vicinity of Cape Horn.

Hidden in a beautiful bay in Beagle Channel, far south of the Strait of Magellan, framed by an impassable barrier of jagged, glacial-capped mountains, Argentina maintains in this out-of-the-world spot a penal colony of murderers and felons, with its little mushroom settlement composed mainly of prisoners on parole and adventurers. This is the southernmost town in the world—Ushuwaia, they call it, retaining the old Yahgan name of the place.

Except for a couple of sheep ranches along the narrow camp at the base of the mountains on Beagle Channel, a logging camp or two, and a few adventurers, the storm-swept archipelago is inhabited only by the creatures of the deep, a limited variety of land animals, sea birds, and the roving Yahgans.

Few vessels penetrate these regions, and I was fortunate to have been brought south, through special favor of the Argentine navy, in their frigate-rigged warship, the *President Sarmiento,* on her annual cruise through those regions, and

was dropped ashore at that isolated convict settlement.

In Ushuwaia fortune still favored me, enabling me to charter the only boat at that time in the harbor, a heavily built, thirty-five-foot cutter, the *Garibaldi,* run by an Austrian named Beban.

In this cutter he transports sheep from the ranches to Ushuwaia, for the convicts, occasionally conveys miners and their supplies to the outlying islands eastward, or goes south Ponsonby Sound way, and trades rum for hard-earned otter and seal skins of the Yahgans. Sometimes he—well, though Ushuwaia is in Argentine territory, the *Garibaldi* is registered in Punta Arenas and flies the one-starred flag of Chile. The *Garibaldi* carried a cargo of sheep below decks, and the filth and stench of the craft would have made a pigsty blush for shame.

We started south in the gray, gloomy drizzle of low-hanging storm-clouds, as characteristic of Fuégia as its fierce winds and penetrating, humid cold, due to the snow- and ice-capped mountain ranges. Even in the middle of summer blinding snowstorms are often of hourly occurrence, the dangerous winds prevailing from the north and south of west.

Close-hauled, with dripping oilskins reflecting the dull light of the clouds, we shot through Murray Narrows with the current. The intricacy of these channel ways is hardly conceivable except through experience, and on the very latest admiralty charts most of the coast is not only imperfectly plotted, but there are still sections showing the undefined dotted line of unexplored coast. In these out-of-the-way channels and bays the nomadic Yahgan paddles his dugout canoe and pitches his wigwam on their shores. As he eats his staple meal of mussels, he chucks out the shells, covering his sites with their glistening heaps. These kitchen-middens represent the accumulation of untold generations of these canoe people, whom Charles Darwin first considered of such a low order of humanity.

Their rugged, desolate land, ever holding over them the possibility of starvation; their constant fighting against storm, cold, and disaster; their everlasting squatting, haunched in canoes, has

LAUNCHING DUGOUT CANOE FOR THE RIO DOUGLAS EXPEDITION. IN THE FOREGROUND IS A HEAP OF DISCARDED MUSSEL SHELLS—STAPLE FOOD SUPPLY OF THE YAHGANS.

THE BOAT IN WHICH MR. FURLONG CRUISED THROUGH BEAGLE CHANNEL.
ITS GREAT LENGTH AND NARROW BEAM UNFITTED IT FOR ROUGH SEA.

indeed made crude and distorted bodies which otherwise would be well-proportioned and comely. But these same elements have also quickened their powers of observation, made them cunning, cautiously fearless and treacherous.

It is often most difficult to locate these Fuégians. But there was none better able to do this than Beban, the lone trader of these parts. The chances were good for finding some of them on the shores of Rio Douglas, where a lone missionary was ensconced, and so, two days after leaving Ushuwaia, we dropped anchor in the mouth of Douglas Bay. Beban, after setting the whole camp in a turmoil with his "aqua diente," shook me with his horny hand and sailed away for Picton Island. The Yahgans here were, some forty all told, feeding literally, rather than figuratively, on the bread of life from the missionary's scant supply of stores.

My work consisted in studying the life of these people and exploring the neighboring islands and the Rio Douglas in canoes and a narrow boat which had seen its best days. Among these Yahgans there were many interesting individuals, but old Asagyinges and his wife,

shown in the accompanying illustration, serve as types.

With three Yahgans in a canoe I followed up this little river and plotted its course. Shortly after leaving the camp, we passed half a canoe, split lengthwise from stem to stern, cast up on the beach, a reminder of a double murder perpetrated in it the night before my arrival, and now, after their custom, it had been destroyed with the rest of the property of the deceased.

Here and there were other abandoned canoes lying bleaching on the shores. For miles the tide was perceptible, until we reached a point where the river narrowed and became a stream. The receding tide left the rocky bottom quite shallow, and this, with the swift current, forced us to abandon going further with the canoe. Up to this point the Rio Douglas could be considered almost as much one of those narrow arms of the sea as a river.

Leaving the Indians in charge, I pushed through the thick Antarctic beeches and underbrush, or waded in the river, some distance into the forest, far enough to feel sure that the river swings northerly, with its source perhaps in the

ASAGYINGES AND HIS WIFE, TYPICAL FUÉGIANS OF THE RIO DOUGLAS
COUNTRY.

region back of Woolya. There is also a possibility of some extensions or lakes along its course further up, but I found no indications of such.

Certain sections of the Fuégian Archipelago abound with ducks and geese, and in their best feeding grounds, the *lagunâs* (shallow lakes) of the northern half of Tierra-del-Fuégo, they are found in countless thousands; but along the coast they seem to be unusually wary of man, considering the few inhabitants and loneliness of these parts. Rio Douglas abounded with beautiful upland geese, and on the way back I shot, at about two hundred yards, a fine specimen with my rifle.

On our departure, near the camp old Asagyinges was peering at us from some long grass on the river bank. Later, up river, far behind us, another canoe stealthily followed under the shadow of the overhanging evergreen beeches and *linea dura*, then disappeared. On our way back, a bit of red complemented among the green foliage on the bank, and my field glasses revealed old Asagyinges and his wife watching us from where they were hidden in the bushes with their canoe, all of which maneuvering was undoubtedly prompted by simple curiosity.

The days spent in this camp, replete with hard work and daily incident, passed rapidly. The Yahgans, when not squatting in their smoke-filled wigwams with their numerous dogs or mourning over the recent dead, were occupied with the simple affairs of camp life—the women gathering firewood and edible fungus, cooking their scant meals of mussels, fish, birds, or eggs, weaving baskets, and looking after the children; the men occasionally assisted the women to gather wood, or hunted, made nets, spears, or canoes.

My time was occupied making notes, sketches, and photographs. I took numerous hand and foot prints, measurements, and phonographic records of their speech, but neither the efforts of the missionary or myself could persuade one of them to allow the taking of a plaster face mask.

Securing the phonograph records proved most interesting, but it was not easy to induce these aborigines to talk or sing into this uncanny thing. A thing which sang back to them their own voice, shouts, embarrassed laughter, and even the sound of their breathing, was to be approached with discretion. Some of the singers would break down in the middle with a hilarious fit of laughter or suddenly run away altogether from the machine.

The Yahgan responsible for the killing of the two men in the canoe was the most difficult of all. Perhaps he associated the returning voice with evil spirits, which to the Yahgan haunt forest, mountain, and sea, and undoubtedly prey upon the imagination of the evil savage no less than does an evil conscience on the mind of his white brother. With his father, this man had also taken part in the killing of two white men recently on a lonely island in the archipelago.

It was my desire to cross Navarin Island in a north-northeasterly direction from Rio Douglas, coming out north at a Yahgan camp at Mussels Bay on Beagle Channel, then to cross the channel in canoes to Remolino, the westernmost of the before-mentioned ranches, where I stayed between visits to Ushuwaia. But I could not persuade a single Yahgan to accompany me through the deep forests and over the snow-capped mountains. Perhaps, being canoe Indians, they were indisposed and even unfitted for hard land travel; perhaps their superstitions raised up greater barriers to penetrating this land than Nature herself.

The only other apparent way to return north was to wait here, for months, perhaps, for the *Garibaldi,* or venture alone with Yahgans by canoe in one of their clumsy dug-outs. These are frequently overtaken by disaster in a region of gales and fitful whirlwinds, known as williwaws, the terror of the small-boat adventurer.

But, for a third time, fortune came my way. The long boat which belonged to the missionary was placed at my disposal. This craft was obtained from a wreck; long, and of narrow beam, it was essentially a river boat, and quite unfitted for sea work. Old and half water-logged, it was in such a poor state of repair that its owner would not risk its further use to any extent, and understood that a new boat he had long since ordered was due to be left him at Ushuwaia. Arrange-

ments were finally made with four Yahgans to accompany me in this old boat to Remolino.

The introduction of many of the white man's customs and ideas upon aboriginal and Oriental races must ever offend the taste of those who have the least sense of the fitness of things and the picturesque. The clipped hair and dull, ill-shaped, homely garb of the white man, when forced upon the aborigine, I believe, not only take away to some extent his self-respect, but certainly, to no small extent, his health. Pictures exhibited by many well-meaning missionaries of their aboriginal protégés "before and after taking" clothes, as an evidence of improvement, are to me sad spectacles. Among the Yahgans, as among other tribes, clothes affect little the real character underneath. The wearers look less like what they are—Indians, and more like white men. Why should we wish to make Indians look like white men?

"Christian" Names for Natives

But here, too, at Rio Douglas, the Indians who ostensibly accepted Christianity were given an English name by the missionaries, in place of the euphonious picturesque ones bestowed upon them by their parents, usually signifying the place where they were born. They were influenced, too, to disuse and forget the old name, which it was feared recalled their former pagan condition and associations. Two of my four Yahgans I knew by the English appellations of James and Bert, another Yagaashagan, and the fourth I do not recall.

It was with much reluctance that James agreed to go, and then with the understanding that we should cross Beagle Channel well before we reached Mussels Bay, to which I agreed. On inquiring of the missionary the reason, he unwillingly told me that a few months before James was camping in an out-of-the-way inlet, just off Murray Narrows, on Hoste Island, with an Alaculoop and his wife. One day, without any apparent cause, James fired his shotgun point-blank at the Alaculoop, blowing his head off. The woman escaped in her canoe and, after James left, buried the body and

THE GREAT GLACIER IN NORTHWEST ARM, WHOSE FALLING BERGS SEND
GREAT WAVES ROCKING ACROSS TO THE OTHER SHORE,
A MILE AND A HALF AWAY.

paddled two days' journey to Mussels Bay, where she had friends.

Though the Yahgans are without chiefs and are scattered much of the time in the hunt for food, yet they have certain fundamentals of government. The coming of the woman and her charge were insufficient evidence, so, launching their canoes, they paddled way down to Hoste Island and verified her story.

Then, as it is the Fuégian custom for the friends and relatives to take blood revenge, James became a marked man, and he naturally had compunctions against passing along the coast occupied by the Mussels Bay tribe.

It was a beautiful morning when we pulled out of the Rio Douglas, and the sun gave a welcome warmth to the chilly air of regions which have recorded practically a whole year of unpleasant weather and storm. We rounded its northern entrance and passed through a narrow channel between a point of land and a little island. The waters rippled gently against the massive, lichen-covered rocks, out of whose crevices storm-bleached roots of Antarctic beeches, the *linea dura* and winter bark, occasionally poked and twined like great serpents; in dank rich top soil, crowning their tops and upper slopes, were the trees themselves—storm-beaten, twisted, and stunted, like the people trees of Doré's drawings. The weird and oblique shapes of those on the storm line, even in the peaceful quiet of this early morning, were full of potentiality of movement, and to obtain a sense of rest one had to look beyond into the thicker or more protected forest, festooned with light green moss, into which their gaunt arms reached. But, after all, in effect, we might as well have been running through some high-wooded islands off the coast of Maine.

In Open Water

We passed out into the broad reach of Ponsonby Sound. Far away astern, south, Packsaddle Island, Hardy Peninsula, and the Wollaston Islands, which terminate in Cape Horn, stood out in filmy rhythm of blue silhouettes between us and the Antarctic Ocean. Between the Horn and the Antarctic continent sweeps Drake Strait, through the only latitudes where open water encircles the earth's surface without intersecting land.

West, across Ponsonby Sound, Pacha Island humped up its dark, drenched shape like a mighty sea monster up to breathe, and stenciled in dark contrast against the distant, rugged slopes and snow-capped peaks of Hoste Island, the most irregular and indented island, I believe, in the world.

But sifting over its jagged tops were clouds, the forerunners of those terrific Fuégian storms, and that dread of mariners, the "white arch." Nothing but the steady swash-creak of the long oars broke the silence or stirred the placid waters of the sound.

There were two courses to Murray Narrows—to hug the shore of Navarin and follow around the lee of Button Island, or to hit straight across the open reach of the sound. It is rarely wise in these parts to go out on the broad reaches in canoes or open boats, unless the latter are of high free-board and of the stanchest kind. But such a direct course would enable us to go through Murray Narrows that night with the current, and thus save a day. The chances were good for reaching it ahead of the storm, so we took it.

Rarely is such a calm seen in those parts. The water lay still—a perfect mirror. Feathers from the down of kelp geese floated delicately on its surface, here and there strewn with whale spoor. Penguin, duck, geese, mollimauks, gulls, steamer ducks, and other sea birds, fed, swam, and dove in uncontrolled freedom. Beside me a monster sea lion thrust up his bristled snout, and, as he sported, shattered into atoms the mirrored reflection of that massive distant mountain, King Scott. Far away, a monster leviathan lifted from the briny depths to breathe, spurted his jet of water, which showed like a silver thread against the dark, mossy recesses of Button Island. Then, with a mighty dive, flung spray high in the air and sent great, ever-widening rings of disturbance softly spreading over the tranquil surface. He was well where he was, for it was not pleasant to contemplate what one lash of his powerful tail might do to our boat.

By late afternoon we had passed Button Island and were approaching the twist of the channel between Hoste and Navarin islands, known as Murray Narrows. One end of the storm had passed to south of us. We now had a fair breeze and set the small square sail.

The Yahgans contented themselves with mimicking and ridiculing the birds and mammals about us. Now it would be a pensive, indignant, big, black shag whose importunate, disturbed dignity and lugubrious attitude they would mock

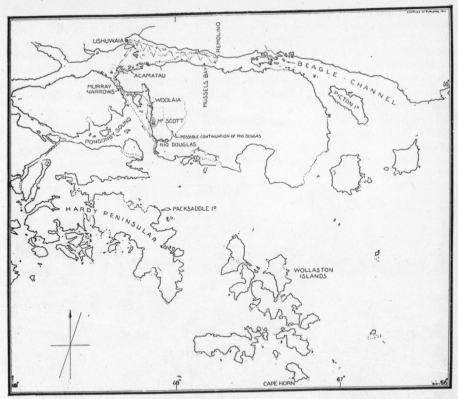

THE EASTERN HALF OF THE FUEGIAN ARCHIPELAGO, FROM BEAGLE CHANNEL
TO CAPE HORN.

Dot and dash lines show Mr. Furlong's course on the *Garibaldi*. Dotted lines show his course with
the Yahgans.

and comment upon; or, with loud shouts and waving of arms, they would scare on at an increased rate of speed an awkward-moving steamer duck, as, with its wings beating the water like paddles, it awkwardly propelled its scurrying flight into one of the many inlets.

My position was at the tiller, and always beside me on the stern sheets lay my rifle. With the wind, an hour more of current with us, and followed by slack water, we could get through the narrow turn in the channel, known as Murray Narrows, that night, and make camp somewhere on the north coast of Navarin, well west of Mussels Bay. The Yahgans were informed of this, after which they lapsed into a spell of moody silence, then gathered nearer together in low conversation.

From the stern thwart, the murderer, James, leaned toward me, and in the ex-

pression of those deep-set, wolfish eyes, could be seen things which caused me to grip my rifle stock as I inclined toward him. Yonder, he said, he had a camp where we *must* go for the night. I answered "no." By the fierce scowl which clouded the broad, flat face, it was well that my hand rested on my gun. Recognizing the place as being the site of the murder, I had no desire to spend a night in that obscure inlet, surrounded by dank, thick forests.

These people are very susceptible to their surroundings, and here there were too many recent associations to stir their imaginations in unpropitious channels for me to experiment too far with the psychology of this particular crew. The boat was swung in a bit to see closer into the place, and then, to James's particular annoyance, we sailed by, and I headed cross current to the Navarin side.

His apprehension was evidenced by his furtive glances ahead for strange canoes, and once, when a guanaco up on a hillside suddenly let loose his idiotic-sounding neigh, his keen eyes snapped quickly in that direction. Without that wonderful, stoical self-control of the Yahgan, he would have been visibly startled.

The clouds were now piling up fast toward our course. Luckily, we had a good breeze, for I doubt if the Yahgans would have rowed away from this point hand, cocked, and from my hip, pointing full at the breast of the third man, who sat amidships in the gap they had opened up, down which I looked at the barbed point of a heavy seal spear. His left hand lightly steadied the whalebone head, in their manner of throwing. But the man in front had moved a second too soon, for the weapon was poised in that preliminary position, but, thank Heaven, not drawn back. By way of subterfuge, he toyed with the loose end of a piece of

USHUWAIA, SOUTHERNMOST TOWN IN THE WORLD. IT IS A YAHGAN WORD MEANING "MOUTH OF THE BAY."

had it been necessary for them to use the oars.

When in the field, it is remarkable how keen and subconsciously sensitive the mind becomes to every sound and sight about one, doubly so to anything visual or otherwise not in attune with what seems to be the natural order of things. While my attention was fixed on the further opening of the narrows, I was not unmindful of every movement of the Fuégians on the four thwarts in front of me. The nearer ones blocked my view of those forward.

The first man scanned me closely, leaned carelessly to one side over the starboard gunwale, while the second lolled over to port. Before he had fully completed this action my rifle was in my sinew about the spear head and shaft, as though to fix it. Then, slightly disconcerted, he put down the spear. It was too accessible for my peace of mind, and he was ordered to stow it away under the thwarts.

We reached the turn, a scant quarter mile in width, and shot through the narrows, where for untold centuries has passed to and fro the canoe of the Yahgan. It has passed here more often and in greater numbers, probably, than through any other one place of the Fuégian Archipelago, for Murray Narrows is the only artery south of Tierra-del-Fuégo which permits direct access from Beagle Channel to those islands and sounds south, which offer the Yahgan not only more in the way of his scant food supply, but, what is more important, the furthest seclusion and protection from the white man.

Had Nature projected that little, rocky, tree-clad point which we had but just rounded, a scant four hundred yards further across the little valley we had sailed through, raising here a mountain instead of depressing a valley, it would have greatly affected existing conditions. In that case, to reach the center of the southern maze, the Yahgans would have,

from which this tribe has derived its name.

But for these narrows, I do not doubt that the decimation of these people by contact with white men through this most accessible thoroughfare of Beagle Channel would have been greatly reduced, and that to-day, instead of the small remnant of about a hundred and seventy-five, they would number several hundreds.

But the narrows existed, to which fact

MR. FURLONG'S YAHGAN CREW. THE MAN IN THE FOREGROUND IS JAMES WHO KILLED THE ALACULOOP.

perforce, to paddle their canoes a full hundred miles eastward, circling the rounded end of what is now Navarin Island, or double the distance about the jagged, stormy coast of what is now Hoste Island to the westward. In each case it would necessitate exposing their tiny dug-outs (averaging about sixteen feet in length, three and a half feet beam, and two feet free-board) either to the open reaches of the South Atlantic or Southern Pacific Ocean, which pound in upon the shores some of the most terrific seas of the world.

The importance of these narrows as a Fuégian thoroughfare is also evidenced by the fact that in the channel on the Navarin side was Yahga, the most important settlement in these parts, and

I awoke very suddenly when a squall, without warning, dropped upon us from the highlands. Then the wind veered so as to force us to beat our way to the northern point of the narrows, Cape Mitchell. Here we encountered a strong head sea beating down Beagle Channel from the east.

Few boats could head up Beagle Channel in that sea; certainly not our craft, with its narrow beam, broken rudder-head, and poor condition, so the sail was lowered and the Yahgans, still sullen and moody, manned the oars, and we swung in a lee through a little archipelago. As we pulled through almost land-locked bays, only occasional wind gusts dropped over the hilly islands, giving little idea of the weather without.

At the head of the first bay I found the abandoned Yahgan camp site of Aca-matau, where was also a log hut and some fencing long since deserted by an adventurer. Landing here, we had an *asado* of mutton and some fresh spring water. Some seven or eight miles further

Copyright, 1911, by C. W. Furlong.

TYPE OF YAHGAN AT ASSASAWYIA.

westward, at another abandoned Yahgan camp site, called Assasawyia, I had heard there was a white man, the mate of a wrecked vessel, living with a Yahgan wife. Though with difficulty I got the men to continue further westward, Assasawyia was preferable to spending the night alone with my four men under the existing conditions.

Thanks to the long Antarctic twilight, there were still a few hours before darkness. Suddenly one of the Yahgans leaned over the gunwale and pounced upon one of those beautiful dark vermilion crustacea, a lobsterlike crab, indigenous to the Magellanes and known to the Spaniards of Punta Arenas as *centolla*. They are delicious eating, tasting like lobster, though more delicate. These crabs measure as long as two and a half feet between outstretched claws, and often are found, like a myriad of other

sea life, in that remarkable Fuégian sea-weed, kelp (*fucus giganticus Antarcticus*).

This kelp has been known to reach its long, snaky tentacles over a hundred and twenty feet from sea bottom to the surface, where it spreads out its broad leaves and pods. The avoiding of this kelp claimed our attention, for it grows in patches so thick as to sometimes check the passing of a boat, and it is an ill fate that awaits the swimmer, though near shore, who may be capsized in its meshes. This dull, yellow-green seaweed takes root from rocks, so serving as a good warning to those who cruise in these parts. To its long, finger-thick stems Yahgan women often make fast their canoe lines while fishing. Flocks of birds often alight on kelp patches, which paint the blue water with spots of dull yellow, green and amber. In a gale of wind the long-pointed, lifting, lipping leaves greatly modify the action of the waves near shore, as we found when we rounded another point into the full force of the gale.

In a bitter wind, which cut through one like a knife, now occurred for some two miles the most strenuous pull of the day—two long, hard hours of it before we brought under the lee of an island, given on both British Admiralty and American charts as a peninsula. This puzzled me somewhat, but the Yahgans gave me to understand that in this inlet was Assasawyia, and we slowly felt our way in the thickening storm and premature darkness, until, passing a slope of beach, the keen-sighted Yahgans perceived the loom of a dusky figure. He was a member of two Yahgan families living here. The white man, who had gone to Ushuwaia, seven miles across channel, had been held up by the gale.

My outfit was carried up the slope to an end compartment of a three-roomed hut. As I entered, a squaw thrust her unkempt, black-haired head through a doorway leading to an adjoining room, then withdrew, and the door was closed. The Yahgan who met us on the beach had sighted us far up channel. Bringing me some water, this sinister-looking chap then joined the others in a near-by wigwam.

I piled a rough-hewn table and one of

A GROUP OF PONSONBY SOUND YAHGANS IN WIGWAM OF BEECH BOUGHS.
SECOND WOMAN FROM THE RIGHT WEARS A FACE MASK.

my heavy camp bags against the outer door, and deposited the other across the door leading to the next room, when I noticed that it opened outward. In its center was a small hole, and I well knew that, if but for curiosity alone, there would be a Yahgan eye on the other side of it. So, out of range of it, I withdrew the stout rawhide lacing from one of my camp boots, doubled the middle into two half hitches, slipped them over the improvised handle of the door, and made the ends fast to the handle of the bag below. Now only with difficulty, and not without awaking me, could either door be opened.

Spreading my guanaco skins and blankets in the middle of the room, I blew out the candle, then quietly shifted my bed to the farther corner. This put me farthest from the doors, and would have deceived anyone who had been watching me, as to where I slept. This was by way of precaution, for they have an unpleasant habit in these parts and Patagonia of shooting through the house when they know where a man bunks. The wind and rain shrieked, beat, and roared, but I was soon asleep.

The next day brought no cessation to the gale, which, during the night, shifted southwest and drove down from the Pacific all day, sending a mean, quick sea boiling through Beagle Channel. For a small boat these channel seas are perhaps the most dangerous known, particularly with wind against current.

This blow literally tore off the waves, and foam-strewed their tops like streaks from a mammoth spider's silver web. The geese hunted during the day were unusually wary and took on the wild character of the storm. It is occasionally impossible for weeks at a time to cross Beagle Channel in an open boat. Time was of the greatest value, and as, in the late afternoon, the gale moderated, I decided to take a chance.

In the Fuégian twilight the men carried the outfit to the boat and shoved off. Not, however, before I had reinforced the oar locks and, with a piece of beechwood, securely wedged the tiller on to the half-rotted rudder head. Rough though it was, the waves were regular and the southwest wind in our favor as we raced along free, diagonally across channel, directly abreast Mussel's Bay now, but well off shore. James's black eyes, furtively, constantly, scanned the coast of Navarin, where, less than three miles away, were men who some day would undoubtedly have his blood upon their hands.

High up over the glacial, rocky crags of the regular, Nature-chiseled peaks of the Martial Mountains, angry dark violet clouds bulged over them from the northwest. The low-hidden, setting sun shot cold, silver shafts of actinic light radiating through them, here gilding their fringes with green silver, there selvedging them with saffron gold, which showed their edges in a double brilliancy through the clear, cold atmosphere of the Antarctic, where they lined against the blue turquoise of a single gap of sky. The whole *cordillera* of southern Tierra-del-Fuégo, as it ranged westward, stood out in a great panorama of scintillating beauty. The white, snow-crowned, glacial-capped peaks caught the light on their western slopes and reflected it in a glistening sheen of pinks, their eastern shadow sides contrasted in dark blue green, merging lower down into deeper blues and the somber blue-violet shadows of rock and forest.

The glow also caught in high lights on the coppered faces of the Yahgans, and glittered from their keen, dark eyes, now gazing fixedly toward the wondrous spectacle. They were concerned with certain lowered, faster-moving clouds, knowing well that shortly they would bring with them a very hurricane of wind, and they also realized only too well the unfitness of our craft to stand it. Far away and above us swiftly rolled down the sea of clouds, under it bore down the white yeast of a foaming sea of waves.

The Place of the Williwaws

From the north another danger threatened. Sweeping here and there cross channel were fitful, dreaded williwaws, those swirling miniature whirlwinds which suddenly drop down over the mountains with cyclonic force and sweep terrifically over the water, picking it up in aërial whirlpools and spinning the revolving spray along in their courses. So tremendous is their force that they will cause an anchored steamer to surge at her chains or capsize an anchored sailboat under bare poles. I cruised later on a small vessel in Last Hope Inlet, whose pinnace was lifted bodily from the water by a williwaw, spun around a few seconds on its painter, like a top on a string, then shot below the water and sunk.

Often the only warning one has of the approach of these, when near shore, is by seeing whole areas of trees falling on the mountainside like ninepins, so fiercely does the williwaw strew its path. We dodged these williwaws, and just before the gale raced down on us, standing up and steadying the tiller between my knees, I obtained a photograph of that inimitable scene; not forgetting, however, when I turned my back on the Fuégians, to keep cognizant of their movements. A blow with a heavy oar or a shove of a powerful arm would send me forever into the icy waters.

Rush-h-h! and the gale struck us. I headed the boat before it, then brought her up a little, for to make Tierra-del-Fuégo it was necessary to quarter. Her sail, being stepped too far forward, coupled with her great length and narrow beam, made her fail to respond quickly to her tiller and caused her to head too much into the wicked, short sea. The sudden changing of the wind against a southwest sea and a strong opposing current, when it first struck, stirred things into a veritable maelstrom.

Never have I experienced a wilder sight; the four Yahgans facing me were the very epitome of stoicism and grim courage. They sat firmly holding their places, clinching thwart and gunwale, their black hair blown and whiffed by the wind. Their jetty, beady eyes, lit with the internal fire of self-control, watched the dangerous seas boiling down on our quarter from behind. Occasionally their eyes would shift to me; once Yahgaashagan's lips parted and a short-cut grunt issued through his glistening white teeth, warning me that an extra bad comber was bearing down upon us.

Twice they visibly clinched their holds more tightly to keep from being thrown out, and fixed their gaze more intently upon me. How could any white man qualm before such splendid nerve and fortitude? The vicious wave bore down, struck, turned, and twisted us, seemingly both ways at once, then, in a last spasm, threw the boat on her beam ends. Those were anxious moments when things hung in the balance; less than a minute determined whether the passing wall of water would leave us mere specks, struggling for a few minutes until numbed stiff in the bitter, icy sea. With the greatest difficulty I held my position and handled the tiller. How we ever righted is a marvel, and, had I failed to have wedged the tiller head before starting, this account would not have been written.

In the darkness of the storm we eventually made out the gloom of great mountains above us, and shot thankfully in under their lee. It was after midnight when we landed in the little bay at Remolino, the Lawrence's ranch, where I had previously made my home. The whole lot of shepherd dogs rushed like a wolf pack down upon us as we landed, growled, snarled, and yelped at the Fuégians, but leaped about me and licked my hands in friendly recognition. I saw the Yahgans comfortably housed in a log rancho, and in half an hour was sleeping soundly in one of the most hospitable homes in the world.

Some Old-Time Yacht Matches
(1901)

THE *CONSTITUTION*, BUILT TO DEFEND THE *AMERICA'S* CUP, 1901.

OUTING

SEPTEMBER, 1901

SOME OLD TIME YACHT MATCHES

By W. J. Henderson

THE history of yachting in the United States begins with the history of the New York Yacht Club. No record exists of a representative yacht or yachtsman before 1844, the year in which the club had its origin. And if one looks over the list of nine starters in the first regatta in 1845, he will discover only one name which can be set down as having had a direct influence in the development of yachting in America. This is the name of J. C. Stevens, who owned the smart little schooner *Gimcrack*. They had quaint schooners in those days. There were no foretopmasts, no jib topsails, no fore staysails, no club topsails, no balloon maintopmast staysails. Three or four sails seemed to be enough for a schooner. But the sailormen sailed their own yachts. The rules of the club specified that only members were allowed to sail or handle boats. Under such rules Mr. Stevens became the commodore of the club in 1846, and the owner of the celebrated sloop *Maria*. In that year *Maria* was the winner in the club regatta and sailed with the schooner *Coquette* in October the first race over an outside course. It was twenty-five miles to windward, from the Gedney channel buoy and back, in a dusty northeaster. The schooner won.

In 1847 James M. Waterbury came forward with his thirty-nine-ton sloop *Una*, one of the wonders of her day. It has been said that her model suggested that of the *Puritan*. *Maria*, which was rated at 160 tons, won in her class in the annual regatta, while *Una* was the victor in hers. *Maria*, like all subsequent big sloops, was finally altered to schooner rig. These two yachts, with their owners, were the chief factors in the advancement of yachting sport in America till the now historic days of 1851. In that year the schooner *America* was built and crossed the ocean. She was the work of George Steers, the builder of the victorious *Una*. Commodore Stevens was one of the most active of her owners, of whom there were several, and his name stands as her owner on the famous cup which she brought to this country, and which is still here. *America* went to Europe without any definite prospects of a race, and she entered the regatta of the Royal Yacht Squadron for a cup open to yachts of all nations simply because she could not get any other good races. She won the cup handsomely, and she is a pretty good boat yet, after fifty years of wear and tear.

In 1857 the owners of *America*, Messrs. J. C. Stevens, Edwin A. Stevens, Hamilton Wilkes, J. Beekman Finley and George L. Schuyler, gave the cup to the New York Yacht Club to hold as a perpetual international trophy. It was eleven years, however, before any one on the other side of the water thought it wise to come over after it. Meanwhile the racing of yachts and the development of the sport was going on. In 1854 the famous sloop *Julia*, afterwards turned into the schooner *Nirvana*, appeared, and proved to be one of the smartest yachts in the fleet. In 1855 W. E. Burton, the actor, who owned a place at Glen Cove, started racing there by giving cups for a regatta. This was the beginning of yacht racing on Long Island Sound. The New York Yacht Club had already visited Newport and subsequently went farther east, sailing races off New Bedford. This was the origin of the later custom of going to New Bedford on the annual cruise.

In 1858 came the first race around Long Island, and with it there comes into the history of yachting in America the name of James Gordon Bennett, Jr. He was the commodore of the New York Yacht Club and the owner of the sloop *Rebecca*. He made her famous in this race by cutting through

course, for any amount. In August, 1859, he raced *Rebecca* against the schooner *Restless* from Brenton's Reef Light to Throgg's Neck for $500 a side, and lost by twelve minutes. In 1860 he sailed *Rebecca* against *Julia* twenty miles to windward and return for $250 a side, and lost by thirteen minutes. On September 11, 1865, he raced his new schooner *Henrietta*, 230

MR. JAMES GORDON BENNETT.

Plum Gut, contrary to the conditions of the contest. *Una* started also in this race, her owner then being W. B. Duncan. Thus it may be seen that W. B. Duncan, Jr., comes naturally by his racing blood. Mr. Bennett did more than any other single man of his time to further the sport of yachting. He was always ready, like Caldwell Colt in later years, to race any one, over any

tons, against George A. Osgood's schooner *Fleetwing*, 206 tons, from Sandy Hook to Cape May, the first race over that course. Again Mr. Bennett lost, but on October 16, of the same year, he raced his schooner against *Palmer* and won. Later in the autumn *Henrietta* defeated *Restless* for $500 a side from Sand's Point to Bartlett's Reef Lightship.

The next year Mr. Bennett was at it again. In October he raced *Henrietta* against *Vesta* from Sandy Hook to Cape May and back in an easterly gale and was defeated by fifty-six minutes. These matches led to the great ocean race of 1866. The yachtsmen of those days would have despised our modern racers. What they regarded as the true sport was a test not only of speed, but of weatherly qualities and endurance. To smash around the outside of Long Island in a hard blow was the sort of thing they liked. They preferred reefs to balloon canvas, and nothing short of a twenty-knot breeze was fit for their sailing.

Henrietta won, sailing 3,106 miles in 13 days, 21 hours, and 55 minutes.

In all the history of yachting in this country there have been no brighter names than those of the men engaged in this race. They all had the finest sporting spirit. They were sailormen themselves, and they loved yachting for its own sake. A match race of any kind, certainly of enough importance to attract public interest, is a great rarity in these days, when everything is centered in the *America's* Cup, and racing shells with titanic sail spreads slip over summer seas within easy reach of the land and the ever

Photo by N. L. Stebbins, Boston.   THE *DAUNTLESS*.

And thus it came about that the owners of *Henrietta*, *Fleetwing* and *Vesta* came together in a transatlantic contest. The match was first made by George and Franklin Osgood, owners of *Fleetwing*, and Pierre Lorillard, owner of *Vesta*, for $30,000 a side, the course to be from Sandy Hook to the Needles in the English Channel. Mr. Bennett asked to be admitted to this race, and his request was granted. *Vesta* did the best sailing of the three, but lost through an error of her navigator and another by her channel pilot.

attendant tug. The days of the racing of the cruising yacht, in which a man spends his summer, are gone, and such skippers as ramping, roaring Sammy Samuels, cracking on sail in the teeth of a northeaster till all was blue, are visions of the past.

In 1867 appeared the famous schooner *Sappho*. She was built by the Poillons as a speculation. She was a keel schooner and her defeats by the *Palmer*, a centerboarder, deepened the erroneous impression, so prevalent in early days, that the centerboard was

THE *AMERICA* IN HER ORIGINAL RIG.

against *Mischief* for the honor of defending the *America's* Cup when the Canadian sloop *Atalanta* was the challenger. She was defeated, but her racing career did not end till about fifteen years ago. Many a splendid contest have I seen her in with the old skimming dish *Fannie* and the noble Harvey cutter *Bedouin*, the latter the property of Archibald Rogers, as fine an amateur sailor as ever trod a deck.

But this is anticipating. About the *Gracie's* time appears the name of John B. Herreshoff in the list of owners entering boats in a regatta. The mere mention of this is enough to recall to the mind of the reader the long series of developments with which the name of Herreshoff has been associated. I note also in the records of those days the name of Franklin Osgood as the owner of the schooner *Magic*. Mr. Osgood was still active in the sport and continued to be for some years. *Magic* was in the following year the first successful defender of the *America's* Cup, for in 1870 the first challenger, James Ashbury's *Cambria*, arrived to try to

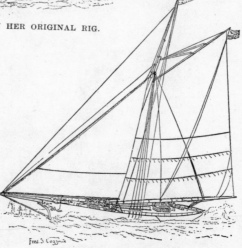

THE *MARIA*.

the secret of the excellence of the typical American yacht. *Sappho* was not a success at first, and the Poillons at length sent her to England in hope of finding a market for her. But again she was easily defeated, and came back to this country still on the hands of her builders. Finally, she was bought by William P. Douglas, vice commodore of the N. Y. Y. C., and altered by Robert Fish. From that time onward she proved a flyer, and she and Mr. Douglas must be set down in the list of yachts and owners who did their share toward developing the sport in this country.

In 1868 in the autumn regatta of the New York Yacht Club appeared the noted old sloop *Gracie*. She was a centerboarder in the seventy-foot class, and was first owned by William Voorhis. She passed from his hands into those of William Krebs, thence to those of John P. Waller, and then to those of Joseph P. Earle, under whom she did her most famous work. It would take a volume to recount the exploits of the *Gracie*. She was one of the competitors

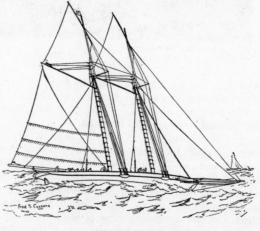

THE *CAMBRIA*.

take the cup back home. Her crossing of the sea brought the indefatigable ocean racer, Mr. Bennett, forward once more. He was now the owner of the new and subsequently famous schooner *Dauntless*, and he matched her against *Cambria* for a race from England to New York. Sam Samuels commanded *Dauntless* and Mr. Bennett crossed on her. She was beaten by 1 hour 17 minutes.

Mr. Ashbury, an Englishman, did his share toward developing yachting, or at least, preserving the splendid spirit of the times, in this country. He kept a standing challenge

self with glory in that first race, but afterward, under the sail-carrying policy of Samuels, she proved to be one of the terrors of deep water. Her owner during her days of greatest glory was C. J. Osborn, one of the old breed of sporting yachtsmen, ready to race anyone anywhere for any amount. In 1872 Mr. Bennett established the Brenton's Reef Cup as a perpetual challenge trophy, open to yachts of all nations. It was last raced for in this country in 1885, when Sir Richard Sutton's cutter *Genesta*, the Cup challenger of that year, defeated *Dauntless*, then owned by Caldwell Colt, in a nasty gale

From a painting by W. Marsh. By the courtesy of the New York Yacht Club.

THE *JULIA*.
Modelled and built by George Steers.

out while he was here to sail any schooner afloat for fifty guineas a side. He found many takers and the days of his stay were full of yachting sport. He went home without the cup, but he came back for another try at it the following year. The season wound up with a series of matches off the Hook, in which *Sappho* and *Dauntless* each beat *Cambria*. Then the two American schooners had it out together. *Sappho* won and was christened "Queen of the Seas."

In the season of 1871 in a race to Cape May appeared the historic schooner *Dreadnaught*, owned by A. P. Stockwell and sailed by Captain Samuels. She did not cover her-

of wind over the long course from Sandy Hook to and around Brenton's Reef Lightship and return. In October, 1874, I note the great match between William H. Langley's *Comet* and W. T. Garner's *Magic*. It was the same old *Magic*, but with the advent of Mr. Langley came the new spirit of the Atlantic Yacht Club. For years Mr. Langley was one of the most ardent yacht racers in this country, and to his energy not a little in the development of the sport is due. He still owns *Comet*, and she is still a tidy little schooner, though no longer in the racing class. In 1875 there was a race for steam yachts around Long Island, and one of the

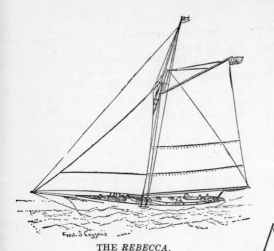

THE *REBECCA.*

THE *GRACIE.*

D. Smith. But she had been outclassed, and soon disappeared from yachting chronicles. Archibald Rogers, too, owner of the *Bedouin*, must be named again; James D. Smith and the *Estelle*; Rufus Hatch and the *Resolute*; J. R. Busk and the *Mischief*; *Schemer* and *Oriva*, and C. Smith Lee—afterwards lost in the ill-fated yawl *Cythera*—Lester Wallack and the *Columbia*; James Stillman and the noble old schooner *Wanderer*; Roosevelt Schuyler, the most ardent and persistent advocate of the cutter model, and his smart cutters *Yolande* and *Devlin*; Robert Center, who, with his iron keel sloop *Vindex*, kept the seas in wintry weather and was always a true sailorman, and who ably seconded Mr. Schuyler in pushing the merits of cutters; Henry S. Hovey and his fine schooner *Fortuna*; Latham A. Fish and the famous *Grayling*; the rattling matches of *Gracie*, *Fanny*, *Bedouin* and *Oriva*, off the Hook in 1883, the dawn of the new era in yacht designing in 1885, when *Puritan* was built to race with *Genesta*; the splendid contests

competitors was, of course, Jacob Lorillard. This gentleman owned and built more steam yachts in his time than any other one man, and he was really the father of steam yachting in America.

Names of men and yachts crowd upon me from this year forward, for it was in 1876 that I first began to be personally acquainted with yachts and yachting in this port of New York. It would not be possible for me to recount the exploits of all the representative men since that time, but a few may be mentioned.

Among them must not be forgotten E. M. Brown, who owned the smart sloop *Julia*. He was afterwards (in 1896) commodore of the New York Yacht Club. *Julia* was so good in her day that in later years she was schooner rigged and brought out by James

THE *SAPPHO.*

THE *MAGIC*.

building defenders of the trophy of yachting supremacy, the old *America's* Cup.

The outward aspects of yachting have indeed changed, but we must not fancy that there is no longer any sporting blood. Like many another old-timer, I myself would jump with joy at the announcement of a challenge to race two or three big schooners from Sandy Hook to Cape May or Brenton's Reef Lightship and back; but after all is said and done, such races are not satisfactory as tests of yachts. They are rather tests of men, and we are testing these just as severely in other ways in our days.

between C. Oliver Iselin's seventy-footer *Titania* and J. Rogers Maxwell's *Shamrock* — all these names and events played their part in bringing American yachting to the place where it now stands, at the head of all the yachting of the world.

But there is no room for full accounts of all these persons and yachts now. Suffice it to say in closing that to-day the old match-racing spirit seems to have died out. Racing is now confined to racing machines, and these have become so expensive to build and maintain that only a few persons are able to indulge in the sport. Men of the type of Mr. Bennett, Mr. Colt, Mr. Douglas and Mr. Osgood, instead of racing with one another for $500 or $1,000 a side, now put their money together into one fund for

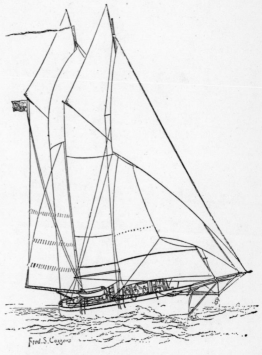

THE *HENRIETTA*.

The Trend of Steam Yacht Building (1901)

THE TREND OF STEAM YACHT BUILDING

By S. W. Barnaby

(Of the Messrs. Thornycrofts)

THE line of progress in the construction of steam yachts, both large and small, has been, generally speaking, in the direction of increase of speed. Thirty years ago with the exception of one or two very large yachts like the *Mahroussa*, designed by O. W. Lang for the late Khedive of Egypt, which attained the high rate of speed of 18.5 knots, the large majority of seagoing yachts had a speed of about 10 knots. The *Mahroussa* was 400 feet in length over all, 42 feet in beam, and 29 feet in depth. She drew fifteen feet of water, and had the oscillating paddle engines introduced by Messrs. John Penn & Sons, surely the most interesting type

of engine to watch in motion ever constructed. They developed 6,400 horsepower with a steam pressure of thirty pounds and ran at twenty-six and a half revolutions per minute. The boilers were of course of the old tank type. Nine hundred and fifty tons of coal were carried. She was considered a marvelous success in her time, but her load displacement was over 4,000 tons, and the price of such a vessel put her beyond the reach of all but very wealthy people.

It was thought to be impossible at that date to drive small launches at a very high speed. With the proportion of length to beam, which was then in fashion, common observation had shown that the power re-

MR. J. PIERPONT MORGAN'S *CORSAIR III.*

Copyright photo by James Burton, N. Y.

MR. HOWARD GOULD'S *NIAGARA*.

quired to force them to a high speed grew at an alarmingly rapid rate. After a certain speed was reached, which was roughly equal to the square root of the length, that is, say seven knots in a fifty-foot boat, or ten knots in a 100-foot boat, increase of engine power seemed to have but little effect on the speed.

It caused the boat's bow to stand up on end, and produced large waves, in the creation of which the engine power was uselessly expended.

In 1872, Mr. John I. Thornycroft surprised everyone by the results he obtained with the *Miranda*, a steel steam launch built

Photo by McClure and McDonald

MR. A. J. DREXEL'S *MARGARITA*.

MRS. GOELET'S *NAHMA*.

for Lord Clarence Paget. These were first authoritatively announced to the world by Sir Frederick Bramwell, who had made experiments with the launch which he described in a paper read before the British Institution of Naval Architects. Although only fifty feet long the *Miranda* attained a speed of nearly nineteen miles an hour, which said Sir Frederick Bramwell, "even in these days would be considered very good for the finest seagoing steamers, and has hitherto been regarded as impossible unless the vessels were at least two hundred feet in length." The speed was achieved by adopting a suitable proportion of length to beam, by building the hull of very light steel plates and angles, the latter being specially rolled in sections not hitherto in the market, by using very fast running engines, five hundred and fifty revolutions per minute, of very light construction with wrought steel columns, quite novel at the time, high steam pressure, and, perhaps most important of all, by introducing a type of boiler which had up to then only been used on railways, and known as the "Locomotive." All these devices, however, although they were an enormous advance on what had been done before, would not have sufficed to enable a small boat of the size of the *Miranda* to attain such a high

MR. JAMES GORDON BENNETT'S *LYSISTRATA*.

BARONESS ROTHSCHILD'S *GITANA*.

speed if it were not that a change takes place in the behavior of the vessel when forced very hard, which at that time was not suspected.

It was known that a curious phenomenon occurred in connection with towing light barges in a canal. If the horses were whipped up to a canter, the barge was caused to ride upon the top of a wave which traveled along with it, and the resistance was then much less than at a considerably lower speed. But this "canal" wave, or "wave of translation," as it is called, can only be formed in a confined channel or in shallow water. Under special circumstances, when the depth of water under the keel of a boat bears a certain relation to the speed, the boat will travel more freely as it runs on the crest of a wave of translation something like the canal barge does, although the usual effect of shoal water is to increase the resistance and cause the boat to drag more heavily.

The improvement which takes place in the behavior of small vessels, forced at a high speed in deep water, is due to a different cause. The rate at which the resistance of the vessel increases with the speed undergoes a change after a certain stage has been reached. Every additional half-knot after that point has been passed becomes easier to get, instead of more difficult. The *Miranda* was the first boat to get over the hill, which it was supposed would continue to get steeper and steeper! Many people think that the improvement is due to the boat lifting herself partly out of the water. There is no doubt that boats built of a suitable form could be made to rise in the water and skim upon the surface, as an oyster shell will do, if sufficiently powerful engines could be put into them to give them a speed high enough in proportion to their length. The punt-shaped boats, with flat bottoms, used on Canadian water shutes are a familiar example. The velocity given to them during their descent of the incline is sufficiently

THIRTY-FOOT LAUNCH BUILT FOR THE GRAND DUKE ALEXANDER OF RUSSIA.

great to make them skim the surface and buck along the water for many yards, and small boats can be towed at a speed which will make them do the same thing, the displacement being very much reduced, and the pull on the tow line being actually less than at lower speeds before lifting takes place. Model boats have been driven in this way on the surface by a rocket tube discharging over the stern. A cannon ball which ricochets along the surface may be likened to a vessel having an enormous speed in proportion to its length. It has indeed been well said by Lord Kelvin that "If a horse could gallop fast enough it could gallop over the surface of the sea without sinking in." We may yet see steam launches approaching this condition when engineers have succeeded in getting much more power out of a ton of machinery than is got at present.

M. Raoul Pictet, the French chemist, built a vessel intended to skim upon the surface, but he failed because the power he could obtain from a given weight of machinery was altogether inadequate. The bottom of his boat was formed of three wedges, the idea being that the inclined surfaces would cause the boat to rise. If this is ever achieved it will only be in smooth water, and there will always be some danger of capsizing as the stability when skimming is not very great, as can be seen in the before-mentioned water-shute punts.

Although it is possible that a lifting occurs in some degree at the speeds now attained, there seems to be little direct evidence of it. No doubt there is a rising of the boat above the undisturbed water-level, due to her being lifted on the back of a wave which the bow sometimes overhangs, in such a way as to be clear of the water altogether, as shown in the photographs of yacht pinnaces at full speed, but it does not follow that the displacement of the boat is actually less. It seems more probable that the improved performance at high speed is due to there being less wave making after a certain critical speed has been passed. What the criti-

cal speed is depends upon the length and form of the ship. Sir Nathaniel Barnaby has thus described what takes place: "The propelling power in the ship is largely expended in making trains of waves. The surface water put in motion by the passage of the ship reaches the position of rest in that way, and the ship has to pay for the re-arrangement. The wave-making expenditure increases within certain limits at a very rapid rate, as the speed of the ship increases. When the limit is reached there is an apparent change in the behavior of the fluid through which the vessel is forced. In a vessel 185 feet long this change for the better begins when the vessel reaches a speed of 24 knots. The longer and heavier the ship, the higher is the speed at which nature begins to favor the engineer in his attempts to fly. In what way she makes this apparent change in her methods is not easy to explain. Sir William White says 'the boat travels

MR. WM. WALDORF ASTOR'S *MIGNONETTE.*

upon the back slope of a wave having the same speed as herself.' She is seen to rise in the water, the bow is eventually lifted out of it, and the vessel settles down to speeds gained with comparative ease under the new conditions. Rails appear to be laid for the boat, length by length, before her forefoot, when the power in the control of the victorious engineer can no longer be denied."

The *Miranda* was the forerunner of a large number of river launches of similar type. The *Mignonette*, for instance, built for Mr. W. W. Astor, for use on the Thames, where high speed is now prohibited, has a speed of 18 miles per hour. Still more recently the *Bedouin* was built, very like the *Mignonette*, but having a draught of water of 11½ inches only. She is driven by a special

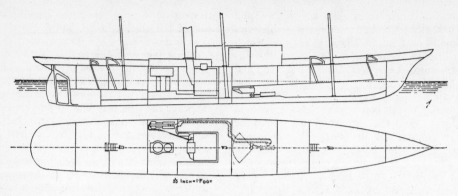

STEAM YACHT *CECILE* FITTED WITH STEADYING APPARATUS.

form of propeller known as the screw-tur-bine. It is placed in a tunnel under the boat's stern, the crown of which rises above the level of the water, so that the screw can be of larger diameter than would otherwise be possible. The screw blades are completely protected by a tube which surrounds them.

The *Gitana*, a steam launch, was built for the Baroness Rothschild, for use on Lake Geneva, and for very many years was the fastest vessel on the lake. She is 86 feet long, and 12 feet 9 inches beam, and has three cylinder compound condensing engines developing 460 horse-power. Her speed was 20½ knots. She was originally fitted with a locomotive boiler but that was afterwards changed for one of the water-tube type, which occupied less space. In 1897 the late Mr. Henri Say of Paris had built by the Messrs. Thornycroft a steam yacht much smaller than the *Gitana* which must nevertheless beat her in speed. Notwithstanding the time which had elapsed since the *Gitana* was built, this was by no means easy to do, but the *Sevillana* reached a speed of 21.44 knots. The Baroness Rothschild was not content to take second place, and she immediately ordered a much larger yacht even than the *Gitana*, practically a first class torpedo boat, and this vessel now holds the record on the lake.

The comparative smallness of British rivers and the amount of traffic upon them has checked the development of speed in river launches in that country. In America some very high speeds have been attained.

In seagoing yachts the tendency seems to be always towards higher speeds and greater capacity for making extended cruises. The large two-masted schooner *Nahma*, which was designed by G. L. Watson, and built at Clydebank for Mrs. Goelet is a case in point. Her dimensions are, length 289 feet, beam 36.7 feet, depth 17.7 feet, tonnage 970. This vessel has a speed of 16½ knots, and can carry 500 tons of coal. Her consumption is 24 tons per day at a speed of 12 knots, and 38 tons per day at a speed of 14 knots. With coal for 20 days steaming she could undertake any voyage required of her. The bridge deck extends for 184 feet amidships. The *Nahma* carries five boats and two steam pinnaces.

The *Margarita*, also designed by Mr. Watson, for Mr. A. J. Drexel, is 288 feet by 36.6 feet, and draws 16.6 feet of water. Her engines of 5,000 indicated horse-power drive her at 17 knots. This horse-power is equal to that of the White Star liner *Britannic*. She has a continuous double bottom and ten water-tight compartments. Sixty-eight men form her complement. The coal capacity is 550 tons. She carries eight boats, among which are a steam launch and a liquid fuel launch.

The *Lysistrata* by the same designer, and owned by Mr. J. Gordon Bennett, has a length of 286 feet, beam 39.9 feet, 2082 tons measurement. Her engines are of 7000 indicated horse-power, and she has attained the high speed of 19.5 knots. Her crew consists of 100 men.

These represent some of the best modern fast yachts. They are as a rule fitted with marine type boilers, but there is a tendency now to divide the power between marine boilers and water-tube boilers of the small tube express type, with a view of getting greater maximum power in a given weight of machinery, and also of getting up steam more quickly, and thus avoiding the necessity of banking fires when lying for a short time in harbor.

The boat shown on page 670, 30 feet long, and constructed of wood, was built for the Grand Duke Alexander of Russia. The engines are triple expansion working with 250 pounds of steam, and at 550 revolutions per minute. Her speed was $13\frac{3}{4}$ knots.

A few years ago an interesting experiment was made by Mr. Thornycroft by fitting moving ballast in the hold of a yacht for the purpose of reducing rolling in a seaway. The yacht upon which the apparatus was fitted, the *Cecile*, page 672, was not very suitable for the purpose, as she was a vessel of great stability, and her excessive stiffness not only caused her rolling motion to be very rapid, but made it necessary to employ a relatively large moving weight in order to keep her upright in the waves. The *Cecile* was 230 tons displacement, and the moving ballast, amounting to eight tons, represented about $3\frac{1}{2}$ per cent. of the displacement. Although this weight was only sufficient to incline the vessel two degrees when moved out as far as possible from the center-line, it had a very marked effect in reducing the rolling. The illustrations show how the ballast was fitted. The eight tons of lead, in the form of a quadrant, was pivoted on a vertical shaft, below the cabin floor, and was free to turn completely round. It was thus quite out of the way, and the installation of the whole apparatus was effected without any alteration in the accommodation of the yacht. The movement of the shaft was controlled by a hydraulic motor, fitted with a valve for distributing water under pressure. This valve was controlled by an automatic device in such a way that the weight was caused to move either to one side of the ship or the other, as was necessary to keep her upright among waves. The automatic device worked admirably, and although the weight was insufficient to completely counteract rolling, it very greatly reduced it.

The amount of weight required to obtain a perfect balance can easily be estimated for any vessel among waves of any given size. Suppose it is wished to balance a ship among average Atlantic waves, which may be taken as about 180 feet long. Such waves have a maximum slope of about seven degrees. If such a weight is provided that when out to the fullest extent of its travel on one side of the centerline of the ship it will incline her seven degrees in still water, this weight will suffice to keep the vessel quite steady among any waves having a slope not exceeding seven degrees. But the ameliorating effect of a very much smaller amount of weight than this is considerable. Suppose, for instance, the weight employed is only sufficient to incline the vessel $3\frac{1}{2}$ degrees in still water, the roll due to a wave slope of seven degrees would be reduced by one half. The heavy rolling occasionally met with in Atlantic steamers and in large yachts, which are made tender for the purpose of making the motion easy, is not caused by waves of a very steep slope, but by a succession of waves keeping time with her swing, and this can be stopped with a very much smaller weight than would be necessary to heel the ship over to the large angle sometimes attained; in fact a very moderate weight would suffice to prevent it.

More Power
for the Motor Boat
(1911)

MORE POWER FOR THE MOTOR BOAT

BY LAWRENCE LARUE

Illustrated with Photographs

LET the motor boatman not be deceived for a moment into thinking that we are about to divulge some secret formula whereby he may increase the power developed by his engine and thereby surprise his friends with two or three miles an hour added to the speed of his craft. Such formulas do not exist, and while some speed maniacs may recommend "dope" in the fuel tank, the addition of any stimulant is almost certain eventually to result in a weakened motor. The power developed by a motor that is in perfect condition cannot be increased, and it is wasted time to labor with an engine that is doing its best. The gasoline motor is not like the steam engine, the power of which can be increased by added steam pressure, and its limitations are sharply defined by its bore, stroke, compression and efficiency of its joints, packing, air passages and bearings.

This would seem to indicate that a new motor offers no opportunity for improvement except during the first few weeks of running required to "wear it in" and increase the efficiency of the moving parts and that no attention will be required by it until the time for the first spring overhauling. This should be true, and every man who has spent time, thought and money on the selection and purchase of a new motor has the right to expect that all adjustments have been made and all faults remedied at the factory and that his acquisition will develop its maximum power and run at its highest efficiency from the outset.

No factory is absolutely infallible, however, and even though the motor may have been in perfect condition when it was shipped, the knocks and jars of transportation, loading and unloading may loosen some of the parts or shake them out of adjustment. Added to this, the amateur may make some mistakes at the outset when trying to start his new motor, and even though the results of these mistakes may not be apparent for some time, they may contribute to a decided decrease in the power of the machine. Then, too, a poor quality of cylinder oil may have been used which has become gummed during the long interval between the final factory test of the motor and its trial by its new owner; and dozens of other troubles and accidents may contribute to the poor performance of a power plant from which great feats have been expected—and can be obtained when the seat of the disturbance is reached and matters remedied.

Secure in the belief that his motor is up to specifications because "it runs," many an owner may be perfectly satisfied with the performance of his new boat, when in reality he may not be getting two-thirds of the power and efficiency to which he is entitled. If his craft is guaranteed to maintain a certain speed and he finally discovers that she falls below this mark, the disgusted owner may be tempted to return the entire outfit to the factory—for the contrast with his feelings when he was under the impression that he was "getting his money's worth" will give him the 'sensation that he has been duped. But to ship a boat or a motor back to the factory entails correspondence, waiting and "red tape" galore and may result in

FIG. I. A MOTOR OF THE SOLID HEAD CYLINDER TYPE, WITH CYLINDER RE-
MOVED IN ORDER TO REACH THE RINGS

a boatless owner during the remainder of the season. The trouble may be due to his own carelessness as much as to any neglect on the part of the manufacturer, and it is to the owner's interest at least to determine if he cannot remedy matters for himself.

Assuming that the motor runs, let us suppose that it does not develop the power for which it was designed. With good gasoline and a "fat" spark, this loss of power nine times out of ten will be due to faulty compression. Power cannot be obtained without sufficient compression in the cylinder, for it is upon this that the force of the explosion depends and a leak allows this useful energy to escape and be wasted absolutely. The compression, of course, can be felt by the resistance offered to turning the flywheel when all valves and cocks in the cylinder are closed. If there is more than a single cylinder, the one offering the least resistance is certain to be that in which the trouble will be found, for under normal conditions the compression should be the same in all on the up-stroke of the piston.

If the motor has but one cylinder, its compression-retaining ability may be determined by turning the flywheel until the point of greatest resistance is reached and then holding it there until it can be moved past the "dead center" easily. If the motor possesses good compression an appreciable time will elapse before the resistance is reduced sufficiently to enable the flywheel to be turned over, but it must be remembered that even in the best of engines the compression will escape eventually. But if the flywheel may be turned over slowly without meeting any vigorous resistance, it may safely be assumed that good compression is a negligible quantity in this case.

The average compression in an ordinary gasoline engine is about sixty pounds per square inch, which would amount, in a four-inch cylinder, to a total resistance of about 750 pounds. But if the flywheel by which the piston is moved is two feet in diameter and if the crank is two inches long (assuming a four-inch stroke), the actual force necessary to be applied at the rim of the flywheel would be but 125 pounds; and if momentum has been attained by giving the flywheel a swing, this resistance can be overcome comparatively easily and the force of compression will not be found to be as formidable as the figures would have it appear. But by keeping the comparative values of these figures in mind and remembering that even the strongest compression will gradually escape past the piston rings if the piston is held near the top of its stroke, even the rankest amateur can learn to distinguish between good and poor compression.

It is to the piston rings that most of the loss of compression can be laid. These rings are supposed to form a tight joint between the cylinder walls and piston, for the latter, having to move freely and being subject to variable expansion due to the heat, cannot be machined to a perfect fit. The rings, on the other hand, being springy, can adapt themselves to any temperature that will be found within the cylinder walls—provided they receive sufficient lubrication.

The majority of motors are tested after manufacture and are shipped to the purchaser with the piston and rings thoroughly oiled and a certain amount of lubricant in the base. In the case of a new machine, however, the moving parts of which are liable to be "stiff" at first, it is better to be on the safe side and introduce plenty of fresh oil into the crank case and to the piston and rings before the motor is started.

But in spite of these precautions, one of the rings may have become "stuck" in its groove so that it no longer automatically fits the curvature of the cylinder walls and consequently the compression and the exhaust gases of the explosion are allowed to escape past it. There will probably be three or four rings on each piston and the motor may run with the remainder of these in working condition, but the best results cannot be obtained unless all are loose in their grooves. Consequently it is for a stuck ring that the owner is to search first when he finds that one cylinder fails to hold its compression as well as its companions.

The only certain way of locating and remedying the trouble is to "get at" the rings. In the case of a motor having a solid cylinder head, this may be done by removing the entire cylinder casting from the base of the machine, thus leaving the piston and rings exposed. If

the motor has a removable head the connecting rod may be loosened from the crankshaft by reaching through the hand-holes generally provided in the crank case and unscrewing the nuts that hold the two halves of the bearing in place. After this has been done the piston may be pulled out through the top of the cylinder and the rings will be ready for inspection.

A Place for Careful Work.

Each ring should be loose and should not bind in any portion of its groove, whether it be pushed in or out or be turned either way as far as the pin forming the stop at the notches in the end will allow. If it is found that a ring is stuck in its groove it is probably due to a deposit of carbon and gummed oil rather than to any mechanical defect. Great care should be taken in loosening the ring and the gummy substance should be dissolved by the application of kerosene or gasoline at every accessible portion.

Then a small screwdriver may be placed under one of the free portions between the ring and its groove and gradually worked around until the remainder is loosened (Fig 1); but the ring should never be bent out from its end, as this would be almost certain to snap it in two. A broken ring is not only useless, but will do actual harm if the motor is allowed to run under these conditions, and as it is not a particularly easy matter to fit a new one in place, rings should be removed only with the greatest care.

Even though the sticking is caused only by a small amount of gummed oil that can easily be dissolved, the ring should be removed in order that it and its groove may be scraped out and cleaned thoroughly. The ring should be thoroughly loosened before any attempt is made to remove it and then it should be worked out gradually in sections, wedging each part out with a stiff wire to prevent its return to the groove. When the ring gets entirely out of its groove it may be slid along the outside of the piston and off at the end, but if more than one ring is removed at a time care should be taken to distinguish them, as each should be returned to its own groove. If the motor is small and the ring is not too stiff, the latter may sometimes be removed by pulling a piece of stovepipe wire between the ring and piston and following this action with the fingers of one hand to push the ring up on the piston as it leaves its groove.

It may be that the ring has been hur-

need grinding may be determined. If it is found that the ring is a comparatively tight fit in its groove so that absolute freedom of motion cannot take place, it may easily be ground down with a piece of fine emery paper. This emery paper, or cloth, should be laid on a flat surface and the ring placed upon it (Fig. 3). Then, by pressing firmly upon the ring with the fingers and giving it a rotary

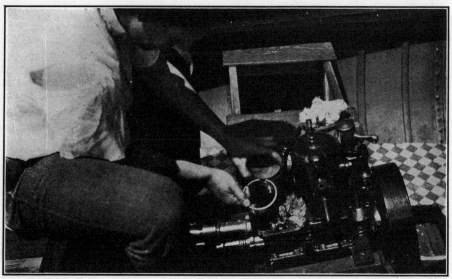

FIG. 2. TRYING THE RING IN ITS GROOVE TO INSURE A PERFECT FIT

riedly fitted at the factory and put in place without having been properly finished. This will cause it to stick in its groove, even though the oil has not gummed, and consequently it should be tested for a good fit before being returned to its place. After the carbon and gummed oil have been removed the ring may be tested for size without returning it to its groove by rolling it around in the groove so that each part will come in contact with the portion of the groove in which it ordinarily rests. In order to have these portions "register" the ring should be held upside down and started with one end placed against the pin forming the stop in the groove (Fig. 2).

Whenever there is the slightest binding between the sides of the ring and the groove such portions should be marked in order that the parts that

sweep with the hand over the rough surface of the emery cloth, the side that is lying down will be ground off slightly.

If the ring seems to be too thick throughout its entire length the pressure of all of the fingers should be evenly distributed, but otherwise only those portions at which the binding takes place should receive the greatest weight. By alternately testing the ring in the groove in the manner already mentioned and grinding the thick portions as described above, a perfect fitting ring and one that should do its share in holding compression for a long time to come may be obtained.

If the entire cylinder has been removed to reach the piston a little care will need to be exercised when assembling the parts. After the rings are in place the piston should be moved to the bottom of its stroke and held in a vertical position with the engine bed while the cylinder is slid over it. The lower edge of the cylinder walls will probably be beveled to allow it to slide easily over the rings as they project from their grooves, but the cylinder must be set on very slowly and not forced, for any undue pressure will mar the edges of the rings and result in scored walls and eventual leakage of compression from the cylinder.

Care should also be taken to keep the rings in their proper position with their notched ends, or joints, surrounding the small pin provided in each groove. If the ends of any ring move around beyond this pin forming a stop the joints of all rings may eventually fall in one straight line, in which case an easy escape for the compression would be furnished. The joints of adjoining rings should always be placed on opposite sides of the piston.

Getting the Piston Back in Place.

If the cylinder has a removable head and the piston has been withdrawn in order to repair the rings, its return to its place may be greatly facilitated by a device, the use of which is illustrated in Fig. 4. The piston will set easily into the cylinder until the first ring is reached, after which it will be evident that each ring must be compressed tightly in order to fit within the cylinder walls. The device in question consists merely of a piece of annealed stovepipe wire—which is flexible and yet strong— about a foot longer than the diameter of the piston. Each end of this should be twisted around the middle of a wooden handle, which may be cut from a broomstick.

By crossing the wire near the handles a loop will be formed which should be placed around the ring that it is desired to compress after the piston has been set in position. When this is done a steady pull on the handles will furnish a leverage that will easily serve to compress the ring so that the piston will drop into place until stopped by the next ring. By dealing with all rings in the same manner the piston of even a large motor may be set in place in its cylinder in

a surprisingly short time and with but very little trouble.

If all of the rings have been examined and it is found that the cause of the loss of compression does not lie with them, it is probable that some of the packing has been loosened or blown out, thus furnishing a vent for the escape of some of the gases. Of course, it is possible that the spark plug is not a good fit or that the relief or priming cock valve has loosened, but the escape of compression and exhaust gases from such an outlet would be so apparent when the motor is running that even the tyro would not look farther for the leak and would tighten these parts before examining the rings.

Escape of compression through the packing of the cylinder can only occur in those motors having detachable cylinder heads. But such trouble is easily remedied and should not be considered as an offset to the many advantages possessed by this type of motor. When it is found that there is a leak in the cylinder packing the head should be unbolted and both surfaces thoroughly cleaned. The old packing that cannot be picked or torn off should be first soaked with kerosene or gasoline and then scraped with a putty knife or other flat, broad-bladed instrument, until the top of the cylinder and the bottom of the cylinder head are perfectly smooth.

Although the packing of the cylinder head is not directly exposed to the heat of the exhaust gases, the walls and surfaces between which it rests will become rather hot through conduction. But this "gasket" also serves as a packing for the water jacket between the cylinder and its head and consequently the joint must be waterproof as well as able to withstand an appreciable amount of heat. Asbestos and rubber packings are made especially for this purpose and either will give satisfactory service when cut to the proper size and shape and held securely in place by the bolts that pass through the cylinder head.

One of the most efficient packings, however, and one that is the easiest for the amateur to apply, can be made from heavy, tough brown paper or drawing paper. Such a gasket will prove to be

FIG 3. USING EMERY CLOTH TO SMOOTH DOWN A RING THAT BINDS IN ITS GROOVE

gas and watertight and will not be affected by the heat of the iron surfaces of the cylinder and its head between which it is placed.

The best manner in which to apply such a gasket is as a sort of shellac-and-paper sandwich of the "double-deck" variety, composed of several layers of each ingredient. In order to cut each piece to exactly the proper shape and size the paper should be laid over the top of the cylinder on the surface on which the gasket is to be placed. By holding the piece firmly in place and tapping the edges and outlines of the iron surface through the paper with the round or "peening" end of a machinist's hammer, the paper will be cut to the proper shape. The edges of all bolt holes and water jacket openings in the surface should also be tapped in this manner, as shown in Fig. 5, but care should be taken not to strike so heavily that the threads of the bolt holes will be injured. The tapping should be sufficient to break the paper and care should be taken to prevent the gasket from moving before the entire outline is finished.

Three or four gaskets should be made in this manner and then a coat of shellac should be applied to the surface of the top of the cylinder. On this should be laid a gasket in exactly the same position as that in which it was cut so that all outlines, holes and openings will "register" and then the gasket itself should be shellacked. This should be continued until all gaskets are in place, each being separated from the others and from the iron surfaces of the cylinder and head by a layer of shellac.

The gaskets should be laid in place quickly before the shellac will have an opportunity to dry. After this "sandwich" has been "built up" and the last gasket has been treated to its coat of shellac, the cylinder head should be bolted in place as tightly as possible. The motor should not be run for a few minutes until after the shellac has had an opportunity to "set."

The above treatment is almost certain to cure any case of leakage of compression from the cylinder proper and the renewal of this packing may cause an increase of from ten to twenty-five per cent in the power developed by the motor. But there is another source of trouble which is oftentimes overlooked in the search for the missing horsepower. This is the crank case compression, or the compression formed in the base by

FIG. 4. A GOOD WAY TO COMPRESS THE RINGS SO THAT THE PISTON MAY BE SET DOWN IN THE CYLINDER

the *down*-stroke of the piston and used to force the charge upward into the cylinder. This is the principle used on what is known as the "three-port" type of two-cycle motor, and while this compression does not amount to more than from ten to fifteen pounds per square inch, the escape of even a small part of it is vital, for it is the actual explosive mixture in its most concentrated form that is lost.

Practically everyone who has had experience with this type of motor is familiar with the "crank case explosion" that occurs whenever too weak a mixture is admitted to the engine. As a rule, such crank case explosions are more startling than harmful, but occasionally the force of the pre-ignited gases will blow out a part of the packing between the crank case and removable base plate with which nearly all motors are provided in order to render the connecting

rod bearing accessible. If it is found that this gasket has been so damaged a new one may be cut out in the same manner as that described for the cylinder head packing, but it is better to use only one layer of heavy paper rather than several gaskets of a lighter weight.

As it is frequently necessary to reach the interior of the crank case by removing the base plate, the gaskets for this portion should not be shellacked. This gasket, however, is not subjected to high pressures and does not need to be absolutely watertight and consequently the application of oil or grease on both sides of the packing will serve the purpose almost as well as will shellac and at the same time will prevent the gasket from sticking to the base plate or crank case when the former is removed.

As a further precaution against the escape of crank case compression, none of the plugs, oilers and pipes leading to the base of the motor should be allowed to jar loose. It may sometimes happen that the valve on an oil cup will become stuck and allow the compression to force its way back against the lubricant, but such a condition will generally be indicated by a very apparent spluttering and bubbling.

It is not only the fact that a leak in the crank case allows a part of the incoming charge to escape that reduces the power of the motor, but the dilution of the remaining mixture, as well, will cause irregular running of the engine. On the up or compression stroke of the motor, a partial vacuum is formed in the crank case. This vacuum should be filled only by the incoming gas, which has already been properly mixed at the carburetor, but any leak in the crank case will furnish an entrance through which air will find its way and thus dilute the explosive charge.

With the rings, gaskets, oil cups, and oil-hole plugs in good condition, there is only one route by which air can be taken into the crank case, other than by way of the carburetor. This is through the crank shaft bearings, for if these have become loosened or worn, an easy passage is formed for the escape of the gas and the admission of the outside air. The crank shaft bearings, of course, cannot be set too tight, or they will bind and soon become worn, but on the other hand, there should be no perceptible "play" between the crank shaft and its bearing surfaces.

Under proper conditions, the film of oil that should be kept on the bearings from the lubricator or from the crank case will serve to make an air-tight joint between the shaft and the surfaces on which it turns. But let even one bearing run for only a short time without oil, and the softer bronze or babbitt metal will become worn, "chewed," or "burned out" in an astonishingly short space of time; and even though the normal supply of oil be resumed, a new bearing will almost certainly be required. This furnishes, to the amateur, one of the most puzzling causes of loss of power in a motor, and while the installation of a new bearing will render the engine as sturdy and vigorous as ever, the inaccessibility of this part of the motor makes the bearing the last place to which the motor boatman will look for power leakage. It is only when he has exhausted every other resource and has proved to his own satisfaction that the rings, packing, and other joints are tight that the novice will realize the important part that properly set crank shaft bearings play in the behavior and general good condition of his two-cycle, three-port motor.

Many an owner has claimed that he has obtained greatly increased power from his motor by a change in carburetors, but, as a rule, this is probably due as much to imagination as to any material advantage gained. When a good motor leaves the factory, it is supposed to be provided with a carburetor of the proper size and type, and, as a rule, the less "monkeying" with this part of the engine, the better. But the carburetor equipment is designed for a certain normal speed of the motor, and it may be that, owing to a slight change in the pitch or size of the propeller, the motor will "turn up" faster than was the case in the factory trials. In this event, the carburetor with which the motor was originally provided may not have a sufficiently large air opening to supply all of the cylinders with

FIG. 5.   CUTTING OUT GASKETS TO PROPER SIZE AND SHAPE BY TAPPING WITH MACHINIST'S HAMMER

enough mixture at this increased speed, and in consequence the engine may "starve."

The remedy, of course, lies in the change to a larger carburetor, but this should not be installed until it is made comparatively certain that the motor really is "starving." A motor suffering from this ailment will run well when throttled, but on the high speeds will miss and backfire and seem to suffer from lack of fuel in somewhat the same manner as has doubtless been noticed when the gasoline supply is about to become exhausted.

These few hints on the common causes of the loss of power in a new motor should not make owners dissatisfied with their purchases and wonder if they are "getting their money's worth," for "leave well enough alone" is a motto that could be applied to good advantage to many a power boatman who sets out to discover the source of a supposed loss of power, only to find that his craft was doing its best in the first place and that his hoped-for improvements turn out to be serious handicaps. There are cases, however, in which it is very evident that the best results are not being obtained, and, in such instances, a common-sense investigation of the possible reasons for the trouble may not only save the owner time and expense, but will give him the pleasure of "knowing his motor" better, as well.

The Lesson of
the America's Cup
Races
(1886)

FIRST DAY OF AMERICA'S CUP RACES — THE START.

THE LESSON OF THE AMERICA'S CUP RACES.

In taking a retrospective view of the events which occurred here during the last season, we see the one which to the yachtsman overshadowed every other in interest was the sailing for *America's* cup. Notwithstanding that this contest had been preceded by many others, of a similar kind, it had features which distinguished it from those before it, and aroused for it an extent of attention, and a degree of interest which surpassed that exhibited for any former ones.

It is especially gratifying at this date to look back at all the events which were connected with these races, and the preparation for them, from the time when the first challenge was received until the stranger had left our shores on his return; and to know, as every yachtsman who is acquainted with the history of the matter does know, of the very excellent spirit, no less than the generosity and enterprise, shown by all the parties who had the preparation for these races and their management in charge. The only apparently untoward event, the carrying away of the *Genesta's* bowsprit, was, perhaps, a most fortunate incident, since it served to show most unmistakably and promptly the fairness and generosity of both parties under trying circumstances.

It seems more than probable that on no other occasion since the sea has been sailed upon has there been seen such a spectacle as was presented to the eyes of the fortunate viewers of these races. In the spirited picture which accompanies this article the artist has succeeded in depicting admirably all that the eye could take in of such a crowd of steamboats and other followers; but upon the occasion of the first race, especially, the tug-boats, and other craft which followed the two races in close order, were too numerous to count, and suggestive of an immense flock of birds following two of their number.

In no other port in the world perhaps could such a number of vessels under steam be mustered, and for no other event, of which the writer knows, has anything like this number been brought together.

These events showed that not only was the yachting community deeply concerned, but that men and women who ordinarily are indifferent about yachting matters regarded this as more than an opportunity for an outing, and were keenly excited as to the issue of the contest.

In making a comparison now between the *Genesta* and our own yachts, more particularly the two which were built to meet her, and in seeking to learn anything from our added experience, due to her visit, it may be well to look at some matters commonly lost sight of, and to take into consideration whatever is conspicuously favorable or otherwise to the contestants on either side. If we do not do this we shall most certainly be liable to make miscalculations which may unfavorably affect the preparations for future competitions of a similar kind.

It seems to be all but invariably taken for granted that the *Genesta* is the best yacht that English yacht-designers could produce, and an English owner could bring over here. Such an assumption is entirely without warrant. The *Genesta*, at the time she left England, had been shown to be the equal, or nearly the equal in speed to any racing cutter of her size and class; but the *Genesta* was not built to come to America or to race under our rules of measurement. She was built to sail under rules which impose such a restrictive influence on beam that never, so far as the writer can discover, has any yacht been built in Great Britain for racing purposes since the *America* won the cup, that has escaped the crippling influence of the rules.

That the yachts built there for cruising purpose have commonly had greater proportionate beam than racing yachts is, of course, quite true. The distinction, however, between a racing and cruising yacht is there greater than here. The model, sail plan, ballasting, etc., of a cruising yacht is usually made subordinate to other requirements than those of speed; and the English yacht-designer may be said to have had no opportunity in the last half century to design, ballast, and equip a yacht as a racer in English waters, and free from hampering restrictions. That, built under such conditions, a yacht has been produced and brought over here and tested against the best craft that we could produce, with the result of being beaten only by 1m. 38s. in a race over a 40-mile course, and in the best racing weather that the boats were tried in, affords no cause for any claim for great superiority seems clearly manifest. It will probably suggest to some minds, as it has to the writer's, that the race might have resulted differently if the *Genesta* had been built expressly for racing under the rule then sailed under, or under less cramping conditions than those imposed upon her designer.

It is, perhaps, not likely that any Englishman will be inclined to build a yacht for the express purpose of attempting to capture the cup. It may not be more likely that any number of Englishmen will emulate the zeal and enterprise which have been shown here, and club together for that purpose. Such a craft would necessarily be a departure, to some extent, from the style of yacht which is best calculated to win prizes in British waters, and would, in consequence, be unfitted to participate in the races there. The opinion has, however, been expressed to the writer by more than one English naval architect of distinction, that a yacht might be built under a length and sail area rule, which would be faster than the vessels now built of the same length. While there is no reason to suppose that a yacht will be built in England for the express purpose of competing for the cup, with greater promise of success, there appears constantly in the columns of the chief English yachting journal a mass of correspondence which shows a great degree of dissatisfaction with their present rule of measurement, and a cry for amendment. Along with this there appears an appreciation of the fact that it is possible to have too much, even of so good a thing as depth, and that beam is not wholly a worthless or undesirable dimension.

It is not inconceivable that the issue of the prevailing feeling of dissatisfaction there may result in more than mere discussion, and that the issue may be a change in the rule of measurement, which will relax the present unreasonable tax on beam, and permit greater liberty of design. In such case it will no longer be prudent or safe to rely upon such a yacht as *Puritan*, good as she has proved herself to be. In taking into account, as the writer has done, the disadvantages under which the *Genesta* came into the contest, he does not leave out of view the fact that these were not all on one side.

At the time the *Genesta's* challenge was received no one-masted vessel of her size had been built and equipped here for a quarter of a century. Old methods of ballasting, sparring, and rigging such as had been used upon smaller boats were seen to be unsuitable, and insufficient to meet a professed racer, in the fitting up of which a well-tried experience had governed the adoption of every feature, and their perfection had been proved by a season's experience. New departures had to be made, and features introduced, which had their sanction rather in the enterprise and judgment of the designers than in the warrant of experience; and it seems highly probable that to the designers of both *Priscilla* and *Puritan* the experience gained has given valuable lessons, and fitted them to meet with increased efficiency any demand upon their skill which may be made for a similar kind of vessel in the future. For some reasons it is to be regretted that as two yachts were built to meet the *Genesta*, greater dissimilarity was not introduced into their relative proportions; that one of them, for instance, did not have more depth and somewhat less beam, so that in the three competing yachts we might have seen good examples, three types, say of eight and thirteen feet draught and one intermediate. But it appears to me that a little study of the diverse qualities and performances of the two boats, *Priscilla* and *Puritan*, almost identical as they are in draught and beam, sailing together, as they did on so many occasions, until their relative excellence on different points became well established, is capable of affording a possibility of suggestion and instruction which should not be allowed to pass unnoticed.

It is a rare opportunity for the observant yachtsman, to find two vessels sailing together, and their performances accurately recorded, which have their main elements so nearly identical or so easily comparable.

It did not take long, after the two yachts commenced sailing together, for the conclusion to be pretty commonly accepted that *Puritan* was the best to windward, especially in a blow, and that she carried her canvas better.

It appeared to be equally well established that *Priscilla* could sail faster off the wind in any weather that the two were tried in. A careful scrutiny of the records, from the date of the first meeting of the yachts to the date of the third and final trial race, will serve to bear out these conclusions. That *Priscilla* should sail faster off the wind was to be expected, as she is practically four feet longer ; but, on the occasions that were most conclusive, her gain in reaching and running was greater than any time allowance scale or theory of corresponding speeds would account for ; while on all occasions, exclusive only of the last, the *Puritan's* advantage in windward work was even greater.

For the sake of making clear the foregoing statements it may be well here to note in a brief way the relative times of the two boats, it being understood that in each case referred to, the difference in the elapsed time is stated as taken from the accounts published at the time, and that to correct the *Puritan's* time for smaller measurement, 1m. 14s. should be deducted for a forty-mile course, and 10s. more for a forty-five mile course. It should be further stated that on the first run from New London to Newport, it is claimed for the *Priscilla*, that though her time is taken as starting 4m. 23s. before the *Puritan*, she in reality waited for the latter boat, so as to go over the course as from an even start. An allowance for this would require that 4m. 23s. should be deducted from *Priscilla's* time on this run, as hereafter given. It should also be noted that on the run from New Bedford to Vineyard Haven *Puritan* lost some time through the giving way of something connected with her throat halyards, and the coming down of her gaff. The first day's run from New London to Newport, distance about forty miles, good breeze well aft, dropping now and then to very light wind, *Puritan's* elapsed time was 34s. less than *Priscilla's*, subject to correction already stated.

The next event was the race for the Goelet cup, which came off in a breeze and sea which caused many mishaps, and obliged several yachts to retire from the course. Here under housed topmasts to windward the *Puritan* proved the abler craft, and gained a signal victory over her rival ; the difference of time at the windward turning-point being recorded as about 12m. In the run to leeward, however, which is something like two-fifths of the whole course, *Priscilla* gained 1m. 43s.

The next sail was from Newport to New Bedford, distance a little under 30 miles. It was performed partly under spinnakers, and with a free wind all the way. Here the *Priscilla's* time was 11m. 16s. better than her rival's.

The next trip was to Vineyard Haven, distance about 25 miles, partly a beat in a strong wind, and was practically a win for *Puritan*, as, notwithstanding some delay by an accident already alluded to, she took only 2m. 44s. longer to do the distance than did *Priscilla*. Next came a trip to Newport, the first part of which appears to have been made in a light head-wind, followed by a calm, and succeeded by a good sailing breeze, free for the remaining distance. This trip is perhaps less determinate of any distinctive quality in the two yachts under consideration than the others ; but the honors were unquestionably *Puritan's*. So far as the records show us, her time was 6m. 10s. better than *Priscilla's*. This ended all opportunity of comparing the speed of the two yachts for the time, but was followed a fortnight later, namely, August 21st, by the first of the trial races to windward and back, over a 40-mile course, with a moderate wind and sea ; and here again with a regularity which savored of monotony, the distinctive qualities of the two boats were shown up, and these did not appear to have been decreased any by some lightening up that had been effected in *Priscilla*, by removal of stores and useless weights, and by the shortening of her lower mast and increase of topmast.

We find that in the 20 miles to windward *Puritan's* time is 12m. 37s. better than *Priscilla's*; and again *Priscilla's* time to leeward is 2m. 39s. better than *Puritan's*. This race appears to have been made in a true wind, and without flukes to favor either yacht.

We next come to the triangular race, which was made in a light wind and some sea. Here again in the windward work, done along the second side of the triangle, the *Priscilla* appears by all accounts to have had no advantage, where the wind was even to both yachts ; though there appears to have been no sufficient weight in it to tax her stability, and she did better than on previous occasions ; but two legs of the course being done with a free sheet, her elapsed time at the finish was 6m. 28s. better than that of her rival. Now we come to the last opportunity that has occurred of comparing the speed of these two yachts over a race-course. In this case the course was that of the New York Yacht Club, which, as most yachtsmen know, takes the boats over lines retraced ; which, with some slight deviations, corresponds very closely with the lines formed by the base and perpendicular of a right angle triangle, the perpendicular being in this case about three-fourths the length of the base. The race commenced with a close-haul along the base of the triangle, a run and close-haul with one tack coming back over the second leg of the course, and a quartering wind from this point to the finish. This was the most interesting of the trial-races; it was made in a good breeze. The *Puritan's* actual time over the 38 miles, 3h. 52m. 37s., is the best ever made over the course by a one-masted vessel, and within twenty seconds of that made by the schooner *Montauk* in 1882. The interesting feature of this race was its closeness, and the fact that while *Priscilla* did no better with *Puritan* than formerly off the wind; indeed she failed to keep the full measure of her advantage in this kind of sailing; on the other hand, the *Puritan* did not, in her customary manner, get away from her on a wind. A marked change had been effected in some way, and it may well repay us to try and find out what the improvement in windward sailing was due to. The difference in the time taken by the two boats to reach the first mark on their way out was 1m. 20s., advantage to *Puritan*. Running from buoy ten to light-ship the *Priscilla* made the best time by 11s. only. Coming back close-hauled, and making a tack near the point of Sandy Hook, *Priscilla* suffered some disadvantage by the carrying away of the iron strap attached to the block connected with her topmast back-stay. *Puritan* makes the best time, but only by 31s. From buoy ten to the finish, with the wind aft the beam, *Priscilla* made best time by 59s.

It will be seen, by an examination of the figures given, that in a beat of 20 miles to windward, in the first trial race, the *Puritan*, in a good sailing-breeze, was 12m., 37s. faster than the *Priscilla*, and that in the last race, in a close-haul with one tack, in a similar breeze, over about nine miles of water, the *Puritan* was only 31 seconds better. It may be seen, also, that while, in the first trial race, the *Priscilla* beat the *Puritan* in the run of 20 miles to leeward by 2m. 39s., in this last race, in a 9-miles run to leeward, the *Priscilla's* time was only 11 seconds better than the *Puritan's*. We now come to the question of *Priscilla's* inferiority in going to windward, and her superiority in reaching and running as compared with her rival, and why, in the last trial race, her windward qualities

showed such a vast improvement, and her speed off the wind appeared to be somewhat lessened, but not to the same extent.

As has already been stated, such an opportunity of comparing the speed of yachts and the influences affecting their speed, is too seldom obtained to allow of this one being passed by unnoticed. I shall, therefore, examine some of the facts and features which present themselves, with a view to make them interesting and instructive. That there was a vast difference in the sailing of the *Priscilla* on the occasion of her last trial-race is very evident, and the only cause that has come to the writer's knowledge that will account for the improvement, and also for the slightly diminished speed off the wind, is to be found in the fact that some four tons of extra ballast were put into her. But here comes up the most interesting question connected with the subject; and it is one which has a much wider significance than as it affects the *Priscilla* alone, or than as it affects the *Priscilla* and *Puritan* relatively.

Why should not the *Priscilla* stand up to her canvas and go to windward as well as the *Puritan*, without an extra four tons of ballast put into her to enable her to do it? If this were a question which involved the discussion of nice varieties of form, or of the superiority of water-lines, sections, sail plans, or other more or less indefinite features, or of architectural skill, or artistic taste, the writer might refrain from dealing with it. It is, however, as he regards it, a question involving none of these subjects in any uncertain way.

If the *Priscilla* failed to go well at high speeds, where the necessity comes in for a shape that is capable of being urged through the water fast, then the question of her defects might be an intricate one.

If she slid off to leeward, when hauled upon a wind, this would account for her failure to go well on this point of sailing; but there appears to be no suspicion that her board is not ample, and that the defect lies in her deficient stability is made plain by observation, and by noting the improvement of her, in windwardly sailing, by the addition of four tons to her ballast. To some of those who have studied the forms of the two yachts, *Priscilla* and *Puritan*, it may have appeared strange that *Priscilla* should not have carried sail, at least as well as the shapely and symmetrical *Puritan*.

As the writer believes, the reason why she did not carry sail not merely as well but much better than *Puritan*, is to be shown by nothing more abstruse than common arithmetic, and a reference to some of the elementary rules used by naval architects.

The difference between *Priscilla* and *Puritan*, in respect to stability and the superiority of the latter, to be made evident by means just referred to, consists in the *Puritan's* ballast plan and in the distribution of weights. In arranging these matters, Mr. Burgess made a bold departure from customary usage. It has been a common belief that ballast in large quantities cannot be used low down, in boats of the moderate draught of the *Puritan*, and that moreover it cannot be stretched along so far fore and aft as he used it; and that both of these features, introduced into the *Puritan*, or other yacht of her size and type, would be ruinous to speed and seagoing qualities in anything like rough water. No doubt any experienced seagoer could state facts that would apparently furnish good ground for the expression of such an opinion; but I have not heard anything said against the *Puritan;* and that she can go to windward very fast in hard weather, and in water that is far from smooth, needs no proof at this date.

I am prompted to deal with this subject because in my hearing it has frequently been discussed, and the shortcomings of *Priscilla* have been referred to causes which, in point of fact, did not exist; while the features which did exist, and were capable of yielding the explanation, did not seem to be even suspected.

These things have, as a usual thing, been made features in comparison with *Puritan*, and her superior ability has been referred to greater beam, shorter bow, longer side, fuller water-line, low rig, etc.

With the possibility of having another international race, in the coming summer, and of preparing more than one boat to meet the *Galatea*, or other British yacht, it seems desirable that some comparison of the features of the two yachts should be made.

The figures necessary for this have been obtained from the designers of the two boats mentioned, or from the New York Yacht Club. Before going further it may be well to explain, for the benefit of such readers as have not given much attention to methods used for calculating the stability of vessels, and their consequent power to carry sail, that this power is dependent on the weight of the boat, and the distance which transversely separates this weight, or its center of gravity, from the center of buoyancy of the vessel, at any angle of inclination. This distance multiplied by the weight of the vessel constitutes the righting moment of the vessel. This depends upon the height relative to the center of buoyancy at which the center of gravity of the vessel is to be found, and the length and bulk of the immersed and emersed wedges. The length and bulk of these depend upon the beam of the boat, the fullness of the water-line, and the fullness of the cross-sections of the boat immediately above and below the water-line; that is at such parts of her as are put into or taken out of water by inclination in sailing. It will thus be seen, in the case of any craft under consideration, that, if the boat's weight be greater, the water-line and cross-sections fuller, and the center of gravity as low down, in its relation to the center of buoyancy of the boat, such a boat must be stiffer, and able to carry more sail, with an equal angle of heel; or that she ought to carry the same sail at a smaller angle of heel.

It will be also seen that if it can be shown that the weight of the boat is larger, and that the immersed and emersed wedges are also larger at the same angle of heel, but the position of the center of gravity in its relation to the center of buoyancy in the two boats is not definitely known, and that the yacht which has the advantage of the other, in respect to the known quantities, does not carry as well the same amount of sail as the other, then the explanation is to be looked for in the undefined features.

I shall proceed now to give some particulars relative to these matters, but before using figures I may state in a general way, and without drawings before me, that both yachts have a similar and ample extent of freeboard; that the midship sections of the two, measured to garboard, are almost identical in depth; that the greater depth below this is due to *Puritan's* outside lead keel. The character of the sections is nearly the same, the *Puritan's* having a smaller area, owing to turning in a trifle earlier below the water-line, and running inside the line of *Priscilla's* until near the keel, making a somewhat hollow floor; where the *Priscilla's* is only a slight variation from a straight line. If *Puritan* was put down in the water 2 or 3 inches, the turn of her bilge at the midship section would be the same as *Priscilla's;* as it now is it is slightly leaner.

I now give some of the measurements of the two yachts : —

	Puritan.	Priscilla.
Length on water-line	81.1 ft.	85. ft.
Breadth on water-line	21.8	21.6
Extreme breadth	22.7	22.5
Sail area, measured as per rule	7981.	7378.
Height from main boom to topsail block	102.1	101.
Area of immersed midship section	80.	86.5
Area of load water-line	1100.	1187.10
Mean breadth of water-line	13.56	13.96
Proportion of area of water-line to circumscribing parallelogram	.622	.646
Displacement in long tons	100.	114.
Ballast in long tons	40.	45.
Ballast in long tons, outside	27.	

If *Priscilla's* sail area were as much larger than *Puritan's* as the difference between the lengths of the two yachts would make proportionate, that is, if the sail areas were in the same proportion as the squares of the lengths of the two boats, there might be a question whether (the centers of gravity being located in corresponding relations to the centers of buoyancy in the two craft) the *Priscilla* could carry sail as well as *Puritan*, with her beam less in proportion to length, and an increase only in the weight of displacement to set off against this. The fact is, however, that *Priscilla* has practically the same extreme beam as *Puritan*, that the average beam is about 5 inches greater in *Priscilla*, owing to her fuller water-line, and that the midship section being somewhat fuller also just below water, the emersed wedge would doubtless be greater than *Puritan's*, even if *Priscilla's* frames were to be put up closer together, so as to bring her down to *Puritan's* length.

As it is, the extra length of *Priscilla* should give her greater stiffness, as it adds to the volume of the immersed and emersed wedges, and also to the displacement of the boat. *Priscilla's* sail measurement, however, is actually less than *Puritan's*. It is also less than *Genesta's*, though both of these boats are nearly 4 feet shorter than she is. These measures, taken by the method used in the New York Yacht Club, show *Priscilla's* area to be 603 feet less than *Puritan's*, and 9 feet less than *Genesta's*. If we compare *Puritan's* and *Priscilla's* sails as proportionate to their lengths merely, and exclude other dimensions as being practically the same in each, we should have, accepting *Priscilla* as the standard, 7,040 feet for *Puritan*, as against 7,378 for *Priscilla;* or, accepting *Puritan* as the standard, we should have for that vessel 7,981 square

feet, and for *Priscilla*, 8,365. A consideration of the foregoing figures, without any more detailed and complete calculations, such as only the possession of the plans and of facts that the writer is not acquainted with would enable him to make, will show pretty conclusively, I think, that *Puritan* is ballasted better than *Priscilla*, and that in this, and in the distribution also, very probably, of weight in the hull and spars of the two boats ; in other words, in the arrangement of those matters which determine the position of the centers of gravity, is to be found the reason that *Priscilla* never sailed evenly with *Puritan* on the wind until 4 tons had been added to the weight of her ballast. In this connection it may be suggested that the ballast on *Puritan's* keel, while it apparently pays well for its use there, is probably the cause, in part, of the yacht's inferiority to *Priscilla* off the wind, and of her need of a larger sail plan than would otherwise be required, as the surface subject to friction is by the lead keel considerably increased. Before leaving this part of our subject it may be well to look a little into one or two matters connected with the use of iron for the construction of yachts. It has frequently been urged, among other advantages, that they were, size for size, lighter ; and it has been believed by those who should know, that the thin plating, greater room between the frames, and absence of cumbrous bulk about the trunk box admitted of *Priscilla's* ballast being stowed inside with as much advantage as was *Puritan's*, since that part of the ballast which the latter had to put inside was much higher than *Priscilla's*.

This opinion the writer feels that he must regard with deference, because of the competency of those from whom it issued to form an opinion. He has, however, never been able to regard it as free from the suspicion of miscalculation. One thing is clear : that of 40 tons of ballast in *Puritan*, 27 tons, or two-thirds of the whole weight, are outside ; and the highest point of this must needs be lower, relative to the center of buoyancy of the yacht, than the lowest of the *Priscilla's* ballast.

The center of gravity of this part of the ballast is of course much lower still. As only 13 tons, or about 40 cubic feet, are required above the 3-inch planking, against nearly 140 cubic feet in the *Priscilla*, above her thin iron plating, it would seem that the utmost contrivance could not stow *Pris-*

cilla's ballast to the same advantage as *Puritan's.* To leave this part of the subject, and devote some attention to the weight of the yachts themselves, including their rig and equipments,—for of course the height and position of every part of these have an influence in determining the location of the center of gravity of the vessel, and the consequent measure of her stability, and a needless hundred weight aloft will require much more in the hold to compensate for it.

It may be found, by referring to the figures already given, that *Puritan's* total displacement is 100 tons, that 40 tons of this weight are due to the ballast; and it follows, of course, that the *Puritan* without ballast weighs, with all her equipment, just 60 tons. By a like calculation we find that *Priscilla* weighs, with her somewhat smaller equipment, just 69 tons. But she is longer than *Puritan;* and, to find out how these two vessels compare in weight, we must reduce the length of one or increase that of the other. As has been before stated, for such a purpose as we have here, every other dimension than that of length can be left out of the calculation, as the breadth and depth are practically alike in both yachts. If, then, we take the weight of *Puritan* without ballast, multiply this by *Priscilla's* length, and divide by her own, we have 63 tons, but *Priscilla* weighs 69 tons. If in place of doing this we take *Priscilla's* weight, multiply it by *Puritan's* length, and divide it by her own, we have 65.75 tons as the weight of an iron *Puritan*, or 5¾ tons more than the present *Puritan* weighs. The iron *Puritan* would really weigh something over this, for we have been comparing the boats by the water-line measure, and they do not have the same amount of overhang; that of *Puritan* being several feet longer than *Priscilla's*, though considerably lighter. The inference from these calculations is, that *Priscilla* has 6 tons and over of weight in her, distributed somewhere between the mast-head and the keel, which she would not have if built as *Puritan* is; that it adds to her displacement and resistance, but does not yield the equivalent in stability which it would if absent from where it is and present in the ballast.

So far as the writer can see, every prominent feature of *Priscilla*, apart from the location of the center of gravity, would indicate her superiority in windward work. As a further evidence of this the area of load water-line may be again referred to. Using the proportion of *Puritan's* water-line to its circumscribing parallelogram, namely .622, we find that *Priscilla* with such a water-line would have 45 square feet less area than at present, and that *Puritan* with a water-line as full as *Priscilla's* would have 43 feet more than at present. Other facts and figures might be used to amplify the proof which I have been engaged upon, if necessary, but what has been written may be sufficient for the purpose; and to those who decry the use of figures and formulas in yacht-designing it may afford some proof that these are not without value, if these remarks serve to prompt a use of proper remedies in the case of *Priscilla*, and if these should prove in some degree practicable, and in a like degree effective.

It is a matter of no small moment to yachting interests, both here and elsewhere, that within the last few years yacht-designing has become a profession, and that a class of educated men have adopted it as such,—men whom education and association have made capable of distinguishing between patriotic zeal and vulgar sentiment. The presence of such men among yacht-designers anywhere, and everywhere, furnishes the best augury and hope for improvement in the speed and quality of our yachts.

Assuredly the man who puts a brand of nationality upon ideas, and refuses all that are not of his own, has no business in any race for improvement.

There are those whose counsel, had it been taken, would not have permitted of such boats as *Puritan* and *Priscilla* being produced, and the contest would in all probability have ended very differently. It would have been a sufficient objection to outside ballast, double-head rigs, long topmasts, mast-head runners, long gaffs, and perhaps even an iron hull, that in the use of these things the British yachtsmen had preceded us. If the American yachtsman can only properly use such features and appliances in his yacht as no one of any other nationality has at some time thought it worth while to use, he is in a pretty bad fix. He could not in this case use a center-board; and if the Englishman should adopt similar restriction I am not quite sure that he could use outside lead; probably he could. Commodore Stevens, of Hoboken, used a weighted board and a heavy fin on the sloop *Maria* somewhere about 1848. I do not think much use was made of outside lead in England for twenty years after this.

Probably in this matter the boy was " father to the man ; " for, as far back as I can recollect, boys and others who took delight in sailing models nearly all put the ballast upon the keel. Even in respect to this, however, the modern yachtsman who objects to ballast on the keel had his prototype, and so late as twenty-seven years ago, the model yacht sailor could be found who would advocate inside ballast, and even water ballast, and adduce facts in support of his views.

The opportunities had in the eastern ports of this country within the past few years, of comparing the sailing and properties of yachts of widely different types, have probably not been enjoyed in like measure by yachtsmen of any other nation. Our ideas ought to grow, and our prejudices disappear faster, in consequence.

It is to be regretted that our experience, and that the experience of yachtsmen generally, has been very little with the medium draught boat ; such as is represented by *Puritan* and *Priscilla*, and also somewhat deeper. There has been little to show us here or elsewhere of what such craft are capable.

It has been a quite commonly entertained opinion among our most active and influential yachtsmen that only the extremely wide and shallow, or the extremely narrow and deep, boat was good for speed ; and the opinion was difficult to oppose by demonstrative argument, as attempts at speed by experienced designers were usually made only with these two classes. The English rules confined their designers to experience only in the deep and narrow class ; while ours was mostly with the opposite class.

The simple length rule of measurement, still unfortunately in favor with some of our prominent clubs, tends as much perhaps to perpetuate the extremely broad type of yacht, and to confine experience to it, as does the English rule to the absurdly narrow and extravagantly deep kind. The man whose experience has been wholly in the production of either of these styles, and who attains success and mastery in his own line, necessarily, perhaps, becomes less confident of the result of working under new conditions.

The advent and success of *Puritan* and *Priscilla* have doubtless directed a large amount of attention to yachts that are not of extreme dimensions, and as doubtlessly given an amount of confidence in this class of yachts that was not had before. The fact that yachts varying so widely as did these yachts from *Genesta* could be brought to race with her with anything like an even chance of success is promising for freedom in yacht-designing.

The fact that the largest rigged yacht could well afford the tax put upon her for it, in racing with the other two, is assuring to the timid ones who are afraid that they cannot spread sail enough to suit themselves.

The further discovery that the largest yacht built to put against *Genesta*, and some four feet longer than that yacht, had a smaller sail area than the cutter, must give assurance to those who are afraid of the rule being too favorable to yachts of the latter class.

It is greatly to be hoped for the promotion of advancement in yacht-modeling, and also in the interest of yacht-racing, that yacht-clubs everywhere will seek to exclude from their rules everything which will prevent the free and fair development of every desirable feature, and of every type of yacht. There appear to be ample spaces not yet filled in between the lines of experience in yacht-designing. One of the matters in which we have perhaps much cause for congratulation in connection with the recent international contest is, that in the *Genesta* the best possibilities of that extreme type of vessel, within the rules which governed her construction, appear by comparison of her with others of her class to have been pretty nearly attained. Everything has been done that is practicable to compensate for narrowness of beam by placing all her ballast upon the lower side of her keel.

What possibilities may yet be reached by the type of vessel opposed to her none can say. The experiment has not yet been tried. The future is promising. We may warrantably be expectant and reasonably hopeful.

J. Hyslop.

Western Yachts
and Designers
(1897)

OUTING.

APRIL, 1897.

MINNETONKA YACHT-CLUB HOUSE.

WESTERN YACHTS AND DESIGNERS.

By Arthur James Pegler.

THERE was a time, and not so very long ago either, when yachting in America figured as solely a salt-water sport, in which only residents along the seacoast could hope to attain any great measure of success or distinction. There remains to some extent that feeling of unbelief in fresh-water craft and the fresh-water sailor, which has ever been met with among those yachtsmen whose habitat lies within hail of old ocean ; but in the light of some recent results of Western designing it appears that our crack builders of racing craft may ere long go to school in the West with profit to their own models.

In New York and Boston the news is received with good-natured incredulity that Nat G. Herreshoff's latest and best has been utterly and ignominiously beaten at a game she was specially designed to win, by a boat the name of whose builder touches no familiar chord in the memories of either Eastern or Western sailfact that the *Tartar*, de-built by An-terson, o f

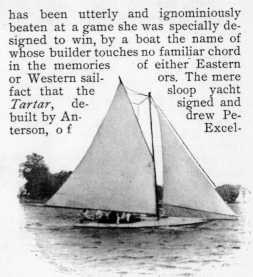

ors. The mere sloop yacht signed and drew Pe-Excel-

ALFREDA.

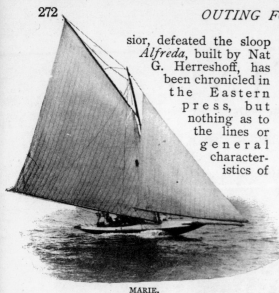

MARIE.

sior, defeated the sloop *Alfreda*, built by Nat G. Herreshoff, has been chronicled in the Eastern press, but nothing as to the lines or general characteristics of sailors have not forgotten either *Grilse* or *Apukwa*, both of which succeeded in winning a majority of their salt-water engagements.

Of all inland yachting organizations, that recognized, for the last few years at least, as the most progressive is the Minnetonka Yacht Club, of Lake Minnetonka. During the last five seasons some remarkable results have been achieved both at home and abroad with boats designed and built on the shores of this picturesque lake. Among the first really important achievements of Minnetonka builders was that of Arthur Dyer, who constructed the sloop yacht *Onawa*, which boat proved so fast under almost any conditions that the old-style sloops, with their square bows and sterns, were absolutely out of it from that time for-

TARTAR.

this really extraordinary craft has been offered to yachting enthusiasts beyond the shores of Minnetonka. The impression, therefore, may yet remain that the *Tartar* won her series against *Alfreda* by chance. Had the *Tartar's* remarkable showing been made anywhere along the Atlantic coast, she would have been much more widely exploited. Minnetonka boats are not entirely unknown either in Boston or New York waters. New Yorkers will remember Mr. George Work's twenty-one-footer, *Minnetonka*, whose remarkable sailing along the East coast attracted attention three years ago; and Boston ward. It that to nized in tion of owing of is not questioned principles recognized in the construction of this boat is a great part the progress

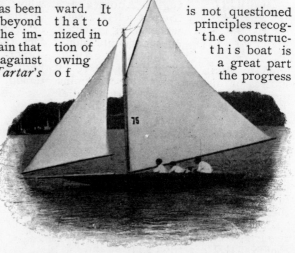

DORIS.

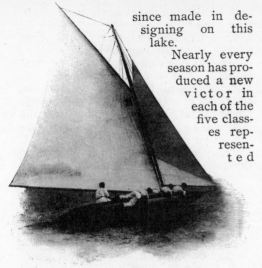

BEATRICE.

since made in designing on this lake.

Nearly every season has produced a new victor in each of the five classes represented in the Minnetonka Club fleet, but never in the history of the organization has there been such a spectacle as that presented when *Tartar*, the winner of the first-class sloop series of 1896, came across the line and won her final race. The event was won in a gale, just such weather as suits both the boat and her owner ; and it seemed as this black-hulled Peterson creation swept by the club-house on the final leg, that nothing was touching but her centreboard. The club-house, docks, and verandas were crowded that day, and many a dainty bit of cambric went fluttering off in the wake of Captain Peet's victorious sloop, for his victory had been a popular one, and the women who interest themselves in Minnesota yachting are very enthusiastic.

Before the close of the season *Tartar* had not only beaten all the local boats, with time to spare, but had run away as well from Herreshoff's twenty-three-foot production, beating her by six minutes in one race, and seven minutes in another. The St. Paul owners of the White Bear Yacht Club's champion, *Alfreda*, seemed scarcely able to realize that their boat, by so famous a designer, had been beaten in such hollow style by the pro-

duction of an old Norwegian A. B., whose principal claim to knowledge of designs lay in practical experience as a sailor of the sea ; but the fact remained.

When the sailing regulations for each year are adopted early in November, Minnetonka yachtsmen begin casting about for likely looking models, and without much delay place their orders for new boats, with that secrecy characteristic of the yacht owner, who invariably believes that at last he has secured the winner in his class. Every season finds from eight to a dozen new boats added to the fleet, some of them from Eastern yards, but the majority the work of local designers and builders.

At the opening of last year, even before there was a sign of activity about any of the boatyards, a rumor was afloat in club circles that six contracts had been let for first-class sloops, which boats should classify in length from twenty-one to twenty-three feet measured three inches above the water-line, and carry from six hundred and twenty-five to seven hundred square feet of sail. About the same time it was learned that the White Bear Yacht Club had forwarded an order to Herreshoff for a sloop of similar measurement, which boat, it was understood, had been ordered with the express intention that if she turned out as fast as expected she should defend White Bear in the inter-lake series of races, occurring in the autumn between the winning boats of each fleet. In fact,

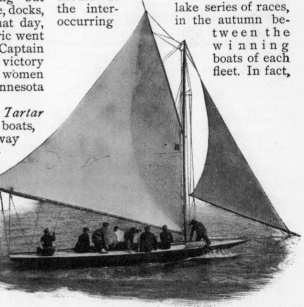

TARTAR.

LUCIAN SWIFT, JR.

it was confidently expected that Herreshoff would be able, when given *carte blanche*, as he was in this case, and furnished with measurements of the Minnetonka sloop *Marie*, the fastest boat of the previous year, to turn out something speedier, at least, than could be produced by any of the local builders. Some degree of consternation was felt among the loyal coterie that leads progression in the Minnetonka Yacht Club, when the fact was established that such a boat had really been ordered for the White Bear.

Already it was rather late in the season, and practically nothing had been done toward provision for a Minnetonka cup defender in 1896. However, within a week after Herreshoff's receipt of the White Bear order, quiet little meetings were being held in Minneapolis, with a view to providing against defeat in the approaching contest for the Minnesota sloop championship cup. As a result of these conferences a syndicate was formed consisting of three well-known members of the Minnetonka Yacht Club, viz., William H. Dunwoody, Thomas B. Janney and William Peet, Jr., all active men in yachting and owners of well-known racing craft. These gentlemen pledged subscriptions for a sufficient sum to obtain the fastest racing sloop of her inches that could be bought for money East or West. Mr. Peet, who is an old member of the club, and one of the best small-boat sailers in the country, was authorized to receive bids for this boat and order her upon his own approval. Many models were submitted and carefully studied before a decision was reached. It was generally understood, in the first place, that the order would go either to Herreshoff or Arthur Dyer, of Deephaven, the builder of *Marie*, *Onawa* and many other celebrities. As it turned out, Dyer's design

met with the greatest favor, and on the strength of his successes, not alone on Minnetonka, but as well in Eastern waters, with *Apukwa*, *Grilse*, *Exile* and others, a decision in his favor was reached. But there's many a slip 'twixt the cup and the lip, and a complicated condition of affairs arose, involving the terms of the contract under which the boat was to be constructed. Just what the actual details of the misunderstanding may have been is not important in this connection. It is sufficient that the intention to give this order to Dyer was canceled and the entire project abandoned, at least for the time. In fact, so much delay had been occasioned through this misunderstanding with Dyer, that it was deemed altogether too late for placing an order in any Eastern yard ; and, to speak plainly, there was not sufficient confidence felt in either of the other local builders on their previous performances to justify placing so important a commission in their hands.

While no boat was being built by Dyer with the express design of figuring as a cup defender, there were three new first-class sloops on the stocks in his yard for members of the club, one of which was the identical model previously approved by the syndicate, and subsequently ordered by the Walker brothers, who are known as among the most enterprising owners on the lake. The *Swift* was also built for Lucian Swift, of Minneapolis, with an eye to the cup championship, while the *Reveille* ordered by the Donaldson brothers, was expected by them to get a good position in the club series. However, none of the trio fulfilled the expectations of her owners.

It was very late in the spring when Andy Peterson, the Excelsior builder, strayed into Mr. Peet's office one day, his bearded countenance ablaze with animation. If a yacht owner is

COMMODORE W. H. DUNWOODY.

mysterious, a yacht designer is mystery personified. Peterson carried very tenderly a paper bundle. There was a good deal of unwrapping to do ere the contents of this parcel were displayed before the interested gaze of the *Kite's* captain. Then for the first time he beheld a model of the *Tartar*. This model was one that Peterson had whittled out during long winter evenings in his little shack on the lake shore, and its merits were at once apparent to so capable a critic as Peet, though it was scarcely to be believed that this common sailor had been able to produce under such conditions anything capable of competing with the work of so distinguished a designer as Herreshoff, or of equaling the work of McLeod, Clapham, or Dyer. Mr. Peet looked at the model, curiously at first, then carefully, then earnestly, and at last eagerly. It was a fast-looking model, but, fast as it looked, the syndicate hesitated to intrust such an order to a man who had up to that time achieved but little reputation for building fast boats. Peterson, somewhat piqued and confident of the correctness of his theory, offered to build the boat for bare cost, and, on her completion, to sail a series of three trial races with the *Kite*, a Herreshoff sloop, recognized as one of the fastest on the lake, and sailed by Mr. Peet himself, while Peterson should handle his new candidate. The understanding was that to complete the sale of his boat he must win two out of the three races at least, whereupon he was to receive for each race won a handsome bonus. The fairness of this proposition to all parties concerned appealed to the syndicate, and the boat was ordered.

Like Palissy, the potter, Peterson put every stick he had, and every atom of energy he possessed, into this work. He labored on the *Tartar* from dawn till dark, and visited the boat-house, if all reports are correct, several times each night, to make absolutely certain that there was no danger from fire or any other source, which might imperil or injure the chances of his favorite. At last, the boat was launched, and a great crowd of interested spectators turned out to witness a first trial race between the aristocratic Herreshoffer and this lowly craft, whose gleaming black hull seemed, as she lay there at the dock, to belie her origin. I venture to assert that if these races had occurred in the East, they would have formed the subject of much lengthy newspaper comment, for the performances of the *Tartar* were such as to carry conviction that there was something new under the sun. In fact, Peterson had fulfilled his boast. The Herreshoff sloop was completely outclassed on every point of sailing. It is not necessary to add that *Tartar* immediately became the property of the syndicate, and that her designer and builder found his pockets bulging with good negotiable currency of the United States.

The apparent peculiarity in the construction of the *Tartar* consisted in her divided stern, an effect produced by cutting out a section of the stern three feet long and one foot wide. During her first races the boat provoked an immense amount of criticism from rival owners of yachts, among whom the opinion seemed to have been formed that *Tartar* owed much speed to her after innovation. The boat was even referred to, in some quarters, as a freak, though there was nothing freakish in the fair, true line of the craft that finally won this season's honors. Never was a boat so criticised on the lake, with the possible exception of *Onawa*, champion of 1893. Nor was this surprising, as the impression obtained, on first looking at her, was without doubt the extraordinary character of her stern. It took closer examination to recognize at its true value the strong, perfect and simple way in which she was put together. *Tartar* is planked with one-quarter inch Michigan cedar, canvased inside, with long, narrow battens covering the inside seams from stem to stern, and wide, thin ribs fitting closely together, making up a construction combining lightness, strength and tightness. The model combines power, being especially powerful well forward. The boat has long, easy, straight lines, shallow draft, and a general air of completeness which cannot escape the eye of the critic. Peterson realized the necessity of perfect rigging, so he fitted the *Tartar* with the best sail and outfit that could be bought. Her centreboard is a steel dagger, weighing two hundred and fifty pounds.

The first club race in which she appeared occurred on June 27th, when, in a good full-sail breeze, she won by six minutes and four seconds over *Marie*, the champion of 1895. The next race, on July 4th, was sailed in a light wind, and *Tartar* won it by only thirty-two seconds over *Charlotte*. On July 11th and 25th she won easily in whole-sail winds by ten minutes and twenty-five seconds, and five minutes and fifty-seven seconds, respectively. Again on August 15th, in light weather, she won by one minute and twenty seconds.

The only boat that beat *Tartar* during the entire season was *Charlotte*, when, on August 1st, the latter craft won, in a fair wind, by the narrow margin of six seconds. Thus the *Tartar* captured the championship, winning five out of six races, her easiest victories being won in good full-sail breezes. It had been predicted by many of the knowing ones that in a blow she would be beaten ; but it took more than a mere assertion to convince Captain Peet that his new acquisition would not do better in heavy weather than under any other conditions, and he insisted that the harder the wind blew the better his boat would handle. He was given an opportunity to prove the truth of this theory in the inter-lake races that followed.

The inter-lake events, which occur annually between the champion sloops and cats of Minnetonka and White Bear lakes, constitute the grand climax of the yachting season on these two lakes.

THE SWIFT.

Three years ago the White Bear Club, with headquarters at St. Paul, offered jointly with the Minnetonka Yacht Club a silver cup to be sailed for at the close of each season by the champion sloops of each organization. Subsequently a cup was also offered in the cat class. In 1895 the races were sailed on White Bear Lake, and as this was the first inter-lake regatta, tremendous enthusiasm was displayed. The White Bear clubhouse was ablaze with gay colors, and the fashion and bravery of the two cities combined to make the scene an inspiring one. The *Marie*, champion of that year in the sloop class, was sailed by Hal P. Watson, of Minneapolis. White Bear's representative was the *Corona*, designed and handled by Dr. James M. Welch. *Marie* lost the first race, purely on a fluke. In the second, when five minutes ahead she lost her jib, thus giving the series to *Corona*. It was freely admitted, however, that *Marie* was easily the fastest boat on either lake at that time. In the contest between the champion cats of the two lakes, sailed on the same days, the Minnetonka boat, *Pinafore*, owned by L. R. Brooks, won her races handily.

The cups are contested for until one club has won two out of three in the series. Last year the races occurred

KATRINA.

on Lake Minnetonka and belief ran high in Captain Peet's black-hulled phenomenon. Nothing was heard about freaks at this stage of the season, for *Tartar* was generally recognized to have won her races without benefit from the "bloomer stern," which had excited so much adverse criticism earlier in the year. The White Bear clubmen, on the other hand, were absolutely confident that their white sloop from Bristol, designed especially for sailing under such conditions as were called for in these races, would be able to carry off the honors of the season without difficulty.

These races occurred during the last week in August, and the club-house in St. Louis Bay was thronged with spectators from all round the lake, as well as from both cities. Nothing had been neglected which could possibly conduce to the success of the events, either from a sporting or a social point of view. The interior of the club-house was a perfect maze of vivid coloring, while from the exterior a thousand flags and pennants fluttered gaily in the gale—for it was a gale that blew that day, such as Minnetonka sailors had not experienced throughout the entire year. The few seconds time allowance was in favor of *Tartar*, but she never needed it. The race was sailed in a double-reef west wind, necessitating a dead beat to windward on the first leg of the triangular course. It was instantly apparent that

the *Tartar* would have all the better of it in that weather. She stood up like a house and fairly chewed into the wind, while *Alfreda* labored heavily in the squalls, and proved unequal to the strain. On the next leg, running abeam and coming home with the wind on the quarter, the boats were more evenly matched, although *Tartar* had slightly the better of it. The last two circuits of the triangle were mere repetitions of the first, *Tartar* increasing her lead on each leg, and romping home a winner over the 10-knot course by more than seven minutes.

On the following day the wind had blown itself out completely, and the race of that occasion became a drifting match until it was called off after they had gone once around the course. The third day, however, it blew a gale again, the wind being almost as strong as in the first race. Each boat carried single reefs, and *Tartar* beat *Alfreda* on every leg, her superiority being especially noticeable going to windward. She won this race by over six minutes.

There was general regret that one of the races could not have been sailed in a good full-sail wind, as it was recognized that the boats would have been more evenly matched under such conditions. *Alfreda* is beyond question a very speedy boat in fair weather, but in a reefing breeze she lacks the stability for windward work. This boat reminds

ONAWA.

me, in fact, of Herreshoff's latest fin-keel models, without the fin.

There were other boats built and sailed with distinction in the fleet last season, of which mention should in justice be made. Chief among them is the *Charlotte,* owned by the Breezy Point Syndicate, and built by the Spalding St. Lawrence Boat Company, of Ogdensburg. She was designed by H. C. McLeod, of Chicago, who figured that the majority of races on Minnetonka would be sailed in light weather and built his boat accordingly, wherein he proved a much better designer than weather prophet. In fair winds she shared the honors with *Tartar,* the latter having slightly the advantage, but the Ogdensburg craft proved too tender for heavy winds, having plenty of beam but insufficient bilge.

The *Katrina,* owned by T. B. Janney, was another fast one turned out of the Peterson yard last year. She acquitted herself well in all sorts of weather, and could be relied on to finish close up to the winner in each race, but she was not quite fast enough to win, though as Mr. Janney wanted her for cruising purposes he expressed himself as thoroughly satisfied. She is certainly the handsomest boat on the lake, if not the fastest. Of the three Dyer boats, *Reveille, Swift* and *Alcyone,* while all of them were good-looking craft enough, not one came anywhere near championship form. The *Swift,* for instance, has the benefit of first-class handling, with William D. Morse at the tiller, and William G. Gale at the jib, but even with two such crack men to handle her she proved a total failure as a racing craft; and neither *Reveille* nor *Alcyone* did much better. The fault to be found with the Dyer boats last year was that the designer had gone to an extreme in cutting away forward, the result being that they were all down by the head. The boats were fast on a free run, but when it came to windward work they labored and could not be made to travel.

There was much of an interesting nature, too, in the contest for championship honors between the second-class sloops. Races were won by W. T. Rolph's *Bird,* built by Herreshoff several years ago, F. B. Long's *Tomahawk,* T. A. Sammis' *Answer,* and the Wilcox Bros.' *Beatrice,* which boat, designed by

Peterson, at last captured the honors in her class.

Perhaps the most interesting feature of recent development on Minnetonka consists in the growing tendency of owners to design their own boats. Each year finds some new boats on the lake built by amateurs. Probably the most successful of these launched during the last few years was one from plans prepared by Harry N. Whittlesey, a young student of naval architecture, whose home is in Minneapolis, but whose studies are being pursued on the Clyde. He launched his tiny sloop *Doris,* put up for William M. Tenny, when the season was more than half over, and by winning four races in succession captured the pennant in the special class. The cat honors for 1896 were gathered in by Theodore Wetmore's *Varuna,* an old-style, square-sterned boat, with an immense spread of canvas and conspicuous ability in windward work.

The *Siren,* owned by T. A. Sammis, and the *Varuna* are the latest of the old-style boats to continue racing, as the spoon-bows of recent seasons have taken the life out of these more ancient craft, though they are still used for cruising and general pleasuring, wherein they prove infinitely more satisfactory than the newer types. Almost any one of the older yachtsmen can be induced on slight provocation to tell a story in which the old *Pinafore, Susie Bell, Pearl, Catherine, Mary Lee, Peerless, Ida* and other ancient types, that would startle the critics nowadays, figure as champions. They carried all the sail they could crack on, had outrigger planks to hold them down, sandbags by the dozen, and unlimited crews.

When a few years ago Herreshoff introduced his famous forty-footer *Gloriana,* it became at once apparent that the old-style, hollow-lined boats would soon be known no more forever, at least so far as racing was concerned. Before this innovation, Captain J. B. Brooks, who came to Minnetonka from Bridgeport, Conn., was turning out all the winners on the lake, but the old chap never took kindly to "that new machine."

It was in the summer of 1893 that the first of the new-style models appeared, and they were well represented. In that year Edmund J. Phelps bought the famous Herreshoff sloop *Alpha,* a boat that had beaten everything in her class the year before on the Eastern coast, and Messrs. Peet and Dunwoody had ordered the *Kite* from the same designer. When these boats were launched at Minnetonka few dared to doubt that one or the other would win the season's championship, but here a local builder jumped into the breach as Peterson has done in the present season. Arthur Dyer, of the Deephaven yard, turned out for Mr. Ward C. Burton, the famous *Onawa*, better known as "The Wraith of Deephaven." The history of this boat for the season was one continuous line of victories. She won five straight races, defeating *Kite* and *Alpha* in hollow style, the two latter fighting it out for second place. *Onawa* won her races by anywhere from seven to sixteen minutes, though it should be stated here that the boat was built to take every advantage of the rules for that year, and she received nearly ten minutes' time allowance over *Kite* and *Alpha*.

In the following year the rules were so modified as to greatly reduce time allowance in all classes, as a result of which most new boats were built up to the limit, and the change proved thoroughly satisfactory all around. At this the *Onawa* withdrew from racing, and in 1894 the *Alpha* and *Kite* contested for first honors. *Kite* won the championship with four races to her credit, while *Alpha* captured the cup by winning three. The *Marie*, Dyer's latest creation at that time, would have won the championship in all probability, but

she was in charge of an almost totally inexperienced man with a green crew, and was, therefore, unable to do much good. However, she redeemed herself in 1895 by defeating both *Kite* and *Alpha*, handily winning both cup and championship.

In determining the rules of the past few years the club has kept chiefly in view the idea of placing the boats in their respective classes on as nearly an equal basis as possible with reference to time allowance, also that of decreasing the crews to a number sufficient only for the management of the boats.

Minnetonka is fifteen miles long, its shores for the most part being taken up with summer homes of Minneapolis and St. Paul people. Carefully trimmed lawns slope gently to the water's edge, while dense growths of elm and maple form a picturesque, irregular background of hues that are ever changing with the season's advance. The coast covers 120 miles. There are innumerable bays and inlets, each possessing its distinctive charm and contributing additional fascinations to this paradise of the Western yachtsman. Well has the poet sung—

Minnetonka, scene of peace,
    Thou home of beauty and of dreams—
No haven in the isles of Greece
    Could chord the harp to sweeter themes.
For houris haunt thy leafy glades,
    While scented zephyrs cool the air,
And looking down from azure skies
    The angels smile—thou art so fair—
        O Minnetonka!

CHARLES B. EUSTIS.   WM. PEET, JR.   WM. D. SAMMIS, SEC. AND TREAS., M. Y. C.

A Corinthian Cruise (1897)

A CORINTHIAN CRUISE.

LAKE CHAMPLAIN TO NEW YORK.

By Ralph Bergengren.

IT was high noon of a rainy, sultry summer day, one of those days when the weather seems to hesitate between a good cry and a hearty laugh, and ends in a maudlin drizzle. On the surface of Lake Champlain the morning wind had raised an insurrection, and an army of tireless little waves charged against the pier of the Champlain Yacht Club and our craft, the *Wanderer*.

The *Wanderer* was a sixteen-foot yawl, lap-streak, copper-riveted and built for salt water, provided with a pair of sweeps, a pair of light oars and two small sails. We had traveled in her before and knew how to utilize every inch of room. Boxes had been built to fit under the seats and provided for ice, food, camp utensils and a couple of oil stoves. Four canvas bags, fat with our personal luggage, hung along the sides, inside the rail. Under the bow grating was the ice-box, and under the forward seat stood the oil-stove boxes, with the cook-box sandwiched in between them. In the centre of the boat stood the grub-box. The inventive Fred had devised for the stern a snug lounging place, padded with the blankets and sweaters. On these reclined Harry, a picture of comfort, with pipe in mouth, legs crossed, feet in the air, and his bony hand on the tiller. John sat in front of him while I found room to manipulate the other sweep. The sails were folded along the side, the rubber blankets tucked carefully over all things wetable, and Fred, when he had thus made everything shipshape, was compelled to stow his own long body as best he might. Then we started.

Behind us the town of Burlington, with its spires and house-tops, and the tall tower of the University of Vermont soon lost itself in the gray mist. Along the west shore lay the Adirondacks, an indistinct outline, while ahead of us the lake rolled itself against a wall of fog which gave to it the effect of an ocean perspective. Out of this fog, some miles south of Burlington, rose the peculiar form of Dunder Rock, poking through the general gray like a small black iron-clad. As we drew nearer the illusion vanished and Rock Dunder stood for what it really is—a shrubby, patchy, little island with a hump like a camel's rising out of its tangled shrubbery.

Some miles south of Rock Dunder the wind shifted and we set mainsail and foresail of rakish cut, a compromise between lateen and spritsail. The wind was capricious, one moment bowling us merrily along, the next trying to head us off our course, always turning propitious again when we got out the oars. The mist we had left behind us.

About the time when we began to figure upon where we should pass the night, we ran across a man pulling a heavy scow leisurely northward. Would he tell us where we were? Not he. Was there a farmhouse near where we could get some milk or eggs? No reply. At least, was there a place near where we could camp for the night? To which he finally answered, "Vessel-dere," pointing a skinny forefinger at the next bluff. Then he rowed away from us.

Around the bluff we found the pier of the Seward-Webb estate, and beside the pier the steam yacht *Elfrida*, her masts clear cut against the sky, her brasses polished and her decks well holy-stoned, a sight to please the eye and rejoice the heart. At the shore end of the pier was a small cottage and on the piazza of the cottage sat the captain of the *Elfrida* in his shirt sleeves, smoking a short pipe. Could we camp near there for the night? Certainly, and he would be very glad to offer us the unoccupied loft of the cottage, which contained bunks. And so matters arranged themselves, and we thankfully accepted the loft. And later we fraternized with the crew who came in and played cards and smoked much tobacco and were jolly good fellows all.

It was seven o'clock when Fred routed us out. The morning was beautiful. The sun shone brightly; the birds sang in the trees and the little waves of the lake danced merrily as though they were shouting in their own fashion, "Come, play with us. Come, play with us. We'll wake you up if you'll give us half a chance to."

Harry was the first to accept the invitation. For a moment he poised on the edge of the pier. Then he went down—plunk—and came up in a moment with a handful of mud for the rest of us. As there is only one way to rid oneself of the effects of a volley of mud, we plunged in after him.

Ah, that morning plunge! How good it is! You roll from your blanket with your eyes half open and creep down to the waterfront. You stand a moment with the music of the morning in your ears and the cool breeze sending shivers all over you. You plunge, and a cold thrill shoots from your finger tips to the tips of your ten toes. And then you come up again and stand rubbing yourself down in the warm sunlight and feel that you are a man and are glad of it.

Two hours later, as we reluctantly pulled away from the hospitality of the *Elfrida*—hospitality that had taken the form of lodging and breakfast and stories and good-fellowship generally— the clouds were piling up to the south and west, and before we had lost sight of the boat-house, rain was falling. Nearer came the storm; west and north we could see it rolling along the mountains and sweeping across the lake, while the downpour steadily increased. Hill's Point seemed the nearest place to camp. As we reached it rain was falling heavily, but within five minutes the sun was again shining.

From Hill's Point we crossed the lake diagonally to Split Rock, where the cliff from which the spot is named marks the outlet of a small bay into the lake. The flash of the water was almost too dazzling and we turned our

bow instinctively to the quiet purple shadow of trees and rocks above which the white wall of Split Rock Light rose in sharp contrast with the cool, green foliage. Split Rock Mountain here comes down steep to the very edge of the lake, a giant Narcissus to a giant pool, and in its shadow we skirted mile after mile along the west shore. Then the dusk came and the sun like a great disk of fire went slowly down behind the dark mountain as we once more crossed the lake to Basin Harbor, and pitched our tent for the night.

Fred, the genius, was the man of importance when we pitched camp. It was he who had made the ice-box which fitted under the bow grating and of which to quote John, "only the top and one side were parallel." Fred had also originated the oil-stove boxes of peculiar shape and many virtues—and some vices—which lurked under the second seat. If you stood them up one way, there they stood, safe and sound, beautiful to see and pleasant to think about, but if you stood them up any other way —and there were eight other ways— little streams of oil would come rushing out, each little stream trying to come out quicker than its neighbor, like so many children stampeding from a school-house.

Fred was a worker by nature. He had been born so and had never avoided the results by learning to smoke, that sure refuge of those who fear to overwork themselves. We others smoked, and so we allowed Fred to do the extra work as the best means of putting in his leisure. So when the dinner was over and the dishes washed and the pipes lighted, Fred would take a knife and the hammer and a few sticks and nails and would go away by himself and begin tinkering at some contrivance of utility or comfort.

Next morning the wind still blew from the south, and of course it rained. The man of ingenuity therefore rigged an awning that protected the oarsmen and allowed us to keep on, and about noon we rowed into Arnold's Bay. We landed at a point where there was no shade and the sun, noting our position with the eye of a general, pushed aside the clouds and poured the fury of his rays upon us. Out on the lake the beautiful ever-changing water turned from gray to blue and the raindrops on the foliage along the shore danced and sparkled.

Port Henry is a small lake shore town and of course the toughest part is along the waterfront. Southeast, about six miles, lies Crown Point and the ruins of two old eighteenth century fortresses on the shore of Bulwagga Bay, and about opposite the traditional site of Champlain's famous battle with the Iroquois. We pitched our tent with the ruined forts behind us and the sun sinking behind Bulwagga Mountain. Before us lay the stretch of lake and mountain north and west, the mountains dark with the increasing twilight, the lake and sky colored to gold and pink and blue and purple by the Midas touch of the setting sun. Long after the sun had vanished, a patch of cloud high in the sky still glowed with the magic of his paint box and when this too faded away, it was only to give place to a full moon pouring over mountains, lake and ruins a glorious flood of untarnished silver.

About a ruined fort, as about anything that man has built and nature is slowly demolishing, there is a melancholy and yet not unpleasant interest. When we obtain the picturesque we must pay the artist's price for it, and Artist Nature demands that man shall have contentedly given his labor that his grandchildren may see it passing picturesquely away. So with Fort Frederick and with its sister fortress. Where once the feet of uniformed companies trod the earth to a barren level, the tall grass waves and repeats in nightly whispers what the dead men say who sleep underneath; on the parapets where men struggled and killed and died the young tree shoots out its green branches and revels in very joy of life with every passing breeze. And at night the moon lengthens the shadows in the old barracks and lights new fires in the long cold fireplaces until one seems to hear again the tread of the sentinel, or the laughter of the guard-room, the clatter of arms and rush of preparation as the news comes that an enemy is at the gate.

We ate breakfast to the music of distant church bells, and an hour later found us wrapped in rubber blankets that left only our heads visible and our corn cobs, and the rain pouring. The wind held fair, so, in spite of the rain, we kept on, traveling with the storm, while clear weather was plainly visible ahead, and the sun was shining on the hills five miles behind us.

Everything was wet by the time we got ashore, but the storm had ceased and a fire and pile of straw from a neighboring barn made things comfortable. Hot steak, black coffee, bread and country butter and cold milk from the ice-box soon made it a memory to laugh over.

That night the mosquitoes held high carnival. They came early, and most of them brought their friends. And so we sat in our dry straw, and with Fred in the middle, smoked mightily till bed-time, and then I, who knew from sad experience that there was no sleep for me, refilled the "Tramp" and settled down comfortably as possible for a night of it. It was not the first night I had spent that way, nor was it the first night that the Tramp had been my companion in a mosquito siege.

The Tramp is my favorite pipe. Years ago I picked him out from a dozen of his fellows. At that time I was a tramp myself, and so I christened him another, and since that day we have passed through many joys together— and perhaps some sorrows. How many only he and I know—and he never talks to anyone but his master.

Monday morning we drove to Lake George along the rough, picturesque, history-saturated road where the British marched in 1758 on their way to Ticonderoga and a French defeat, past the scene of Lord Howe's death and Ambercrombie's overthrow. The morning was beautiful, clear and crisp. The rains of the day before had cleared the atmosphere and deepened the beautiful greens of the foliage, and the transparent blue of the lake. The little creek, where Lord Howe met his death, seems even now to wear a deserted aspect, and one would hardly be surprised to hear the crack of a murderous rifle.

We even penetrated into the old magazine, remarkably well preserved, much to the scandal of our shore clothes, donned in honor of the drive. And then out along the crumbling, grass-grown parapet that one great nation built to be the bone of contention between two others, captured and recaptured again and again, garrisoned by the soldiers of France, of England and of the new-born Continental Congress, and held at last by nature and exposed only to the unresisted forays of the relic hunter. Then, after a comfortable dinner, we sailed away from Ticonderoga.

Ah, those breakfasts and dinners and suppers, when one has drunk deep of the open air as an appetizer! Many things can be accomplished with an old oil-stove if you but know how. And there are not many dishes to wash, and what we had were tin ones, which a little loose sand, or gravel, or rotten wood, or ashes, or dried grass, or what not, scoured till they shone again.

The run to Putnam took about three hours, and we left Putnam just before sunset under a light wind. As the sun set the wind died away, leaving only the smallest possible breeze, and under this we floated slowly southward. The moon rose over the dark hills, and we wrapped ourselves in our blankets and settled ourselves as comfortably as might be. Over everything was the deep uneasiness of night in the woods, the silence that seems one moment to cover all nature as with a woolen blanket and is broken the next by innumerable little sounds, the cry of the whip-poor-will, the grumbling of frogs along the shore, with now and then the snapping of a twig or the distant call of some lonely night-bird.

In time we saw far ahead of us and slowly approaching, a long line of dark objects, two abreast. It was our first tow of canal-boats, and the sight was one long to be remembered. Each barge had its light at stem and stern, and save for these lights there was no sign of human occupancy. As they passed us, each huge bulk cutting in its turn the crystal bar of moonlight, they seemed a spectral train born of the night and returning into it.

Soon after passing the tow we entered the Narrows. High banks, alternating with low marshy shores, prevented any immediate camp, and so we drifted along to the music of frog and whip-poor-will, burning much tobacco, and sometimes trying the echoes with our favorite song—wonderful echoes that tossed the chorus back and forth and up and down in words and sentences and simple, unintelligible shouts, as though the buccaneers were all alive again and rioting among the hills.

At one o'clock we made fast to an old pier opposite the sleeping village of Dresden and arranged things for the night. It was nearly noon when we breakfasted preparatory to starting for our last day on the lake, which had now narrowed to the dimensions of a beautiful river. The afternoon was intensely hot, but a light breeze served to carry us to Whitehall and the beginning of the Champlain Canal, where the gate of our first lock shut behind us.

Our first camp on the Champlain Canal was about two miles south of Whitehall on the west bank. In front was a sleepy little bay, a mere spoonful of water after our experience with the lake; overhead the heavy smoke of a smudge hung, through which a horde of canal mosquitoes strove vainly to penetrate. It is not pleasant eating in a thick smoke, and so we hurried the ceremony and hustled through the dish-washing and got ourselves as quickly as possible on the other side of the mosquito netting which guarded the door of the tent.

We covered the distance from Whitehall to Waterford in hot clear weather, with no breeze except that made by the motion of the boat. Almost immediately upon entering the canal we abandoned oars and took turns on the towpath. Nor was towing hard. The *Wanderer* was very light, and one could walk along the level path hardly feeling the pull of the boat at the other end of his tow-line.

Our progress was almost a triumphal march. Everywhere we met with friendly greetings. Our passport allowed us a speed of four miles an hour, and we just about made it. To be sure our "mule" was the object of much comment, but canalmen—pleasant enough fellows though they are if you take them right—are only human. The hat for the mule we had bought at Port Anne for twelve cents—a broad-brimmed straw that added the one touch to complete the animal's picturesqueness. And as he strolled along

"WE TOOK OUR TURNS ON THE TOW-PATH."

"THE WANDERER WAS MADE FAST TO THE STERN."

the tow-path with the "mule hat" upon his head, a cob pipe in his mouth, and a sixteen-foot boat hitched to his belt by a thirty-foot line, who could blame a passing boatman for a joke or two? Usually they offered to trade mules with us.

For three days we glided peacefully between the banks of wild flowers that sometimes almost hid the mule from view. All three days the sky was a cloudless field of blue. In the stillness of the clover-scented air we could hear the lazy drone of the summer insects, and here and there the mule would stir up a troop of yellow butterflies, and these would rise and flutter a moment about his white-robed figure before taking to flight. Cool bridges spanned the canal at intervals; huge canal boats poked lazily into view around the bends ahead of us and disappeared as lazily behind, and now and then we drifted past a herd of cattle wading out into the cool water and rubbing their heads affectionately together under the over-hanging trees.

Three days we towed thus along the canal and through its many locks, camping at night on the bank and defying the mosquitoes with smudges and netting.

There is something decidedly tomb-like about a lock (and we passed some twenty of them) as one sits in a small boat and the water comes tumbling, rushing in, sometimes turning your boat completely round before it raises it to the surface of the higher stream

outside. Still more impressive is it when you seek a lower level and the falling water drops you inch by inch into the well, while the dark, cold walls rise slowly about you and the patch of sky above your head grows smaller and smaller, until at last the heavy gates at the end of your prison swing open and you see the shining level of the stream flowing gently away under its quiet bridges and between its flowered-covered banks.

At Port Edward the Hudson river begins to run parallel with the canal. It would have been possible by making a carry at this point, to have immediately taken to the river, but we were all in love with the canal and felt that we must leave it all too soon even when it joined the Hudson at Waterford.

It was night when we finally passed from the canal into the river. The moon had not yet risen, but the four-mile stretch from Waterford to Troy was alive with pleasure boats and the laughter and gayety sounded strange to our ears after the quiet of the canal and lake. By the light of the moon we dined on milk and crackers, and then, when the dinner was over, we found that Fred had spilt the remainder of the milk down the open throat of " General Utility."

(The General was the small traveling bag which carried all our odds and ends, and got full every night and had to be straightened out every morning. And so it was that he happened to have his mouth wide open and Freddie tipped the milk-can into it.

While we were busy working over the General, a canoe, belonging to one of the local clubs, glided up, and the occupants, finding that we were strangers, offered to find us a camping place, an offer we gratefully accepted.

Next morning we sailed with a fair breeze past Troy, past the laundries, past a small beach and a flirtation between two coal heavers and a party of laundresses, and then out into nature again leaving smoking factories and crowded houses in the distance.

The wind was fair and strong and growing rapidly stronger. Soon the river began to get on its white caps and a few tugs plowing up stream left behind them wakes whose proportions warned us to beware if we should meet larger craft.

The wind increased in violence and the growing darkness warned us to get ashore. Cedar Hill was near at hand and here we ran the boat aground.

Sunday morning we drew away from Cedar Hill under a light breeze. The river was calm and we sailed quietly between low green hills and past small villages and single, pleasant-looking residences. As we passed the village of Stuyvesant Landing we could hear plainly the notes of the organ in the small square-towered church on the hill. We dined on board the boat.

About one mile north of Athens we camped for the night beside an enormous ice-house. South of us and opposite the village of Athens were the twinkling lights of Hudson, and now and then a steamer anchored there sent the white glare of her search-light streaming across the river.

Shortly after leaving Hudson we saw the Catskill Mountains rising bold and blue and rugged against the western clouds—"the mountains of the sky" indeed. Ah! those Indians! when they named a place they named it. No Thompson's Mountain or Jones' Creek, but "Beautiful Shining Water" and "Mountains of the Sky." All day we ran along in the shadow of the hills.

Late in the afternoon a heavy mist rose and we ate supper in the tent, the rain falling heavily. When we awoke in the morning the first sound to greet our ears was the same gentle patter that had lulled us to forgetfulness.

While we were at breakfast, Harry happened to glance up the river.

"By Jove, fellows," he exclaimed, "there comes our carriage!"

A big tow was coming down the river.

"We've got to hustle if we're going to get that," said Fred, beginning to gather up his traps.

Down came the tent in a wet unwieldy mass, and like so many ants we hustled back and forth to the boat, dropping our traps any way to get them in, and ourselves on top of the whole, seizing oars or tiller, whichever was nearest, and so out after that string of canal boats. We came up beside the

SOLID COMFORT—ON THE SHORE OF LAKE CHAMPLAIN.

last boat but there was no one there to take our line and we dropped behind.

By the time we had put the boat in order and were really ready for business

"MADE FAST TO AN OLD PIER."

another tow was visible through the rain. This time the race was easily won. The painter of the *Wanderer* was lengthened and made fast to the stern of the last boat and, as the rain ceased and the sky cleared, she entered upon the last stage of her journey. The "canallers" we found to be right pleasant fellows when we got acquainted—kind, cheerful, hospitable, a bit rough in their manners, perhaps, as men who swear naturally and without knowing it.

The tow consisted of thirty-four boats towing four abreast, a floating village with its houses and families and small children, some of the boats laden, many of them empty. Looking from the rear boat the spectacle was a curious one, the procession of barges stretching far ahead lead by a single steamer, a smaller one acting as convoy, dropping a boat here, taking on another there while the great whole never paused in its steady onward march.

After supper we sat with the crew of the canal boat and smoked our pipes, watched the stars come out and told or heard stories. Stories of the Brazilian Rebellion, where one of our hosts had served on a cruiser and made much prize money and spent it all in one wild month in New York afterward. Stories of accidents, of the breaking up of tows, of the Great Blizzard, and finally yawns and good nights.

I awoke just before sunrise. We had left the Highlands and the crescent moon was still trying to hold her own against the growing pink of daylight. Presently over the low hills the sun rose clear and very hot, and laid a long finger of fire across the water.

And then we cooked our last breakfast and ate it sorrowfully, shook hands with our friends the "canallers"—may good luck attend them—and climbed back over the rudder.

An hour later, when the Wanderer had been tossed and buffeted and thrown about by many wakes large and small, we helped to pull her out of the water and her cruise was over.

Champion Canoes
of Today
(1897)

W. C. NOACK, WINNER OF PADDLING TROPHY.

CHAMPION CANOES OF TO-DAY.

By R. B. Burchard.

THERE are two schools of canoeists, and the pendulum of their respective popularities swings now in one direction, now in the other. hold its original power, probably for the reason that the demands upon the racing man had become too exacting as the sport had grown more refined.

There is no prettier work afloat than canoe handling ; but, as it is now, it requires the mental skill of the boat sailor with the physical skill of the gymnast, and unfortunately there are few possessing the ability who are willing to devote themselves to so absorbing a sport. So long as there are half a dozen devotees who practically live in the canoe houses

Neither of them is likely to entirely supplant the other, for each of them in its own sphere meets distinct want. There be those of the old school to whom the canoe is the faithful companion and friend on all the silent highways ; who turn to it, year by year, as the trusty and well-loved transport to the heart of nature. On the other hand, there be those whose inventive skill is constantly exercised in the development of the highest form of naval design, and whose adventurous seamanship is satisfied with nothing but the excitement of personal prowess, the do and dare of fierce competition and the glory that crowns the successful contestant. But this impulse, during the past four years, had somewhat overreached itself, and had failed to

" MAB," SHOWING SAIL PLAN.

293

MAB," SHOWING STEERING-GEAR—FLAT SLIDING-SEAT.

tion, light displacement and shoal draught, and being sailed by one of the best canoe sailors, easily defeated the older and heavier canoes. There are many novel and interesting points about this canoe. It was designed and built by N. Gilbert, of the Gilbert Boat Company, of Brookville, Ontario. The length of the boat is sixteen feet over all, the beam thirty inches, and the depth eleven inches inside, amidships. The flat floor, common in racing canoes for many years, is abandoned, and the new boat's 'midship section shows a marked dead-rise, as was the case in Mr. Barney's famous *Pecowsic*. The keel is nearly straight, the bottom plank almost straight. The stem and stern posts are plumb, and they both meet the keel at nearly a right angle. The stem is out of water when the canoe is at rest.

The widest part of the canoe is at the fore end of the well, or about eight feet from the bow. There is no sheer to the deck-line, the gunwale being nearly the same height above the water amidships as it is at the bow and stern. The sliding-seat is five feet three inches long,

from the spring thaw to the autumn frost, the occasional sailor has no chance in the trophy races. He drops out of racing altogether, and is apt to adopt that method of canoeing which affords him the most fun at the least expenditure of effort. The incentive of emulation being gone the racing canoemen became lazy.

This state of things in the canoe world naturally roused apprehensions in the minds of those to contests most inclined, and the rule makers attempted to correct its tendency by limiting sail area. The result was similar to the effect of like restrictions in yacht racing; it did but stimulate the construction of a type of boat to meet the new conditions, and the restriction of sail area brought into existence the boat of lighter displacement.

It was these circumstances which, at the American Canoe Association meet at Grindstone Island last season, brought out the *Mab*, owned by Charles E. Archbold, of the Royal Canadian Yacht Club. This boat having been built of the lightest possible construc-

" PIONEER," SHOWING TRUSS SLIDING-SEAT.

UNDER REEFED SAILS.

and is raised eight inches above the deck.

The foremast is stepped about eight inches from the stem-head, and therefore, being shallow, it is supported above the deck by a circular wood block or collar, about eight inches in diameter and three inches in thickness. The sails, which are of union silk, are of the standing bat's-wing pattern, fitted with two battens from luff to leech, the total sail area being 126 square feet. The storm sails contain ninety square feet. As in nearly all the modern racing canoes, the sails neither reef nor lower. The spars are hollow, the pine sticks being cut in two, vertically, the two halves gouged out and then fastened together.

The hull is of ribband-carvel construction with white-cedar planking and deck, there being three planks to a side, running from end to end, one-eighth of an inch in thickness (three-sixteenths before finishing).

The centerboard is a thin plate of steel of the Linton Hope pattern.

Everything about the boat is studied with a view to lightness, the weight or ballast consisting of the crew, who is perched outside of the boat to windward, on the end of his five-foot sliding-seat, and manœuvers the craft by means of a five-foot thwartship tiller.

The ability to carry sail in such a light contrivance, depends entirely upon the skill of the canoeman; and so long as the boat carries sail and is held right

side up, it will skim over the water, borne by a breath that would scarcely move a heavier boat.

The *Mab* is built with the modern small shallow cockpit, whose floor is above the centerboard trunk, so that any water which enters runs out through the centerboard trunk. The cockpit is three feet long, eighteen inches wide, and five and a half inches deep. The centerboard slot bisects the whole cockpit, and runs twenty-five and a half inches forward of it and five inches aft. The centerboard itself is a Linton Hope dagger, straight on the fore edge and curved on the after edge. It, as well as the rudder, is made of fourteen gauge steel, tempered and trued. The board is three feet six inches long and eighteen inches wide. The centerboard trunk is made long so that the board may be dropped at any desired point, forward or aft.

A noteworthy feature of the construction of the *Mab* is her high sliding-seat, which is raised upon strong supports to a height of eight inches above the deck. The stationary part of the seat is supported not only in the usual method on the deck itself, but also upon blocks inside the coaming of the well, which rest upon a truss-work, that is in turn supported upon bases which rest upon the ribs of the boat in either bilge.

The Butler tiller slides in a horizontal collar which is, in turn, fastened to a

BELAYING SHEETS.

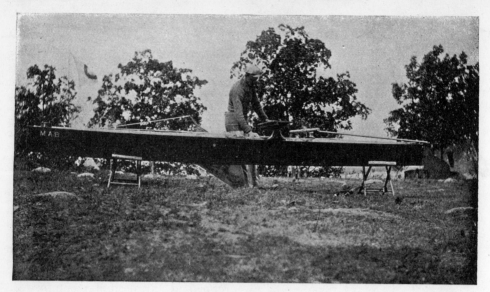

"MAB," SHOWING SHEER PLAN.

vertical collar which encircles the mizzen mast after the usual fashion. The construction of the brass collar is original, however. The photograph of the canoe, stern on, shows the arrangement of the sliding-seat, the deck tiller, and the "Norwegian" tiller. The latter is a device adapted from the Norwegian fishing boats, a number of which were on view at the Chicago exhibition. By this contrivance, instead of rudder lines or chains, a long stick is toggled to one end of the rudder yoke; the other end reaches away forward in the boat, so that the occupant thereof may grasp the stick and steer the craft from any part to which the steering stick may reach.

In the *Mab* and other canoes employing this device, the stick is toggled at one end to the rudder yoke, and at the other to the collar of the deck tiller. The advantage is that it is always taut, and never hanging loose; and it may be pulled or pushed, so that a single stick upon one side will serve the purpose of two rudder lines.

The fittings of the *Mab* are original, varnished rawhide frequently taking the place of brass. The fair leaders on deck are simply brass thimbles bound with rawhide. Stiff pieces of rawhide are also found to serve as cleats.

The rig of the *Mab* is so simple as to need no explanation, the photographs being self-explanatory. The sails being fast to the mast, there is only one line

to each. This is the sheet, which is double-ended, reeving through fair leaders so as to be readily reached from the sliding-seat upon either side of the canoe. The sheet is held by a cam cleat, the cam being provided with a long lever which may be operated by the toe of the skipper when he is so far out on the seat that the canoe can only be reached by that member. Thus, when a squall strikes, he leans far out on the end of the seat which has been extended far over the seething water. If he sees that, even with the leverage of the whole seat, he cannot hold up the canoe, he may slip a cam cleat with his toes, let the sheet go, and ease the vessel while the flaw passes.

The paddling trophy also was won by a newcomer with a new method, W. C. Noack, of the Detroit Boat Club and the Western Canoe Association, though some famous paddlers, including D'Arcy Scott, the champion of '93, and R. O. King, then the holder of the trophy, were in the race.

He defeated Mr. King by 38 seconds; Mr. Scott, by 1m. 22sec.; Mr. Bickerdike, by 3m. 22sec., and Mr. Plummer, of the New York Canoe Club, by 3m. 22sec. The course was laid out for a mile, but it was probably longer. Mr. Noack asserts that he paddles five hundred and twenty strokes to the measured mile, and this course was two hundred and forty strokes in excess of that.

Mr. Noack began canoeing in 1893,

and he has never been defeated in an open race. His first race was won in an open regatta, the tandem canoe race of '94, of the Northwestern Amateur Rowing Association. He was one of the winners in the same event in '95, winning in the record time for a half mile, 3m. 40sec. He again won in the same event in '96. Thus he has been one of the holders of the Northwestern Amateur Rowing Association tandem championship for the last three years in succession. Mr. Noack won his first single-canoe open race in '95, when he succeeded in securing the Northwestern Amateur Rowing Association championship, making half a mile in three minutes and twenty seconds, but sixteen seconds slower time than the record tandem event was paddled in. That time also is record time. Mr. Noack claims to have made the full mile, measured, in seven minutes and forty-three seconds against a head wind, in practice, without being pushed. He also won the championship in '96, thus holding the Northwestern Amateur Rowing Association single-canoe championship for the last two years. Last summer, at the meet of the Western Canoe Association, he won three first prizes, viz., the Minnehaha championship paddling cup (being the single-canoe championship of the Western Canoe Association), class one paddling, and the hurry-scurry. This last race was as follows: run twenty-five yards, swim twenty-five yards, climb into the canoe and paddle twenty-five yards, capsize, climb into the canoe again and paddle twenty-five yards to the finish.

The winning of the American Canoe Association trophy was Mr. Noack's tenth successive victory of the season.

His style of paddling and position are different from those of other canoeists. He is a firm believer in the sitting position. The position which will do away with as much lost motion as possible is, in his opinion, the best position; and the more steadily the canoe rides the less energy it requires to push it along. The Canadian paddler kneels, while Mr. Noack sits on the bottom of the canoe on a couple of cushions, his legs underneath the center thwart or cross-piece, so that his abdomen comes within about three inches of the thwart. The knees are raised, so that the thighs brace upward against the thwart. The feet are set against a light toe or foot brace on either side of the canoe, very little pressure being exerted against these braces.

It is claimed that, kneeling upon one knee, the paddler is enabled to take a longer stroke than in any other position; but he has that longer stroke on but one side, the right side, should he kneel on his right knee. This is not so on the left side, however, for, with the long stroke, he incorporates a body movement—a body roll sideways turns the upper part of his body to the right; but this he cannot so readily do when his stroke is on the left side, for then his kneeling position (his left knee being upward) prevents him from drawing his paddle as far back as on the right side. All this assuming that he paddles with a double blade. So the advantage, if any, of the long stroke, is found on but one side. By assuming the kneeling position, the paddler also cannot begin to keep his canoe as steady as if he were to sit in the bottom of his craft; and, therefore, he has a greater amount of lost motion to overcome. Lost motion means lost energy—means an expenditure of more power to propel the canoe; it means harder and more work for the paddler, and slower progress for the canoe.

The advocates of the kneeling position also claim that in that position an advantage is gained while paddling with the wind, in that the body of the paddler presents a greater surface to the wind. It is true that the wind will help the boat along; but it will also make the canoe more unsteady, and the advantage is doubtful. But, should the paddler encounter a head wind, it is wholly unnecessary to state that one in the kneeling position will be retarded vastly more than the sitting paddler, whose body offers less resistance to the wind, and whose canoe, by reason of his lower position, rides much more steadily and subject to less lost motion.

The sitting paddler, likewise, can extend his stroke far backward, if he wishes; but, when any paddler extends his stroke beyond a certain angle, back of the center of his body, he raises and carries water, and that means a waste of energy, with corresponding results. And by turning his body sideways, to extend the stroke, he throws his canoe from side to side—makes her ride more unsteadily: and that means lost motion, to overcome which additional energy is necessary. So it becomes apparent that the long stroke, extended far backward, is not so advantageous as it would appear. Paddling is not to be compared with rowing. The rower pulls with both arms at the same time, while the paddler dips his paddle on but one side at a time. It will be seen from the accompanying picture that, by assuming Noack's position, the paddler is firmly seated and braced, and, by so being, does away with all rocking—lost motion—of his canoe. His center of weight being lower, his canoe does not become top-heavy, as does that of the kneeling paddler, whose body is much higher, and therefore subjects his craft to become top-heavy.

A canoe is not a rowboat, and one cannot as readily do gymnastic feats therein as in the latter. The kneeling paddler is therefore obliged to devote some attention to balancing his canoe, a thing the sitting paddler is not obliged to do. The latter can devote all his attention and energy to propelling his canoe.

The god of winds is not always so obliging as to remain at home and give the paddler perfectly calm water. He is more apt to be attending to business, and buffeting the little canoe upon the opposing waves.

Mr. Noack's stroke is also radically different from that of other paddlers. It is an arm and shoulder movement, almost straight forward and back, with no body movement to speak of, his body being nearly rigid.

There is no recovery to his stroke, as with a body swing. He reaches far forward, dips but the width of his blade, all power being applied at the commencement of the stroke, the stroke not being continued beyond an angle of thirty degrees back of the center of the body. The paddle is held at an angle of about forty-five degrees, and it is pulled with the right arm and pushed with the left arm simultaneously, the center of the paddle being as if on a pivot. The paddle is turned on the half (one end of the blade horizontal and the other vertical), to save windage, and the blade feathered by means of the usual wrist movement.

The paddle used is of second-growth mountain spruce, eight and one half feet long. It has spoon blades, something like those of an oar, so that it will not carry water, but will grip the water almost at the moment it enters.

Mr. Noack's canoe is an open Canadian racing canoe, built of white cedar with Spanish cedar trimming, and weighing twenty-five pounds. It is 16 feet in length over all, 30 inches beam, and 10 inches in depth amidships; at the bow and the stern it is 15½ inches deep. It is provided with a very short deck at either end, like most Peterborough canoes.

Just as among the larger craft all are yachts whether propelled by sail or steam, so the standing-sail, sliding-seat contrivance is called a canoe as well as the paddling racer. All who go to the meets are canoeists. Perhaps it is just as well that all are not racing men. To him who will persevere until he may compete creditably in the races of the American Canoe Association there is opened a world of ecstasy such as few sportsmen realize.

"MAB," DOWN THE WIND.

The New Twenty-Footers (1897)

KENNEU.　　　　　　　　　　DAD.　　　　　　　　　　ASTHORE.

THE NEW TWENTY-FOOTERS.

By R. B. Burchard.

INTERNATIONAL competitions are always stimulating to any form of sport. That seems to be a platitude, but there are many estimable members of the opposition party around the yacht-club houses who pretend to deny it. Let them attend any of the races on the programme of the Long Island Sound Yacht Union and watch the performances of the eccentric fleet of small sailboats which have been hatched in the heat of international emulation during the past winter, and they will behold types of racing craft and witness a quickness in handling together with a speed in footing hitherto undreamed of in the annals of small-boat sailing. If one has followed the history of the competitions for the Seawanhaka Yacht Club challenge cup, if he has been one of the enthusiastic few who saw the *Ethelwynn* beat the *Olita*, and then the *Spruce IV.* in 1895 ; the *El Heirie* carry away the palm from the *Paprika*, the *Riverside* and the *Vesper*, only to suffer defeat at the hands, or rather at the heels, of the Canadian *Glencairn* in 1896, he has kept abreast of the times in boat-sailing, and he is prepared for almost anything in the way of freak or monstrosity that the present season may bring to light. But if the crews of the old-time sloops *Dare*

Devil and *Lily R.* could cast their weather eyes over their musty piles of sand-bags and behold our "jib and mainsail" sloops of 1897, they would see something to "make their two eyes start like stars from their spheres."

Racing restrictions always bring out eccentric types of boats, varying among themselves according to the ingenuity of the designer in his effort to make the largest boat out of the given measurements. But let the same rules stand for a few years, and the fleet will gradually become all of one general type. In all types of racing yachts the light-displacement canoe hull now has the ascendency, the at one time popular idea of deep hulls and accelerated momentum having become exploded. No better demonstration of the superiority of

DAD.

301

the light-draught and unballasted sail-boat over the deep, heavy one has been given than in the thrashing which the fifteen-footer *Paprika* gave the celebrated Bermuda dinghies last winter. These boats, which were described in OUTING, March, 1896, like certain cutter and canoe fleets on the other side of old ocean, for years enjoyed a world-wide renown for their speed, anterior to their lining up against boats of another type. The dinghies are ballasted with a cargo of lead, and when they fill they sink like lead. After a capsize and sinking the lead is fished up, and the boat, freed from its weight, rises to the surface. *Paprika* was taken to Bermuda and was sailed against and around these famous boats by Mr. Irving Cox, one of the New York designers.

An interesting problem will be solved this year concerning the best means of ballasting these small boats. Among the half-raters it was clearly proved that the best form of ballast was crew-ballast laid along the weather-deck, and that every pound of lead in a keel was a pound of useless cargo. From the manner in which *Glencairn* and *El Heirie* were sailed with their crews at times perched on the weather-topside, their legs waving wildly over the water, it would seem that the limit of size for a boat sailed on canoe principles had been

DAD.   KENNEU.

reached. Had "hyking" seats been permitted, the performances of these boats might have been amusing if not seamanlike. This year a restraining element upon freak development has been introduced by the mutual consent of the clubs interested, in limiting the sail-area to five hundred square feet. Although those who framed the agreement of which this rule is a part are acknowledged to be among the most skilled talent in practical boat-handling, there comes a wail from the discontented: "A tax on sail is a tax on skill." If we interpret the spirit of the Royal Canadian-Seawankaka competition correctly we understand it to be a match in boat-sailing and not in boat acrobatics; not that we have any wish to condemn the latter, for there is no prettier sport than canoe racing.

These races of small sailboats are designed by the yacht-clubs who patronize them to develop a new generation of amateur sailors; and that the international competitions inaugurated by the challenge of Mr. J. Arthur Brand have already served a valuable purpose toward this end is evident. The young Corinthians who frequent the waters where these boats have appeared, especially on Long Island Sound and the St. Lawrence River, have attained a skill in boat-handling which is probably unsurpassed. These spry little boats are not without their critics, however; and one of the Boston journals has attempted to throw the whole scheme into disrepute and ridicule, notwithstanding the fact that the American representative last year, Mr. Clinton H. Crane, the owner and designer of the *El Heirie*, is a graduate of the Boston Institute of Technology, and that his famous boat was built in a Boston yard.

Perhaps prejudice has been engendered by the innocent attempt to add these little boats to the yacht-club classifications, and to call them *yachts*. Such boats used to be called sailboats, and boat-sailing used to be considered a form of sport quite as distinct from yachting as is canoe-handling. The New York Yacht Club, last winter, in all its ponderous dignity, declined the proffer of an unequal union of the large fleet with the small one, in refusing to enter a union of small yacht clubs; but this course should not be construed as expressive of their disapproval of the

F. B. JONES AND W. IRVING ZEREGA.

sport of boat-sailing. This brings up the generic question, "What is a yacht, anyhow?" The old sailor's definition was comprehensive, though libelous: "A yacht is any kind of a vessel, from a dinghy to a full-rigged ship, where they carry liquor for a cargo and have a devil of a time." If all kinds of pleasure craft are yachts, then these little racing-boats are yachts, for they do certainly occasion a form of pleasure unsurpassed in sportsmanlike activity, and I doubt if the contestants in these races would exchange their place at the helm or sheet for the Sybaritic luxury of any steam-yacht afloat.

The Seawanhaka Yacht Club, however, in fostering the development of these swift sailboats, and in admitting young men to its club membership at a liberal discount from its membership dues, has augmented rather than compromised its dignity as a yachting organization; and if a new school of gentlemanly and skilled Corinthian sailors has been developed on Long Island Sound, it is because this powerful club has dignified the sport.

The Seawanhaka challenge cup, which Mr. Brand and his half-rater, *Spruce IV.*, failed to secure for the Minima Yacht Club of England, in the match races with the *Ethelwynn*, now is enshrined in the parlors of the Royal St. Lawrence Yacht Club, in Montreal, because of the superiority of Mr. G. H. Duggan's *Glencairn*, over Mr. Crane's *El Heirie*, the best of the American fifteen-footers of last year. That it may be borne back in triumph to its natural home in the Seawanhaka Yacht Club is the earnest wish of every member of that club, and of all the enthusi-

astic coterie of small-boat sailors on the Sound from College Point to Milford. The earnestness and spontaneity of this purpose was evinced in the prompt delivery of the American challenge last year, for as soon as the cheers that hailed *Glencairn*, the victor, had subsided, a launch put off from the flagship to deliver a challenge for the coming season to the Canadian representatives on the Committee boat.

The two years of racing in the little fifteen-foot boats in which the victory went once to American and once to British talent, have expounded a wholesome lesson to the participants in the more conspicuous international matches, by showing that yacht-races may be so well managed by good executive and committee work, as to leave little opportunity for subsequent dispute, and that the victory may be lost or won without acrimony.

It is a weakness of yachtsmen that they are never satisfied with what they have, and it should be a source of satisfaction to the happy owner of a small yacht that he is no worse off in this particular than he who owns a steamer or a schooner-yacht. There is always more room wanted for this, or more power for that; and it is probable that desire will keep ahead of wealth and invention into the infinities of time.

As soon as the fifteen-foot class had proved to be a success, and the smaller clubs had begun building one-design fleets, and the racing spirit had become

LE ROY DRESSER AND "SHARK."

KENNEU.   ASTHORE.

kindled, the insatiable desire for larger boats commenced its insidious work, and therefore the coming races for the international cup will be sailed in the twenty-foot class.

The following conditions have been determined upon by the two interested clubs, the Royal Canadian Yacht Club and the Seawanhaka-Corinthian Yacht Club of New York. The boats must not exceed twenty feet racing length by the Seawanhaka rule. According to this rule the racing length is determined by halving the sum of load-waterline length and the square root of the sail-area. The draft of keel must not exceed five feet, and a centerboard when it is down shall not exceed six feet. Centerboards must be constructed so that they may be fully

KENNEU.

housed, but the use of weighted boards is permitted. All ballast must be fixed, and no outriggers or sliding seats are allowed.

The total number of persons on board is limited to three, and the helmsman must be an amateur. The sails are limited to mainsail, jib and spinnaker; and the area of the mainsail and jib ("fore triangle") is not to exceed under the circumstances five hundred square feet.

The races are to be sailed without time allowance and with a "one-gun" start.

The necessary result of a limit to sail-area is the production of a boat of the lightest construction possible, designed so as to offer the least possible resistance to the water through which it is driven.

The boats entering this year's races

will probably be all of one general type as to hull-saucers and skimming-dishes; the principal distinction between them being that of fin-keel and centerboard. For stability, the former will depend upon a bulb of lead, probably of about seven hundred pounds weight, attached to the bottom of the fin, and the latter will be held up by the acrobatic powers of the crew. Of course the further the crew are capable of extending their bodies, arms, legs, shoes, anything of weight to windward the better. The sailor of slow motion and dignified disposition would better confide his reputation for social gravity to the vessel that rides over a fin-keel; the actively inclined will enjoy cable-car athletics in hanging on to the slippery bilge of an egg-shell center-boarder.

Nearly all of the boats will be fitted with a balanced rudder; such a rudder is hung below the hull, independent of the keel, and a small portion of the blade extends forward of the rudder-post. The effect of this contrivance, when fitted to a shallow hull, is to make the boat wonderfully sensitive to the helm, so that these boats fly about like ice-boats, doubling on their course like

SHARK.

a pursued hare. The drawback to the balanced rudder is that in light weather the helmsman is deprived of all mutual understanding between himself and the tiller. He can tell nothing by the pull of the helm, for there isn't any pull, and his eye must be constantly on the water and the sail. The consequence is that a race is a far greater strain upon the nervous resources of the helmsman than of old; but the boats have a quick-

ness in handling which was unknown before the days of the balance-rudder.

In anticipation of the coming contest there are two fleets of these little racing boats now preparing, one on Long Island Sound, the other on the waters of Lake St. Louis. The former are to compete for the distinction of upholding the challenge of the Seawanhaka Yacht Club, and those of the Canadian fleet are striving for the honor of defending the cup for the Royal St. Lawrence Yacht Club. The American trial races will be sailed at Oyster Bay on July 12th and two succeeding days, and the Canadian races will take place on the club course near Dorval, beginning August 2d. The international races will take place at Oyster Bay, Long Island Sound, on August 14th and the succeeding days. The preparation on the part of the Canadians, so far as the building of the fleet is concerned, is for the most part under the direction of Mr. G. H. Duggan, the successful designer and skipper of the *Glencairn*, which won the coveted cup last season. No less than seven boats have been built for different Canadian yachtsmen under Mr. Duggan's direction. These will sail against one another, and then against the Cuthbert boats from Toronto, and such others as are entered. The best of all will be chosen as the Canadian defender.

The preparatory work thus being guided by one experienced hand, the best results of unified effort are secured. Mr. Duggan will thus be enabled to work out his various ideas and to compare his various boats together under the best possible conditions. Such a method should accomplish a great deal for the science of boat-designing in two such active seasons as the last and the present have been upon the St. Lawrence. The American yachtsman who have followed the races of these sprightly little fleets know well enough from the defeat they suffered last year that they have an adversary of the finest mettle to contend with. The American representative of last year, Mr. Clinton

Mr. W. P. Stephens's designs, he having built the successful *Ethelwynn*, and being one of the most skillful designers of small boats.

Some of the more prominent of these boats are described in detail in our Monthly Review at the end of this magazine. At the early part of the season the owners are very canny, and perhaps unduly timid in giving out information concerning their boats, and somehow only a fairly general descrip-

ASTHORE.

H. Crane, of Boston, is pursuing the same method in the construction of three boats, but otherwise it is each man for himself on the American side.

Good boats will be built for the American challenge. Boats have already been turned out by Gardner & Cox, Charles Olmstead, Clinton H. Crane (the owner of the fifteen-footer *El Heirie*), L. D. Huntington, Jr., and R. E. Fry. It is also rumored that Mr. Paul Butler is quietly building a twenty-footer. It is remarkable, that no one of the new fleet has been built from

tion can be published before the racing has commenced.

The races promise good sport, and will tend to inculcate the idea that the best fun is often obtained in the smallest craft.

There are undoubtedly many "dark horses" still to be heard from, and as was the case last year, the best boats may appear only at the last minute and bear away the palm. The sport will be spirited and interesting, and neither the Canadians nor the Americans will be content with defeat.

The Challenge
of the *Shamrock*
(1899)

THE CHALLENGE OF THE "SHAMROCK."

BY A. J. KENEALY.

WM FIFE, JR.,
The designer of *Shamrock*.

THE cheering news of a challenge for the *America's* Cup caused yachtsmen to rejoice on both sides of the Atlantic last summer. Now that challenger and defender are nearly completed, both countries are eager for the contests and anxiously watch for every fragment of information concerning the *Shamrock* and her rival.

Frankness and fairness characterized all the preliminary negotiations from the issue of the challenge to its acceptance. The conditions of the race were agreed upon by a delegation from the Royal Ulster Yacht Club, which assumed the challenge of Sir Thomas Johnston Lipton, and they were ratified by the Committee of the New York Yacht Club. There was a gratifying desire for a rattling good race, which reminded all hands of the days when Lieutenant Henn, the generous, the chivalric, brought over his "tin-frigate" *Galatea* to sail against *Mayflower*.

The Royal Ulster Yacht Club is a thoroughly representative and sportsmanlike body. Its commodore is the Marquis of Dufferin and Ava, who as Governor-General of the Dominion of Canada did much to cultivate cordial relations with the United States. He has been for many years an honorary member of the New York Yacht Club. The Marquis is a thorough yachtsman, and one of the best handlers of small craft to be found anywhere. He is a good sportsman and traveler, and his "Letters from High Latitudes," containing a vivid description of a polar voyage in the *Foam* in 1856, show high literary qualities. He is a member of the Royal Yacht Squadron.

Sir Thomas Lipton is a self-made man. He was born in Ireland, brought up in Scotland, and is a citizen of the world. He is a wealthy merchant, and

has large interests in this country. Though by no means a representative racing yachtsman, he has long taken a general interest in the sport. He joined the Royal Ulster Yacht Club in 1897 in order, it is hinted, to induce that club to challenge in his behalf for the *America's* Cup.

Sir Thomas is the third Irishman who has challenged for the cup, the first having been Lieutenant William Henn, R. N., and the second Lord Dunraven. The Royal Northern, a Scotch club, fathered Lieutenant Henn's challenge, while the Royal Yacht Squadron acted for the Earl of Dunraven, as it did also for Sir Richard Sutton, whose cutter *Genesta* was beaten by the *Puritan*.

Genesta, *Galatea*, *Thistle* and the two *Valkyries* were built on the Clyde, the first two from the design of Mr. Beavor Webb, an Irishman, and the other three from the design of Mr. George L. Watson, a Scotchman.

When the challenge was sent, Sir Thomas announced that the *Shamrock* would be a 90 foot cutter from the design of William Fife, Jr., of Fairlie on the Clyde. His intention at that time was to have her built at Belfast by Messrs. Harland & Wolff, the famous firm that constructed all the White Star fleet, including the *Oceanic*, the largest steamship afloat. This firm, however, does not make a specialty of yachts, and the order for the hull was placed with the Thorneycrofts, of Chiswick and Blackwall on the Thames, a firm celebrated for torpedo boats of rare velocity.

Immediately upon the receipt of the challenge Commodore John Pierpont Morgan, of the New York Yacht Club, ordered the Herreshoffs to build a yacht to meet *Shamrock*. He also prevailed upon Mr. C. Oliver Iselin to superintend the building of the yacht and also to "tune her up" for the cup races. Mr. William K. Vanderbilt, who is now the sole owner of *Defender*, placed that famous craft at the disposal of Mr. Iselin, as a pacemaker, but it is understood that the expense of repairing, fitting out and running *Defender* will be borne by Commodore Morgan, who also refused to allow any of his brother yachtsmen to contribute toward the cost of the new vessel.

The circumstance that some form of manganese bronze in conjunction with nickel steel has been used in the hulls of challenger and defender would seem to indicate that in the important matter of lightness there will be little difference between the two yachts.

Valkyrie III. is a composite vessel, with steel frames and wooden planking, and she is thus considerably heavier than the *Defender*, whose bronze underbody and topsides of aluminum composed the ideal combination of lightness and strength, being as far ahead of *Valkyrie III.* in this important particular as *Vigilant* was in advance of *Valkyrie II.*

Mr. Fife, by going to a crack firm of fast torpedo-boat builders for the hull of *Shamrock*, has shown excellent judgment. The success of the firm has been great in turning out strong, light and remarkably fast steam vessels. The experience of the Thorneycrofts, extending over many years, has, no doubt, been utilized by the talented designer of *Shamrock*, and I have no doubt that the challenging yacht is at least as light as Commodore Morgan's defending vessel.

So far as form is concerned, with all the cup challengers and defenders before him—in addition to the lessons learned from his own experience with *Calluna* and *Ailsa*—the *Shamrock* will doubtless be a down-to-date racer in all that the term implies. These are some of the reasons that lead me to believe that this year's contest for the cup will be replete with interest. I also believe that the challenger has a fighting chance of winning the cup, having formed this opinion from the reports of competent judges who have had the opportunity of examining the design of the *Shamrock* and are enthusiastic in its praise. These men are, moreover, not of the kind likely to "go off at half-cock."

Much speculation has been indulged in with regard to the shape of the new Herreshoff champion. It may safely be presumed that Mr. Herreshoff, recognizing all the advantages of a big boat, has built as close as he dared to the 90-foot limit. Equally certain is it that he has embodied the principle of the fin keel into the model as far as he possibly could. Bearing in mind that all the Fife boats are very fast off the

wind, an attempt has been made to improve on the reaching qualities of *Defender*, the triangular courses giving many opportunities for that branch of sailing.

Defender was a remarkably stiff boat. I saw her caught in a heavy squall in one of her early races against *Vigilant* off Sandy Hook. *Vigilant* dowsed her club-topsail in a hurry, and kept her lower sails lifting with a fisherman's luff until the worst of the puff was over. *Defender*, on the contrary, started neither halyard nor sheet, but kept all sail set and was allowed to drive through it with everything clean full. I saw her in another squall off Newport when she carried away her gaff, which prevented her from winning the Goelet Cup, which was won that year by *Vigilant* This was the cause of her being fitted with the steel gaff and the steel boom which she carried during her races with *Valkyrie III.* and which answered thoroughly. Mr. Iselin approved them highly, and the new craft will be rigged with them also.

Expert sailmakers speak in praise of the special brand of duck manufactured for the sails of Commodore Morgan's yacht. It has been so woven as to guard against the uneven stretching which caused so much trouble with *Defender's* "muslin." If it is true, as I hear, that the new craft's boom will measure in the neighborhood of 110 feet, the mainsail will be a "regular whopper" and no mistake. It will be recalled that *Defender's* racing main boom was 105 feet in length, the same as *Valkyrie's*, and when that dimension was reached it was thought that the extreme limit had been arrived at.

To sum up, Nat Herreshoff has aimed at a lighter craft than *Defender*, one equally stiff, a better reacher and faster runner, and one quite as able in windward work.

Whether all these objects have been attained will soon be known, for the races between the new craft and *Defender* will be eagerly and critically watched by experts. There is sure to be great rivalry between the Scandinavian crew of *Defender* and the seamen from Deer Island, Me., that will man Commodore Morgan's vessel. It was, I think, a capital idea of Mr. Iselin to arrange to have the two boats sailed by men of different nationalities, the object being to arouse the keenest competition. The crews are to get prize money in all the races that occur between the craft, so that there will be the most powerful incentive possible for really smart yachtsmanlike work.

It is needless to expatiate on the fillip to yachting generally that the rivalry between the *Shamrock* and her Yankee opponent is sure to engender. Let us concede that the boats are useless except as racing machines; that when the contest for the *America's* Cup is concluded the careers of both craft

his courage in issuing the challenge, which means the expenditure of a vast sum of money and the enduring of a heavy weight of responsibility. Commodore Morgan, in assuming all the expense of building a cup defender, has shown that he is well and plenteously equipped with patriotism and sportsmanlike spirit.

JESSICA, DESIGNED BY FIFE.

are over; that because of their excessive draught of water they cannot possibly be used as cruisers, and that, owing to their great expense to keep in commission and the lack of class competitors, there is no future for them in the sport of racing. But, granted all this, when we consider the patriotic enthusiasm aroused in two great seafaring nations, the keen rivalry excited between the yachtsmen of Great Britain and the yachtsmen of the United States, who is there bold enough to proclaim that the game is not worth the candle? In my opinion Sir Thomas Lipton is entitled to the gratitude of all yachtsmen for

There are two yachting factions on the Clyde. One worships at the shrine of George L. Watson, who designed the *Britannia* for the Prince of Wales, the *Meteor* for the Kaiser, and the three *Valkyries* for Lord Dunraven. The other bows down before the altar of William Fife, Jr.

Watson has by far the larger *clientèle*, having designed, in addition to his squadron of superb racing craft, a large fleet of magnificent steam yachts for American and European millionaires. But there are hundreds of canny Scotch experts who, in spite of the shortcomings of *Calluna* and the ill-luck of *Ailsa*, believe that Mr. Fife can, if he tries really hard, produce a faster cutter than Mr. Watson.

The name of William Fife, Jr., is quite as familiar to American yachtsmen as it is to the devotees of the grand sport on the Clyde, where so many of the racing cracks of the past half century have been launched from the famous old yard at Fairlie, in Ayrshire. The advent of the 53-foot cutter *Clara*, which arrived in New York in 1885, was made interesting by her subsequent successful racing career, in which she sailed away from nearly all the American craft that were bold enough to enter the watery lists against her. Her performance against the shoal centerboard yachts that were so popular hereabouts some dozen years ago did very much to demolish the high estimation in which that type was held.

All doubts concerning her sea-going abilities were dispelled by the fact that she sailed across the ocean under her own rig, reaching port without a strain, although she had been subjected to the stress of more than one Atlantic gale. Thus she had cogently demonstrated that it was possible for a long, narrow boat with a small lead mine on her broad keel to cross the Western Ocean in perfect safety and comparative comfort. As a matter of fact, *Clara*, when hove to under her trysail in mountainous seas, rode their steep sides with duck-like buoyancy—easy as an old shoe. So much for her seaworthy qualities.

With regard to speed there was only one boat—the *Anaconda*, designed by Phil Elsworth—that could put up any kind of a race against her, and then only in moderate weather. Whenever it blew hard the "lead-mine" ran away from the "skimming-dish." The American experts pondered much, but the general custom was to sneer at and ridicule what was termed the "cutter craze." This, too, in spite of the ten-ton cutter *Madge*, designed by George L. Watson, Fife's rival, which, in 1881–2, beat the three best American boats that could be found to sail against her, scoring six wins out of seven starts.

In 1888 the 40-footer *Minerva*, a cutter also, designed and built by young Fife, boldly sailed across the Atlantic and beat the whole fleet of Burgess boats in the same class, maintaining her superiority for two seasons and eventually succumbing to *Gossoon*, a keel craft of higher power, designed by Mr. Burgess especially to beat her. Charles Barr, a young Scotchman, sailed her with ability in all her contests.

It may fairly be urged that no two other racing boats that ever visited these waters from transatlantic ports excited so much keen rivalry on the part of New York and Eastern yacht designers and yacht owners as did *Clara* and *Minerva*. It may also be advanced without fear of contradiction, that these two Fife fliers had a great influence in improving the type of the American racing yacht, in abolishing the "splasher," the "skimming-dish," the "sandbagger," and other vicious and dangerous classes that were then in the heyday of their popularity and renown.

It is as a designer of comparatively small racing yachts that William Fife, Jr., has gained most fame. George L. Watson and he are close rivals in the 20-raters and 40-raters. The first large modern racing cutter turned out from Fife's board was the *Calluna*, built in 1893, simultaneously with *Valkyrie, Britannia* and *Satanita*. She was owned by a syndicate of Scotch yachtsmen, headed by Mr. Donaldson, and was built with a view, if she proved fast, to challenge for the *America's* Cup. She was, however, a disappointing boat, starting in thirty-six races and winning only two firsts and eight other prizes. She sailed several races in which the American *Navahoe*, owned by Mr. Royal Phelps Carroll, competed, but the Yankee craft was on the whole faster than she.

Yachtsmen may be interested in the circumstance that in that season of 1893 *Britannia* had in forty-three races, three new lower masts, one topmast, two bowsprits, and one gaff; *Calluna*, one new lower mast, one main boom, and one gaff; *Valkyrie*, one new lower mast, one topmast, one boom, and one bowsprit, and *Satanita* one new bowsprit and one boom. The season seemed to be a very trying one on spars, and consequently on the bank accounts of the yacht owners.

The next large vessel that Mr. Fife designed was the racing cutter *Ailsa*, which was built for Mr. A. Barclay Walker, to beat the Prince of Wales' cutter *Britannia*. She sailed her maiden races in the Mediterranean in the spring of 1895, and won some valuable prizes. Her subsequent performances in British waters during the same season were less gratifying. She is 126 feet over all, 89 feet on the load water-line, with a beam of 26 feet, and a draught of 16 feet. This year she is rigged as a yawl.

Capt. Tom Jay, who sailed her across the Bay of Biscay, when questioned as to whether, with a forefoot so much cut away, and a stern-post so raking, she was not an awkward craft to handle in a seaway, said :

"Believe me, sir, it's not always so much the craft that's awkward as the people that's in her. Of course, being so easy to drive, craft like *Ailsa* reach faster than the old-fashioned vessels, and that makes them drive harder into the seas, but that is mostly a matter of the canvas you set. Of course, the worst time is when you're sailing a point or two free, because then they go their ten knots, and that means that they throw it about a bit."

He gave the interviewer the general impression that *Ailsa* was a thoroughly good sea-boat, even if a little afflicted with the habit of throwing the spray about a bit in a piping breeze.

On the occasion of Lord Dunraven's last challenge for the *America's* Cup, he was granted the privilege of substituting for *Valkyrie III.* another vessel of approximate dimensions. He obtained this concession because the Fife cutter *Ailsa* was at that time deemed a most formidable vessel. Her victory over the Prince of Wales' cutter, *Britannia*, in her maiden race at Cannes, on March 7, 1895, when she made her début in a suit of sails imperfectly stretched, and with a topmast so defective that a jib-topsail could not be properly set, gave the Watson contingent a great scare.

This scare was not diminished when, in a subsequent race off Nice on March 29, *Ailsa* again beat *Britannia*, winning a handsome trophy valued at $2,500, presented by James Gordon Bennett. The trophy was a punch-bowl of silver, with a capacity of fifty quarts, made by Tiffany, of New York.

Ailsa raced during her second season in the Mediterranean, making the record passage from the Needles to Gibraltar in five days twelve hours. She returned in May, her passage from Gibraltar taking nearly twenty-one days, having head winds all the way. She sailed up Southampton Water flying twelve winning flags.

In spite, however, of her brilliant victories in the Riviera events, *Ailsa*, like *Calluna*, never distinguished herself in home waters, *Britannia* getting the better of her in an exciting series of races.

Experts from this country who have examined *Ailsa* profess to see a number of characteristics of *Vigilant* embodied in the Scotch yacht. This is probably correct, as yacht designers, like authors, learn from each other and are apt to adapt good ideas wherever encountered.

There is little doubt that *Vigilant* or *Defender* would find it an easy task to defeat *Ailsa*. But Mr. Fife has, no doubt, profited by the mistakes he made in *Calluna* and *Ailsa*, and the new *Shamrock* may be expected to prove a formidable rival. So far as the quality of the *Shamrock* is concerned, expense has been a minor consideration. We may thus look forward to a contest with a craft of highly scientific construction, propelled by sails of irreproachable cut and fit, sailed by the best amateur and professional talent that Great Britain, famous for its yachtsmen, can produce.

Mr. Fife will also have an extra incentive for designing a winner, in the fact that Mr. Watson, his chief professional antagonist, has made three successive failures—*Thistle, Valkyrie II.* and *Valkyrie III.* having been beaten, respectively, by *Volunteer, Vigilant* and *Defender*. This may have stimulated Mr. Fife to excel himself, and in that case a very superior vessel must be encountered.

It may be mentioned that Mr. Fife has already made a successful début in international yachting, having designed the *Canada* which beat the Chicago craft *Vencedor* in the race for the cup offered by the Toledo International Yacht Race Association, in 1896, at Toledo, Lake Erie. The *Canada* was a forty-foot fin-keel craft similar to the Fife 20-rater which raced against *Niagara* the same season in British waters. *Vencedor* was practically a duplicate of the Herreshoff boat *Niagara*. Three races were sailed, the first being called for lack of wind to finish, *Canada* winning the second by 23 m.,

34 s., corrected time, and the third by
26 seconds, corrected time. It was
pointed out to the winners that the
Dominion ought not to claim too much
honor for the victory, as the *Canada* was
a Scotch boat in every respect. It was
also urged that Chicago need shed no
tears, as *Vencedor*, by the wildest stretch
of imagination, could not claim the
Windy City as her true origin. As a
matter of fact *Vencedor* was designed
by Mr. Theodore Poeckel, who, for a
number of years, was associated with
the Herreshoff Manufacturing Company
of Bristol, R. I., and who had the advantage of intimate acquaintance with the
plans of Mr. Howard Gould's *Niagara*,
which had raced so successfully against
the British 20-raters. Thus when ana-
lyzed it will be seen that the contest resolved itself to a virtual battle royal
between Fife and Herreshoff, with victory to the Scotchman.

It is worth recording that the frames
of *Canada* were got out at the Fairlie
yard, that the sails were made by Ratsey
& Lapthorne, and that the standing and
running rigging were prepared under
Fife's direction; and that all these were
shipped from the Clyde to the Andrews
shipyard at Oakville, near Toronto,
where the lead keel was cast already, so
that all that remained was to set up the
frames, and plank and deck the boat
according to Fife's specifications. Thus
in less than ten weeks after the boat
had been ordered by cable she was
launched and had sailed her maiden
race against *Zelma*.

Among the boats designed by Mr.
Fife, Jr., for Canadians may be mentioned *Cyprus, Zelma, Vox* and *Vidette*.
These craft were so successful as to insure him a wide popularity on the Lakes.
Among the vessels of his design that fly
the stars and stripes are the 53-foot cutter *Clara*, owned by J. Howard Adams,
of New York; the 40-foot cutter *Minerva*, owned by Joseph E. Fletcher, of
Providence, R. I.; 42-foot cutter *Uvira*,
owned by Clifford V. Brokaw, of New
York; 46-foot cutter *Barbara*, owned by
C. H. W. Foster, of Boston; 33-foot cutter *Delvyn*, owned by M. Roosevelt
Schuyler, of New York; 46-foot cutter
Jessica, owned by Joseph M. Macdonough, New York; 43-foot cutter *Kestrel*,
owned by J. B. Miles, of Bristol, R. I.;
41-foot cutter *Ulidia*, owned by W. Seymour Runk, of Philadelphia; 36-foot

cutter *Yama*, owned by Allan Ames, of
Oswego, N. Y., and the 36-foot yawl
Albicore, owned by Seymour J. Hyde,
New York.

The only yacht designed by Mr. Fife,
Sr., that is flying the flag of the United
States, so far as I can discover, is the
91-foot schooner *Lady Evelyn*, launched
in 1870 and brought to this country by
Sir Roderick Cameron, and now owned
by A. E. Towner, of New York.

For three generations or more the
Fife shipyard, at Fairlie on the Clyde,
has flourished. Mr. R. T. Pritchett, the
well-known British yachting writer, has
recorded that the steamer *Industry*,
built by Fife, plied some sixty years between Greenock and Glasgow unceasingly, and was still in existence, but lying on the mud at Haulbowline, in 1886.
This goes to show that good work and
good material were the grand characteristics of the old shipyard then, as they
are now.

It may be mentioned that in addition
to his accomplishments as a naval architect the younger Mr. Fife is a skillful
mechanic and one of the smartest amateur boat sailers on the Clyde. Briefly,
he can design a yacht, build her and
steer her to victory. Mr. Watson can
compete with him creditably in all these
arts. Mr. Beavor Webb, in his younger
days, had the reputation of being one
of the best amateur helmsmen in Great
Britain. It is somewhat remarkable
that the three British naval architects
who designed the five cup challengers
are not only experts at the drawing-
board, but also thoroughly familiar with
the practical part of yachting from the
construction of the hull to the rigging
of the boat, the setting of the sails and
handling the craft to the best advantage
under canvas in light or heavy weather.

Mr. Edward Burgess was also an expert at the tiller or wheel, and few pro-
fessionals can teach Nat Herreshoff any
new "wrinkle" in the sea-jockey's lore.

Mr. William Fife, Sr., after fifty-five
years almost constant work in a shipyard in the building of yachts and small
vessels, was greatly interested in the
bulb fin when it came out first. The
boys of Fairlie made several models of
the famous Herreshoff craft, *Dilemma*,
and sailed them with much zeal. Some
of the naval architects and shipbuilders
also tried their hands at whittling out
fin keels and racing them for modest

From a photograph by West, Southsea.

"AILSA," DESIGNED BY FIFE.

wagers. Mr. Fife competed likewise, his craft being a three-foot model of his first big cutter, *Cymba*, built in 1853. The old gentleman was delighted that he was able to beat the very best of the "fins" in going to windward.

There was a representative collection of models of Fife-designed boats at the English Yachting Exhibition of 1897. Among them was the cutter *Gleam*, designed by William Fife, Sr., in 1834, which, by her speed, brought much fame to the Fairlie shipyard. The *Tiara*, 1850, and the *Cymba*, 1853, showed the progress made in design and construction in twenty years. The famous *Fiona*, *Foxhound* (1870), *Bloodhound* (1874), *Sleuthhound* (1881), the last-named three being celebrated forties, designed by the firm for the Marquis of Ailsa, also bore evidence of yachting development, while the almost invincible *Annasona* and the *Isolde*, *Hester* and *Saint* brought the history of the firm almost down to date. Not that this list enumerates one tenth of the yachts for which the Fifes, *père et fils*, are responsible, but it is fairly representative of the splendid type of craft turned out.

The crack forty, *Isolde*, in two seasons won for her owner, Mr. Peter Donaldson, no less than £2,162 in prizes, while *Annasona*, built in 1881, in her second season won more than £1,500, being skippered by O'Neill. *Annasona* was (and still is, I believe,) the flag-ship of Major Bogle, Commodore of the Royal Torbay Yacht Club. She is perhaps the most celebrated forty-tonner ever built. In 1894 the Fife twenty-raters, *Luna*, *Thelma*, *Zenita* and *Dragon*, won forty-four first and thirty-five other prizes, valued at £1,125, against the twenty-seven first prizes, and forty-three other prizes, valued at £589, won by *Asphodel*, *Deirdré*, *Inyoni*, *Stephanie* and *Audrey*, designed by Mr. G. L. Watson, Mr. C. Nicholson, Mr. C. P. Clayton and Lord Dunraven respectively.

These few instances give an idea of the kind of man the New York Yacht Club will have to encounter; and no doubt the senior and premier yachting organization of the United States will make the requisite arrangements, as in the past, to insure a series of interesting races and to successfully defend the cup.

It has been the custom of the New York Yacht Club to select as champion the best boat available, and with that end in view it has held trial contests open to the craft of all recognized American clubs, that might be suitable for the defence of the historic trophy. For three proud seasons Boston bore off all the glory of the international races, the Burgess yachts, *Puritan*, *Mayflower* and *Volunteer* having beaten *Genesta*, *Galatea* and *Thistle* in 1885, 1886 and 1887. To meet Lord Dunraven's *Valkyrie II.*, Boston built two vessels, the *Jubilee* and the *Pilgrim*, which proved less speedy than Herreshoff's *Vigilant*. In the last cup race, in 1895, Boston had no representative trial boat, *Defender* being probably considered good enough to tackle Lord Dunraven's big cutter.

The contest this year will be between the new Herreshoff boat and *Defender*, both of which will be raced persistently and continually. Yacht designing is not an exact science, and *Defender* has not yet had her capabilities fully developed. Many yachtsmen believe that the new boat will not defeat *Defender*, especially in windward work. They are convinced that in any event the old champion will put up a capital race and distinguish herself in 1899 as she did in 1895. Finally, the American nation may be assured that every possible effort will be made to keep on this side of the ocean the cup which the schooner *America* won so gloriously in 1851, and which our British rivals have made since then so many gallant efforts to recapture.

The New Yachts
of the Year
(1899)

THE NEW YACHTS OF THE YEAR.

BY A. J. KENEALY.

THE steam pleasure fleet of the United States may be said to have been destroyed in the late war, though happily not by the Spaniards ; it was depleted by Uncle Sam, and an important aid it was in the national crisis. The removal of so many of the largest and fleetest yachts from the ranks of pleasure has made much activity in shipbuilders' yards, and the cheerful tap on the rivets has enlivened many a seaport long unfamiliar with the sound. Then, too, there is general prosperity in the air, and when things are financially prosperous the well-to-do American who dwells near navigable salt or fresh water feels that he must go yachting. So he straightway buys or builds a craft if he does not already possess one, while if he is a yacht owner he hauls the old boat out and equips her, trig and trim, for the joys of the season.

The present year has witnessed quite a well-marked revival in the yacht-building industry, not only in large steam vessels to take the place of those acquired by the Government, but in the smaller fry, propelled by sail or motor, in which a man of moderate means may indulge his nautical propensities at reasonable cost.

This year promises to be the largest and most successful in contests, too, since the pastime was introduced in organized shape by Commodore Stevens in 1844; and the position yachting occupies as compared with that period could not be better emphasized than by the contrast between *Gimcrack*, the first flagship of the New York Yacht Club, owned by Commodore Stevens, and the new flagship *Corsair*, owned by Commodore Pierpont Morgan, which, as I write, is being fitted with her machinery at Hoboken, under the shadow of the hill on which the Stevens mansion stands. It is hoped that she will be in commission a few days after these remarks are printed in OUTING, and those who have an opportunity of seeing her in all the pride of her panoply,

MR. RICHARD STEVENS' "AILEEN."

319

with her seagoing finery attached, will I think agree with me that she is a worthy flagship for the Club. *Gimcrack*, though a saucy little bucket, would look as insignificant alongside of her as a Jamaica bumboat at the gangway of the battleship *Oregon*.

I think I would endure all the annoyances inseparable from the lot of a millionaire just for the joy of calling the *Corsair* mine. I am not envious in the least, as a rule, but there is something about the "yachty" look of the handsome vessel that makes me covet her and want to steal her in spite of certain scriptural injunctions to the contrary. I know it is sinful, but I can't help it.

A description of *Corsair* has already been given in OUTING, but the bald dimensions of a yacht, giving details of materials, convey no idea of a vessel's beauties. Like a gorgeous sunset a fine yacht must be seen to be properly appreciated. Her picture connot be appropriately painted in words no matter how brilliant the writer. There are certain subtleties which can be seen only, and not adequately expressed. When Sir Thomas Lipton sees the *Corsair* from the deck of his steam yacht *Erin*, he will frankly admit that the Americans know how to build steam yachts. He may, however, find some consolation in the circumstance that her grace and beauty are owing to the artistic eye of one of his countrymen, for Mr. Beavor Webb, her designer, is also an Irishman.

A few days before this story was written there came into the port of New York the fine, new, steam yacht *Aphrodite*, built at Bath, Me., for Col. Oliver H. Payne. This vessel was designed for sturdy, deep-sea cruising and not for mere showy flaunting about the coast in stilly summer seas. When one is told that a cruise in her round Cape Horn is one of her owner's intentions he can well understand what her massiveness means. A high, flaring bow ensures comparative dryness forward; bilge keels, 24 inches deep and 140 feet long, will doubtless give her sufficient stability in a seaway and prevent her from excessive rolling, while a noble freeboard will keep the water off her decks and make her as buoyant as a tightly corked empty bottle.

The *Aphrodite* is a big vessel built of steel, 303 feet over all, with 35 feet beam

and 16 feet draught. Her hull is divided into 15 water-tight compartments with 9 athwartship steel bulkheads. Her decks are of steel covered with yellow pine planks. She has a deck-house of steel 160 feet long, but this is sheathed with polished mahogany. Below she is luxuriously fitted up. Her machinery is exceptionally powerful, being capable of driving her at a speed of 18 knots an hour under forced draught. This was demonstrated on her trial trip. Under natural draught she goes 16½ knots with ease. Should any mishap befall her engines she has sufficient sail area to banish all alarm. She is rigged as a bark and carries 17,000 square feet of duck. She is in every way an admirable deep-sea cruiser and reflects credit on Mr. Charles R. Hanscom, who designed her, and on the firm that built her. Criticasters have raised the objection that she is not so beautiful as her name would imply—nothing about her to suggest the goddess Venus, born of the sea. This may be true in a certain sense, but it should be remembered that an oak and a palm are both beautiful though their styles may be different.

Another seagoing craft of noble proportions is the auxiliary brigantine-rigged vessel now well under way in the Robins yard in the Erie Basin. She was designed by Mr. Clinton H. Crane for Messrs. D. W. and Arthur Curtis James, who did so much cruising in the famous schooner *Coronet*. She will be 160 feet over all, 130 feet on the water-line, beam 26 feet 9 inches, with 14 feet draught. Like *Aphrodite* she is intended for deep-water work and when completed will be fit to navigate the globe. She is divided into six water-tight compartments. Her owners, who are capital seamen, will rely principally upon sail as a motive power, using steam only when necessary. Her sail spread, exclusive of flying kites, is 13,000 square feet. This, in all probability, will be found to be a trifle more than she will be able to carry. The machinery is compactly stowed away. It consists of two water-tube boilers, triple expansion engines, with three cylinders, 9 inches, 14 inches and 23 inches in diameter, with 18-inch stroke. The propeller is of the feathering variety, and the smokestack is telescopic so that when under canvas nobody would suspect the existence of a "tea-kettle." The deck-house is erected between the masts and occupies nearly all the space longitudinally. In this is the dining saloon. The craft has a topgallant forecastle and a poop deck. The crew's quarters are forward. Below decks the quarters are commodious and the space is admirably utilized. There is no gingerbread work in the vessel, everything being neat and in good taste. She will be christened *Aloha*.

Mr. Arthur Curtis James, who is a good navigator and seaman, will command the yacht, which is expected to be completed some time next month.

Another strictly deep-water cruiser is a vessel now in course of construction at Lewis Nixon's shipyard, at Elizabethport, N.J., for Mr. J. Harvey Ladew. The craft, which has not yet been named, has a hull of similar design to that of the United States Coast Survey steamship *Pathfinder*, built at the same yard. Mr. Ladew used to own the steam-yacht *Columbia*, a remarkably fast boat, rechristened *Wasp* when bought by the Government last spring. The new craft doesn't look nearly so slim or fairylike as the *Columbia*, but she will be a stout, serviceable, seagoing craft, with a brigantine rig and canvas enough to drive her at an eight-knot gait in a whole-sail breeze. The vessel is of steel, extra strong, with double decks, and a bunker capacity of 250 tons, with which she may steam 6,000 knots, or even further at a pinch, without recoaling.

Her dimensions are 200 feet over all, 165 feet on the water-line, 33 feet 6 inches beam, and a draught of 11 feet. Her machinery is constructed with a view to bad weather. She has two Scotch boilers, each 11 feet in diameter, and 11 feet long, which will supply steam at a pressure of 170 pounds to the square inch to a triple expansion engine with cylinders of 18, 27 and 45 inches diameter, with a stroke of 28 inches. It is estimated that she will be able to go 12 or 13 knots an hour, and maintain that rate of speed as long as her coal lasts.

The yacht is fitted with living quarters on both the main and the berth deck. There are five suites, each consisting of a sitting room, bedroom and bath. There are a large saloon 16 by 32 feet, a dining-room 18 by 30 feet, and a large stateroom 14 by 24 feet. On the berth deck aft, there are staterooms for eight guests.

After the international races are over next October, Mr. Ladew will start on a cruise round the world. The yacht can accommodate a party of twenty-four with ease. The *Pathfinder* was built for service in Alaskan waters, and for that reason her scantling is strong. Mr. Ladew's yacht has been built of equal strength. She will cost more than $200,000.

It was the late Lady Brassey who did so much to popularize deep-water yachting, but she would be surprised if she could only know what an immense influence her charming stories of cruises in the *Sunbeam* have exerted on American yachtswomen and yachtsmen.

The popularity of the auxiliary steam yacht is shown by the number of new craft building, and by the conversion of "old-timers" into auxiliaries by fitting

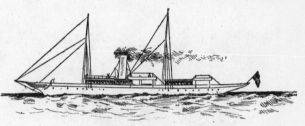

MR. EUGENE TOMPKINS' "IDALIA."

them with some sort of motor with which they can rise superior to the dismal fate inseparable from a dead calm. A man can stand a stiff breeze right in his teeth. In fact he thoroughly enjoys it, as it gives him an opportunity to test the weatherly qualities of his craft, and to enjoy a rattling thresh to windward. But the depressing effects of a calm make his heart sick. There is no more disagreeable sound at sea than the creak of the blocks and the flap and the slat of sails, as with no breeze to steady her the vessel wallows and plunges on the heaving ocean. Any old sailor will tell you that he prefers a howling gale off one of the stormy capes, with all the accompanying disagreeable incidents appertaining thereto, to the weather, met with generally in the equatorial regions, known as the "doldrums." The sun streams down in blinding rays on the deck; the pitch boils and bubbles in the seams; the yards are trimmed to every faint breath of air that seems to promise a breeze; there is nothing but backing and filling and box-hauling, until the sweat-soaked mariner, with hands chafed with pulling and hauling on sheets and braces, realizes what a tarnation fool he was to go to sea in a "windjammer," instead of a nice steamship, which is never becalmed except when her machinery happens to get disabled.

But the moment the vessel crosses the belt of calms and "bald spots," and gets within the magical influence of the glorious trade-winds, with white fleecy clouds sailing across a beautiful blue sky and the azure sea capped with foaming crests, with dolphins sporting across the bows and flying-fish scurry-

water, whose surface no breeze ruffled, and in which a little fleet of Larchmont yachts were suffering the tortures of the becalmed, praying for wind, scratching the mast, cursing the calm, and meanwhile consuming stores in excess of even the needs of the occasion, in the vain hope of appeasing the clerk of the weather.

These are the reasons why the auxiliary vessel is growing in favor. Three or four years ago a New York yachtsman clapped a boiler and engine into the fine old schooner *Hildegarde,* which used to belong to the Prince of Wales, and was brought to this country by Mr. George Gould. The result was satis-

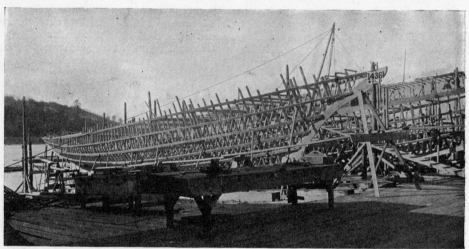

MR. G. M. ALLEN'S 80-FT. TWIN-SCREW NAPHTHA YACHT.

ing away from the voracious bonitos, why, then he will thank his stars that he is aboard a sailing vessel and away from the smoke and the smell and the monotonous throbbing of marine boilers and engines.

The moral of this is that an auxiliary motor is an excellent device for bridging over that distressing interval of calm that frequently separates two exhilarating breezes—notably on Long Island Sound. There I have seen vessels bound to the eastward, going down the Connecticut coast, impelled by a nice breeze off the land, while at the same time a westward-bound fleet was hugging the Long Island shore, and making good progress with a wind of some pretensions. Between these two divisions, however, was a long and thick streak of

factory, and the example was followed by many owners of small yachts. This season the grand old schooner *Palmer,* which for many years proudly carried the private signal of Mr. Rutherford Stuyvesant, will appear with a smokestack and an engine capable of driving her at an eight-knot gait. Mr. Stuyvesant used to be an earnest devotee of sails alone, but he has now realized the advantages of the auxiliary type. His splendid vessel, *Arcturus,* carries a large sail spread, and also a powerful boiler and engine. Such has been the marvelous progress in the engineer's art that machinery takes up only a fraction of the space it used to do, so that the installation of an auxiliary plant in a vessel does not very greatly encroach upon the living quarters of the owner.

MR. PIERPONT MORGAN'S "CORSAIR."

Following the example of the *Hildegarde*, the new owner of the *Palmer* will depend principally on sails for his motive power, but in the event of the wind falling light he will be able to make port in good season. This to a business man is sometimes of vast importance.

The schooner *Halcyon*, though not so celebrated as the *Palmer*, nevertheless has a certain fame that will ever cling to her. She is the craft in which General Paine, of Boston, conducted so many scientific experiments in the way of trim and tuning up, with the result of converting quite a slow old coach into a rather speedy vessel. Mr. George

Work, who recently purchased her, will convert her into an auxiliary. She is a roomy, comfortable craft, and is thoroughly fit for summer cruising. There is quite a fleet of these old-timers now hopelessly outclassed so far as racing speed is concerned, which, if fitted with what shell-backs call a "tea-kettle," might afford lots of pleasure to yachting fogies whose racing days are over, but who still have a liking for the fragrant breath of the ocean and always think it fresher and spicier and more abounding in health-giving ozone when it is inhaled off soundings.

The modern steam yacht is almost

MR. JOHN P. DUNCAN'S "KANAWHA."

essential to the down-to-date man of wealth and fashion. Yet the pastime of steam yachting may be said to have become popular only during the last decade. On the Atlantic Coast there has been built a great fleet of steam pleasure craft of moderate size, which give much enjoyment and healthy rec-

MR. P. A. WIDENER'S "JOSEPHINE."

reation to their owners and guests. These small vessels have now been perfected so that comfortable cruising may be had aboard of them at moderate cost. So far as the machinery is concerned, the saving in fuel has been great as compared with the costly consumption of coal in vessels of the old type. Smell, smut, smoke and vibration, which used to be serious drawbacks, have been reduced to a minimum.

Then, again, ingenious naval architects have utilized every fragment of space at their disposal, and have given much attention to ventilation, plumbing and all other sanitary safeguards. Thus the steam yacht of to-day is luxurious as a lady's boudoir. Ice-making machines, electric-light plants, spacious refrigerators and other scientific devices for enhancing the pleasure of existence have made life afloat far more agreeable than it is ashore. To that reason is owing the growth of the American steam-yacht fleet, both on salt and fresh water.

Surprising also is the increasing popularity of the launch propelled by the numerous admirable motors now on the market, each of which seems to have some special quality as recommendation. It seems not altogether improbable that they will soon be as plentiful on the water as the bicycle is ubiquitous ashore.

There is great activity at the works of the Gas-Engine and Power Company and Seabury Company (Consolidated), Morris Heights, where a large force of men are engaged on nearly a hundred

vessels, from the torpedo-boat destroyer *Bailey* of 6,000 horse-power and a speed of 30 knots, to a tiny naphtha launch. The vessel which takes the yachtsman's eye and charms him at the first glance by her beauty is the large steam yacht *Kanawha* which the firm is building for Mr. John P. Duncan, to replace the old vessel of the same name which was purchased from Mr. Duncan by the United States Government for war purposes.

The new craft is considerably larger than the old, her dimensions being 227 feet over all, 192 feet on the load water-line, with 24 feet beam and 15 feet depth. She will draw only 10 feet of water, which is the ideal draught for a coastwise cruising yacht, making it possible for her to enter almost every harbor frequented by yachtsmen. The vessel has twin screws propelled by two triple expansion engines, the cylinders being 14, 24 and 42 inches in diameter, with a stroke of 24 inches. It is expected that she will make more than 20 miles an hour under natural draught. The *Kanawha* will be rigged as a three-masted schooner and fitted with all the latest scientific appliances.

Well under way at the same yard is a twin-screw steam yacht for Mr. Louis Bossert, of Brooklyn. She will be christened *Mayita*, is of composite construction, 135 feet over all, 111 feet on the load water-line, with a beam of 16 feet, a depth of 9 feet 6 inches and a draught of 6 feet 6 inches. This type of yacht is very popular, there being quite a fleet of vessels of similar dimensions which the firm has turned out. They are of good shape, well put together, and quite fast. *Mayita* will be fitted with Seabury boilers and triple expansion engines, and will be rigged as a two-masted schooner.

A boat of similar type is the *Aria*, ordered by Mr. Edward H. Blake, of Bangor, Me. Her dimensions are 145 feet over all, 117 feet on the load water-line, with 17 feet beam, 10 feet depth, and 7 feet draught of water. Speed and seagoing ability are the combined qualities aimed at in this vessel, which will be rigged similarly to *Mayita*.

The largest naphtha yacht in existence is also being built. She is 80 feet long and will be propelled by twin screws. This shows the advance of the naphtha craft, the first vessel of the type being a ten-foot craft.

Space will not permit me to give even casual mention to the squadron of launches, steam and naphtha, auxiliaries, tenders and other boats which are fast being prepared for launching by this firm.

Mr. J. Rogers Maxwell, who has taken his pleasure in sailing craft ever since he was a small boy, has succumbed to the fascination of the "kettle," and this year will be seen in a handsome steam yacht which his trusty ally, Mr. Wintringham, has designed for him, and which is being built by Pusey & Jones, of Wilmington, Del. She is 146 feet over all, 117 feet on the load water-line, with a beam of 18 feet 6 inches, a depth of 11 feet 2 inches, and 7 feet 3 inches draught. This vessel is intended principally for cruising on Long Island Sound. She will be called *Kismet*.

Mr. Maxwell's friends, who are aware of his devotion to sailing craft, will be much surprised if he can refrain from indulging in his favorite recreation. They expect to see him spend much of his spare time in the 30-foot knockabout being built for his eldest son by the Greenport Basin and Construction Co., from a design by Mr. Clinton H. Crane. This type of craft, intended for cruising and class racing, is very popular in Eastern waters. As will be seen from the plan, there is good accommodation for such restricted dimensions. The sail plan is quite moderate.

At Roach's yard, Chester, Pa., a fine steam yacht is being built for Mr. Eugene Tompkins. She is of steel, and will be christened *Idalia.* Her dimensions are 176 feet over all, 146 feet on the water-line, 21 feet 6 inches beam, 13 feet deep and 10 feet draught. Her machinery consists of four water-tube boilers, and a triple expansion engine with four cylinders, 12½ inches, 20 inches, and two of 22½ inches diameter, with 18 inches stroke. She is expected to develop a speed of 17 knots. She has two deck-houses, the forward one containing a dining-room and pantry, and the after one a smoking-room, buffet and deck saloon. From this a companionway leads below to the main saloon, which is spacious. The interior arrangements are luxurious. The vessel was designed by Messrs. Gardner & Cox to take the place of the *Illawarra*, which Mr. Tompkins sold to the Government last year.

At Roach's yard is also being built, from plans by the same naval architects, the steel steam yacht *Aileen* for Mr. Richard Stevens, of Hoboken. She is 122 feet long on the keel, with 20 feet beam, and a depth of 12 feet 6 inches. She has triple expansion engines, the cylinders of which are 10, 16 and 25 inches in diameter, with 16-inch stroke. The engines will be driven by two water-tube boilers.

At Roach's there is also building, for Mr. J. Gardner Cassatt, of Philadelphia, the large steam yacht *Eugenia* to replace the boat of the same name which was bought by the Government and rechristened *Siren.* The new craft is 140 feet on the water-line, with 21 feet beam, 13 feet 9 inches depth, and 200 tons gross burden. She is of steel, and will be a regular floating boudoir of luxury.

At Neafie & Levy's yard, Philadelphia, a new *Josephine* is being built to replace the old craft of the same name, but now called *Vixen*, which Mr. P. A. Widener sold to Uncle Sam. The craft is 257 feet over all, 216 feet on the water-line, 30 feet 3 inches beam, 19 feet 6 inches depth, and 14 feet 6 inches draught of water.

J. HARVEY LADEW'S DEEP-SEA CRUISER.

It is imposssble, within the limits of an article of this kind, to give more than a few hints concerning the fleet of new vessels, but it may be said in a general way that the club in which each of the vessels mentioned is enrolled has reason to feel proud of the craft that will so soon fly its burgee.

With regard to the outlook of the season's sport in Great Britain, our sprightly contemporary, *The Yachtsman*, has the following interesting editorial remarks relating *inter alia* to another American-owned boat : " There is every prospect of 1899 being a most notable year in the history of yachting, for, besides the splash made by Sir Thomas Lipton, it will witness the launch of the largest sailing yacht and also the largest steam yacht ever built for private individuals. Both these vessels are of Mr. G. L. Watson's design, and of the two, perhaps the steamer will attract the more attention, for she differs in many ways from the usual run of pleasure vessels.

MESSRS. D. W. AND ARTHUR CURTIS JAMES'
AUXILIARY BRIGANTINE " ALOHA."

"This new yacht is to be built to the order of Mr. J. Gordon Bennett, at Dumbarton, by Messrs. Denny, and she will be some ten feet longer than *Mayflower*, but considerably broader. It is stated that she is to be the fastest steam yacht in the world, and, judging from her ownership, we believe this is more than probable. But her chief distinction will be her remarkable appearance. Our Clyde correspondent informs us that he knows, as an actual fact, that the new vessel will have a straight stem and only one mast. The position of this mast is also uncommon ; it is to be placed abaft the funnel.

" The result, we should say, will be a craft of very piratical appearance, for nowadays we associate these outward and visible signs with quick-firing guns, stores of cordite and other unpleasant commodities. What part the Spanish

war has played in forming Mr. Bennett's taste we are of course unable to say; but it appears certain that the new yacht gives expression to the same feeling of emulation which prompted our forefathers to build their yachts on the prevailing man-o'-war type of the day.

" Mr. Bennett's yacht will be distinctly progressive; but it appears that the other notable vessel—Mr. James Coats's s c h o o n e r — is rather the reverse. In appearance she is more old - fashioned than her predecessor, *Rainbow*, and it is whispered that Mr. Watson has embodied his admiration for the famous old China clippers in his design.

" The building of *Rainbow* and Mr. Coats's new ship puts an end to the idea that steam will ever entirely supersede sail in yachts. The development of steam propulsion has been enormous during the last twenty years, whilst that of sailing yachts has practically stood still. Of course various measurement rules have produced different types to suit each, and each has taught something in the way of design; but, to all intents and purposes, the *bona-fide* cruiser built to-day is very much the same as what was turned out twenty years ago. It is therefore a most healthy sign that men should be found who still prefer the large sailing yacht to the palatial kettle. It is the instinct of the true sailor to prefer canvas to steam, but we are bound to say that steam as exemplified in such a yacht as *Mayflower* might pervert even the most enthusiastic salt."

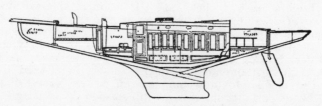

J. ROGERS MAXWELL, JR.'S, KNOCKABOUT.

Drifters
Out of Lowestoft
(1901)

Harbor lights, Lowestoft.

DRIFTERS OUT OF LOWESTOFT

By Walter Wood

ILLUSTRATIONS BY M. J. BURNS

SCARBOROUGH CASTLE, grim and ruined, tops the hill which overlooks the gray North Sea between Flamborough Head and Whitby Abbey, where Caedmon, founder of English poetry, was a monk, and not far from which was the monastic home of the Venerable Bede, father of English learning. When Baeda and Caedmon were alive they watched the early fishers sail away to catch and bring ashore that marvellously prolific creature which was and is of all fish the unchallenged king. They went and came, these small crude craft, when wind and sea permitted, and to-day, twelve centuries later, the men of the East coast put to sea, also at the will of wind and wave, to gather some of its abundant harvest.

The Lowestoft drifters have come south after their voyage north to accompany the herring in that mysterious migration which begins at the Shetlands, the unnumbered living mass advancing almost as the Gulf Stream goes on its appointed way.

We sailed from Scarborough on a Sunday as the bells were chiming for the morning service, knowing that when they rang for even-song, we should have shot our nets and be drifting at them, and that with her catch the vessel would run to Lowestoft and work from that, the home port, until the herring had inscrutably vanished for the season.

These Lowestoft vessels are only part of that vast fleet which is known as herring drifters, and includes the small boat containing two or three men and the steamer with her round dozen. There are ketches, like the Lowestoft drifters, and a great variety of other rigs, such as yawls, dandies, luggers, mules, Zulus, keelboats, yaffers and sploshers. The "Lowestoftman"—it is typical of the North Sea fishing industry that boats are spoken of as "men" of their ports: the "Hullman," the "Fileyman," the "Grimsbyman," and so on—is a well-found craft, some eighty feet in length and seventeen or eighteen in beam. They are honestly and stoutly built, and when they come to grief, it is through stress of wind and sea, and not because of owners' carelessness or fishermen's incapacity.

The drifters carry nets enough when they are fastened together and suspended in the sea to make a wall which may be a mile long, or even more, and several yards deep. The upper edge, called the "back," has a great number of corks which keep the nets upright, and to afford the necessary buoyancy barrels or great leather floats are used. The nets are shot over the quarter just before sunset, while the vessel sails slowly along. When all the nets are overboard the swing-rope is paid out; the boat is brought round head to wind, the ordinary sails are taken in, the foremast is lowered till it rests on the crutch of the

witnessed many centuries ago. It was at night when the herrings were caught, and night on the vast and melancholy waste of water hides that modernity which only day reveals. There are other riding-lights, and here and there, the mast-head and side-lights of a steamer going north or south; but the steel and iron hulls are only guessed by some chance glimmer from a port or deck-house.

And the men have changed but little,

We sailed from Scarborough on a Sunday morning.

mitch-board, the drift-mizzen is set to keep the vessel head to wind, and the fishing-lights are shown—the lantern on deck which can be seen in clear weather for five miles round, and a light at the head of the mizzen-mast. A watch is set, a solitary man, and the rest of the crew turn in until he hoarsely calls them up to haul.

The Lowestoft fishermen say that the method of catching herrings has scarcely changed during the last thousand years or more, and that their nets must be the same in principle as those which were employed before Richard the Lion-hearted and his Crusaders sailed for the Holy Land. The statement has much of truth in it, and when we drift at our nets on the lonely sea, with our great lamp-like riding-light burning steadily amidships, we present much the same spectacle that could have been

surely! Their dress for work is primitive, hiding all that is suggestive of the modern landsman. There is the jumper which the skipper and crew wear—a garment made of stout canvas and barked with the sail-cloth. It covers the arms and trunk nearly to the knees, almost as the coarse smock garbed the serf of old, and the men of his rank who would alone, in those days, go to sea to fish. The jumper in its long variety is like a night-dress. Its short form is generally favored, but skippers often use the long garment, as the covering keeps the cold out, and skippers, being leaders, have spare time in which to feel the draughts that invade all unprotected crevices. There are rough, thick, woollen stockings, and boots which may be thigh boots, or half boots, or clumpers, according to the weather, and as for head-dress, that is anything in the

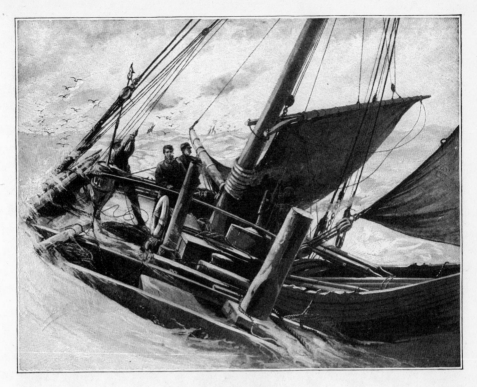

On the grounds.

way of covering which comes handy; but mostly a cap, except in bad weather, when it is the sou'-wester.

Our own skipper is a man who has followed the drifting for thirty years. His very life is wrapped up in the herring and its possibilities, for upon the success of the fishing his income depends. He is learned in the lore of herringing. You may try to turn him from the topics of the sea and drifters, but he will invariably come back to the herring, and you listen contentedly to his talk by the hour, for he has a subtle knowledge of his subject. He has much time to spend at the tiller, and in giving orders when the nets are shot or hauled; and there are the odd moments, too, when we assemble in the cabin aft, with its lack of light and air, and ways of life that are reminiscent of the customs of the Middle Ages.

When we get clear of the harbor and beyond the sad cadence ot church bells, I volunteer to relieve the skipper at the tiller, asking for the course.

"Nor'-east-by-east, quarter east," he

says. "She's a quick steerer, an' you wouldn't really get to feel her for a day or two. Not so much to starboard, sir; that's better. Now a bit to port, so, as she goes. She's like a wilful woman, an' needs humorin'; but she'll obey if you make her. Would I give women votes? Well, it's an odd question; but I wouldn't—an' I reckon I'd take away most o' the votes 'at men have got, for they've no qualifications to use 'em." From that we get to other subjects; but always return to herrings, drifters and the sea and fishermen.

The mate after a while takes the tiller and we go below to dinner. George, the boy, who is the skipper's son, has laid the feast. There is no waiting, no helping, no ceremony. A leg of mutton is in a tin dish on the cabin floor; another dish, big and oblong, contains gravy—a small lake of it; a third is heaped up with potatoes, and a fourth is filled with Norfolk dumplings. They have been boiled, and consist of flour and water and baking powder. On the Dogger, rolled out flat and baked, they would have been called "busters." George is proud of his cooking skill, and explains that he can make the dumplings better and richer by the addition of suet. We pour out tea, a heavy, sickly liquid, sweetened with condensed milk and much sugar, all boiled together with a mass of used leaves which have not been removed from the kettle. We help ourselves from the joint with our own little knives and two-pronged steel forks, and with a long, common, pewter spoon, scoop up such gravy as we can

crews at sea, but never with a kinder and cleaner-speeched than this.

"Now," says the skipper at last, knocking his pipe on the locker and clambering to his feet, "I reckon it's gettin' pretty nearly time to shoot." So we climb on deck, and just as the worshippers ashore are making ready for even-song we shoot our nets.

No confusion exists as to duty. The skipper controls and takes the tiller. The hawseman has to be forward to make fast

Drifting.

catch between the drifter's rolls and pitches, and if we want a dumpling we annex one with a fork-plunge. All of us can reach with ease, for our sea boots are mixed up with the dishes. It is very crowded in the cabin, and we are thrown against each other with the lurches, and our lake of gravy partly mingles with the cinders of the stove-pan, while our enamelled mugs overflow into our jumpers. George, with folded arms, gazes steadily upon me from a corner near the oil-lamp, and at times he smiles. I know what is passing through his mind, and assure him that I have been out on the North Sea many times and have never yet been mastered by it. "You're sure you aren't goin' to be turned up, sir?" he says, and the men laugh hilariously but kindly. I have been with many fishing

the seizings of the warps; amidships is the whaleman, paying out the nets, while the net-ropeman also pays out and hauls in, holding the net-rope; the work of the net-stower is to pay out the nets from the net-room, which is a large chamber forward; the younker, being the man of all work, helps anybody who calls for his assistance, while the boy has all sorts of odd jobs to do, as well as the cooking and washing up.

The nets are floating near the surface, indicated by a mile-long line of bobbing barrels and buoys which mark the quarter, half and three-quarter lengths of nets, and we go drifting at the will of wind and tide. The sea, week day and Sunday, appears to be evermore the same, but, although we are toiling on the deep as harvesters, we know that it is Sunday. Westward, dimly

Drift-net fishermen—heaving the nets.

A new type of Keelboat.

seen, is the high land of the Yorkshire coast, with Caedmon's old monastery crowning the cliff at Whitby, and there returns to mind the picture of the men who on these same waters plied the craft of herringing more than a thousand years ago—pretty much in principle as we are doing now.

When we are slowly drifting we assemble in the gloomy cabin aft and take our tea. There is the kettle on the floor, and near it some enamelled mugs; accompanied by a great stack of bread and butter, a dishful of wedges of cheese; a dish of sliced cucumber and another dish of sliced onions. The cucumber is part of my addition to the menu; also some bananas and oranges—and we Dutch the fare.

George has climbed into a cupboard-like bunk, which he is sharing with the whaleman, and though he feigns sleep, yet, from time to time, he makes sepulchral observations. He has determined in his heart that I shall be distressed, and for aught I know to the contrary, he has some fearsome medicine that he wishes to inflict upon me.

A typical North Sea fishing boat.

An old type of the "Lowestoftman."

I am as stubbornly resolved that I will have none of it.

The skipper strips a banana cautiously, rather distrustfully. He does not seem fully to understand, and after the first bite says that he has never before eaten a who do the most work don't get the most pay. The dealer an' the middleman comes in and sees that that don't happen. We used to sell the herrin' by the hundred, count in' of 'em an' givin' a hundred an' thirty-two to the dealer as a hundred. The

A Lugger.

A type of Scotch herring boat.

banana, and thought it was a thing containing seeds. "Fishermen don't often eat fruit," he explains. "They don't seem to need it—and fruit's dear. But it's good —like a meller apple, I reckon. Yes, sir, I'll take another. I could learn to like 'em. Landsmen have a lot to be thankful for, when they can get things like that to eat, and why they should ever come to sea for pleasure, is a thing I can't understand."

"I reckon," says the whaleman, with a sigh, "'at no man but a fool or who wasn't forced, would go fishin'. It's sixteen week since I left my wife—an' I'm pinin' to see her again. She'll be goin' to church by this time. An' there's so much work to do an' so little for it when it's done."

"Yes," proceeds the skipper, "the men thirty-two were 'over-tail,' an' belonged to the dealer, who got nearly a third of the profit of the catch for just a-handlin' it ashore, although he hadn't to do any o' the hard work o' fishin'. We sell by measure now, a cran bein' a thousand herrin', but it's the dealer first an' the fishermen a long way second. That don't seem to be right, nohow, but then there's so many puzzlin' tangles in this queer world. Think what it means for fishermen and dealers when there's been an extryordinary catch—as sometimes happens. Only four year ago, in November, a fleet of us was kept out o' Lowestoft by fog. When the fog lifted, four hundred drifters, sail an' steam, crowded in, an' all had big catches, too. It was Sunday, but special permission was given to use the market, an' thirty thousand crans were landed—thirty million o' herrin'. Think of the 'over-tail' in that lot! Most of 'em went off to Russia—an' I wonder what'll happen to us if Russia doesn't take our herrin', but buys from the Japs? Them little colored men are wonderful, an' we've had several of 'em out in the fleets with us, learnin' our ways, so that they can buy drifters an' catch herrin' for themselves off the Japanee coast, I take it.

"There's so many stories told of fishin' that aren't true, an' so many people come an' bother you with foolish questions. One tale that's made such a lot of is the death-cheep of the herrin'. They'll tell you that when the herrin' are caught an' shaken out of the nets an' are wrigglin' an' lashin' about, they'll squeak just like wee little kittens. Well, sometimes they do, but not often, an' that's only when they're full of wind an' you step on 'em or pick 'em up an' nip 'em.

"Then there's land people who come an' bother you with foolish questions. I try to put 'em off, but can't allus do it. There was an old lady who worrited me past endurance with her questions, askin' if the herrin's were caught in the barrels, as she'd sometimes seen 'em that way in the shops. I told her no, an' then she aggravated me to that extent that I told the only fib I ever spoke in my life—for I larned a lot about the Scriptures at Sunday-school. 'How do you kill 'em when you've caught 'em?' she asked, an' I answered, 'We bite their heads!' She looked at the catch o' herrin's we had, an' murmured as she walked away, 'Lor'! How tired your poor jaws must be!'

"There's a wonderful lot o' luck in the herrin' fishin'. I like it best when we can have a good clear sweep of sea to ourselves —an' that comes earlier in the year, say in June, when we go away North, and come down with the shoals till we start to make Lowestoft our head-quarters. That's a better time than this, when we're all so crowded that there isn't room enough on the sea for us, and we get bunched up an' foul our nets, and sometimes lose them an' our fish as well. I've known us lose a hundred nets, costin' three pound each—three hundred pound altogether.

"You were askin' about the Dutchman that we saw comin' away from the North— it allus seems so strange to me how them old boms make their way out and home again—they do things so leisurely, you see. He hadn't even got his tawps'ls set. I reckon 'at the Dutchmen are poor fishermen; the French are better, an', of course, Lowestoft men best of all. I once saw some Dutchmen with a catch of herrin' so big that the nets looked just like a solid mass, an' the Dutchmen were three days in haulin'. They had to get the foremast up an' rig halyards, an' they shook the herrin' out like apples from a tree. The Dutchmen were three days in haulin', but I daresay we should ha' done the work in fourteen or fifteen hours. It's cruel hard work when it comes to a heavy haul, because there's no stoppin' for meals when we once begin."

"No," observes the hawseman, "there's just a mug o' tea an' then breakfast, which may be served at five or six in the mornin', or the same time in the afternoon—an' that's the fisherman's best meal. He don't take no count o' dinner, nor yet supper, so long as his breakfast's got. Old Skip there, he don't want no more nor two herrin' for breakfast, I reckon; an' I don't care for more nor eight or so; but the old net-stower, he çan't be satisfied nohow wi' less nor a dozen, an' I do know fishermen who manage to get through nearer a score—an' herrin' are wonderful good things to eat, they say."

"There's no question, to my thinkin'," pursues the skipper, "'at herrin's get to know when you've come amongst 'em. They feel the loss o' their comrades an' swim away. An' I think that that's as wonderful as their want o' sense in not goin' astarn when they're meshed. If they did they would escape, many o' 'em, but they allus drive ahead, an' keep stuck. They've no chance, what wi' the drifters an' the dog-fish an' the cod, which carry off enormous numbers. The dog-fish are cruel an' destructive creatures, doin' a lot o' harm to our nets, but in the case o' the cod we do get something for our pains and loss, for we bring 'em on board. With the dog-fish we can do nothing but bang him on the head— an' we allus do that, givin' him a wide berth, for he's fair poison if he gets his teeth into you. I've seen cod that thick about the nets that they've been like a flock o' sheep, an' that crazy after herrin' 'at they just jump up out o' the water alongside an' beg for 'em, as a dog will beg for a biscuit.

Hauling the nets.

You see, we get to understand fish, us fishermen, just as you gentlemen ashore know the ways o' dogs an' horses. Now, sir, I don't know about you, but I'm goin' to turn in. Take my bunk there, if you'd like it. I can manage on the locker."

"I think," I answer, "that I will lie down on deck."

George peeps from his dark cupboard and smiles broadly. The skipper gives me a coverless pillow and a couple of rugs and I climb the straight short ladder to the deck. "Take up thy bed and walk," says George, as a forlorn hope, and the laughter which greets the sally does not die till I am stretched on the planks, with the raw wind striking across my face and the roughening water from the pitiless and sullen Dogger lapping against the drifter's hull, telling its tales of hardship and suffering; bringing back oppressive memories, and resurrecting that nameless fear which comes to all who understand the North Sea and the smashing fury of its waves, when gales sweep landward from the east or north. I cannot rest, and rise and join the lonely watch-

man, and, holding by the riding-light and smoking, we converse in low tones, pausing at times to listen to the spouting of a blowfish which is swimming around the drifter, whose presence is interpreted by the watchman to be a sign of herrings. Always our talk is of the sea and drifters and herrings. Insidiously there comes up from time to time some tale of loss and sorrow and I call to mind the wrecks that I myself have seen. You cannot get away from the gloom and pity of it. The North Sea has you in its grip—and the grip is merciless.

"It's one o'clock," I tell the watchman in answer to his question. We rouse the crew, and in the darkness, sleepy, silent, heavy, oil-frocked and sea-booted, and in most cases wearing woollen mittens, they come on deck to start the long, laborious work of hauling the nets, which may last four or fourteen hours. George reels against me, owlish but incorrigibly hopeful. "Still tawpside-up, sir? That's good. Like these old drifters—they're all right so long as they keep afloat, aren't they? There's tea in the galley, and there'll be breakfast by and by." With that he tumbles down a little square hole forward, to stow the warp as the nets are hauled in, and I see him no more until the herrings have been shaken from the nets, and are slatting slimily about with the drifters' heavy roll.

Four hours' hard hauling, shaking, stowing and packing—and twenty thousand herrings as the pay for all the work. Not a heavy catch, not an overwhelming profit —ten pounds for owners and skipper and crew, with all expenses first to be deducted, but still something for the night's rough work; and so, with thankfulness that matters are no worse, we raise the foremast, get all sail on, and surge away to harbor on the rising sea, with the water washing inboard almost rail deep, and the breeze drumming through the rigging and sweeping out at the foot of the sails. The skipper takes the helm till breakfast is ready; then, willingly obedient to the summons, we tumble below again and fall hungrily upon tea, bread and butter and herrings—herrings freshly caught, gutted, beheaded and deprived of tails, slashed with jack-knives latitudinally, so that when the huge dishful of them is placed on the floor, piping hot from the boiling fat in which they have been fried, we can bend down and help ourselves, and with our fingers strip the crisp, delicious morsels from the bones and eat them. Savage, certainly; but cutlery is scarce and space is cramped, and there is no table, no ceremony. And do we not ashore, in splendid halls of banqueting, eat plovers' eggs, asparagus, and such like things as Bombay duck in just the same crude fashion?

Competition is as merciless in drifting as in other walks of life, and only the fittest of the fit survive. The drifter is seen at her best when she is running for market in a smart breeze, not the "smart breeze" of the North Sea smacksman, which means a dangerous gale; but the strong wind in which the Lowestoftman can carry all his canvas and crack on with tautened gear and deck awash. That is the time when skipper and crew enjoy the triumph of success of toil, and run to port with some of the sea's good harvest. These Lowestoftmen claim that their craft are the hardest-driven of any in British waters, and this may well be so, for on both main and mizzen they carry enormous jackyard topsails, and the

Lowestoftman will hold on to these in strong winds which make it needful for lesser sails to be taken in.

When all expenses are paid the owner of the vessel receives half of what is left, and the remaining half is divided amongst the crew according to their rank, less three shares, which go to the owner. The skipper takes one and eleven forty-eighth shares, the mate one and a quarter, the hawseman one, and the rest lesser shares, the boy receiving a half share. "It sounds pretty well," the skipper says, "but I've worked a whole year at the driftin', reckonin' the lost time ashore in winter, an' for all I've done I've made only thirty-four pound. It's a bare, hard livin' at the best.

"Yes, these drifters are fine boats, an' bein' what they are, we are pretty safe in them, an' when it breezes up too much, we can run in to port an' get away from the weather. The deep sea trawlers can't do that; they're out on the Dogger and have to stick it through, be the weather what it will. No, I've no mind to go. All my thirty year have been spent in driftin'—beginnin' in June or so, goin' north to meet the herrin', an' followin' on 'em south back to Lowestoft, an' workin' 'em till Christmas. It's bitter cruel work in the cold late autumn an' the winter, an' I've had many a narrow squeak. I've seen drifters founder with all hands; but I've allus got safe back. It's no good stayin' out when the wind an' sea are too strong, for you lose both nets an' labor; but competition gets that fierce you're forced to do as others do—an' some of 'em hang on to the weather till there's scarcely no chance to get away in safety. An' when they hang on you've got to hang on too, for fear o' bein' left. It would never do to run back without herrin' an' find 'at other fishermen had stuck on an' got some."

The wind falls just before we reach the harbor, and we pull in slowly with our sweeps. As we labor on a steam-drifter comes past, with her fussy little compound engine making a hundred and forty-five revolutions of the propeller a minute.

Her skipper, a black-bearded giant, leans out of the wheel-house door and shouts a friendly taunt at our own master, his mellow Suffolk drawl and cadence coming over the water like a song.

"Can't you get in, Jarge? Won't you be

Drawn by M. J. Burns.

Off for market.

Scotch herring boats, entering Lowestoft Harbor.

late for market if you don't hurry up?" He waves his hand and laughs triumphantly.

Our skipper does not answer the genial giber, but to me he says, with a look of distrust of the future in his clear blue eyes, "Don't you see it for yourself, sir? Steamers is sweepin' sailin' boats off the herrin' grounds, an' soon there won't be one of 'em able to make a livin' out of driftin'. An' then what's to happen to some of us?—for we can't all go into steam."

When the drifters used to go to sea the urchins followed them along the haven, singing:

> Herrings galore;
> Pray, Master—

> Gay Master—
> Luff the little herring boat ashore.
> Pray God send you eight or nine last;
> Fair gain all,
> Good weather,
> Good weather,
> All herrings—no dogs.

The boys continued their crude and unmelodious ditty until they were pacified with biscuits which were thrown to them by the crews.

There is no singing to sea nowadays, but when the herrings are landed, the ragged urchins follow the baskets and, swooping down, seize the fish which fall to the ground, claiming them as loot.

The Herreshoffs and Their Boats
(1895)

THE

NEW ENGLAND MAGAZINE.

JULY, 1895.

"VAMOOSE."

THE HERRESHOFFS AND THEIR BOATS.

By Henry Robinson Palmer.

Illustrated from photographs by N. L. Stebbins.

WHILE the new yacht *Defender* has been in process of construction at Bristol, Rhode Island, public attention has been attracted in no small measure to that town and to the man who has designed and built the craft. It is only a few years ago that Edward Burgess was regarded as the greatest yacht designer of the day; and when he died, in 1891, the prediction was freely made that his equal would not soon be developed. Other men might be found who would design fast yachts, but the chances were that if the British yachtsmen should challenge for the *America's* trophy again, the cup would presently be on its way to the other side of the ocean. At least that was the conclusion at which a great many pessimistic observers arrived when they learned of the untimely death of the man who had created the *Puritan*, the *Mayflower* and the *Volunteer*. But almost at the moment of Mr. Burgess's death the victories of the *Gloriana* were pointing unmistakably to "Nat" Herreshoff as the designer upon whom the task of producing another international champion might profitably be imposed.

The Herreshoffs have been boat-builders and sailors for generations, and the

343

designer of the *Defender* has made and sailed craft of all sorts and sizes from his boyhood up. On their paternal side, as the name indicates, the family are of German descent, one of their ancestors having emigrated to this country in the last century and entered the employment of John Brown, a famous merchant of Providence. Subsequently he married Miss Sarah Brown ; and thus the present generation of Herreshoffs at Bristol are enabled to trace their ancestry back to Chad Brown, one of the original settlers of the state, who took up his abode in Rhode Island shortly after the arrival there of Roger Williams. During the Revolution the Browns were known far and wide through the colonies for their intense and serviceable patriotism. It was John Brown who

the same family of Browns, it may be added, came the benefactions which led the corporation of Rhode Island College to change the name of that institution to Brown University.

The grandfather of the present Herreshoffs turned to agriculture in his later years, and settled on " Popasquash " or " Pappoosesquaw " Point, across the harbor from Bristol. His son, Charles Frederick, the father of the designer of the *Defender*, was born there in 1809, and

NATHANIEL G. HERRESHOFF.

JOHN B. HERRESHOFF.

provided the boats, on the night of the memorable burning of the *Gaspee* in 1772, to carry the plotters down the river to where the British vessel lay fast aground ; and after the war it was one of his vessels which first bore the stars and stripes into Chinese waters. His interest in everything pertaining to the sea was naturally great, for he had a fleet of forty ships. It is related of him that he frequently went down the bay to meet these incoming vessels, having that fondness for the water which has manifested itself in so many of his descendants. From

like his sons after him early showed a great love for the sea. At twelve he was master of a sail-boat which he had himself constructed, and which he could sail with the skill of a veteran helmsman ; and two years later he was known throughout the vicinity as an expert mechanic and sailor. He graduated from Brown at an age that seems strangely early to us of a later generation, and returning to Bristol, found his chief delight in building and sailing boats. Many of these were very fast and won more than a local reputation ; and even after the present Herreshoff Manufacturing Company had been formed the active members of the firm received much valuable assistance and counsel from the elder Herreshoff. He

"CUSHING."

died a few years ago, and is remembered as a cultured and attractive old man, "who never said ill of anybody," to quote Captain Albert C. Bennett of Bristol, his life-long friend. One amusing story relating to his boat-building career is that he always named his craft "Julia," in honor of his wife. No amount of argument could induce him to give any of them another title. Mrs. Herreshoff is still living at Bristol, and occupies the homestead on Hope Street, opposite the shops of the company. She traces her descent from the Boston Lewises, a seagoing family; so that John B. and "Nat" Herreshoff, her sons, come fairly by their love of the water, on both sides of the house.

Charles Frederick Herreshoff had nine children, seven sons and two daughters, all of whom are yet living. The two daughters are Mrs. Chesebro and Miss Sarah Herreshoff, both making their home at Bristol, the latter with Mrs. Herreshoff at the homestead. Charles Frederick, one of the sons, lives at the yet older family homestead on Popasquash Point, being a farmer, but interesting himself in boat-building and sailing as well; and Lewis lives with his mother and sister. He is of a literary turn of mind, and has written many articles for the newspaper periodicals and magazines, although he has been totally blind for some years. Some strange malady of the eyes has overtaken no less than four members of the family, among them John B. Herreshoff, the president of the boat-building company, who was stricken at the age of fifteen. Julian Herreshoff

has conducted a school of languages at Providence, and alternates in his residence between that city and Bristol. His musical taste and talent are perhaps his chief characteristics. The other sons are Francis, James B., who studied at Brown University and has attained a considerable reputation as a chemist and engineer, John B., already referred to, and Nathaniel Greene Herreshoff, the designer of the yacht which in all probability will defend the *America's* cup against the British challenger next fall.

The president of the Herreshoff Manufacturing Company, John Brown Herreshoff, was born in 1841, and, like his father before him, manifested an early interest in boats. He was an expert sailor in his early teens, and if blindness had not overtaken him at the age of fifteen he might have become a phenomenal marine designer. As it is, he has a wonderful knowledge of speed qualities in a boat, and by passing his hand over a model can tell more about its value than most men who have the use of their eyes. His part in the company, however, is chiefly of a business character. He can carry accounts in his head to a surprising degree; and one story that is told of his experience with the representatives of a South American country who had been despatched to New York to contract for three American-built torpedo boats illustrates his mastery over details. The South Americans summoned him to New York to figure on the craft, and after describing them to the blind man, asked him what his price would be for the construction of them. "I shall require

THE HERRESHOFF BROTHERS' FIRST SHOP.

some time to consider the matter," said Mr. Herreshoff. "But how much time?" he was asked. The craft were of a novel pattern and possessed some features that made the task of calculating their expense especially difficult. "Half an hour," said the builder; and at the expiration of that interval he presented figures that were so satisfactory to the South Americans that the boats were ordered. In due time they were built and delivered according to the agreement.

Mr. Herreshoff has been married twice, and has one daughter by his first wife. He lives in a comfortable home on High Street, Bristol, at the head of Burnside Street, near by the machine shops of the company and within sight of the workshops at which the crack sailing yachts are built. He is a familiar figure on the streets of the town, going about freely, but always accompanied by an attendant, sometimes a member of the family. He makes frequent journeys away from home

THE PRESENT SHOPS.

in connection with the business of the company, and in spite of his affliction is as shrewd a business man as could be found in many a long day. His advice is sought in the construction of most of the boats that are built at the Herreshoff works; but it is upon "Nat" that the burden of the designing and constructing comes. Indeed, so far as the *Defender* is concerned, it is doubtful if the members of the syndicate who ordered her have had any transaction with the president of the company. It is with the younger brother that they have had their dealings, and to him will be due whatever credit may accrue to the boat.

John B. Herreshoff has now been building boats more than thirty years; and in that time a great fleet of vessels, steamers and sailing craft has been launched at Bristol.

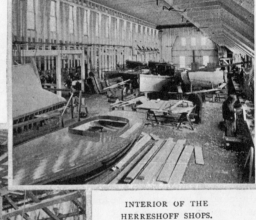

INTERIOR OF THE
HERRESHOFF SHOPS.

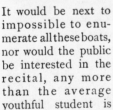

It would be next to impossible to enumerate all these boats, nor would the public be interested in the recital, any more than the average youthful student is anxious to master the Homeric Catalogue of Ships. But there have been certain epoch-making craft produced at the Herreshoff yards which are worth the study of every intelligent American. Nobody can note the record of the *Gloriana* and the *Wasp* without feeling that the Bristol designers have done something more than copy and elaborate

the work of their predecessors. They have not merely availed themselves of the achievements of Mr. Burgess and those who went before him, but have struck a new vein, so to speak, and one which has already produced most plentifully.

While his elder brother was building up his business gradually at Bristol, "Nat" Herreshoff was preparing himself for his future career there by study at the Massachusetts Institute of Technology, a prenticeship at the Corliss Engine Works in Providence, where he had a hand in the construction of the great engine which moved the machinery at the Philadelphia Centennial Exposition, and a course in engineering abroad. He visited some of the best-known ship-yards in Europe, and on his return to this country was well qualified to enter upon the work that has since kept him so busily employed in his

"SHADOW."

native town. But all his boyhood had contributed to this result. Like his brothers and his father before them, he had been a boat-builder and a sailor while scarcely in his teens, and even as a little child, if he could not be found about the house, he was sure to be discovered at play on the shore of the harbor. During his boyhood he employed himself much of the time in guiding his blind brother, and the constant association of the two naturally resulted in a mutual understanding which has been of great value to them in the years of their business partnership.

It was shortly after his return to Bristol in 1877, when he was about twenty-nine years of age, that "Nat" Herreshoff brought out his famous catamarans. Catamarans had been constructed before; but he made use of a novel idea in the method of joining the two sections of which these queer craft are composed, and revolutionized their construction. Hitherto they had consisted of two hulls united by an unjointed series of braces; but he introduced a joint, by means of which the hulls acted almost independently of each other. They accommodated themselves to the waves in much better fashion; and the result was that "Captain Nat" beat nearly every craft he encountered. One

day he lay in wait off the mouth of Bristol harbor for the steamer from Newport. When she came abreast, the wind blowing briskly up the bay at the time, he headed his novel yacht in the same direction, and beat the steamer to Providence so badly that the fame of his boat spread far and wide. It is said that on one occasion he made twenty-one miles in an hour over a measured course in one of these catamarans. At another time, on the occasion of a yacht race off Sandy Hook, he hung about the starting line with his double craft until all the contestants had gotten far down the course. One of the crew on board the boat which the older Herreshoff, the father of "Captain Nat," was sailing, says that they saw the queer craft putting out long after they had set off on the race, and watched its progress with interest. Nearer and nearer she came, and before long had passed not only this particular boat but every yacht in the fleet. This was one of "Nat's" quiet little jokes.

He is very quiet, by the way, and seems to like his own company better than the association of many friends. His head is evidently full of new plans, and he does not have to depend on anybody but himself for entertainment.

Judging by the number of new ideas he has evolved and published to the world in the course of his eighteen years of work at Bristol, he must be "thinking up" something new during most of his waking moments. He walks along the street with his head inclined forward, as if he were in search of some novel notion, though there is a local saying that he acquired the habit from watching his rivals in his races, craning his head in order to see them from under the boom.

father and son, a greater number of times, probably, than any other one man. He says he never saw "Nat" excited in a race but once. It was in a race in Gowanus Bay, and the future designer of the *Defender* was at the helm. The breeze slackened, and it was thought advisable to raise a top-sail, but in the course of this operation one of the corners got away from the crew, and the sail went

"GLORIANA."

Captain Bennett, already referred to, a Bristol veteran who went to sea for the first time as long ago as 1826, and has crossed the ocean sixty-four times in sailing vessels in the course of his long career, has sailed with the Herreshoffs,

flapping high into the air. Captain Nat took off his cap and flung it down on the deck, and the language in which he indulged himself for a moment is said to have been extremely forcible. "But that's the only time," says Captain Bennett, "that I ever saw him when he seemed to be excited." As the yachting public knows very well, he is uniformly cool and

" WASP."

careful in a race, sailing his craft for " all she is worth," and making few errors.

On one occasion he was steering the *Ianthe* in a race in the vicinity of New York, when the breeze almost deserted the boats and left them idly moving in the direction of home, but at a snail's pace. There were two or more classes of yachts in the fleet, but the skipper of the *Ianthe*, steering wide of his comrades, ran into a little breeze he had seen far to starboard, and beat all the classes over the finish line. It is by carefully observing the possibilities open to the wide-awake helmsman in every race that he has won his great reputation as a sailor.

Captain Nat's home at Bristol is a comfortable one. The house is a spacious structure at the foot of Hope Street, not far from the workshops of the company, and with its back to the street. It has been said that its isolation and the fact that it fronts the water are indicative of the attitude of its owner toward the general public. He likes to be let alone, and his chief inspiration has always come and always will come from the sea. His windows look far down Narragansett Bay, with Popasquash Point stretching to

the south, and Prudence Island in the foreground. It is a picturesque bit of scenery, and as Captain Nat has an interesting family it is no wonder that he is satisfied with his home. Five of his six children are boys; and some day, he says, he is going to man a boat of his own construction with these youthful representatives of the Herreshoff family. Mrs. Herreshoff was Miss Clara De Wolf of Bristol.

One of his most famous inventions is his coil boiler. He has given much attention to the designing of the machinery for the steam craft he and his brother have built, and in the course of his long years of work and experiment has made many improvements in the engines with which they have been equipped. One of the earlier Herreshoff steamers to make a name for itself was the *Stiletto*, which created a sensation ten years ago. She was a long, narrow craft, and so promising were her speed trials that she sought out the *Mary Powell* on the Hudson and challenged her to a race. The *Powell* had long been known as the fastest steamboat in this country, but the *Stiletto* kept on even terms with her, and at the end of the course, if memory serves, she ran across the bow of her big rival. The speed of this audacious little vessel pleased the government officials, and they purchased her for a torpedo boat. She has never been fitted out with torpedoes, but has served the authorities at Washington as a despatch boat, as has the *Cushing* also, which was ordered for the Navy from the Herreshoffs on account of the fine work of the *Stiletto*. The *Cushing* is said to have struck a thirty-mile gait on one occasion, and on her official

been called the fastest steam yacht in the world, and it is certain that she is at least one of the very fastest. Efforts have been made time and again to race her against the speedy *Norwood*, but the match has never occurred. Probably if she were beaten, "Nat" Herreshoff would stop work on his sailing craft long enough to attempt the construction of a steamer that would be unquestionably the fastest yacht afloat. The construction of steamers, it should be noted, was for many years his chief concern. His

" VIGILANT."

trial trip covered twenty-three or twenty-four knots an hour. She is 138 feet in length, with a beam of 14.6, draught, 3.7, horse-power, 1720, and tonnage, 115. She carries three guns, and her cost is put at $83,000.

Among the other famous steam productions of the Herreshoffs are the yachts *Now Then*, *Say When*, *One Hundred*, all of these three craft being built primarily for speed qualities; the *Henrietta* and the *Vamoose*, the latter ordered by Mr. Hearst of California. The *Vamoose* has

work at the Institute of Technology, the Corliss shops and abroad had all been calculated to increase his interest in steam craft and make him more proficient in building them and their machinery. As long ago as 1876 he produced a torpedo boat for the torpedo school at Newport, which was only sixty feet in length, but achieved a speed of twenty miles an hour. The officers of the school called it the *Lightning*, and compared with the average naval vessel of the day it deserved its title. It is recalled that on the trial trip of the craft the designer was at the engine, showing that he could manage a steamer as well as a sail boat, if the necessity arose. Indeed it has been said that he knows more about high-speed engines than any one else in the country.

His years of study along this line away from Bristol were supplemented by several years of valuable experience there, during which the government stationed a staff of officers at the Herreshoff works for the purpose of experimenting with high-speed machinery, no other firm in the country making a specialty of that grade of production at the time. Chief Engineer Benjamin F. Isherwood and a

investigators from Washington left him superior, in his own particular line, to any other American boat-builder. It is no wonder, when we consider his natural genius, that his steam craft have proved speedy vessels.

There is money in the construction of fast steam yachts; and that fact probably accounts for the comparatively recent development of the big sailing yacht at the Herreshoff yard. John B. Herreshoff is a shrewd business man, and he has been more anxious to put by something for a rainy day than to win glory for himself or his brother by building swift sailing vessels. It is said that when a yacht was needed to

" BALLYMENA."

number of naval colleagues were at Bristol intermittently for four years, studying compound and triple expansion engines, the arrangement with the Herreshoffs amounting practically to a partnership between them and the Navy Department. The government furnished the expert knowledge required for the investigations, and the Herreshoffs supplied the shops and the other requisite facilities. There can be no doubt of the value to the younger Herreshoff of these years of association with the government experts. He had already become a master mechanic with few equals, and the hints he received in the course of his intimate acquaintance with the experienced

meet the *Genesta*, back in 1885, Mr. Herreshoff was approached and asked for figures on such a boat. The price he set was $30,000, as the story goes, and the prospective purchasers, considering the amount too high, placed their order with Edward Burgess, who designed the *Puritan* for them. What seems strangest about this story is that $30,000 should have been regarded as too great a price to pay for a cup-defender. The Vanderbilt-Iselin-Morgan syndicate will be out of pocket many times that amount when they have settled for the new aluminum and bronze vessel from Bristol.

During his long years of work in build-

"COLONIA."

"Nat" Herreshoff yearned, without doubt, for the time to arrive when he would be able to show the world what he could do with a big racer of modern design. And as all things come to him who waits, this opportunity at length arrived. Now that the Herreshoffs are possessed of a reasonable competence, the designer is able to give as much time as he desires to the development of any notion that may come into his head, though it ought to be added that in the case of the *Defender* the notion pays very well.

The "cat yawl" is a Bristol variety of boat. Not that there are no cat yawls anywhere else, but at Bristol they flourish like the traditional green bay tree. Captain Nat built one of these for Commodore Edwin D. Morgan some years ago, and so pleased was the latter that he ordered a twenty-six-footer constructed along the same general lines. As the result, the *Pelican* was launched in December, 1890, and on the seventh of that month the designer and his brother Lewis made a trial trip in her, although the gale in which they sailed was one of the severest of the winter. The craft proved stiff and fast, and it was seen at once that her model was a success. The

ing boilers and hulls for steam yachts, Captain Nat was by no means uninterested in sailing craft. He kept storing up ideas for future development, and no doubt he felt that some time he would have an opportunity to turn to the construction of a sailing yacht of sufficient size to bring him into the first rank among the designers of such boats. He had been known before as a successful sailboat designer; his *Shadow* of the early seventies had taken more prizes, perhaps, than any other sailing craft ever built. But there is a certain prestige attaching to the construction of a successful big yacht that does not attach to the construction of smaller racing vessels. Edward Burgess's name became widely known for the first time when he had created his fast ninety-footer, although he had been building fast boats for a good many years.

"HANDSEL."

history of this boat is important because the *Gloriana,* racer of glorious memories, was the direct outgrowth of the *Pelican.*

Mr. Morgan recommended the Herreshoffs to Royal Phelps Carroll, who was intending to build a boat for the season of 1891, and the result was that the order for a forty-six-footer, the future *Gloriana,* was placed at Bristol. Meanwhile Mr. Carroll married and went to Europe, and this event changed his plans for the season to such an extent that the new yacht was ultimately constructed for Mr. Morgan. It has been said that the *Gloriana* was a lucky accident; but those who are familiar with the care and thought that the designer put into her are aware that such a notion is entirely erroneous.

up before him. And that, in a word, was precisely what he did. The *Gloriana* was a success from the start, and at the end of the season was confessedly the swiftest and ablest boat of her size on this side of the ocean, if not in the world.

The launch of the famous craft took place early in May, Mr. Morgan having gone to Bristol in a special car to witness the event. Four or five hundred people watched her as she glided into the harbor; and while her model was seen to be peculiar, there was something about it that suggested speed even to the untrained eye. Her name was suggested by a line in Spenser's "Faerie Queene," "That greater, glorious queene of faery land;" and when she won the race

"CLARA."

roneous. Here was a turning-point in the career of Captain Nat. If he failed to build a fast boat, it would be said of him that his forte was the construction of steam craft, and that he would best stick to that branch of marine architecture in the future, at least so far as craft of large size were concerned. On the other hand, if he should produce a boat far and away superior to the existing vessels of her class, unlimited possibilities would open

against the *Beatrix* off Newport in August, her trophy was a beautiful silver cup designed and made by the Whitings, on which a feminine figure was engraved, representing Her Majesty of the faery race.

The *Gloriana's* chief characteristics are her raking stem and overhang stern, which make her look very different, viewed broadside on, from the racing yachts of former days. Instead of the perpendicular bow of her predecessors,

"POLLY."

it is scarcely an exaggeration to say that she has almost nothing forward, everything being reduced to the minimum at this point in order to give the least possible resistance while she is gliding through the water. She seems to sweep over the sea rather than push it to either side of her, and her deep keel enables her to get a "grip" far down below the surface, while at the same time her displacement is not increased. It might be supposed that with almost no forefoot it would be difficult to keep her from falling off in a strong wind; but the reverse is true. She hugs the breeze in a way to delight the soul of the old salt, and minds her tiller as quickly as could be desired. In her first race around the Scotland lightship, when she started home on a reach, Captain Nat, who was at the tiller, called a member of the crew aft to assist him in case of necessity. But no necessity arose. The boat responded to the slightest touch, and the skipper sailed her the entire distance home with only one hand.

The season of 1891 will long be remembered for the series of races between the forty-six-footers. This class of yachts had succeeded, in natural sequence, the forty-footers, and the contests between them were among the most interesting in the history of the sport. It is worth while to notice that among all the aspirants for honors, only one boat of any importance, the Burgess yacht *Beatrix*, was a centreboard. On account of this fact it was desired, from the beginning of the

season, that the *Gloriana* should encounter her; and as race after race occurred and they did not come together, the popular interest in their ultimate meeting increased. In the first race in which the *Gloriana* started, on June 16, she was pitted against the *Nautilus*, *Mineola* and *Jessica*. The regatta was under the auspices of the Atlantic Yacht Club; and the Bristol craft beat the *Mineola*, her nearest competitor, by eight minutes and seventeen seconds. Two days later, in the New York Yacht Club regatta, there were six starters, but the *Gloriana* won from all her rivals. Two of the contestants were designed by Burgess, two were Fife boats, and a fifth was from the Wintringham shops; but the second boat at the finish was half an hour behind the Herreshoff wonder. In this race there were wind and rain in plenty, the breeze blowing at the rate of twenty miles an hour.

On the twentieth of June occurred the Seawanaka Corinthian Yacht Club regatta over the lower bay course off New York. A heavy mist overspread the water, and the yachts were invisible at a short distance. The rivals in this race were the *Nautilus* (Wintringham), *Jessica* (Fife), and *Gloriana*, the *Jessica* getting away nearly two minutes ahead of the Bristol boat, but the latter soon forging to the front and ultimately winning. On the succeeding Monday, the *Sayonara*, another Burgess craft, the *Jessica* and the *Uvira* contested with the *Gloriana*, and were handily beaten; and on Tuesday, in a light breeze, the undefeated yacht won a fifth time, securing a handsome cup, valued at $500, which had been offered as a prize by Vice-Commodore David Banks of the Atlantic Yacht Club. In these races Captain Nat was constantly in evidence, and a large degree of the success of the boat may be attributed to his wise seamanship, although in later seasons, without his presence, she has continued her former successful record.

In her sixth race, on August 7, for the Goelet cup, off Newport, the *Gloriana* won again ; and on August 13 she secured

was again at the helm, and again the glorious craft crossed the finish line a winner, beating the Burgess boat *Oweene* by a little more than a minute, and the *Beatrix* by more than five minutes. This was the only time that the two rivals met during the season ; but it was sufficient to give the *Gloriana* the undisputed championship in her class. She had won eight straight races, and in so doing had called general attention to her designer.

In the NEW ENGLAND MAGAZINE for September, 1891, a writer referring to Burgess, who had just then passed away, quoted this stanza : —

" CONSUELO."

another $500 trophy by defeating all the other boats of her class in a race designed especially for the forty-six-footers, though her margin on this occasion was only twenty-eight seconds. But as yet the *Beatrix*, which had been winning races in eastern waters, had not made her appearance against the Herreshoff boat, so that when the two finally met in the *Gloriana's* eighth race off Newport on the seventeenth of the month, popular interest was at its height. Captain Nat

" Ah, who shall lift that wand of magic power,
    And the lost clew regain?
The unfinished window in Aladdin's tower
    Unfinished must remain."

But there were already indications that the dead designer's work would be carried forward to triumphs which he could scarcely have predicted. It was at the time of the *Gloriana's* great successes that a newspaper man went to Bristol to see " Nat" Herreshoff, and came away with this impression of him :

"The Bristol inventor by no outward sign shows the pride or exultation which would be justifiable in view of his success. He is the same quiet, business-like, industrious man that he was last April, when the *Gloriana* was on the ways and an 'unknown quantity.' If he has changed the style of yacht architecture for the whole world, one would never suspect that he realized the magnitude of what he has accomplished." Thus at the moment of Edward Burgess's untimely death, Herreshoff, who was of the same age as the Boston designer, was at the threshold of his widest fame. The one had put aside his pencil and paper forever, while the other was beginning to attract the notice of yachtsmen all over the world.

The success of the *Gloriana* revolutionized yacht-building. Everybody went in for the receding bow which had been made so familiar during her career, and the overhang stern, which in her had been carried to the extreme. In the fall of 1891 the *Dilemma*, a fin-keel boat and obviously an attempt to utilize the good points of the *Gloriana* in a superior creation, was launched at Bristol, and in the succeeding year the "new *Gloriana*," or *Wasp*, as she was ultimately named, was built for Mr. Archibald Rogers. The *Dilemma* proved to be a fast boat, and had a successful career until a few months ago, when she was wrecked at the entrance to a Long Island harbor. A local designer has reconstructed her since this catastrophe, being compelled to reproduce one entire side, and it will be interesting to note whether or not he has succeeded in preserving her original lines sufficiently to allow her to win races as before.

The career of the *Wasp* during the season of 1892 was in large measure a repetition of that of the *Gloriana* in 1891. She met the latter frequently, and in a majority of instances won from her simply because she embodied the result of the observations of the designer on board the *Gloriana* during her first season. The *Wasp* retained the good points of her predecessor, and added certain new ones which made her easily

the fastest forty-six-footer ever produced. She is larger than the *Gloriana*, though belonging in the same class, her length being between seventy-one and seventy-two feet over all, while the *Gloriana* is a few inches shorter. Her keel runs practically parallel to the water line along its entire distance, and at the forward end there is an abrupt break, the broadside view showing a direct rise for several feet, after which the stem continues to the bow in a straight line. The water lines forward are fuller than they would be if the stem were permitted to reach direct to the keel, and the stem has a greater rake even than that of the *Gloriana*, the lead being farther aft. The races between the two craft have afforded much interest in every season since they first came together; and last year, out of fourteen meetings, the *Wasp* came off victorious ten times. Thus it is fair to argue that yacht designing, despite the critics who called the *Gloriana* a lucky accident, is a real science and art at Bristol.

Early in 1893 Mr. Royal Phelps Carroll had the satisfaction of seeing at last a Herreshoff boat of his own afloat. She was eighty-four feet on the water line, and a hundred and twenty-six over all, emphasizing thus the peculiarities of the smaller yachts that had preceded her on the ways at Bristol. She was designed to win the new international trophy abroad, the Royal Victoria cup, and to bring back to this country the Cape May and Brenton Reef trophies, which had been won in 1887 by the British cutter *Genesta*. The preliminary trials of the *Navahoe* were not entirely encouraging, and her subsequent career in British waters was not equal to the hopes of her designer and owner. But one of her contests was as remarkable a race as was ever sailed. She started with the *Britannia* on the twelfth of September, in competition for the Brenton Reef cup, the course being from the Needles to Cherbourg, France, and return, a total distance of one hundred and twenty miles. Wind and sea were both heavy, and during most of the race the yachts were within a minute of each other. It had been predicted that the American craft would be at her worst in just this kind of weather, but she won the race by two minutes and a half second, and the trophy in consequence. Her competitors at various times during the summer were the *Britannia*, the *Valkyrie*, the *Satanita*, the *Calluna* and the *Iverna*, and out of nineteen starts she won but three first prizes. Six seconds were placed to her credit, however, five thirds and two fourths, and in one race she was disabled. The percentage of victories won by the *Britannia* was 52.63, of the *Valkyrie*, 41.66, and of the *Navahoe*, 15.78.

After this experience the American yachtsmen began to regard the situation in respect to the approaching international regatta with increased seriousness. The *Vigilant*, another Herreshoff boat, had proved her superiority to her competitors on this side of the ocean; and yet the Herreshoff *Navahoe* had not shown up encouragingly in British waters. The *Valkyrie* left England on August 23 to sail for the cup in the autumn races off New York, and observers were not lacking on this side of the ocean who predicted her success. But the *Vigilant* had given great promise in her preliminary contests. Four boats had been built for the purpose of defending the trophy, — the *Pilgrim*, launched at Wilmington for Stewart A. Binney of Boston; the *Jubilee*, a South Boston fin and centreboard combination boat, designed by John B. Paine and owned by General Paine, the veteran yachtsman; the *Colonia*, ordered from the Herreshoffs by a New York syndicate with Archibald Rogers at the head; and the *Vigilant*, launched at the Herreshoff yard on June 14, and owned by another syndicate including Commodore Morgan and C. Oliver Iselin. The *Vigilant* is a centreboard yacht, combining with that type, however, some of the best features of the keel model, and having a coating of Tobin bronze. The *Colonia* is a larger *Wasp*, being of the familiar keel variety of later seasons and possessing great depth. Following are some statistics of the four craft : —

	Length over all.	Beam. ft. in.	Draught. ft. in.
Vigilant,	124 feet.	26	14
Colonia,	123 "	24	16
Jubilee,	123 "	22 6	13 6
Pilgrim,	122 "	23	22 6

During the early season the *Vigilant* had indicated her superiority as an all-around boat, although the *Colonia* showed up well, and many people believed that with some slight changes in her rig the *Jubilee* might exhibit her heels to her rivals. The official trial races began on September 7, off Sandy Hook, when the *Pilgrim* and *Jubilee* were disabled, and the *Vigilant* won on actual time, the race going to the *Colonia* by six seconds, however, on time allowance. The course in this contest was fifteen miles to windward from Scotland lightship, around the stakeboat and home. Two days later, in the second trial, the course was a triangular one, ten miles to each leg. The *Vigilant* won over the *Pilgrim*, her nearest competitor, by two minutes, nineteen seconds, and the *Colonia* was fourth. In the third and last race the course was the same as in the first. The *Vigilant* won with ease, and the *Colonia* came in second, about seven minutes behind. The *Vigilant* was accordingly chosen to defend the *America's* cup against the *Valkyrie;* and the Herreshoffs had the satisfaction of seeing their other boat, the *Colonia*, selected as the alternate defender. That was considerable glory for one season, despite the comparative failure of the *Navahoe* to accomplish the purpose for which she had been built; but there were greater glories to come. Captain Nat was anxious to show the British yachtsmen that his latest creation was superior to the *Valkyrie*, notwithstanding the defeats of the Carroll boat.

The length of the *Vigilant* on the load water line was officially determined as being 86.19 feet, while that of the *Valkyrie* was 85.50. Thus the American boat was compelled to allow her rival one minute and forty-eight seconds in each contest. The first of the series occurred off Sandy Hook on the seventh of October, the attempt to sail two days previously having ended in failure. The course was fifteen miles to windward and return, but unsteady wind rendered the race a series of alternate beats and reaches. Captain Nat was at the helm of the American craft, and at the finish she was five minutes and forty-eight seconds ahead of her competitor, corrected time. Such a fleet of steam and sailing vessels as were on hand to witness this contest had perhaps never before been assembled; and when the victorious yacht crossed the line a winner by nearly six minutes, she was greeted with an uproarious demonstration.

The second race of the series was the most successful one from the Herreshoff point of view. The wind was strong at the start, and increased until it blew at a rate of thirty-two miles an hour at the finish. The course sailed was a triangular one, and at the end the *Vigilant* was ten minutes, thirty-five seconds in the lead. When the day for the third race arrived, the sea was high and choppy and the east wind was blowing half a gale. The yachts were sent to windward fifteen miles and return, and the *Valkyrie* was ahead of her rival at the turning mark. On the run home, however, the Yankee craft began to gain, and at the finish she was forty seconds ahead on corrected time. The *Valkyrie* sustained several mishaps on the homeward run, and if she had not split her silk spinnaker at a critical moment there is no telling how the race would have resulted. Lord Dunraven, her owner, was not satisfied with the result of the series; but the *Vigilant* had won in three straight contests, and the cup stayed on this side of the sea. There are a great many " ifs " in yacht racing, but the boat which holds together at critical moments is entitled to some credit, whatever it may be supposed her competitor would have accomplished if she had not met with this or that misfortune.

The career of the *Vigilant* last year is familiar. Mr. George J. Gould purchased her to race in British waters, and in June she crossed the ocean in the short time of fourteen days, seven hours and fifty minutes, — the best time, it is said, ever made by a sailing yacht over the same distance, with one exception; the exception, moreover, was when the *Henrietta*

beat the *Fleetwing* in a race across the ocean, with all possible sail set, of course, while the *Vigilant* proceeded under short canvas. The American champion was distinctly a disappointment on the other side of the sea. Captain Herreshoff was at her helm in many of the races she entered, but owing to one cause or another she came in first in only four contests, while the *Britannia*, which was unquestionably the swiftest British yacht of the season, owing to the sinking of the *Valkyrie*, won twelve firsts. It would be profitless to discuss the reasons for the failure of the American yacht on these occasions; but in general it may be said that she was built for sailing in American waters, free from the shifting winds and currents of inland bays, and that in her career in the United Kingdom she was constantly at a disadvantage on this account, the British skippers knowing their ground thoroughly, and the British boats having been constructed with a view to racing under just such conditions as prevail over most of the English, Scotch and Irish courses.

This year the construction of the *Defender*, the yacht which in all likelihood will meet Lord Dunraven's *Valkyrie III.* in the fall, has drawn the eyes of the yachting world again to Bristol. The greatest secrecy has been maintained regarding her lines; but it is known that she is a keel craft of great beauty, plated above the water line with aluminum for lightness and below with manganese bronze. She has been ordered by a syndicate composed of Messrs. Iselin, Morgan and Vanderbilt; and her cost has been estimated as high as $180,000. She has a bow that is cut away even more than her predecessors at the Bristol shops, and her stern is in large measure of the familiar type of recent seasons. She is an improved *Gloriana*, *Wasp*, *Colonia* and *Vigilant* all in one; and if she does not sail away from the latter yacht in the preliminary races this summer the public will be treated to a genuine surprise. She measures about eighty-nine feet on the water line, and her spread of canvas will undoubtedly be greater than that of the *Vigilant*. Captain " Hank " Haff, the hero of numberless yacht races, will be in command of her; and her crew, which is composed of " down-easters " from Maine, will be as fine a lot of American seamen as can be found anywhere. For weeks they have been cruising on the *Colonia* in preparation for the races of the season; and by the time the *Defender* enters her first contest they will be able to work together with precision and confidence.

Thus the latest and finest product of the Herreshoff works and of the keen mind of Captain Nat Herreshoff enters upon her career. Her surroundings during the months which have brought her into being have been humble, for the Herreshoff shops are not pretentious structures by any means. But she is, to all appearances, the greatest sailing yacht ever designed, and we shall all be grievously disappointed if she does not prove her title to the international championship. May prosperous winds go with her, and her races prove her, as our fondest hopes already proclaim her, the unquestioned Queen of the Seas!

The Evolution
of the
Forty-Six Footer
(1892)

8

Fred.S.Cozzens

Painted for OUTING by Cozzens.

Engraved by Hoskin.

GLORIANA.

THE EVOLUTION OF THE FORTY-SIX-FOOTER.

BY GEORGE A. STEWART.

EVERY yachting novice knows what a revolution has been wrought in the science of yacht-designing during the past ten years, a development of which the *Puritan* was the leading exponent; how the battles of beam combined with small displacement against depth with low and heavy lead keels, and the fight of "sloop" versus "cutter," have been waged, and how the "compromise" boats have been evolved, both in America and in England. The *Puritan-Genesta, Mayflower-Galatea* and *Volunteer-Thistle* campaigns have been wonderful educators in the science of the sea, and they have gone far to solve many vexing questions of naval architecture.

With the attention of the yachting world riveted on the greater actions of this period, it is not surprising that the minor panorama should have passed comparatively unnoticed. Yet the events and competitions which have led up directly to the *Gloriana* and her swift sisters are no less interesting than the international competitions which overshadow them, and the results are fully as instructive to the student of naval science. In fact, the value of big international competitions lies not so much in the races themselves as in the stimulus which they give to yachting in general, fostering a wholesome growth among the craft of all classes and sizes.

The most conspicuous of the results of the *Puritan* era are the 46-footers, and during the past Summer these famous craft have received an amount of attention which is second only to that given to the national champions themselves. Yet the origin of the class is a very modest one, its growth dating back to the international year of 1887. In that year the Adams Brothers, Messrs. George C. and Charles F. Adams, 2d. commissioned Designer Burgess to furnish them with a 36-foot water-line keel sloop. She was to fit no particular racing class, and, indeed, was designed chiefly as a cruising yacht; and that size was chosen as it appeared to be the smallest in which a stateroom could comfortably be built and ordinary cruising comforts obtained.

Though such was the modest origin of the *Papoose*, as the new yacht was called, her construction attracted no little attention among yachtsmen. Though the "cutter cranks" had been temporarily silenced by the success of the centerboard compromises, *Puritan* and *Mayflower* against the "out-and-outer" *Genesta* and *Galatea*, they were by no means convinced. The state of public opinion at that time was still chaotic and not unmixed with prejudice. The victory of the *Puritan* had

Fred. S. Cozzens
86

SHADOW.—THE PROPERTY OF DR. JOHN BRYANT.

done much to appease national pride and to soften the national heart toward foreign ideas. But whether the 3 - beam *Papoose* should be classed as a cutter, or as an American keel sloop, was a vexed question, and the question whether so much beam could be successfully combined with a 10-ton lead keel was also vigorously discussed.

Up to this time the question of

Centerboarder *Vixen* had "tanned" the cutter *Maggie* unmercifully in two races at Marblehead. *Thetis* and *Stranger* had had their fling, and while the cutter won the series, the *Thetis* rested proudly on her record of having "drowned out" the cutter in a beat around Cape Cod on a wicked night. A subject, therefore, of a good deal of speculation, *Papoose*, was launched in the Spring of 1887. She had a beam of 12 ft. on a water-

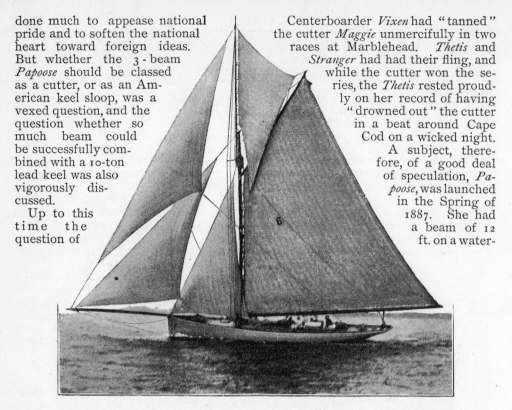

PAPOOSE.—FORMERLY OWNED BY GEO. C. AND CHAS. F. ADAMS, 2d, NOW BY JOHN T. MOTT.

type among the smaller classes of yachts had, in the bouts between "cutters" and "sloops," resulted more or less in a "stand-off." Before the year 1880 honors in New York waters had been borne off by the wide, shoal type of centerboarders, *Wave* and *Schemer* being perhaps the two most widely known. In Eastern waters the centerboarder *Shadow* had enjoyed practically a monopoly of the racing honors since her building in 1871.

The arrival of the Scotch 6-beamer *Madge* in 1881 shook the complacent confidence of the Yankee in his wide sloop. The *Madge* carried everything before her till she met the *Shadow*, which yacht succeeded in fighting the foreigner to a draw, each yacht winning one of two races. The series, however, resulted in a practical victory for the centerboarder, as its conclusion found the *Shadow's* owners eager for a third race, while canny Captain Duncan preferred to rest on the laurels already won rather than risk them in a decisive bout with this tough customer from the East.

line length of 36 ft., and drew 7 ft. 6 in. of water. What a remarkably successful production she was for an experimental boat is shown by her subsequent racing with the 40 - footers. Probably no American craft has shown a better distribution of displacement than the *Papoose*, combined with fair lines, as her disturbance of the water, when driven at high speeds, is remarkably small, and under such conditions her absolute speed was barely inferior to that of the 40-footers, in spite of her more than three feet of inferiority in length.

The first public trial of *Papoose* was made in the open regatta of the Dorchester Yacht Club, at Nahant, June 17, 1887. The début was made all the more interesting by the presence of the *Shadow*, and of the Watson 6-beam cutter *Shona*. The *Shona* had beaten the *Shadow* once the preceding Fall in a light air with rolling sea—true "cutter" weather. Consequently there was considerable rivalry between the centerboard sloop and the cutter, while the presence of *Papoose* made a triangular contest of rare interest at that time.

It was a light southeasterly breeze, and the *Papoose* did not get a quick start, on account of the big fleet crossing the line. Skipper Adams gave her a good head, however, and she slipped through the lee of her rivals amazingly fast. Soon she had head-reached them all, *Shadow* included, and showed to the front of the fleet. Then she began to show what she could do in the pointing line. When she took starboard tacks for the Whistling buoy off the Graves, she had gained such a commanding lead that the others were out of it. She kept on gaining before the wind, and especially on a reach, and the breeze increasing on the second round of the course served but to emphasize her superiority. The *Shadow* defeated all the remaining competitors with her old-time ease, the *Shona* doing very badly, partly owing to a new and ill-fitting suit of canvas. This made the *Papoose's* victory all the more noteworthy.

At this distance of time it is possible to look back and discount some of the *Papoose's* victory, as she was two feet longer than the *Shadow* and a considerably more powerful boat. But in those days the *Shadow* was considered well-nigh invincible by anything under 40-feet water-line, so that the *Papoose's* victory gave her great prestige. It certainly was a most creditable performance, and showed that a new type had been found that was far and away faster than anything that had gone before.

The success of the *Papoose*, like that of the *Puritan*, went far to put an end to the sloop-cutter controversy. It was

CHIQUITA.—THE PROPERTY OF AUGUSTUS HEMENWAY.

apparent that the 6-beam cutter could not stand before the new "compromise," while it was equally plain that the "skimming-dish" centerboarder was doomed. *Papoose* continued to win all through this year, usually having about half an hour to spare over her nearest competitor. This of course established her as a very fast craft, and made hers the type which should be imitated in future productions. From *Papoose*, in a direct line through the 40-footers, can be traced the improvements which have given us the wonderful 46-footers of last year. The sequence is direct, and a most interesting one. The speed, combined with cruising comfort, that the *Papoose* possessed attracted owners to the sport, and the next year saw half a dozen 40-footers in the lists.

Papoose had held the honors in 1887, but the record in 1888 was pretty well distributed through the fleet. At the close of the season perhaps the *Chiquita* might be selected as a shade the fastest 40, though the margin from first to last was very small.

About the same time with *Papoose* the *Banshee*, a centerboard 40-footer, was designed by Cary Smith. Like *Papoose*, *Banshee* was intended for a cruiser, but showed good speed, and a number of races were sailed between the two craft in New York waters. The keel boat won most of the races, part of the time being helped out by the never-failing "*Papoose* luck."

The racing between *Papoose* and *Banshee*, and the fact that these boats combined advantages never before reached in American designing, led naturally to the building up of a 40-foot class in 1888. For the first time absolutely non-capsizable boats were possible for Americans if they chose the keel type, while practical non-capsizability was attainable if they should prefer the centerboard. The new style craft differed from the old in that they were much better sea-boats, were built and rigged much more strongly and contained accommodations that were a vast improvement on anything that had preceded them.

The international racing, culminating in the victory of the *Volunteer* over the *Thistle*, spurred up great interest in the sport, and attracted new converts. As was natural, Designer Burgess had the most of the designing to do at this time,

and the new craft were all from his draughting board. The year 1888 saw the production of the centerboard forties *Nymph* and *Chiquita*, and the keel boats *Babboon* and *Xara*. These, with *Papoose* and *Banshee*, made quite a respectable fleet, and as all were evenly matched, the victories were well divided among them. This served to keep the interest unflagging till the very end of the season. In fact, some of the best races of that year were sailed in September.

In the four new boats of that year Mr. Burgess tried several different types. The *Nymph* was a fairly wide centerboard sloop, her beam being 14 ft. 6 in., though she was a compromise to the extent that she had a heavy lead keel and drew six feet of water. The *Chiquita* was one step more of a compromise, narrower and deeper than *Nymph*, being 13 ft. 8 in. wide, and drew 7 ft. 6 in. of water, while her centerboard did not hoist above the cabin floor. This last was a very desirable feature, as the cutting of the cabin by the centerboard trunk is one of the disagreeable features of the centerboard type.

The *Xara* was an enlarged *Papoose*, but she was never so successful as her prototype. In fact, later experience has shown that the *Papoose* was herself too wide for the best results, and Mr. Burgess always regretted that he had not given the *Xara* the same absolute beam as the *Papoose*—12 ft., instead of the 13 ft. 4 in. which she actually had. It is evident now that the *Xara*, with 12 ft. beam and the lines of the *Papoose*, would have been a better boat than any of her rivals of that year.

The Adams boys, having disposed of *Papoose*, were out with a new keel Burgess boat. Following their usual penchant for the lucky seven letters and the double "O," they christened their new ship the *Babboon*. She was practically the same dimensions as the *Xara* and about the same type of boat, except that, following the new fashion set by *Volunteer*, she had an overhanging bow in place of the straight stem. *Babboon* was rather a disappointment, probably because the success of her owners with *Papoose* led people to expect more of her than of the others. She had the faults common to all the keel 40-footers of that year—of too much beam and a defective keel plan. This gave a boat of great resistance, but lacking the power to carry sail enough to make her fast in spite of this resistance.

The commonplace record of the *Babboon* was relieved by her performance in the attempted race during the New York Yacht Club cruise at Vineyard Haven. This was the day, it will be remembered, which gave the schooner *Alert* much prestige. It was a wicked day, indeed, and a heavy southeasterly gale with thick rain squalls was excuse enough for any yachtsman to keep within the shelter of East Chop.

The smaller yachts thought it wiser to keep inside the harbor, and few even of the big craft showed their nose-poles outside of East Chop. The wonder of the regatta committee on the *Electra*, then, can be imagined, as the little *Babboon*, with single-reefed mainsail and second jib set, flew by the flagship, close-hauled on a wind and making splendid weather of it at that. The sea was tremendous, and the little forty seemed to jump clear out of water as she rose on the crest of a heavy wave. Spray flew across her in sheets, and life-lines were stretched fore and aft to prevent her crew from being washed over-

board, but still the little ship stuck it out, and her crew never gave up till the signal was given that the race was postponed. The work of the *Babboon* and her plucky crew that day was the theme of admiring comment throughout the fleet for the rest of the cruise.

A new impetus was given to the sport in 1889, which may be called the banner year of the forties. More than a score of yachts of this size, all built within two years, and all with more or less pretension as racers, were afloat, and the prospect for hot and close contests was excellent. The surprise of that year was the wonderful sailing of the Fife cutter *Minerva*, which put to rout the whole fleet of American forties, winning with such ease that her title as champion for the year could not be questioned.

The year 1890 marks the decadence of the 40-foot class, though that year was rendered memorable by the appearance of the swift 40 *Gossoon*. Few of the forties of 1889 had the courage to renew their hopeless battle with *Minerva*, and the advent of *Gossoon* went still further to drive the older craft off the race-course. After a wonderfully close fight, each yacht, indeed, winning half the battles in which they were engaged together, the *Gossoon* on her public form had a trifle the better of the struggle, and the year closed with the Burgess boat acknowledged the champion of her class.

MINERVA.—FORMERLY OWNED BY ADMIRAL CHARLES H. TWEED, NOW BY CHARLES LEE CARROLL.

BY GEORGE A. STEWART.

SECOND PAPER.

"HELEN," OWNED BY MR. EDGAR SCOTT.

THE *Papoose* having been practically alone in the racing in 1887, it was natural that her new owners, Messrs. Bayard Thayer and John Simpkins, who had bought her almost as soon as she was laid up in the Fall, should enter the racing season of 1888 with plenty of spirit.

In 1888 the racing began at Larchmont, and *Papoose* went on to the races there. All of the forties were under-rigged for racing, and as they all had approximately the same amount of canvas, they fought it out very closely together, the differences in the designs coming out in the different conditions of weather. The victories were distributed quite impartially through the fleet. *Chiquita* had rather the largest sail-plan, and she was, on the whole, perhaps the fastest of the fleet. *Nymph* was probably next in ordinary racing weather, while *Babboon* and *Xara* had it nip and tuck. Little *Papoose* plugged along, being rarely far out of her allowance and winning her share of first prizes. On the cruises she dogged the

leaders all day, occasionally going to the front in a not-to-be-denied fashion, and in general making life a burden for the owners of the 40-footers, which should have beaten the 36-footer easily by reason of their greater length.

In the Fall of 1888, without much heralding, a little black cutter sailed across the Atlantic and anchored in Boston harbor. This boat was destined to work a revolution in the forty-foot class, and to make an unsurpassed record for a foreign yacht sailing against the fleet in strange waters. Needless to say, this yacht was the *Minerva*, designed by Fife, of Fairlie, Scotland. She was built for a cruiser, and was what would have been considered on the other side a powerful sail-carrier, though of small power compared with the American type. The *Minerva* was a "sweet-looking shippy," and her graceful lines excited much favorable comment. There the wise-heads stopped, however, as Americans were so wrapped up in their belief in wide beam and big sails that they had no fear of a craft which was

"MARIQUITA," OWNED BY MR. HENRY F. LIPPITT.

only 10 feet 6 inches wide and carried several hundred square feet less canvas than the yachts she would have to meet.

The *Minerva* was not raced that Fall, but she followed the racers at times, and the way in which she would keep up with the forty-footers in light winds, when without light sails and towing a dinghy, was afterwards remembered. But at that time little was thought of it.

added the flush-deck centerboard racer *Gorilla*, and William Gardner turned out the keel *Liris*, the biggest-powered craft of the fleet. Burgess designed the centerboard *Verena*, an improved *Nymph* with bigger sails; the keel *Tomahawk*, a steel craft with 12 feet beam and 10 feet draught; and the keel *Mariquita*, the widest boat in the fleet, set upon a spindling lead keel. "A high center of buoyancy and a low center of gravity" was the motto that year. But while the high center of buoyancy was undoubtedly obtained, it is clear now that a great

"NAUTILUS," OWNED BY MR. J. ROGERS MAXWELL.

"Cutters always sail fast when they are not racing," was the comment, and nothing more was thought of it.

But with the year 1889 a change was inaugurated. The presence of the *Minerva* had absolutely no effect on the designing, and American designers simply tried to outvie each other in the matter of power and big sails. The interest excited by the forties the year before increased the building, and a big crop of new boats was the result. This time Burgess was not alone, as Cary Smith

failure was made in obtaining a low center of gravity. Designer McVey added the *Helen* and *Alice* to the list. These boats, while creditable to their designer as first ventures, failed even more than the Burgess boats in getting the requisite stability, though *Helen*, with some improvements, showed up very well the next year.

The season of 1889 reached the high-water mark in the history of American yachting. Never has there been a year in which the outlook for sport was so inspiring, and the season fulfilled anticipations. A score of 40-footers were booked to do battle with each other; the three crack 70-footers *Titania*, *Katrina* and *Shamrock*, improved to the last degree, were breathing fire and slaughter at each other; while throughout the clubs of the country a general awakening was evident among the smaller yachts. Until its record is surpassed by a better, the year 1889 will stand as the banner year in American yachting.

The racing of 1889 was one long triumph for the *Minerva*. Blow high or blow low, in smooth water or heavy seas, it was all the same to the wonderful little Scotch cutter. She beat the fleet with perfect ease, at times distancing her competitors, and showing an all-round superiority which put her in a class by herself.

Little was thought of the *Minerva* as a racer at first, and Mr. Tweed, her owner, had no intention of putting her on the circuit. A delay in preparing the *Liris* for the first race in New York led the crew of the Gardner cutter to ask for the loan of the *Minerva*, in order that they might not go unboated. The natural speed of the Fife cutter was so apparent in this first race that thereafter Mr. Tweed could not resist the pressure brought to bear upon him. So the *Minerva* came to be a racing cutter pure and simple, and her owner, who never sailed in her in a race, was able to get only one or two sails in his yacht that year.

A queer ending for a yacht built for a "cruiser!" but Mr. Tweed's experience is not unprecedented in the racing fleet. Unlucky indeed is that owner who loves not racing, but who owns a fast yacht. He is looked upon as little better than a criminal if he keeps his ship out of the races, and at last he yields to the importunities of his friends, and sadly stays ashore while his yacht is sailed to victory by some one else. Such an owner has no salvation except in building a boat so slow that no one of his friends would compromise his reputation by sailing her in competition with the cracks.

After a fairly successful "Spring opening" in New York the *Minerva* came to Marblehead, where she electrified Bostonians by winning two races right off the reel. Back to Newport, with just the same result. "*Minerva* first, the rest nowhere," usually described the racing where the conditions were equal. During the season the *Minerva* won nine races out of twelve starts. In one race she broke down, and she was beaten but twice, once by the *Nymph* in the Seawanhaka Spring race, and once by the *Liris* at Larchmont.

The *Minerva's* best contests of that year were given by the *Tomahawk*, *Liris*, *Verena*, and *Papoose*. The *Tomahawk* was a big-powered craft, but with too narrow a keel, so that she did not get as much power as she should have had. She had a big wetted surface, and was not particularly fast off the wind. But

"GOSSOON," OWNED BY MR. CHAS. A. MORSS, JR.

on the wind she was the best boat in the American fleet, and was very nearly as good as the *Minerva* on that point of sailing. With the *Minerva's* greater speed on the other points of sailing and her time allowance, however, the Scotch cutter was always safe to win. The *Liris* displayed spurts of speed at times, especially in smooth water, and she beat the *Minerva* once that year. Light construction and light rigging were carried to a greater extent in the *Liris* than in her competitors. Her rig was fatally light, and her series of breakdowns hurt her record.

In light winds the *Verena* was probably about as fast as the *Minerva*, but in two trials she did not capture a race from the narrow cutter, while in all-around weather she certainly was not equal to the Scotch boat. Little *Papoose* hunted the *Minerva* as hard as any of the American forties did. With an enlarged sail-plan

deal had been expected of her, and, in fact, her lines were capable of high speed, as was afterwards proved. But her lead keel was woefully thin, which brought its center of gravity so high that she failed to carry her big sails, so she simply lay down on her side and "wallowed" in strong winds. Cary Smith's *Gorilla* was not up to the first notch in light winds, but she was a splendid sail-carrier and made her best performances in hard weather. In the special New York Yacht Club race at Newport she caused much admiration by carrying her full mainsail and jib home to windward in half a gale of wind without parting a rope-yarn.

The year 1889 taught many valuable lessons in lightness of construction, lightness combined with

"GORILLA," OWNED BY MR. WM. KENT.

the *Papoose* kept close after the champion at all times, and she worried Captain Barr more than any other boat, as she was the only one to which he had to give time allowance. It was hard work for the American forties to give *Papoose* her time, and in the races she was often placed either second or third.

The *Mariquita* was a grievous disappointment in her first year. A great

strength of rigging, etc. The best steel wire was demanded, and every superfluous ounce was whittled off spars, blocks and upper iron-work. The saving in weight and windage was considerable, and compared with the forties of 1888, those of 1889, and especially those of 1890, showed a vast improvement in rig. Sails also received a looking over, and many improvements were made in cut and material.

The racing record of the 40-footers for 1889 was as follows :

	Per cent. Starts. Firsts.	Number of Times. 1st. 2d. 3d. 4th. 5th. 6th. 7th. 8th.							
MINERVA .. 12	75	9	2	0	0	1	0	0	0
VERENA ... 5	60	3	0	1	1	0	0	0	0
NYMPH 9	44	4	2	1	2	0	0	0	0
LIRIS...... 13	35	4	4	4	1	0	0	0	0
GORILLA ... 21	24	5	2	4	5	1	4	0	0
PAPOOSE ... 11	18	2	5	2	1	1	0	0	0
TOMAHAWK. 6	17	1	1	2	0	1	0	1	0
CHIQUITA .. 7	14	1	2	1	2	1	0	0	0
MARIQUITA. 15	0	0	6	3	4	1	0	0	1
BANSHEE... 5	0	0	2	0	2	1	0	0	0
HELEN..... 5	0	0	1	1	1	1	1	0	0
ALICE 10	0	0	1	2	1	5	0	1	0
XARA 4	0	0	0	2	1	1	0	0	0
LOTOWANA . 4	0	0	0	1	2	1	0	0	0
AWA 2	0	0	0	0	1	0	0	1	0

In the design of the yachts, too, the season of 1889 effected great changes. During the preceding two years the tendency had been toward abnormally large sails, which brought in boats of big resistance. The success of the light-powered *Minerva*, and the graceful ease with which she would slip round a course, while her big-powered rivals struggled and panted in a hopeless effort to keep up, led our designers more to a consideration of easy lines. The hollow water-lines and hard bilges went out, and the tendency was toward fuller lines and more displacement.

Designer Burgess was primarily a cruising man. He took more interest in that side of yachting where two or three friends take a sturdy little cruiser and knock about the shore on a cruise than he did even in the racing. His natural inclination was for wholesome boats, strongly built and not over-sparred, and he frequently deplored the competition which drove designers to an undue skimping of weights and to racing appliances which savored of the "machine." He had to go with the stream, however, and his productions of 1889 were as extreme and "machinish" as those of his competitors.

The influence of the *Minerva* was plainly visible in the *Gossoon*. While adhering to the big sail-plan which characterized the American yachts, Mr. Burgess narrowed the beam of the *Gossoon* to 12 feet, and gave her a less crooked midship section than her predecessors had. More displacement, and especially a thicker lead keel, made up for the power lost in beam, and the success of the *Gossoon* seemed to approve the value of the changes.

Minerva's unquestioned superiority in 1889 relegated the other forties of that year to the cruiser class, though Mr. Belmont, with characteristic pluck, had extensive alterations made to the *Mariquita's* keel-plan, and had a new try at the racing. The alteration worked wonders. From being fatally "tender," the *Mariquita* became one of the most powerful boats in the fleet. She was now able to hold up her sail-plan, and her good lines brought her well to the front. It was a great victory for Mr. Belmont's perseverance when, in the Seawanhaka Yacht Club race, in a heavy breeze and sea, the *Mariquita* beat the *Minerva* over the course, though losing to her on time allowance.

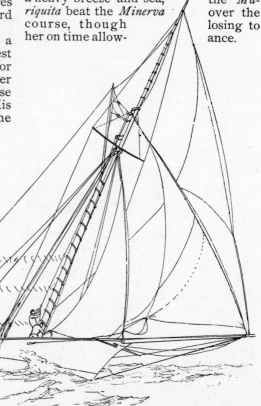

"LIRIS," OWNED BY MESSRS. SAMUEL MATHER AND C. W. WETMORE.

THE EVOLUTION OF THE FORTY-SIX-FOOTER.

BY GEORGE A. STEWART.

Completed.

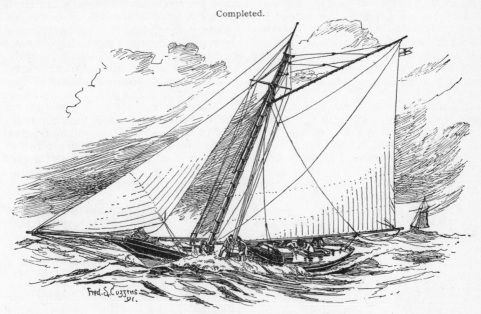

BARBARA. — OWNED BY C. H. W. FOSTER.

THE yachtsmen of Marblehead, accustomed to seeing the *Minerva* leading the fleet home by margins varying from five minutes to half an hour, could hardly believe their eyes when they saw the champion of 1889 following half a mile in the wake of the newcomer. *Gossoon's* position was at once established, and though there were many close races between these two leaders of the fleet, the superiority of the *Gossoon* was not doubted by the majority of racing men. Tough struggles they were, every one, the *Gossoon* fighting all day to get far enough ahead to give her less-powered rival her time allowance, and many times just failing in the attempt.

The *Gossoon's* time allowance to the *Minerva* was usually less than two minutes over the course. The closeness of the racing is shown by the fact that, although in ten races the *Gossoon* failed but once to beat the *Minerva* on actual time, the Scotch cutter finished within her time allowance in half the races. Two victories, awarded to the *Minerva* by two seconds, further attest the closeness of the racing. The record of the year, as finally made up, showed a practical tie,

five victories to each, but it was generally agreed that the *Gossoon* was a trifle the faster craft — an opinion which was concurred in even by Capt. Charles Barr, who sailed the *Minerva* so doggedly in her uphill fights.

Two other 40-footers were built in the year 1890, both from the hands of Designer Burgess. Both were centerboarders, and both succumbed to the keel *Gossoon*. But for this the centerboard type should not be held strictly to account, as each embodied experimental ideas which had not before been associated with the fastest order of centerboard craft.

One of these boats was named *Moccasin* and the other *Ventura*. The *Moccasin* was an attempt to combine the idea of small sail-carrying power with the centerboard type. She was narrower than the other centerboarders, having a beam of 13 ft. 6 in., as against *Verena's* 14 ft. 6 in. *Moccasin* showed a fair turn of speed, but was not raced as keenly as her competitors. Many who followed the *Moccasin's* career feel assured that with careful attention she would have followed close on the heels of *Gossoon* and *Minerva*.

NOTE.—For illustration of *Gossoon* and *Nautilus* see OUTING, May, 1892, of *Minerva*, OUTING, April, 1892.

Ventura was still more of an attempt to combine the narrow beam of the keel yacht with the shoal draught of the centerboarder. She was but 12 ft. wide, and her board did not hoist above the level of the load water-line. This produced a craft that offered exceptional advantages for cruising, as she had large cabin accommodation under flush deck, with shoal draught. If speed could have been added, she would have been perfect. But while the *Ventura* sailed some very good races, especially in light winds, it was apparent that she was not up to the level of *Gossoon* in all-around racing.

The year 1890 marked a considerable change in the method of building racing yachts. Heretofore the wooden construction had usually been considered good enough for yachts of the size of 40-footers, though the experiment of building *Tomahawk* of steel had been quite successful, and *Liris* had been composite built, with double skin. Iron floors and steel strengthening-plates had been used generally; but in 1890 all three of the new 40-footers were of composite construction, part of the frames and deck-beams being of steel. Lightness of hull and rigging were still more carefully considered, and attention to details played a large part in *Gossoon's* success. How strong she was, in spite of her lightness, is shown by the fact that although her club-topsail was carried through every race in which she competed, she finished the season with but two breakdowns.

The record of the 40-footers for 1890 was as follows.

Yacht.	Starts.	Per cent. Firsts.	—Number of Times—					
			1st.	2d.	3d.	4th.	5th.	6th.
CHISPA . .	1	100	1	0	0	0	0	0
MINERVA .	23	65	15	5	1	2	0	0
GOSSOON . .	13	54	7	4	2	0	0	0
HELEN . .	4	25	1	1	0	2	0	0
VENTURA .	10	20	2	4	1	3	0	0
CHOCTAW .	8	13	1	3	1	1	2	0
LIRIS . .	14	7	1	5	7	1	0	0
MARIQUITA .	14	7	1	5	6	1	0	1
TOMAHAWK .	3	0	0	2	0	0	1	0
MOCCASIN .	5	0	0	0	2	1	1	1
PAPOOSE .	1	0	0	0	1	0	0	0

The year 1891 was devoted to the building of the wonderful 46-footers.

OWEENE.—OWNED BY A. B. TURNER.

The success of the *Gossoon* drove all the other forties, *Minerva* included, into retirement. Mr. Bayard Thayer had lodged with Mr. Burgess an order for a 40-footer to beat the *Gossoon*, but Mr. Belmont wished more accommodation than the *Mariquita* afforded, so he gave Mr. Burgess an order for a new yacht in the 46-foot class. The *Alga* had for several years demonstrated the value of the 46-footer as a cruiser, and in the year 1890 there were a number of good contests between the 46-footers *Milicete*, *Thelma* and *Alga*. Mr. Belmont's order turned the tide in the direction of the 46-foot class. It seemed a pity that what building there was should be divided between two classes ; so Mr. Thayer was prevailed upon to build a 46-footer instead of a 40. This established the 46-footer as the coming class, and nine new yachts of that size were built for the season's sport. Thus the sequence beginning with *Papoose*, continuing through the 40-footers and culminating in the swift *Gloriana*, is seen to be a direct and natural one.

The *Mineola* and *Sayonara* were Burgess boats, and a third Burgess production was the *Oweene*, ordered by Mr. A. B. Turner. Mr. C. H. W. Foster added to the excitement by ordering the cutter *Barbara* from the Scotch designer Fife. A strong tide was now setting in the direction of the 46-foot class. Mr. John B. Paine, son of Gen. Paine, had the design of a 40-footer completed, but realizing the trend of events, he changed his intention and designed the 46-footer *Alborak*.

New York thus far had not taken a hand in the designing, but now Mr. J. Rogers Maxwell came to the front and commissioned Designer Wintringham to build the *Nautilus*.

Vice-commodore Morgan had not been very lucky in his Burgess productions *Tomahawk* and *Moccasin*, so he decided to try a change of luck. He commissioned the Herreshoffs to build him a 46. The Herreshoffs had a reputation as builders of fast-sailing craft which dated back well into the sixties. Of late years they had devoted most of their attention to steam yachts, but the success of the *Gloriana* proved that the Bristol builders had not allowed their minds to grow rusty regarding the elements of speed in sailing-craft.

Mr. Charles A. Prince added much to the yachting outlook by ordering a centerboard 46 from Designer Burgess. The success of *Minerva* in 1889 and of *Gossoon* in 1890 drove all the other owners to the selection of a keel yacht to carry their racing colors, but Mr. Prince's faith in a wide centerboard boat had not been shaken. The success of the *Beatrix* went far to prove the soundness of her owner's reasoning. She was probably the fastest among the Burgess boats, and at the close of the season was fit to push the *Gloriana* to her very best paces. Mr. Cornelius Vanderbilt ordered the *Ilderim*, a Burgess keel 46 ; but as her owner went abroad, this yacht did not go into commission.

Such was the unexpectedly large fleet which offered promise of grand sport for 1891. Nine new 46-footers, representing a cost value of over $100,000 and combining the efforts of five different designers, furnished a class which has never been surpassed.

The four Burgess keel boats were all practically of the same type, their beam varying slightly from that of the narrowest, *Sayonara*, to that of the widest, *Mineola*, and their displacement varying inversely as their beam, so that all had approximately the same sail-carrying power. All had large sail-plans, the *Sayonara's* being enlarged from the original plan in order to make her a particularly good light-weather boat. The *Oweene* was a compromise between the *Sayonara* and *Mineola* both in beam and displacement, and her design, combined with skillful attention, brought her out ahead of her sister craft. Still all the Burgess keel boats were so similar in type that it was inevitable that any yacht which could beat one of them handily would defeat them all.

The centerboard *Beatrix* was quite a beamy craft, as she was 16 ft. wide, as against *Oweene's* 13 ft. 4 in. The *Beatrix* also carried a heavy lead keel, and the combination of ballast and beam made her the most powerful of the Burgess boats. The Fife cutter *Barbara* showed a fine-cut section, with considerable flare to her topsides. She was the smallest powered boat in the fleet, barring *Jessica*, having several hundred feet less sail than the Burgess boats.

The Paine cutter *Alborak*, as was to be expected, was the most powerful boat in the fleet. She was the widest of the keel boats and carried the most lead.

While designed by John Paine, she represented the General's idea of power, and was a strong experiment in that direction. The *Nautilus* was a well-turned boat, but she had not power enough to carry the sail needed to make her a winner.

In the *Gloriana* the Herreshoffs hit the mark. Her peculiarity was a very full set of water-lines, which gave her a powerful shape. The tendency of recent years had been from the very hollow forward water-lines to lines practically straight; but Herreshoff took a step beyond and made his entrance water-lines quite full and convex. This sort of a bow the builders had tried the preceding Fall on the cat-yawl *Gannet*, and had proved its efficacy.

The Burgess boats carried from 3,900 to 4,000 square feet of sail by the measurement rule — a big sail-plan for a 46-footer. The *Gloriana* carried 4,150 square feet, and the Paine cutter over 4,300.

The *Barbara* had only about 3,600 feet of sail, and it seems a curious anomaly that with this small sail-plan she should have been very fast in light winds and not so good in a breeze. The explanation is probably to be found in her flaring section, which gave a boat practically narrower than the others in light winds, while she had not sufficient power when heeled over in a breeze.

It is also worth consideration that the *Jessica*, with only about 3,000 feet of sail, could sail so near to her competitors, which spread one-third more canvas than she did. The *Alborak's* huge sail-plan was a serious difficulty in the way of getting the highest speed, and in fact throughout the year it was impossible to hold her sails in shape sufficiently well to bring her up to the highest standard in windward work.

In construction the 46's were full of interest. Of them all the *Barbara* showed the best construction, though she had a trifle too much weight of material. All the boats were composite, part of the frames and deck-beams being of steel, while in the *Gloriana* all the frames were of steel. The *Gloriana* had a partial system of diagonal strapping, while the *Barbara* showed a complete and strong system of diagonal straps. Vice-commodore Morgan indulged in the luxury of double planking for the *Gloriana*, which added to his yacht's strength.

The Burgess boats, while cleverly constructed in the main, were too light in particular spots, and their records suffered much in consequence. At the beginning of the season the *Mineola* and *Sayonara* met the *Gloriana* in New York before the defects in their construction had been remedied, and suffered disastrous defeats.

The *Gloriana* was too weak originally in her deck construction, but this fault was remedied before the Spring races. From the first the *Gloriana* showed remarkable speed, and as she caught her competitors off their form, she established a reputation in her New York races even greater than her speed warranted.

After their rout in New York the *Sayonara* and *Mineola* went into the repair-shop. The result was that they were much better and faster boats on the New York cruise than they were in the Spring. At Marblehead the *Oweene* and *Beatrix* established themselves as the best of the Eastern boats, and the New York cruise was looked forward to to establish the amount of *Gloriana's* superiority to *Oweene* and *Beatrix*, as it was generally considered that the Bristol yacht would win.

It was a disappointment that Mr. Morgan decided not to send the *Gloriana* on the cruise, contenting himself with races sailed at Newport. Much of the *Gloriana's* speed was due to her condition, as she was handled like a race-horse, while her competitors were harnessed up for the family driving. The *Gloriana* was carefully attended to at her moorings at Newport between races, while the other 46's went on the cruise, racing day in and day out, wetting sails and stretching them out of shape, breaking down and not taking sufficient time to repair, tiring out crews, and, in general, taking the handicaps which a yacht cruising suffers when pitted against a yacht which sees no service except on race days and days devoted to preparation for races.

Gloriana won the Goelet cup for sloops —a remarkable honor for a 46-foot yacht. All her competitors suffered accidents in this race; but the *Gloriana* would have won had there been no accident. This race, with her five straight wins in New York, gave the *Gloriana* her record of great superiority to her mates, for there was nothing in her last two races to in-

Painted for OUTING by Cozzens.   Engraved by Connolly,

BEATRIX (NOW HARPOON).—OWNED BY G. C. AND C. F. ADAMS, 2ND.

dicate that she had any considerable margin over her competitors.

The special race of August 13th was an unsatisfactory affair. The *Oweene* was out of it for some much-needed repairs, and the *Beatrix* did not start, as neither of her owners was a member of the New York Club. It was a fluky

The Corinthian Yacht Club sweepstakes was looked forward to to settle the question of superiority and to give a true line on the *Gloriana's* speed. This was the only race in which the *Beatrix* met the Bristol boat, and it was the centerboarder's misfortune to carry away her throat halliard block just before the start, which gave her adherents a loophole of escape when the end of the race found her well astern of the champion.

That race was a very close fit between the *Gloriana* and *Oweene*, the Herreshoff boat winning by 51 seconds actual time and 1 minute 21 seconds corrected time. On the eight miles of windward work

MINEOLA.—OWNED BY AUGUST BELMONT.

day, with a shift of wind, and the race would have been won by the *Sayonara* if she had stuck to the *Gloriana*. But *Sayonara* and *Mineola* split tacks with the leader and made an unnecessary tack, the wind canting so that they could have fetched home without it. The *Gloriana* saved herself by 28 seconds.

the *Gloriana* beat the *Oweene* only 19 seconds. It was hoped to arrange some further races between the *Gloriana* and *Beatrix*, but Commodore Morgan decided to lay his boat up.

The success of the *Gloriana* was due to the excellence of her design throughout. She had a novel feature in her very full bow, and her building has added considerably to the knowledge of the best lines for speed. She was very powerful also, and the increase of sail which she had over her Burgess competitors was sufficient to account for her superiority in light winds, while the Herreshoff boat's power enabled her to carry off her big sail-plan in a breeze. The excellent care which *Gloriana* received added also to her sailing qualities; and the question as to just how much she was superior to her nearest competitors under even conditions will never be known. What she will do in the coming season, now that she has become the property of Dr. W. Barton Hopkins, of Philadelphia, a member of the New York Yacht Club, and is to be raced by John Barr, as skipper, remains to be seen.

The 46-foot class, even excluding *Gloriana*, was the fastest class which has ever been evolved. Their actual speed, under ordinary conditions, was almost equal to that of the 70-footers. Even in strong breezes, so long as the water held fairly smooth, the 46-footers were practically as fast as the 70-footers.

A comparison of the dimensions of the 46-footers cannot fail to be of interest. Such comparison is given in the following table:

Yacht.	Owner.	Length over all.	Length L. W. L.	Beam.	Draught.
		Feet.	Feet.	Feet.	Feet
GLORIANA	E. D. Morgan	70	45.3	13.1	11.2
BEATRIX	C. A. Prince / Dr. John Bryant.	63	45.8	16.0	7.5
OWEENE	A. B. Turner	62	45.8	13.3	11.0
SAYONARA	Bayard Thayer	62	45.8	12.8	10.5
MINEOLA	August Belmont	62	45.8	13.5	10.5
BARBARA	C. H. W. Foster	63	45.9	13.0	11.7
ALBORAK	John B. Paine	65	45.9	14.2	10.8
JESSICA	W. O'B. McDonough	61	46.0	10.2	10.4
NAUTILUS	J. Rogers Maxwell	62	46.0	13.5	10.2

The record of the 46-footers in 1891 was as follows:

Yacht.	Starts.	Per cent. Firsts.	Number of Times							Did not Finish.
			1st.	2d.	3d.	4th.	5th.	6th.	7th.	
GLORIANA	8	100	8	0	0	0	0	0	0	0
BEATRIX	11	64	7	3	1	0	0	0	0	0
OWEENE	19	26	5	8	3	1	0	0	0	2
JESSICA	19	26	5	7	3	1	2	1	0	0
SAYONARA	25	24	6	8	8	1	1	0	0	1
MINEOLA	24	17	4	6	5	2	2	0	1	5
BARBARA	10	10	1	1	1	4	0	0	0	3
ALBORAK	8	0	0	3	2	2	0	0	0	1
NAUTILUS	12	0	0	2	3	5	1	1	0	0

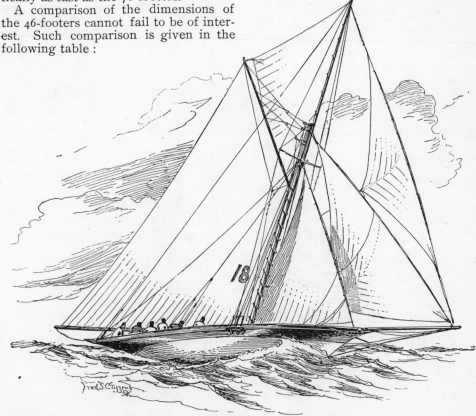

JESSICA. — OWNED BY W. O'B. MACDONOUGH.

THE LATE EDWARD BURGESS.

it is probable that the experimental class of the future will be somewhat smaller, as the expenditure of from $15,000 to $20,000 for one season's racing would confine the sport to a very few owners.

The outlook for the present Summer is an interesting one, though no such fleet of racing yachts will contest as in 1891. Several new experiments in the way of hanging lead ballast will be tried, and the racing of boats with ballast-fins and, possibly, with weighted centerboards against extremely wide and shoal center-board craft carrying little or no ballast, will be tried in the smaller classes.

The evolution of the 46-foot class, as will be seen by any one who has had the patience to read this description to the end, has embraced a large part of the yachting history of the years from the conclusion of the late international era to the present time. All the problems of naval architecture which have been solved during these years have been applied to the 46-footers and their fore-runners, and a large part of the growth of the science has sprung from these comparatively small craft. Though the present season will be rather a quiet one compared with some of the exciting years which have preceded it, still a great deal of interest will be taken in the events that do occur, and with the solution of one or two important problems, the smouldering fire will be apt to kindle anew another year.

It must be said, however, that the 46-footers did not come up fully to the expectations which had been formed as to their serviceability. It was expected that they would furnish more cabin room than the 40-footers did, but this they failed to do. They got an extra stateroom, to be sure, but this was given up to the sailing-master, and the big crew which their sail-plans demanded necessitated a large part of the yacht's accommodations being given up to the forecastle. They were very expensive boats for their size, and

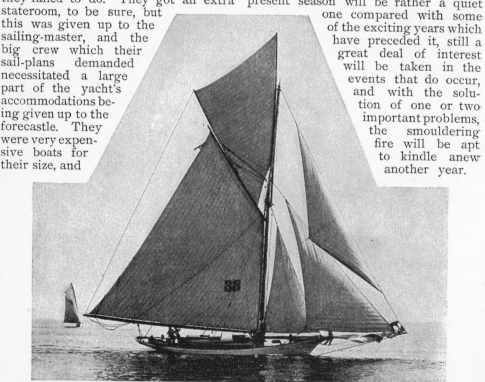

VERENA.-- OWNED BY ARTHUR AUSTIN.

The Great
August Cruise
(1899)

THE GREAT AUGUST CRUISE.

BY A. J. KENEALY.

FOR more than half a century the squadron cruise of the New York Yacht Club has been considered the chief aquatic event of the year. From the point of view of Dame Fashion and of Sport alike, it has been looked on as preëminent. This year's cruise will be sure to surpass in brilliancy even the proudest of the past, for is not the America's Cup to be fought for in October, and will not *Defender*, champion of 1894, measure her strength against the redoubtable *Columbia* for the glory of meeting Sir Thomas Lipton's *Shamrock?*

These sunny August days will be fraught with stirring deeds afloat, for the yachting fever is epidemic, and the followers of the sport of both sexes are "tuned up" to the height of patriotic enthusiasm, naturally eager that the representative of their own loved land shall vanquish the Scotch yacht with an Irish name that we shall soon welcome so warmly.

The cruise of the club has come to be regarded with singular favor by the American girl—so omnivorous of aquatic events. Some, indeed, after reveling in the delights afforded by the Larchmont week, will "take in" the cruises of the Atlantic and Seawanhaka Corinthian Clubs and finish up with the squadron cruise of the New York Yacht Club with an insatiable zest that compels admiration. But should our nautical girl fail to participate in the enjoyments so lavishly offered at her shrine by the Larchmont, Atlantic and Seawanhaka organizations, no earthly power can persuade her to do social penance and keep aloof from the attractions of the great squadron cruise.

The fact that we have been victorious in war and that our pleasure fleet coöperated right bravely with our navy in the inspiring events of last year, has also been conducive toward the great yachting revival, the like of which surpasses all my experience in American and British waters.

When Commodore J. C. Stevens, the day after founding the New York Yacht Club in the cabin of the little schooner *Gimcrack*, off the Battery, started out on a cruise to Newport, he could have had no idea what an annual stately marine pageant he was inaugurating. It will be recalled that there wasn't a single steam yacht in existence. His squadron was limited in size and insignificant as to tonnage, but the founders of the sport were built on correct lines, and the pastime so auspiciously inaugurated has taken a firm grip on our people and has become national and popular.

Gimcrack, Commodore Stevens' flagship, was launched in June, 1844, from the yard of William Capes, in Hoboken, where she was built from a design by George Steers, who later made the model of the famous schooner *America*. I regret to say that, so far as I am aware, there is no authentic model of her in existence. Her general appearance, however, is familiar to members of the New York Yacht Club from antique lithographs that adorn the walls, but her shape is missing from the superb collection in the model room. I gather that she was about 51 feet long over all, 49 feet on the water-line, 13 feet 6 inches beam, 5 feet 2 inches deep, and 7 feet 6 inches draught of water. A very modest vessel, it is true, but, for all that, famous, because she was the first flagship

of the New York Yacht Club. She acted as flagship for three years, when her place was taken by the celebrated *Maria*. In the end she was broken up at Oyster Bay, L. I.

But *Gimcrack* led the fleet of the newly formed club, and the squadron, consisting of the *Spray*, thirty-seven tons, Hamilton Wilkes; *Cygnet*, forty-five tons, William Edgar; *La Coquille*, twenty-seven tons, John C. Jay; *Dream*, twenty-eight tons, George L. Schuyler; *Minna*, thirty tons, James M. Waterbury; *Mist*, forty tons, Louis A. Depaw; *Petrel*, sixteen tons, George E. Rollins, and *Ida*, James Rogers, sailed off to Newport on a cruise by way of Long Island Sound. They arrived at their destination on August 5th, having touched at Huntington, New Haven, Gardiner's Bay and Oyster Pond, now known as Orient Point.

Newport in those primitive days was a quaint old fishing town, with nothing of architectural beauty except the Scandinavian windmill and a few ancient houses. No stately palaces crowned her magnificent cliffs, and her simple inhabitants never dreamed of the splendor and glory that were to come. But our early yachtsmen appreciated the conveniences of the harbor and were not blind to her natural beauties. It was thus that Newport began to shine as a modest rendezvous for yachts, and it

became the objective point of the club in its annual squadron cruise. In those days none but members were permitted to sail and handle their yachts, no paid hands being carried by those sterling salts.

It was no wonder that Newport had rare attractions for the members of the club. There is generally a breeze to be found off Brenton's Reef, the starting point of some of the most exciting races in the annals of the sport, and then the water is so clear and deep, and the air so fresh and pure, and the scenery so romantic and charming, that none can resist its marvelous and varied fascinations. The old-timers sailed many rattling match-races off this delightful port. They indulged in many deep-sea fishing expeditions when cod and haddock abounded in the waters near by. They speared the swordfish off Block Island's shore, and trolled for bluefish in their season.

For the first ten years in the club's history women took no prominent part in its celebrations beyond attending the "Amateur Corinthian regattas," which used to be started off the old club-house in the Elysian Fields, Hoboken, N. J., which Commodore Stevens built. The first of these events was sailed on October 6, 1846, the course being from a stake-boat anchored off the club-house, thence to and round a stake-boat anchored off Fort Washington Point, thence to and round a stake-boat anchored in the Narrows (off Fort Hamilton), thence to Southwest Spit, and return to the place of starting. Whole distance, forty miles. The race was for a silver cup, subscribed for by members, and the occasion, the first of its kind, attracted a big crowd to the Elysian Fields, at that date a sweet sylvan retreat much frequented by New Yorkers in summer time. The schooners *Gimcrack, Dream, Spray, Cygnet, Siren* and *Cornelia* and the sloop *Una* started, the time allowance being forty-five seconds a ton, Custom House measurement. The cup was won by *Una*, owned by Mr. J. M. Waterbury. *Dream, Gimcrack, Cygnet* and *Cornelia* did not finish.

This was the first regatta ever sailed in New York, and although there were no yachting reporters in those days the newspapers mentioned the circumstance and chronicled the large attendance of both sexes. In the regatta on October

12th, in the following year, the *Maria*, the club's new flagship, sailed her maiden race. The tide at starting was the last of the flood and the wind strong from southwest. *Maria's* competitors were the sloop *Lancet* and the schooners *Siren*, *Cygnet*, *Spray* and *La Coquille*. *Maria* won with remarkable facility, beating the *Siren* (second), by 58m. 15s.; actual time. The sailing committee consisted of George L. Schuyler, Andrew Foster, Jr., and William E. Laight. These races being the first of their kind proved interesting. The speed of *Maria* was surprising. It used to afford her owner pleasure to meet the steamers coming into port and describe big circles round them. The greatest speed she ever logged was seventeen nautical miles an hour. According to the chronicles in the club archives the *America* used to get shamefully defeated whenever she sailed against *Maria*. The last-named would have been sent to England during the World's Fair of 1851, but it was concluded that she was not exactly fit for deep-sea voyaging and *America* went instead. After the death of Commodore J. C. Stevens, *Maria* became the property of his brother Edward, who lengthened her seven feet and rigged her as a schooner. She was then sold and used in the fruit trade, plying between New York and Honduras. In October, 1870, while on her passage to New York, laden with cocoanuts, she was caught in a gale off Hatteras and was never heard of afterward. Better fortune attended her rival, *America*, which is in as good condition as she was a quarter of a century since, and which is to be seen during the cruise and in New York waters during the international races if the present plans of her owner are carried out.

The influence of Commodore John C. Stevens on the development of the racing yacht by means of *Maria* and *America* was undoubtedly great. If it had not been for these two great racing yachts, *Defender* and *Columbia* might not have been possible. But remarkable as was this influence on the sailing yacht it had its parallel too in steam. A primitive launch was designed by John Stevens in 1804. It was of the twin-screw variety and her machinery was of course quite crude, but from her was evolved not only the steam yacht *Corsair*, the present flagship of the club, but also the great *Oceanic*, the biggest

steamship afloat. John Ericsson, our famous engineer, took hold of the crude idea of Mr. Stevens and developed the screw propeller, the *Robert B. Stockton*, built by him, being the first vessel driven by a screw to cross the Atlantic in 1839. People that take part in this August cruise may well ponder on what the Stevens family has made possible, not only in yachting but also in ocean navigation.

Commodore James Gordon Bennett, of the New York Yacht Club, was one of the first to realize the capabilities of Newport as a social as well as a yachting center. He was the earliest colonist and cottager and much of its world-wide popularity is due to his efforts. He persuaded many of his fashionable and wealthy friends to settle there and the city grew apace. The naval station became an important one, and this was another powerful incentive to its growth, as a "swell" resort for the officers of the United States Navy seems to have an almost magnetic attraction for the American girl and her matchmaking mamma.

Mr. Bennett, in the *Rebecca, Dauntless* and the *Henrietta*, made Newport his yachting headquarters, never weary of commending its beauties and sounding its praises.

It is rather peculiar that until comparatively recently Newport has had no

:NEWPORT·HOUSE:

yacht club. That defect has, however, been remedied, and the resort now boasts of a prosperous club. The races of the 30-footers, that ever popular class, have been sailed in Newport waters for three years, and it may be said that there is no finer sheet of water in the world for small craft to disport themselves in than Narragansett Bay, where the breezes are brisk and the water smooth. In the open sea, either in the direction of Block Island or toward Gay Head, no better conditions are possible for testing the speed of large yachts, as the speed and set of the currents are well known and accurately charted, and thus no advantage is likely to accrue from special local knowledge of the tides such as obtains in other waters on the Atlantic coast.

My readers must pardon me for expatiating on the growth of Newport, but it is really associated with the progress of yachting. What Cowes is to British yachtsmen so is Newport to the American contingent. The establishment of the station of the New York Yacht Club on Sawyer's wharf was a great convenience to the fleet, the landing stages being perfect. The house is picturesque, admirably arranged, and provided with all facilities. In the height of the season the scene is brilliant. Fashionable equipages laden with wealth and beauty dash down to the station. The occupants alight, and boarding trim gigs or dainty launches are ferried off to the fleet. Sometimes the harbor is so crowded with pleasure craft that a considerable number of yachts are forced to anchor outside. Always during the cruise the Fall River steamboats have difficulty in threading their way through the clusters of craft to their docks.

The yachts have made it a rule of late years to "dress ship" on one of the days of the club's visit to Newport, and the fleet, bedecked with bunting, with snow-white decks, gleaming brasswork and shining varnish, with rigging taut and trim, makes a splendid marine spectacle, full of animation, steam launches darting hither and thither, handsome gigs pulled by brawny oarsmen, smart as paint in their Sunday rig, colors flying—all this, I promise you, is well worth seeing, and once seen is graven for life on the receptive tablets of memory. I have often wondered why some marine painter of real ability does not make the spectacle the subject of a great picture. Photography, it is true, gives a vivid idea of the spirited scene, but it requires color to do full justice to the August visit to Newport of the great squadron.

It will well repay a sightseer with a big bump of curiosity jutting out from his cranium to turn out early in the morning and watch the yacht stewards doing their marketing in busy Thames street. Every known delicacy and comestible is on sale in the great marts that here abound. Huge sides of beef, car-loads of fish, fruit and poultry, are quickly disposed of, and conveyed in groaning wagons to the landing stage. Once there the stores are seized by the sailors and stowed away in the boats, whose gunwales are brought down almost to the level of the water's edge. The great cargoes of ice that are taken aboard are such as to astonish one. Also is the immense quantity of lobsters that leave the shore bound out to the yachts. The Newport lobster is fat and juicy, and the yachtsmen fully appreciate him. No wonder that the Newport tradesman looks fat and sleek and prosperous!

At eight o'clock in the morning, on the signal of a gun from the flagship, eight bells is struck and the colors displayed. The morning scene on the day of a great race, such as that for the Astor cups, is especially brilliant. The yachts get under way early, and the white-sailed procession leaving the spacious harbor for the open waters of Narragansett Bay is almost bewilderingly beautiful. The scene is watched from every point of vantage ashore. Excursion trains and excursion craft bring hordes of interested spectators from city and country. The ubiquitous catboat dances cork-like on the bounding waves, and is in evidence in hundreds. And out to Brenton's Reef, where the start is generally made, the squadron of steam and sail proceeds, the racers stripped for action, the steamers bearing deck-loads of animated guests eager for the sport to begin. With but few exceptions the races for the cups presented annually by the late Captain Ogden Goelet were sailed in good breezes, the competitors being noted craft. Of course, there were occasions when the complete success of the contest was marred by unfavorable weather conditions — notably in 1893, when a fluke made futile the race between *Jubilee, Colonia, Vigilant* and *Pilgrim.* But as a historical fact, it must be conceded that these annual contests sailed for so many years off Newport were highly conducive to the progress of the sport.

Captain John Jacob Astor, in offering valuable trophies to be raced for annually off Newport under similar conditions governing the Goelet cups, has earned appreciative thanks from his fellow members. The only right he reserves is the privilege of inviting any foreign yachts visiting these waters to compete for the prizes. The nominal value of these cups is $1,000 for the

view of the squadron, a large excursion steamer being chartered for the purpose and an interesting race being arranged. Glen Cove is, however, a rather stagnant part of the Sound, so far as breezes are concerned, and the races that were started in that vicinity were not always remarkable for their brilliancy. I remember how strongly former Commodore Gerry opposed the substitution of Glen Cove for New London. He pointed out that the members of the club who hailed from Boston, and at that time owned the majority of the finest sailing yachts afloat on this side of the Atlantic, could scarcely be expected to come so far west as Glen Cove to join the fleet, and that New London was in all respects a more

THE YACHTS "DRESS SHIP" AT NEWPORT.

schooner trophy and $500 for the sloop prize; but it is a matter of fact that the cups are far more costly than the amounts named. The Goelet prizes were much valued and eagerly competed for, the natural result being to stimulate interest in the sport. The same object is sure to be achieved by the Astor trophies, for one of which *Columbia* and *Defender* will race in a few days.

As I write it is pretty generally understood that the squadron will rendezvous this year at New London, a favorite resort of the club since its inception. During the past few years the squadron was mustered for its cruise at Glen Cove, on Long Island Sound. This was in order to afford the non-yacht-owning members an opportunity to get a good

suitable and convenient rendezvous. But all his eloquence was wasted. Glen Cove was chosen, and ever since *Vigilant's* first year the fleet has come together there (except in 1898, when, because of the war, there was no squadron cruise). The change back to New London will be gratifying to most members.

New London proper is as quaint an old town as Newport. The squadron, however, comes to an anchorage off the Pequot Colony, where the club has a regular station and landing stage. The fleet is always accorded a fervent welcome by the hotel, the casino and the cottagers, the festivities comprising a dance and fireworks, which are returned by hospitalities aboard, the vessels being illuminated. The citizens of New London highly appreciate the visit of the yachts, and come down *en masse* from the city by trolley and by water to inspect and criticise the new craft of the year. Along the Connecticut beaches sea lawyers and marine critics are plentiful, and keen and captious are their criticisms. Their exuberance generally takes effect in the hiring of the civic brass band, which embarks in a steamer and serenades the squadron. The fleet, while giving the citizens a sort of free marine circus, incidentally leaves many dollars behind, for stores of all kinds are purchased there, and the hostelries also reap a bounteous harvest.

Only one day is spent at New London usually, as the first squadron run is started on the morning following the rendezvous, the start being from a mark off Sarah's Ledge, near the entrance of the harbor, and the finish off Brenton's Reef, Newport. The club, by the offer of costly prizes, does its best to stimulate the emulous rivalry of its members. Trophies are offered to yachts in cruising and racing trim, and a vessel may elect to sail in either trim, skinned for action, with nearly everything superfluous sent ashore, or else in actual cruising condition, with nothing removed.

The runs of *Columbia* and *Defender* will be the interesting features of the cruise, for by that time both vessels will have been "tuned up" for real racing, and Commodore Morgan's craft should then be in her true form. It is safe to prophesy that all New London that can afford to take a holiday will be seen afloat off Sarah's Ledge to see the start of these two famous flyers. I remember when the *Volunteer* came to New London for the first time she was met by two tiny boys in a dory driven by a sail made of burlap, and handled in really creditable style. There was a fine breeze from the southward and quite a lop of a sea, but these brave little youngsters, nothing daunted, tacked about in their little boat like old tars, exciting admiration aboard the steam yacht on which I was a guest. I merely mention this little incident to show what enthusiasm prevails among the Yankees. It beats hollow that of New York. From New London to Cape Ann all the seafaring population talks yacht.

If the squadron is favored (as it generally is) with a spanking southwester,

the clippers of the fleet will hum past old Point Judith at a gait that will try the "tea kettles" of the older types of steam craft to keep up with them. As for *Columbia* and *Defender*, under the condition above mentioned, driven by proud and lofty pyramids of duck, they will leave the bulk of the fleet hull down astern, and swoop into Newport with only a few of the very fastest steamers able to keep them company. Their reception is sure to be right royal, with a large flotilla to meet them and convoy them to port.

Martha's Vineyard is, I understand, to be the next objective point after Newport. The sail through the Sound is generally delightful, the shore, from Gay Head to Cottage City, and on the other side past the Elizabeth isles, presenting many picturesque features. There is usually a spanking southwester blowing in the afternoon which wafts the fleet gayly along to the anchorage at the Vineyard, where the club owns still another station and landing stage. The club has a host of friends at Cottage City, where the Oak Bluffs Club, which owns one of the coziest snuggeries in Massachusetts, receives them with open arms, offers them prizes to sail for, and in a hundred hospitable ways tries to make their sojourn pleasant.

Cottage City is another quaint and charming resort for yachtsmen, cool and pleasant and restful. The fleet will probably stay at the Vineyard two nights and a day, and may sail through Wood's Holl into Buzzard's Bay, and into the famous old whaling harbor of New Bedford, dear to the hearts of all seafarers, whether sailing for bread or pleasure. This is another "stamping ground" for yachtsmen, who find there hearty greetings. From New Bedford the fleet will make its way back to Newport, where other races may be sailed before the squadron disbands.

It will be seen that the cruise thus promises to be exceedingly pleasant. Secretary Oddie thinks that the fleet that will participate in it will be large. Many vessels that haven't been in commission for years will fit out for the sole purpose of joining the squadron, and all the vessels new this year are, of course, to be finished in time for this great yachting function, which is preparatory, in a measure, to the cup contests in October.

The Story of the
New York Yacht Club
(1901)

THE STORY OF THE NEW YORK YACHT CLUB

By A. J. Kenealy

JOHN C. STEVENS,
THE FOUNDER OF THE CLUB.

FOR more than fifty years the first home of the New York Yacht Club was a landmark of rare historic interest to yachtsmen. It occupied, when first built in 1845, a conspicuous place on the New Jersey shore of the Hudson, with the lovely Elysian Fields of Hoboken at its back, and it was the cradle of a sturdy infant sport destined to grow to gigantic dimensions. Hoboken was rural and sylvan in those days. Picturesque farmhouses of Dutch and German types dotted the green meadows, watered by purling brooks, and no prettier spot could have been chosen for a yacht club.

The devotees of the sport were then few, racing was confined to matches for a modest stake or wager and these were rare. The few pleasure craft in existence hailed from New York and Boston. One of these, the schooner *Gimcrack*, was owned by John C. Stevens, the father of American yachting, and the first commodore of the Club. This gentleman had boated from his boyhood. The first craft he owned was built by himself in 1802, and was

christened *Diver*. She was nine feet long, three feet deep and three feet wide. The *Maria*, his last and most famous craft, for many years flagship of the Club, flew her pennant one hundred and fifty feet above sea level.

Mr. Stevens was the first to realize that the sport of yachting needed organization. He consulted with his friends and won them over to his opinion that the time was ripe for an American yacht club. The failure of the Boston (so called) Yacht Club, which had been founded in 1835, with Captain R. B. Forbes as commodore, but had only lasted two years, did not appear to be a case in point, for the Boston club had for flagship and fleet the schooner *Dream*, of twenty-eight tons custom house measurement, and its chief pleasure was fishing. It exercised no influence on yacht building, cruising or racing. It was only a

CUP WON BY CYGNET IN FIRST REGATTA
OF N. Y. Y. C., JULY 17, 1845.

yacht club in name, composed of members who loved to sail in pleasant weather and indulge in old-fashioned chowder and card parties. The club went quietly out of existence in 1837, a year of commercial panic.

Mr. Stevens on July 30, 1844, called a

pointed: John C. Stevens, George L. Schuyler, John C. Jay, Hamilton Wilkes, Captain Rogers. On motion it was resolved that the club make a cruize to Newport, Rhode Island, under command of the Commodore. The following yachts were represented at this meeting: *Gimcrack*, John C. Stevens; *Spray*, Hamilton Wilkes; *Cygnet*, William Edgar; *La Coquille*, John C. Jay; *Dream*, George L. Schuyler;

THE FIRST CLUB-HOUSE—ELYSIAN FIELDS, HOBOKEN, N. J., 1845.

meeting of yachtsmen, which assembled aboard his schooner *Gimcrack*, anchored off the Battery, New York. Nine yacht owners responded. What happened on that occasion I transcribe from a treasured document in the archives of the Club.

" Minutes of the New York Yacht Club on board of the *Gimcrack* off the Battery July 30, 1844, 5 p. m. According to previous notice the following gentlemen assembled for the purpose of organizing a yacht club, viz.: John C. Stevens, Hamilton Wilkes, William Edgar, John C. Jay, George L. Schuyler, Louis A. Depaw, George B. Rollins, James M. Waterbury, James Rogers.

" On motion it was resolved to form a yacht club. On motion it was resolved that the title of the club be the New York Yacht Club. On motion it was resolved that the gentlemen present be the original members of the club. On motion it was resolved that John C. Stevens be the Commodore of the club. On motion it was resolved that a committee of five be appointed by the Commodore to report rules and regulations for the government of the club. The following gentlemen were ap-

Mist, Louis A. Depaw ; *Minna*, James M. Waterbury; *Petrel*, George B. Rollins; *Ida*, Captain Rogers. After appointing Friday, August 2, at 9 a. m., the time for sailing on the cruize the meeting adjourned.''

In this business-like manner the keel of the Club was laid. Next day the little fleet started on the first squadron cruise ever sailed in the United States, touching at Huntington, New Haven, Gardiner's Bay and Oyster Pond, known now as Orient Point, and reaching Newport on August 5th, where they were joined by ex-commodore Forbes, of the defunct Boston Club, Col. W. P. Winchester, of the schooner *Northern Light*, and David J. Sears, all of Boston. These were the first Bostonians that were elected to membership. This cruise was the forerunner of many others. Newport, at that time a mere fishing village, from its splendid harbor was naturally appreciated by seafaring men, but that it would in time become the

MODEL ROOM OF THE FIRST CLUB-HOUSE.

yachting center of the country, probably never occurred to the owners of the little fleet that anchored there in 1844.

In the light of subsequent events it is interesting to note that the flagship *Gimcrack* was a tubby craft of twenty-five tons custom house measurement, and that the united tonnage of the whole fleet was less than two hundred and fifty. *Gimcrack* in spite of her apple bows and her cockle-shell dimensions will always be famous as the prototype of the modern fin keel, for she was fitted with a fixed fin of heavy plate iron, four feet deep and fifteen feet long—lacking only the bulb of lead at the base to make it a twentieth century device.

The first election of officers took place at Windhorst's, New York, on March 17, 1845. John C. Stevens was chosen Commodore; Hamilton Wilkes, Vice-Commo-

SECOND CLUB-HOUSE—ROSEBANK, STATEN ISLAND, 1865.

dore; John C. Jay, Recording Secretary; George B. Rollins, Corresponding Secretary; and William Edgar, Treasurer.

The first club-house was built by the brink of the Hudson, on ground the use of which was given by Commodore Stevens, who also paid the builder's bill. Modest and unpretentious, it was opened in 1845, and from the anchorage off the club-house the first regatta was started on July 17 of that year. So far as I can discover after a good deal of research it was the first yacht race worthy of the name held in the United States. It was an event so unique that according to the newspapers of that time a crowd of many thousands

Schooners also set a single headsail, a gaff-foresail and mainsail and a small main gaff-topsail. Foretopmasts were rare at that date. Sometimes when the wind was dead aft or on the quarter, a squaresail of modest expanse was bent to a yard and set flying. Spinnakers and club-topsails were of a later growth. But the nine boats made the best of the brisk sou'wester and the strong young ebb. They sailed a gallant race, rounded the Southwest Spit and homeward ran, the schooner *Cygnet*, owned by William Edgar, winning the cup and gaining the plaudits of the people who had lingered in the Elysian Fields to see the victorious yacht sail home.

In this unpretentious manner the sport of

THIRD CLUB-HOUSE—STAPLETON, STATEN ISLAND, 1875.   (NOW ON GLEN ISLAND.)

flocked to the Elysian Fields to see the start. There were nine competitors, the prize being a silver cup, which cost $45, the amount being made up from the entrance fees of $5 per boat.

At a signal from the club-house anchors were hove up aboard the contesting craft, sails were hoisted and amid cheers from the populace, the yachts started for the Southwest Spit, the outward boundary of their course.

In those primitive days no "ballooners" bothered the crews, and the era of professional jockeying was happily unknown. Sloops carried one headsail only—a jib with a bonnet in it. The after canvas consisted of a mainsail of moderate dimensions, and a jib-headed gaff-topsail set on a stumpy spar.

yacht racing was introduced to the inhabitants of the island of Manhattan and their neighbors in New Jersey. The growth of the glorious pastime has since been concurrent with the progress and prosperity of the Club.

Its founders and early members loved the sport for the enjoyment and pleasure it yielded. There was no society end to yachting in the youthful times I write of. People of fashion took no interest in either racing or cruising. Commodore Stevens and his clubmates generally were seamen and navigators. They handled their own craft in sailorly style. As a proof of this I cite a regatta held by the club on October 6, 1846, in which the competing yachts were manned by club members solely, the regular crews being left ashore. This was the first Corinthian yacht race sailed in America, and the prize was a cup subscribed for by the club. The starters were the sloops *Maria*, J. C. Stevens, and *Lancet*, G. B. Rollins; the schooners *Siren*, W. E. Miller; *Cygnet*, D. L. Suydam; *Spray*, H. Wilkes, and *La Coquille*, John C. Jay. The course was from the flag-ship *Gimcrack*, anchored off the club-house, thence to a stake-boat off Fort Washington Point, thence to another stake-boat in the

THE RECENT CLUB-HOUSE, MADISON AVE., N. Y.

Narrows, and back to the starting point, the whole distance being forty miles. The time allowance was twenty-five seconds per custom house ton. The wind was strong from south-west. *Maria* won with ease, beating the schooner *Siren* (the second boat) by fifty-eight minutes and fifteen seconds actual time.

The sloop *Maria* is famous among yachts-men all over the world. As the second flag-

ship of the club she is part of its history. She had as much influence on yachting in this country as the schooner *America* exerted on the yacht builders and sailmakers of Great Britain, which was vast. She came into existence in the following manner: The crack North River sloop in 1844 was *Eliza Ann*, whose skipper's veins were full of sporting blood. When he learned that the fleet of the newly formed club was going on a pleasure jaunt to Newport he decided to go also, and show them how fast a North River sloop could sail. Without going into particulars, it is sufficient to say that the *Eliza Ann* beat every yacht with much ease in each daily run from port to port. Commodore Stevens was impressed by her speed. At his request the Commodore's brother, Mr. Robert Livingstone Stevens, took off the lines of *Eliza Ann* and improving upon them, designed *Maria*, which was built in the same year by Mr. William Capes, of Hoboken. On her maiden sail she nearly capsized in a squall off the Stevens Castle. A ferry-boat steamed to her rescue and towed her to her dock, where her redundant rig was reduced and her monstrous wings were clipped. After that she beat every craft she sailed against, including steam vessels.

Maria will ever be remembered as the yacht whose owner originated many devices which at the present time masquerade as modern. Even as *Gimcrack* possessed the germ of the fin keel, so was *Maria* the mother of outside lead, the weighted centerboard and hollow spars. When Commodore Stevens formed the syndicate which built the schooner-yacht *America*, as an exhibit from this country to the World's Fair held in England in 1851, Mr. Robert Steers, her designer and builder, agreed to charge nothing for her if she did not defeat *Maria*. The reverse happened. *Maria* actually sailed round the *America* many times. The syndicate absolved Steers from his compact and paid him in full. But so disappointed were the members with the performance of *Amer-*

ica that they almost decided to send *Maria* to England in her stead. A certain notable experience of the big sloop in a nasty sea and a northeast gale, when she met with her only defeat in a race against the schooner *Coquette*, a much smaller vessel, demonstrated that she was not adapted for blue water work. So *America* crossed the Atlantic, being the first American yacht to sail over the western ocean. She won the cup which has made her name renowned among all maritime racers.

It is not generally known that the first international race between America and England was sailed in 1849. Particulars are lacking. Only the bare record remains that the Yankee keel schooner *Brenda*, flying the burgee of the New York Yacht Club, sailed against the Marquis of Anglesey's famous cutter *Pearl*, beating her by fifty-five seconds. The length of the course is not given. *Pearl* was the first yacht with the distinctive cutter rig. She was built at Wivenhoe in 1820, and was for a long time the fastest yacht in Great Britain.

The Club in its second year had 122 members, but only ten yachts in its squadron. The building of a pleasure craft in those days was quite a serious undertaking, not because of the cost, which was far less then than now, but for some other reasons which cannot easily be explained. Perhaps because yachts were considered too luxurious for the simple tastes of our forefathers. It may be concluded that the victorious visit to England of *America* had not been without a certain amount of fruition, for we find that in 1853 the membership had increased to 153 and the fleet to fourteen. Commodore Stevens remained in command of the Club until 1855, when

failing health compelled him to retire. An enthusiastic yachtsman, a generous gentleman, liberal, opulent and popular, he established the sport on an enduring basis. He suggested the visit of *America* to England, defraying the lion's share of the expenses.

THE NEW HOME, WEST FOURTY-FOURTH STREET, N. Y.

While there he tried to induce British yachtsmen to engage in other races with his schooner but the way the Yankee terror flew away from their fleetest yachts in the ever memorable race for the Royal Yacht Squadron Cup, scared off the faint-hearted English.

Commodore Stevens spent at least $100,000 —a vast sum in those days—in building *Maria* and in subsequent alterations. In every possible manner he showed his devotion to the sport. Yachtsmen mourned sincerely when he died at the age of seventy-two at his home in Hoboken in June, 1857.

The third international yacht race between America and England was held in 1852. Mr. Robert M. Grinnell, of the New York Yacht Club, commissioned Bob Fish to build him

STAIRCASE AT THE ENTRANCE.

the twenty-one-foot centerboard sloop *Truant*. The craft proved fast. She was taken to England on the deck of the *New World*. She raced against yachts double her size, winning handily seven races out of eight—four times on the Mersey, once at Kingstown, and twice on the Thames. Her only defeat was on Lake Windermere, when she lost by six seconds. In the following year the English made a rule that centerboard yachts should sail by themselves. As *Truant* was the only yacht of that type in Great Britain, her racing career was thus brought to a sudden close. The war on centerboard yachts was waged with great bitterness in England until 1893, when Lieutenant Henn induced the Yacht Racing Association to abolish all restrictions on centerboards, thus making possible the racing in British waters of Mr. Royal Phelps Carroll's *Navahoe* and Mr. George Gould's *Vigilant*.

For many years the house in the Elysian Fields was the headquarters of the Club. From its porch many exciting finishes were seen. In the model room the members met, and smoked, and spun rare yarns. There was no club uniform, no pipe clay and no red tape. There was however, a sturdy and admirable simplicity, an exact sense of honor among the old salts in every way commendable. When the war broke out in 1861, the Club had 488 members, and a fleet of 75 schooners and 22 sloops. In that year the annual regatta and cruise were omitted. The Club met with its first reverses during the years of the war. Its membership dwindled and its fleet decreased. In 1865 the Club was incorporated. Hoboken began to hum with industry. Its natural attractions were marred by the encroachments of commerce. In 1868 the Club abandoned its home in New Jersey and leased a villa on Staten Island, near Fort Wadsworth. Its fleet then numbered 42 boats and the members were 278. The old house was occupied later by the New Jersey Yacht Club. Subsequently the New York Yacht Club occupied another house at Stapleton, Staten Island. In 1871 city quarters were taken at the corner of Twenty-seventh street and Madison avenue, the Club having on its roll 452 members, 37 schooners, 14 sloops and 8 steamers.

It is violating no confidence to mention that the Club had its share of adversity and in fact that its very existence was imperilled in 1877, for lack of money. Things were so bad that the Club resolved to give up its New York quarters and its Staten Island home, meanwhile storing its models and other property until times improved. Happily this course was not necessary. Some rich men stepped into the breach and saved the day. Ever since then prosperity has attended the organization. In 1884 the Club moved into No. 67 Madison avenue, with 309 members and a fleet of 108 yachts. This was its home until 1901. Here its triumphs over Sir Richard Sutton, Lieut. William Henn, Vice Commodore Bell and Lord Dunraven were celebrated. On the occasion of its semi-centennial, in 1894, it dawned upon the Club that its quarters were too cramped for comfort. At every meeting new members were elected and when special functions were held the house was crowded so that there was standing room only. At that time there were 1,038 members and its squadron consisted of 85 schooners, 84 single stickers and yawls, 122 steam yachts and 12 steam launches. A larger house was imperative, but the Club is conservative and deliberates before it acts.

The present magnificent house in which the Club begins its second century is on West Forty-fourth street, between Fifth and Sixth avenues. It is in startling contrast to the first club house, which was demolished last year. The land on which the present building stands was a gift to the Club from ex-Commodore J. Pierpont Morgan. The members subscribed liberally to the building fund and the result is a mansion in every way worthy of the Club. In the style of the modern Renaissance of the French school it is simple, substantial

and handsome. The employment of Indiana limestone with artistic carving gives a massive appearance to the exterior. The three windows in the second story modelled after the sterns of Spanish galleons, afford the requisite nautical flavor.

The interior is superb in every way, combining all the luxuries and conveniences of this sybarite age. Two apartments are striking, the model room and the grill room. The first is a lofty room

FIREPLACE IN MODEL ROOM.

of noble space on the second floor, finished in carved oak, elaborated with representations of sea monsters. The grand marble fireplace is a work of art. The mantel weighs forty-five tons. A fine gallery runs round the north, east and west sides. And on the walls of this room is displayed the most notable collection of yacht models in the world. Some of the whole models, fully rigged, of yachts that have added luster to the Club, are in glass cases and stand in alcoves. The display shows the progressive growth of the American and the British yacht. The arrangement so far as possible is chronological in order that an intelligent study of yacht evolution may be easy. The models of *Maria* and *America* have a commanding place as well as those of *Julia*, *Rebecca* and other famous old craft.

Historic ocean races conducted under the flag of the Club are recalled by models of the schooner *Dauntless*, which when owned by James Gordon Bennett was beaten by Mr. James Ashbury's schooner

yacht-naval architecture. The models of the modern school, beginning with that epoch-making yacht *Minerva* and the equally remarkable *Puritan*, supplemented by *Gloriana*, *Vigilant*, *Defender* and *Columbia* complete the story.

With regard to steam yachts the collection is not so rich. The first steamer that flew the Club's burgee was the paddle wheel steamer *North Star*, owned by Cornelius Vanderbilt; a yacht only by courtesy. It is only within the last twenty years that steam yachts have been popular in this country, although as a matter of history the first steam yacht races held

THE GRILL.

Cambria in a race from Ireland to New York, by one hour and seventeen minutes; by models of the three schooners *Henrietta*, *Vesta* and *Fleetwing* which faced the boisterous Atlantic in midwinter, in 1866, for a purse of $90,000, which *Henrietta* won. Another great ocean contest is recalled by a model of the schooner *Coronet*, owned by Mr. Bush, which beat *Dauntless*, owned by Commodore Colt, in a race across the Atlantic, sailed in March, 1887. The model room is impressive when it deals with the glorious past. It is a never-ending source of joy to the student of

in this country were managed by the Club in 1875. On the roll of the Club to-day are the largest and most magnificent steam yachts in existence. The cruising schooner on which the Club once prided itself has given way to steam. Sails are too slow for the rapid life of the twentieth century. A wise provision of the Club which makes it compulsory for a person entering a yacht in a Club race to furnish a model of the craft insures the growth of the model collection.

The grill room is built after the fashion of an old wooden ship, with beams and

EX-COMMODORE J. PIERPONT MORGAN.

knees. It is plainly furnished in oak and is of the sea salty.

The library, though not large, is rich in the literature of the sport. It is added to continually. Rare old prints, engravings, lithographs, portraits in oil and yachting scenes in water colors, as well as modern photographs adorn the walls in artistic profusion.

The most precious treasure owned by the Club is the cup won by *America* sailing against a fleet of fifteen in the regatta of the Royal Yacht Squadron round the Isle of Wight on August 22, 1851. The trophy was presented to the Club by Messrs. J. C. Stevens, George L. Schuyler and Hamilton Wilkes on July 20, 1857, to be held as a perpetual challenge cup for friendly competition between foreign countries. The principal proviso was that the cup should always remain in the custody of the Club winning it, and not become the property of the members or yacht owners.

The Club accepted the trust, and subsequently assumed the control of the races sailed for it by Mr. James Ashbury's schooners, *Cambria* and *Livonia* in 1870 and 1871, and also in the Canadian challenge by Major Charles Gifford's schooner *Countess of Dufferin* in 1876, and Captain Cuthbert's challenge with the sloop *Atalanta* in 1881.

The *Atalanta* was a very inferior craft. She was signally defeated. In spite of this

drubbing, Captain Cuthbert threatened to challenge again with her the following year.

The Club on December 15, 1882, resolved to return *America's* Cup to Mr. George L. Schuyler, the only survivor of the winners of the trophy. Mr. Schuyler embodied some new conditions in another deed of gift, the principal one being a clause forbidding a defeated vessel to compete again for the cup until two years have elapsed. Thus Captain Cuthbert was headed off, and the real object of the new deed of gift was attained.

The New York Yacht Club up to 1885 had assumed the duty of defending *America's* Cup against all comers. In that year, Sir Richard Sutton challenged with the cutter *Genesta*, and the Eastern Yacht Club interested itself in the contest. Mr. Edward Burgess, of Boston, was a young ambitious naval architect with original ideas. His yachts, all of moderate size, had proved highly successful. The Eastern Yacht Club determined to be represented in the trial races. Accordingly, Mr. J. Malcolm Forbes and some of his friends, commissioned Mr. Burgess to design *Puritan*, and this he did with rare skill and judgment. To the generous beam and centerboard of the American

CUP PRESENTED BY THE CLUB
TO MR. MORGAN.

type he added the outside lead of the British and also the cutter rig. So artfully did he combine these powerful factors that *Puritan* proved vastly superior to the New York boats in the trial races, and was chosen to defend the Cup, which she did quite handily defeating *Genesta*.

When Lieutenant Henn challenged in 1886 with *Galatea*, General Charles J. Paine, of Boston, commissioned Mr. Burgess to design *Mayflower* to beat *Puritan*. The result was that *Mayflower* did beat *Puritan*, and also *Galatea*. In 1887, Vice-Commodore Bell challenged with *Thistle*, and was beaten

ler, the sole surviving owner of the Cup, and he once more transferred it to the Club.

Divested of legal verbiage, the deed of trust conveys *America's* Cup from George L. Schuyler to the New York Yacht Club in trust as a perpetual international challenge cup to be sailed for by yacht clubs having an ocean course. Competing yachts, if of one mast, shall be not less than 65 feet nor more than 90 feet load water line; if of more than one mast, not less than 80 feet nor more than 115 feet load water line. Ten months' notice must be given by the challenging club, as well as the name, rig and following dimen-

SOME CLUB TROPHIES.

by General Paine's *Volunteer*, another Burgess centerboard.

Owing to the water line length of *Thistle* being found to be several inches in excess of the figures given by Mr. Watson, her designer, the New York Yacht Club decided that still another deed of trust was necessary to guard against a similar error in the future. Mr. John H. Bird, who was at that time secretary of the Club, accordingly drew up a legal document known as the "Deed of Trust, 1887." By this the Club again returned the trophy to Mr. George L. Schuy-

sions: length on load water line, extreme beam and draught of water, which dimensions shall not be exceeded. Challengers must cross the ocean under sail on their own bottoms. No restriction on sliding keels or centerboards.

As soon as the provisions of the new deed were published, a storm of hostile criticism burst from the British press. Complaints of "sea-lawyerism" and "sharp practise" were plentiful. The reason for the wrath evoked was the dimension clause, which was supposed to give too much advantage to

EDWARD M. BROWN.

E. D. MORGAN.

ELBRIDGE T. GERRY.

SOME EX-COMMODORES.

the club defending the trophy. Lord Dunraven was especially bitter in his denunciations. So much so that his first challenge in 1889 was recalled. The New York Yacht Club pointed out the following clause in the deed of trust: "The club challenging for the Cup and the club holding the same, may by mutual consent make any arrangement satisfactory to both as to the dates, courses, number of trials, rules, and sailing regulations, and any and all other conditions of the match in which case also, the ten months' notice may be waived."

This provision seems to be broad and fair to an unprejudiced person. Lord Dunraven was induced to alter his views. The Club agreed to accept the length on the load water line, as the only dimension required and on that basis Lord Dunraven challenged again and yet again, and was beaten twice. Under the mutual agreement clause, Sir Thomas Lipton's challenges were ar-

ranged, and yachtsmen generally admit that under the deed of trust, in spite of its reading like a mortgage, a perfectly fair and sportsmanlike match can be made.

It is certain that the keen international rivalry for the possession of the Cup has been of boundless benefit to yachting. The schooner *America* opened the eyes of the English, and wrought a revolution in the hulls and the canvas of their racing yachts. Enemies of the great ninety-foot sloops decry them because of their immense cost and their utter worthlessness after their racing careers are finished. One might as well run down a race horse for not being able to haul a coal wagon, or draw a plough, after the turf has seen his finish. Or a racing automobile for its uselessness for business purposes.

Modern competitors for *America's* Cup are racing machines, if you will, but they are the most graceful fabrics that human art has devised. The glorious memories of their achievements will live in history though their hulls are sold to the junkman after their deeds are done. The stimulus afforded to the cleanest and healthiest of all sports by the Cup races is worth more to the nation marine—in a word, of our salt water supremacy.

The growth of the sport has been phenomenal in the last decade. Society has taken up the pastime. The girls love it. The

THE MODEL ROOM.

than the money and effort expended. It induces in young men a love for the ocean. It keeps alive the glorious traditions of our navy and of our once magnificent merchant squadron cruise of the New York Yacht Club is one of the great events of the season. Few fashionable people care to miss the race for the Astor cups. Fewer the international contests; yet on the roster of the Club, figure the names of men who do not know one end of a yacht from the other. The most exalted foreign personage in the honorary list is King Edward VII. The admission of women as flag members was a popular step. The receptions to ladies are always well attended. The yachting girl is very much in evidence, and has come to stay.

The Club prides itself on its stations established at points along the coast from Atlantic Highlands to Martha's Vineyard. Each has a fine float and landing stage which does away with the old unpleasant practice of shinning up a slimy wharf when desiring to go ashore. The yachtsman finds a long distance telephone at all the stations, a comfortable room to read and lounge in, a mail box and other conveniences. The station at Newport is the largest, but all are well adapted for the purposes for which they were devised. The cost of establishing these stations was about $18,000, and the expense of keeping them up is about $7,000 a year. The Club permits other yacht clubs to enjoy the accommodations of these stations. This privilege is highly appreciated by foreigners, and also by members of American clubs, who enjoy it every day during the yachting season.

The members of the Club are more benefited by these stations than they would be if there was only one large club-house near the water front. Though it seemed wise to have a town house in the very heart of clubdom, whence a start may be made for any place on earth, and stations at Whitestone, New London, Newport, and other places frequented by members.

The Club will begin its fifty-seventh yachting season under the happiest auspices. With a handsome club-house, a magnificent squadron of 424 vessels, a membership of 1,619, and a large balance at the bank, and, above all, with a history of which it has reason to be proud, it may thus look forward with confidence to maintaining its praiseworthy prestige of being the premier yachting organization of the United States, if not of the world.

The coming summer will be a busy one, and an anxious one for members of the Club, for there can be no doubt that Sir Thomas Lipton, and his designers and advisers, have benefited by the past experience in our waters, and that in his present challenge for that time-honored trophy of the Club, the *America's* Cup, he will be represented by the best designed, and built, and equipped, and handled boat that has yet crossed the Atlantic in quest of this much-coveted symbol of yachting supremacy. All the ability that money can command will be backed by the determination of a very persistent opponent.

The preparations being made on this side, too, are marked by an equal spirit. Two boats are being built to determine which is the better to meet *Shamrock II*. One of them, for a New York syndicate headed by Mr. August Belmont, is being designed and built by the Herreshoffs; and the other for Mr. Thomas W. Lawson, of Boston, is from designs by Crowninshield, and is being built by Lawley. Nothing has been spared which money can procure or ingenuity invent to assure that either of these boats shall be capable of successfully defending the Cup. They will, in a short time, be ready for preliminary spins, and in the early summer they will contest in a series of races for the supreme honor of becoming the chosen one to meet the challenger.

Natural interest will be accentuated by the local pride of the two great yachting centers of the Atlantic seaboard, and yachtsmen are assured of a summer of unusual, indeed of intense, interest.

What the result will be never admits of a doubt within the walls of the New York Club, where the spirit and confidence which animated its founders still runs strong.

Sea Cookery for Yachtsmen (1901)

SEA COOKERY FOR YACHTSMEN

By A. J. Kenealy

THOSE who go a-sailing for pleasure in small craft, frequently suffer hardships, or at least inconvenience, in the way of meals, because of their lack of knowledge of the provisions to take with them, and of simple methods of preparing wholesome and appetizing dishes.

Sea cooking differs materially from shore cooking, inasmuch as the stove in a house

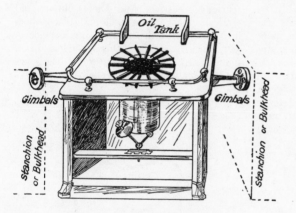

FIG. 1. A YACHTSMAN'S STOVE

is erected on a floor that is both stationary and stable. The yachtsman who has a cosy galley with a fixed stove that burns coal or coke or charcoal, and which draws well, has reason to bless his fortunate stars.

There have now come into vogue several varieties of the blue-flame wickless cooking stove. In the accompanying illustration, Fig. 1, I have depicted a stove which I have found to suit. It is wickless and burns the ordinary kerosene oil. To suit sea conditions the stove is slung on gimbals like a ship's compass, so as to yield to every motion of the vessel. The railing round the top prevents pots and pans from sliding to lee-ward. Fig. 2 shows the finest fry-pan ever invented for an oil stove, on which broiling is impracticable. It acts as a broiler or fryer at will. The raised bars prevent the steak or cutlet from being soddened with fat, the result being equal or nearly equal to a gridiron. If frying is required put

the necessary quantity of oil, butter or fat in the pan. Let it come to a boil and then immerse in it the article, fish, flesh, fowl, reptile or vegetable that you wish to cook.

With a stove having only one lid or burner the sea-cook might often have some difficulty in keeping three utensils on the boil at once. Luckily ingenuity has surmounted the obstacle and Fig. 3 shows three stewpans of small size that will fit over the burner of the stove shown in Fig. 1. They are in the market, but it took me a long time to find out where they are for sale. In one you may cook curry, in the second rice, while clam broth may simmer in the third. In good sooth a very cerberus of stew pans!

Some sort of a contrivance for storing ice so as to keep it solid as long as possible is indispensable. Such a device is shown in Fig 4.

For sea picnics buy as many of the thin wooden plates (costing only a trifle) as you may require. These after being used may be thrown overboard. Take nc crockery ware or china to sea in a small boat. Cups, saucers, plates and dishes can be obtained made of enameled steel. These are unbreakable and cleanly. Stewpans, kettles, pitchers, coffee pots and fry-pans are also made of enameled steel, and they cannot be surpassed. Cooks' furnishings depend on the size of the boat and the hands she carries. I suggest the following, but leave the sizes to the discretion of the purchaser who knows about how many mouths he has to feed. One kettle for boiling water for tea or coffee, one deep fry-pan, one iron pot with tight-fitting cover for boiling meat, fish or cooking chowder. One teapot, one coffee-pot, a soup ladle, a long iron two-pronged fork (known aboard ship as the cook's tormentors), two stewpans for cooking vegetables, one broiler (if the implement can be used), one cook's knife, one vegetable knife, one swab for washing pots, pans and plates, and dish towels for drying them, soap, cups, plates, dishes, knives, forks, spoons, glasses, *quant. suff.* Do not forget a galvanized iron bucket for the cook, a can opener and a corkscrew. Also matches in an airtight can or glass. Fuel in either fluid or solid shape should not be omitted.

FIG. 2.
THE IDEAL FRY-PAN.

When we come to the question of the food supplies to be taken aboard, much will depend upon the individual. Hard tack, salt tack, flour, beans, corned beef, salt pork, bacon, hams, canned meats, sardines, canned fruit and vegetables, cornmeal, lard, butter, cheese, condensed milk, sweetened and unsweetened coffee, tea, cocoa, chocolate, pepper, salt, mustard, vinegar, poultry seasoning, sugar and rice are some of the staple comestibles that suggest themselves, but these may be added to or subtracted from according to circumstances.

A ham is one of the most easily procured comestibles. Pick out a small one, not too fat. If you want it tough as leather boil it furiously for a couple of hours then haul it out of the pot and eat it. If you want a delicate, tender and juicy ham soak it in a bucket of fresh water for twelve hours. Then scrape it well and pop it into a big pot full of cold fresh water. Let it come slowly to the boil. As soon as the water reaches the boiling stage, regulate the heat so that a gentle simmering, the faintest possible ebullition is kept up for five or six hours, according to the size of the joint. Then take it out of the pot and skin it. The rind will come off as easy as an old shoe. Then return it to the water in which it was boiled and let it remain until it is quite cold. Next dish it, drain it and put it in the ice box to harden. Cut in very thin slices with a sharp knife and you will admit that cooked after this scientific formula, ham is mighty fine eating.

FIG. 4. ICE TUB.

Corned beef cooked after the same fashion will also be a success. The secret is a simple one of chemistry. Hard boiling hardens the fibers and tears the meat to rags. Gentle simmering softens the meat while allowing it to retain its juices.

The navy bean at present in use, though much may be said in its praise, is far inferior to the lima bean. This legume if substituted for the insignificant (by comparison only) little bean on which Boston breakfasts every Sabbath morn will be found so palatable that the lesser variety will never again be used. Procure a quart of lima beans. Pick out all that are shriveled or discolored. Soak them all night in plenty of cold fresh water and in the morning you will find them plump and tender. Wash them well and place them in a pot on the fire with a square piece of salt pork weighing three-quarters of a pound, simmer them gently till they are tender, but not till they reach the porridge

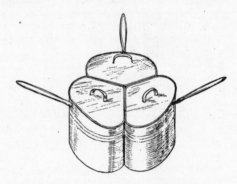

FIG. 3.   A NEST OF STEWPANS.

stage. On the contrary, let each bean be separate like the soft and swelling grains of well-cooked rice. Strain through a colander, saving a pint of the water in which they were boiled. Pack in the bean pot. Bury the chunk of pork in the beans. Season the pint of water reserved as mentioned above to your liking. Pour over the beans in the pot and put in the oven to bake. The flavoring of beans depends upon the taste of the cook.

Sirloin steaks are a good staple viand. Make the butcher cut them not less than two inches thick. If you cannot grill them heat your fry-pan almost red hot. Put no fat in the pan. Place your steak cut into convenient chunks into the hot pan. Let one side sear for a minute or so to keep in the juices. Then turn it over. It will be cooked sufficiently for most palates in five or six minutes. Place on a piping hot platter, spread some fresh butter on the steak, sprinkle with pepper, and pipe to grub. Chops may be cooked in the same way.

Meat may be roasted in an iron pot if the cook has no oven. Moderate heat, continuous care to prevent burning and frequent basting are the three requisites of a successful pot roast.

So far as beverages are concerned, useful hints in that direction are given in Fig. 5 which shows a picturesque and shipshape vessel to carry when a-cruising.

There is no daintier dish than a fresh, fat lobster, generous and juicy, just hauled from the pot in which he was caught. Pick out a particularly lively specimen of medium size but heavy. The cock lobster may be distinguished from the hen by the narrowness of the tail, the two upper fins of which are stiff and hard, while the tail of the hen is broader and the fins soft. The male has the highest flavor, the flesh, too, is firmer and the color when boiled is a deeper red. The hen is well adapted for lobster *a la* Newburg, but for eating on the half shell a male in prime condition is far preferable.

The secret of cooking lobsters is to plunge them in a pot of furiously boiling sea water and to keep the water in a condition of fast ebullition for just twenty minutes. Fresh water to which salt is added will not do so well. Salt water fresh from the ocean is indispensable. It brings out the correct flavor and imparts an indefinable zest to the lobster. Hard shell crabs may be boiled in the same way, but ten minutes will be ample time.

All fresh vegetables are, in the opinion of the writer, improved in flavor by cooking them in sea water fresh from the ocean, not from a harbor contaminated by noxious influences from the shore. All vegetables should be immersed in boiling water and cooked till done. Potatoes will take about half an hour to boil, but cabbages, carrots and turnips much longer. I should not advise the cooking of the three last named esculents aboard a small craft. Canned asparagus, French peas and string beans take little time to prepare and are excellent if a reliable brand is purchased. Open the can, drain off the liquid and throw it

away. Wash the vegetables, strain the water off, place in a stewpan with a lump of butter and heat throughly. The liquid of canned vegetables is unfit for human food.

Hard clams or quahaugs are plentiful at any port during the boating season. The recuperative qualities of the small variety served ice cold on the half shell with a dash of tabasco sauce and no other seasoning are beyond praise. Now while the little clam is excellent eating just as soon as opened from the shell, taking care to waste none of his precious juices, his elder brother also has inestimable gastronomic values.

The easiest and simplest method of preparing clam broth is to scrub the clams well and wash them in several waters. Put them in an iron pot, without any water or liquid. Let them remain on the fire for twenty minutes. Then strain the juice, into which put a little fresh butter, a small quantity of milk, and a dash of red pepper. Drink while hot.

Never add water to clam broth and never let it boil after the milk is added, as it will curdle nine times out of ten.

To make clam soup clean the clams as for broth. Place them in an iron pot on the stove. As soon as they open take them out of their shells and chop very fine. A hardwood bowl and a two-bladed chopping knife is the best apparatus for this job. Strain the clam liquor, return to the pot, add minced onions to taste and the chopped clams; simmer gently for one hour, thicken to taste with cracker dust, season with sweet herbs and pepper; let it boil fast for ten minutes, take off the stove and add some hot milk and a lump of fresh butter. Serve.

Clam chowder is an old sea dish whose popularity seems never likely to wane. It is a simple dish to prepare, although many cooks make a mystery of it. Cut half a pound of streaky salt pork into small cubes. Fry in an iron pot together with half a dozen medium sized sliced onions until they are a light brown. Chop fifty hard shell clams fine. Peel and slice thin a dozen large raw potatoes. Break up four sea biscuits and soak till soft in cold water or milk. Scald and peel and slice six ripe and juicy tomatoes. Put these ingredients into the pot in layers, pour over them the strained juice of the clams. Season with red and black pepper, sauces and herbs to taste. Cover an inch with hot fresh water and simmer for three hours. A pint of sound California claret added just before serving is an improvement. An old hen makes tip top chowder cooked in the same fashion.

Fish chowder may be prepared in a similar way. Cod, haddock, sea bass and bluefish are good made into a chowder.

The soft shell clam makes a delicate stew or broth. The tough parts should be rejected from the chopping bowl. Boiled for twenty minutes and eaten from the shell with a little butter and pepper they are also very appetizing. A big potful soon disappears.

There is no excuse for the yachtsman neglecting to enjoy the delights of fish fresh from the sea. Fishing tackle should always be carried. Bluefish and mackerel may be caught by trolling and if you have fisherman's luck once in a blue moon a Spanish mackerel may fall to your lot. If so that day must be marked by a white

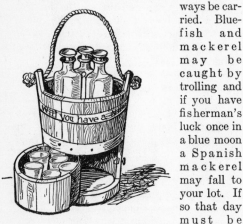

FIG. 5. A TRAVELING COMPANION.

stone for a Spanish mackerel transferred in about two shakes of a lamb's tail from the fish hook to the fry-pan or better still, if your arrangements permit, to the gridiron or broiler, is good enough for the gods to feed on. Two axioms should be borne in mind, namely, to fry in plenty of boiling fat or to plunge into boiling water. Never humiliate a fish by placing him in a cold fry-pan or into a cooking pot of cold water.

Before frying fish dip in well beaten egg and then sprinkle with bread crumbs or cracker dust, dip in egg again and then add more bread crumbs or cracker dust. This is for epicures. For ordinary seafarers if the fish is rolled in yellow cornmeal without the egg the result will be nearly the same. Cut up large fish into suitable sizes, but fry small fish whole.

Soft shell crabs should be cooked in boiling fat. When brown they are done. Ten minutes is usually enough to cook them thoroughly.

Always when you boil fish of any kind indigenous to salt water or fresh put them in boiling water either from the sea or fresh water well salted. A little vinegar added is good. A two-pound fish should cook sufficiently in fifteen or at most twenty minutes. Fish with white flesh take longer to boil than those with dark.

An excellent sauce for boiled fish may be made thus: Put a piece of butter as big as an egg in a saucepan or a tomato can. Heat till it bubbles, add a heaping tablespoonful of flour, stir till quite smooth, pour slowly into this, stirring continually a pint of the water the fish was cooked in and add two hard boiled eggs chopped fine. This may be flavored with anchovy sauce or a few drops of Harvey or Worcestershire. Some prefer the addition of a little lemon juice or even vinegar. Every man to his taste!

When a very little boy I sailed in the *Derwent*, a small schooner engaged in carrying bottles from Sunderland to London. The bottles were taken in from the factory where they were made, stowed in the hold of the schooner and transported to a wharf at Wapping. Bottles are a clean kind of freight, and our skipper being a very particular kind of a man the *Derwent* was kept as bright as a new pin outside and inside, alow and aloft. Of this dashing little vessel I was cook and cabin boy. There was no regular galley on deck, simply an iron cooking stove erected on the foreside of the mainmast and on that in storm and calm I boiled and baked for a crew of four for more than a year—in fact till I quit the coasting trade and signed away foreign. My skipper took me under his special guidance. The grub had to be well cooked and the deck kept spotless or I used to suffer. Skipper and mate were epicures after a fashion, so I had to keep my weather eye open.

My experience in merchant vessels and pleasure craft, has fitted me to write with some small assumption of authority on the subject of sea cooking. Some of my methods may seem queer and perhaps grotesque, but condemn them not till you have tested them in the crucible of experiment.

Cruising up the Yangzte (1899)

CRUISING UP THE YANGTSZE.[1]

BY ELIZA RUHAMAH SCIDMORE,

Author of "Jinrikisha Days," "Java, the Garden of the East," etc.

WITH PICTURES BY HARRY FENN AND OTTO H. BACHER, FROM PHOTOGRAPHS.

ABOVE Hankow the Yangtsze River tests all of a fresh-water navigator's skill and patience; and changing to small, light-draft steamers, we were three days in accomplishing the four hundred miles to I-chang, sounding and feeling the way among sand-bars by day, and anchoring at night. The picturesque old walled town of Yochau, at the edge of Tung-ting Lake, was declared an open port in April, 1898; but its people have a bad name, and its future only a stormy promise. The Hunan brave is the most disorderly of all Chinese; Hunan literati have sent out the shameful pamphlets and led the anti-foreign crusades for years; and Hunan has so reeked with the blood of martyred priests for a century past that, had France been so disposed, she might have taken possession of the whole province, and, indeed, all the provinces of China, *more Germanico*, long ago. The opening of Yochau, with the free navigation of this inland sea of three hundred square miles, secures great prosperity for the region, and some illumination for its bigoted and unreasonable people. An old trade route crosses from the lake by the Meiling Pass to the river above Canton. On great Kiu Shan, or Golden Island, tea-culture has been made the finest art, and this tea, possessing, along with other virtues, the gift of longevity, is all reserved for the Emperor of China. The first crop of this choice tea of immortality would be worth eight Mexican dollars a pound, by commercial estimates, if it could be bought; but the priests guard each sacred leaf-bud, and send it all to Peking, though, by common gossip in the Purple Forbidden City, the emperor drinks something less rare. The argument in that imperial topsy-turvydom is that, as the emperor never visits any one or drinks any one else's tea, he cannot know the dif-

ference, and that if the Kiu Shan tea was ever exhausted, heads would fall when a substitute was offered.

Above the outlet of Tung-ting Lake, the Yangtsze is a broad, shallow, wandering stream, half the volume of the river being diverted through the lake by a canal at its western end. The lead was swung, and the monotonous chant of the man at the line rang all afternoon, and the tiniest of steam-launches skimmed the surface like a frantic water-insect, the pilot probing the mud with a bamboo pole, and marking the six-foot channel by a line of staves.

The next day there were the same monotonous mud-banks again, protective dikes that run for three hundred miles above Hankow. Country-folk used the embankment as a highway, processions of men, women, and children, buffaloes, pack-horses, carts, and sledges filing along in silhouette against the sky. Lone and ragged fishermen inhabited burrows in the bank, or from a platform over the water worked big, square dip-nets by levers; and for fifty times that I watched the big, square cobweb drop beneath the waters, once a small silverfish was dipped up. Children with flying pigtails, as near to young apes as their earliest ancestors could have been, shrieked at the fire-boat, and ran along to watch the foreigners on deck. "Look! see! Look! see!" they screamed joyfully; and "Foreign devil! oh, foreign devil!" they bawled, with menacing gestures. "Oh, give me a bottle! Quick! Give me a bottle, foreign devil!" other frantic ones cried. Chinese passengers on the lower deck found amusement in holding out bottles to induce the poor, tired little apes to run for miles along the mud-banks, only to have the boat veer away to the baboon laughter of the inhuman teasers of the wretched little country-children, to whom a glass bottle is a treasure. In revenge, the children have learned to fasten a mud ball on the end of a bamboo, and with a quick jerk shoot the pellet to the steamer-decks. The fusillade

[1] See also "The River of Tea," in the preceding number of THE CENTURY.

is unpleasant, often dangerous; and as the young imps master the science of projectiles, there are bits of inshore navigation beset with uncharted perils.

We came to larger towns with stone embankments, conspicuous temples, and yamuns where inverted fish-baskets on tall poles proclaimed the official residence. When we reached the Taiping Canal, which cuts away to Tung-ting Lake and drains the Yangtsze of half its flood, the lonely river was enlivened. Here two great trade routes, the land route from north to south, and the river route from west to east, cross. Great Szechuen cargo-junks came down with the current, their chanting crews steering by a broad projecting sweep or oar at the bows, and great junks went up, sailing and tracking, with gangs of ragged creatures straining at their bricole thongs, like the beasts of burden they are. Brown sails and blue-and-white striped sails ornamented the water, and hills beyond hills rose in the west, with needle-spired pagodas pricking the sunset sky, and bold headlands coming to the river's bank. It was six o'clock and all blue-black darkness when we crept close to the twinkling lights of Shashi's bund, and dropped the heaviest anchors. The current races there at the rate of several miles an hour, and passenger-boats that ventured out for prey came whirling at us broadside on, stern first, bow first, any way at all, and banged the steamer's hull alarmingly. A hundred boatmen squawked, screeched, and chattered madly, and if one of them failed to grapple the chains and lines along the free-board at the moment, the current swept him astern and far down-stream before he could recover headway with the oars. The frantic ki-yi-ings of these disappointed ones, swept away into distant darkness, filled the night air along with the noises on shore.

Shashi is an old city with a deservedly bad name. The opening of this port was secured by the Japanese in the treaty of Shimonoseki (1895), and as soon as a Japanese consulate could be built, the Shashi spirit broke out and the building was destroyed, the four ringleader assailants afterward executed, the consulate rebuilt at local expense, and further concessions granted in reparation. The customs officers, occupying house-boats moored to the bund, barely escaped with their lives, and the floating British consulate was set adrift and with difficulty rescued from burning. The town is behind the embankment, and one sees only a few roofs to tell of a city of seventy-three thousand in-

habitants; but Shashi is, after all, only the port and place of junk transhipment for King-chau, the provincial capital, which lies back from the river a mile above the rowdy water-town.

We had toiled three hundred miles upstream to reach this great cross-roads of provincial trade, yet we could have returned to Hankow by a hundred-mile journey, either on foot or by boat, through a line of creeks and small canals. For a last day we had bright, mild December sunshine. Mud-banks gave way to clay and gravel banks, and conglomerate, red sandstone, and limestone cropped out. Fields were green with winter wheat, tallow-trees glowed with rich red autumnal foliage, and men in dull blue garments at work on those trees added another color-note to the picture. Pagodas spired the crests of near and distant hills. Temples, dagobas, and shrines told of the great religion which came by this route from Tibet and India. The Yangtsze is a broad, deep stream in this upper limestone region; the landscape is attractive; and the Tiger Tooth Gorge, first in scenic attractions, was followed by a remarkable natural or fairy bridge spanning a ravine between two rocky hills. Four miles below I-chang and a mile back from the river, a palisade wall rises a sheer thousand feet, extends for a mile or more, and the Chih Fu Shan monastery crowns a pinnacle rock that is joined to the palisade wall by a masonry bridge. This neglected old Buddhist fane is as remarkable as any of Thessaly's "monasteries in the air," and one needs a clear head and steady nerves to walk, or be carried in an open "hill-chair," up the narrow goat-path on the rock's face and along a knife-edged ridge, and across "the bridge in the sky" to the needle rock. There is a dizzier path still up rock-hewn staircases around to the monastery door. A few miserably poor and ignorant priests crouch on the summit of the rock. The altars are stripped and deserted, and imagination must supply any legends or splendors attaching to this aërial shrine.

A great graveyard extends from I-chang's city walls for a mile along the river-bank and a half-mile inland, and the foreign settlement is in the midst of this gruesome suburb. French, Scotch, Canadian, and American mission establishments, the consulates, customs buildings, and a few hongs, all solid brick-and-stone buildings in high-walled compounds, constitute the settlement, which dates from 1887, although conceded as an open port in the Chifu convention of 1876. The foreigners even manage to play golf in this graveyard, a course of a thousand bunkers and hazards, with fine drives insured from teeing-grounds fixed on certain superior mandarin mounds.

I-chang, one thousand miles from the sea, and in the shadow of the great central mountain-range, which crosses China from Siam to the Amur, is the head of steam-navigation and port of transhipment for all the products arriving from the provinces beyond the range. The famous gorges and rapids of the Yangtsze begin there, the river running through the Mountains of the Seven Gates, as its flood has cut seven deep cañons through the uplifted rocks, and carved their walls to a scenic panorama for the four hundred miles between I-chang and Chung-king. Despite conventions and promises, I-chang remained the end of steam-navigation for twenty years after the privilege of such navigation was conceded on the Upper Yangtsze. Obstructive mandarins resorted to every subterfuge and device to prevent the march of progress and the inevitable end of their extortions, and even that arch-pretender to progress, Li Hung Chang, gravely assured negotiators that the monkeys on the banks would throw stones at the steamers in the gorges, and he could not let foreigners run such risks! The privilege of steam-navigation on the upper river was again conceded in the treaty of Shimonoseki in 1895, but clumsy junks and *kwatsze* continued to mount the rapids at the end of bamboo tow-ropes, with all navigation suspended in the weeks of flood, until, in March, 1898, Mr. Archibald Little, who had clung to the intention for twenty years, took a small steamer to Chung-king. In June, 1898, the free navigation of all waterways was enjoyed through British diplomacy, and steam-whistles have echoed in all the great gorges.

The prize in view on the Upper Yangtsze has been the trade of Szechuen, the richest, most fertile, and best-governed province of China, the twenty million inhabitants of which have been praised by every traveler from Marco Polo to the present day of Lord Charles Beresford's commercial mission. Szechuen's fertile plains and valleys have earned it the name of "the Granary of China," and proverbs relate that "Szechuen grows more grain in one year than it can consume in ten years," and the boast is made that "you never see an ill-dressed man from Szechuen." It is one of the great silk provinces, and the seat of opium-culture in China, patches of poppies flaunting in the gorges, and great plains and valleys above ablaze with the seductive flowers which furnish three fourths of China's opium-supply.

With the assistance of all kindly and hospitable I-chang,—and they offered and brought, sent and lent and gave, every possible thing that could be thought of for our comfort,—our kwatsze, a lumbering Noah's ark of a house-boat, got away late in the afternoon of our first day ashore. On a flatboat fifty feet long a two-room cabin had been built amidships, leaving a space at the bows for the crew to work, cook, sleep, and eat, and a space behind the cabin where our boy and cook lived and worked, dodging the sweep of a giant tiller, which reached up above the roof of our cabin, where the master stood to command the craft. A projecting cabin at the stern, the most ridiculous flying-poop, was the captain's cabin, where he immured a rather pretty, flat-faced wife with small feet and a dirty blue coat, whose life seemed spent in sitting on a stool and smiling at space.

This tipsy, top-heavy, crazy craft was ours for so much each day that we chose to keep it, and a crew of ten men were engaged to take us the thirty-nine miles to Kui, through the three greatest scenic gorges and back, any farther travel a matter of fresh bargain, the whole expense of boat, crew, provisions, and gratuities for the week's trip being less than thirty dollars in silver. All books of Yangtsze travel are full of delayed starts and long waits by the way because of the dilatory and missing cook, and we were complacent at sight of our chef smilingly picking duck-feathers as we poled out into the stream, to cross and tie up far from city temptations, and enter the I-chang Gorge at sunrise. While we had tea the boatmen crept up and in among the maze of junks off the city-front, and began to make fast for the night. Then we found that a cook in the boat was not everything. The captain was not on board—buying rice, the substitute said, and plainly intending to put us through all that our predecessors had endured of missing crews and delayed starts. The captain's "cousin," a Szechuen soldier with the word "brave" sewed in gory red letters on the back of his coat, was playing captain overhead, and, at our discovery of the situation, went leaping along from junk to anchored junk to find his relative. We held parley with our companion kwatsze, and to the amazement of the crew, they found themselves rowing across the river and tying up to the bank beyond the other fishers' village. We had a delightful dinner on board, as regularly ordered and perfectly served as if on shore; and in our snug fore-cabin, with its carved and gilded partitions and window-frames, our rug portières and American oil-stove to offset the pitiless drafts of river-damp, we congratulated ourselves on a first naval victory. At daylight the lost captain himself roused the crew, the octogenarian fo'c's'le cook dealt them bowls of rice and green stuff, the braided bamboo ropes were uncoiled, and the draft-creatures began hauling us up-stream. The captain greeted us smilingly, without embarrassment or apologies, and no strained relations followed the incident of the night before; but the Szechuen soldier with his red-lettered, decorative back was missing, still hunting for the lost captain on the other shore.

The first or I-chang Gorge begins two miles above the city, the river, narrowed to less than three hundred yards, flowing for nine miles in a deep chasm five hundred and a thousand feet deep. Two great conglomerate cliffs form an entrance gateway, at one side of which a torrent has cut out the picturesque San Yu Tung Ravine, at the mouth of which I-chang residents maintain a summer club on a large house-boat moored in the cool drafts of the gorge. There is a cave-temple of great antiquity in the side-wall of this ravine, and by following a path along rockhewn shelves and through tunneled archways that furnished three gateways of defense in militant times, one comes to the broad balustraded space at the front of the shrine, a noble *loge* commanding a set scene of classic Chinese landscape, the very crags and clefts and stunted trees of ancient kakemono. The cave arches back in a great vault with a central column or supporting mass, and in the farther darkness there is a sanctuary full of gilded images, guarded by carved dragons, gnomes, and fantastic bird-creatures, that peer out from dark crevices. Poems and inscriptions are carved on the walls, and incense-burners, urns, and bells tell of better days when Buddhism flourished from Tibet to the sea. The few poor priests boil their miserable messes of pottage, and live in small chambers at one side of the vaulted hall—mere dens and caves, which, half lighted on that sunless side of the ravine, are comfortably cool in summer and as cold as Siberia in winter.

The I-chang Gorge cuts straight westward for five or six miles, and then turns at a right angle northward, an arrowy reach between gray, purple, and yellowed limestone walls overhung with the richest vegetation. Tiny orchards and orange-groves are niched between the buttresses of these storied strata walls, and cling to terraces; quarries and lime-kilns show, and mud houses are left behind, stone huts and houses being cheaper beside the quarry than the wattle and dab of the plains. Brown junks floated in midstream, and junks with square and butterfly and striped sails were dwarfed at the foot of the cliffs. All day our trackers strained at the braided bamboo ropes, crawling up and down and over rocks where bamboo hawsers have cut deep, polished grooves in the conglomerate and limestone banks by the friction of centuries. Lookout men at the water's edge kept the line free from rocks, throwing it off from any projections, and wading out to release it from hidden snags. Where foothold was wanting, the trackers scrambled on board and rowed around the obstacle or across stream to tracking-ground again. Their whole performance was the burlesque of navigation, the climax of stupidities, and nothing ingenious or practical seems to have resulted from the three thousand years of "swift-water" navigation on the Upper Yangtsze. The ridiculous, top-heavy, tilting kwatsze is wholly unsuited to such a flood-river, and the trackers tow by a rope fastened to the top of the mast, as on the Peiho, the mast shivering, springing, and resounding all the while. They rowed us with poles, round sapling stems held to the gunwale by a string or straw loop, and it was a marvel that the kwatsze responded to these bladeless oars, even when all hands, including the cook, rowed madly, screaming and stamping in chorus, and the captain on the roof raging and shrieking, and threatening to drop through upon us. The kwatsze would reel and wabble, gain by inches, and round the ripple or point, and the ragamuffin crew would drop off with the tow-line and fasten it by a flat metal button at the end of their bricole thongs. With a deft loop, that can be detached with the least slackening, the cotton thongs hold firmly to the slippery cable. In all these thousands of years they have never learned to "line up," either by a capstan on board or a winch on shore, nor to invent other compelling swift-water fashions of the Nile, the St. Lawrence, the Snake, the Columbia, or the Stickeen. Some years ago Admiral Ho was ordered to these river precincts, where lawlessness had been rife, and he, unprecedented in this century in China, took an interest in his work, and attempted to better things. He established a system of life-boat patrol in the gorges, and his little red rowboats waiting above and below rapids and eddies, and moving alongshore to render assistance, had a salutary effect on the wild river-folk. Any traveler of distinction,—and all foreigners are that,—or "explorer" in the by-parts of Asia, can have a life-boat detailed to accompany his kwatsze through the gorges, adding to his prestige, compelling precedence, and insuring safety at the river-towns, where the scum of the Yangtsze rob and batter at every opportunity. Admiral Ho, moreover, compiled a "Traveler's Guide to the Upper Yangtsze," which pictures the river's surface from I-chang to Chung-king, with the profile of each bank as seen from the water, and gives pilots directions for every rock and eddy.

We varied our time in the lower end of I-chang Gorge by many walks ashore, where familiar flowers and leaves grew among the strange plants, and bouquets of bittersweet, wild chrysanthemums, asters, and maiden-hair ferns went to our cabin tables. Where the water trickles through beds of spongy sandstone, the whole rock face is covered with a fine mantle of ferns, and this soft stone, cut off in slabs, makes a fairy fern wall or wainscoting in garden-spaces and conservatories at I-chang. In midsummer, when the river is in flood, and the accumulated rain and melted snows cannot race through the gorges fast enough, weeks pass without a craft showing off Pin-shan-pa, as deserted a river as the Fraser in its cañons, although the Yangtsze above I-chang presents no greater difficulties than the Snake, the Upper Columbia, the Stickeen, and other swift-water rivers of the United States, and the sheik of the first cataract of the Nile and a Lachine pilot would scorn the small ripples in these Chinese gorges.

The I-chang Gorge seems to end in a cul-de-sac, a vertical barrier-wall blocking the cañon squarely; but we turned a sharp point, and saw a narrower and deeper gorge cutting straight to the face of another transverse barrier. This upper end of I-chang Gorge, flooded with the golden sunlight of an autumn afternoon, each bank lined with processions of striped and tilting sails, and the great walls rising sheer two or three thousand feet, was one of the most beautiful pictures that I can remember. The western wall was bold and precipitous, the eastern barrier broken by fantastic pinnacles, needles,

spires, and arches, with natural bridges, cave-temples, and great rock inscriptions on its face. The natural or fairy bridge, from which a pious hermit flew directly to the sky, once led to a great temple, which marked where the ancient four kingdoms met. The steep wall of rock at the end of the gorge was topped by a second ridge, and a further, higher pinnacle aspired to the very sky, capped with a white temple that played hide-and-seek with us among the gorges for the next three days.

As there was no foothold on the rock walls of the upper gorge, sail was spread, and the ridiculous oars went hit and splash to a frenzied chorus, every man stamping and shrieking, and the captain on the roof outdoing them all as we worked against the current. A puff of wind filled the sail, and the crew dropped their pole-oars, and crouched on their heels to rest. Suddenly a mournful " Ki-yi," the wail of a Sioux brave, was given by the most leather-lunged ragamuffin of the lot; and all the rest let off ki-yis and war-whoops, together, singly, and at intervals, without moving from their "stand-at-ease" position. "Why do they make that noise?" I asked our boy; and after much gabbling with the band of water-braves, he answered for them: "To make wind come. He talkee wind-joss." But the wind-joss was inattentive, and at every swirling stretch they had to row and stamp their way again.

The I-chang Gorge has an even finer gateway entrance at the upper end than where it opens to the Hu-peh plain; and as we passed through the stupendous gates, the great columnar "Needle of Heaven" spired the north bank, and the last of sunset glory filled the valley ahead. Beyond Nanto village, where the smooth, oily river was olive and purple as it swirled around black boulders, we crossed the sheeny stretch, and made fast bow- and stern-lines to stakes driven in the sandy shore. The kwatsze was braced off from shore by the longest poles to guard against a sudden fall of the river in the night grounding us on sharp rocks that would pierce the thin hull. We dined in quiet after the exciting day of landscapes and navigation, having covered twelve miles in twelve hours of frantic exertion. The trackers had a fifth round of rice and greens, rigged up a mat awning over the bows, produced some ragged quilts from the hold, and laid themselves in close mummy rows on the deck-planks for the night.

In early starlight a cock, which was part of our live provisions in the forecastle's depths beneath the sleeping crew, let off a resounding pæan from its dark prison, and we could hear old Wrinkles, the venerable river-cook, snap the twigs, start his charcoal fire, and begin his day's routine of washing and boiling rice. In that deathly, breathless stillness every sound told, and we could follow his processes as well as if we saw them.

many rocks, and from the breakfast-table we watched the trackers straining at the lines, heads hanging forward and arms swinging uselessly from their brute bodies as they hung in harness. Surely, in all the scale of lower humanity, no creature can be sunk to such a mere brute life and occupation as a Yangtsze tracker.

HALF-TONE PLATE ENGRAVED BY C. SCHWARZBURGER.

THE FOREIGN SETTLEMENT OF I-CHANG AND THE GRAVEYARD GOLF-LINKS.

Later we saw red life-boats and fishermen's boats hanging around the rocks in the stream, and a gray-and-white stork, posing on single leg, stretched itself and idly floated away; another and another stork launched itself off, until their line in the sky against the crags completed the ideal Chinese landscape picture. Huge cargo-junks came by, veritable ships or caravels of Columbian cut, with seventy and a hundred trackers straining in leash and yelping as they ran, their masters or drivers running beside them, beating the air and the sand, with feints at belaboring them, and rivaling our captain in the flow of frenzied vituperations. Their tow-lines cleared our mast by a toss, or were dropped and drawn under our keel with a drubbing noise that was a novelty to nerves in navigation. There was swift water there among

In this Egyptian valley of sand and boulders our dahabiyeh came early to the temple of the red dragon, Hwang Ling Miao, built high above the sand-levels, with an attendant village spread below it, where all the wants of junks and trackers may be supplied. Sand terraces held rows of houses, sheds, and booths on stilts, where bean-curd, dried fish, meat, fowls, eggs, rice, vegetables, and charcoal tempted one, while rope-weavers on high platforms like dove-cotes or martin-boxes braided stiff bamboo strands into the shining yellow ropes that are so nearly indestructible. Bamboo ropes do not rot or fray like hemp or cotton, and water and dampness only improve their qualities. The strands for weaving and the coils of finished cable are kept buried in wet sand, and it is usually only the old, dry, and brittle bamboo rope that snaps under sudden strain. The country-people carried their burdens in deep baskets on their backs like Koreans. An old priest took us in the temple's side-gate, and showed us the great columned hall, with its gilded shrine guarded by carved dragons writhing in chase of jeweled balls. There was an inner sanctuary and court, with curious plants, a few fine vases, and incense-burners before the altar; but the living spark, the splendor and dignity of the great religion, had departed from Hwang Ling Miao.

The autumn nights were chill and damp in the gorges, but the days were those of the most perfect Indian summer, a mild, warm, golden air filling all space, soft September hazes hanging in the distance; and after the radiant, glowing yellow afternoons there were sunset pageants that lifted the Yang-tsze gorges to higher scenic rank in one's mind than they perhaps deserve.

over and between great rocks. Our turn came, and we swung out and crept up the foaming incline, and all afternoon we inched along up this reach of rapids, with moments of suspense and hairbreadth escapes; and just as we rounded the danger-point, with a last tug and yell from the trackers, the mast at our door-sill gave way, toppling shoreward with the strain, and nearly carrying the cabin with it. Then bedlam was ten times let loose; but somehow, in the general chaos of things, we were drawn slowly inshore and on into a snug little bight cut back into the high sand-bank. It was then sunset, the glowing west hidden by the purple precipice walls that rose three thousand feet to the splendid sky-lines overhead, the east all melting rose and blue, and the great gray Yosemite walls southward dim in shadows.

A dense fog shut us in until ten o'clock the next morning, when we poled out from our sand slip, ran along the bank a bit, and

APPROACH AND MASONRY FRONT OF CAVE TEMPLE NEAR I-CHANG.

Where the river turned almost at a right angle again, we came to the first rapids, the Siau Lu Chio and the Ta Lu Chio (the Little and Great Deer-Horns), and swung into line behind other craft, and waited our turn to be dragged up a short mill-race that ran

were at the foot of the Ta Dung, or Otter Cave, Rapids. As we grappled and were hauled up a chute between two rock masses, a figure came leaping along the boulders, made a desperate slide down a rock shelf, and landed on our deck—our long-lost, red-

SAILS IN THE GORGE OF I-CHANG, WITH A RED LIFE-BOAT IN THE FOREGROUND.

lettered Szechuen soldier, who had followed by foot-paths and short cuts overland from I-chang, hunting the kwatsze with the flowery flag.

We worked through another narrow mill-race among the rocks, swung across to another bit of compressed current, and, with thumps and bangs along every plank of the kwatsze's infirm old body, reached the foot of the real rapid, and lined up behind big junks hung over with coils of rope, crates of cabbages, and cackling fowls. A junk swung out, and had just begun to work up the white-capped incline when a big boat came speeding down-stream, sixty or eighty men chanting at the sweep. The resistless current spun it around like a toy, shot it this way and that way, and after three whirls in mid-stream, sent it, head on, in air-line toward the junk hanging in mid-rapids at its tow-ropes' ends. Just when we should have heard the crash, and both junks should have gone to splinters, when all the air rang with Chinese yells, the runaway veered off at an acute angle, and was soon diminishing in far perspective.

Old Wrinkles was in command forward; the Szechuen soldier was on deck; even our silk-clad boy lent a hand; and during certain seconds, or seeming hours, of agonizing suspense, when our bow-line caught, and a

tracker with a life-line around him swam out into the lashing waters to disentangle it, our cabin cook woke from his opium dream, clambered to the roof, and outyelled the captain on his own stamping-ground. Then a red life-boat rowed across our sunken line, which, suddenly tautened, gave the rescue corps a shock of which they volubly informed the village, the valley, and the whole welkin space. The captain's pretty, moon-faced wife crept from the coop of a cabin, lifted up the deck-planks, and sat ready to bail out with a wooden scoop clumsier than anything Fuegians or prehistoric man ever used.

We triumphantly breasted the stiff flume, all whitecaps and billows for a hundred yards. Then the din ceased, and the trackers drew us in beside a sandy reach covered with patches of raw cotton salved from two wrecks, whose masts alone were visible. Other wrecks were laid up on the sands, with all hands mending ribs, calking seams, spreading piece-goods out to dry, and dip-netting tufts of cotton down from eddies and back-water pools.

All the mellow, radiant afternoon, from rock to rock, we banged along among incipient rapids, the shaky old kwatsze miraculously holding together, the trackers in and out of water splashing stork-like in long,

ENTRANCE OF I-CHANG GORGE, UPPER END.

single files through shallows, or scrambling like a pack of beagles over sand and boulders. Through it all old Wrinkles went on boiling rice, the most restful, delightful old creature in China.

We tied up at the end of this exciting day below Lao Kwan Miao, an ancient temple on a terrace, where five white stone cube and pyramid pedestals used to show fire-beacons to tell benighted travelers of another temple stage in the river journey, as at Hwang Ling Miao.

They had bailed the boat every few hours that day. The captain had gone below with a candle, and stuffed rags and pitch into the yielding seams of the boat, and twice in the night he came to examine the hold. While we waited for the dense morning fog to clear, I took a look below, and found that the severe knocking about that the old kwatsze had endured, in the two days' straining up the valley of rapids, had loosened seams from stem to stern along one whole side, through which the water slowly seeped. A transverse partition had sagged away two or three inches from the side-frames when the mast wrenched loose, and only the special prov-

idence that keeps crazy Yangtsze craft afloat had saved us as we bumped and banged our way along the rocky shores. It was madness to think of straining the kwatsze up any more rapids, and there was risk enough in rowing through the great Liu-kan Gorge to Tsin Tan village, where we could repair or secure a new kwatsze. It depressed my spirits and dulled all anticipation and realization of this finest of all the Yangtsze gorges to see it at such risk of life, and every eddy and jutting rock and swirl of current made my heart sink deeper as we tracked up toward the towering entrance cliffs. A turn, and we were within the deep-cut, dull red and purplish cliffs towering perpendicularly one, two, and three thousand feet, and the muddy river swirling at their base. For two miles there is no ledge or shelf or tracker's foothold within that royal gorge, that closely approaches that of the Arkansas above Cañon City.

The men had rowed frantically into the deep cañon, the body of the infirm kwatsze shivering and rocking as if about to fall apart; but when the upward draft of a breeze caught our sail, we went silently upward against the flood through a cañon worthy to match with the Fraser's and the Arkansas's best.

The great walls part for a space, and make room for a sloping hillside, which the village of Tsin Tan climbs in rock-piled terraces, stretching along for a half-mile's length. A temple and a few houses cling to the steeper opposite bank, and between the Yangtsze roars and dashes over a ledge of rocks, where a steep fall in the river-bed causes the Tsin Tan Rapids, the most dreaded of the river's obstructions. Above the echoing roar of the river the cañon resounded with the beat of gongs and the wild chant of trackers on each shore, as junks hung quivering in the rapids.

We did not need to watch the straining trackers and the junks in the rapids, or to see two junks part cables and sweep back, for us to know that one long pull at our masthead in that current would scatter the kwatsze planks like jack-straws. As the crew had been definitely engaged to go as far as Kui, two or three days farther in time, we dreaded mutiny, or at least "bobbery," when we announced that the kwatsze should go no farther, since the Chinese mind is always aflame with suspicions at any deviation from an original plan or bargain—at anything that does not "b'long custom." We were willing to pay a pacifying indemnity, even, for releasing them from the contract to track and row those additional miles to Kui; but knowing the lingual possibilities of the captain, it required courage to break the decision to that inflammable person. His looks were lowering, storm-signals flew from each eye, and the blue-cotton Szechuen turban had a contradictory twist and cant. He was told that we would not risk our lives any farther up-stream in his kwatsze; that he could have a day to calk and pitch and mend, and must then return to I-chang; and the face was illumined, the master mariner more relieved than we. "The kwatsze stays here. We will take a light sampan with a sail at the other end of the village, and push as far beyond Mitsang Gorge as we can in a day"; and the captain leaped with joy, and the crew begged to man the sampan.

Tsin Tan is so picturesquely placed, with the lines of the Liu-kan and the Mitsang gateways both in view from the village, that when steam-navigation is the regular thing Tsin Tan's outlook will be far-famed. Rows of village women gaped and grinned at us,

HALF-TONE PLATE ENGRAVED BY J. W. EVANS.

DESCENDING TA DUNG RAPIDS.

OLD WRINKLES, THE FO'C'S'LE COOK.

the boy answered that the cook and crew were all on board. We counted ten men at the bows gobbling down their first rice, and the captain was told to shove off at once. Then our boy said with embarrassment, "One piece cook no have got." The piece of a cook had just gone up-town to get some money that a cousin owed him, he said. We waited a quarter of an hour, then ten minutes of the soft, still, warm, early day, smoke rising straight in air from each village, and every detail of cañon walls and distant peaks exquisitely clear in that pure, pale light. No one was in sight on the shining shingle, and we told the captain to let go, he incredulous, and the crew grinning in foolish amaze at the idea of white travelers severed from a cook.

their children's red, green, and orange coats the only touches of color in town, save for the heaped oranges and pomelos for sale by the river-bank. Swine roamed everywhere, and men staggered up and down steep paths with baskets of coal and country produce on their backs.

Once embarked on the river above the rapids in a sampan, that seemed to skim like a bird after the clumsy creep of the kwatsze, we could enjoy the wild scenery without distraction or panic. When well within the walls of the Mitsang (Rice-Granary) Gorge, the breeze took the sail and floated our speck of a boat up the flooded crevice between stupendous cliffs.

When we had shot down-stream in the late afternoon, and into the gulf of blue gloom within the Mitsang's steep walls, the wind, in regular Alaskan williwaws, played with our sampan alarmingly. Gusts struck spray from the water, made swirls, and bored eddies that sucked down our bow and sent us reeling down the cañon. We met many such small maelstroms, rowed through chow-chow water in stretches, but finally reached Tsin Tan beach, and the protection of the American flag in our kwatsze beyond. The relic had been patched and mended a bit, tacked and pasted together, and we promised presents all round if, starting at six in the morning, the crew could reach I-chang by six at night.

When the early tea-tray was pushed in,

Although bewildered, they bent to their poles, and, once in mid-stream, the boy recovered from stupefaction and admitted that the cook had gone ashore the night before, to return before daybreak, and that the debtor-cousin story was a fiction and excuse of the moment. The cook was probably asleep in some opium den, the boy said, as he had smoked and slept all the way upstream, leaving the boy, with the aid of the captain's wife, to do nearly all the cooking; thus the miracle of our well-served dinners was all the more amazing. While the boy and the captain's wife looked to coffee, toast, and bacon, one of the little mud stoves of the country was brought to the front, its lumps of charcoal glowing, and in that primitive chafing-dish eggs scrambled in boiling milk at last materialized. While I stirred the frothing mass, the whole crew watched agape, and the captain's head hung down from overhead to witness the amazing spectacle of a foreigner acting as cook. It was a cheerful ship's crew all day long as they urged and drove the kwatsze on toward their extra gratuities, and at the very mention of cook all burst into laughter, and old Wrinkles wiped tears away.

There were such pale-blue mists and lilac lights in the Liu-kan Gorge that the splendid precipice walls were transfigured, the great cañon far more impressive than when we had passed through before, dejected, in a sinking kwatsze. We raced down the valley of rapids in contrast to our toilsome ascent, whizzing past rocks and through mill-races, plunging and spinning around as we had enviously watched other downward craft do when we were hanging inert at the ropes' ends. We made a headlong dash at a junk in Ta Dung Rapids, shot away one second before the collision was due, and went pirouetting down-stream. The crew worked a great sweep-oar rigged at the bow to keep the kwatsze's head on its course, the captain swung the clumsy tiller-beam without exhortations, and the current did the rest.

By noon the upward wind was felt. Gusts swooped down from the heights, spun the kwatsze round, and bored whirlpools at our bows. We had retraced five days' journeys then, and while we drifted in aimless circles the crew fortified themselves with a vegetarian lunch, bowl after bowl of cabbage-soup and rice restoring their brawn and tissue. Then they laid to their oars, or hop-poles, with a will, even a pale Szechuen scholar, who was working his passage down-stream, stamping with the rest. Once an oar snapped, and it took a miserable quarter of an hour to put about and manœuver to recover it in that bottomless gorge where none dared swim. Old Wrinkles squared the splintered ends with his cleaver, spliced them firmly, and the crew resumed chant and stamp, vexing the Yangtsze with their broken strokes until the current caught us. It was the rarest of all our autumn days, and we basked in the sun, and feasted eyes again on the splendidly splintered and buttressed walls, the caves and high-hung temples, the bridges and rock inscriptions on the walls, and the procession of striped sails creeping at their feet. We dipped the ensign and flew past Pin-shan-pa customs station, behind which the palisade of seamed and broken marble strata, overgrown with vines, so easily suggests a tropical temple ruin. We passed the gateway at full speed at sunset hour, and were fast at I-chang jetty at the appointed time, ready to kneel with flag in thanksgiving, like Columbus in the picture.

At ten o'clock the next night the boy came grinning to us. "That cook want money; just now come." And then it was related how the cook, strolling down to Tsin Tan's shore at his leisure, found the kwatsze gone hours before. Giving his coat as security for his passage-money, he embarked on a downward junk, sure of finding us tied up and waiting around some corner for the cook to prepare the tiffin. He had dealt with foreigners before, and knew their feints and helplessness. Another garment went to a second and swifter craft, until, changing from junk to junk, he had arrived shivering in his last thin garments, a full day behind us, but asking to be paid for that day and his down-stream traveling expenses.

While it was swift and easy to descend the Yangtsze by kwatsze, our difficulties began with steam-navigation. It was *difficilis descensus* Yangtsze then. After vexatious delays, we twice embarked, twice had the machinery break down, and twice were taken back to I-chang, arriving finally in Hankow on a third steamer, which lost one propeller on the tedious down trip. From palm-trees and orange-trees in the gorges of the far interior range, we traveled to snow-striped hills around Nanking, and to hard frost at Shanghai, 31° 15′ N., which latter lies thirty-three seconds north of and a thousand miles nearer the sea-coast than I-chang, 30° 42′ N.

TRACKERS ON THE UPPER YANGTSZE.

A Cruise on the Norfolk Broads (1895)

The Century Magazine.

OCTOBER, 1895.

A CRUISE ON THE NORFOLK BROADS.

WITH PICTURES BY JOSEPH PENNELL.

BETWEEN the sea beaches of Yarmouth and Lowestoft, the grainfields of Wroxham, and the crowded river-wharves of Norwich, lie the plains and valleys through which flow the Bure, the Yare, and the Waveney. Before losing themselves irrevocably in the sea, these rivers turn aside, as it were, now and then, from their more serious duty of providing a watery highway, to frolic in a series of wild lakes and meres. These limpid waterways have been used for generations by the homely Norfolk barges. For generations also it has been an open secret to sportsmen and anglers that in summer the Broads are an angler's paradise, and that in winter wild ducks are almost as numerous as thrushes in August. In time the secret was whispered abroad. Following in the footsteps of the men of the gun came others with palette hooked on thumb; and once the smoke from an anchored house-boat — the artist's improvised studio or the journalist's den — rose up among the reeds and grasses to rival the vaporous column circling skyward from the fenman's cottage, the land of the Broads was summarily annexed to the domain of pure romance. This its magnet still holds good; and now, as one may see during the whole of the long summer, the sails between the meadows are almost as thick as cabs on Piccadilly.

For more than a decade cruising on the Broads has taken a foremost place in the long list of sports and pastimes yielded by that amazing little island where, by utilizing every rill and rivulet, every hill and upland, man has doubled the size, and tripled the pleasure-giving capacity, of the stretch of earth he calls his England.

I.

WOULD you hoist sail from the heart of a rustic village? There is Wroxham, set upon the river Bure seven miles from Norwich, an admirable collection of thatched cottages, tall hedges, rose-gardens, rustics, and clucking hens. This yachting-station in a meadow is one of the favorite points of departure for a cruise on the Broads. But if you are one of those who must have the scent of the sea in the nostrils, Great Yarmouth, down upon the coast, will send you forth as well equipped for an inland voyage into poppy-land as for the rounding of the Cape. Lowestoft, farther south, will rival that perfection, with the added attraction to fishermen of offering a swift approach to Oulton Broad and its fresh-water catches.

We were in pursuit, not of fish, but of adventure, and therefore it was that Wroxham had cast its spell upon us. We were curious to see how an inland village, of strictly agricultural habits and rural traditions, would arrange the *mise-en-scène* of a yachting-station.

The booths and shops of the highroad running from the railway at Wroxham to the Bridge displayed their tawdry flannels and cheap yachting-caps with naïve, rustic ostentation. Peddlers were dancing fish-hooks in the eyes of dragon-flies, and offering worms in tin boxes. Butchers' shops led the way to an inn, and some farmers' carts starting forth from the stable-yard showed us the road to the Bridge. Beneath the latter flowed a river,—a stream, rather,—along the banks of which were grouped the promised village beauties of rose-vines, thatched roofs, and bits of emerald turf, set in a frame of golden grain-fields. A blackbird, singing on a reed-stalk, sent his song forth as if in invocation to the beauty of this pastoral landscape. Would any marine mind, in full possession of its nautical faculties, have looked to find a yachting-station in such a setting? Yet where there seemed barely room for a wave, there a fleet lay at anchor, or was hoisting sail. Twenty or more yachts, yawls, steam-launches, barges, and smaller sailing-craft gave to the river an animation commonly associated solely with the sea. The scene could hardly have been gayer under an Italian sky, and there was in the very air a gala note that made this pool that had become a yachting-station, and these yachts that were sailing forth to cruise between the meadows, assume an aspect of unreality.

Meanwhile, both on the yacht decks and on shore, the preparations for immediate departure were being carried on with great bustle and gravity; this cruise among the grasses was obviously undertaken with all the seriousness of a genuine sea voyage. Dinghys and row-boats were spinning about, carrying luggage and passengers to the more distant crafts. Hand-carts and wheelbarrows were being trundled over the Bridge, for the Norwich train was in, and the new arrivals were in haste to be off. Shouts, commands, orders crossed and recrossed one another from deck to shore, sailors, rustics, grooms, and yachtsmen all talking at once. The river was busy with a multitude of reflections: the limpid blues would be obliterated by the whites of flapping sails, and the blacks of painted hulls as quickly replaced by dashes of crimson or streaks of cobalt-blue — movable dashes that followed the figures of the yachtsmen, the placing of deck pillows and of cushioned chairs. All the while the soft gold of an English noon was flooding the scene, the overarching sky carrying its own argosies of sun-whitened clouds.

About a certain low shed close to the river-bank, where the yachts lay thickest, we stood watching the putting forth of the boats on their river journey; noted the dexterous storing away, in lockers and cabins, of the mounds of trunks, portmanteaus, boxes of provisions, guitars, banjos, fishing-gear, and "silhouettes," or vast-rimmed straw hats. Imperceptibly the hubbub and noise had died out; the strong-voiced young yachtsmen, the agitated parsons, and the ladies in distress over missing pieces of luggage, had all sailed away, re-lapsing into composure now that the sails, in their turn, had begun to flutter in the breeze.

It was noon, and it was now quiet on the river. A flock of white ducks were swimming into the very middle of the stream; their quack, quack made a pleasing recitative to the accompaniment of the lapping water. A figure, coatless, hatless, lean of shape and keen of eye, stood beside us. The lean man had crossed his arms, for now at last he had a moment of leisure. It was for that moment we had been forced to wait, that our inquiries concerning boats and dates might be answered.

"Sorry indeed I am, sir; but there's not a boat left. Those two are off to-morrow. The very last boat I had was that yawl yonder." The man's eyes followed the boat, now going down stream, as they might the vanishing shape of a friend.

This was a dispiriting announcement. It was certainly not the one we had come up from London to hear; and J. Loynes, owner of cabin yachts, yawls, and wherries, "fitted with every convenience for cooking and sleeping," was now paying us the compliment of showing a disappointment as keen as our own. Presently he proffered a seat on the top of an overturned barrel, that we might be the more at our ease to be lamented over and sympathized with. Then he began again, with cheery civility: "An' now we must see what can be done about a boat. If it was only to the Hook you were going, I've a beauty in — just the very thing." The Hook? An illuminating smile upward toward the low shed was our enlightenment; for on the shed we read: "Yachts for Holland, the Hook, and Zuyder Zee. On hire. To be had of J. Loynes." Once more we looked at the river, at the simple, nodding grasses, at the lily-pads, and the ducks swimming through them. Were expeditions for the north pole also fitted out in this amazing little stream? Loynes had caught the question in our smile, and was answering it.

"You see, sir, it's as easy to do the Hook and Holland as it is the Broads, an' in a way, as you may say, it's a better business; for Holland's better known. It's been more writ up; an' there's nothin' like writin' up a country to make it known." In Loynes's mind, at least, literature had its solid uses. "There's a gentleman, a painter, whose writin's have made Holland very fashionable — a Mr. Boughton. You may have heard of him. An' now the Broads is beginnin' to be writ up, and business is gettin' better every year. In the heavy season, as you see, there ain't a boat to be had. I'm more sorry than I can speak it, I am, I can't oblige you; but—" here he paused suddenly, and unhooked his lean arms, clutched at his

YACHTING-STATION, WROXHAM.

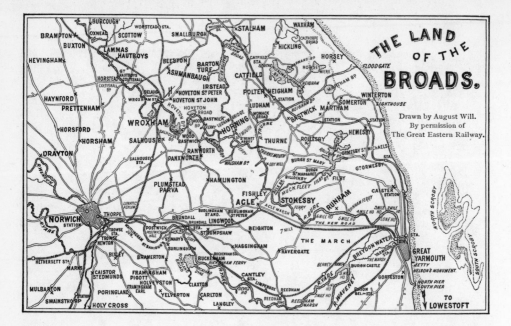

The Land of the Broads.

Drawn by August Will.
By permission of
The Great Eastern Railway.

long beard, let his eyes sparkle a little, and cried out exultingly—"but there's the *Vacuna*, I do believe; Jimpson has her to let." With the excitement of his discovery still strong upon him, Loynes hailed a man just then crossing the Bridge. "I say, Mills, bring round the jolly-boat, will you; and—Jimpson—I've got a party looking for a yacht—tell Jimpson." And in due time the mysterious jolly-boat, with the unknown Jimpson in it, was duly brought round.

Meanwhile Loynes was hurrying us along the river-bank. He began a swift enumeration of the yacht's merits: she was small, but she was fast; she had, indeed, been built for the Broads. Being only a five-tonner, and carrying just the right amount of canvas, she was particularly quick in coming about, a great feature in sailing these narrow rivers. A moment later, and we were boarding her. She was a beautiful little toy of a yacht, with a neat finish of woods and brass mountings to announce her as a Brahman among her kind.

Another short half-hour, and she was ours. Jimpson himself, owner of the King's Head inn, and the letter of the yacht, had come up in the jolly-boat to witness the signing of our lease. After the formalities of the law had been attended to, we were informally asked to assist at a short council. "Now that the boat suits you, sir, have you thought of provisioning her?" We were forced to admit that we had not; and thereupon our counselors grouped themselves about us. Loynes promptly chose the deck-rail; a brown piece of paper stretched across

his knee became his improvised tablet. Jimpson, a large man, was already comfortably seated on the cabin. One other figure, a silent one, lent its presence to the proceedings: it was that of the sailor who had brought the jolly-boat and Jimpson up from the inn gardens.

He had swung himself from the dinghy to the yacht's deck with the air of a man who was taking possession of the boat. He was indeed the *Vacuna's* skipper, and we were to be his "party" during the week's cruise. From the forward hatchway, into the depths of which he had slid his sinewy body, his searching blue eyes were now fixed upon us; they were taking a series of purely professional observations. "As handy a man as is to be found on the Broads," was Jimpson's commendatory introduction at the other end of the boat. "He's known from Lowestoft to Norwich, an' from Norwich to Wroxham Broad—is Mills of Yarmouth. A family man, ma'am, an' as handy with a rope as he is civil an' steady. An' now, sir an' madam, there's the essentials, if I may so name them—tea an' coffee, sugar, a bit of flour, an' marmalade. If you're lookin' for a tasty bit, sir, there's nothing like bacon an' a cut of good ham. But salt beef, that's the thing you'll want by you, first and last, for the men, sir." Salt beef, it was agreed, should be the bed-rock of our supplies. "Jimpson," asked Loynes of the innkeeper, "is there anything else?" Jimpson quickly responded, without reflection: "There's the beer—for the men. The King's Head can supply you, sir, an' Mills will see it's put aboard. An' a fowl or two cooked, an' some fresh lettuce, is tasty the first day or so out. The missis will see to that, sir. Mills, is there anything else?" Mills, still within his hatchway, took a moment in which to make the tour of his memory; with no inn ledgers on his mind, he approached the momentous subject with the caution of a family man. "Who's to go with me?" he finally asked, lifting his head inquiringly. "I'll send Grimes along," Jimpson answered slowly, as if the gift of Grimes cost him an effort. On Mills's face was written the patient acceptance of the inevitable; all the spirit went out of his voice. Resettling his chin on his crossed arms, he answered, "I believe there is n't any potatoes." And with the additional entry of the neglected potatoes the council came to an end.

II.

Now at last the great moment had come. Our sails were set, the two-foot gang-plank had been lifted, communication with the shore was at an end, and we were drifting into mid-stream. Now that we were fairly afloat, there was an instant of speculative suspense. Would the yacht fit into the river? The width of the deck would surely fill the stream, and its rails overlay the grassy banks. Yet, narrow as was the watery highway, a boat under full sail was coming up stream; she was to be met and passed. Again there was a curious mounting of the pulse-beats. We passed the up-coming boat without so much as grazing the bank. Imperceptibly all the while we were floating farther

and farther out upon the river; fainter and fainter grew the faces of Jimpson, of Loynes, of the farmers and plowboys assembled to see us start forth; and between the bushy tree-boughs the outlines of the Wroxham houses were soon merged in the blur of the blue and green distances.

Meanwhile, from the first moment of our starting forth there had been pregnant signs of trouble aboard. Mills the skipper and his mate were at odds. The mate was a buttonless stable-boy with a face and smile as open as his shirt. Ten minutes before we started he had been rubbing down a sweating roan. But neither the lad's boyish smile nor his deftness in the art of stowing away had power to soften the sharp edge of our skipper's dislike; he took no pains whatever to conceal his scorn of stable-boys playing at sailoring. We had barely gone a dozen yards on our way before there came the deep growl of his displeasure; for our sails were hanging as limp as wet linen, and the infant mate was ordered to test his strength at quanting. Against his shoulder he had promptly proceeded to plant one of the long poles that lay along the cabin; securely fixing its padded leather top against his narrow chest, he then began slowly to walk the deck, pressing the long pole into the mud of the river-bed.

"Here, take the helm! A little more strength's what's needed over that pole," Mills cried out, with a note of impatience in his voice, after watching the lad's purpling face. But even under the pressure of his own

SAILING ON THE BURE.

strong muscles the yacht was still crawling at a snail's pace. Another ten minutes, and Mills had hailed a man going up-stream in a rowboat. "Davy! I say, Davy! Give us a start, will you?" The man stopped rowing, swung his rope aboard, and himself immediately after. Without a word he seized the remaining pole, and began walking the deck on the port side. For a good fifteen minutes there was only the sound of the men's deep breathing to be heard. "We don't get a true wind till we get to the open," puffed Mills in an explanatory aside. In another moment we had swept clear of the green shores. A fresh breeze, blowing across the meadows, now filled our sails; the poles came presently to a rest, and Mills was once more at the helm. "You see, sir, I had to have help round that first reach. That 'ere," and Mills, with a dig of his thumb in the air, contemptuously indicated the figure of Grimes bending over the ropes in the stern — "that 'ere ain't no more use 'n a baby — for polin'." Then the lad was sharply ordered to "stand by the ropes."

But with the advent of the wind came also our skipper's good humor. The mere study of tides, a patient acceptance of the caprices of the wind, and knowing one's river as a man knows the face of his own child — these are only the rudiments of a science every skipper must master before he is counted worthy to sail a boat. But sailing on the Broads demands the finishing grace of an art. A Norfolkman, on these rivers of his, must feel himself to be both host and guide: his courtesy must be lined with conscience. We had gone only a short quarter of a mile when Mills, in an opening speech, gave us the text of his sermon on the ethics of nautical conduct.

"You see, sir an' madam, if you 'll allow, this is how I looks at a cruise on the Broads. It all depends on the skipper, I says. You may never see me again, sir, or you, madam; but as sure as I 'm talkin', the pleasure of a party on board a yacht is in the skipper's hands. If he 's rusty or crabby, your pleasure 's void an' your money 's wasted. Grimes, my lad, you may bring me a glass. I drinks to our voyage an' your good healths. An' lively, mind, Grimes, for there 's a boat comin' up to windward."

Deep was the glass in which the success of our cruise was drunk, and swift was the tossing of the foamy beer by our skipper's practised hand; for there was not only one, there were a number of boats, coming up to windward. The river was a thronged highway. Yachts, barges, yawls, rowboats — such was the flotilla riding between the meadow-banks. With the sunny whiteness of the bulging sails was con-

trasted the novelty of the prevailing background: trees, farm-houses, hay-ricks, garden walls, herds of cattle, windmills — a landscape through which the moving sails seemed to play the rôle of winged figures. Gradually the charm and beauty of this river life began to work their spell. The zigzagging of the yacht from shore to shore was soon accepted as a novel way of getting into closer touch with a river-bank, the narrowness of the river and the low, close shores giving one the sense of being at one and the same moment on land and on water. All the usual signs and sights seen and looked for from a yacht's deck must be forgotten, to be replaced by fresh and novel experiences. For the usual horizons seen from aboard a yacht, there were fringes of larches behind which the blues of the hills and of the sky came together; to test the course of the wind one looked at the tossing of tree-boughs, and to note its strength there was the waving grain to take the place of foam-capped water. The sails we met came from behind barns, and the bows rounded the bark of tree-trunks. To speak a ship one had only to shout across the meadows. As far as the eye could see, the landscape was dotted with white wings. Rarely above the low shores did the river show its sunned face, and the boats in the narrow channels seemed to walk upon the meadows. The church spires of Horning and Hoveton crowning the hilltops alone appeared stable, for the ever-moving sails gave to all the landscape a shifting and fluctuant aspect.

And now the breeze had strengthened. Our sails were full, and for a good fifteen minutes or more we had a true bit of sailing. Along with the wind the tide of our skipper's spirits had risen. In his eye there shone fresh life and vigor; his shrewd face, with its long, thin nose, and the clever wrinkles on brow and chin, was set about with smiles. A sun high in the heavens, a fair wind springing up, full lockers, and only two cabin passengers — what could man or sailor ask more? Mills's voyage from shore to shore, as the *Vacuna* tacked and came about, was a saunterer's gay meeting with succeeding groups of friends and acquaintances. I have rarely known a man whose bowing acquaintance was at once so large and varied. No bargeman passed us but it was, "Hallo, Jim! Any news down Yarmouth way?" or it was, "How are you, sir? Glad to see you down so early this year," to two elderly gentlemen sailing their own yacht. It is certain if any man could humanize an English river, could thaw its reserve into a Gallic fervor, it was Mills. For rustic on shore and for bargeman, for the fisherman mending his net and the girls working in the fields, Mills had his smile and his jest. He was as full of gossip as a provincial

A FARM IN THE BROADS.

SAILING ACROSS THE FIELDS.

newspaper, and as generous with his news of the day as a street bulletin.

For my own part, I had never been on such intimate terms with an inland country. We brushed the reedy banks as if the grasses were a friend's garment, and the branches of the trees, in their turn, swept the puffing cheeks of our sails. Geese and swans betrayed their hiding by sailing forth from their ambush to menace and, if possible, affright; and finding we meant no harm, ranged their battalions in line, forming a winged escort. The cows, lying or standing, took their place in our talk; they would lift their heads as we bore down upon their clover-patch, raising their mild eyes as they stopped to listen; and then once more we would hear the sound of their slow breath upon the grass, and the rhythmic switching of their tails. The open cottage doors took us into the privacy of family life; the farmer, shouting to his plowboy across his garden patch, told us dinner was ready; and the voices within denoted the exact temperature of the mistress's temper. Rustic calling to rustic proved the Norfolk preference for continuing a strictly apostolic succession in the matter of name-giving. As for the houses themselves, when you have sailed into a man's front door, missing it by a mere matter of a few feet; when you have managed to graze the side of his barn in lieu of demolishing it; when your bow has swept his wife's milk-cans hanging on the fence — why, for the life of you you cannot help feeling that somewhat close re-

lations have certainly been established between your boat and the shore.

All the while the wind and river between them were taking us on with quickening speed. The outlook changed with kaleidoscopic swiftness. A sweep of turf with grazing cattle would be replaced by a fenman's cottage blocking the sky-distance at the head of a dike; and then a thatched farm-house, with its wall-spaces abloom with roses, would be succeeded by the Georgian Gothic gables of a gentleman's seat; on the next tack a daub-and-wattle hut beneath a thick growth of trees was a significant reminder of those more economical builders in brushwood and clay, with their more strictly utilitarian purposes.

"It's a bit ticklish, this wind — a bit ticklish," Mills suddenly broke out. "I don't like the way it's dodgin' about. It's wery treacherous — full of variety, that's what it is. It's a good deal like women, beggin' your pardon, ma'am." And he brought his helm round with a quick turn. A reach farther on there was a "quieter bit of sailin'," as the skipper termed a steadier wind; and then he went on with what was still in his mind.

"Variety! Lord bless you! No woman as is worth havin' but is full of it. There's my wife. God bless her! I would n't part with her for all the gold in England. But you'd have all the variety you'd want on a washin'-day when it's wet, an' neuralligy is a-settin' in. I've been through all that, I have. There's nothin' like it — for variety. An' when you come in yourself, wet to the skin, an' lookin' forward to a bit o' rest an' warmth by your own fireside, an' you see your wife's head tied up, an' she a-bendin' over the wash-tubs, you know what's before you,—you do!—an' you just haul in your sheet an' drop anchor, you do. An' you do it wery quiet. I've been through all that, I have. Lively there, my lad, lively! I've a bit of tackin' to do just here—wery ticklish she is." And Mills, with his eye on his sail, relapsed once more into silence. The silence was soon broken; the wind sent us headlong into an eel-hut, and only Mills's skill in a quick handling of the ropes kept us clear of the bank. No sooner were we fairly started on our course amid-stream than Mills had brought his tiller round with a mighty sweep, and was shouting to Grimes:

"Let go your jib! Let her go, I say! Can't you see there's a boat comin' up to windward?"

III.

THE boat that was passing us to windward was a sight to enchain the eyes. It was a huge craft, yet it was riding the narrow waters with a swift and confident ease that put to shame the paces of our own deft *Vacuna*. As the full, mahogany-tinted sail bore down upon us, for one dark moment its convex surface made a brown tent between us and the sky. Then the tent sailed by, and the foreground was clear once more. The boat itself, we then saw, was as myriad-hued as the plumage of a tropical bird. Crude, strong colors had been lavished on hull, cabin, and mast; even the poles lying along the ocher-tinted deck were a vivid cobalt-blue. The boat's deep crimsons, greens, and yellows presented strangely un-English color contrasts, and the sober grays and greens of the landscape were all at once surprisingly intensified. A caique strayed from the turquoise blue of the Adriatic and adrift among these Norfolk lily-pads could scarcely have brought to the eyes a greater surprise than did this survival, doubtless, of the old Norse love of the barbaric in color.

Meanwhile our skipper was giving the boat and its crew his customary greeting. "How are you, Cross? How's the missis?" The man at the helm gravely returned the salute. Standing waist-high above the low cabin, with hand on tiller, he might have been cut in bronze. Only his eyes seemed alive. Mills, the set of our sails, Grimes tugging away at the ropes, those of us grouped along the stern — all these details had been taken in at a glance, with that swiftness of vision which is the gift of birds and mariners. The skipper gave no more concern to his own full sail, which was tied, than if it had been a solid piece of nature rooted in the meadows. A single passenger was to be seen on deck. On a mound of nut-brown silken pillows, close to the mast, reclined at full length a young and lovely girl. As she lay there, her eyes fixed on the pages of a book, her hair, a light-brown glory, was spread about her, drying in the breeze. The other accessories to the pic-

DRAWN BY JOSEPH PENNELL.

HOVETON CHURCH.

WHERRIES.

ture, the pale, esthetic silks curtaining the cabin windows, the glimpses of rugs and hangings within the cabin, a mandolin lying on the low divan, a blur of pink roses massed in a huge blue vase—all these were only insignificant details beside the one compelling presence, that of the young beauty lying on her bed of pillows, with the tendrils of her hair afloat in the wind.

"She's only a pleasure-wherry," was Mills's somewhat contemptuous comment. There were others, "true" wherries, he would have us know, that for centuries past had been the merchants' carriers. Up from Yarmouth and Lowestoft they had made their way by day and by night through these winding river-courses. It was only of late years that something of their dignity as a commercial flotilla had been lowered by some of the newer, later-built craft having been turned into pleasure-boats.

"The wherry's built for trade, an' not for pleasure, I hold," Mills broke forth, with a vigor of condemnation in his tone. "They goes light over the water, that I can't deny; they rides the water like a bird. But a yacht seems more shipshape for a gentleman's pleasure, I always says. They're a wonderful handy craft, an' 'll sail as close to the wind as any ever I did see, an' they 're just made to order for these 'ere reaches an' rivers, sir. You see, sir, it 's the way a wherry's mast is stepped that makes her handy—that an' the sail's bein' without a boom. Her mast yonder is to the extreme for'ard. An' the length of her, an' the breadth,

—they runs from forty-five to fifty feet long, with a beam of ten to twelve,—an' the lowness of her hull, it all helps. Just look at that 'ere wherry roundin' that reach. Ain't she a purty sight ?"

The wherry that was rounding the reach was evidently no light "pleasure" craft: this was the "true" wherry. Its patched and darned sail had an unmistakable professional seriousness; the man at the helm, as we came alongside a tack or two farther on, was as patched and darned as his sail. Both the skipper and his craft told their own story: it was one of long days' and nights' sailing in open and narrow waters; of innumerable loadings and unloadings at the crowded Norwich and Yarmouth quays; of a life lived in a perpetual round of weighing anchor and hoisting sail.

Mills had his usual interchange of river courtesies with the rough-featured helmsman. Then, as the breeze went light, our skipper set his foot once more upon the seat, resting his body against the tiller as he held it lightly with one hand. By these signs we knew that the gift of speech was once more to descend upon Mills of Yarmouth.

"Many 's the long month I 've wherried it," he now mused, "along these rivers. Man and boy, I 've lived my life on the Broads, all but the seven years I was at sea; an' long years they was, though a man ought to see the world, whatever it costs, I 've always held. Well, sir an' madam, if I may make so bold, I 've known what it was to sweat an' shine like the darky cooks we 'd take aboard on the Florida coast; an' my beard an' hands have been froze with the cold in the Russian seas; an' I 've been lyin' like a dead man with the yellow Jack in African waters: but for poorness of livin' an' hardship, give me a Norfolk wherry. Poorest fodder on record, is it, on board a wherry. A piece of sour bread an' an onion, a red herring with no head on an' no gills, that 's what it is week in an' week out. If I got a piece of sweet pork I felt I was a magistrate; a cup of tea without milk, I was a mayor; a bit of homemade bread an' cheese, and no king was happier. Grimes, my lad, another glass. That breeze do bring a thirst to a man."

It was no breeze that was imparting the bibulous impulse to our skipper: he was only toasting the present moment of prosperity. There was an entirely honorable elation and a desire to prolong the lyrical moment in the knowledge that with the dark winter he had turned his back on such a past of hardships. And what more hospitable or kindly than for one at a full table to wish to share the good things of the feast with his brethren that were passing him by?

Mills had hardly finished his glass before a wherry was seen slowly creeping up stream. The lowered sails told us what we knew already, that both wind and tide were against the boat.

"You 've the wind dead ahead; it 'll be better further on," was Mills's spirited greeting.

Two bronzed, bearded faces were lifted, for both men were at the poles; and both began to speak in the unintelligible Norfolk jargon. The quants came to an abrupt rest, and presently the eyes of the two giants glistened as if with some fever of anticipation. It was a form of fever that appeared to move to compassionate interest not only Mills, but Grimes, who disappeared, to reappear on the instant with two foaming glasses of beer. The quanters sat themselves down on their cabin, the glasses were emptied at a single toss, and as they wiped their beards they rose to send across the water the civilities common to men the whole world over when drinking at another's expense. A sentence or two more of the jargon, and the wherrymen were again bending over their quants.

In point of beauty I have never seen a craft, whether made for man's pleasure or for the furthering of his commercial intercourse, more exactly to my taste than a Norfolk wherry. Far across the meadows a wherry might be seen lying among the tree-boughs, or it might be creeping or sailing or flying before the wind. Whatever its office or its attitude, to look upon a Norfolk wherry was for the eye to rest on the most picturesque thing afloat. Not the least among its qualities was the way in which a wherry did its hard work: it had an artist's grace, or that ease which comes with a perfection of adjustment in making labor take an outward festival aspect. Not even the most ancient and weather-worn of wherries ever appeared

DRAWN BY JOSEPH PENNELL.

THE MOUTH OF WROXHAM BROAD.

aware of the sobering fact that it was earning its living.

IV.

" GRIMES, my boy, tie your sheet, an' bring me a glass. We 're on the Broad the next tack, an' there 'll be some sailin', then, there will!" and Mills emptied his glass. A moment later he took the *Vacuna* so close to the tree-boughs that our sail swept the whole breadth of the green façade. The next instant there came a thunderous command: " Ease your mainsheet! Ease her, I say! Can't you see there 's a boat comin' off the Broad? We 'll have to make another tack. Quick with your jib!" We were more than half-way about before Grimes had loosened his sheet; for in moments of emergency the space between Grimes's ears and his intellect seemed lengthened to stellar distances.

"That lad ain't worth tuppence, he ain't," was Mills's growl as he watched the infant mate's leisurely fingering of the ropes. Grimes greeted this low commercial view of his marine abilities with a serene smile.

Mills meanwhile had steered our boat sharp to the right, and with a swift turn had sent us flying through a narrow opening. The river was left along with the bushes guarding the gateway, and we found ourselves entering a wide, open space of water. The water-piece was an inland lake the glittering surface of

portions of a captive sea. To sail to the distant upper end was surely to undertake a voyage of formidable length; and doubtless, if one chose the spot with care, one might have the luck to run the chance of a drowning adventure. Wide and long was the stretch of the water, and few and distant were the signs of man's habitation. The beauty of the Broad consisted in this remote and isolated aspect: it was a bit of wildness set in the finish of English lawns. Beyond the screen of the trees yonder there lay another world; this wide lakelet seemed set apart as a home for wild birds and a watery refuge for the coyest fish. To one of us, at least, the moment had brought exhilaration in its train.

"Ha-ha-a! This is sailin', this is! Grimes, my lad, get me my racin'-cap. You may tie your mainsail. No more miserable dodgin's in and out between banks o' daisies and willow-boughs." Now it was that the true mariner in Mills's stanch sailor's soul came to life; eye and hand were as quick in response as an instrument to the touch of a master. The red of the racing-cap framed a face aglow with delight; and it was impossible, I think, for a man to look more lovingly at a full sail.

" Sailing on the ocean —
  Sailing on the sea — a——

Seven years of it, sir, and then back to old

DRAWN BY JOSEPH PENNELL.   IN A NARROW CHANNEL.

which seemed overbrimming earth's shallow cup; for the shores were low, their level lines accentuating the breadth of the liquid acreage. The lake was Wroxham Broad.

In America, on Long Island, this pretty inlet would have seemed a water-piece of fairly respectable area. Here, in this tight, compact little island, Wroxham Broad took on the pro-

Yarmouth. That 's right, my bird! Go, fly — on with you, *Vacuna!*"

What with the height of Mills's spirits, and the surprise of his breaking into song, we had barely noticed the fairly racing speed our cutter was showing. Her sails were in the water, and below there was an ominous rattle of glasses and crockery. With the quickening of

AN OLD MILL.

our pace Mills broke out again as we took our second turn across the lake.

"As I was sayin', sir, this is a grand piece of water, this is. She 's rightly named the Queen of the Broads. There 's none to match her." Then he went on to explain that the shape of the Broad was peculiarly adapted for sailing, being oblong, with rounded corners. "A wessel can sail right round it and back, with a jibe or two, an' no tackin' needed. An' you should see the water frolic on her when the regatta 's on, an' all the banks as crowded with craft as a Yarmouth quay. That 's a sight! Ah! but it 's grand sport, a Wroxham regatta!"

Of the crew and passengers of the *Vacuna* Grimes alone had remained unmoved. During this hour of free, swift sailing he had sat with an impassive serenity, with his hand on the ropes and his eyes fixed on the most distant points. When the order came to go about, he awoke as if from a trance.

"That boy ain't no more a sailor than I be a corpse," was Mills's contemptuous growl.

"What is it, Grimes? What do you see?"

"Them 's eels, ma'am, them is. He 's a-skinnin' 'em. I likes eels," and in the eye of Grimes there was the hunger of the growing boy. Bread and jam from the nearest locker, it was suggested, might be made to suffice as a temporary substitute for eels.

On our next jibe we came about in a hurry, for a lively breeze was churning the lake into a little racing sea; and as we scudded through the water the figures on shore seemed by contrast as immovable as statues. The skinner of the eels might have been an automaton. Farther on there were yards and yards of the filmy lace of a fisherman's net hung on poles; through this lace the landscape became suddenly idealized, as a woman's features assume a more perfect unity through the harmonizing meshes of a veil. Near by a pale townsman was holding forth a fishing-rod with the rigid solemnity of the amateur. He had cautiously chosen a still and glassy surface. According to Mills, the spot was one backed by a reputation of past good "catches," and yet nothing was biting. As we swept by Mills had his fling at the townsman's ignorance. "Them tofts ["toft" is Norfolk for "swell"] comes down from the cities, an' think the flingin' of a rod over a boat is the whole history of fishin'. Their empty catches ought to teach 'em, but they don't never l'arn anything."

The *Vacuna*, meanwhile, was making her very last trip up to the farther end of the Broad. The wind had strengthened, and our decks were wet, and so were we. But what was a dashing of spray when one could feel the swift flight of the boat through the water; when the waves were of a height to make the yacht dance; when our sails were stretched to their utmost limit, and the breeze was whipping the cheek till the whole frame was aglow? The geese and ducks were doing their sailing closer in to the shore. Overhead, snipe, sea-gulls, and wood-pigeons beat the air with their wings, circling and swirling, and the sportsman among us was certain he had heard the whistle of a pheasant in the grasses.

Now upon the hills the hay-stacks were beginning to cast a warning length of shadow. Mills took one glance at the hills, and a ringing order to "come about" followed the glance. A skilful handling of the sails and some practised steering sent us flying through the narrow gateway, and no fewer than three sails were near to do justice to the grace and dignity of our exit. Once upon the river, there was again the quiet lapping of the water along the fringe of grasses, the breeze was coming puffily, fitfully, and the shores seemed to close in about us. The trees were again our neighbors, and the round, full eyes of the gentle cows looked at us above the low bushes.

Across the meadows the giant arms of a windmill could be seen pawing the air. Another reach, and this picture gave way to one of more romantic aspect: a strip of water, separated from the river only by a band of tree-trunks, was covered with water-lilies; it was gravely announced as another broad — Little Salhouse Broad. It was a bed of lily-leaves. Close to its inlet two fishermen were bending over their rods with the fixed tension which true passion for a sport brings to sinew and muscle. What to them was the loveliness of the low rising of the hillside behind them, or the lovely massing of the greens in this Goose Island with the yellow of the mustard-fields? Some snipe flew out of the bushes; a pheasant made a great stir among the reeds, heavily winging its low flight to the opposite shore; some water-hens were riding the stream; and above, high up, dipping into the blue of the sky-spaces as a swallow dips into water, there circled and swirled a company of black-birds.

All the while the river itself was a marigold-bed, and the landscape was lighted with delicate tones. Had we not known the hour, we should soon have been told it by the signs abroad on the river. A sail-boat, lying under some willow boughs, was having its deck turned into a temporary banqueting-table. Two girls in broad hats and loose blouses were pouring tea for two curates. As we sailed past, London "at homes" were brought suddenly very near. The air was filled with the tones of the clear English voices, and with certain questions and answers which seem as much a part of English interiors as the wall-paper. "Do you take cream or lemon?" and "The cake, please." "Thanks, awfully; I don't mind if I do." A river-bend, a dash of shade, a boat and two white ties—where is the English

maiden who, in India or in the wilds of America, could not manage with such surroundings to set up a little temple of Home, with a hissing kettle as a form of incense?

"At Hornin', ma'am,— Hornin' Ferry," was the skipper's answer to an unuttered, but none the less expressive question; and Grimes visibly brightened.

There was still a broad or two to pass before the bubbling of water beneath our bow could be exchanged for the bubble of water in a kettle. Hoveton Broad, like Salhouse Broad, shone through the trees, a-glitter with the sparkle of shallow waters on which the lily-leaves rose and fell in ceaseless motion. The river, between its banks of yellow buttercups and purple irises, gallantly made an upward turning, as if to salute the pretty lakelet, and as quickly dropped away to the southward, to take broader sweeps and a fresh outlook over wide marshes. From one of the more desolate, wilder plains some hundreds of gray and white wings were beating the air, and out of the medley of cries there came the unmistakable squeal of sea-gulls. The heavens were peopled with them; the marshes were alive with the tremor of beating wings and moving claws; and the river was flecked with the down of their feathers. Across our bows a troop of youthful swimmers were taking a trial trip, and our masthead moved amid the mass of beating wings. Mills was making the most of the moment. "It's the close season now, sir; the gulls spends their summers here along with their young. It's fine feedin' they gets on the reeds, and the marshes is what the young ones need. There's thousands of 'em every year here at Ranworth Broad. They 're all at sea in the winter."

The swirling and circling of the big white wings had hardly ceased to darken the sky when a cluster of red roofs told of man's habitation. Rows of straggling houses, a windmill set high on a hill, a series of gardens brimming over with pinks and hollyhocks running parallel with the river—if anything could make one feel at home in Horning, it was the pretty ways and graces with which it came out to the very edge of the river to meet one.

A row of children suddenly filled the river-front. They seemed to come forth, as if at a pre-concerted signal, through the low doorways and over the narrow door-steps of the Horning cottages. Without further delay they burst into a song. They were in excellent practice, for the words of the song were made quite clear.

> Ho, John Barleycorn!
> Ho, John Barleycorn!
> All day long I raise my song
> To old John Barleycorn.

A NORFOLK WHERRY.

When the song was done some twenty-four childish eyes were fixed on the strangers in the boat.

"They always sings — Hornin' 's famed for that. Two hundred years, they say, the children o' Hornin' have sung to the passin' boats. But it 's the yachts that they makes their money off of," was Mills's unblushing introduction of the waiting choir. Something of the youth and freshness of those clear, high voices, that only a moment ago had mingled so deliciously with the pinks and the rose scents in the homely, old-fashioned gardens, had gone. The chil-dren, after pocketing their pennies, had turned unnaturally incurious backs on us and the river. They had learned already, apparently, to take a strictly professional view of the world as it passed. There were still two miles of sailing, and much jibing and tacking, before a picturesque grouping of sails, trees, and houses proclaimed that we were nearing one of the favorite river-stations.

"Let down your jib! Let her go! An' do it tidy; don't want no blunderin'," Mills was shouting out, for the eye of his world was upon him. A yacht, a lugger-rigged boat, and two

HORNING

wherries, some open sheds, two low thatched houses, and a group of rustics—such was the world we had come upon as we rounded the tree-boughs. Just below the thatched houses Mills brought the yacht round with a swing.

"Is your anchor ready? Is it ready, I say?" he was shouting again, as he flung himself against the tiller, heading the yacht bow on to the meadows. Grimes answered the shout by a plunge overboard into the grasses; another second, and he had buried the anchor in a mound of daisies. And thus it was that we made our first port; for this was Horning Ferry.

Our arrival, meanwhile, was making a mild stir along the shore. The life and movement among the boats and on the river-banks recalled the animation we thought had been left behind at Wroxham. On the decks of the boats there was much moving about; people were getting into jolly-boats, or were already amidstream rowing across to the inn. Two Cambridge boys came out of their cabin to take a look at the newcomers. Of the two wherries one had the look of a friend: it was the "pleasure" craft we had met just after leaving Wroxham Broad. The beauty was still on deck; she was seated now on her mound of pillows. A group of men gathered about her, and they were serving her from a tray filled with a tea-service, as they might a queen. Her gurgling, girlish laughter came across the water, filling the air with its youthful music. To those cadences succeeded a grinding noise as of ropes working on rusted iron. It was the noise of raft-pulleys working a rusty chain, for the raft was being ferried across the stream.

On the raft was a particularly smart-looking trap; a groom was standing at the horse's head, and a girl was on the box seat, her perfection of attire recalling the Bond street tailors. The rustics gathered about the ferry-landing watched the approaching equipage with slow, dull gaze. A few seconds later they were fixing the same glance on us as we were boarding the jolly-boat, for Mills had brought the boat round quite as a matter of course. "That kettle takes an hour or more to boil," had been his sole explanation of our trip across to the inn.

The little inn was as modest a tavern as had ever set itself up in the business. It boasted the trimmest of gardens, the neatest of barmaids, the most irreproachably bare of sitting-rooms. But one of us, from the river, had seen a church tower among the trees on the hillside; and not even the august names in the visitors' book, of the Marquis of Lorne and party, and of the late Duke of Abercorn, and of the more familiar and home-sounding name of our own Mark Twain, could keep us indoors in a stuffy inn coffee-room.

Once on the road, the perfume of the woodbine in the hedges seemed of a superfine essence of sweetness. All the earth scents were doubly good to breathe after the salt in the air along the river-marshes. The road behind the inn stables took us between fields of the blondest of oats and the most bridally attired buckwheat. The hedges were gardens full of hawthorn and sweetbrier; and the blackbirds, the thrushes, and the twittering wrens made the wild seafaring notes of the gulls of half an hour ago seem as far away as the sea itself. Through the trees beautiful were the river-distances: over the tree-tops and through the tree-boughs the river made a series of radiant lakes and ponds in which the shores were mirroring their tranquil loveliness. Horning Church sat on the top of a hill, looking down upon this scene. It was set like a jewel in its crown of green trees. But for all its flowery, foliaged adornment, the church had a separate, abandoned appearance. The village had forsaken it, as many other river villages have forsaken their churches; it had wandered down the hill to the shore, where it might the better earn its livelihood, leaving its church alone. We ourselves were soon taking our journey across the river on the raft. Returning to the yacht, we found the table set for tea; the cake and jam were flanked by huge bunches of wild flowers. The tea was excellent: perhaps the concert of blackbirds in the bushes, and the butterflies among the blue corn-flowers, gave to the little feast an extra flavor. It is only on a yachting cruise on the Broads that one can always be so sure of a flower-garden and an open-air orchestra. Half an hour later Mills was sounding the growling note of his displeasure. "We sha'n't be able to get that boy down the hatchway: he's

ticklish bit of wind, an' she won't last long," was our skipper's warning comment as once more we swung out into the channel. And so soon does the mind take on the garment of habit, wearing it with ease, that the yacht's motion and the being under sail seemed by far the most natural methods of getting on in the world.

"The breeze is fallin' away." This had an ominous sound at six. "It 's fallin' wery light. We 'll never get to Acle Bridge. We 'll be caught at Hornin' Hall."

Acle Bridge, Horning Hall, the end of the world — were they not all alike to us? Was not this the loveliest, the most perfect moment of the day? We were sailing through a land of pure gold, with horizons dipped in purple; the river was turning from saffron to palest violet, and every goose and swan was a transfigured creature, clad in dazzling plumage; cows, yachts, windmills—we were drifting past them as one who passes things seen in a dream. The slowness of the speed was a part of the charm of the hour; one had a sense of floating, of being borne onward by means unseen, unfelt; and the languor of the breeze was an indolent music in tune with the softness of the sunset hues.

DRAWN BY JOSEPH PENNELL.

THE VILLAGE OF HORNING.

takin' in his winter provisions, he is; an' here 's the wind goin' light!"

Grimes was rescued from the jam-pot in time to help in the hoisting of the sail. Some of the fleet about us were gone already, for the wind was beginning to drop with the sun. "It 's a

Suddenly we had stopped; once more we were bow on to a meadow piece. Again our anchor had been flung forth into a mound of daisies; and Mills was furling his sails.

"It 'u'd 'a' come to polin', an' I doubt if we could have made the reach roun' the abbey.

A MISTY MORNING ON THE BROADS.

An' at the Hall we 're sure of our milk in the mornin'."

Two yachts, and our old friend the pleasure-wherry, had also been "caught" at Horning Hall. They lay just below our own boat, and some of their passengers were abroad upon the meadow-banks, awaiting their dinner. One by one the groups were recalled to their respective boats, the appearance of the skipper on the gang-plank being the Broads form of announcing dinner. We took many a turn from the farm-house dike to where the path sank into the marshland before Mills's rosy face was beckoning us aboard. As we entered the cabin the hand of Grimes was again seen in the arrangement of the lamps and the floral decorations. As a sailor he might be a failure, but he had in him the soul of a born butler.

The stars were well out before our coffee was served beneath them. The sunset had all but died out along the marshes. Through the trees, as the night fell, along with the light of stars there came the glow of farm-house interiors; and upon the river there trailed the reds and yellows from the yachts' lanterns and their open port-holes. And as we "turned in," from the boats' decks there came the noise of college and music-hall songs and the strumming of banjos.

V.

WE awoke next morning to an ominous sound of falling raindrops. One look through the opening of our tent-like awning, and we knew what was before us: it was as wet a prospect as the eye could light on even in England. The skies seemed to have come down several thousands of miles nearer the earth, as if to make their downpour the more effective. The river had lost all its spirit; whatever turning of the tide it was, the river itself, under that merciless pelting of the rain, had come to a dead standstill. Trees, shrubs, reeds—all were in floods of tears; and the landscape in general had the same look as the cows out in the open—that of standing about with the great patience of animal resignation. After so dreary a prospect the cabin seemed a little corner of warmth and coziness. The discovery that Mills made French coffee sent our spirits up several degrees above the zero of disheartenment. In spite of the gloom without, there was an early-morning spirit of contentment within. Both the cabin and the library — the latter unopened until now—had been singularly neglected: within certain closed boxes there was the best of company. Alas! our reading was enlivened by a painstaking series of well-planned interruptions. To Mills, indeed, as to so many true men of action, books and reading were so poor an occupation that any man possessing rudimentary organs of compassion must do his best to mitigate the evil; by the bracing effects alone of cheery and continuous conversation could a man be expected to get through his page. Finally, down the hatchway the news that the "fish was bitin'" was followed by the moving appeal:

"Have a line, now; do, sir. There's a scud goin' by." When he found fishing in a pelting rain failed to rouse us to action, he turned in despair to giving us news of the weather. "It's lessenin'; the clouds is breakin', and the wind's risin'. We'll have a fine day — there's a bit of blue now." And with that news even our heroine was left incontinently to her fate. After luncheon it cleared in earnest. The clouds were rolling up their white curtains, and the face of a soft, melting summer noon came from behind them. On deck the breath of the wet, moist earth, laden with the vigor of an unbreathed sweetness, swept the nostrils; and in every bush and tree the thrushes and blackbirds were singing as if to burst their throats with gladness. The river in a twinkling had become a bed of radiance.

Presently a voice sounded from below the deck-railings. Mills was calling upward from the seat of the jolly-boat, which he was holding alongside. "I'm goin' for milk and eggs, ma'am, to the Hall. Perhaps it'u'd be your pleasure to take the trip up the dike." A moment later, and we were gliding across the sunlit river. What could be better, after a morning in a stuffy cabin, than a trip in an open boat, and a descent upon an English farm-house? One or two skilful strokes of Mills's oars sent us skimming from the brilliantly lighted river surface to the quiet of a placid creek: it was like turning from a busy highroad into a lane. The green waterway

seen leaning over a rustic stile. It was a traditional pose in which to discover feminine rusticity; but the living loveliness of the girl's fair face, and the soft, animal wonder in her hazel eyes, made one oblivious of all other less genuine models. "Is it milk or cream?" was her strictly professional question. "It's milk, my lass, an' eggs, if you've got 'em fresh." Mills was obviously entirely at his ease with the rustic divinity. With a long, sailor-like lurch forward he took his place beside the girl, leaving us to follow. "An' the guv'nor, how is he? An' your aunt, an' the stock?" we heard him say as the two bent their steps toward the back of the farm-house. Mills took his way to the barn while the girl seized our own moment of indecision to grasp the milk-jug and cross the courtyard. As we stood watching her, noting her young, fresh loveliness, why was it that suddenly other equally fair and comely shapes took their places beside her — that Maggie Tulliver, Hetty Sorrel, and Tess of the D'Urbervilles should also be crossing that sun-flooded courtyard, trailing before our eyes the memory of their tragic fate? The peace, the perfect stillness of the farm-house inclosure, the wet and dewy earth shining through the tree-boughs, the herds of cattle and the droves of sheep moving under the fresh sunlight yonder, the very drone of the bees in the bushes, had brought vividly to mind those immortal types of women whose histories seem forever interwoven with such homely notes as the pour-

DRAWN BY JOSEPH PENNELL.

ST. BENET'S ABBEY.

seemed to have captured the secret of perpetual twilight, the day finding its way only through the dense arch woven by the osiers and willow-boughs.

Presently stood forth through the glistening tree-trunks the fair façade of a stout, substantial mansion mantled in ivy. It was Horning Hall. Close to the farm a girlish shape was

ing of milk into tin cans, and the rhythmic thud of the churn. The farm maiden meanwhile had filled our milk-jug, and Mills's visit within the barn had come to an abrupt end. We were about to depart when, in an inspired moment, we ceased gazing at a live picture and dwelling on tragedies to confront both in one. As we turned toward the dike a stone building rose up before us. It was as unexpected a building to meet in a remote country farm as might have been, say, the Tower of London or the New York Produce Exchange. The structure was sturdily buttressed; it had beautiful early-English traceries in its regularly spaced windows; and although its porch and belfry had long since disappeared, it was as unmistakably a chapel as if rows of choristers were still intoning within its vaulted roof, instead of the impatient stamping of the beasts stalled within its walls.

"It 's a barn, ma'am. A chapel? Yes, ma'am; it was St. Benet's chapel. But it 's been a barn since before ever I was born."

Here Mills announced abruptly: "The wind won't hold, sir; it 'll be fallin' light as the day wears. We 'll never get to Acle Bridge." The threat brought us to our senses and also to the boat.

It was good to be under way once more, and pleasant it was to hear again Mills's familiar refrain: "Ease the mainsail; let out your jib! Ease her — start her — shake her up! Oh, ho! now I think we have the weather-gage — an' as fine a day as one can hope to see on the river. We 'll make Acle in no time."

The chapel proved to have been part of the old abbey, and we soon sailed past what was left of it. The marshes to the left were an unbroken plain. Out of the tufts of grass there rose up suddenly the huge outlines of an ungainly draining-mill, from the lower, southern side of which blossomed a lovely Gothic portal. Clearer and clearer became the shape and form of it; here and there within the portal were bits of time-worn border traceries, tottering canopies, and a pile of shapeless capitals and rib-vaultings. The bank along the river showed faint traces of broken bits of walls, of sunken towers and ramparts, now but mounds of turf.

For many a turning and twisting in and out among the river-marshes were the outlines of the mill and the abbey portal to mark for us the brevity of human grandeur.

VI.

WIDE and flat were the marshes that led on to Acle Bridge. The reaches were longer, and the sailing was smooth and free. Below the mouth of the Thurne the land was one vast plain, broken by the dim outlines of distant windmills, of church spires, and clusters of farm-house roofs. In such a breadth of earth man and his works played an unimpressive rôle. Far away in the dim perspective of a narrow dike, strange, primitive craft bore down toward the river; the men poling the high-heaped mounds of flags and rushes seemed to be navigating haystacks. In the rich, warm light these moving rafts lent a singular charm to the river life; their shadows in the clear streams were dense and soft, for land and water were being lighted by the glow of a perfect English afternoon.

DRAWN BY JOSEPH PENNELL.

STOKESBY.

The sails we met were drifting toward one goal. From dikes and streams, yawls and lateeners were quanting toward the Bridge. Presently there came the stirring notes of a vigorous command:

"Let down the jib! Do it tidy! Don't want no blunder here! Is your anchor ready?"

Once again, as at Wroxham and Horning, the river had widened suddenly below an arched bridge. A fleet of yachts lay moored along a grassy river-bank. Here also the boats' decks were crowded with figures — with girls in sailor hats, with sunburned youths in frayed "silhouettes," and with bronzed sailors in their yachting-caps. Several hundred of these heads were lifted as we sailed by. Another tack, a bearing down hard on the helm, shouts and some inarticulate profanity from Mills, and we had come to our moorings at Acle Bridge.

The inn was set close to the river, and although the highroad ran a mile farther inland, the Angel inn had the air of having seen more stirring times. The little inn sitting-room was parlor and taproom in one; its chairs opened friendly arms, bits of old silver gleamed on the mantel-shelf, and low settles, cupboards, and tables of antique make were suggestive of the dead-and-gone figures that had peopled the cozy room. In the smile of the genial host there was the welcome which imagination lends to mine host of the coaching period.

As the preparations for dinner were going on below deck, we wandered up toward Acle. The town was a wandering assemblage of houses, with shops that gave themselves metropolitan airs. But a church dedicated to as mythical a personage as St. Edmund the King was more alluring than the sight of London fashions abbreviated to the timidity of provincial taste. Pretty suburban villas, perfectly kept lawns, and trim gardens, led the way to the church, the tower of which had turned its back on the town, the chancel facing the street. The quaint Norfolk structure was placed in a perfect setting; for the cemetery was a garden where the gravestones seemed decorative slabs in high relief amid the sober gaiety of the flowers and the blooming shrubs.

Through the trees the sunset was pouring a flood of softened light, and the river, as we crossed the bridge, lay beneath our feet, a bed of gold. Every bush and weed was of a transfigured beauty, and the cows, as they came down to the shores, seemed to be drinking, not water, but a Pactolian stream. The wide marshes were now at their best, suffused with light, while above them arched a sky that was one vast cup of coral.

Aboard there were the miseries of a belated dinner written on Mills's anxious brow. "You

DRAWN BY JOSEPH PENNELL.

YARMOUTH BEACH.

see, ma'am, I 've five courses — soup, an' fish, an' chops, an' 'taters, an' hot plates; an' this 'ere stove is the wery de — I beg pardon! But it 'u'd try the patience of a wery saint." His explanation given, Mills and his red racing-cap — his signal-flag of exultation or of distress — disappeared with a Jack-in-the-box quickness into the hatchway depths. There were worse things than waiting for dinner, we agreed, with such a sky and earth for entertainment. These failing us, there was still the inn. It was the hour when taverns the world over do a prosperous business. There was an endless procession of farmers' and carriers' carts stopping before the tavern door; beer or something stronger was handed to the less sociably inclined rustics, while within the tap-room a crowd of sailors, yachtsmen, and ruddy-faced farmers were standing about, or were grouped along the benches. London drawing-room tones, the boyish tenors of Cambridge students, the rough jargon of the Norfolk dialect — these sounds poured out through the door, making a strange babel.

To us on deck, long after dinner had been eaten, the noisy little inn continued to send forth the sound of its prosperity, while the noise that rose from the yachts was neither mystic nor devotional: the twang of guitars and banjos, the jingle of pianos out of tune, and a discordant chorus of after-dinner voices, made an early "turning in" out of the question. No sooner were the stars fairly out than a rival show of fireworks made the river a blaze of yellow and crimson lights. The yachts and

THE QUAYS AT YARMOUTH.

their passengers and crews, the cows lying in the meadows, the furled sails, and the ropes of the rigging — again and again did this world abroad upon a river-bank spring out of the dark, unreal and of an amazing brilliance, to be as swiftly engulfed in the abyss of night.

VII.

WE were up and away so early the next morning that the cows were still at rest in the meadows. The inn shutters were as tightly closed as the yachts' awnings. Not a sign of a reveler was discernible; we alone had kept good our engagement with the dawn. We might have made a meal of our boastful pride if we chose, for we had no other for a good hour at least. The wind was already abroad upon the meadows, and was blowing in the right quarter. With Yarmouth twelve miles off, and the dreaded prospect ahead of several hours' poling if the breeze should fall away, the gnawing of the early-morning hunger affected Mills as little as an appeal to a wooden idol. The getting of his boat "tidily" through Acle Bridge, the restepping of the mast once we were on the lower side of its stone arch, the hoisting of his sails, the *Vacuna's* swinging into the channel, and our subsequent swift running before the wind — these were acts and events which made our skipper sublimely indifferent to a breakfastless state. We were of

less heroic mold: coffee and rolls at seven in the morning assume an importance out of all proportion to the part they play in the rest of one's day. We turned a cool eye on the fair earth, and, wrapped in our cloaks, sat on deck, hugging the grievance of our hunger. Stokesby would be more beautiful to look upon than in the early morning, for there our breakfast was promised us.

No town dweller, I presume, who is a lover of nature ever remains wholly insensible to the charms of a sleepy earth throwing off its night mists. Acle Marsh, just below the Bridge, stretched its breadth to the horizon with such an alluring early-morning freshness as to stir even our spiritless state. The cows were now walking about in search of their meal. Long lines defiled slowly between the few widely scattered trees and windmills. The skies were full of clouds, and the clouds as full of light; they were traveling across the zenith as fast as we were scudding through the water.

"Stokesby 's round that 'ere reach. We 'll be layin' to in a jiffy. But it do seem a shame to lose such a wind, it do!" was Mills's plaint as at last the roofs of the village began to define themselves among the trees. Stokesby was set close to the river, upon a low and fertile marsh. A windmill beckoned us onward through a light ambuscade of trees, and close beside the ambuscade we dropped our anchor. The time of our lying to was brief; doubtless the spires of Yarmouth were beckoning Mills onward, for we were out again upon the river before the table was cleared. We had gone but a brief quarter of a mile on our way when Mills began to apostrophize his native town. "Yes, sir; it's Yarmouth town we'll see inside of an hour or two. Her chimbleys and church spires 'll be lookin' out for us. Lord! but the years they've been my beacon lights, with Polly Ann waitin' along with 'em! Yarmouth 's a great town— few finer. An' the Rows—they 're a great show if you 're not used to 'em; an' so is the herrin'-quays. Haul in the main, my lad, an' when you 've tied your sheet bring me a glass. I 'll drink to Polly Ann, bless her! Here 's to Polly Ann!"

Long and frequent were the toasts to Mary Ann, and nearer and nearer drew Yarmouth town. Out of the dull wastes of the marshes the dim, dusky mass that lay along the southern horizon slowly resolved itself into the outlines of a city. There were the signs of its movement and life abroad upon the river long before we swept its quays. Grammar-school boys, with Eton caps and wide collars, trooped along the low, rising shore; soldiers were lounging beneath the trees; and the river was alive with shipping, with floating flags, and the pennants of yachts.

Here at these Yarmouth quays must end for us the sweet return of the day's rising over river-banks, of the floating between the reeds and flags, of the soft-colored halcyon hours beneath the blue of the sky and the starry nights. To replace such joys, would Yarmouth send forth to greet us the people we have thought of and loved as peopling that islanded city? Would Little Em'ly stand upon the marshes, shading her soft eyes? Would Peggotty's boathouse be there? Would Steerforth's wraith rise out of the sea to wave its helpless arm in air?

Along the quays there lay a Sabbath stillness. The hush of the old town was broken only by the clangor of St. Nicholas's chimes. But louder than the roar of the ocean, stronger than the blare of trumpets from unseen barracks, from the beach there came upon the ear the mighty murmuring of a great multitude. It was only some thousands of pleasure-seekers crowding the Yarmouth quays and sands. Then it was we knew for a certainty we had indeed come back to the world of cities.

Anna Bowman Dodd.

DRAWN BY JOSEPH PENNELL.

Racing Schooners
(1896)

RACING SCHOONERS.

By R. B. Burchard.

"Oh, happy ship, to rise and dip
With the blue crystal at its lip!
Oh. happy crew, my heart with you
Sails and sings and sings anew!"

IF there is anything that is typically and conspicuously American, it is the American schooner. She is a characteristic and distinguishing feature of the scenery along our seaboard, just as the lugger is on the English coasts, the lateen in the Mediterranean, or the junk in the China seas. Though an incidental note merely, she is as indispensable to the landscape as the hansom to the London street scene, the camel to the desert, or the gondola to the Venetian picture. You are accustomed to her conventional outlines everywhere—in the art gallery, the shop window, the pictured panels of the rural omnibus. Travel to the uttermost West and her chromoed presentment, in calm, or storm, or wreck, greets you as a matter of course from the papered wall of tavern or homestead. Wherever it may be, just a little schooner will make a whole landscape American, though the sea, the atmosphere, the coast itself might do as well for Spain or Borneo.

A well-founded tradition tells us that the first schooner was conceived and contrived by one Captain Andrew Robinson about 1713. Where? Why, at Gloucester, of course! And the story says, as the little vessel slid from the stocks into the water, an enthusiastic Yankee cried out something like, "Gee! See how she scoons!" and the new type was forthwith named schooner for all time. The New England boys of that period, like all boys from Cain and Abel down to us, had a trick of whirling little flat stones over the surface of the water so that they should skip from little wave to wave, cutting the tops as they sped. Little Praise-God Barebones and the young Winthrops and Brewsters used to call the game "scooning"; we call it "scaling." For myself, I do not believe that the "schooner" expression was evoked at the launch. I can, however, readily imagine the line of old salts with battered cocked hats and queues done up in marline, sitting along the string-piece of Gloucester dock watching the two big fore-and-aft sails of the new "critter" as they cut curves through the air or went eating up to windward; then I can appreciate the application of the utterance, "See, how she scoons!"

The handiness of the fore-and-aft rig, divided into two nearly equal portions, made that arrangement of canvas popular from the start; and now nearly all of the coastwise fishing and carrying vessels are of the schooner family. Vessels of from 200 to 250 feet in length, or from 1,000 to 1,500 tons burden, which a few years ago would have been *bark* or *ship* rigged, are now built as three or four-masted schooners; and occasionally we are surprised on the watery way by the appearance of such a vessel as the five-masted schooner *Governor Ames*,' built in Waldoboro, Maine, 1888; 245 feet long, 49.6 broad, 21 feet draught, and 1,690 tons burden."

The advantages to the coaster of the fore-and aft over the square rig are: first, economy of hands in working; second, quickness in handling, and third, windward power. A well appointed three-masted schooner with a small steam-engine and winches for hoisting sail, heaving up anchor, and

Photo J. S. Johnston, New York.

EMERALD.

handling cargo, can be worked with a third of the crew required on a bark of the same size. In working in a crowded throroughfare, or tacking in and out of frequent harbors, the handiness of the fore-and-aft rigged vessel with her sails flinging from side to side at the helmsman's will is an obvious advantage. Along the rocky shores of Maine and New Brunswick, one meets fleets of fishing boats in which the jibs are dispensed with, the foremast being stepped in the bow, and whose two sails are nearly or exactly of the same size. A boat of this sort is called a periauger or pirogue. It is ugly to look at, but it is handy for one or two men to manage.

While there seems to be no limit to the scope of utility of the fore-and-aft rig, I think its picturesqueness belongs only to the conventional two masted schooner. The periauger is unsightly on the one hand, so is the three-masted schooner on the other. But to my mind there is nothing afloat less than a bark or ship rig so beautiful as a wellplanned schooner. A Sandy Hook pilot schooner is a fine boat; a well-kept Gloucester fisherman is a beauty, and a first-class schooner yacht is a delight to look upon.

AMERICA, 1851.

The Spanish Armada, arrogant with guns and streamers; the Venetian fleet, with carved hulls, banks of oars, and sails dyed and blazoned with brave devices; the little fleet of Columbus, familiar to us through their modern fac similes at Chicago; Lord Nelson's squadron at Trafalgar—these, in the mind of him who loves the sea and its beauty and romance, form a succession of pictures as vivid as the tapestries of Bayeux. But the golden medieval days are but a tradition now; the ships of the line have passed away in turn, and the queenly clipper ships of a generation ago are superseded by unsightly aggregations of machinery which are about as pleasant to look at as a fleet of floating boiler foundries. The sea is despoiled of its romance and its sport. If one is in search of the picturesque on

the deep, he must needs hunt up the infrequent merchantman of the old type or follow the luxurious pleasure fleets of England and America. These should be painted on a smaller canvas than are the ancient glories of the sea, and from a less brilliant palette, but they have a refined beauty and a virility of their own. In your marine gallery, after your galleys and galleons, and caravels, and double-deckers, and swift clippers, you may place your great cutters and schooner fleets. Those who come after us will say that maritime beauty ceased at that point and that the age of steam succeeded. Our fleet of schooner yachts of two decades ago, gathered for a great race off Brenton's Reef or Sandy Hook, was a sight worthy of commemoration : cracking on sail after sail—towering club-topsails, main-topmast staysails, balloon jibs or bellying spinnakers— until each ship became a flying cloud of canvas ; shifting, breaking out or trimming home as the white meteors flashed around the appointed mark—these were the yachtsman's delight and will continue to be unless ill-advised rules bestow all the honors upon the swift but useless "freak" and close the entry lists to livable yachts.

As compared with "single-stick" vessels —the sloops and cutters—the schooner has still the advantage of ease and economy in handling. It is a well-established principle of yacht-building that the more the canvas is condensed—the less the *number* of sails in a given area—the closer the boat will sail to the wind. Thus a catboat will sail closer than a sloop of similar hull and sail-area ; and a sloop will sail closer than a schooner. Prior to 1859 sloops and schooners were raced together, time allowance being based on tonnage, the sloops always having the advantage. In 1863 yachts were again classed by tonnage regardless of rig, and the schooners were placed at such a disadvantage that the following year the yachts were again divided according to rig.

A sloop, however, has advantages in handling over a catboat (unless the boats are small); and a schooner is easier to work than a sloop. A load which is too heavy for one to handle in bulk, he may carry in sections; and if one has two or three hundred yards of canvas to hoist aloft, he may be glad if it is divided into two or more sails. " Tailing on " to the main-sheet to trim in is another occasion when one appreciates the advantage of the schooner rig. Again, your schooner may be bowling along in company with your friend's sloop, under full sail; there is a little rain cloud astern, but you conclude that it amounts to nothing. Presently sky and water are black, and down comes the squall. Your topsails are "clewed" up ; you lower away your foresail, and you go comfortably through the flurry, while your friend's sloop is hove to with lowered peak, and all hands aboard are falling over one another in the general scramble to haul on the reef-pendant and tie in reef points.

The racing crews of large sloops are more than double the number of those on schooners of equal size.

Of the nine original members of the New York Yacht Club who met aboard the schooner *Gimcrack*, July 30th, 1844, to effect the organization of the club, seven owned *and sailed* schooner yachts. There was only one large sloop represented, viz., the 40-tonner *Mist*, the other being a smaller boat. The racing freak, it is true, came with the beginning of things, and on the first cruise of the club during the same year appeared the sloop racing-machine, Commodore Stevens's famous *Maria*. She beat the fleet out of sight, of course. This yacht was ninety-two feet on deck, and was fitted with two centerboards and carried outside ballast.* For years she was as much of a wonder as *Defender* is now ; she readily defeated everything, including the famous *America*, although the latter was a larger yacht. She was an untractable brute to handle, like her latter-day progeny, and was hardly safe in a heavy sea. She was finally sunk in the Gulf of Mexico.

There were two causes, I think, which led to the subsequent popularity of the schooner yacht : first, the advantages of

AMERICA, 1893.

comfort and of easy handling, herein pointed out ; and second, the impetus given to yacht building in general, and especially to that of schooners, by the victory of the *America* in 1851. There were in the early days, as there are now, a large and wealthy class of yacht-owners, to whom the chief attraction in a boat was the comfort and relaxation which it afforded, and who had a genuine love of sailing. Racing was an important but not the controlling element. The majority of such men are now weaned away by the steam-yacht luxury. There have also been two causes which have put a check upon the increase of the schooner fleet : first, the development of the steam yacht, and secondly, the fact that all the first-class racing of recent years has been done in sloops or cutters. The first steamer enrolled in the New York Yacht Club was Commodore Vanderbilt s *North Star*, built in 1853. This vessel was used partly as a trader, so that the first real steam yacht was the *Firefly*, launched the following year, and owned by J. A. Robinson. In 1866, the year of the great ocean race, there were only three or four steamers enrolled, while to-day there are one hundred and fifty-five steamers and seventy-two schooners on the club's list.

Subsequent to the famous exploit of the *America*, the production of schooner yachts led to the formation of an ideal fleet of pleasure craft, not racing-machines, but safe, comfortable vessels, beautiful to look upon and affording racing sport which has never been excelled. The schooner became popular in England for a time, but the same causes have operated there, so that the racing men have always held to cutters while many of the others have taken to steamers.

Among the schooners which have been famous in the annals of sport are *Julia*, 1854 ; *Magic*, '57 ; *Henrietta*, '61 ; *Fleetwing, Palmer* and *Phantom*, '65 ; *Vesta*,

Dauntless and *Halcyon,* '66 ; *Sappho,* '67 ; *Madeleine,* '68; *Tidal Wave,* '70; *Columbia, Dreadnaught, Rambler, Wanderer,* and *Enchantress,* '71; *Peerless,* '72; *Clio* and *Atalanta,* '73; *Comet,* '74; *Clytie,* '77; *Intrepid,* '78 ; *Mischief,* '79 ; *Crusader,* '8ᵣ *Norseman,* '81; *Montauk,* '82; *Gray*-ᵢnd *Fortuna* '83.

The principle which unfortunately is becoming dominant is that a racing yacht cannot be built so as to be adaptable to cruising and living purposes. The history of the old schooner fleet is a forceful negation of that proposition. The yachtsmen of the past generation—a *coterie* of such spirits as Commodore Stevens, Messrs. Bennett, Osgood, Hatch, Voorhis, Douglass, Lorillard, Stebbins and General Butler—were sportsmen of sterling qualities, which it would be difficult to equal and impossible to excel. The narrative of the palmy days of schooner racing constitutes a chapter of unrivaled brilliancy in the annals of sport. The winter race across the Atlantic of 1866, ᵣot to mention the subsequent ocean races of 1870 and 1887 ; the numerous matches, some of them between a dozen schooners, on the three hundred mile course between New York and Cape May; the spirited contests year after year on the Brenton's Reef and Sandy Hook courses—such events kept continually

1870, in which the *Cambria* made the first attempt to recover the *America's* cup. Besides the English yacht there were twenty-four schooners entered, of which seventeen started. Of these, nine came in ahead of the *Cambria,* the old *America* being fourth.

The history of those spirited days has been ably narrated in Lieutenant Kelley's "American Yachts," and in the books of Captain Roland Coffin and Captain Keneally, which originally appeared in the numbers of this magazine.

The schooner racing fleet, though now comparatively small, has thus far been unspoiled by the entrance of the "freak" in its lists ; and the present owners are pre-eminently of the same metal as their illustrious predecessors.

Among schooners which have been successful in recent races are *Ramona* (the old *Resolute*), *Constellation, Colonia, Emerald, Mayflower* (cup defender), *Merlin, Ariel, Lasca, Marguerite, Iroquois, Amorita, Elsemarie, Shamrock, Viator* and *Quisetta.*

The *Emerald* is a steel center-board vessel, designed by H. C. Wintringham. She was built by the S. L. Moore & Sons Co., at Elizabethport, N. J., and launched May 10, 1893. She is owned and sailed in all her races by J. Rogers Maxwell. Her first season's

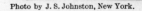

Photo by J. S. Johnston, New York.   COLONIA.

ablaze the enthusiasm which seldom glows nowadays save on the occasion of an international race. The owners were always on the alert for a match, around Long Island, fifty or five hundred miles out to sea, anywhere, against anything, from a rival yacht to a clipper ship. The high average of excellence attained is illustrated by the regatta of

work was not equal to her later performances, for the reason that her canvas was not in good shape nor was the yacht tuned up to racing trim. During the following winter her bow and ballast were altered, her foremast, moved forward, and her sail-plan increased. These changes perhaps led to the assumption that the original form was not satisfactory. The original bow was of the clipper type, with straight lateral lines. The modern convex stem came in vogue during that season, and when the finishing work was taken in hand the opportunity was offered to shape the bow in conformity with the new idea. She was then given a rounded bow, the downward curve of which has a greater convexity than that of any other yacht of her class. It is not *praam* or spoon shaped, however, although these terms are often applied in descriptions of yachts of this type. Looked at bow-on, the cutwater is seen to be sharp its entire length; the sides of the bow are seen to be clean and wedge-shaped; there is no hollow and very little fullness. From the side the stem shows the segment of an ellipse curving downward from the stemhead to the water-line. Below the water, the fore-foot

is there any outside ballast. The centerboard which is 20 feet, 6 inches in length, is hung at the forward end of the keel, so that the line of the fore-foot and bottom of the board may be made almost continuous and straight from the water-line to the aft end of the center-board. The board, in use, drops about ten feet, but it has an extreme drop of four feet more. It is wholly of wood, excepting, of course, the straps and fastenings.

The cross section of the yacht shows

Photo by J. S. Johnston, New York. EMERALD.

is almost a straight line from stem to keel, at an angle of about thirty degrees to the water-line and extending aft over a third of the submerged length. The keel is long compared with all of the modern boats, except *Vigilant*, being 44 feet with a water line of 86 feet. It is straight and nearly parallel to the water-line throughout its entire length; it is flat on the bottom, turning into the side with a radius of about six inches, and about thirty-three inches across at the widest part, tapering to fore-foot and heel.

There is no bulbing to the keel, nor

strong bilges, fuller than *Colonia's* and *Ariel's*, with considerable hollow below; the fullness of the bilge is carried well aft. The stern-post rakes about forty-five degrees; the rudder contains about forty square feet of surface. The stern overhang is not excessively long; the counter is not flat underneath but has a fair deadrise; the wide transom rakes almost in line with counter, and the stern is wide enough to permit of an ample quarter-deck. Unlike those of other modern racing yachts the deck of the *Emerald* is protected by bulwarks sixteen inches in height. On the wind these are a drawback to the vessel's speed which is not wholly inconsiderable, opposing as they do a surface of over 150 square feet on each side when the lee rail is out of the water ; and, when the lee bulwarks are plowing through the sea, there is considerable drag. Many racing yachts are built without bulwarks, and their decks are fitted with long, light cleats or battens to which the crew may hang by heels or fingers as best they can.

The *Emerald* is built entirely of steel, the plates being laid so that the bottom of each is fitted over the plate below as in a clinker-built boat, a system of construction which has been used but twice in this country, in the *Emerald* and *Free Lance*. In the *Defender*, *Colonia* and many other new boats the plating is set on so that one row of plates has both upper and lower edges inside, the next below having both edges outside, and so on alternately. The lead ballast of this yacht, of which there are fifty-five tons, is wholly inside the hull ; it was originally in blocks, but it has recently been molded into the vessel. The dimensions of the *Emerald* are as follows :

Over-all length............................	118 feet
Water-line length.........................	86 "
Fore overhang.............	14 "
Aft overhang..............................	18 "
Beam...	22 "
Draught.....................................	10 "
Length of keel............................	44 "
Least freeboard...........................	3 " 9 inches
Height of bulwarks.............	1 foot 4 "
Length of center board.................	20 feet 6 inches
Drop of center-board.....................	12 "

Spars—mainmast, deck to mast-head, 74 feet ; main boom, 71 feet ; main gaff, 41 feet ; main-topmast, above mainmast-head, 33 feet ; foremast, 63 feet ; fore-boom, 31 feet ; fore-gaff, 32 feet ; fore-topmast, above fore-mast-head, 29 feet ; bowsprit outboard, 33 feet.

The interior accommodations of the *Emerald* show that she was not designed to be a racing-machine. Descending the companion steps the guest finds himself in a comfortable saloon, about 14 feet by 21 feet, with 6 feet 8 inches head - room. The forward partition is built to the end of the center-board trunk, and abaft the companion steps on the port side is a door leading into the owner's cabin, which has a berth on either side, and a bureau against the after-bulkhead. This stateroom is shut off from the lazarette by a steel bulkhead through which there is no opening. The saloon is lighted from a skylight above and ports in the vessel's sides. The joiner's work is ash, mahogany and quartered oak. On either side are broad. transoms, with berths in

either bilge. The four corners of the saloon are devoted to lockers and bookcases. Abreast of the companion way are a bath-room on the starboard and a guest's wash-room on the port side.

The center-board trunk serves as a partition separating the officers' quarters on the port side from two guests' state-rooms on the starboard side, and there is a passage along the port side of the trunk.

At the fore end of the center-board trunk there is a wood bulkhead, forward of which are the pantry, kitchen, etc. In the bow of the vessel is a steel bulkhead which divides the forecastle from the galley. In the event of injury to either end of the vessel the steel bulkheads would probably prevent disaster. With plumbing outfit, which includes a bath, eight wash-basins and five closets, with generous kitchen appliances and ice-boxes, and comfortable furniture, and with steel bulkheads for safety, and in view of her great speed withal, the *Emerald* is a material and veritable protest against racing rules which encourage the introduction of empty and untenantable shells into the yachting fleet.

The *Emerald* has now been raced persistently for four seasons, during the second and third of which she was easily the best in her class and in fact the fastest of all schooners. In the Goelet cup races of those years she defeated the pick of the schooner fleet, beating the larger ones even without time allowance. Her first formidable rival was Commodore George H. B. Hill's *Ariel*, which, though a smaller vessel, and sometimes sailed in a class lower than that of *Emerald*, throughout the season of '94 gave Mr. Maxwell's schooner many a lively chase for the laurels.

In '95 the *Ariel* was raced only in the squadron runs of the New York Yacht Club near Newport, and the other schooners seldom gained points on the *Emerald*. In 1896 the *Colonia* was converted from a keel cutter into a center-board schooner, and she and *Emerald* fought it out all summer, the majority of the cups going into the lockers of *Vigilant's* swift sister, who now, for the first time, had an opportunity to show her true worth.

The long keel under the *Emerald* affords her great speed down the wind. Until this year the *Emerald's* best work was to windward ; reaching she is about even with *Colonia*, but to windward the Herreshoff boat has the advantage of five feet greater depth.

From the beginning of her career the *Emerald* has had a worthy antagonist in the *Ariel*, owned, as we have said, by Commodore George H. B. Hill. During

draught, 3 feet 3 inches least freeboard. Her gross tonnage is 101.17 tons and net tonnage 96.12 tons.

She is a beautiful yacht in appearance, with a pleasing sheer to her rail from stem to stern. She has long graceful overhangs and sharp bow. In her racing days she was painted black and

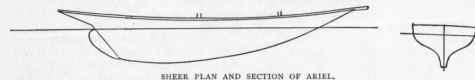

SHEER PLAN AND SECTION OF ARIEL.

the season of 1894 they raced together on every possible occasion, though in many regattas the *Ariel* sailed in a class lower than her rival, each yacht generally winning in her class. At that time the *Ariel* was the flagship of the Seawanhaka - Corinthian Yacht Club. She was splendidly commissioned and well handled ; her owner was fortunate

her sides shone with a burnished luster. She and her white rival, the *Emerald*, both in perfect condition as to hull, decks, spars and rigging, with their novel convex stems and generally thoroughbred appearance, caught the eye wherever they sailed or dropped anchor.

The keel of the *Ariel* forms a graceful curve from the stemhead to the heel

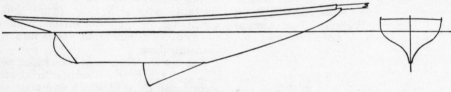

SHEER PLAN AND SECTION OF EMERALD.

in having the assistance of such skilled Corinthians as Robert Center, J. F. Tams and Theodore Zerega. The *Emerald*, however, won in the majority of their contests. During the season of 1895 the *Ariel* was entered only in the races of the New York Yacht Club cruise near Newport, and since then she has not been raced.

of the stern-post. A glance at the accompanying diagrams will show the dissimilarity from the *Emerald* on the one hand and from the *Colonia* on the other. The deepest part of the keel is considerably aft of amidships, and there is a rise of nine inches from that point to the heel. The bilges are rounder and lighter than those of the *Emerald ;* there is no hollow

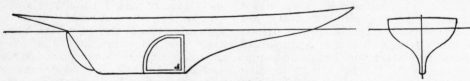

SHEER PLAN AND SECTION OF COLONIA.

The *Ariel* was designed by A. Cary Smith and was launched at the works of the Harlan & Hollingsworth Company in June, 1893. She is a steel center-board schooner : 109 feet over all, 79.85 feet water-line, 15 feet fore overhang, 17 feet aft overhang, 21.10 feet beam, 13.9 depth, 10 feet 6 inches

underneath the bilge, and there is considerable deadrise above the keel. The topsides are straight amidships with a very slight tumble-home.

The *Colonia's* early history has been recorded in these pages. She was built in 1893, for a syndicate headed by Archibald Rogers, by the Herreshoffs, and side by side with her victorious rival the *Vigilant*. There are many points of similarity between the two boats, and also marked differences. *Vigilant* is a center-board yacht. She is built of Tobin bronze. The keel boat is steel throughout. *Vigilant's* keel is long and straight; *Colonia's* is shorter. The bows are similar but the sterns are unlike, *Colonia's* being rounded on deck while that of the *Vigilant* is straight. The bilges of the latter are full where those of the former are more slack.

The *Colonia's* dimensions are as follows: over-all length, 122 feet; waterline, 86 feet; fore overhang, 17 feet; aft overhang, 19 feet; beam, 22 feet; depth, 16.4 feet; draught, 15.4 feet. Her keel is bulbed, carrying 80 tons of lead. Her topsides are high, the least freeboard being 4 feet 6 inches; the rail is very low. She is very similar to the 46-footer *Wasp* which was owned by Mr. Rogers.

The bow of the *Colonia* is of the same general type as that of *Emerald* but longer and more pointed, having seventeen feet overhang to fourteen in that of *Emerald*. The keel of the *Colonia* is rounded at its forward end where *Emerald's* keel turns at an angle. The forefoot of the former is cut away and rounded upward where that of the latter is straight. Her stern overhang is only a foot longer than that of *Emerald* but it is of different shape, the deck terminating in a long instead of a broad oval, and the counter goes straight up to the deck, omitting the transom.

In the trial races in 1893, although she was ably handled by Captain Haff, the *Colonia* was beaten by the *Vigilant*, as follows: First race, *Vigilant* beat *Colonia* by 14 seconds elapsed time, but *Colonia* won by 6 seconds, double time allowance. Second race, *Vigilant* won by 12 minutes 14 seconds corrected time. Third race, *Vigilant* beat *Colonia*, 6 minutes 43 seconds.

Last winter the *Colonia* was purchased by Clarence A. Postley, vice-commodore of the Larchmont Yacht Club. She was converted into a center-board schooner by A. Cary Smith, the work being done at the works of Nixon & Son, Elizabethport. A slot was cut through the deep keel, and a steel trunk built into the boat to receive the wood board. There was no change made in the hull save removing some lead which Captain Haff had added to the keel. The new rig is the largest yet put on a schooner of the *Colonia's* length, and, by the New York Yacht Club measurement, is one thousand square feet more than the *Emerald*.

In the early races of the New York, the Atlantic and the Larchmont Yacht Clubs, the *Emerald* beat the *Colonia*, the latter yacht being handicapped by the fact that the center-board was jammed in the trunk and that the new sails had not yet been fully stretched.

The work done by the *Colonia* at the Atlantic race, June sixteenth, which she sailed without her board, and on the Goelet cup race, August seventh, sailed with the board, shows a difference of about one minute per mile in favor of the board. After being tuned up she has won a majority of the schooner races.

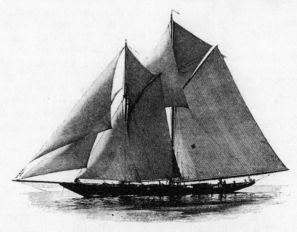

ARIEL

Photograph by R. B. Burchard.

AMORITA.   QUISSETTA.

RACING SCHOONERS.

By R. B. Burchard.

Photograph by J. S. Johnston.

MERLIN.

PART II.

"Build me straight, O worthy master!
   Stanch and strong, a goodly vessel,
 Which shall laugh at all disaster
   And with wave and whirlwind wrestle!"

THE modern racing yachtsman
would hardly couch his order to
a designer in the terms nor
in accordance with the lines of
the good Cambridge poet. The racing
yachts built nowadays are not expected
to do any wrestling with the storm and
the whirlwind. Races, for the most
part, occur in the summer time, and are
usually sailed in light airs and on
smooth water, and these conditions are
carefully considered by the successful
designer. It is fairly evident that under
the rules in vogue the creation of greater
speed than that attained by the existing yachts can be accomplished only at
a further sacrifice of sea-worthy power
and comfort. The time has come when
under a further pursuance of these rules
racing yachts must of necessity constitute a class by themselves. This is
clearly the case among the smaller
yachts, although the larger ones, even
the most extreme of them, are serviceable for knocking about in such sheltered waters as Long Island Sound.
Whether one would care to be caught
in a gale off Nantucket in the best of
the modern flyers is another question.

It is "a short life and a merry one"
with the up-to-date racer. Unless she
is first in her class she is nothing, and
the proud champion of last season is
cast off the next. The racing fleet of
twenty-five years ago, however, are
nearly all in use to-day,—comfortable
yachts and fit for ocean service. Of
what use will this year's champions be
ten years from now?

Ten years ago Mr. A. Cary Smith designed the *Julia*, now the *Iroquois*, the
queenly little flagship of the Seawanhaka-Corinthian Yacht Club. She was built
as a cruiser for Chester W. Chapin and
sailed by him to Nassau and the Windward Islands. She was entered in only

one race by her first owner, who sold her to T. Jefferson Coolidge of Boston. Subsequently under the ownership of Ralph N. Ellis and Commodore Henry C. Rouse she has done some creditable racing. Last season she won first prizes over *Clytie* in the New York Yacht Club annual regatta ; over the *Sachem* in the Atlantic Yacht Club regatta ; over *Marguerite* in the New York Yacht Club run to New London, and again in the run to Newport. Racing with a class larger than her own she won second prizes, the first going to *Amorita* and *Elsemarie*, and she also won several seconds in her own class. Just before the great blizzard of 1888, four schooners, including a New York pilot - boat

signed by the self-same hand. Would the modern yacht, with her long overhangs and short keel, have ridden out such a gale ? Could it have been possible to hold her "hove to" at all in such a tempest ? Or would the very qualities which constitute her quickness in turning and her speed to windward have rendered her powerless to wrestle with the whirlwind ?

There are a large number of men who would sail racing yachts provided such craft were adaptable, as were the schooners of the past generation, to all-round purposes. There are a limited number who are willing to maintain costly yachts suitable only for racing. A racing sportsman wants the fastest yacht in her class. That is right ! He should have it. He orders the designer to lay down the fastest boat possible in accordance with the rules. The designer works up to the full of his abilities, and that also is right. If the resulting masterpiece turns out to be a craft of such a character

Photograph by J. S. Johnston, N. Y.

ELSEMARIE.

and a down-East smack, and also the stanch yawl *Cythera*, sailed out of New York Bay within a few hours of each other. All were lost in that fatal storm. The little schooner *Iroquois* rode through the fearful fury of that tempest and was hove-to riding to a canvas drag for a couple of days, oil being pumped the while from her bows.

Last year the swift *Amorita* was launched from the yards where the *Iroquois* had been built, having been de-

that, her races having been sailed, she must needs be dismantled and laid up until the next great contest shall call her out, then there is that much treasure, for the meantime, anchored to the bottom, that much sport lost to somebody. If yachtsmen consider that the ideal craft shall be such as are capable of flying with the greatest possible speed in smooth water over the little triangles in Long Island Sound and useless for other purposes, that is their affair. But if such is the case, why not remove the present restrictions and admit catamarans and proas?

If it is true that the new prize-winners are undesirable boats, it is no fault of the designers. The responsibility rests solely with the rule-makers. The racing formulas under which yachts are constructed are made for two purposes, viz., to restrict the type of boat and to afford a fair basis for computing the time allowance which shall be given by a larger yacht to a smaller one. If they have failed in either of these purposes, it goes to show that skill in rule-making has not fully kept pace with skill in yacht designing.

After nine years' study and experience on the part of her designer, does the *Amorita* represent his mature idea of a perfect yacht as compared with his earlier conception as embodied in the *Iroquois?* Probably not. What the yacht does represent is his idea of the fastest boat conceivable under the given restrictions.

IROQUOIS.

The *Amorita* was designed by A. Cary Smith, and built for William Gould Brokaw, by Harlan & Hollingsworth at Wilmington. She was launched in December, 1895.

She is of steel construction. Her under-body shows a deep rockered keel of the *Valkyrie* type, the fore-foot from the water-line to the center-board being almost straight. Just under the water-line, where the stem joins the fore-foot, there is a slight upward curve. The ballast is all inside, cast in a gutter keel. The centerboard houses below the cabin-floor, permitting of an arrangement which places the saloon amidships in the deepest and widest part of the vessel. The extreme draught, without the centerboard, is thirteen feet, or three feet greater than that of *Emerald* and only 2.4 feet less than that of *Colonia*. She has a good beam for a yacht of her type, with slightly flaring top-sides and a rather slack bilge. The chief characteristics of the *Amorita's* form, however, are her bluntly rounded bow, her long, heavy stern-overhang, and the fullness of her bows and quarters above the water-line. Comparing the line of her stem, from water-line to stem-head, on the sheer plan, with the same line on *Emerald* or *Colonia*, the stem of the *Amorita* has a heavy rounded curve approximating the quadrant of a circle where the others approach a straight line. It looks as though the bow had rammed something hard. The fore-overhang of the *Amorita* is over a foot shorter than that of her successful rival, the *Quissetta*, though the latter is a shorter boat; while her aft-overhang is nearly three feet greater than that of *Quissetta*. The *Amorita's* stern ends in a heavy oval transom, where in most of the new yachts the sterns are fined away into a long and slender overhang. She is an attempt to build a boat as large as possible above the water-line, on the least possible displacement. A comparison of the general dimensions of this vessel with two earlier yachts of the same designer shows the modern shortening of water-line and deepening of the keel:

	O. A. L.	W. L. L.	Beam.	Draught.
Iroquois, 1887	96.3	80.6	21	10
Elsemarie, 1893	91	69	21.2	8.6
Amorita, 1895	99.6	70	20	13

The internal arrangement of the *Amorita* is also original, and calculated to make the most of all the space which her constricted under-body allows.

Until a few weeks ago the *Amorita* was the fastest boat in her class. Last year, she and the *Emerald* were the fastest schooner yachts afloat. Between the two they swept everything before, or, rather, left everything behind them, in their respective classes. *Amorita* made her *début* at the beginning of last season and at once proceeded to gather in *all* the prizes in the seventy-five-foot class. She was never outsailed by a yacht of her own class, and during her first season, she was beaten only by the larger vessels *Emerald* and *Lasca*. She sailed sixteen races, of which she was first in thirteen, second in two, and third in one. The last instance was the event of the Goelet Cup race, August second, on the Block Island course, where in a moderate wind and on smooth water, *Amorita* was beaten by *Emerald* and *Lasca*. The latter yacht had just returned from a ten-thousand-mile cruise in foreign waters, and in this race she made the best actual time over the course.

The *Emerald*, however, won on allowance. *Amorita* was third by actual and corrected time, in a fleet of ten schooners, which comprised these three, followed by *Mayflower*, *Marguerite*, *Elsemarie*, *Merlin*, *Loyal*, *Neæra* and the big *Constellation*. On September twenty-first, in the race for the Colt memorial cup at Larchmont, the *Amorita* was defeated in very light weather by the *Emerald*, and two days afterward she was beaten in a moderate breeze by the same yacht. Truly remarkable is the career of a vessel when one is prone to record her defeats rather than her victories, as noteworthy events.

During the first two months of the past season she continued her unbroken record in her own class, and was beaten only by the larger yachts *Colonia* and *Emerald*. During the Larchmont race week, she defeated *Colonia* by time allowance two out of three races: on July twenty-second she beat *Colonia*, and two days later she defeated *Colonia* and *Emerald*. In the latter race she was beaten by *Emerald* only one minute and four seconds actual time.

While the *Colonia* was engaged in her successful attack upon the supremacy of the *Emerald*, a new craft was being fitted out which was destined to eclipse the prestige of the *Amorita* in its mid-day splendor.

The *Quissetta* was launched July sixth, and she was towed into Larchmont Harbor on July twenty-fourth, having just been delivered to her owner. It had

been given out that she had been designed for a cruising yacht. Her racing length was four feet below the limit of her class, while it is a generally accepted notion that the nearer a yacht is built to her class limit the better will be her chances of success in racing. The *Amorita* measures quite up to the class limit, while *Quissetta's* racing length is 71.13 feet, or 3.87 feet below it. The new boat has two feet less beam, and two less draught than last year's champion; she is 2.4 feet shorter on the water-line, and has 3.6 less over-all length.

Quissetta also carries six hundred square feet less sail than *Amorita*. When her graceful overhangs were noted and her fine appearance appreciated, it was remarked that it was a pity she had not been built up to the racing limit.

The owner of the new yacht modestly made no pretensions, but on August third, in the first race of the New York Yacht Club's cruise off Huntington Harbor, when *Quissetta* beat *Amorita* in a light breeze by four minutes eighteen seconds, boat for boat, over a twenty-one mile course, yachtsmen knew that something had happened. On the following day, after the tedious run in light and fluky airs from Huntington Harbor to New London, the reporters made a scramble for the telegraph offices with the news that *Quissetta* had beaten *Amorita* fourteen minutes thirty-five seconds, actual time. It was then evident that the new boat was a wonder in a light breeze. On the run from New London to Newport, after a close race in light and variable winds, the *Amorita* defeated her new rival. During the Goelet Cup race the *Quissetta* carried away a throat-halyard block and withdrew.

In this race *Amorita* was beaten by *Colonia*, but she beat *Emerald* on allowance and all the other schooners on actual time. On the following day *Quissetta* beat *Amorita* on the drift through Vineyard Sound;

AMORITA.

Photograph by J. S. Johnston.

QUISSETTA.

and on the return to Newport, after a good race, *Quissetta* crossed the line six minutes forty-one seconds ahead. On this, her first cruise, she won the Walrus Cup, which was awarded to the schooner winning the most runs.

After the start of this race the wind flattened, and all of the yachts drifted and sailed in and out of the harbor as the tide took them or a puff carried them on. Then they all anchored about the starting line so near together that a biscuit could have been thrown from boat to boat. If a man was seen to go forward near the windlass of either boat, the others followed suit. When they got under way again it reminded one of the old-time races in which the contestants got up anchor and started at the signal.

Quissetta was absent from the Seawanhaka Yacht Club races August twenty-ninth and thirty-first, and the wind being very light, *Amorita* did not finish in either race. In the American Yacht Club regatta, September nineteenth, *Quissetta*, having grounded,

withdrew when *Amorita* was away in the lead, giving the other boat her only victory over the new flyer.

The work done on the New York Yacht Club cruise convinced many that the *Quissetta* had supplanted the *Amorita* as the champion of the seventy-five-foot class. There were as many others who contended that all of the successes of the new schooner were on squadron runs, excepting the race for the Commodore's Cups at the beginning of the cruise, and more races were needed to prove that *Amorita* was a beaten boat. Mr. Brokaw was too good a sportsman to admit the defeat of his now famous yacht without a desperate struggle for the supremacy. The matter was the subject of daily controversy among the experts of the "Rocking-Chair Fleet" at Larchmont, and matters finally came to a head. The club offered a cup for two out of three races, and Chairman John F. Lovejoy, Fleet Captain George A. Cormack and W. H. Hall were appointed a committee to take charge of the races. So it happened, just at the close of the season, when most of the yachts had been laid up, the few enthusiasts who lingered on the Sound after the vacations of most men were over, were favored with the spectacle of a great match contest which equaled in sportsmanship, if not in brilliancy, the famous races of the past generation.

The two yachts began their remarkable duel on September twenty-fourth. The course was laid out on a fifteen-mile triangle off Larchmont, to be sailed twice round. The *Quissetta* was handled by Captain Norman W. Terry, the well-known skipper of the *Grayling*, and the associate of Captain Haff of the *Defender*. Commodore H. M. Gillig, E. M. Lockwood, the owner of *Uvira*, Mr. Hall of the committee, and Captain George Gibson of the *Ramona*, were also aboard. The talent on the *Amorita* in addition to her owner were Captain Ed. Sherlock, who held the wheel, Captain Haff of the *Defender*, who trimmed sail, Vice-Commodore

Postley, owner of the *Colonia*, Designer A. Cary Smith, Herbert B. Seeley, the owner of *Microbe*, Al. Comacho, the Corinthian skipper of *Raccoon*, and Hazen Morse, the famous cat-boat sailor,—a formidable array of talent in truth.

Captain Haff had the wheel of *Amorita* at the start, and placing his boat well to windward of the *Quissetta* he made a dash for the mark-boat on the weather end of the line. Captain Terry gave the *Quissetta* a wonderful hitch to windward under her rival's stern, and within a few feet of the mark-boat, placing her on the weather quarter of *Amorita*, and made a plucky attempt to pass her to windward. There was but eight seconds difference between the yachts in crossing the line.

The two yachts started on a broad reach across the Sound, under club-topsails, maintopmast staysails, jib-topsails and reaching forestaysails at the start, and sailed for miles so near together

Photograph by J. S. Johnston.

AMORITA.

that in the distance they looked like one vessel.

They rounded the mark on the opposite shore with spinnaker booms lowered, sixteen seconds apart ; but instead of breaking out spinnakers they started off on a luffing match, *Quissetta* struggling hard for the weather berth. Halfway down the leeward leg, *Quissetta* gave up the attempt for a time, broke out her spinnaker, and bore away under her rival's stern. Terry had hung with a bulldog grip to the *Amorita's* weather quarter, but Haff and Sherlock had shaken him off. With such evenly matched vessels, and with skippers whose skill has never been excelled, this race, even with its untimely termination, displayed the acme of yachting sport. The *Quissetta* gained three seconds on the run, *Amorita* rounding the leeward mark thirteen seconds ahead. After rounding the mark, *Quissetta* broke tacks with her rival. *Amorita* promptly followed suit, and bore down upon the windward side of the other boat. *Quissetta* holding her course, began to make up her difference to leeward, and called upon the *Amorita* to luff. The latter failing to respond to the demand, *Quissetta*, in an attempt to tack under her stern, carried away her own bowsprit on the *Amorita's* main boom. The latter boat continued round the course. The committee decided that by the act of her bearing out of her course in the way of *Quissetta*, the *Amorita* became disqualified. *Quissetta* had not finished the course, and consequently there had been no race.

By the following morning the broken bowsprit had been replaced, and the struggle was resumed. During this race *Amorita's* bobstay slackened, and her bowsprit snapped off. Mr. Harris, whose boat had been in the lead, refused the barren victory to be obtained by continuing alone, and the second day's work

MARGUERITE.

was lost. On the next day, September twenty-sixth, the first race was sailed, *Quissetta* winning in a moderate sailing breeze by four minutes fifty seconds actual time, and eight minutes six seconds corrected time, over the thirty-mile course. The *Quissetta* beat the *Amorita*, boat for boat, two minutes forty-two seconds in the twelve miles of windward work, and two minutes and eight seconds in the eighteen miles of reaching.

The second and final race was sailed September twenty-eighth in a moderately light wind, *Quissetta* proving her superiority on every point. She won by five minutes forty-five seconds actual, and by nine minutes one second when her time allowance is added.

The details of these races are given in the " Monthly Review" at the end of this number.

The *Quissetta* was designed by Gardner & Cox, and built by Thomas Marvel, at Newburgh, N. Y. She is owned by Henry W. Harris, of Orange, N. J., a young man recently graduated from Yale College, who was previously owner of the forty-footer *Nymph.* While in college Mr. Harris was commodore of the Yale Yacht Club. The yacht is built entirely of steel, and is a beautiful example of flush plating, her sides being smooth and highly polished. Her topsides are black, while the *Amorita* is painted white.

The *Quissetta*, like the *Amorita*, embodies a combination of deep lead-laden keel and centerboard, but the boats are very dissimilar, especially in the character of keel, rudder and stern-post and bow- and stern-overhangs. The bottom of the keel of *Amorita* is rockered ; that of *Quissetta* is flat, and it is cut away at both ends with an almost circular concave sweep. In this, as in other points, there is a marked similarity to the fast little cutter *Norota.* The lead ballast of the *Quissetta*, of which there are twenty-seven tons, is bolted on in four pieces. There is no inside ballast. The keel is eighteen inches wide amidships, and it tapers fore and aft. It widens a trifle at the bottom. In the older boat the rudder-stock follows the stern-post all the way down to the bottom of the keel in the usual way ; the after-line of the rudder following a general elliptical curve with the keel. The stern-post of the *Quissetta* has a very slight rake aft, and it is cut short at about half the depth of the keel, but at, approximately, the real depth of the hull. A great circular sweep forward from the foot of the stern-post to the end of the keel cuts off what would otherwise be an inordinately long keel. The rudder drops aft below the stock, and is almost round instead of deep and narrow. Perhaps the cleverest work in the design of the new schooner is the treatment of the bow and entrance. The line of the forefoot, under water, in the *Amorita* is almost straight up to the water-line, turning downward again above water as it turns into the downward curve of the bow. This gives the effect of a reverse curve right under the forefoot.

In the case of the *Quissetta*, the convexity of the stem is carried under the water, and the curve is not reversed until it is a good distance aft and under water. The bow of the *Quissetta* is long and fine ; that of the *Amorita* is comparatively short and full. The older boat in sailing throws a considerable wave and looks as though she pounded. Many of the smaller-class boats whose bows are of this type, make a great fuss under their bows, and in light airs or calms they slap and pound with a great noise, but they go right along all the time, contrary to orthodox notions. It is quite likely that the trifling disturbance under the bow of the fleet schooner is harmless. Be this as it may the *Quissetta* parts the water under her bows without the slightest disturbance. The bilge of the *Quissetta* is hard, the floor more hollowed out and the keel more like a fin than that of *Amorita*. *Quissetta's* topsides are straight where *Amorita's* have a slight flare, and the latter has less freeboard than the former. The quarters of the older boat are cut low over the water, and the transom is deep ; the counter of the *Quissetta* rakes high and the stern is fine and graceful to balance the bow. The transom rakes far aft, so as to almost follow the line of the counter. The transom of the *Amorita* is deep and at an angle with the counter. The *Amorita* was evidently designed so that the water-line and the power would be increased as soon as she began to heel from the perpendicular. The overhangs of the new boat are fair, fine and graceful.

The following are the general dimensions of the two yachts :

	Amorita.	Quissetta.
Over-all length	99.6 feet.	96. feet.
Water-line length	69. "	66.6 "
Fore-overhang	12.8 "	14.2 "
Aft-overhang	17.8 "	15.2 "
Beam	20. "	18. "
Draft	13. "	11. "
Least freeboard	3. "	3.3 "
Sail area	6400 sq. "	5800 sq. "
Sailing length	75.06 "	71.29 "

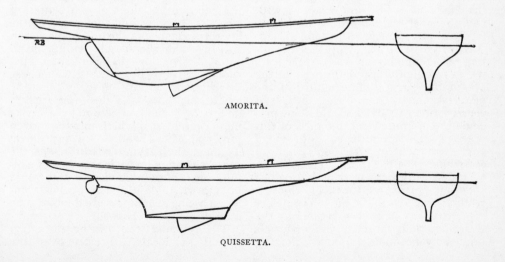

AMORITA.

QUISSETTA.

Photograph by J. S. Johnston, N. Y. A LARCHMONT START.

RACING SCHOONERS.

By R. B. Burchard.

THE large expenditure of money and brains on yacht-racing during the last quarter of a century has elevated the craft of yacht-designers among the ranks of scientific professional men. In old times the designer and builder were one and the same man. A block model was whittled out and submitted for approval ; it was then sawed into sections, the lines taken off and "laid down," and the boat built more or less accurately in accordance with them.

After the trial-trip, a process of cutting off and adding on was commenced, which frequently lasted throughout the life of the yacht. The nature of the materials now used, and the methods of construction employed, would alone preclude the unlimited continuance of this practice, although in the case of some of our finest yachts we frequently hear of experimental alterations. These, however, generally apply to trim and ballast and that portion of the keel which is really extraneous to the hull. The nicety of calculation in such a vessel as the *Defender*, built largely from materials previously not thus employed, floating exactly upon the predetermined waterline, and carrying her enormous sailspread at about the expected keeling angle, is a triumph of scientific procedure.

The construction of the sail-plan is quite as important as that of the hull. A mast "stepped" a foot or two out of place will always be a source of trouble. When hulls were boxes such points made little difference, save in the strain on the arms and backs of the helmsmen ; but in the yachts with short waterlines and deep fins, an error in figuring the relative positions of the center of effort of the sails, and the center of the lateral resistance of the hull to the water, will result in the vessel's sailing in all sorts of directions independent of the rudder. In the little boats, which are, in their way, affairs quite as scientific as the big ones, the designer tries to dodge the difficult problem by contriving a centerboard which may be moved fore and aft as well as up and down. To meet the varying conditions as the centers change on various points of sailing, this is a useful device ; but it would be impracticable in the large boats unless a racing-machine were devised such as man has not yet seen.

Theoretically the center of effort should be located directly over the center of lateral resistance. But designers depart from this rule in accordance with their originality and their experience, and the location of the centers is the last of the secrets to be divulged concerning a yacht. If a schooner is planned and trimmed so as to have a weather-helm in a light air she will wear out a man an hour in ordinary sailing. If she trims while sailing on the wind so that her owner may gracefully handle her with one hand and without breaking his starched collar, the vessel must have a slight lee-helm in very light airs. This means that the center of effort has been moved forward.

But these centers, so readily located on the plans, do not remain fixed in the vessel herself. Therefore, all calculations are more or less approximate. As the momentum of the vessel increases, it is found that the center of resistance moves aft, and of course the center of the sails varies with every varying position of the boat. This is one of the reasons why yacht-designing must always be an art as well as a science.

Everything about the form of a boat—sail-plan, hull, keel, centerboard, rudder—rounds up in the problem of the location of the centers. The trial-trip is an event fraught with anxiety even to the most expert, and happy is the designer whose vessel "hangs" and "trims" right from the start. Certain it is that the work done in the last two or three years has been wonderfully accurate in this regard.

After the yacht is finished the troubles of the skipper begin, and there are many of them which he keeps locked in his stalwart breast, only to be unfolded in the confidences of the cabin. For racing-yachts are like mettlesome horses, and have tricks to be mastered which are frequently unsuspected and difficult to explain. More than once have yachts of the largest and swiftest types been known to take the bit in their teeth, so to speak, and run away with their astonished skipper, until they were rounded up by letting all the fore-sheets fly.

Sometimes a boat with an obedient

SHAMROCK.

weather-helm on a beam wind will, when the wind blows hard over the quarter, take a notion to do surprising things in the way of yawing off in a perilous fashion, and sometimes becomes unmanageable. This was noticed years ago, especially in the very deep, narrow cutters which were developed under the old English measurement rule. The deep, fin-keels of latter-day build are said to occasionally be guilty of the same perverseness. Some of the old schooners were terrors to steer down the wind and at times required two or three men on the wheel. The yachts of the new type, in ordinary sailing, steer easier and truer ; but it is the unusual conditions that are dangerous, and one is safer not to vex the capricious dispositions of the modern beauties with the annoyances of the high-seas.

Among the modern schooners which embody a happy combination of speed, comfort and seaworthy power the *Lasca* is a notable example. Her dimensions are as follows : Over-all length, 119 ft.; water-line, 89.9 ft.; beam, 23 ft.; draught, 10.8 ft. Her gross tonnage is 121.23, and net tonnage 115.17 tons. The *Lasca* is a steel centerboard schooner, built by Henry Piepgras at City Island in 1892, from the plans of A. Cary Smith. That this yacht is not of the type whose value is cut in two or quartered as soon as they are beaten on the racing-course is evidenced by the fact that after her owner, Mr. John E. Brooks, had had four seasons' use of her, during which he had cruised over 15,000 miles in American and foreign waters, he sold her to Mr. James S. Watson, of Rochester, N. Y., for nearly $40,000.

The *Lasca* was designed as an ocean cruiser, and was therefore built with great fullness at the lower part of the cross-section. She has an easy bilge with nearly straight lines from water-line to keel, or with no hollowing out under the floor. This form is radically opposed to the latest idea of speed and stability as exemplified in the newest racing-yachts, but it is essential in a seagoing yacht. Such a vessel will ride the sea with ease where a boat which has hard bilges and is cut hollow underneath the floor would be in a precarious condition. The yachts of the latter type are popular for the present, because, when ballasted by a deep keel, they are fast in smooth water. Caught, however,

in a heavy sea with no wind to steady her, a boat of this type would be in a fair way to "slat" her masts out.

The *Yampa* is another example of A. Cary Smith's seagoing yachts. She is practically an enlarged *Iroquois*, and was built for Mr. Chester W. Chapin, the former owner of the latter yacht. Her dimensions are : Over-all length, 134 ft.; water-line, 110.9 ft.; beam, 27 ft., and draught, 14 ft. The *Yampa* is now owned by R. Suydam Palmer, and was, last season, chartered to Edward Browning, of Philadelphia. Her frames, like those of the *Lasca*, make a straight V from keel to water-line, and she is a very comfortable vessel in a seaway. That she is fast under favorable conditions is shown by the record of a run, under full lower sail and topsails, of 595 nautical miles in fifty hours, from Teneriffe to Cadiz.

The last of the remarkable fleet of schooners designed by A. Cary Smith previous to the building of the *Amorita* is J. Berre King's *Elsemarie*.

The *Shamrock* was the forerunner of the *Emerald*. She was built in 1887 as a sloop, four years after the *Grayling* and the *Fortuna*, and six years before the *Emerald*.

The form of her hull indicates the transition between the old yachts and the new. She has the long, low, rockered keel of the old type, but all her ballast (about thirty tons), excepting a little trimming lead (about a quarter of a ton), is on the outside. It is distributed throughout nearly the entire length of the keel, running aft to the sternpost. She has a long clipper stem of the old type, with hollow bow lines. There are only 4.4 ft. fore overhang, and this measurement is taken well out on the figurehead. The aft overhang, however, is 9.1 ft. The stern is narrowed down to 8 ft. in width. The extreme beam of the yacht is 20.3 ft. The topsides tumble home from abaft amidships to the stern.

The *Shamrock* was designed by her original owner, J. Rogers Maxwell, and she, with the *Sea Fox*, designed by A. Cass Canfield, are notable examples of modern racing-yachts which have been both designed and sailed by Corinthian yachtsmen. Mr. Maxwell has sailed in nearly all of the important regattas in New York Bay and Long Island Sound since 1865. His first boat, the 30-ft.

sloop *Black Hawk*, was originally a cat-boat built by Harry Smedley, then a noted builder, for Harry Haydock. This boat was of the type then popular, with straight stem and transom, measuring the same on the water-line as on deck. Mr. Maxwell's second boat was the cabin sloop *Black Hawk*, which was 34 ft. water-line and 38 feet over all. Next he owned the sloop *Peerless* ; then the open sloop *Carrie*. He built the sloop *Daphne*, 48 feet over all, in 1868. She was sold in 1871, and re-named *Christine*. The same year the 54-ton sloop *Peerless* was built, and afterwards changed into a schooner. Mr. Maxwell built the schooner *Crusader*, 118 tons, in 1880. She was dismasted in a race off Sandy Hook, and then rebuilt. He owned the sloop *Daphne*, which he sold in 1887 to Commodore G. C. W. Lowrey, so that she became subsequently the flagship of the Larchmont Yacht Club. It was therefore with no 'prentice hand that Mr. Maxwell undertook the designing of a great racing-sloop in 1887.

The *Shamrock* was originally a wood sloop, built by J. F. Munn and H. C. Wintringham at South Brooklyn, from the designs of her owner. She was subsequently altered into a schooner by Mr. Wintringham and her form somewhat improved. She was given a new bow, being entirely rebuilt for about fifteen frames from the stern. Her water-line was lengthened about two feet, and she was given a harder bilge. To accomplish the latter alteration the planking was taken off and a crescent-shaped piece secured to each timber. She proved to be a remarkably fast schooner, although beaten by the *Elsemarie*. She was sold in 1893, when the *Emerald* was built, to Willard P. Ward, of New York, who is her present owner.

To show what a slight increase of sail will do for a boat, the cases of *Elsemarie* and *Shamrock* may be cited. The *Else-marie* at first had a very short main - topmast, and in a race with *Shamrock* was beaten to windward. The reason was that the club - topsail was set too low down, and the peak could not be set up as it should be, because it would at once spoil the topsail. The consequence was *Shamrock* beat her easily. The betting was at once on *Shamrock*, for it was known that she could beat *Elsemarie* on a broad reach, or before the wind. At once a new foretopmast was made for the *Elsemarie* eight feet longer than the old one, and so much more sail put in spinnaker and balloon jib-topsail. At the same time a No. 2 jib-topsail could be set in the place of the "baby." The next meeting the *Elsemarie* ran away from *Shamrock* before the wind.

The *Marguerite* is a centerboard schooner built in 1888 for R. Suydam Palmer by G. Lawley & Son, Boston, from the designs of the late Edward Burgess. She is now owned by Henry W. Lamb, of New York. She is 96.11 ft. over all, 79.11 water-line, 21 ft. beam, and 11 ft. draught. In 1895 she beat *Mayflower* and *Mon Reve*, July seventeenth, Eastern Yacht Club, on actual and corrected time, winning the first prize of the club and the Puritan Cup. She was second to *Emerald* at Larchmont, July fourth, and also at the American Yacht Club on the following day. She was fifth in the Commodore's Cup race July twenty-ninth, and on the following day she was beaten by *Ariel* and *Iroquois*. On August third she defeated *Iroquois*, but lost to *Ariel*. On August fifth she was second to *Ariel*.

The *Elsemarie* like the *Iroquois* is a little vessel in which one might cruise in comfort, anywhere along the coast, without a twinge to his nerves when the wind whistled through her rigging o' nights. In fact she was built in 1893 for a cruise to the Bay of Fundy. Out of forty-five races she has won thirty-two. During the season of 1895 she sailed eighteen races, of which she was first in two, second in ten, third in two, sixth in one, and in one race with *Amorita* she did not finish.

LASCA.

The Seagull
(1899)

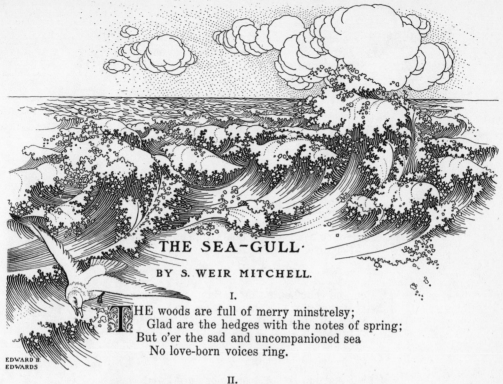

THE SEA-GULL·

BY S. WEIR MITCHELL.

EDWARD B.
EDWARDS

I.

THE woods are full of merry minstrelsy;
    Glad are the hedges with the notes of spring;
    But o'er the sad and uncompanioned sea
      No love-born voices ring.

II.

Gray mariner of every ocean clime,
    If I could wander on as sure a wing,
Or beat with yellow web thy pathless sea,
    I too might cease to sing.

III.

Would I could share thy silver-flashing swoop,
    Thy steady poise above the bounding deep,
Or buoyant float with thine instinctive trust,
    Rocked in a dreamless sleep.

IV.

Thine is the heritage of simple things,
    The untasked liberty of sea and air,
Some tender yearning for the peopled nest,
    Thy only freight of care.

V.

Thou hast no forecast of the morrow's need,
    No bitter memory of yesterdays;
Nor stirs thy thought that airy sea o'erhead,
    Nor ocean's soundless ways.

VI.

Thou silent raider of the abounding sea,
    Intent and resolute, ah, who may guess
What primal notes of gladness thou hast lost
    In this vast loneliness!

VII.

Where bides thy mate? On some lorn ocean rock
    Seaward she watches. Hark! the one shrill cry,
Strident and harsh, across the wave shall be
    Her welcome—thy reply.

VIII.

When first thy sires, with joy-discovered flight,
    High on exultant pinions sped afar,
Had they no cry of gladness or of love,
    No bugle note of war?

IX.

What gallant song their happy treasury held,
    Such as the pleasant woodland folk employ,
The lone sea thunder quelled. Thou hast one note
    For love, for hate, for joy.

X.

Yet who that hears this stormy organ voice
    Would not, like them, at last be hushed and stilled,
Were all his days through endless ages past
    With this stern music filled?

XI.

What matters it? Ah, not alone are loved
    Leaf-cloistered poets who can woo in song.
Home to the wild-eyed! Home! She will not miss
    The music lost so long.

XII.

Home! for the night wind signals, "Get thee home";
    Home, hardy admiral of the rolling deep;
Home from the foray! Home! That silenced song
    Love's endless echoes keep.